MW00991364

# Quality Management with SAP®

SAP PRESS is a joint initiative of SAP and Galileo Press. The know-how offered by SAP specialists combined with the expertise of the Galileo Press publishing house offers the reader expert books in the field. SAP PRESS features first-hand information and expert advice, and provides useful skills for professional decision-making.

SAP PRESS offers a variety of books on technical and business related topics for the SAP user. For further information, please visit our website: *www.sap-press.com*.

Markus Kirchler, Dirk Manhart
Service with SAP CRM
2009, 382 pp.
978-1-59229-206-6

Susanne Hess, Stefanie Lenz, Jochen Scheibler
Sales and Distribution Controlling with SAP NetWeaver BI
2009, 250 pp.
978-1-59229-266-0

John Hoke, Lorri Craig
Maximize Your Plant Maintenance with SAP
2009, 372 pp.
978-1-59229-215-8

Karl Liebstückel
SAP Enterprise Asset Management
2008, 552 pp.
978-1-59229-150-2

Michael Hölzer, Michael Schramm

# Quality Management with SAP®

Bonn • Boston

**ISBN 978-1-59229-262-2**

3rd Edition 2009
4th German edition published 2009 by Galileo Press, Bonn, Germany

Galileo Press is named after the Italian physicist, mathematician and philosopher Galileo Galilei (1564–1642). He is known as one of the founders of modern science and an advocate of our contemporary, heliocentric worldview. His words *Eppur si muove* (And yet it moves) have become legendary. The Galileo Press logo depicts Jupiter orbited by the four Galilean moons, which were discovered by Galileo in 1610.

**Editor** Eva Tripp
**English Edition Editor** Jenifer Niles
**Translation** Lemoine International, Inc., Salt Lake City, UT
**Copy Editor** Julie McNamee
**Cover Design** Jill Winitzer
**Photo Credit** Masterfile/Royaltyfree
**Layout Design** Vera Brauner
**Production Editor** Kelly O'Callaghan
**Typesetting** Publishers' Design and Production Services, Inc.
**Printed and bound in** Canada

# Contents at a Glance

# Contents

# Preface

Quality management has regained its importance with the rise of globalization. Companies are increasingly using integrated SAP functions to support process-oriented quality management, and so there is great need for real-world information. This has proven to be particularly significant in global companies when the parent company and the subsidiaries or joint-venture partners build up common IT structures and then must structure the processes of quality management in similar ways.

This book focuses in particular on SAP ERP 6.0. We'll describe in detail the interrelationships with the quality standard ISO 9001. Dr. Berthold Eilebrecht of the Dr. Eilebrecht SSE company, expertly supplemented our information in the important area of connecting subsystems to SAP ERP, providing valuable details in Chapter 7, Quality Inspection. This area is discussed in almost every QM project. With SAP ERP, the methodology of FMEA (Failure Mode and Effects Analysis) and the control plan, which is prevalent in the automotive segment, has become part of the standard functionality. We therefore rewrote the corresponding subchapter and assigned it to Chapter 6, Quality and Inspection Planning. During the regeneration, Dr. S. Matz provided intensive support, as well as Dr. M. Schulz and Dr. G. Kicherer, who all work for SAP AG.

We would also like to thank Mrs. Beate Lindqvist of SAP AG and Mrs. Yvonne Lorenz of Itelligence AG, who provided us with real-world experience and supplements on SAP NetWeaver BI for Chapter 10, Information Systems and Evaluations. We would like to thank Mr. Dransfeld of Vetter Pharma, who provided a comprehensive report and valuable tips on LSMW for data transfer of inspection plans, which supplemented Chapter 14, Migration Concepts. This topic has become standard repertoire of every QM project.

The high importance of audits in everyday business is addressed in Chapter 12, Audit Management Using SAP. Here as well, Mrs. Yvonne Lorenz made considerable contributions for which we would like to thank her once again.

**Michael Hölzer**
**Michael Schramm**

# Introduction

This chapter describes the structure of this book and how you can make the best use of it. It describes the groups of readers for whom the book is intended, along with a short overview of each subsequent chapter and their interrelationships.

### Target Groups

This book is geared toward all those interested in how SAP ERP supports quality management. It is suitable for newcomers to SAP ERP, those changing from a legacy system, and those experienced R/3 users who want to change their existing systems to SAP ERP or want to expand the quality management module (SAP QM). Those already using the QM module will learn more about its functions and options and will find suggestions for its extended use and optimization. Consultants from other module areas will get an overview of the functionality of the QM module, and consultants for the QM module will find useful tips for their work.

As prerequisites, readers should understand the basic concepts and processes of quality management and have a practical knowledge of a PC system with menu-driven user programs.

### Topics Covered

Although the subjects of quality management—along with quality planning, quality inspection, and quality control—are the actual focus of the book, we also will describe in detail the points of contact with other components in the SAP ERP system and the business processes in which quality management plays an essential role. You will get tips on how you can map your quality management system with SAP ERP and structure and describe your business processes. The important functions of vendor evaluation and test equipment monitoring will also receive in-depth treatment. Although these are assigned to other SAP ERP modules, they are still closely connected to quality management.

**Tip**

We will at times highlight points of particular interest in this way. This sometimes involves menus that are hidden, suggestions for mapping your processes, or alternative implementation options, if a direct solution is not available through SAP ERP. These tips have emerged from the practical experience of the authors, and with their help, a few problem cases have already been solved. The tips are mainly aimed at users.

**Customizing Tip**

In contrast to the target group referred, this tip is geared toward specialists who are able to change the Customizing settings. Otherwise, the same explanation applies as for the Tip feature just described. Important recommendations based on the authors' practical experience have been highlighted in this way. This gives you the chance to employ the most elegant and quickest implementation option for your processes.

### Structure of the Book

The book is structured so that you do not have to read all of the chapters in sequence. The chapters generally begin with the presentation of a general and business-related problem and the requirements of a management system. After that, we describe the solution options using the SAP system, and then elaborate on these with scenarios and examples.

If you have had very little experience with SAP software up to now, you should initially read **Chapter 3**, Overview of SAP ERP. However, even if you have practical experience with SAP, you will definitely find some interesting information there.

**Chapter 5**, Quality Management in the Supply Chain, links topically with Chapters 6, 7, and 8 and therefore should be read before those three chapters.

**Chapter 6**, Quality and Inspection Planning, **Chapter 7**, Quality Inspection, and **Chapter 8**, Quality Control, are thematically linked so you should read these in conjunction with one another.

The remaining chapters are, for the most part, stand-alone chapters, and you can read them independently of each other.

### Contents of the Chapters in Brief

#### Chapter 1, Implementing Management Systems with SAP

The demonstration of a quality management system is generally based on norms.

Different norms and developments are explained, as well s the requirements that emerge from the norm ISO 9001 and the options for implementing them with SAP ERP.

**Chapter 2, Modeling QM Business Processes Using the EPC Method**
In this chapter, you learn how you can map your business processes by paying particular attention to quality management with the SAP system. Event-driven process chains (EPC) are introduced as a suitable tool for modeling and describing flows. Examples are included to show how to apply EPC.

**Chapter 3, Overview of SAP ERP**
This chapter provides an overview of SAP AG. The SAP ERP system and its modules are described as necessary for the interaction with SAP QM. The structure of typical SAP work centers is addressed, as is the organization of the implementation project, the transfer of data from the legacy system, and the interfaces to external systems. A section is dedicated to the further developments of SAP ERP. The connectivity of SAP ERP on the Internet and intranet is further extended with SAP NetWeaver. The new strategies are introduced and explained. In this chapter, you learn, in particular, how quality management can benefit from these new technologies.

**Chapter 4, Operating SAP ERP**
This chapter gives you a basic introduction to using the SAP interface. This chapter mainly addresses less-experienced users and those who are new to SAP ERP. The explanations are mainly general and refer to all modules. However, the examples and screenshots were mostly selected from the QM module.

**Chapter 5, Quality Management in the Supply Chain**
This chapter is an introduction to the subsequent central chapters, Quality and Inspection Planning, Quality Inspection, and Quality Control. It shows how quality management is present in each step of the supply chain and acts as a common thread for the supply-chain process. Studying this chapter makes the context of the subsequent three chapters clearer and easier to understand.

**Chapter 6, Quality and Inspection Planning**
This is the first of three central chapters of the book. It contains a description of the necessary basic data and master data, the different task-list types — routing, inspection plan, and reference operation set — and the relevant catalogs. You are provided with a detailed description of the creation and function of sampling procedures, sampling schemes, and dynamic modification rules. The control charts

and the batch inspection are also included in this chapter. The applications in Materials Management, in Production, and in Sales and Distribution give you an insight into practical use. With FMEA (Failure Mode and Effects Analysis) and the control plan, this chapter is supplemented by two methods for planning and risk minimization, which are absolutely indispensable for the automotive industry.

**Chapter 7, Quality Inspection**

This chapter describes how to create inspection lots and how you can perform planned (and even unplanned) inspections. You learn how you can implement your inspection strategy using SAP QM. Quality inspections are run based on practical examples, and the characteristics of Materials Management, Production, and Sales and Distribution are emphasized. At the end of the chapter, you will find information on the integration of subsystems in quality inspection with SAP ERP.

**Chapter 8, Quality Control**

This chapter provides different options for initiating and tracing management and improvement actions using SAP QM. First, we describe in detail the use decision, which functions not only as a completion of the quality inspection but also contains the short-term controlling actions such as sorting or post-processing. A central topic in this chapter is vendor evaluation, which can be used to create ranking lists of vendors that have been evaluated according to different criteria. You can plan actions to improve quality and evaluate their success afterward. In addition, the tools Quality Level, Dynamic Modification, and Statistical Process Control (SPC), as well as the recording of quality costs, are presented in detail.

**Chapter 9, Quality Notification**

This chapter describes with precision how you can make optimal use of this exceptional tool in your company. Quality notifications not only allow you to transfer or archive information but also to plan and trace activities and actions. You can make long-term use of the quality-notification data through convenient evaluation options. This chapter also describes the stability study, which is critical for the process industry.

**Chapter 10, Information Systems and Evaluations**

The various evaluation options using the different information systems represent one of the strengths of the SAP ERP system. This chapter provides an overview of the comprehensive options to retrieve and process data. Finally, SAP NetWeaver Business Intelligence (SAP NetWeaver BI) is introduced on the basis of some examples.

**Chapter 11, Test Equipment Management**
Test equipment is very important for planning and performing inspections and also for complying with the requirements of the quality standard. This chapter introduces solution options for managing your test equipment and planning and documenting calibration with the SAP ERP system.

**Chapter 12, Audit Management Using SAP**
Planning, executing, and evaluating audits is supported by SAP Audit Management, which is a component of the SAP Business Suite. This chapter describes the tools and objects used in SAP Audit Management.

**Chapter 13, Customizing**
Customizing refers to the menu-driven adjustment of the SAP system to your company's requirements. Although this chapter is not to be regarded as formal Customizing training, it does provide you with an overview of how to make the necessary settings when you customize your SAP ERP system. Knowledge of this subject is not an absolute prerequisite, but the content described here will help you to better understand the system and its Customizing options.

**Chapter 14, Migration Concepts**
If another EDP system was used prior to the implementation of the SAP system, or an existing CAQ (Computer Aided Quality Assurance) system is replaced by the QM component of the SAP system, the issue of consistent data transfer immediately arises. This problem area is also referred to as migration. This chapter provides you with useful tips on how to plan such a data transfer and what needs to be considered.

**Appendix A, Glossary**
An extensive glossary explains concepts from quality management in general, and the SAP system and the Quality Management module in particular.

**Appendix B, Abbreviations**
A detailed abbreviation directory provides quick help with abbreviations that are used in this book and that appear in the SAP help texts. However, you will find the module abbreviations in Chapter 3, Overview of SAP ERP.

**Appendix C, Bibliography**
You can find an overview of the sources or get information about the supplementary literature available for the individual topics.

*Certified management systems are a prerequisite for industrial enterprises and many other industries to ensure economic success. Based on some examples, you learn how SAP ERP supports you in setting up and documenting a management system.*

# 1 Implementing Management Systems with SAP

Until a few years ago, only some industrial companies — mainly from the automotive sector — implemented and documented quality-management systems and had themselves QM-certified. Since then, this has become normal business practice, as the population of companies that maintain quality-management systems has expanded widely. Building companies, trading concerns, service companies, care establishments, hospitals, handicraft businesses, and finally even government agencies and doctors' practices became certified according to ISO 9001-9003.

Today, you usually talk of management systems because the concept of quality management was only the starting point. Numerous enterprises have introduced environment management systems according to ISO 14001 and enhanced these with existing quality-management systems to create "integrated management systems." Even before Basel II, banks and insurance companies required the implementation of risk-management policies in companies they worked with. So, it makes a lot of sense to integrate these enhancements into an existing management system because this already contains many needed elements and must only be extended to meet the additional requirements.

Since the introduction of ISO 9001:2000, everything is directed toward process management, in which the entire range of business processes is described (see Figure 1.1). An essential goal of the revision of standards was to replace the existing 20 elements with a process-oriented management model that could be used in practice within companies. A consistent process organization supports the further development of an organization and improves its competitiveness. Recommendations from ISO 9004 have been included in ISO 9001:2000. A strong focus on quality-relevant processes was replaced by a holistic consideration of the flows and business processes. An implementation with SAP ERP is an ideal solution because quality management is strongly integrated in the logistics core processes in SAP ERP.

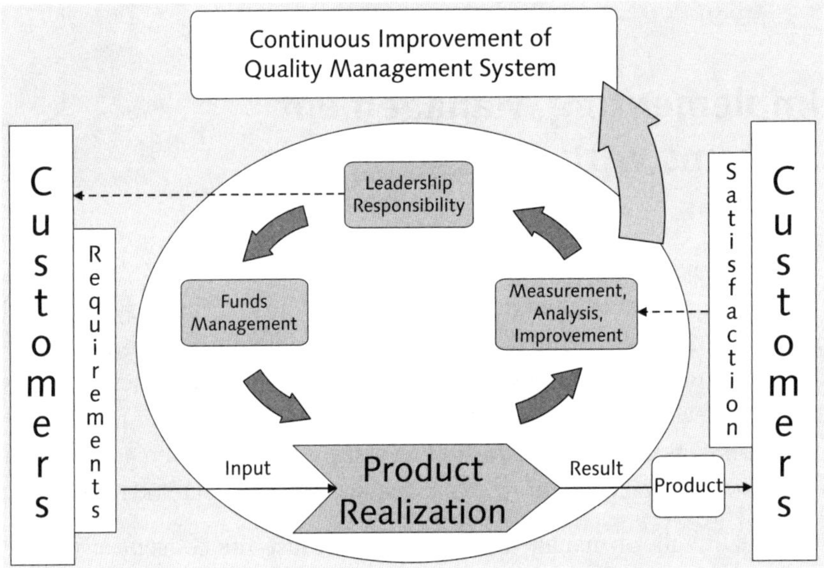


**Figure 1.1** Model of the Process-Oriented Approach According to ISO 9001:2008

## 1.1 Basic Principles

This section initially describes the rules for management systems and then the implementation of a QM system.

### Rules for Management Systems

A quality-management system (QM system) cannot be standardized, given that the requirements for businesses and products differ substantially from case to case. The only thing that is standardized is a model to document the QM system. There are few compulsory guidelines set for the implementation of a QM system, but there are minimum requirements for achieving it.

The requirement to create rules for quality management originated in the 1950s in the United States. This development was supported by the strict quality requirements for the military and for construction of nuclear power stations. These rules took shape with the introduction of the MIL Q 9858 standard in 1963, which was further developed at the beginning of the 1970s to become NATO rule AQAP (Allied Quality Assurance Publications). And, in the automotive industry, Guideline Q101 issued by Ford for quality-assurance systems soon became the accepted standard.

Due to the fact that in the 1980s increasingly different country- and industry-specific rules emerged, an ISO committee (International Organization for Standardization) took on the development of a uniform and globally usable standard, which was published in 1987 and was accepted by most of the ISO member countries. This standard is now recognized everywhere and comprises the standards series ISO 9000-9004. In Germany, for instance, according to the European harmonization and implementation in the national standard, it is called ISO 9000-9004.

Despite the harmonizing and still dominant influence of the ISO 9000 series of standards and those that follow, the specific sets of rules have been maintained and further developed. So, the military standard AQAP still exists, however, the requirements of the standards series ISO 9000 and those that follow have been integrated. The U.S. automotive industry developed Rule QS 9000, based on Q 101 and integrating ISO 9000 and those that follow. QS 9000 further extends the requirements of the ISO 9000 series. The German automotive industry developed a similar standard with the updated rule of the VDA (Association of German Automobile Manufacturers). The multiple certification according to QS 9000 and VDA 6.1, is now being replaced more and more by a certification according to the more comprehensive standard ISO/TS 16949.

To prove to a third party that these rules are being observed, you can be certified by an accredited company. This can be done, for instance, according to the standards ISO 9001, VDA 6, QS 9000, or ISO/TS 16949.

A common feature of all sets of rules is the proof of existence of certain elements and the documentation of flows and processes. This becomes your advantage when you use the SAP ERP system. It supports your management system throughout the entire supply chain (see Figure 1.2). It also helps you structure and comply with a management system in your company and performs numerous tasks for documenting the management system according to the corresponding standards. Because SAP ERP is an integrated system, it is also ideal for supporting the entire management system with its various business processes.

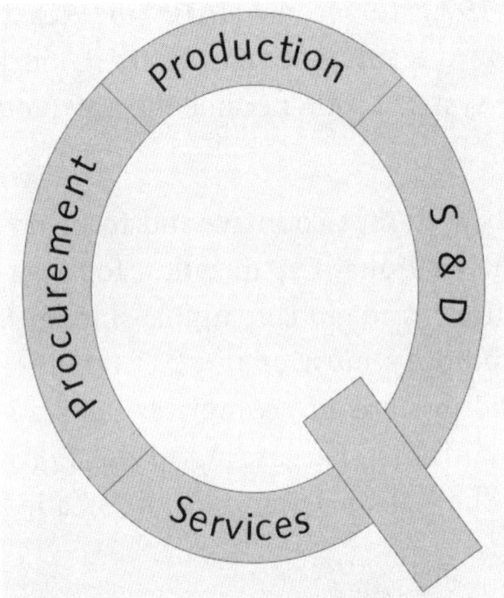


**Figure 1.2** Integrating the Management System in the Supply Chain

The management system is not merely a matter for the quality department, but rather the organization's entire management is responsible for maintaining and improving the system. The support for the management system by SAP ERP is therefore not only limited to the SAP QM module but also is completely integrated in the entire SAP ERP system because the management system is integrated in the entire business process.

#### Implementing a QM System with SAP ERP

Regardless of whether you have already implemented a QM system or are planning to do so, you will benefit from implementing your processes with SAP ERP. If you have already designed a management system in your company, it will be much easier for you to describe the business processes for the SAP ERP implementation because you can rely on the existing management documentation and procedures. Your interfaces are also already defined there, along with a description that provides your SAP consultant with a better starting point than if he had to first "sift" through all of the information. However, don't forget to incorporate all of the necessary changes in your processes (which automatically arise) in the management documentation and processes after the SAP ERP implementation.

If you are planning to design a QM system after introducing SAP ERP, you will receive multifaceted support from the SAP ERP system. This doesn't mean that the introduction of the SAP ERP system replaces the development of a management system. However, it does supplement and facilitate this. If you take the requirements of a management system into account while implementing SAP ERP, you can save yourself much additional effort at a later stage. For one thing, this means that the flows of your business processes (and their documentation, for example, with the EPC method) can be transferred without any problem into your management documentation or in your process descriptions (see Chapter 2, Modeling QM Business Processes with the EPC Method).

## 1.2 Quality Elements

When describing the options for adhering to the standard requirements by using the components of the SAP ERP system, we will limit ourselves to the quality elements of the ISO 9001 standard. There are corresponding ways of adhering to the rules QS 9000, VDA 6, and ISO/TS 16949.

Table 1.1 shows which components, in addition to SAP QM, are suitable for implementing the requirements from the corresponding standard chapters. The selection of elements is still somewhat geared toward the older edition of the ISO 9001 standard.

| Standard Chapter | Element | Mapping in the SAP System |
|---|---|---|
| 4 | Quality-management system | QM, PP, PS, PM |
| 4.2 | Documentation requirements, control of documents, and records | QM, MM, PP, Document Management System |
| 5 | Responsibility of management | QM, PM, HR, CO |
| 6.2.2 | Capability, consciousness, and training | HR |

**Table 1.1** Relationship Between Elements and SAP ERP Modules

| Standard Chapter | Element | Mapping in the SAP System |
|---|---|---|
| 7.2.2 | Evaluating the requirements with regard to the product (contract check) | SD, MM |
| 7.3 | Development (design control) | PP, PS |
| 7.4 | Procurement | QM, PM, PP |
| 7.5.1 | Controlling production and services (process control) | PM, PP |
| 7.5.3 | Identification and traceability (inspection status) | QM, MM |
| 7.5.4 | Property of the customer (products provided) | QM, PM, MM |
| 7.5.5 | Product maintenance (storage, etc.) | SD, MM |
| 7.6 | Control of monitoring and test equipment (test equipment monitoring) | QM, PM, PP |
| 8.2.2 | Internal audit | QM |
| 8.2.3 or 8.2.4 | Monitoring and testing processes and products (inspections) | QM |
| 8.3 | Control of defective products | QM, CO |
| 8.4 | Data analysis (incl. statistical methods) | QM |
| 8.5 | Improvement (corrective and preventive action) | QM, PM |

**Table 1.1** Relationship Between Elements and SAP ERP Modules (Cont.)

Table 1.2 shows the elements of the ISO 9001 standard and the options for implementing them with SAP ERP. Only a few essential standard requirements could be dealt with here because a complete text analysis of the standard with all its requirements would go far beyond the scope of this table.

| Standard Chapter | Standard Requirement (Abbreviated) | Implementation Option with SAP ERP |
|---|---|---|
| 4 | **QM system**<br>Processes must be identified and defined; the system must be documented, and documents and records must be controlled. | You have identified and defined the processes through the introduction of SAP ERP and the selection of components, especially QM. The documentation of your implementation, which is required anyway, can also be used for the documentation of your QM system, or it can be partially referred to for this reason. |
| 4.2 | **Documentation requirements**<br>The documentation of the management system must adhere to certain requirements. Documents and records must be controlled. | The entire SAP ERP system is designed in such a way that this item is fulfilled. Each creation and modification of documents and records (as long as they are processed through SAP ERP) is recorded with user name, date, and time. This means that relevant proof is always available. The release after inspection is implemented via a status concept, and the appropriate personnel is defined through the authorization concept and the responsibility for certain processes. Special authorizations are to be implemented using a digital signature. The document-management system is particularly suitable for implementing this standard requirement. |
| 5 | **Management responsibility**<br>Organization: Responsibility and authority must be specified and documented, resources must be provided, and QM evaluation must be performed. | The implementation of SAP ERP, the use of the required modules, the responsibilities for the mapped processes, and the authorization concept ensure that numerous requirements are met directly.<br>The SAP ERP information systems provide access to nearly all facts you require for the QM evaluation. |
| 6.2.2 | **Capability, consciousness, and training**<br>The training requirement must be identified, necessary qualifications must be attained, and records on the training status must be maintained. | You can meet the requirement to record the training status by using the HR module. There you can manage the corresponding information for each employee. |

**Table 1.2** Fullfillment of the ISO 9001 Standard with SAP ERP

| Standard Chapter | Standard Requirement (Abbreviated) | Implementation Option with SAP ERP |
|---|---|---|
| 7.2.2 | **Evaluating the requirements with regard to the product (contract checking)**<br>Checking the requirements and the capability to meet them — managing contract changes. | This element is supported by your SAP ERP system in different modules. You can manage contracts using the document-management system. The material master data enables you to review a part of the requirements. You can use production planning and storage management to check the capacity. The engineering change management with the change master record (date, processor, etc.) allows you to manage contract changes, and the entire system records all management data. In addition, you can create or supplement records with comment fields in different transactions and by using the notification tool. |
| 7.3 | **Development (design control)**<br>Development and phase planning; defining organizational and technical interfaces; establishing and documenting development entries; verifying, documenting, and validating results; and documenting changes. | These requirements can for the most part be covered by existing components. You can plan a development project and its phases with the Project System (PS). Product Lifecycle Management (PLM) ensures integration in the supply chain and quality management. You will find the organizational and technical interfaces at different points in SAP ERP, and you must define and describe them there. Important interfaces for a development and production company include Purchasing (MM) and Production (PP). |
| 7.4 | **Procurement**<br>The vendor must be evaluated, procurement specifications must describe the requirements adequately, and the procured products must be verified. | SAP ERP also provides complete support in this context. You can find the status of your vendors at any time through vendor evaluation. The suggested criteria not only allow quality evaluation but also the evaluation of quantity reliability or timeliness of deliveries. You can carry out these evaluations for all materials supplied or only for specific ones. For each vendor, you can define guidelines regarding the vendor's QM system or manage the existing ones.<br>The procurement specifications are all available in the system (e.g., material master with individual purchase order texts, purchasing info record, vendor info record, quality info record, etc.), and you can refer to them when ordering, when goods are received, or during incoming goods inspection. For verification, precisely plannable inspections are available in QM. |

**Table 1.2** Fullfillment of the ISO 9001 Standard with SAP ERP (Cont.)

| Standard Chapter | Standard Requirement (Abbreviated) | Implementation Option with SAP ERP |
|---|---|---|
| 7.5.1 | **Controlling production and services (Process control)**<br>Production, assembly, and service processes must be planned and executed under controlled conditions. | Routings provide you with the best options for planning your production and assembly processes or services. You can specify the type of production and service, including the relevant production resources and tools or operating supplies. You can plan the maintenance of your products and production facilities with the Service Module (SM) and the module for preventative Plant Maintenance (PM). |
| 7.5.3 | **Identification and traceability (and inspection status)**<br>The product must be clearly identified during production, that is, the inspection status of a product must be indicated everywhere. | You are quite flexible with regard to the product identification with SAP ERP and can easily meet the standard requirements. In each phase, you can print out the corresponding papers for identification and attach them to the goods, for example, the receipt of goods certificate for the inbound delivery, the production order for production, or the delivery note and the test certificate for the outbound delivery. It is possible to print out labels with a barcode, if required. SAP ERP also supports the management of physical samples and batches. Serial number management enables you to trace individual products, if necessary. The status of the products is documented in the system, for instance, via confirmation messages for certain operations. If required, you can also print out work papers or labels to indicate the inspection status.<br>The system can be configured so that no product can be dispatched without having completed the required inspections and having documented them. |
| 7.5.4 | **Property of the customer (products provided)**<br>The property of the customer must be identified, verified, and protected. | You can carry out verification with SAP ERP, for instance, via a GR (Goods Received) inspection or certificate query. Storage management from SAP ERP is a good solution for the storage area. |

**Table 1.2** Fullfillment of the ISO 9001 Standard with SAP ERP (Cont.)

| Standard Chapter | Standard Requirement (Abbreviated) | Implementation Option with SAP ERP |
|---|---|---|
| 7.5.5 | **Product maintenance (storage, etc.)**<br>Suitable methods and processes for identification, handling, packing, storage, protection, and dispatch must be adopted. | You can adjust your system to these standard requirements with the Materials Management, Storage Management, and Sales and Distribution components. For instance, for methods and processes that have to be adhered to at certain stages of the production process or with regard to product maintenance, you can include detailed descriptions as long texts at any time in routings and inspection plans. |
| 7.6 | **Control of monitoring and test equipment (test equipment monitoring)**<br>Test equipment, provided it is necessary for the fulfillment of quality requirements, must be released and calibrated or verified at regular intervals. Records must be kept on the calibration and verification results. | The combined possibilities of the PM and QM modules of your SAP system enable complete test equipment monitoring. This test equipment monitoring contains the master data for all test equipment, the status (locked, free, etc.), the management (who has which item of test equipment where), and the calibration monitoring, which ensures that each item of test equipment subject to monitoring is regularly recalibrated on the basis of a maintenance plan. As usual, all data on test equipment monitoring is stored in the system database and is available for information or further evaluation. It is also possible to integrate a subsystem that may already exist for test equipment monitoring, which communicates with the SAP ERP system through a dedicated interface. |
| 8.2.2 | **Internal audit**<br>An audit program must be planned — criteria, scope, frequency, and methods must be defined — and records must be maintained. | Audit management is directly supported by the SAP ERP system. You can find solutions in the SAP CRM. You can use the quality notification to document and trace audits. |

**Table 1.2** Fullfillment of the ISO 9001 Standard with SAP ERP (Cont.)

| Standard Chapter | Standard Requirement (Abbreviated) | Implementation Option with SAP ERP |
|---|---|---|
| 8.2.3 or 8.2.4 | **Monitoring and measuring processes and products (inspection)**<br>The characteristics of the product must be monitored, measured, and verified. Only upon completion of the defined actions can the product or service be released. | You can meet all requirements by using the functions inspection planning, inspection with results recording, and quality control from the SAP ERP QM module. Incoming goods checks can be automatically or manually triggered; you can manage provided inspection certificates, define in-process and final inspections in production, or automatically start inspections before delivery. All inspection results are stored in the database, which provides numerous evaluation options. |
| 8.3 | **Control of defective products**<br>Responsibility and authority must be defined, including identification and control of products; evaluation for rework, special release, and scrapping must be carried out; error description must be recorded; and reinspection must be conducted after rework. | You will primarily find tools in the QM module to meet these requirements. The responsibilities are arranged in the authorization concept. Digital signatures also enable the verification of authority here. Evaluation occurs when evaluating the inspection results and usage decision. The inspection description, the error code, different long texts, and the quality notification are available for the error description. You can ensure reinspection by automatically or manually generating inspection lots. |
| 8.4 | **Data analysis (statistical methods)**<br>Data on customer satisfaction, processes, products, and vendors must be recorded and analyzed. | SAP ERP QM provides numerous evaluation options, which should generally suffice. You can determine and graphically analyze the process capability, the average value, and standard deviation;<br>create control charts; and control processes with SPC (Statistical Process Control). You can determine customer satisfaction by evaluating customer complaints (notifications). Vendor evaluation in QM and MM provide statements on quality, quantity reliability, and timeliness of deliveries. The QM information system enables extensive data analyses. |

**Table 1.2** Fullfillment of the ISO 9001 Standard with SAP ERP (Cont.)

| Standard Chapter | Standard Requirement (Abbreviated) | Implementation Option with SAP ERP |
| --- | --- | --- |
| 8.5 | **Improvements (corrective and preventive action)** Corrective measures must evaluate errors, including customer complaints. You will find the direct implementation of these requirements in the QM and PP modules in particular. You can create and trace determine causes, prevent recurring errors, initiate measures, record results, and evaluate measures. | Preventive measures must determine possible errors and causes, prevent the occurrence of errors, initiate actions, record results, and evaluate actions; corrective and preventive actions work directly through error recording for the inspection results and the use decision. You can use your own action catalogs or initiate individual measures or actions using free texts and quality notifications and trace and monitor these over time. All information and quality records are available from in-process and final inspections involving production. You can record customer complaints, initiate corresponding actions, and further trace them via the quality notification. Your SAP ERP system can provide information at any time on all actions, steps, and their processing status, as well as provide information for a QM evaluation. |

**Table 1.2** Fullfillment of the ISO 9001 Standard with SAP ERP (Cont.)

## 1.3 Documenting the Management System

The SAP ERP Document Management System (DMS) provides you with a suitable tool to document your management system.

You can adjust the DMS to your requirements through Customizing. You can save the original documents in the SAP ERP system or store them on your PC systems and only manage them in SAP ERP. You can, for example, record the following data for each document:

- Document number (various options possible)
- Revision (freely definable)
- Storage location (also in external host systems)
- Processing status
- Other management data

You can use this tool to manage and save your management-documentation, procedures, work instructions, quality-assurance agreements, and all other documents related to your management system. An authorization concept allows you to define who can view documents and who can edit them. Each authorized user can thus always keep himself up to date on the current status of the documentation of your management system. This also eliminates the problem of informing all those involved, for instance, about a new issuance of a specific procedure because the current status is always available in the system.

You can also link various documents with BOMs (Bills of Materials), define documents as production resources or tools, assign them to routings or inspection plans, and link documents to other SAP objects such as the material master record. Integration in the SAP ERP workflow provides you with further options for triggering subsequent actions. You can reach the document-management system via the following path: LOGISTICS • CENTRAL FUNCTIONS • DOCUMENT MANAGEMENT SYSTEM.

## 1.4 QM Information System

As you have seen in Section 1.2, Quality Elements, the recording and documentation of inspections and inspection results is always required in the standard. Everything that you enter or confirm in the SAP ERP system must meet these requirements. To find this data quickly and to analyze it further, the information systems are available as described in Chapter 10, Information Systems and Evaluations. One of these information systems is the QM Information System. You can reach this system via the following path (see Figure 1.3): LOGISTICS • LOGISTICS CONTROLLING • QM INFORMATION SYSTEM.

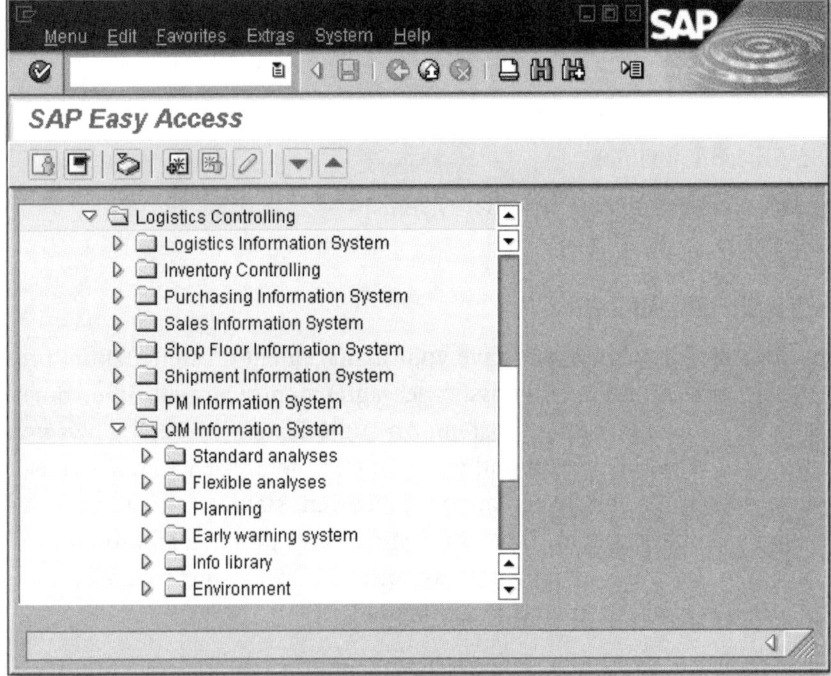


**Figure 1.3** Menu of the QM Information System

There you will find numerous analyses and evaluation options that will help you with quality planning and in evaluating your QM system.

## 1.5 Environment Management

The growing sensitivity of companies and customers regarding environmental problems has led to increased emphasis on environmental management in recent years. For modern companies, environmental protection has become a strategic objective that can be pursued by implementing an environment management system.

The EU directive (EEC) No. 1836/93 and the ISO 14001 standard created a common system for environment management and for environment auditing in which companies can voluntarily participate.

As already mentioned at the beginning of this chapter, the different management systems are beginning to merge more and more, which is why in general only one management system is referred to. Nowadays, this system is frequently documented in a book of its own and is also referred to as an "integrated management system." This development has already taken place in many companies with regard to environment management.

Since the revision to the ISO 9000 series of standards and those that follow in the year 2000, the structure of the ISO 9001 standard has been aligned to the ISO 14001 standard for environment management. The new version of ISO 14001 from 2004 further improved this alignment. This facilitates a common documentation and process description.

Thus the comments in previous sections that were focused on quality management are also relevant to environment management. Many of the hints for implementing standard requirements as they are listed in Tables 1.1 and 1.2 also refer to ISO 14001. Sometimes the elements even have the same or at least similar names such as "controlling documents" or "corrective and preventive measures."

Table 1.3 contains the ISO 14001:2004 standard chapters that correspond to those of ISO 9001:2000. Based on this, you can create the connection to the modules of the SAP ERP system by referring to Table 1.2. This way you will see that you are well supported by SAP ERP in implementing your environment management system.

In addition to the general support of the individual elements, the SAP ERP system also provides a specific environment management component. You can find this component by using the following path: LOGISTICS • ENVIRONMENT, HEALTH AND SAFETY (see Figure 1.4).

| ISO 14001:2004 | | ISO 9001:2000 | |
|---|---|---|---|
| Introduction | – | 0 | Introduction |
| Application area | 1 | 1 | Application area |
| Normative references | 2 | 2 | Normative references |
| Concepts | 3 | 3 | Concepts |
| Requirements to an environment management system | 4 | 4 | Quality-management system |
| General requirements | 4.1 | 4.1 | General requirements |
| Environmental policy | 4.2 | 5.3 | Quality policy |
| Planning | 4.3 | 5.4 | Planning |
| Implementation and execution | 4.4 | 7 | Product implementation |
| Inspection | 4.5 | 8 | Measurement, analysis, and improvement |
| Management evaluation | 4.6 | 5.6 | Management evaluation |

**Table 1.3** Corresponding Elements Between ISO 14001:2004 and ISO 9001:2000

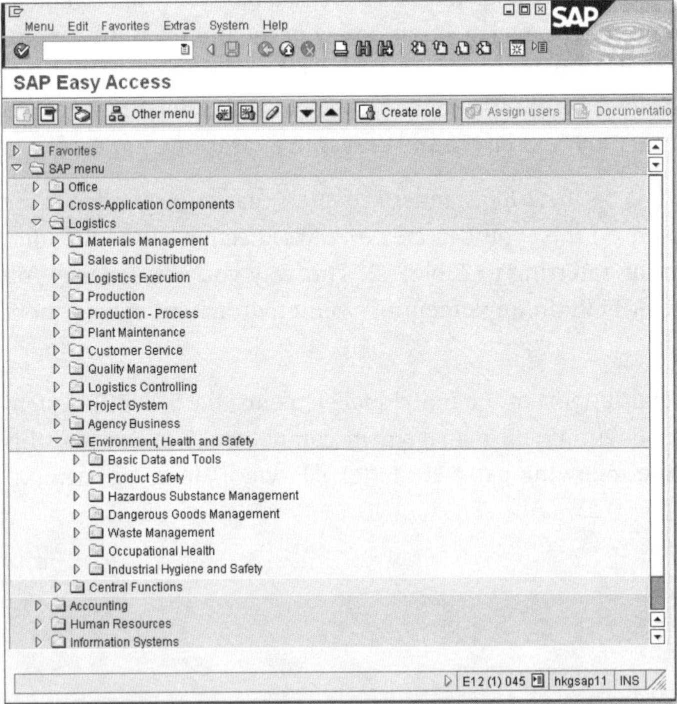


**Figure 1.4** Menu Tree for Environment, Health and Safety

This component refers to the areas of environmental protection, health protection, and safety at work (EH&S). There are several submenus available: BASIC DATA AND TOOLS, PRODUCT SAFETY, HAZARDOUS SUBSTANCE MANAGEMENT, DANGEROUS GOODS MANAGEMENT, WASTE MANAGEMENT, OCCUPATIONAL HEALTH, and INDUSTRIAL HYGIENE AND SAFETY.

With its environmental data management, SAP provides an integration of environmental protection into the SAP ERP system. This link enables you to view the entire lifecycle of products, materials, waste, and residual substances in companies. The aspects of product safety, waste and emission management, and safety at work are integrated in the processes of the entire supply chain.

### Hazardous Substances Management

The Hazardous Materials Management subcomponent contains some functions required for companies that use hazardous substances.

### Product Safety

Via the SAP ERP subcomponent Product Safety (see Figure 1.5), you can access functions that are mainly of relevance to companies that produce hazardous substances. You are provided with a hazardous-substance management and environment, health, and safety data system that enables you to manage all environment-relevant information on pure substances, preparations, mixtures, and residual substances in conjunction with the Substances Workbench. This is generally referred to as substance.

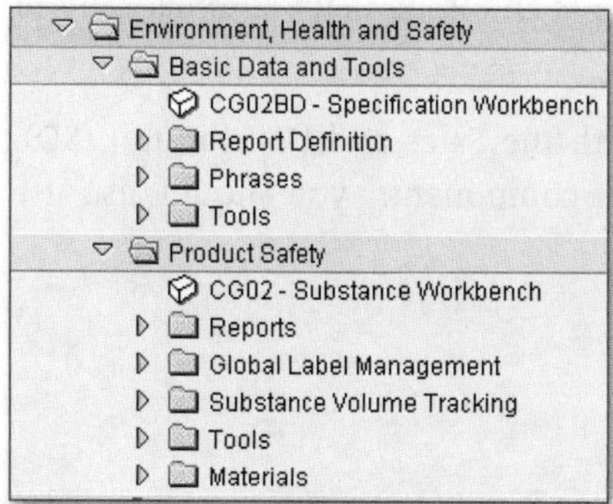


**Figure 1.5** Submenu Product Safety

To manage the data regarding substances, the system provides the following functions:

- **Specification Workbench**
  Data of substances relevant to the environment are managed here, including substance identifications, material assignments, compositions, substance listings, and properties. You can generate the material safety data sheets from the substance database where you can also access phrases.
- **Phrases**
  Standard texts can be managed in catalogs and transferred into reports with little effort.
- **Report**
  An important function of the environment, health, and safety data system is the report. It is generated on the basis of report templates and data from the substance database and can then be managed and automatically dispatched. When creating a report from shipping, it can be supplemented with shipping data. Examples of reports are material safety data sheets, tremcards, labels, and product descriptions. Substance data reports are integrated in document management.

### Dangerous Goods Management

The Dangerous Goods Management subcomponent can do the following:

- Record material data relevant to dangerous goods (dangerous goods master).
- Define dangerous goods checks and execute them in sales and distribution processing.
- Define dangerous goods transport documents and issue them automatically or manually.

Because these subcomponents cooperate with the Sales and Distribution (SD), Materials Management (MM), and SAPscript components, you should also use them in your system.

## 1.6 Laws

In addition to standards, the adherence to which is voluntary in some areas, there are numerous laws and directives. One example is the German Devices and Product Safety Law (GPSG), which came into force on January 5, 2004, and stipulates or intensifies parts of the international quality management standard ISO 9001 with its legal requirements. Let's take a look at one point of the law here: the obligation to execute product observation and to keep a complaints book. This basically corresponds to the requirements for measuring customer satisfaction and recording, analyzing, and evaluating customer complaints under the quality management standard ISO 9001.

Implementing these requirements with SAP ERP is easy because of the quality-notification feature. You can easily analyze and evaluate notifications for customer complaints, and you can record and send actions (see also Chapter 9, Quality Notification).

## 1.7 Outlook

The integration of systems continues to gain momentum. Many companies have already integrated quality-management and environment-management systems, so safety at work and industrial hygiene and safety will follow. In these areas, SAP ERP supports you with some specific subcomponents in EH&S.

With the new guidelines on credit assignment for banks, generally referred to as Basel II, it makes sense to use the existing management system with the help of SAP ERP to generate proof and to enhance it with regard to additional requirements. The same applies to risk management, which is required by many banks, investors, and insurance companies.

Management systems will certainly undergo further development. In ISO 9001 and the EFQM model (European Foundation for Quality Management) for business excellence, the idea of business processes and integrated flows is in the foreground (see Figure 1.6). Because SAP ERP is a process-oriented system, support for these continually developing management systems shouldn't represent any problem in the future.

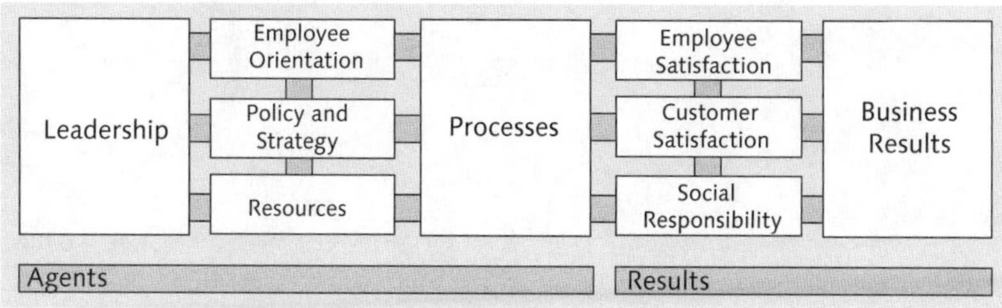


**Figure 1.6** EFQM Model

*Good planning is half the work. Considering this fact, you should take a closer look at the EPC method. This chapter describes how you can model your business processes using this method and how you can plan the implementation in the SAP ERP system.*

# 2 Modeling QM Business Processes Using the EPC Method

The presentation of the business processes using the graphical method of the *event-driven process chain* (EPC) serves as a description and distinction to other processes. This considerably simplifies the mapping in the SAP ERP system while documenting it at the same time.

## 2.1 Basic Principles

At the beginning of an SAP ERP QM project, in addition to the almost unmanageable multiple functionality to be dealt with, core questions always arise concerning each individual business case. Where is the organizational delineation? Who carries out which task with what system support? How are the different SAP ERP components used? How are forms structured? From these questions, another question immediately follows: How can business processes be described, structured, and made visible as simply as possible? You must be able to answer all of these questions clearly to ensure sufficient project stability. In general, a pure textual form – to be meaningful – requires a lot of work and is too time-consuming. A written description of the different contexts is often unclear and difficult to read, and therefore easily becomes merely part of a confusing mass of project documentation.

The solution, which you probably have thought of already, appears quite simple at first glance: You display your scenarios graphically rather than in written form.

On closer consideration, this seemingly simple process actually causes difficulties because each involved person has a different opinion on what is a clear and straightforward graphic. Simply consider the countless flipchart graphics with the equally countless display versions for the same subject, and the different results that can emerge for the same situation!

What, then, is the ideal solution? The ideal solution is a systematic display format that can be easily understood, that is suitable for simple definitions of complex relationships, and that above all stands up to a critical scientific analysis. It may seem like there is no such thing. But take a closer look at the EPC method, and perhaps at the end of this chapter, you will be as dedicated a follower of this method as many of the SAP project team members have become.

## 2.2 Definition of Concepts

Let's first look at the term *business process*.

### 2.2.1 Business Process

The set of standard specifications normally referred to in quality management, such as ISO 9000 and those that follow, QS 9000, or VDA, doesn't provide any clear definition for the concepts *process* or *business process*, although they frequently use these terms. Because we don't need a standardization for all concepts, we take a look at the business process from the business side and then from the technical side. From the business point of view, a process will be considered as a sequential series of actions with identifiable results. A good example of this is quality planning (see Figure 2.1).

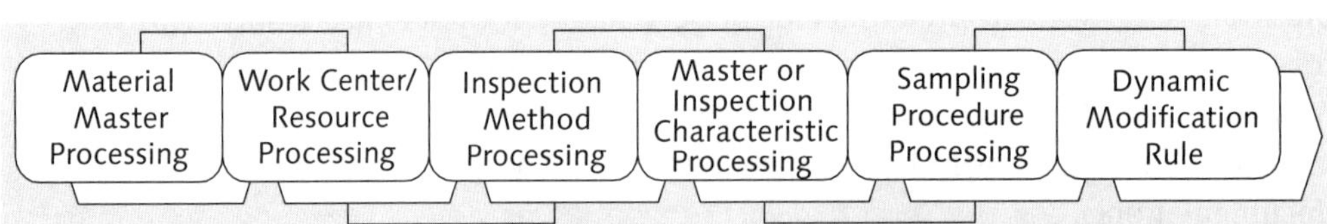


**Figure 2.1** Business Process Quality Planning

From a technical point of view, a process is a procedure that runs in accordance with the laws of chemistry or physics, based on the principle of cause and effect. The industry speaks of process manufacturing if it involves continuous processes. Otherwise, the concept of process in production is used with the business definition, namely that process consists of several sequential actions that result in value being added. When using terminology in a project aimed at producing improvements in a company, the following definitions might be relevant [Keller97].

- A process/business process is a chain of business activities with individual results.
- Different business processes influence each other interactively and trigger other processes.
- Several people or organizational units are involved in one business process.
- Business processes have a defined beginning and a defined end.
- A successful business process must be planned and must coincide with the capabilities of the company.

### Modeling Business Processes

Structuring business processes with the aim of optimizing them has been an issue since the beginnings of industrialization. Formal description and discussion with those involved in the process lead to constant improvement throughout business-process modeling. You can measure the success or failure of a chain of actions by using measurable units. In this context, you can easily draw a comparison to the principle behind quality-assurance systems: Achieving continuous improvement is not possible without continuous process modeling.

In quality management in particular, modeling of existing processes plays a central role when implementing standard software. As quality management is integrated more and more into the supply chain, quality-relevant activities must be integrated more precisely and adjusted to the neighboring processes. This is the only way of ensuring acceptance of total quality management involving the SAP ERP QM.

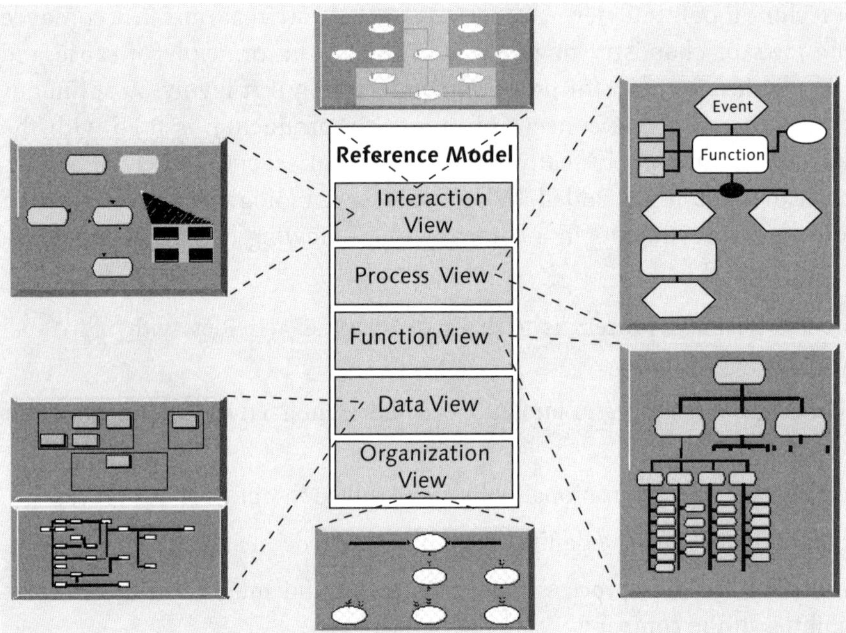


**Figure 2.2** Reference Models

## Business Processes and Reference Models in SAP ERP

Standard business software relies on the representation of generally valid business processes. Based on these processes and process chains, the manufacturer interprets the requirements of the market, which is known from a variety of customer projects. To communicate these experiences and the idea of a business process to the user, SAP provides *reference models* as part of SAP Solution Manager as a knowledge basis (see Figure 2.2 and 2.3). Therefore, we can only advise each project administrator to refer to the reference models stored in the system as a basis for modeling business processes.

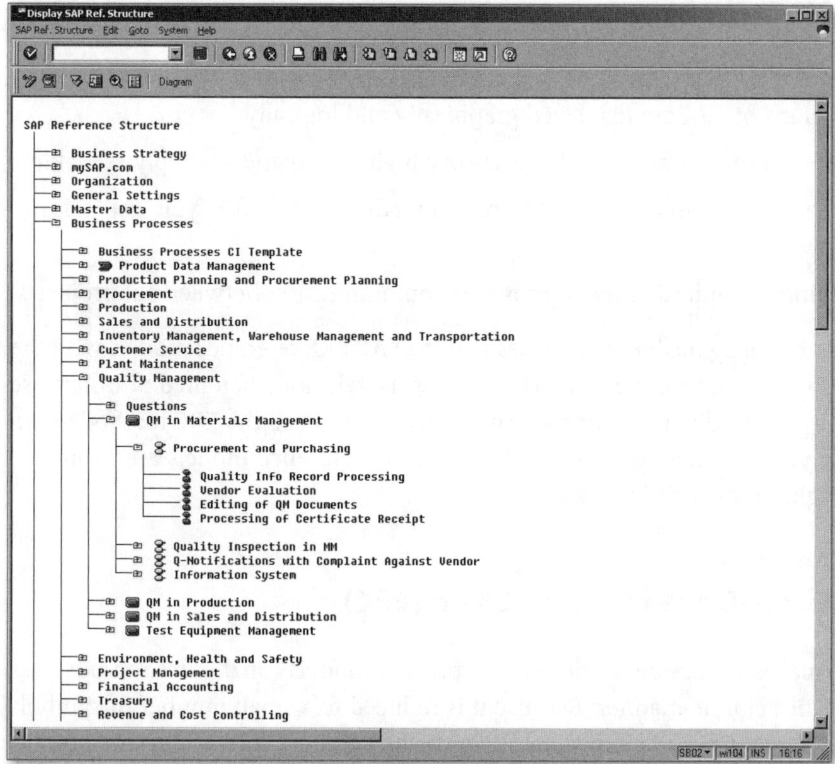

**Figure 2.3** Component View of the SAP Reference Model

All reference models have been designed with the EPC method, which are described in further detail later in this chapter. When setting up your system, you should use the reference models in SAP Solution Manager as an initial solution. It's important to know in this context that process components can be added or left out as necessary. You can call other additional functions in SAP ERP as well as other selection menus from the process-screens view by double-clicking on them. Among these functions are the following:

- The relevant transaction
- Customizing tables
- Data models
- Explanatory texts

The use of reference models has the following benefits for a QM project:

- The standard flow of closely related processes is directly visible.
- The options of QM are displayed graphically and logically.
- The integration character of QM is clearly highlighted and is simply readable.
- You can transfer uncritical processes immediately because you get a faster overview.
- Specifying a standard schema promotes communication between subprojects.

The method to map business processes and the SAP ERP reference models with the EPC is also a development of SAP. The process itself is not a patented or otherwise copyright-protected application, which means you can use the EPC method when modeling your business processes. Of course, all reference models are protected by copyright in the SAP ERP system.

## 2.3 Event-Driven Process Chain (EPC)

The EPC makes it possible to design the process models for the desired business processes in a simple manner. Because it is reduced to a small number of symbols and clear semantics, you can quickly learn the method, and it doesn't present problems to users who are unfamiliar with it. The modeling of processes with the EPC is also particularly suitable for use in team meetings. Especially in the often very lively integration meetings, an accelerated result-oriented work is achieved by focusing on components relevant to inspection.

In sessions with the EPC method, the following questions play a major role:

- When should something be done?
- What should be done?
- Who should do something?
- What information is required to achieve this?

### 2.3.1 Elements of the Event-Driven Process Chain

The elements of the EPC method can be used to map the temporal and logical sequence of a process. The essential elements, events, and functions (actions, tasks) are always presented in chronological sequence, which means that an event is always followed by a function and never by another event. The basic elements of an EPC are easy to describe (see Figure 2.4):

- **Event (hexagon)**
  This basic element describes when a state is to occur. The event is the business state that exists after an operation. This means the event is the central control element within a process. The description of events follows fixed syntactical rules, so that a preceding auxiliary verb is always followed by the perfect participle of the selected verb, such as:
  - Results are recorded.
  - Quality info record is created.
  - Inspection plan is created.
  - Usage decision is made.

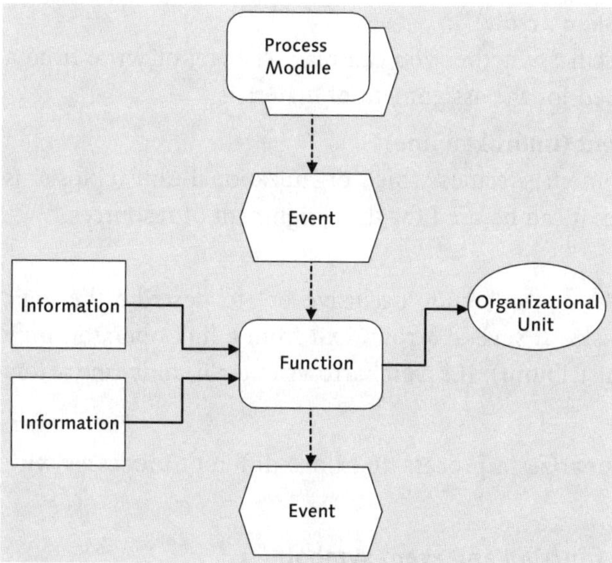


**Figure 2.4** Basic Structure of an EPC

- **Function (rounded rectangle)**
  This element describes what should be done. The function concept describes the operational activity of an employee in a company. For users of a computerized system such as SAP ERP, the function is often the same as a *transaction* in the system.

- **Organizational unit (ellipsis)**
  This element describes who does what. The organizational unit stands for jobs and departments in companies. These can be units assigned according to tasks, objects (market segments, product groups), or processes.
- **Information objects (rectangle)**
  These elements describe which information is necessary to perform the task. Information forms the basis to execute business functions. It is generated in an information system based on specific rules or imported into the system from outside.

The connections between the elements are represented by lines, arrows, and operators:

- **Control flow (dotted arrow pointing downward)**
  The control flow maps the temporal-logical procedure and links the events to the functions.
- **Information flow (unbroken arrow)**
  The information flow specifies whether you can read, change, or write from a function; it can also be used for the assignment of materials.
- **Organizational assignment (unbroken line)**
  The organizational assignment specifies which organizational unit (ellipsis) is responsible for a function; it can be used for the assignment of resources.
- **Link operator (circle)**
  The link operator uses "and," "or," and "exclusive or" to describe the logic between functions and tasks. If several arrows exit from a link operator, only one arrow can enter it (distributor); if several arrows enter it, only one arrow can exit from it (linker).

The following solution summarizes a process and links different processes with each other:

- **Process path (combined function and event symbol)**
  Whereby the function symbol is in the foreground and the event symbol is in the background.

Table 2.1 contains an overview of the symbols used in the EPC method.

| Description | Icon | Definition |
|---|---|---|
| Event | | The event communicates that a business state has occurred that can trigger a function or can be the result of a function. |
| Function | | The function describes the business task for transforming an initial state into a target state. |
| Link operators | XOR ∧ ∨ | The link operator describes the logical connections between events and functions. |
| Control flow | | The control flow describes the temporal-logical dependencies of events and functions. |
| Process path | | The process path displays the connection from a process or to a process (navigation help). |
| System organizational unit | | A system organizational unit describes an organizational unit of the SAP ERP system that enables the mapping of organizational units and structures of the company in the SAP ERP system. |
| Information object | | An information object is a mapping of a real-life object (e.g., business object, entity). |
| Information flow | | Information flows display the data flow between two functions. |
| Assignment of system organizational units | | This assignment describes which organizational unit of the SAP ERP system is required for the execution of a process or function. |

**Table 2.1** Symbols of the EPC

### 2.3.2 Structure of the Event-Driven Process Chain

You can describe complex models on different hierarchical levels with elements of the EPC. An EPC on the lower level is referred to as a process module and contains the functions, the events, the information flow, and the organizational unit. The EPC always begins with an event or a process path and ends with an event or a process path. A process path can contain one or more process modules and thus forms the upper level. EPCs that consist only of process paths, and thus individual process modules, are described as scenarios (the term *scenario EPC* is also used). Process detailing can occur at each of the hierarchy levels. A fully structured EPC contains all of the elements occurring in the syntax.

However, the term *lean EPC* is also used for describing an EPC. Here, you can initially make do without the information flow and the organizational unit. The *lean EPC* consists only of functions and events to which control flow arrows and link operators have been applied. In an even simpler form, the link operators can be omitted from the first step. This form is particularly suitable for sketching models during a workshop or for a consistency check of an operation in the SAP ERP system at the prototype stage.

The formal structure corresponds to a graph-based model made of nodes and edges. Operational methods such as graph grammars or declarative methods with specific languages for graphs are suitable for a scientific description of the syntax. A detailed description of these, however, would go beyond the scope of this book. For the current purposes, the description of the process for creating an EPC on the basis of examples is sufficient. For this reason, an EPC is created for a process module that involves an in-process inspection on a step-by-step basis.

### 2.3.3 Scenario

The following example involves simple inspection-lot processing in a production environment with discrete manufacturing. Goods are produced in lots for individual job orders. A lot-based inspection at the end of each production step is intended to ensure the quality of the goods. The inspection plan is fully integrated in the routing and contains all required information (inspection characteristics, process control) for results recording. If a defect is detected, a quality notification is generated from results recording. The inspection-lot processing ends with the usage decision (inspection-lot completion). The quantity feedback from production takes place via the feedback transaction in the SAP ERP Production Planning module (PP).

#### Step 1

Initially, it is useful to consider all process modules involved in inspection-lot processing in the SAP ERP reference model (see Figure 2.5).

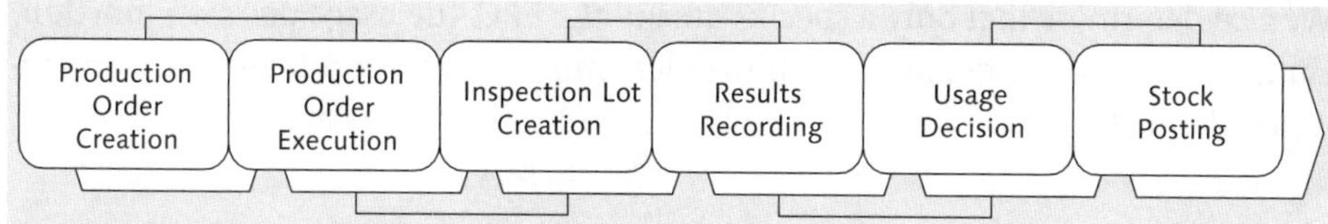


**Figure 2.5** Process Modules for Inspection-Lot Processing

There are two methods available for creating the EPC. Method 1 requires a tool with changeable reference models (ARIS Toolset from IDS Scheer AG or IPW from Intellicorp). You simply use the existing reference model and change it according to your needs (see Figure 2.6). In Method 2, you use a normal drawing program (VISIO, CorelDraw, etc.) to create the required symbols on your own. For the sake of simplicity, let's assume that you use Method 2.

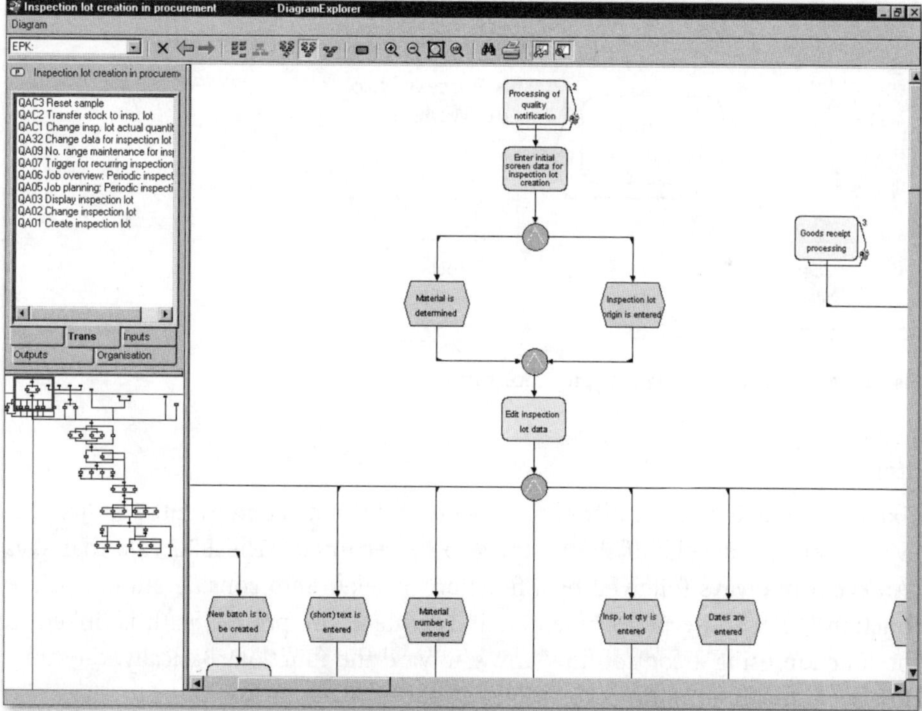


**Figure 2.6** Reference Model for Inspection-Lot Creation

We also determine that only a specific area of the EPC, the usage decision function, contains a particular detailing with the elements "information flow" and "organizational unit."

### Step 2

To begin with, the scope of the process module to be depicted is limited. The incoming process path is placed at the beginning of the EPC (see Figure 2.7); the process paths that end the process module are placed at the end of the EPC. A glance at the reference process module in the SAP ERP system then shows the potential of the individual functions.

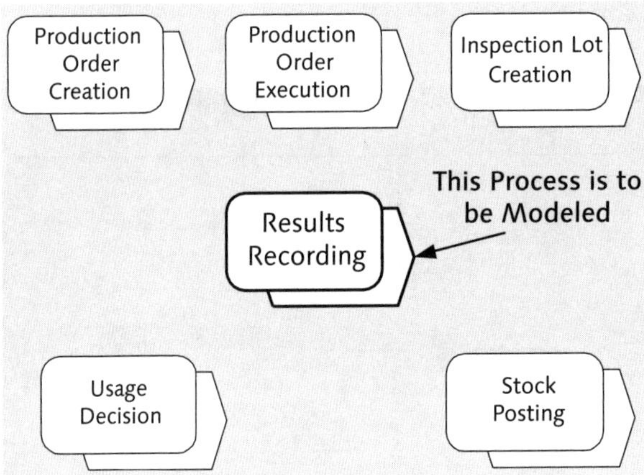


**Figure 2.7** Start of Modeling with the Process Paths

### Step 3

You start modeling at the incoming process paths and set an event. The first relevant event is "Results of the samples to be recorded." The EPC rule that says "An event is always followed by a function" is taken into consideration, and the function "Selection type to be entered" is edited. The process path is linked to the function using a control flow arrow toward the function. Basically, the function provides three options for selecting the inspection lot: You can enter the inspection lot directly, select it using a selection list, or use the report "Worklist for results recording." You must then structure the EPC in a way that allows both functions "Enter Inspection Lot" and "Enter Additional Selection Criterion" to be executed in parallel (see Figure 2.8). The link is effected by means of the function operator "AND." Because you can alternatively select the inspection lot via the worklist for results recording, this path in turn must be linked with the operator "XOR" (exclusive or).

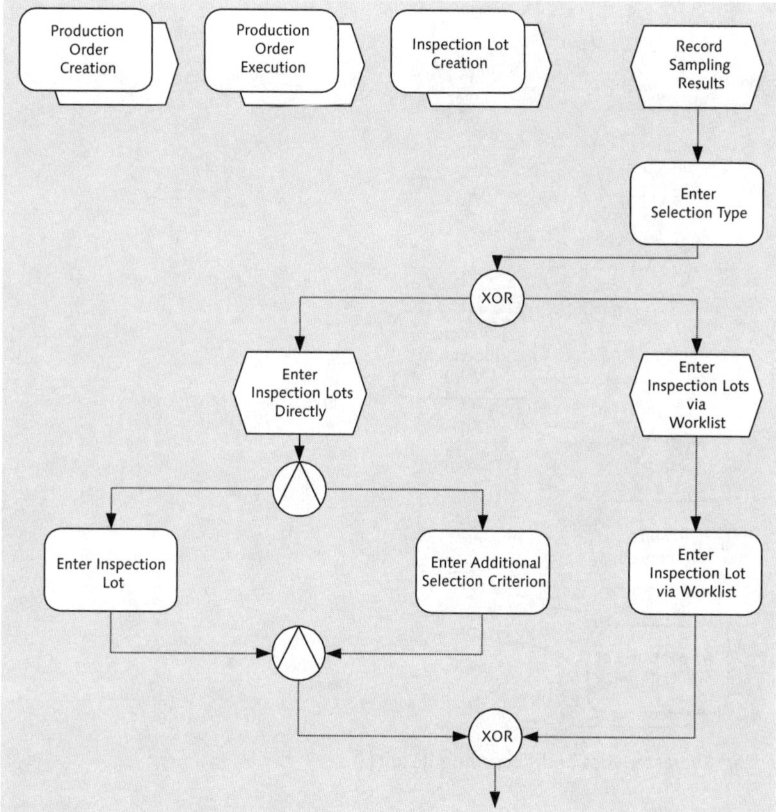


**Figure 2.8** Selecting Inspection Lots

## Step 4

In the next step, you model the process up to the next process path "Inspection Lot Completion," showing the individual steps of results recording in a slightly simplified form (see Figure 2.9).

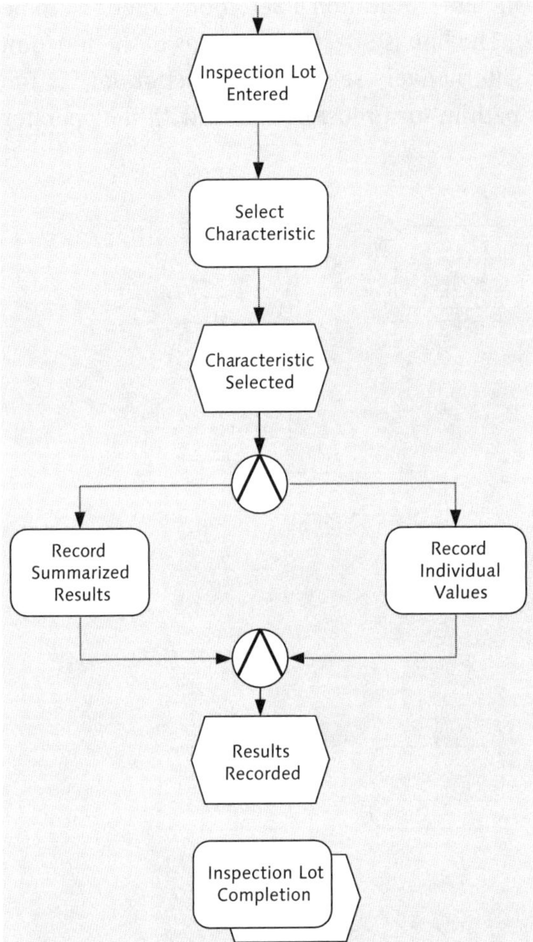


**Figure 2.9** Selecting Characteristics and Recording Results

### Step 5

Let's take a quick look at the possibility of results recording that includes defects recording. *Defects recording* refers to a particular version of the QM module in inspection planning. If a defect is found (characteristic evaluation "rejection"), a defect data record in the form of a quality notification is created automatically. You can then edit the quality notification and use additional functions to send it as an email.

With the subsequent defect recording, you can also depict the process around "Results Recorded" as shown in Figure 2.10.

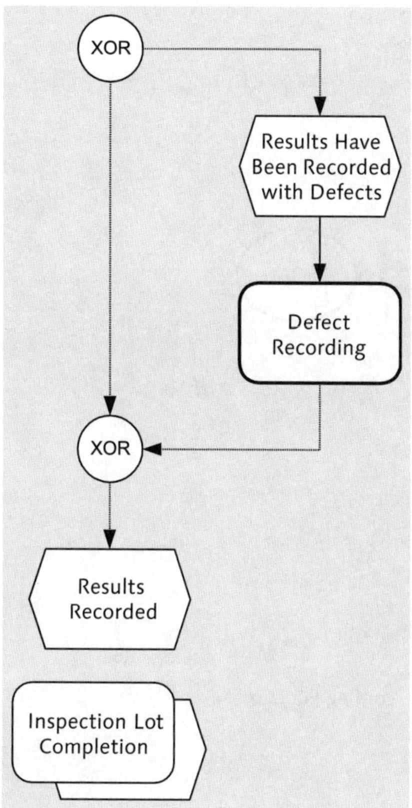


**Figure 2.10** Recording Defects for the Result

### Step 6

The process is now structured and contains all necessary process modules for describing the inspection lot selection with subsequent results recording. Still missing are IT-related and organizational assignments of the functions. These will be demonstrated by using the function for defect recording as an example. There, you can see the data flow for the automatic functions "Create Quality Notification" and "Send Email" as well as the organizational assignment to the "Quality Management" department.

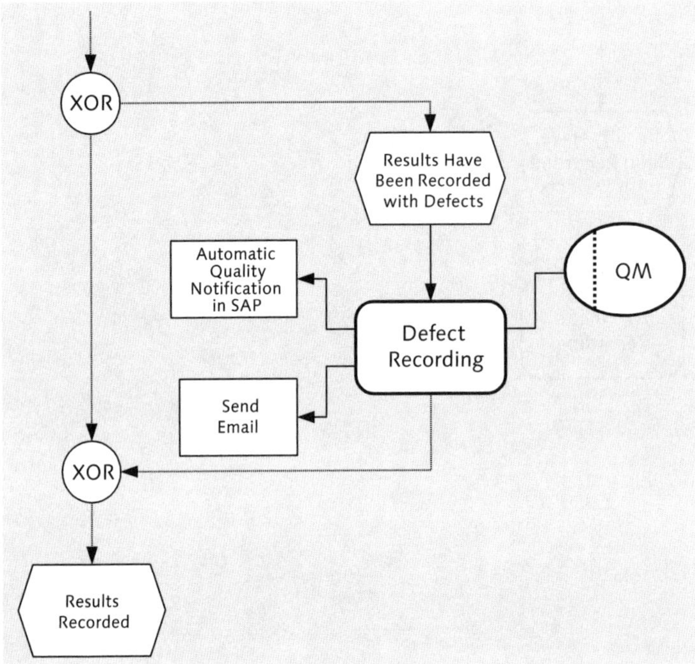


**Figure 2.11** Organizational Assignment of the Defect Recording Function

### Organizational Units

When implementing an SAP ERP system, you must pay special attention to the organizational units (see Figure 2.11). In many cases, the forms, documents, and other data media for information objects in their current state can be omitted. Information can be replaced with the corresponding data structures of the SAP ERP system, which can be edited consistently across process borders. By mapping functions and their organizational assignment together, you can create the basis for authorization in the SAP ERP system.

You always complete the EPC with an event, in this case "Events Recorded." This way you can reach a state that allows the linking to another process module. With the EPC, you now have a roadmap for process prototyping in SAP ERP.

Depending on the level of detailing, such an EPC can almost completely replace a verbal description of the business process, the data streams involved, and the organizational assignment. Furthermore, the EPC is a multi-purposed schedule for use in the following areas:

- Project documentation
- Process visualization
- Process instructions
- Interface maintenance of subprojects

**Advantages at a Glance**

The advantages of using the EPC method are listed here:

- The EPC method of mapping business processes is easy to learn.
- Difficult issues can be laid out clearly.
- Changes to the process, in contrast to prosaic descriptions, can be simply mapped.
- The EPC method is equally beneficial for users and consultants.
- EPC mappings in an implementation project promote cross-department communication.
- Working with the EPC is the best foundation for an implementation with ASAP.
- The step from business process to Customizing is much easier using the reference model.

*This chapter provides an overview of SAP AG and the development of SAP software as well as its releases up to the latest developments. This is followed by the basic information about the Quality Management module and recommendations for implementation projects.*

# 3 Overview of SAP ERP

In addition to important overview information, you get an insight into the concept and some parts of the SAP ERP system that are associated with an implementation project. For total comprehension, this is not only useful but also indispensable.

## 3.1 SAP AG

SAP GmbH ("Systeme, Anwendungen und Produkte in der Datenverarbeitung," or Systems, Applications and Products in Data Processing) was founded in 1976. It replaced the partnership "Systemanalyse Programmentwicklung" (System Analysis Program Development) that had been formed in 1972. The five former IBM employees Dietmar Hopp, Hans-Werner Hector, Hasso Plattner, Klaus Tschira, and Claus Wellenreuther laid the basis of today's corporate software group. In 1988, SAP GmbH was transformed into a public company and listed on the stock exchange as SAP AG. Since 1998, it has been one of the 30 stocks used to calculate the important German stock market index DAX. In 2007, SAP achieved sales revenue of more than $14 billion (10.2 billion Euro), with approximately 44,000 employees worldwide.

## 3.2 Development of SAP ERP

The first standard software developed by SAP was the "System R" in 1973. R stands for real time, signifying that the data input is processed immediately. This set the SAP software apart from the usual batch-processing programs, in which the data had to be entered first and then processed in batches (usually overnight). The results were often only available the next day in the form of computer lists.

The next software from SAP was System R/2, which was developed from 1978 onward. It is mainly used in very large companies and corporate groups. The essential difference of the R/3 program package (developed from 1987 onward) lies in the fact that System R/2 was designed for use on a central host computer with terminals, whereas System R/3 uses so-called client-server technology. In a client-server system, although the main part of the software runs on the central host (server), certain dialog functions, above all the graphical user interface (GUI), are sourced out to intelligent workstations (clients, personal computers). From around 1992 onward, the R/3 system was the driving factor behind the company's breakthrough on the world market.

For a long time, the client was accessed exclusively through SAP GUI. Around 1996, use of the Internet Transaction Server (ITS) and a SAP GUI for HTML made client access via the Internet possible. Between 1999 and 2002, within the scope of a mySAP.com initiative, the Internet functionality was further advanced with features such as XML support and SAP Web Application Server (WAS, since renamed SAP NetWeaver Application Server) for a global exchange of company data up to the integration of Java technology. Since 2005, SAP ERP has been delivered, in which the core functions of R/3 are retained as SAP ERP Central Component (ECC) and are supplemented and enhanced with SAP Business Solutions.

SAP NetWeaver Portal constitutes the full integration with web-based technologies. Combined ABAP Java programming allows for direct access to SAP business logic with browser-based applications. A combination with external data within such an application provides a homogenous environment to the users in which they can fulfill their tasks without having to switch programs. Despite all of these innovations, the user interfaces in the logistics modules are hardly affected by this development. All core components of logistics and the customer-specific enhancements are still retained in SAP GUI without any disadvantages concerning the web technology.

## 3.3 Modules of the SAP ERP System

SAP ERP is designed like a module kit. The central database and the Basis Components (BC) are surrounded by components (also referred to as modules). The SAP

ERP purchaser can choose one of several databases (Oracle, DB/2, Microsoft SQL Server, etc.) and select the modules (components) to be used. Many companies start with Financial Accounting (FI) and Controlling (CO) and later expand their system to Materials Management (MM) and Quality Management (QM). However, if the complete data-processing system of a company is to be changed, you need to implement most of the modules from the beginning.

In addition, you can choose from a wide range of operating systems for the SAP ERP system. There is, for example, a choice among different UNIX derivatives, Linux, Windows versions, and OS/400.

**Tip**

The SAP ERP software has always made full use of all available hardware potential. For this reason, a thorough planning of the IT structure in your company is of special importance. It is no coincidence that there are many jokes regarding the interpretation of the abbreviation SAP, for example, "Search, Activate, Pause" or "Slow Application Program." Always choose cutting-edge hardware components with good performance specifications; otherwise, anticipated savings can turn out to be very costly to achieve in reality!

In addition to the modules, let's take a quick look at the "solutions" provided by SAP. The basic functions and components of the system can be found at the SAP ECC. New functions and system enhancements are added by means of extensions and solutions such as SAP Product Lifecycle Management (SAP PLM).

Although this book only deals with the QM module, it is an advantage to know at least the names of other modules. Abbreviations for modules (in SAP terminology components) are derived from their English names, which is why these are also indicated in Table 3.1.

As you can see from the structure of the chapters, the QM module is not to be seen as an isolated unit. It is closely integrated with other modules. When we talk of quality management in Materials Management, of quality management in Production, and of quality management in Sales and Distribution, we are referring to the applications and close links with the Materials Management (MM), Production (PP), and Sales and Distribution (SD) modules. This is supplemented by links to Controlling (CO) and integration of test equipment management through the Test Equipment Management module (EXM, previously PM). Shared functions of Basic

Components (BC), the different information systems (IS), and, if required, the SAP Business Workflows (WF) are also used.

| Component | English name |
|---|---|
| **General components** | |
| BC | Basic Components |
| CA | Cross-Application Components |
| AC | Accounting – General |
| **Accounting** | |
| FI | Financial Accounting |
| FSCM | Financial Supply Chain Management |
| TR | Treasury |
| CO | Controlling |
| IM | Investment Management |
| ICM | Incentive and Commission Management |
| EC | Enterprise Controlling |
| RE-FX | Real Estate Management |
| **Logistics** | |
| LO | Logistics – General |
| PLM | Product Lifecycle Management |
| SD | Sales and Distribution |
| MM | Materials Management |
| LE | Logistics Execution |
| QM | Quality Management |
| EAM | Enterprise Asset Management (Plant Maintenance) |
| CS | Customer Service |
| PP | Production Planning and Control |
| PS | Project System |
| EHS | Environment, Health and Safety |

**Table 3.1** Names of the SAP Components

| Component | English name |
| --- | --- |
| **Human Resources Management** | |
| HCM | Human Capital Management |
| HR | Human Resources |
| PT | Personnel Time Management |
| PY | Payroll |
| PE | Training and Event Management |

**Table 3.1** Names of the SAP Components (Cont.)

For a better understanding, the next section briefly explains the basic functions of the three modules that are particularly closely related to QM.

### Materials Management (MM)

This module builds the core of the logistic functions. It maps the business process "Materials Management" from requirements planning through procurement to warehousing and storage of goods.

The material master data is stored in a database and can be supplemented with different additional information (material views) after creating the basic data. One of these additional information items is the Quality Management view that determines if a material is, for example, relevant to quality regarding procurement or inspection. The entire procurement process with vendor data and terms of delivery belongs as much to MM as do receipt and warehouse management. Each goods movement takes place as a specific transaction type to which subsequent functions or conditions can be linked. Particularly with regard to transaction type and stock type (unrestricted-use stock, inspection stock, blocked stock), the interaction with QM is very close. Quality-relevant elements such as vendor selection, vendor evaluation, delivery release, or requirements regarding the vendors' quality-management system are assigned to QM in MM because both modules are closely interlocked here.

### Production Planning and Control (PP)

Production Planning and Control (PP) as well as MM are assigned to the application area "logistics." This area provides comprehensive functions for quantity and capacity planning and control of production in different industries. These functions include the following:

- Master data management
- Production planning
- Shop floor control
- Special production methods, including lot, series, and Kanban manufacturing

The PP-PI component (Production Planning–Processing Industry) was specifically tailored to the requirements of the processing industry (chemicals, pharmaceutics, food). You can use this component to manage substances, samples, batches, recipes, and resources.

QM is also closely related with this module. Inspection planning is based on routings, inspection lots can be triggered by production orders, and inspection equipment can be assigned individual work steps as production resources. Quality management involves the planning and execution of in-process inspections and inspections at the end of production, using elements and functions from the QM module.

#### Sales and Distribution (SD)

The Sales and Distribution (SD) module provides the master data (available for virtually every module) and the functions "Sales," "Shipping," "Invoicing," and "Foreign Trade."

The Sales function involves the processing of inquiries and the creation of quotations and order documents with the usual pricing details. Other tasks include specifying the partners involved (besides the selling company, primarily the customer), recording product and service details, indicating price and delivery date, and creating forms (quotation or order confirmation).

For shipping, a powerful tool is available for monitoring deadlines of existing orders. Product availability and creation of the usual shipping forms such as stock notes and delivery notes are taken into account when setting up and handling deliveries. QM comes into play here as well because it can create inspection lots upon goods issue and is responsible for drawing up inspection certificates. Upon completion of delivery, material stocks are updated with regard to value and quantities.

Order handling is concluded with invoicing. Information regarding outstanding debits is passed on to accounts receivable accounting, and invoices are created. Credit and debit memos can be processed, and delivery invoices can be grouped or split up.

For international trade, the Sales and Distribution (SD) module provides different useful functions that are required, including accordingly maintained master data for import and export handling and support for the corresponding documents, such as movement certificate, customs invoice, or the MITI commercial document for Japan.

This way, QM in SD regulates goods-issue inspection as well as inspection certificates related to a delivery. Furthermore, it supports the processing of customer complaints through a specific type of quality notification.

## 3.4 SAP R/3 and SAP ERP Releases

Like any other software, SAP software undergoes continuous development. In SAP terminology, the different software versions are referred to as *releases*.

### General Information on the SAP Releases

Explanations in this updated edition are largely based on SAP ERP Release 6.0; whereas examples and screenshots for the most part have been created with the IDES test system. All the same, most of the information provided is also valid for users of previous SAP R/3 versions 4.0 to 4.7 because many of the functions and options described are available (exactly as explained or in similar form) for all versions up to SAP ERP. In the course of the release upgrade, the SAP ERP logistic core functions, which include QM, were combined in SAP ECC .

If a new version is installed within an SAP R/3 or SAP ERP system, this is referred to as a *release change*. As a general rule, customized settings can be transferred to the new release. New, additionally settings may have to be configured as necessary. You should expect difficulties when specific customer programs have been created or special adjustments have been performed that were not intended in the standard system. In many cases, these need to be revised during a release change.

**Tip**

To achieve a smooth release change, you should avoid non-SAP modifications if possible. For customer-specific enhancements, there are numerous user exits and BAdIs available. Ways to use these BAdIs are explained in the following sections.

### Functional Enhancements and Changes in the QM Module

You can see the exact changes to your R/3 or SAP ERP version through the menu item HELP • RELEASE NOTES. Subsequently, you will find a short history of the most important changes in the area of quality management.

#### R/3 Release 4.0

As of R/3 Release 4.0, the following improvements were available:

- Digital signatures
- Differentiation between manufacturers and vendors (important when making procurements through distributors)
- Quality inspection for external processing under production order (important for extended workbench or job processing)
- Mass change of inspection data
- Improvements in the area of certificate receipt and certificate creation
- New functions for sample management
- Changes to sample due to new inspection specifications
- Histogram and run chart for results recording and evaluation of characteristics
- New quality control charts (np, p, c chart, etc.)
- Interface to external statistical systems (QM-STI)
- Improvements in link-up to the Quality Management Information System (QMIS)
- Test equipment management with calibration planning, orders, inspections, and usage decisions

### R/3 Release 4.5

With R/3 Release 4.5, the following functions have been improved or added:

- Manual inspection lot for physical sampling
- Inspection specification based on batch determination
- Batch input for inspection characteristics
- Defect recording through data interface (QM-IDI)
- Specification of preferred inspection type
- Evaluation or deletion of quality level
- Control charts and results history for test equipment management

The main focus of Release 4.6 was on improving the user interface and more closely integrating functions. Some functional enhancements were introduced.

### R/3 Release 4.6

SAP Easy Access and EnjoySAP are umbrella terms for numerous improvements to the user interface in R/3 Release 4.6. In addition to a redesigned menu structure in the form of a vertically orientated menu tree, noteworthy changes include the increased use of buttons and icons as well as the enhanced tab technology, the user-specific menu selection, the favorites list, and the introduction of user roles. The user roles provide the QM employees with direct access to specific menu trees for their activities. User roles are intended for users such as inspection planners, quality inspectors, notification processors, and test equipment administrators.

Other new functions of R/3 Release 4.6 include the following:

- Integrated maintenance of documents in the quality info record
- Reduced number of data entry views in results recording
- New graphic technology for control charts, histograms, and run charts
- Electronic receipt and issue of certificates
- Solution database for quality notifications

The users of previous R/3 versions (before release 4.6) adapt to the new display very quickly because the changes to the interface are not extensive, and menu paths have for the most part remained the same.

The differences between R/3 Release 4.0 and 4.6/4.7 are shown from the following examples: In Figures 3.1 and 3.2, you can see the search help for a material number in Release 4.0. First, the type of search (in this case MATERIAL BY DESCRIPTION) is selected, and the short description is entered in the entry window that follows.

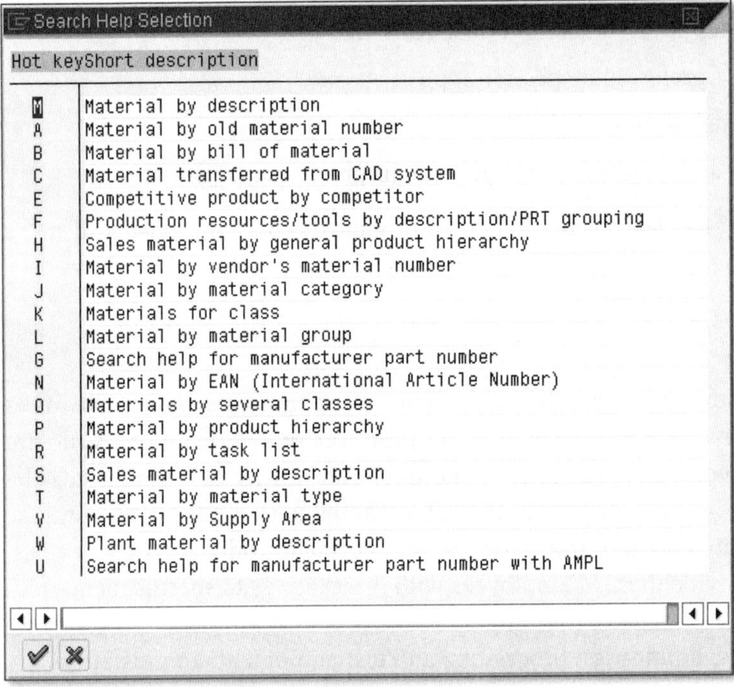


**Figure 3.1** Search Help Selection in SAP R/3 Release 4.0

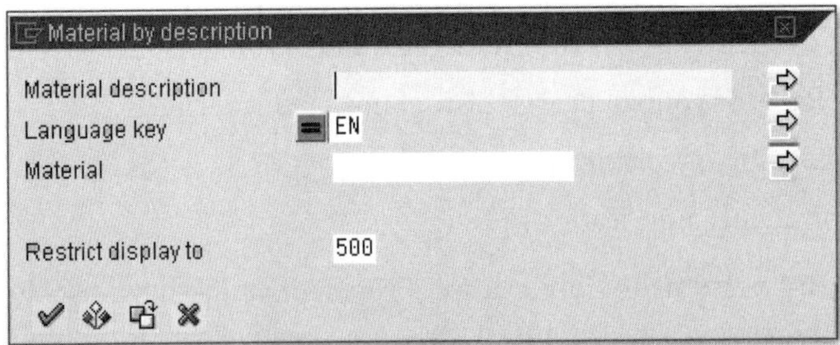


**Figure 3.2** Search with "Material by Description" in SAP R/3 Release 4.0

In R/3 Release 4.6/4.7, a kind of index with tabs appears (see Figure 3.3). Each type of search corresponds to a tab. The search is carried out in the same window as the selection of the tab.

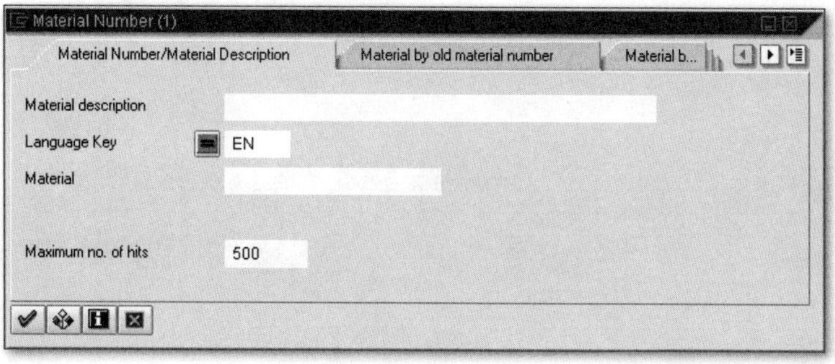

Material Number (1)
Material Number/Material Description | Material by old material number | Material b...
Material description
Language Key EN
Material
Maximum no. of hits 500

**Figure 3.3** Search with "Material by Description" from SAP R/3 Release 4.6 onward

You can see other variants in Figures 3.4 and 3.5. In the RECORD USAGE DECISION screen, toggling the partial views CHARACTERISTICS and STOCKS is implemented in Release 4.0 through a button in the display. From Version 4.6 onward, tabs are used for display. The DEFECTS tab is shown immediately in Release 4.6/4.7, whereas the DEFECTS button in 4.0 only appears after having recorded defects.

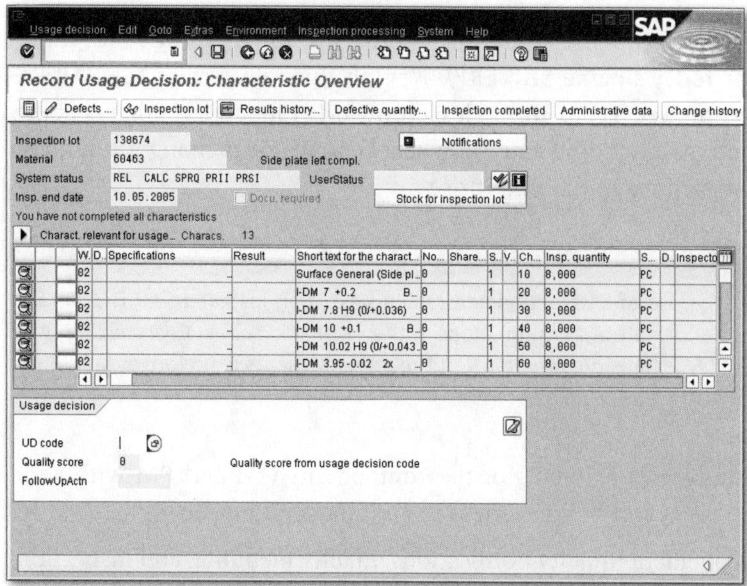


**Figure 3.4** Record Usage Decision Screen in SAP R/3 Release 4.0

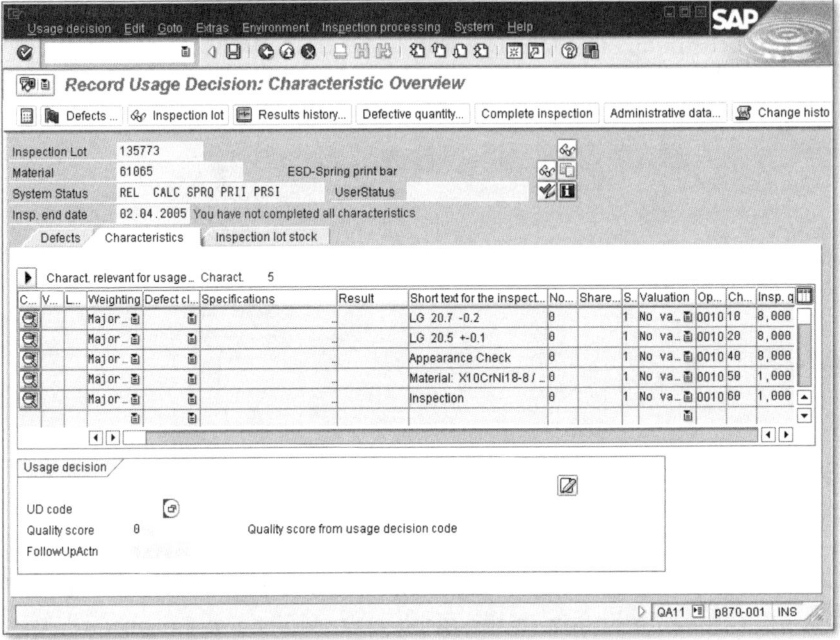


**Figure 3.5** Record Usage Decision from SAP R/3 Release 4.6 Onward

## R/3 Release 4.7

From SAP R/3 Release 4.7, SAP called its system SAP R/3 Enterprise (as a preliminary stage for today's name SAP ERP). New in this release was the SAP R/3 Enterprise Extension Set. From this release onward, functional enhancements were implemented mainly in the extension sets area, whereas changes often also affected the core functions in the Enterprise Core.

> **Note**
>
> A prerequisite for the use of all functions described next is an installed SAP R/3 Enterprise system and the lockout of PLM functions in the extension set via Customizing. After activating the PLM extension, a rollback of the enhancements is no longer possible.

- **Stability study**

  The stability study uses elements of the components QM and PM with additional enhancements and bundles these to an integrated business process.

  - Quality Management (quality notifications, quality planning, and inspection-lot processing)

  - Asset Lifecycle Management (within the area Plant Maintenance, maintenance planning, and scheduling)
  - Materials Management (material master, batch management, and bill of material [BOM])

  The stability study is used to take physical samples at storage conditions and to inspect and manage samples throughout the entire duration of the study at defined points. During these process phases, you can do the following:

  - Flexibly control all process steps in an integrated environment.
  - Make use of the structure of the stability study (mapped by a quality notification), which provides you with multiple tools to perform all necessary activities and process steps during the stability study.
  - Enhance or adjust all process steps in accordance to the needs of your company.
  - Trigger the individual process steps by using the action box in the quality notification.
  - Retrieve a transparent overview of all objects of the study (as recommended in the guidelines according to GMP and FDA).
  - Permanently monitor the process progress.

- **Flexible inspection specifications**
  Flexible inspection specifications allow you to influence inspection specifications, both for inspection-lot creation and within results recording by the following:

  - Flexible specifications selection
  - Flexible specifications amendments

  This function is used if inspections cannot be completely preplanned, for instance:

  - When inspection is a service
  - Inspection of complaints
  - Inspection within the scope of stability studies

The familiar functions for inspection planning remain valid. As with the existing inspection-lot generation, the task list is assigned when inspection lots are generated, and all inspection characteristics are provided in the form of a maximum task list. The selection of relevant characteristics takes place via the transaction "flexible inspection specifications."

The flexible inspection specifications function is first supplied for manual inspection lots for the stability study: You can influence the specifications for lot creation by means of appropriate activities for the study. With a few adjustments (described in the release notes), this function also can be used for other inspection lot origins.

A range of new Business Add-Ins (BAdIs) allows you to implement functional enhancements without modifications. You will find these BAdIs in Customizing under QUALITY MANAGEMENT • ENVIRONMENT • TOOLS • BUSINESS ADD-INS.

- **Enhancements (BAdIs) in Quality Planning**
  - In the engineering workbench, you can maintain customer-specific fields for the inspection plan at the characteristic, operation, and header levels.
  - When saving the inspection plan in the engineering workbench, all plan data on a BAdI is provided.
  - The overview screen in the engineering workbench allows the definition of an additional button for starting your own programs at the characteristic, operation, and header levels.
- **Enhancements (BAdIs) in Quality Inspection**
  - BAdIs support the flexible specifications selection.
  - You can display any data in the inspection lot through additional subscreen areas and change inspection-lot data of the structure QALS_ADDON.
  - Depending on the screen-control key of the sample type, you can activate an additional tab in the physical-sample records transactions.
  - In results recording, a subscreen of the header allows you to display additional data.
  - In a subscreen of the usage decision header, you can display additional data.
  - When saving data in results recording, all inspection-lot data is provided in a BAdI.
  - You can program your own rules for evaluating characteristics and original values.

- **Enhancements (BadIs) in the Quality Certificate**
  - Along with characteristics, you can maintain additional customer-specific fields in the certification template.
  - You can change certification-characteristics data while transferring these into the certification template.
- **Enhancements (BAdIs) in Logistics**
  - In procurement, the criteria to assign quality info records can be influenced.
  - You can replace the monitoring of the required QM system in the procurement process through a specific program.
- **Enhancements (BAdIs) in Quality Notification**
  - At save time, you can make changes to the notification data.
  - You can influence the display and activity of follow-up actions with the action box.
  - Depending on the notification type, you can implement the free reference object screen according to your needs.
  - The document flow chart for quality notification allows you to replace the node attribute of an object. This way, you can display the inspection-lot short text for objects such as "inspection lot" as an attribute. Using the BAdI, you can determine for each notification type if a user status can be changed.
- **New Developments in SAP R/3 Enterprise Core 4.70**
  - The input processing for measured values allows you to control the processing of the measured values.
  - A range of new BAdIs permits the implementation of functional enhancements without modifications.
  - Depending on the notification type, you can now integrate one or several customer subscreens in the notification header.
- **Enhancements in Handling Units**
  - The inspection-lot generation for goods movements of handling units (units of load carrier and the material on these) occurs automatically.
  - You can now specify whether in the case of partial deliveries a specific inspection lot is to be created for each delivery or whether all deliveries are assigned to the first inspection lot.

- **Enhancements in Usage Decision**
  A new BAdI enables you to enter alternative quantity units in the usage decision.
- **Results Copies**
  You can apply characteristic values from earlier inspection lots during inspection-lot processing.

### ERP Release 2004

As of this release change, the name of the system changes once again from SAP R/3 Enterprise to SAP ERP. The release notes for quality management as a component in SAP ERP Central Component (ECC 5.0) provide the following innovations:

- Archiving of physical samples in the sample management
- Expansion of the sample management in the master record by:
  - Withdrawal location
  - Information on the withdrawal location
  - Processor
  - Date of withdrawal
  - Time of withdrawal
- Stability studies within the framework of trial management

### ERP Release 6.0

From this release onward, the following functions have been added or enhanced:

- Objects are integrated with the SAP search engine TREX.
- The quality inspector role is available in the portal.
- Communication occurs with the quality inspection engine of SAP or other quality management systems.
- Structure changes in the IMG of quality management IMG activities have been reassigned and new ones have been added.
- Multiple specifications: Additional information about the suitability or approval of goods depending on various objects, such as country, customer, dispensatory, and so on. It is possible to expand existing inspection plans.

- General QM evaluations: The results recording and quality control include improved evaluation options, for example, comparison of inspection results based on different characteristics or evaluation of current and archived data.
- The process completion is enhanced by an evaluation, including follow-up actions.

## 3.5 SAP PLM and Quality Management

The QM module has been integrated as a solution component into SAP PLM (Product Lifecycle Management), where SAP PLM in turn represents a part of the SAP Business Suite. The entire lifecycle of a product is supported companywide with SAP PLM, from development through production to maintenance. The solution components support product innovations and development, engineering, compliance with regulatory obligations, quality, and maintenance management. SAP PLM enables companies to bring their products to the market — at the right time and at lowest possible costs — and to process and provide consistent information on the product and related processes.

Collaboration across company boundaries is made possible through additional Internet-based technologies and mobile applications. Nonetheless, the QM module remains a component of the "classical" SAP ERP system. SAP PLM enhancements ensure the availability of web-based and other functional enhancements. However, these must be activated separately through the Enterprise Extension Set. Examples are Audit Management and stability studies. The solution map in Figure 3.6 shows the structure of the SAP PLM solution.

| | | | | | | | |
|---|---|---|---|---|---|---|---|
| Lifecycle Data Management | Document Management | Product Structure Management | Recipe Management | Integration | Engineering Change and Configuration Management | | |
| Enterprise Asset Management | Technical Assets Management | Preventive and Corrective Maintenance | Maintenance Processing | Work Clearance Management | | | |
| Program and Project Management | Project Planning | Project Execution | Interfaces | Program Management | | | |
| Lifecycle Collaboration and Analytics | Design Collaboration | Collaborative Project Management | Quality Collaboration | Analytics | Enterprise Portal Content | | |
| Quality Management | Audit Management | Quality Assurance | Quality Improvement | | | | |
| Environment, Health and Safety | Basic Data and Tools | Product Safety | Hazardous Substance Management | Dangerous Goods Management | Waste Management | Industrial Hygiene and Safety | Occupational Health |

**Figure 3.6** Solution Map of the SAP PLM Solution

## 3.6 Project Management for SAP ERP Implementations

This section does not describe project management in complete detail and is not intended to replace the usually necessary support of an outside consulting company. This section is intended to give a rough overview of what has to be considered when managing an SAP ERP implementation project and what has been proven successful in practice. In this context, specific characteristics of the implementation of the QM module are discussed. There are many ways to achieve the goals defined, and a different approach could be equally successful.

Whether you implement the SAP ERP system with all or only a few of its modules or implement the QM module later, a well planned and well organized project management is indispensable. You should not underestimate the scope and complexity of such an implementation and the effort involved. Depending on the industry and company, the implementation of SAP ERP is the largest or one of the largest IT projects that a company must face. In this context, the internal and external deployment of personnel and know-how as well as the commitment of all those involved is as important as strong financial support. Implementation of the new software can mean extensive changes to the entire IT structure: networks (LAN and WAN), repeaters, workstations, and operating systems, including larger monitors and new workstations.

At project kick-off, you need to decide whether the implementation should be performed with or without external support. We highly recommend *external support*, regardless of type and number of modules to be implemented. Even if the internal IT staff or the affected department possesses a lot of know-how, an implementation fully performed by internal personnel is likely to fail.

If you share the view that external support is essential for the project's success, you face the issue of which partner to choose. Many companies offer consulting services related to SAP ERP, and this makes the choice even more difficult. If an implementation of the entire SAP ERP system with all modules is planned, we recommend procuring the services of a company providing consulting for all modules. If, however, the QM module is to be implemented afterward, that is, when other modules are already in operation, you need a consulting company specializing in this module. SAP offers consulting services, as well. In addition, SAP provides the so-called SAP Partner Consulting, which comprises more than 20,000 consultants worldwide. There are also many freelance consultants, many of whom possess extensive expertise. The following questions will help you examine the consulting services available:

- Is the desired extent of consulting services provided?
- What experience and reference projects exist? Who are the contact persons there?
- Which consultants are available for which module?
- Are the consultants available for the entire project duration?
- How many times a week are the consultants available?
- Are the consultants in my area (what would be the travel time)?
- What are the consultants' qualifications?
- What costs are involved?

It is no coincidence that the cost factor is mentioned last. A low-cost offer of consulting services is of little use if the consultants are not available, if they change constantly, and if have such long journeys to make that they are already tired by the time they reach the company!

The quality of a consulting company stands and falls with the *qualification* of its employees. The QM module alone is so complex that a single consultant simply cannot know all of its intricacies and possible uses. In addition, there are the interfaces to other modules whose uses require solid knowledge of the entire SAP ERP system. Less-experienced consultants can slow down progress of the project. You can avoid many problems by requesting proof of qualifications in the form of resumes, training certificates, practical experience in the respective module, years of service in a consulting company, or reference projects. In addition, SAP offers training and qualifications programs to become a SAP ERP Certified Application Consultant. However, this certification is not yet offered for all modules.

While searching for an appropriate consulting company, your organization must structure the project and work out a rough *project plan* that defines the milestones of the project right from the beginning of the consultant search. A project-team structure shown in Figure 3.7 has proven successful in practice.

The core team with the project manager for the company coordinates the progress of the project and the deployment of consultants in arrangement with the project manager of the consulting company. The following project-management tools have proven effective for projects that span several modules:

- **Project manual**
  Description of the project, goals, interfaces, principles, and so on.

- **Project plan**
  Schedule.
- **Controlling information interchange**
  Intranet, email, documentation server.
- **Regular project meetings**
  Meetings with the module project managers.

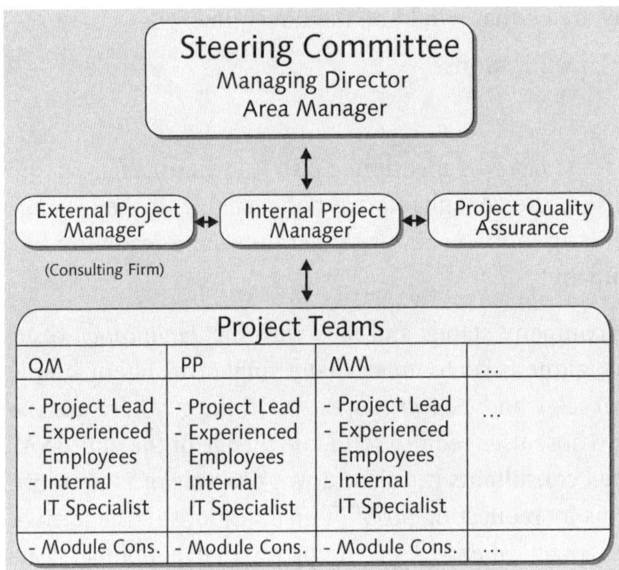


**Figure 3.7** Project Structure for the Implementation of SAP ERP

This list could be extended further still. The last item on the list has proven to be particularly important. It is only through *regular project meetings* for all subprojects that you can discover interface problems at an early stage and introduce countermeasures to solve these problems. The more closely interlocked the modules are, the more important a collaboration between all parties involved becomes. Where necessary, integration meetings should be held to cover important topics in more detail and clarify important aspects among the individual project teams. The QM module is strongly affected by interface issues because it interacts with many other SAP ERP modules. This is often underestimated in the implementation.

It has been shown that having small project teams implement individual modules — in parallel to the core team for the entire project — can be particularly effective. A *project team* consists of:

- A module project manager from the specialist department
- Key users (main users) from the specialist department
- Employees from the company IT department
- Module consultants of the consulting company

This module project team also works according to established practices of project management:

- A project description (project manual) with goals and definition of interfaces
- Schedule
- Logging of decisions, agreements, and so on
- Logging of the project status at fixed intervals (e.g., monthly)
- Concluding report with a description of the scope implemented

Depending on the topics covered, module project team meetings can involve all or only a few team members. The intervals between team meetings depend on requirements and objectives, on the progress of the project, and the dependency on other module project teams.

At project start, the entire IT structure should be available for the project team so that it is possible from the first day to work and demonstrate on the SAP ERP system. An additional presentation system would be ideal, such as SAP IDES. As soon as the IT structure is ready, and a basic implementation in SAP ERP has taken place, the actual work can begin in the module project teams.

Essentially, a project consists of the following *phases*:

- Concept phase
- Customizing
- Test and correction phase
- Training and documentation for the users
- Master-data transfer
- Production phase

Alignment of terminology is very important from the very beginning, that is, in the concept phase. You will soon realize that a specific terminology exists in the SAP ERP system and especially in the QM module. In general, the consultant will have adopted the SAP terminology, while you will make use of the standard descriptions used in your company. For mutual understanding, it is essential to define the terms and expressions used and explain their meanings. Under certain circumstances, this can lead to the production of what amounts to a practical dictionary that lists the company terms next to the corresponding SAP expressions.

After standardizing terms and expressions, the next step is an *implementation workshop* of one to three days duration. The aim of this workshop is to give an opportunity for the consultant to explain the possibilities provided by each module, and for the module project manager and the future users to express their requirements and wishes. During this phase, the scope, goals, and some details of the project can be agreed upon. The results of the workshop are documented in the form of a project manual to give all parties involved access to this information at any time (ideally, the project manual will be published in the intranet).

An existing quality-management system is a great help when working on the project concepts. The process descriptions from the quality management manual and the process instructions provide a good basis for discussion on how these can be implemented through SAP ERP or (to be more precise) through the QM module. To support this, the relevant operations can be documented using flow charts or the EPC methods described in Chapter 2, Modeling QM Business Processes Using the EPC Method, during the workshop and in additional team meetings.

A smooth transition from the legacy system to the new system is essential for user acceptance and thus for a successful implementation of SAP ERP. It is often the little things such as old code keys or number ranges that build up familiarity with the SAP ERP system. Logically combined, *meaningful numbers* are usually easier to understand than a consecutive numbering. Captions and labels can be changed easily to adopt names from the legacy system. This way, the user will immediately find familiar items in the new system. In part, this has to be taken into account at the concept phase (concerning number ranges, internal and external number assignments), although this does not rule out future adjustments during user tests.

Individual integration discussions with the other module project teams during the planning phase are a necessity for implementing the QM module successfully. For example, if quality management is planned for procurement, coordination with purchasing and warehouse management is required. If quality management in production is a central topic, the module project team for Production Planning must be involved as well.

The phases "Concept," "Customizing," and "Test" are not to be understood as a linear sequence but instead form a *control loop* with increasing degrees of detail. Testing is not only a matter of checking the correct settings but also requires a review of the concept. If the approach chosen has proven successful, you normally will need to do fine-tuning during Customizing to improve the performance of the system. However, it can turn out that the concept does not adequately map the business processes of the company or has not taken them sufficiently into consideration. In this case, the concept must be revised, reset, and re-tested until the team has reached the goals defined.

During this iterative process, caution is needed because increasing familiarity with the SAP ERP options in general and the QM module in particular leads to new wishes. Too many "nice to have" functions can endanger the time frame of the project.

One risk during implementation of the QM module lies in the introduction of too many functionalities in the first step. This can jeopardize the implementation itself as well as threaten user acceptance. The complexity of the QM module is easily underestimated. However, it can be divided into the following:

- Quality management in Procurement
- Quality management in Production
- Quality management in Sales and Distribution

This division indicates that the QM module is closely interlocked with other modules that must be fine-tuned, implemented, and used in daily operation. Therefore, we recommend starting off with a less complex system (*lean implementation*) and to expand the functionality step by step later on. Improvements and enhancements can thus be defined, set, and tested continuously and then applied to the production system. Prior to this, a re-engineering of the business processes or subprocesses might be necessary. Due to the clear and easily understandable operation flow, QM in procurement is the ideal starting point for the implementation.

A *continuous testing* of all customized functions, together with a separate completion test and release test at the end of the project cycle, are essential for a successful production start-up. Not only the consultant but also the key users should be responsible for testing the customized functions. Any defects revealed during the test phase can be eliminated before the production start-up takes place. Basic settings for catalogs, sampling procedures, and dynamic modification rules are tested regarding their suitability for daily use. After unfavorable settings have been introduced into the production system and saved in the database system, they are hard to change or delete.

Users from the specialist departments should get involved as much as possible. This cooperation can help to track down defects at an early stage and means that proposals for improvements can be made and considered. The level of acceptance for the system will increase with the involvement of the users. This is of particular importance because the business processes must run uninterrupted after production start-up.

For a meaningful test result, well-chosen test data is essential. Bear in mind that irrespective of a lean implementation, it must remain possible to process special cases and special materials without high overhead. Remember that in a production environment, it is normal to process several thousand cases per day, and it will be of no use when 99% of these cases can be processed without any problem, while the remaining 1% requires a lot of time and effort.

For a smooth production start-up, training of all users is an absolute necessity. Training can be provided by specialized service companies, by consultants, or by the key user(s). Preferable in any case is training on the customized system of the company because this is the only way to get to know the processes that will be used in daily work. If you manage to recruit key users for training, their internal knowledge of the company can be used optimally. Training documents tailored to the company and the customized system should be created and made available.

Before production start-up, the *transfer of master data* needs to take place. Because most companies have already worked with a computer system before the introduction of SAP ERP, the old master data must be transferred into the new system. The same applies to the QM module. The overhead involved in data transfer increases in relation to the extent to which quality management was implemented in the legacy system. This procedure is referred to as data migration or migration from the legacy system to SAP ERP. A transfer of material master data into the SAP ERP system is necessary for the other modules anyway if the data is not already available. If inspection plans were already in use for the legacy system, these plans must be transferred into the QM module. As of SAP R/3 Release 4.5, transactions are available for the batch input of inspection plans. This data transfer must be precisely defined and described in advance (migration description) and performed at a fixed date shortly before production start-up. The time and effort necessary to describe, provide, and transfer the data is not to be underestimated and must be taken into account during project planning and implementation.

Before data transfer to the production clients can take place, basic data must have been provided in the QM module. This includes sampling rules, sampling procedures, dynamic modification rules, and catalogs; otherwise, errors would occur during batch input of inspection plans (which access sampling procedures).

A careful preparation will pay off at production start-up. The first days after start-up, all test cases should be monitored again on the production system and get logged. At this stage, it is no longer possible to run all kinds of tests because in the production system, real business events are triggered and processed. Thus, a review can only be performed on real processes. After thorough pre-testing, however, defects in the production system should be the exception.

SAP ERP supports project management with its own methods. These include in particular the procedural model in Customizing (see Chapter 13, Customizing).

## 3.7 Customizing

Every SAP ERP system is first installed with the shipped software client 000 (standard version). Unfortunately, this standard client cannot be used directly. You first need to set up the software and adapt it according to your company's needs. This process is referred to as *Customizing*. Depending on the size of the company, the number of modules implemented and the number of employees involved, Customizing can take several weeks or even months for each module. However, to give you a better idea of realistic time frames, consider that a company with approximately 500 employees was able to start working with all modules of the SAP ERP system after 12 months. Involved in the project were seven employees of the IT department, an outside consultant for each module, and one or two competent employees from each specialist department.

For the QM module, depending on the scope of the implementation, 20 to 60 consultant days should be assumed. These are shared across concept design, Customizing, briefing and training, testing, troubleshooting, and other tasks. From the specialist department, another one or two employees will require the same or up to three times the amount of time working on the project (depending on the scope and target of the project).

For detailed information on Customizing, see Chapter 13, Customizing. Additional information on master-data transfer can be found in Chapter 14, Migration Concepts. Checklists for testing as well as additional information for registered readers are available on the publisher's website for this book.

## 3.8 Client Concept

A company managed with SAP ERP software is referred to as a *client* and has a specific client number. The client represents the top level of the SAP ERP organizational structure. Each client number stands for a complete system with specific master and transaction data and possibly different Customizing or server hardware. The usual procedure is to create one client for each subsidiary (e.g., private corporation) or foreign subsidiary of a large company. In general, a company only requires a single client (production client). In addition to this, however, at least two clients for software implementation are installed, as described in Table 3.2.

| Client Number | Description | Comments |
|---|---|---|
| 100 | Customizing client | All settings (Customizing) based on the standard system (shipped client 000) are performed. Even after production start-up, all changes are implemented on this client and get transferred to other clients by transport request. |
| 200 | Test client | All changes made during Customizing are transferred to this client by transport request to create a mirror of the first client. After entering master data manually or automatically, you can run business transactions and systematically test them. All defects revealed in this way must *only* be corrected in the Customizing client. Corrections for defects are then again transferred by transport request to the test client. Even after the start of the production system, this client is used to test all changes and enhancements. |
| 300 | Production client | After successful testing with the test client and after having transferred all Customizing settings by transport request, all required master data is transferred into the production client on the key date. From the production start-up on, this is the client with which you will be working. |

**Table 3.2** Simple Client Concept

The explanations in the preceding table should make clear why it is essential to specify the correct client number at logon to the SAP system (see also Chapter 4, Operating SAP ERP).

## 3.9 Organizational Structure

As stated in Section 3.8, Client Concept, the *client* is the top-level element of the SAP ERP organizational structure.

The *company code* is an accounting concept. It is subordinate to the client and represents an independent and self-contained accounting area. A client can comprise several company codes. A company code in turn can be subdivided into controlling areas and profit centers.

Within logistics, the plant is the most important organizational element; it is subordinate to the company code and represents a production location. The company code can contain several plants. Production planning and control mainly takes place at the plant level but can also be implemented across several plants.

The *purchasing organization* is an organizational unit and always assigned to a company code. It can procure materials or services for one or several plants. Vendor evaluation refers to the purchasing organization. If the purchasing organization is responsible for several plants, the vendor evaluation is also cross-plant.

The *storage locations* are assigned to plants and allow inventory management on the plant level.

## 3.10 SAP Work Center

A typical SAP work center consists of one networked personal computer (workstation, client) with a sufficiently large monitor (at least 17-inch). Although virtually all functions can be accessed by using the keyboard, a mouse is essential as an input device. You can choose from a range of operating systems for the workstation. Windows 2000 and Windows XP are popular choices, but Macintosh, UNIX, and Linux are also supported.

The SAP client installed on each personal computer can be used in the same way as a typical Windows platform and provides a GUI compliant with the SAA standard (System Application Architecture), through which the users can communicate with the R/3 system. In SAP terminology, this client is referred to as SAP GUI (SAP graphical user interface). The user can choose between different versions of the SAP GUI. Additionally, we recommend installing Microsoft Excel on the PC because SAP ERP offers a list download and import into a spreadsheet from various screens. In these spreadsheets, you can then perform further processing and evaluations.

For printing jobs, a *printer* is required, which can be connected locally to the workstation or may be available in the network. Ideally, the shared network printer should be located nearby. A local printer can also be used from other workstations. This assumes, however, that the PC connected to the printer must be turned on, and the print data reception program (SAPlpd) must be active. If a printer is used by several users, a network printer is recommended because this is available for use independently of a PC. Basically every type of printer is suitable, that is, dot-matrix, inkjet, or laser printer, although each printing technology has strengths and weaknesses. Prior to activating a printer, the system administrator must set up the printer in the SAP Basis system (BC). A local setup using Windows and Windows printer drivers, for example, does not automatically enable any output in SAP ERP!

## 3.11 SAPscript

The SAPscript editor can be used to design the layout of forms and printed text. SAPscript is a page-description language that you can use to create virtually any kind of form, which is only restricted by the features of your printer. With the SAPscript editor, you can adjust documents such as work papers, inspection plans, or certification forms corresponding to your company's corporate identity.

## 3.12 Reports

A report is an SAP ERP program that supplies you with results in table form that can be output on the monitor or printer. This list contains selected data from your database. The data for a report is selected in a selection screen where you can specify the selection criteria, for example, a material-number range. The selection is started by means of RUN and not by pressing Enter, which also makes it clear that a program is being executed.

The list or report can be viewed onscreen or printed out. Often (not always) a download is possible. You can use this feature to download the list on your personal computer and further process it in a spreadsheet program.

Usually, standard reports can be found in each module, sometimes in the menu item ENVIRONMENT, sometimes in EXTRAS. Unfortunately, this is not unified in the SAP ERP system. Your own reports get a program name and are accessed from the main menu using SYSTEM • SERVICES • REPORTING, indicating the report name. An example for a report can be found in Chapter 11, Test Equipment Management, where the maintenance plan is retrieved in the form of a report using this method.

**Tip**

You should plan the adjustment of your forms and reports at an early stage and allocate sufficient programming capacity for this task.

We recommend following these steps:

1. Create a list of all printouts, forms, and lists that you receive from or create with your system and that you need for your work.
2. Try editing this list by asking the following questions: Which of these reports is really necessary, and which ones can be omitted? Can any of the reports be summarized?
3. Find out (possibly with the help of a consultant), if and where you can find or generate similar reports in your SAP ERP system, and create the sample printouts.
4. Define in which way existing reports need to be adapted and which reports must be reprogrammed, and then delegate this task.

For quality management, think — for instance — of quality notifications to vendors and of *internal quality notification*; think of printouts of inspection plans, inspection instructions, percentage evaluations, or vendor evaluation.

It is important to perform these preliminary tasks at an early stage because experience shows that shortly before production start-up, many requests for report adjustments will arise.

## 3.13 ABAP Programs

ABAP (*Advanced Business Application Programming*) is the SAP proprietary programming language. The applications in the SAP ERP system and the reports referred to were programmed in ABAP. The IT specialists in your company also have access to ABAP programming. The ABAP development workbench can be found in the menu TOOLS • ABAP WORKBENCH. From there, you have access to numerous tools for development and testing ABAP programs. These options are particularly useful to create individual reports.

## 3.14 SAP ERP QM as a CAQ System

CAQ (*Computer Aided Quality Assurance*) systems are used to an increasing extent, especially in the automotive industry. This involves support for tasks of quality management by electronic data processing. The necessity for this results in part from the demands of ISO 9000 standards for systematic inspections and "controlled" quality records, and in part from the increasingly urgent desire of management to be supplied with quality data and analyses of quality-related costs because these are required as a starting point for improvement in efficiency and productivity. Furthermore, only an electronic CAQ system can enable an organization to process, evaluate, prepare, and archive the data quantities from inspection and quality control at an adequate speed.

The typical requirements for CAQ systems are:

- Quality planning
- Quality Inspection
- Inspection-order management
- Quality-data recording
- Quality-data evaluation and reporting

- Quality control
- SPC (Statistical Process Control)
- Test equipment management

CAQ systems often only focus on a few of the mentioned requirements. Specialized systems (e.g., for SPC processing) were to some extent enhanced by the manufacturer to meet the main requirements of the customer. CAQ systems that satisfy all of the needs just listed are usually expensive and complex.

If companies already have a CAQ system, these are individual PCs or PC networks. The advantage of the stand-alone PC solution is that you can make a start at low cost and effort. In many cases, the CAQ system is a SPC workstation situated in the quality lab and is already used for tasks such as planning and evaluation. Depending on the size of the company, decentralized inspection locations will (sooner or later) make it necessary to interconnect several PC workstations and to move to a file server solution. The disadvantage of individual workstations and a network solution is the lack of integration of such a CAQ system into the supply chain of the company.

The SAP ERP QM module is a kind of CAQ system that meets a wide range of requirements. You can benefit from all advantages offered by CAQ systems. A complete integration of quality management into the overall system converts the disadvantages of an external CAQ system into an advantage of SAP ERP. Regarding quality management in MM, Production, and SD, the interfaces to these modules become joints. A seamless data exchange between procurement, goods receipt, production orders, or deliveries allows for productivity and optimized data consistency as multiple recording of data in different systems is avoided. Furthermore, integration into the R/3 system provides capabilities regarding the quality-related costs, which could hardly be achieved with an external CAQ system. A linking to SAP Human Resources (HR), for example, makes retrieving training costs belonging to prevention costs as easy as retrieving inspection and nonconformity costs from Controlling (CO).

However, if you are not willing to abandon your external CAQ system after implementation of SAP ERP, this presents no problem. SAP developed a defined interface (QM-IDI) that allows for connection between external systems and the SAP ERP QM module. For more detailed information see Chapter 7, Quality Inspection.

## 3.15 New SAP Technologies

This section considers some of the new SAP technologies starting with the SAP ERP strategy.

### 3.15.1 SAP ERP Strategy

SAP is currently involved in replacing the previous client-server technology, as it was used in SAP R/3. The new technology is called SAP NetWeaver. In the future, all solutions will be based on this technology, from the core functions in SAP ERP to the enhanced solutions of the SAP Business Suite (see Section 13.5.2, SAP Business Suite) to the non-SAP solutions, which are connected through the communications interfaces of SAP NetWeaver.

The SAP ERP and SAP NetWeaver technology allows for integration of all relevant business processes. As a result, people, information, and business processes can be interconnected using state-of-the-art Internet technology (see Figure 3.8).

| | | | | | | | |
|---|---|---|---|---|---|---|---|
| Integrating People | SAP NetWeaver Portal | Collaboration | | Portal Content | Multi-Channel Access | | Security |
| Integrating Information | Business Intelligence | Knowledge Management | | Master Data Management | Organization of Content | | |
| Integrating Processes | Business-to-Business | Business Process Management | Connectivity | Integration Content | Message Handling | Infra-structure | |
| Application Platform | Production Development | Openness and Interoperability | Reliable Operation | Platform Architecture | Management of Entire Lifecycle | Composite Application Framework | |

**Figure 3.8** Integration of People, Processes, and Information

In SAP ERP, quality management can be found in the area of CORPORATE SERVICES (see Figure 3.9). In addition to the familiar functions, the enhanced communication features of the SAP NetWeaver technology enrich QM to a configurable environment for the exchange of quality-relevant data along the supply chain. You can reduce goods-receipt inspections if both business partners retrieve the inspection data of the relevant products through a shared application on the Internet. Results of current production not only provide the business partner with information on the quantity already manufactured, but also on the product quality.

| | | | | | | | |
|---|---|---|---|---|---|---|---|
| Analytics | Strategic Enterprise Management | Financial Analytics | Operations Analytics | Workforce Analytics | | | |
| Financials | Financial Supply Chain Management | Financial Accounting | Management Accounting | Corporate Governance | | | |
| Human Capital Management | Talent Management | Workforce Process Management | Workforce Deployment | | | | |
| Procurement and Logistics Execution | Procurement | Inventory and Warehouse Management | Inbound and Outbound Logistics | Transportation Management | | | |
| Product Development and Manufacturing | Production Planning | Manufacturing Execution | Product Development | Life-Cycle Data Management | | | |
| Sales and Service | Sales Order Management | Aftermarket Sales and Service | Professional-Service Delivery | | | | |
| Corporate Services | Real Estate Management | Enterprise Asset Management | Project and Portfolio Management | Travel Management | Environment, Health and Safety Compliance Management | Quality Management | Global Trade Services |

**Figure 3.9** Solution Map for SAP ERP

### 3.15.2 SAP Business Suite

The SAP Business Suite was formerly known as mySAP.com. It includes the SAP NetWeaver-based solutions and provides all functions for mapping the core processes within and outside your company, industry solutions included. In addition to SAP ERP, the SAP Business Suite consists of solutions to control mission-critical business processes internally and across company limits. These solutions are SAP Customer Relationship Management (SAP CRM), SAP Product Lifecycle Management (SAP PLM), SAP Supplier Relationship Management (SAP SRM), and SAP Supply Chain Management (SAP SCM) (see Figure 3.10).

Product development and quality management processes can be integrated through SAP PLM. Through a web connection, internal and external partners can be integrated into the operational processes.

SAP NetWeaver, which is intended to be an open application and integration platform, consists of the following elements:

- SAP NetWeaver Application Server (SAP NetWeaver AS)
- SAP NetWeaver Process Integration (SAP NetWeaver PI)
- SAP NetWeaver Portal with Knowledge Management and Collaboration
- SAP NetWeaver Business Intelligence (SAP NetWeaver BI)

- SAP NetWeaver Master Data Management (SAP NetWeaver MDM)
- SAP NetWeaver Mobile
- Composite Application Framework (CAF)

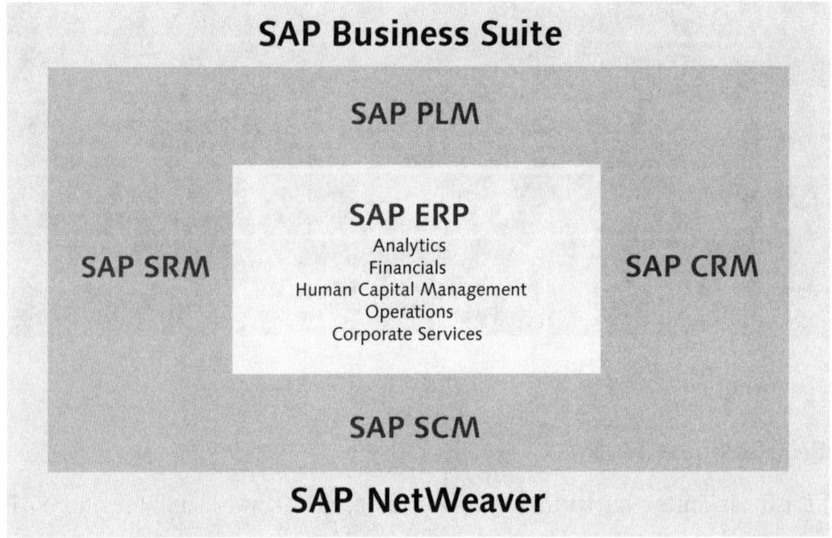


**Figure 3.10** SAP Business Suite and SAP ERP

### 3.15.3 SAP NetWeaver Portal

SAP NetWeaver Portal is an enterprise portal that provides the user with fast, simple, and convenient web-based access to all internal and external applications, including contents and services that they require for their daily work. It supports the employee by providing the right information and applications with the click of a mouse and by means of an interface that is easy to understand, adjust, and use. The portal's main characteristics are as follows:

- Single point of access to applications using a web browser
- Contents and services
- Personalized and role-based user interface
- Convenient integration
- Openness and flexibility
- Access everywhere and at any time

### Single Point of Access with Web Browser

The SAP NetWeaver Portal provides all users with a central starting point. The portal provides access to all functions necessary to perform daily activities. Users can benefit from the advantages of a single integrated company portal through their web browsers.

The SAP NetWeaver Portal provides access to all SAP and non-SAP applications and Internet services. At the same time, users have access to the intranet and self-service applications as well as extranets and existing applications, again with only the web browser.

### Personalized and Role-Based User Interfaces

SAP NetWeaver Portal is preconfigured for a variety of organizational roles (employee, controller, purchaser, order processor, manager) and can be fully adjusted to individual requirements. There are configuration options on all levels: individual, role, company, and industry-specific. This guarantees that the information, services, and functionalities are available that are relevant for the corresponding area of operations.

The users can use different roles to participate in different business scenarios. For instance, a user can create requirement requests using the employee role and automatically participate in the business scenario "E-procurement." Another participant in this scenario can use the purchaser role to execute this purchase order. Depending on the roles used, different functionalities, contents, and services are required. SAP NetWeaver Portal is shipped with different predefined roles that can be used as starting points for a company-specific personalization as shown in Figure 3.11.

### Convenient Integration

SAP NetWeaver Portal allows the user to drag and drop between different applications with the click of a mouse. Internet, intranet, extranet, and other applications tend to overwhelm the user with information and technical possibilities, many of which are not related in any way with the tasks. A lot of the users' time is wasted because they need to remember and enter different passwords for each application, search information and files, and have to toggle between different user interfaces. The lack of integration between web-based resources and business applications impairs user productivity.

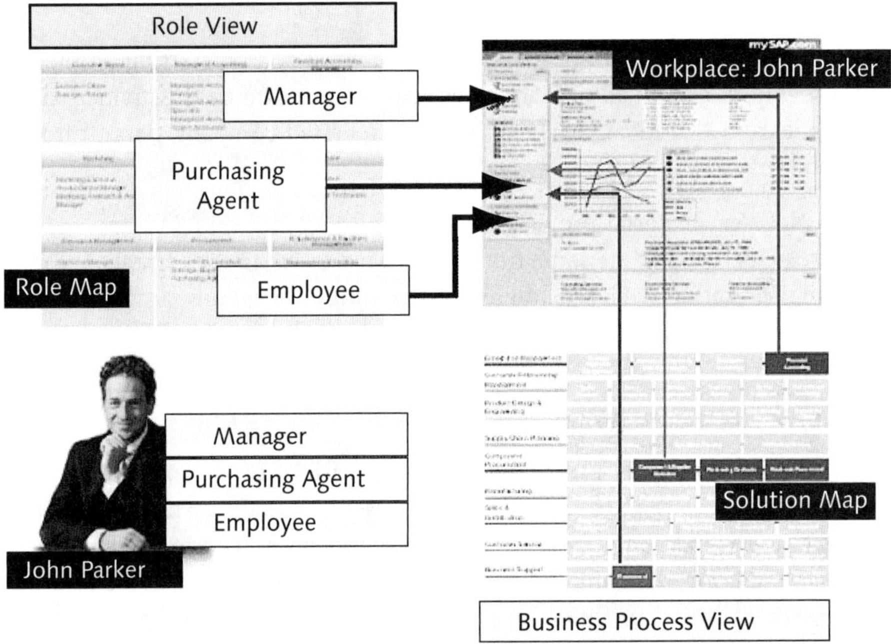


**Figure 3.11** Ergonomic Work Center Configuration

With SAP NetWeaver Portal, a purchaser can, for instance, drag an overdue order onto the icon of an express dispatcher within the same window. The web page of the carrier is automatically accessed to enter all details of the overdue delivery. This integration saves the user several steps because there is no need to open the web browser, enter the web address of the carrier, log on to the website, and enter the order data.

### Openness and Flexibility

An important characteristic of the SAP NetWeaver Portal is an open and flexible infrastructure, which bundles the resources in accordance with the role and the personal requirements of the company user. A centrally located and managed server and very strong security mechanisms provide the user with a convenient single sign-on (SSO). The SAP NetWeaver Portal allows for a collaborative web environment based on the Internet Business Framework. This framework facilitates access, required changes, and collaboration considerably. It is a flexible and open infrastructure for all SAP solutions that is based on web standards and relies on XML-based web messaging and web flow.

### 3.15.4 Using SAP NetWeaver Portal in SAP QM

By using the SAP NetWeaver Portal, users can gain access to the business processes needed, any time and anywhere. The browser enables you to access the functions of the QM system anywhere in the world.

For quality management and handling related tasks, this involves an extended SAP ERP system. It is not just dealing with management tasks in the "white collar" area but with more tangible tasks in the front office or the company's production area. In a raw production environment, operations of a plant-operator inspection should be performed with the same software as in a lab clean-room environment or even in a protected office. In production, such factors as clear measurement-data display from more than one meter and simplified usage components are more important than the latest statistical evaluation.

How can a web-based quality-management portal be useful here? Depending on the range of tasks, there are two different approaches that are both closely connected with the concept of roles:

- Reducing and simplifying the application components that are really needed in a certain situation
- Merging the involved application components in a shared GUI

How are the roles in the different work areas of quality management to be defined? And how can a company portal support these adequately? Let's take a closer look at the QM user roles of a manufacturing plant.

#### Quality Inspector Role

Quality inspector is the most important role in the production process (see Figure 3.12). The speed of access to comparative data and additional information promotes quick and competent decision making. User acceptance can only be achieved through an intuitive and easy-to-use interface. Roles can vary from dealing with only one measurement task to roles where a large number of analysis results must be quickly entered into a table. The inspection results input is often an operation that is entered exactly into cost accounting and to a major extent influences the quality costs. Therefore, an investment in this area bodes well for efficient improvement to the production flow and is definitely on par with the acquisition or refinement of a production facility.

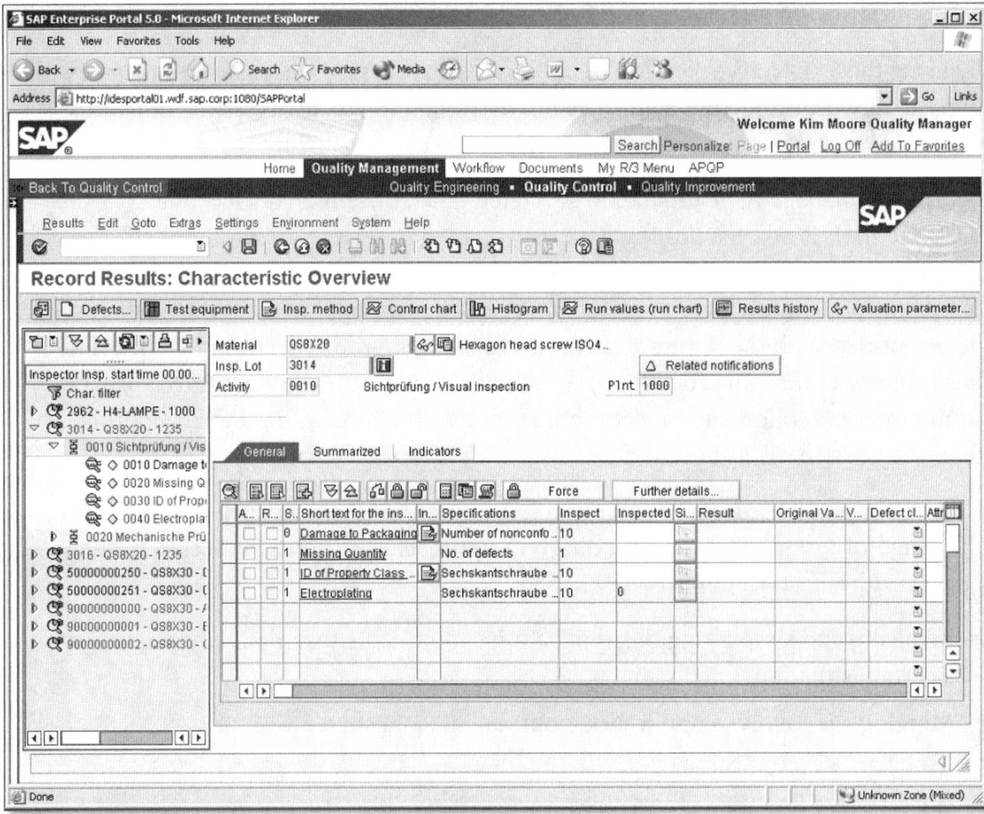

Figure 3.12 Quality Inspector Role

## Quality Planner Role

The role of the quality planner is performed in cooperation with all subtasks for optimal product quality. The quality planner does not just keep track of internal contexts but rather coordinates tasks related to vendors and customers. In the quality planner's workplace, vendor evaluations and multiple analyses from production stability to notification volume can be found. Because this data forms the basic information for company decisions, an integration of the SAP NetWeaver BI is of interest. Additionally, you can integrate other reports generated from within the SAP ERP application easily.

### Inspection Planner Role

In this role, transactions from several business segments are merged. The role of the inspection planner comprises functions from the integrated work scheduling and the actual inspection planning.

Planning tasks require access to CAD and formula data as well as statistics on inspection frequency and error rate. For each measurement task and method of recording, the inspection planner defines which methods — for instance, SPC — or other visualized processes will be used. Access to the document management system is crucial here because the inspection processes, inspection instructions, and additional supporting documents are stored in this system.

### Notification Processor Role

Communication also means to react to important issues in a timely and efficient manner. The notification processor role provides you with a communication tool that you can use to quickly reply to general queries and to solve problems within a company (see Figure 3.13). As a notification processor, you are responsible for smooth process flows: You coordinate the handling of incoming notifications and control the reaction flow by suitable measures. In addition to quality notifications, you are also responsible for general notifications. General notifications enable the users to document simple issues without having to define the type from a business point of view. As a notification processor, you isolate the incoming notifications according to the context and ensure a precise business assignment. This means you provide for quick and targeted processing of a request.

### Test Equipment Manager Role

For quality inspection, reliable test equipment is required. In your role as test equipment manager, you provide for a smooth process flow in your company. A prerequisite is a high availability of test equipment tools and production resources. Your field of action is targeted toward efficient management, maintenance, and calibration of test equipment. By this, you get direct access to test equipment history. If you determine during calibration that a piece of test equipment can no longer be used, the test equipment history clearly shows which characteristics have been tested with this test equipment. And you can immediately initiate the required steps for sustainable quality assurance.

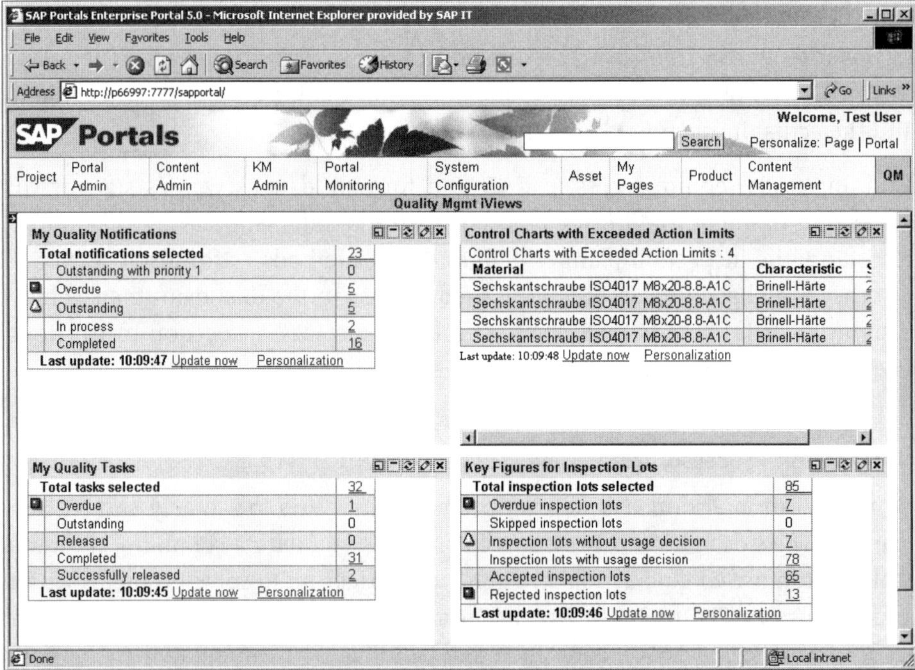


**Figure 3.13** Notification Processor Role

## Quality Manager Role

A quality manager has to face multiple challenges, including smooth production flows, lowest possible quality-related costs, and sustainable quality control. It is essential to efficiently control different operations and to make the right decision at the right time. With the quality manager role, SAP NetWeaver Portal offers you the necessary field of action for your responsible task (see Figure 3.14). MiniApps provide you with useful QM key figures and evaluations at a glance, so you can always re-survey your quality strategy and, if required, adjust it together with the quality planner.

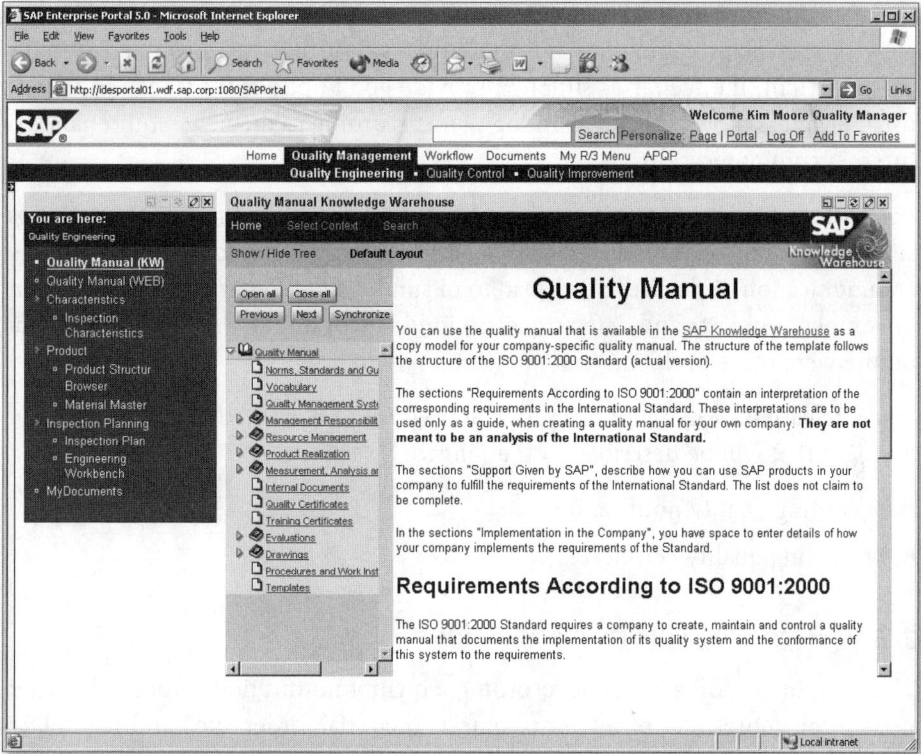


**Figure 3.14** Quality Manager Role

### 3.15.5 Principles of SAP Internet Scenarios

Within the SAP ERP system, you can map and handle numerous business processes through the Internet. Because a dedicated SAP ERP web server for quality management is installed in only the rarest cases, we recommend searching for in-company coalitions regarding Internet usage and developing a joint strategy. If the company is of a certain size, the installation of a separate web server is justified, given the relatively low overhead. The applications shown here are shipped with the system. An Internet connection naturally requires an initial configuration and installation of the web server. In the simplest case, you need a PC of suitable capacity with Microsoft Internet Information Server or an SAP NetWeaver AS and SAP basic tools. The host is integrated through the house network in the production SAP ERP domains. Your customer requires Internet access and the access authorizations provided by you in the form of a user name and password. With this, your customer cannot normally gain access to complaint data of other companies.

Standard Internet applications can be enhanced — as is the case with SAP ERP — with specific programming and therefore cannot be treated as fixed systems. To this extent, the scenarios supplied provide good options for transferring your usual business processes and adapting them according to the new requirements of Internet communication.

In a customer-oriented service society, it is crucial to offer your customers the possibility to handle quality-related tasks over the Internet. Notification processes and communication difficulties often lead to misunderstandings about the assignment of complaint objects and defects descriptions. If working in the same notification on the web, these problems will not arise that often.

Since Release 4.0, SAP ERP has provided two Internet scenarios for quality management that will be described in the following sections:

- Recording quality notifications
- Processing quality certificates

### 3.15.6 Recording Quality Notifications

The most important aspects of recording a quality notification through the Internet are the conformity of reference objects (material, order, etc.) and the defects descriptions. The processing difficulty is considerably lessened through this process, which leads to a faster and "leaner" business case on both sides. The customer can activate the Internet notification at any time and can be notified about the processing status of the notification. Because this form of notification handling is not an industry standard yet, your company can set itself apart from its competitors by using this process, which is in itself a positive side effect.

The quality notification is directly transferred into the SAP ERP system by the Internet application, gets transferred into the corresponding notification type, and is then available there for further processing. The transactional user of the notification is responsible for further processing that can be enhanced by an additional workflow connection to an active processing object (workflow item).

#### Prerequisites in the SAP System

The quality notification is created by an employee of the receiving company. The customer is created in the customer master record of the given SAP ERP system, and the employee is maintained as a contact person.

**Tip**

In Customizing, the start notification type for transaction QM01 (Create Quality Notification/Create Notification) needs to be specified because this is the only way to find the correct notification type during notification creation over the web. The system also checks if the notification was sent to all mandatory partners. As in this case, if the notification type Q1, Customer Complaint, is involved, you must define the sold-to party and the contact person as mandatory partners in Customizing. Additional mandatory partners mustn't be created because these cannot be serviced through the web.

To use the Internet transaction, the contact person in question (this could be more than one) receives a number stored in the customer master record and an Internet identifier of type BUS1006001 (business partner employee). You communicate this number and identifier to your customers, most suitably during a workshop on the subject. If your customers agree, they can immediately benefit from complaint handling by Internet.

**Scenario**

Using an example of a customer complaint described further in Chapter 9, Quality Notification, the alternative of notification handling through the Internet is now described in the following section.

#### Calling the Internet Application Through the Contact Person

After having delivered to a major customer, a defect has been found in the CD casing. Instead of a phone call with additional fax or email, the person lodging the complaint starts the Internet application for notification handling and logs on with his personal number and password. In the next step, the employee determines if he wants to create a new notification or query the status of older notifications. With his logon, the customer only gets access to materials that have been delivered to him or for which you have provided notification handling. The materials permitted need to be defined in advance in the *customer materials info record*.

#### Creating the Customer Complaint

After selecting a material from the proposal list, the customer begins describing the problem. By switching to the web page provided for this purpose, he starts with the defects description in the SAP ERP system used here: by selecting a defect from the defect catalog. With the defect location (also selected from a catalog) recorded and after entry of a text-based defect description, the notification is complete (see Figure 3.15).

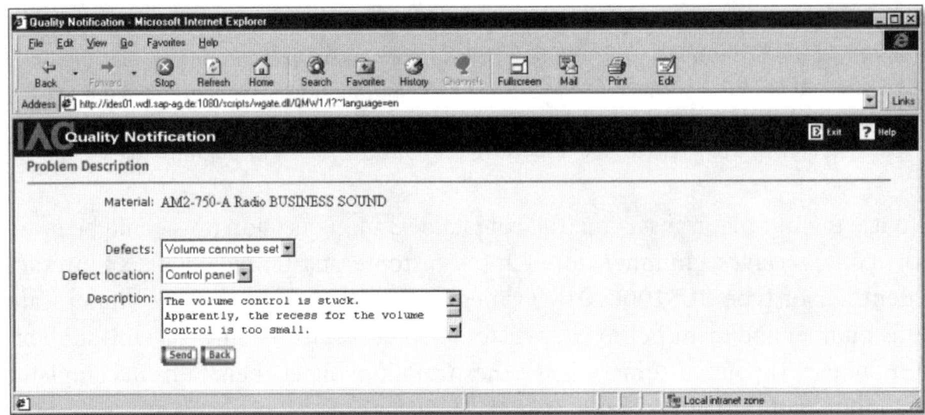


**Figure 3.15** Notification Processing on the Internet

If the process of quality notification handling by Internet was coordinated well, the customer will help to speed up the process by providing a note on the posting document (delivery note or material number). This note will help to identify the delivery in the course of notification handling. In this case, too, the selection options for defect codes and defect locations get assigned to the materials beforehand. For this reason, the customer only sees the codes for defects that were assigned to the materials affected. In the next step, the notification is saved on the web page. After saving, the notification is assigned a notification number that gets displayed to the customer. The customer and the complaint recipient can use this notification number to identify and track the notification.

### Additional Processing in the SAP ERP System

The main goals are to confirm receipt of the notification as quickly as possible, to decide on an immediate action, and to initiate this action. (Figure 3.16 shows the processing of a typical notification. One register is dedicated to document the corrective actions.) With the different lists for the work queue, this presents no problem. For example, the setting of a specific number range interval can distinguish the Internet notifications from all others. By selecting notifications with a certain status, you can select the newly created notifications. If your workflow provides for an hourly reading of newly created notifications, the first step for efficient processing has been performed. It can be necessary in special cases to call the customer by phone or contact him in other ways. In most cases, however, the customer has at least the option to quickly and easily file a complaint that contains all relevant information that is important for further processing by you.

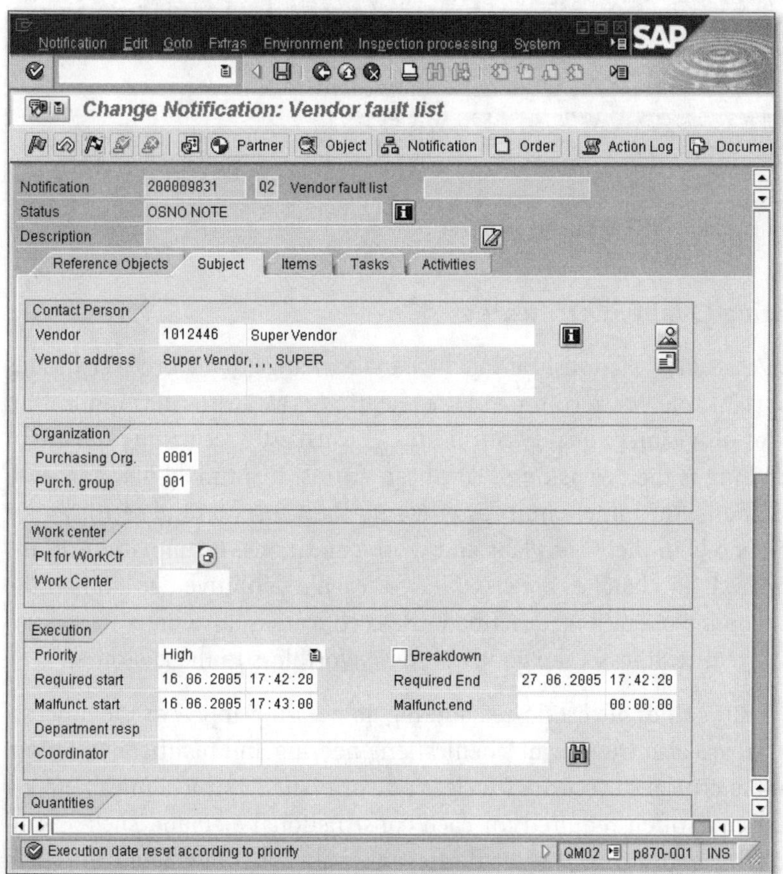


**Figure 3.16** Notification Processing in SAP ERP

## Displaying the Notification Status

The customer can query the processing status by means of the notification number through the web (see Figure 3.17). The list of quality notifications contains all of the information specified by them, such as material, defect codes, and defect description. The defect description can also contain the name of the complaint recipient so that the customer can contact the responsible person to get detailed information on the processing status.

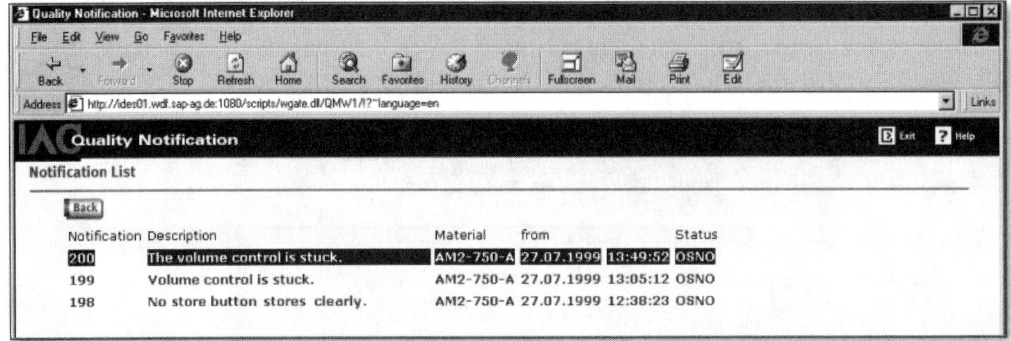


**Figure 3.17** Notification Processing on the Internet

### 3.15.7 Creating Quality Certificates

For all vendor/customer relationships in which the exchange of material certificates plays an important role, we recommend the use of SAP IAC (Internet Application Component) for provision of quality certificates. A constantly recurring problem of certificate handling is the provision of certificate forms, in a timely manner, with the supply of goods. Customers must often verify the values on the certificate or re-analyze the goods in their own labs and work conditions. Examination results are then compared, and batches are classified to reach a definitive decision on the use of goods. For the operations described, the certificate is absolutely necessary; without the correct certificate, the goods become worthless to the customer.

The illustrated difficulties of certificate handling do not only apply for the processing industry but are also true for mechanical engineering and plant construction. In plants that are critical to security (nuclear power plants, petrochemical, etc.), a specific certificate is often required for each constructional element, such as outlets, tube sections, and so on. The certificates must always be available and must be presented upon acceptance of delivery. In some real-world projects, costs for certificates and documentation made up almost a quarter of the project costs.

With the Internet application *Creation of quality certificates*, the customers can conveniently access the agreed certificates by Internet. The reference object for locating the certificate is the *batch*. This concept can — depending on the customer situation — involve an order number or any other identification number of a delivery to let the customer identify the goods affected.

### Prerequisites in the SAP ERP System

The certificate definition from Chapter 6, Quality and Inspection Planning, forms the basis for the operation because it defines the content and appearance of the certificate. It is no problem to use more than one certificate form for certificate handling over the Internet. The certificate profile determination and the certificate contents agreed upon with the customer need to be defined in advance. This way, the customer sees the correct certificate upon selection of a batch. Without implementing a certificate profile determination in the Customizing of the SAP ERP system, a certificate handling over the Internet is not possible.

You need to consider the following settings to allow an employee of the receiving company to display the quality certificate:

- The customer is created in the customer master record of the SAP ERP system, and the employee is maintained as a contact person.
- The certificate profile determination is set up.

### Prerequisites on the Customer Side

On the customer side, a normal Internet connection with a standard browser (Microsoft Internet Explorer, Netscape, etc.) is implemented. To display and print the certificates, a PDF-capable browser is needed. A popular PDF viewer is Adobe Acrobat, a shareware program that can be downloaded from the Internet.

**Scenario**

The example of a gearbox assembly with aluminum casing components is used here. To ensure that in certain areas of application (drilling platform) no corrosion occurs, the specification for a specific alloy part requires a documented analysis per certificate. In the "Drilling Platform" use case, the alloy content must be greater than 1% to guarantee corrosion resistance in sea water. For use case "Mechanical Engineering," the specification is identical. However, the alloy component does not need to be documented in the form of a certificate.

The certificate is to be enclosed for every delivery with the claim "corrosion resistance in sea water."

### Call of the Internet Application by the Customer

The customer logs on with his number and password. With his logon, the customer only gets access to materials that have been delivered to him or for which you have provided for certificate handling.

### Certificate Selection by Batch Number

All certificates must be assigned to a batch in advance. With the Internet application, you do not search for the certificates directly but use the batch number. To search for the correct batch, the following search criteria are available:

- **Product group** (in the SAP ERP system = goods group)
  All batches of a goods group are detailed in a list.
- **Search string**
  In this search type, the relevant material is identified through the short text of the material, a generic search with * (any character string) and + (for a character) is permitted here.
- **Batch number**
  For direct entry.

A combination of the criteria is also possible. The search criteria is then linked together through a logical AND linking.

The search is run by clicking on the FIND button. The results list shows the materials found and the batches assigned but not the certificates. All result lists are displayed with material, batch, and (if applicable) expiration date.

### Certificate Creation

By selecting a batch from the results list, the customer receives a certificate with the contents defined in the certificate profile determination of the SAP ERP system. The template includes formats and results display as required by the client. The certificate is provided as a PDF file and thus can be stored as a file or printed out (see Figure 3.18). Certificates created through the Internet application are identical with certificates of the SAP ERP system in terms of form and content and are exclusively based on inspections already completed. This form of certificate handling ensures an identical data basis and guarantees consistent document contents.

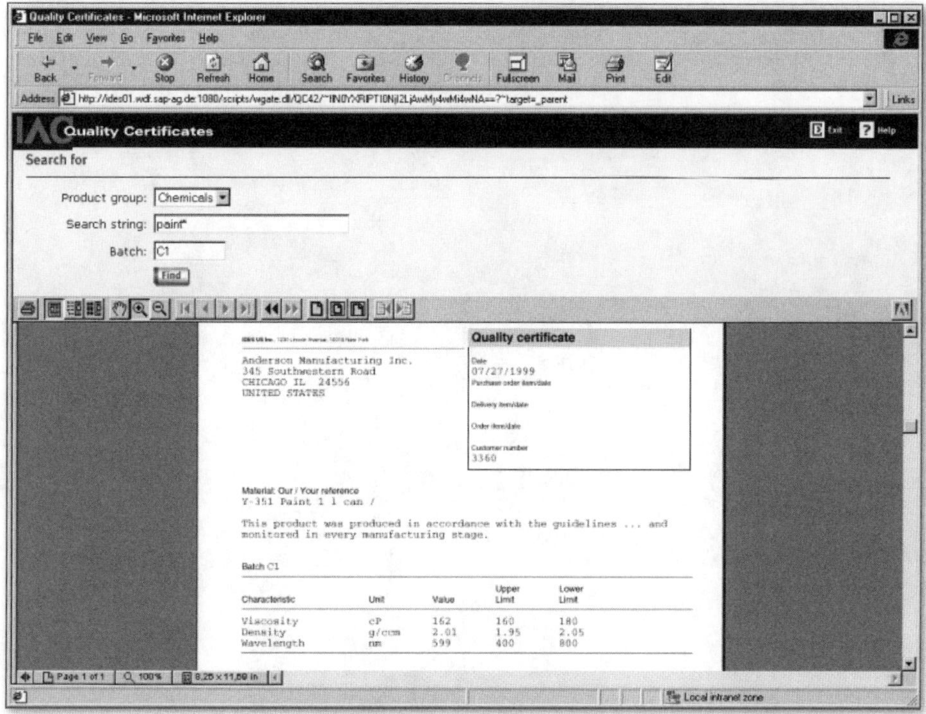


**Figure 3.18** Quality Certificate on the Internet Through IAC

*This chapter provides you with the basics of operating the SAP ERP system. It is mainly intended for first-time users, but experienced users also will find useful hints.*

# 4 Operating SAP ERP

You first learn how you can log on and off in SAP ERP. This is followed by a description of the user interface, including its menus and toolbars. You also learn how to print and to make user settings.

## 4.1 General Notes

The screenshots used in this chapter were created on a test client, and care has been taken to use examples showing the SAP QM module. At the end of the chapter, you find important display options from other components, in particular from the Materials Management module (MM), which will prove useful for your daily work in quality management.

## 4.2 Logon and Logoff

This section considers the logon and logoff to and from the SAP ERP system.

#### Logon

You can start the client and open the SAP logon window by double-clicking the SAP icon (see Figure 4.1). If there are several icons on your desktop, each of them refers to a specific client.

**Figure 4.1** SAP Logon

Two to three inputs are usually required to log on (see Figure 4.2):

- **Client number**
  This often has been entered already, but you must check and overwrite this number if necessary.
- **User name**
  Enter the user name assigned to you.
- **Password**
  Enter your password here. This password is your personal key to the system, and you should protect it from unauthorized access.
- **Language**
  Normally, the language is preset and must only be entered if you want to use a different language from the one set.

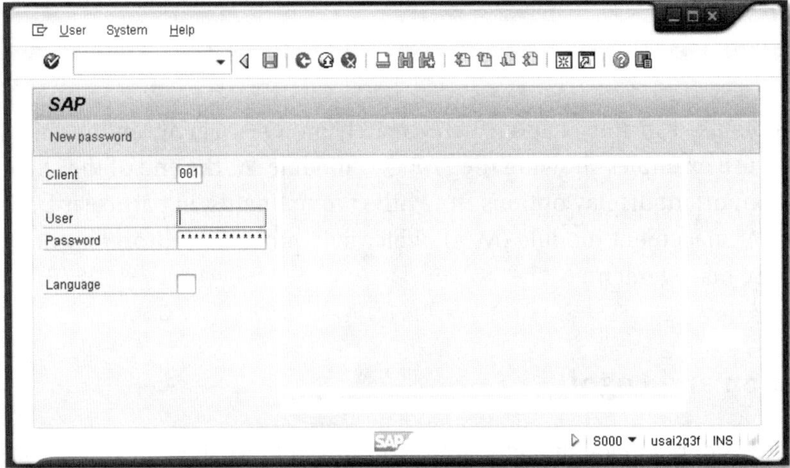


**Figure 4.2** The Logon Window

At logon, your personal settings and your access authorization for the entire duration of the session take effect. For example, your default printer will already be defined at logon. The user settings or the user profile allow the system administrator to define the levels of access for each user, that is, which data can be displayed or edited by the user. The quality manager, for example, is usually not allowed to view any HR or payroll data.

If the SYSTEM MESSAGES and/or COPYRIGHT window appears, confirm with the [Enter] key until you reach the main window (initial menu).

### Logoff

You can log off using the command path SYSTEM • LOG OFF (see Figure 4.3).

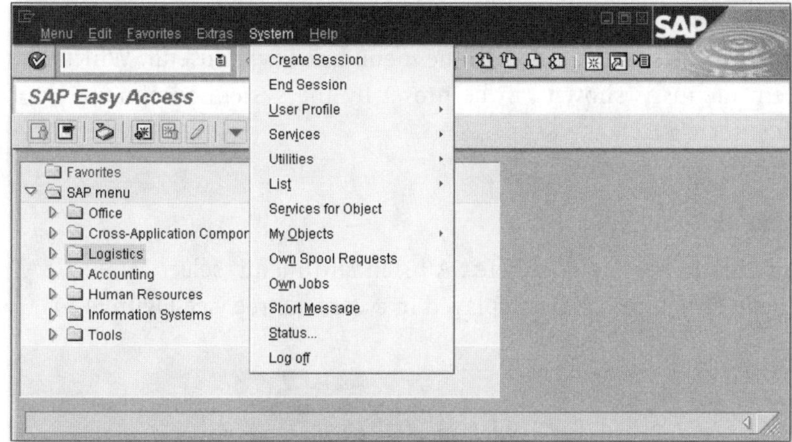


**Figure 4.3** Logging Off from the Main Menu

An even quicker way to log off is to click the "x" in the upper-right corner of the window (as is the standard in any Windows application). This closes each of the SAP ERP windows (sessions) individually. At logoff, a query window is shown, as shown in Figure 4.4.

**Figure 4.4** Security Prompt at Logoff

If you are not sure whether you have saved all of your transactions, click NO.

## 4.3 User Interface

As of R/3 Release 4.6, the interface between the user and the system has been completely revised and is now called SAP Easy Access. The most striking difference is the new menu structure. In previous releases, the menu structure was always displayed in the menu bar. Since R/3 Release 4.6, the general menu items are displayed in the menu bar when accessed from outside an application, whereas the menu structure of the components and transactions is displayed in a menu tree in the main window.

The display of user roles and favorites in the menu tree is very useful. Which one of the different menus is shown can be preset by the system administrator or defined by the user via EXTRAS • SETTINGS.

### Standard Menu

If you are not able to see the complete SAP standard menu, select MENU • SAP MENU. The menu structure will be displayed in a vertical tree (see Figure 4.5).

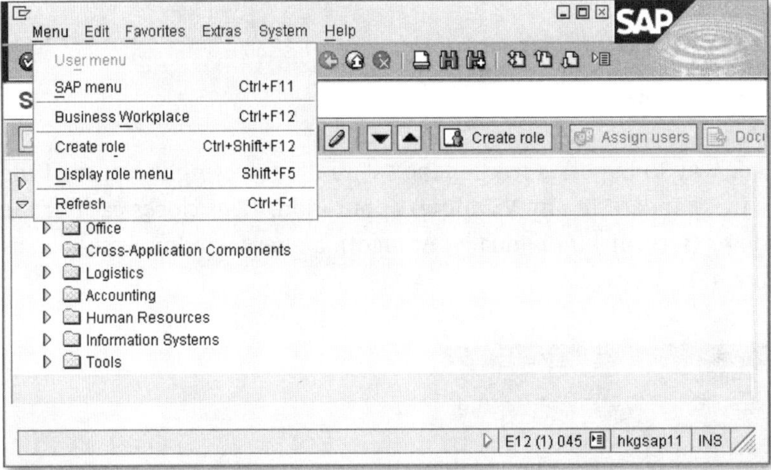


**Figure 4.5** Display of the Standard Menu

### User Menu

If a user menu was set up, you should use this user menu instead of the standard menu. In the user menu, you will find user-specific transactions and reports as well as Internet and intranet addresses for direct selection. The system administrator will usually set up the user menu according to your needs. For this task, the system administrator can select from a range of predefined user roles and enhance or combine these as needed. Typical user roles for QM are inspector, inspection planner, or test equipment administrator.

### Favorites

You are probably familiar with the concept of a favorites list from your Internet browser. In this list, you can add, sort, and remove your preferred transactions and reports as well as Internet or intranet addresses.

### Main Window

After you have logged on, the main SAP ERP window SAP EASY ACCESS will appear. The basic structure with different menu bars is the same for all windows of the system (see Figure 4.6).

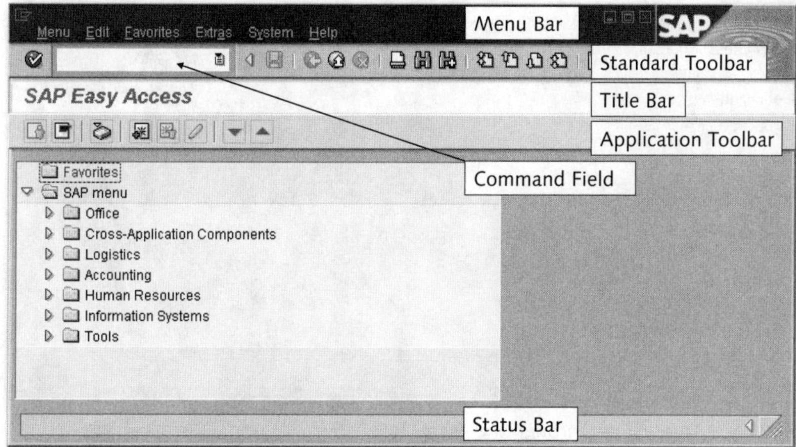


**Figure 4.6** Main Window with Menu Bars

### Title Bar

The title bar displays the name of the window. For example, the title of the main window is SAP EASY ACCESS, and the window titles in inspection planning are DISPLAY INSPECTION PLAN or CREATE INSPECTION PLAN.

### Menu Bar

The menu bar shows all menus that are currently available. If the menu tree is displayed also, the menu bar only contains the general functions because the individual applications are accessed through the menu tree (see Figure 4.7). The menus SYSTEM and HELP are displayed in every window of the SAP ERP system. Selections are made in the same way as in Windows applications, using the mouse or keyboard function key [F10] and the [Up], [Down], [Left], and [Right] arrow keys.

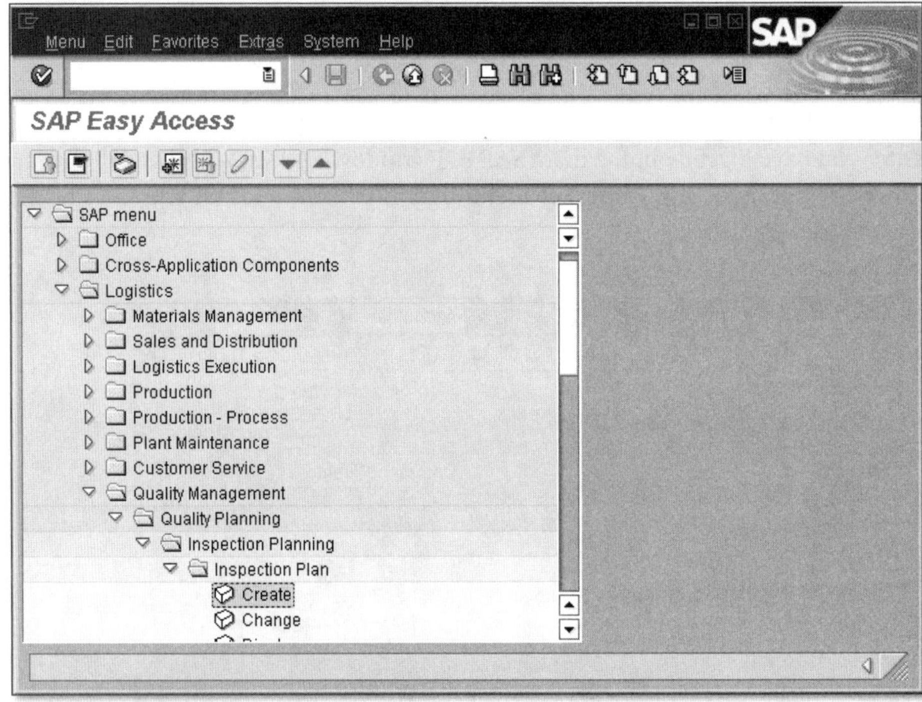


**Figure 4.7** Selecting a Transaction Through the Menu Tree

### Standard Toolbar

The standard toolbar contains icons for frequently used functions, as shown in Figure 4.8. On your screen, the available icons are highlighted in color, and the inactive ones are shaded.

**Figure 4.8** The Standard Toolbar

You can find an overview of the available icons and their meaning in Table 4.1.

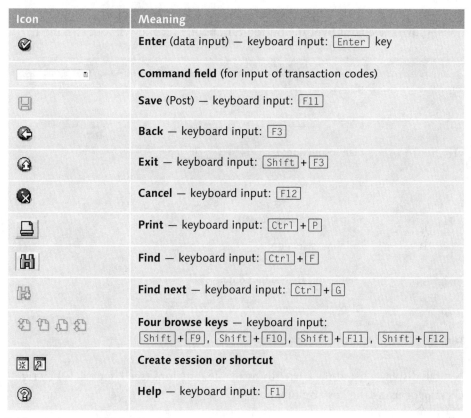

| Icon | Meaning |
|---|---|
| | **Enter** (data input) — keyboard input: Enter key |
| | **Command field** (for input of transaction codes) |
| | **Save** (Post) — keyboard input: F11 |
| | **Back** — keyboard input: F3 |
| | **Exit** — keyboard input: Shift+F3 |
| | **Cancel** — keyboard input: F12 |
| | **Print** — keyboard input: Ctrl+P |
| | **Find** — keyboard input: Ctrl+F |
| | **Find next** — keyboard input: Ctrl+G |
| | **Four browse keys** — keyboard input: Shift+F9, Shift+F10, Shift+F11, Shift+F12 |
| | **Create session or shortcut** |
| | **Help** — keyboard input: F1 |

**Table 4.1** Icons and Their Meanings

### Application Toolbar

The application toolbar is located below the toolbar. It contains some additional buttons for functions that are only available in the current menu (see Figure 4.9). This means the appearance of this menu bar changes according to the currently selected menu.

**Figure 4.9** The Application Toolbar

Frequently used buttons are shown in Table 4.2.

If you are not familiar with a button and want to know something about its functions, move the cursor over the button for about a second without clicking it.

| Button Icon | Meaning |
|---|---|
| | **Run:** [F8] |
| | Delete: [Shift]+[F2] |
| | Plan inspection: [Ctrl]+[Shift]+[F1] |
| | Edit long text: [Shift]+[F4] |
| | Help for selection screen: [Shift]+[F6] |
| | Detail or selection: [F2] |
| | "Hat" indicates header data: [F5] |
| | Display document: [F2] or Select: [F2] |

**Table 4.2** Icons and Their Meanings

You can display a list of the currently available functions (see Figure 4.10) by right-clicking or using the key combination [Ctrl]+[F].

All functions can also be selected using the menu bar of the current window. The icons and buttons provided as well as the functions shown when right-clicking represent a selection that can contain more or less functions than the menu bar.

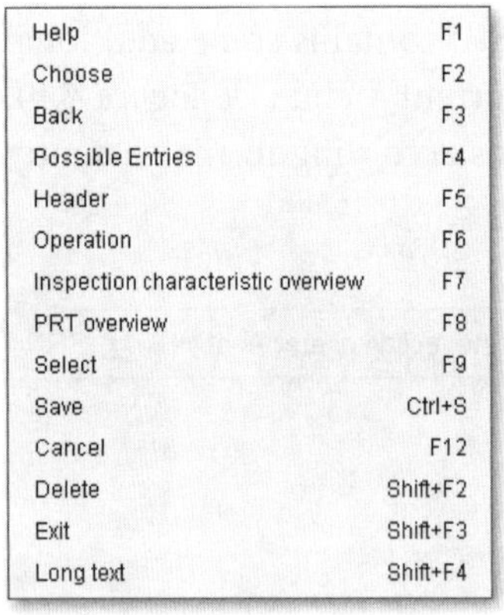

| | |
|---|---|
| Help | F1 |
| Choose | F2 |
| Back | F3 |
| Possible Entries | F4 |
| Header | F5 |
| Operation | F6 |
| Inspection characteristic overview | F7 |
| PRT overview | F8 |
| Select | F9 |
| Save | Ctrl+S |
| Cancel | F12 |
| Delete | Shift+F2 |
| Exit | Shift+F3 |
| Long text | Shift+F4 |

**Figure 4.10** Right-Click Menu

### Status Bar

The status bar at the bottom of the screen consists of an output field in which you are shown SAP ERP system messages that do not open separate windows (see Figure 4.11). There are three types of status messages:

- Information
- Warnings
- Error

**Figure 4.11** Status Message

Moreover, you will find information on the system status (CLIENT, SESSION, SERVER, INSERT/OVERWRITE, TIME). You can set the parameters to be displayed through the SAP GUI.

If a question mark appears in the status bar of a message, you can double-click on the status bar to open the related Help page.

### Dialog Boxes, Checkboxes, and Radio Buttons

An additional element is the dialog box, which is displayed on top of the active window and requires an input or selection (see Figure 4.12). When a dialog box is opened, the status bar often shows a message as well.

You are likely to encounter the status message shown in Figure 4.13 quite often. In some cases, a message box appears instead.

You can close the window by pressing Enter and make the correct entries. In general, required input fields contain a checkmark or a question mark, which tells you that an input is mandatory.

In addition, there are checkboxes (you can choose several options) and radio buttons (you can choose only one option). An example is shown in Figure 4.14.

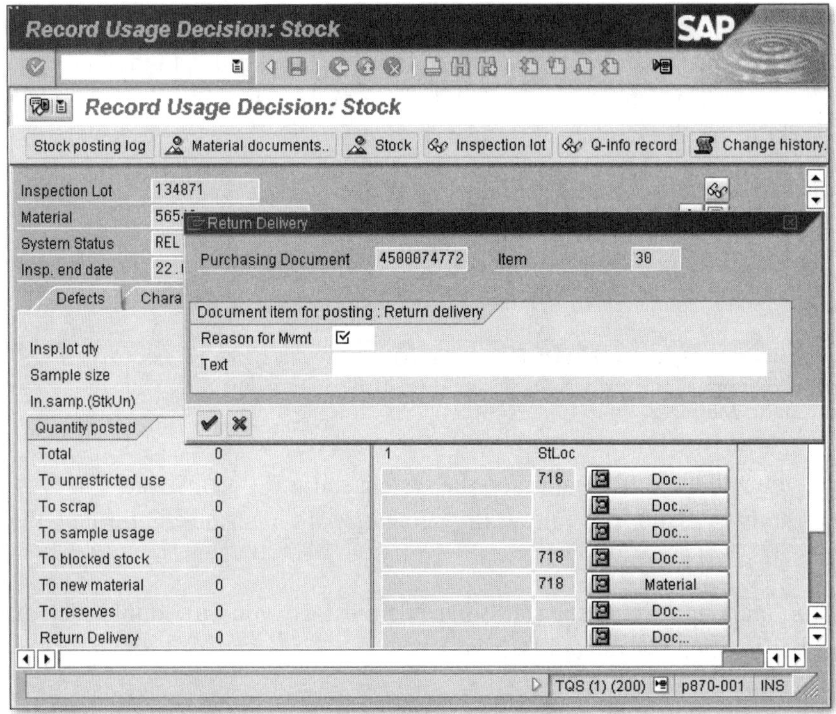


Figure 4.12 Dialog Box

Figure 4.13 Status Message — Error

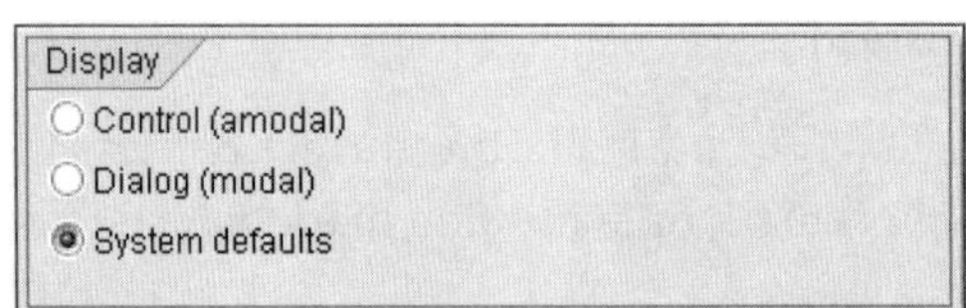


Figure 4.14 Window with Radio Buttons

### Matchcode Search

Whenever the F4 help (input options for a field) contains a list that is too long, the matchcode search is useful.

Wildcards used are "+" for a single character, and "*" for one or more unknown characters. At the end of a word, these characters can be omitted. For example, if you enter the string "*connector*" in the MATERIAL DESCRIPTION field (see Figure 4.15), all materials containing the word "connector," whether at the beginning, in the middle, or at the end of the description, are displayed.

Instead of this direct search, you can press [F4] (input options) to use a search help (e.g., when searching for a material, vendor, etc.). When searching for a material, search helps are provided, as shown in Figure 4.15.

You select a search method by clicking on one of the tabs. If, for example, you want to search by material description, you click on the corresponding tab. A dialog box similar to the one in Figure 4.15 appears. Enter the search term (e.g., MATERIAL DESCRIPTION) here.

If you want to search, for example, for material numbers of the "CD-casing" example, you could enter the search term "CD" in the MATERIAL DESCRIPTION field. The results list would show all material descriptions beginning with "CD," together with the corresponding material number.

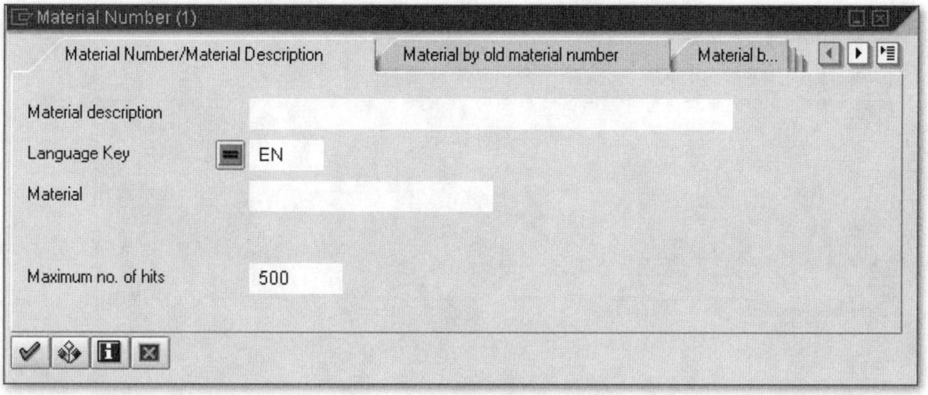

**Figure 4.15** Selecting the Search Help

The selected search (tab), as in this case via MATERIAL BY DESCRIPTION, will be displayed immediately when the search help is opened again later, that is, this setting remains valid until it is changed. By clicking the MULTIPLE SELECTION icon, you can search for multiple values or search within a specified range of values.

## 4.4 Print

This section takes into account the printing of an inspection plan and the output of the screen display.

### Printing an Inspection Plan

The following example shows how to view an inspection plan in print preview or how to print the plan.

Open the Inspection Planning window (path: Logistics • Quality Management • Quality Planning • Inspection Planning), and select Information System • Print Task List (General).

The window Print List for Task List is opened (see Figure 4.16). Enter the material number and select the desired checkboxes. The Run icon or the keyboard input F8 opens the print preview of the inspection plan (see Figure 4.17).

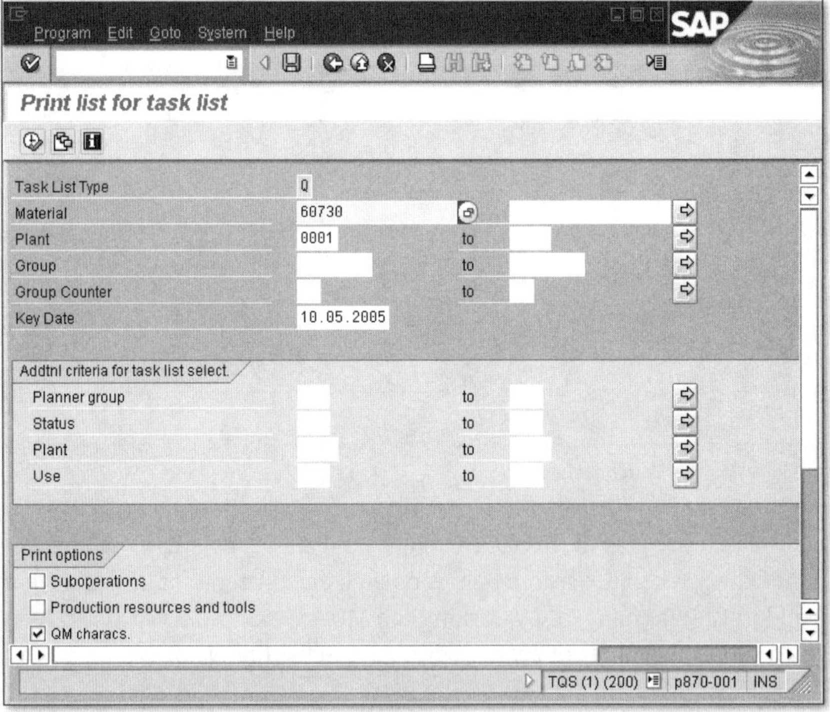


**Figure 4.16** Print List For Task List

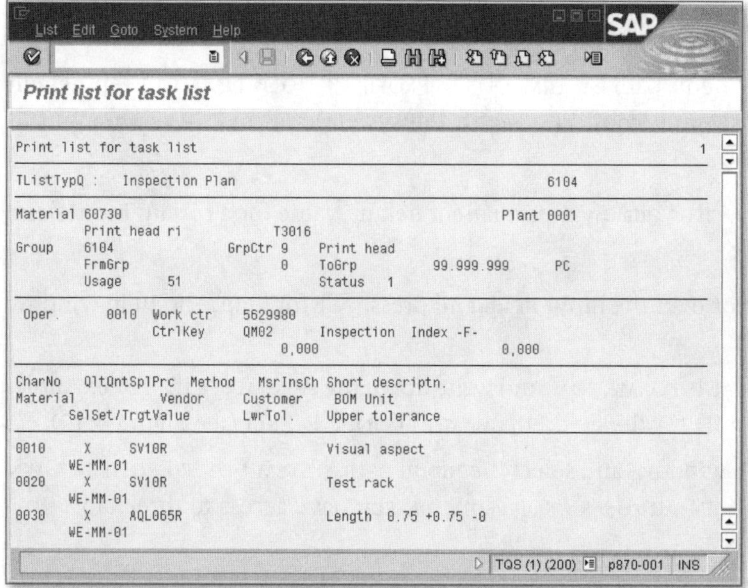


**Figure 4.17** Print Preview of the Inspection Plan

Click the print icon or select LIST • PRINT to print the plan on the assigned printer. Prior to this, the specified OUTPUT DEVICE is displayed. If you want to print the plan to another printer, you can now specify a different output device.

### Output of the Screen Display

Click the icon, and select HARDCOPY from the selection menu. The screen contents are printed to your local default printer (see Figure 4.18).

**Figure 4.18** Screen Print Selection Menu

## 4.5 User Settings: User Profile

You can use the menu path SYSTEM • USER PROFILE • HOLD DATA to keep default values during a session (connection with the system) and reduce the amount of input needed.

If you want to specify your own, permanent default value for a certain input field, do the following:

1. Move the cursor over the input field, and press F1 for help. The Help window appears.
2. Select TECHNICAL INFORMATION, and write down the PARAMETER ID. For example, the PARAMETER ID for the field PURCHASING GROUP is EKO (see Figure 4.19).
3. Close the Help window, and select the menu path SYSTEM • USER PROFILE • OWN DATA. In the MAINTAIN USER PROFILE menu, you have access to three tabs:
   - ADDRESS
   - DEFAULTS
   - PARAMETERS

The ADDRESS view contains personal data (address, title, and department) and contact information (telephone and fax number or email address). These values are used for quality notifications if you want to print telephone or fax numbers with the name of the coordinator (processor).

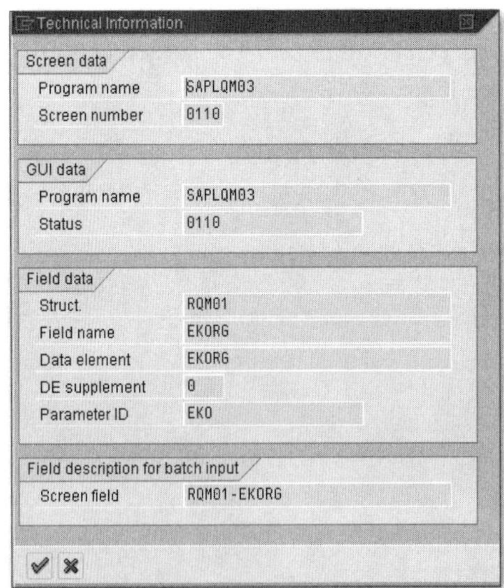


**Figure 4.19** Technical Information

The DEFAULTS view contains information such as the name of the printer or the date format to be used for this user.

Finally, the PARAMETERS view allows you to specify the parameter ID (obtained previously from the Technical Information) as a default value (see Figure 4.20). The list you may find here already can be supplemented with the parameter "EKG" and the desired default value. To complete the operation, save your changes.

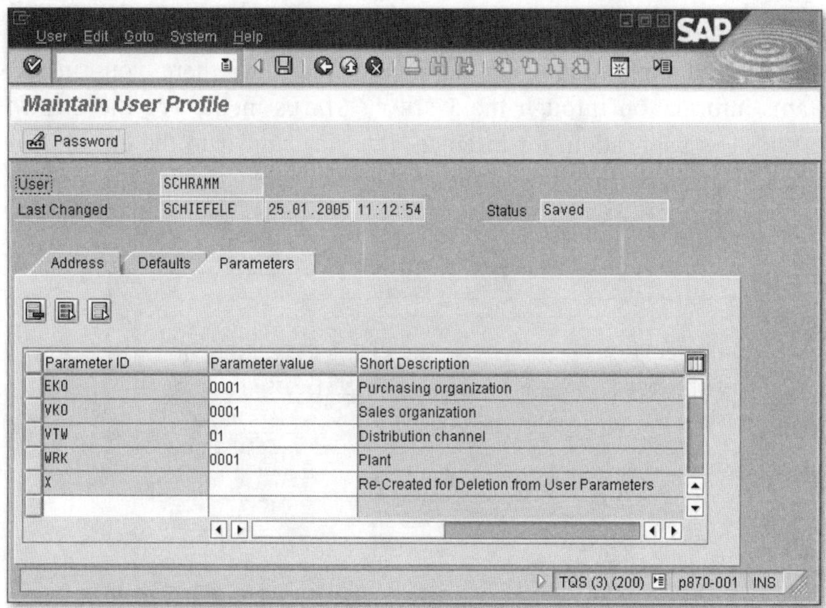


**Figure 4.20** User Parameters

## 4.6 Working with Transaction Codes and Multiple Sessions

To become familiar with the operation of SAP ERP, we recommend accessing all menus through the default menu tree using the mouse. Doing this will make it easier to remember the menu labels, and after a while, you will gain an overview of the menu structure, even if you do not know and use all transactions right from the beginning.

After a few weeks, you can start using the transaction codes as well. These amount to a kind of short description for each processing menu (the transaction). Over time, you will know these transaction codes by heart and be able to switch from one menu to the other instantly, without having to spend several seconds selecting long path names with the mouse.

First of all, however, it is important to find out which transaction code is used for the desired menu. There are two methods to search for transaction codes:

- **Through the status display**
  Select the desired application using the menu paths. Once there, you can display status information through the SYSTEM • STATUS menu. For the CREATE INSPECTION PLAN application, for instance, a display similar to the one shown in Figure 4.21 appears. The TRANSACTION field contains the transaction code (in this case QP01).

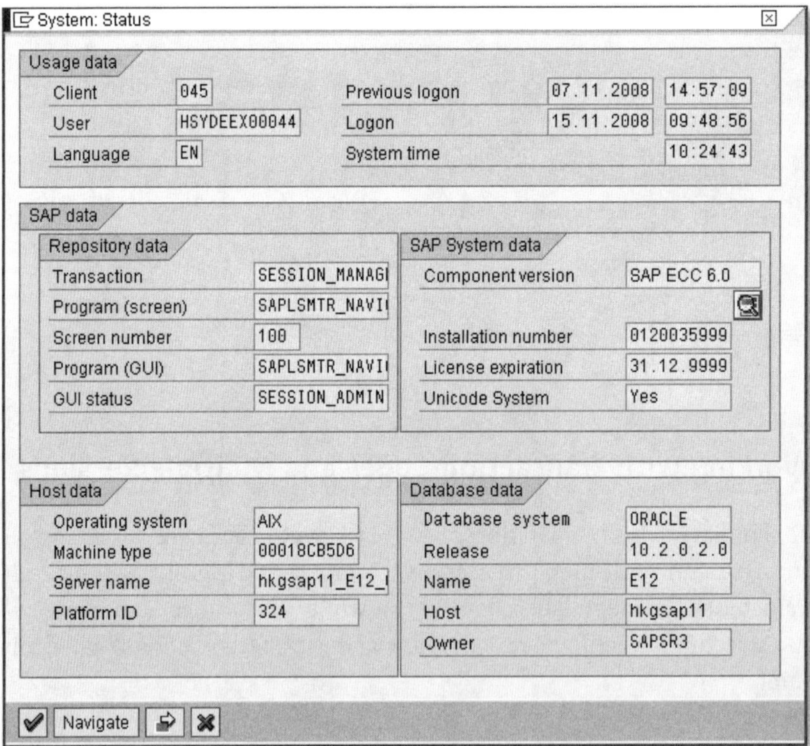


**Figure 4.21** System: Status with Transaction Code

- **Through the menu tree**
  For an overview of several transaction codes for a work area, you can use the menu tree. On the standard toolbar, select EXTRAS • SETTINGS, and click DISPLAY TECHNICAL NAMES (see Figure 4.22).

Click the branches of the menu tree until you reach the transactions (with the cuboid symbol). The transaction codes (TECHNICAL NAMES) will be displayed. The example in Figure 4.23 shows the transaction codes for CREATE INSPECTION PLAN (QP01), CHANGE INSPECTION PLAN (QP02), DISPLAY INSPECTION PLAN (QP03), and others.

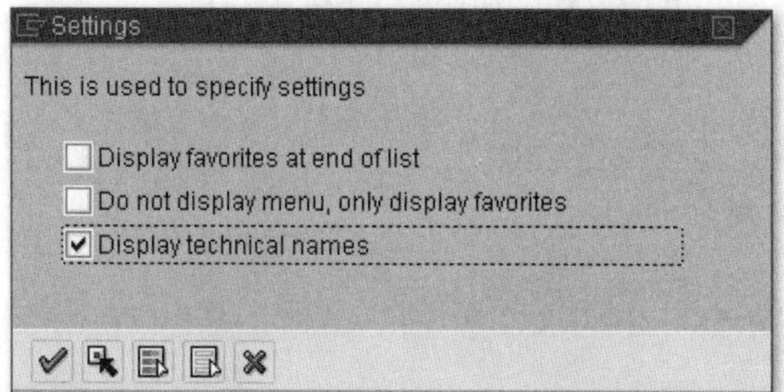


**Figure 4.22** Selection Menu Item Display Technical Names

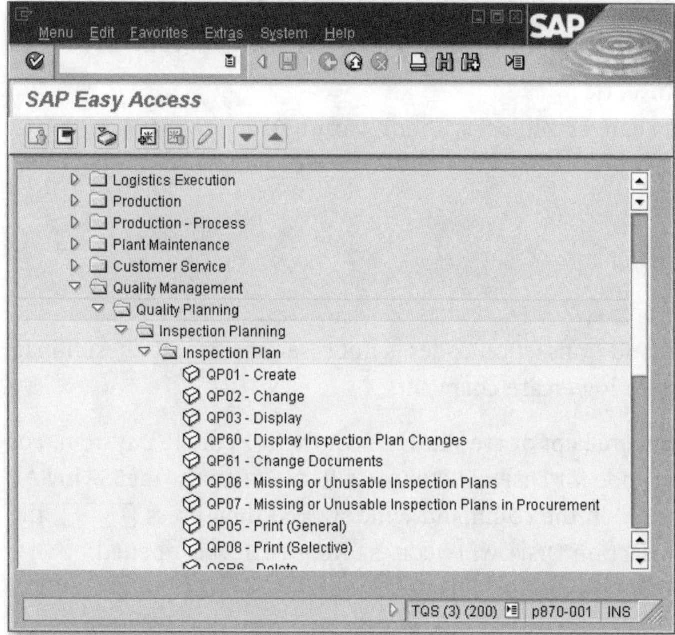


**Figure 4.23** Dynamic Menu

You can work with multiple sessions (display windows) at the same time. You can switch between sessions in the same way you toggle between windows in Microsoft Windows (e.g., with the key combination [Alt]+[Tab]).

The combination of multiple sessions and transaction codes enables fast and efficient work. You can open a maximum of six sessions at a time, keeping in mind that each session consumes a certain amount of system performance.

By using the transaction codes found and the command field, it is possible to navigate quickly from one transaction to the other. To enter commands, place the cursor in the command field of the standard toolbar (see Figure 4.24).

**Figure 4.24** Command Field of the Standard Toolbar

Using the command field, you can enter and trigger the following commands by pressing Enter:

- **Starting a Transaction**
  - In the same session (window), enter: "/nxxxx" (xxxx = transaction code).
  - In an additional session, enter: "/oxxxx" (xxxx = transaction code).
- **Terminating the transaction**
  Enter: "/n" (unsaved changes get lost without warning).
- **Deleting the session**
  Enter: "/i".
- **Generating a session list**
  Enter: "/o".

The input of commands and transaction codes is not case sensitive; it doesn't matter if you use uppercase or lowercase characters.

Many transaction codes were kept or are similar to those from the R/2 system. For example, the transaction code for DISPLAY: PURCHASE REQUISITION is "me53" in SAP ERP. If you enter "/nme53" in the command window and then press [Enter], the initial menu for the transaction DISPLAY: PURCHASE REQUISITION is opened.

> **Tip**
>
> You can, for example, use a session mode to view an inspection plan in the INSPECTION PLANNING menu and at the same time use a second session to display related data in the MATERIAL MASTER.

You can open a new window (session) by placing the prefix "/o" in front of the transaction code, by selecting the path SYSTEM • CREATE SESSION, or by clicking the icon in the application toolbar.

## 4.7 Help in the SAP ERP System

The SAP ERP system provides you with a variety of help options that will be briefly described in the following sections.

In most cases, you will use the *direct help* (F1 help) for an input field. Highlight the text of the input field by clicking it (the text will be shown with a dotted border), or place the cursor in the input field and press F1. A short help text regarding the field will be displayed (see Figure 4.25).

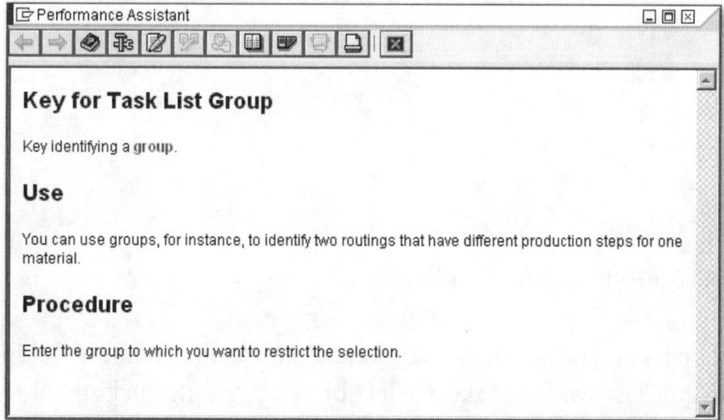


**Figure 4.25** Help Window Called with F1

If this help text does not answer your question, you can click APPLICATION HELP (in Version 4.0 referred to as EXTENDED HELP). However, this requires that you work with the Windows operating system and have Internet Explorer installed on your system because the APPLICATION HELP needs this browser as an interface. Instead of using the F1 key, you can open the HELP menu (in Version 4.0 also referred to as Direct Help) by clicking the question mark symbol in the toolbar. The third option is the *context menu*, which you can open by right-clicking. The first menu item in this context menu is also the DIRECT HELP.

From the DIRECT HELP (in addition to the APPLICATION HELP), you can also select the technical information by clicking the TECHNICAL INFORMATION icon. As described in Section 4.5, User Settings, the technical information provides you with different information such as transaction codes, and field and table names that can be important for troubleshooting.

A further option of the system is the so-called INPUT HELP "Possible Entries" (F4 help). This kind of help is especially useful if you need to enter a value or code but do not know exactly what value or code to enter. Move the cursor over the field and click the arrow to the right of the field, or press F4. The display for the STORAGE LOCATION field is shown in Figure 4.26.

**Figure 4.26** Selection Options for the Storage Location

Select a line by double-clicking it. You can display a calendar for all data input fields by pressing F4. The quickest way to make a selection is by double-clicking.

If there are many input options for a field, a dialog box for further restriction is shown after pressing F4 (see the description of matchcode search earlier in Section 4.3, User Interface). The HELP menu in the menu bar provides different options (see Figure 4.27).

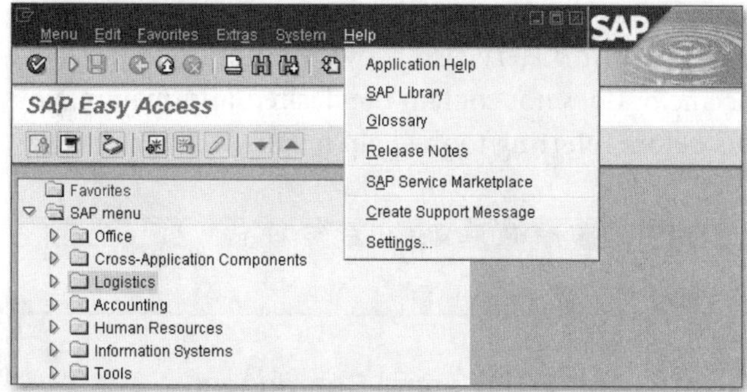


**Figure 4.27** Selection Options in Help

Using the path HELP • SAP LIBRARY, you can navigate to the SAP library. On selection, the browser is opened. Clicking the node in the left part of the window opens the various "books" of the SAP library (see Figure 4.28). If you click the SAP ERP CENTRAL COMPONENT BOOK, a new window appears. There as well, you open the book by clicking the node and the LOGISTICS NODE; there you can find the QUALITY MANAGEMENT BOOK (see Figure 4.29). Another click on this window opens a third window in which you can find the help of the QM module. On the left side, you can see a menu structure and on the right side the respective help text. You can navigate through the tree structure and select the help topics there. The SAP Library provides a detailed explanation for each module and function.

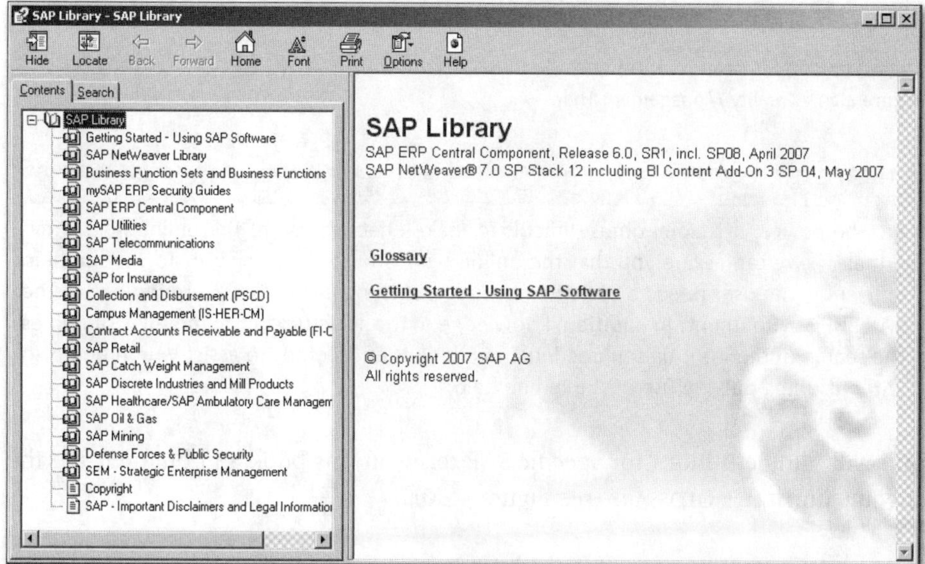


**Figure 4.28** SAP Library

If you are already in an application (and not in the Start menu), for example in Inspection Planning, the APPLICATION HELP also shows the application-related topic. If this topic is too specific or does not contain the desired information, you should go back a few menus before referring to the help menu.

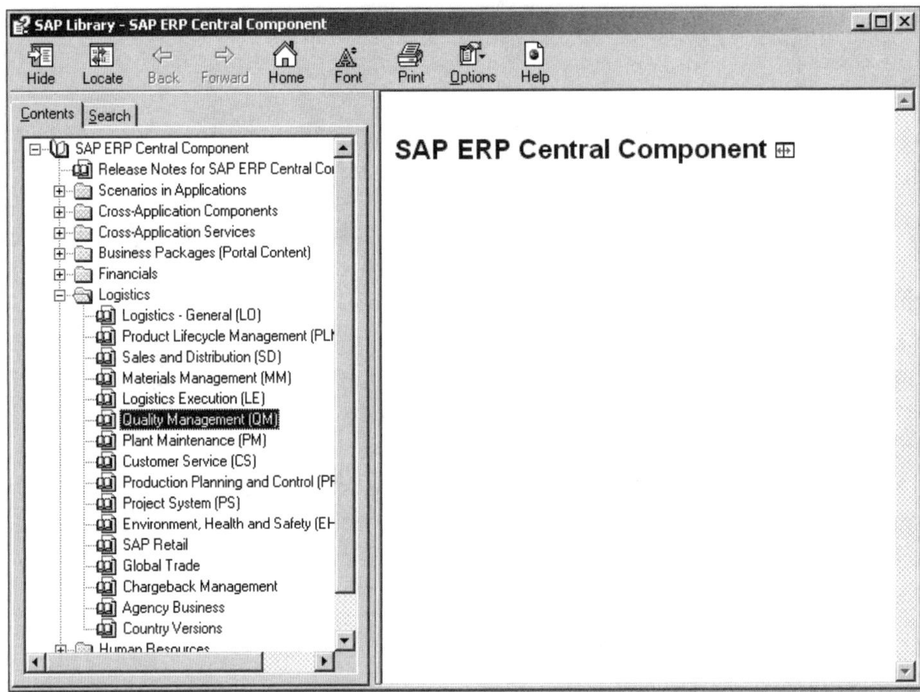


**Figure 4.29** Quality Management Help

**Tip**

For the novice, it is sometimes difficult to make effective use of the online help. Nevertheless, we can assure you that the online help is in fact easy to use. To use the help efficiently, the user needs a certain knowledge of the concepts and terminology of the SAP ERP environment. In addition, knowledge of the structure of the modules simplifies the search of the information needed. This book is an attempt to assist you in doing so without ruling out the use of the online help.

You will find definitions for specific SAP terms in this book and online using the menu path HELP • GLOSSARY (see Figure 4.30).

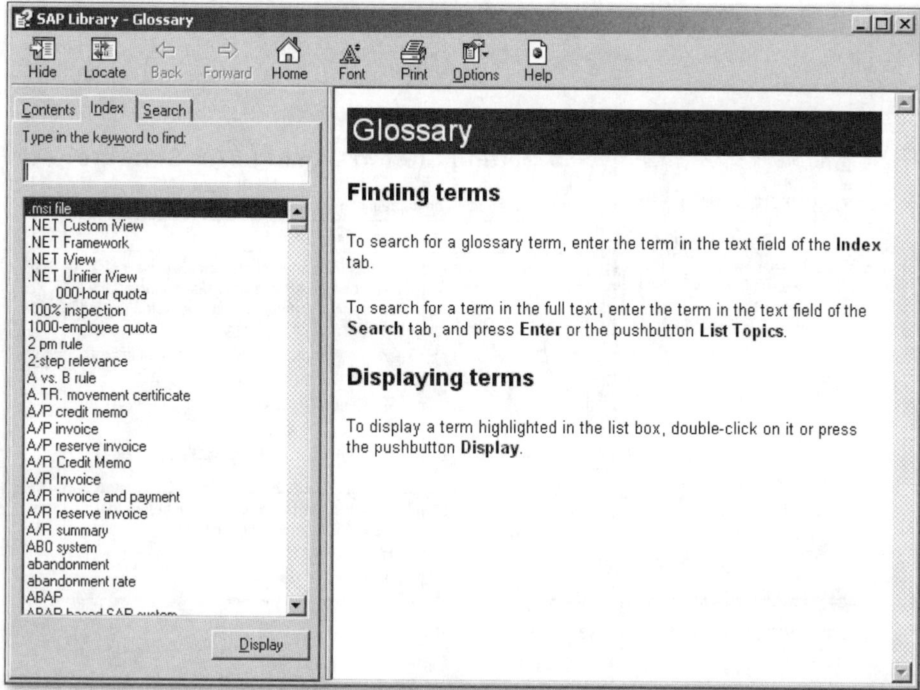


**Figure 4.30** Glossary

The first book of the SAP library is called *Introduction to the Use of SAP Software* (see Figure 4.31). There you can find basic information on the registration, use of the GUI, and the help. You can specify under HELP • SETTINGS if the [F1] help should appear in a normal window (modal window) or using the performance assistant. The type of presentation depends on your personal preferences.

In the submenu RELEASE NOTES, you will find information on what has changed in the respective SAP ERP release. Again, the information is internally structured by application components. This information is especially interesting if you have moved to another release and want to know which changes are important to you.

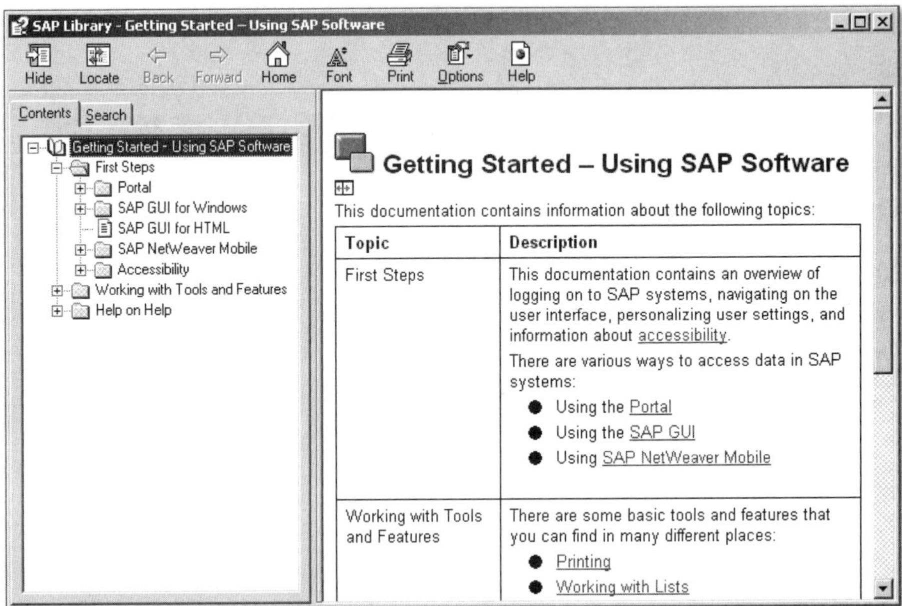


**Figure 4.31** Introduction to the Use of SAP Software

## 4.8 Display Functions and List Displays

This section is intended to illustrate the practical use of some important display functions from the logistics process because these are useful for your work in quality management. More detailed information on display and evaluation can be found in Chapter 10, Information Systems and Evaluations, and in the relevant sections of other chapters.

### Vendor Data

In QM, a good contact to the vendors is especially important. To ensure this, you need address and other contact information. You will find this data in the PURCHASING menu, which you can reach via the following path: LOGISTICS • MATERIALS MANAGEMENT • PURCHASING. From there select MASTER DATA • VENDOR • PURCHASING • DISPLAY (CURRENT) (see Figure 4.32).

After entering the vendor number and the purchasing organization, and selecting the checkmark in the ADDRESS field, the address and communication data is displayed.

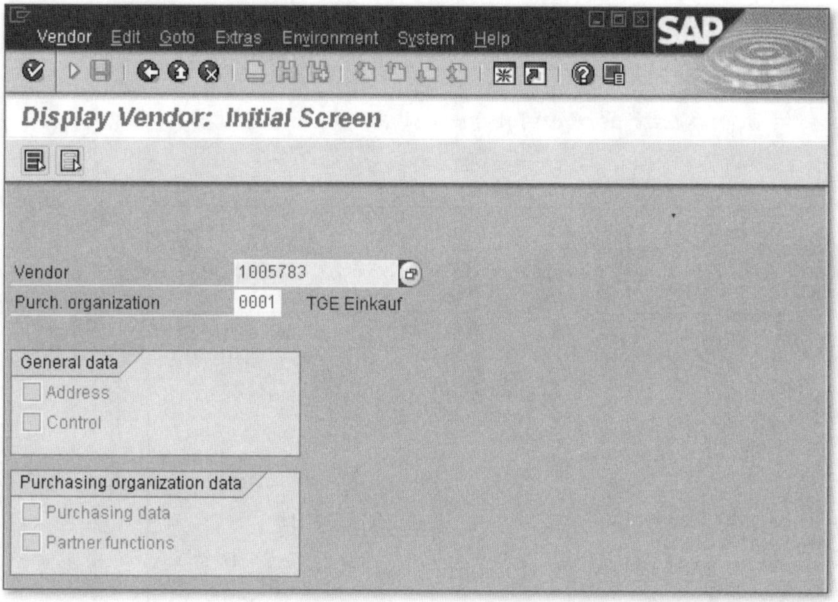

**Figure 4.32** Display of Vendor Address

### List Display: Goods Receipts from the Vendors

It will often turn out that you are not only interested in the current worklist of inspection lots but also in the development of the latest goods receipts of a certain vendor. The list-display function, which can be found at several locations in the SAP ERP system, is suitable for this task. The starting point is the Purchasing menu. There you can select Purchase Order • List Displays • By Vendor to switch to a selection screen titled Purchasing Documents per Vendor. Selection screens are easy to identify because they contain many input fields requiring value ranges "from/to" and the eye-catching Run icon. The input fields allow you to enter different selection parameters such as the vendor number. If you do not know the selection value, you can use the matchcode search described earlier (function key F4). After clicking Run, a display such as the one shown in Figure 4.33 will appear.

If you select the purchase order item and click the PO History button (Purchase Order History), a display will be shown indicating on which date you received which delivery quantities (see Figure 4.34).

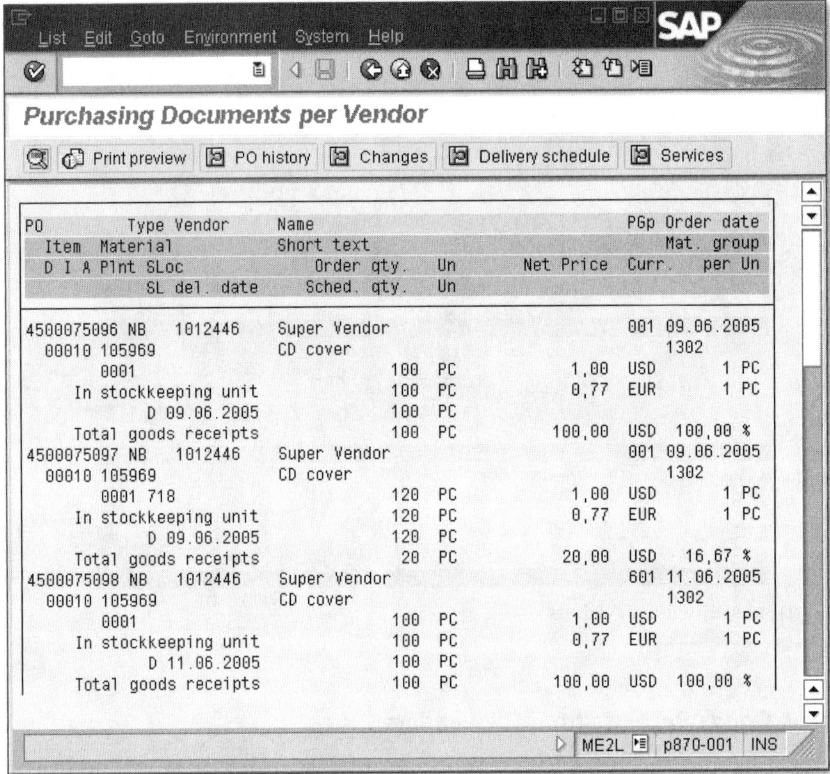


**Figure 4.33** List Display: Purchasing Documents per Vendor

List Edit Goto Views Environment System Help

*Order History for Purchase Order 4500075101 00010*

GR/IR assignment | Order price unit | Blocked stock

| Cat. | Doc. no. | Itm | MvT | Pstg.dt. | Qty.in OUn | | Value in local curr | |
|---|---|---|---|---|---|---|---|---|
| GR | 50249405 | 0001 | 101 | 11.06.05 | 25 | PC | 19,28 | EUR |
| GR | 50249406 | 0001 | 101 | 11.06.05 | 25 | PC | 19,28 | EUR |
| Total goods receipts | | | | | 50 | PC | 38,56 | EUR |

ME2L p870-001 INS

**Figure 4.34** Purchase Order History

### Stock Overview

An information of similar interest is found in the warehouse stock of a material. In the first step, select LOGISTICS • MATERIALS MANAGEMENT • MATERIAL MASTER and then OTHER — STOCK OVERVIEW. In the selection list displayed, enter the PLANT and MATERIAL NUMBER. A display will appear showing the storage location together with information on whether the goods can be freely used or whether they are in inspection stock (see Figure 4.35).

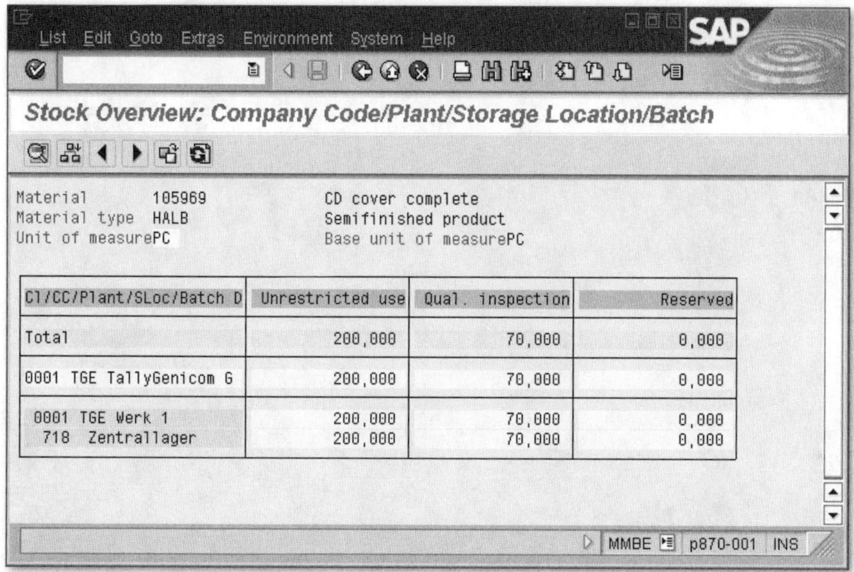


**Figure 4.35** Stock Overview

Of course, there are many more display options from Logistics that could be important to your company. The previous examples illustrated some of the options available. The list displays needed for your purposes can best be defined with your company's purchasing, logistics, and production departments.

*This chapter is intended primarily for quality managers, IT managers, and project managers of SAP ERP logistics projects. You will first gain an overview of the most important accompanying and integrated functions of SAP QM in the supply chain and then find detailed descriptions of the individual modules.*

# 5 Quality Management in the Supply Chain

Initially, this chapter provides the basic information for the quality management in a supply chain. Then Supply Chain Management (SCM) and Materials Management (MM) are taken into account.

## 5.1 Basic Principles

Understanding quality management as a productive component of a company's supply chain is important in recognizing both the basic requirements and potential for process improvement. As soon as the work of QM is seen as a real operational activity, the question of whether it makes sense to implement computer support is no longer an issue.

Within the supply chain, activities relevant to quality are executed internally and externally (see Figure 5.1). A homogenous process design from the point of view of QM, combined with the use of integrated software, enables these activities to be executed at the required level. Further, consistent implementation of the QM system results in an exceptional transparency regarding the quality of the logistics process. The properties of the QM components are essentially based on the quality-control cycle and quality-pyramid models.

**Figure 5.1** QM Elements in the Supply Chain

The quality circle (see Figure 5.2) results from the requirements and expectations of the customer. The customer does not just judge only the product quality here but rather the quality of the entire vendor relationship. Given that vendors today generally audit their customers, a complete QM approach based on the supply chain has a more positive impact on quality evaluation than an approach based on islands of CAQ (Computer Aided Quality Assurance) solutions.

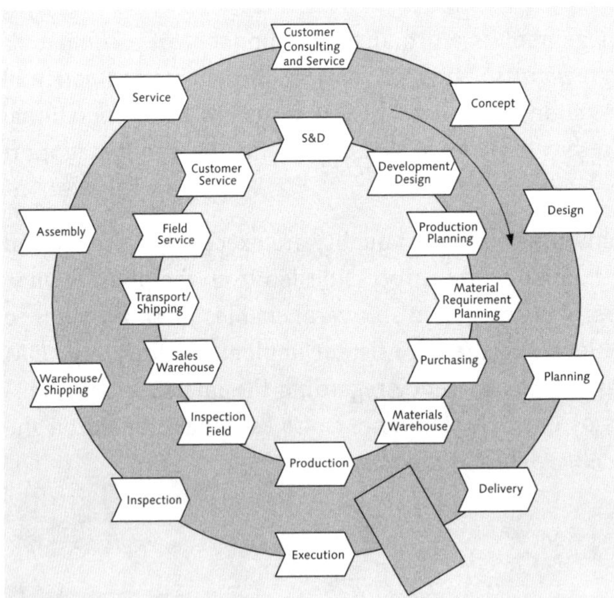


**Figure 5.2** Quality-Control Cycle

## 5.2 Supply Chain Management

Increased competitive and technological pressure causes many companies to focus on core competencies, a trend confirmed by the constant reduction in vertical integration. This development leads to a permanent increase in purchased materials, components, and also services. This makes having efficient vendors increasingly important, if not crucial! In addition to the internal logistical value chain, the interfaces between vendors and buyers contain a great potential for optimization. The Supply Chain Management (SCM) strategy is based on this. Purchasing, often operated as pure "vendor-rating," thus becomes a strategic company function. The differences between traditional purchasing and SCM are detailed in Table 5.1.

| Traditional Purchasing | Supply Chain Management |
|---|---|
| Short-term view, opportunity-based cooperation | Long-term partnership |
| Price-oriented | Total costs |
| Broad vendor basis | Single sourcing, modular sourcing |
| Much vendor change | Very little vendor change |
| Unreliable delivery | Synchronized delivery |
| Functional separation | Functional integration |
| Separated development | Common development |
| Uncoordinated capacities | Uncoordinated capacities |
| Interrupted information flow | Consistent information flow |

**Table 5.1** Comparison Between Traditional Purchasing and Supply Chain Management

The formation of a value-creation partnership requires mutual willingness to improve the efficiency of the cooperation. The basis of every partnership is trust, without which close collaboration can never be successful. To evaluate the collaboration between vendors and customers, SCM uses a number of factors, a few of which are essential for quality management (see Table 5.2).

SCM will certainly gain further importance for quality management in the supply chain. The system functions and processes in the SAP ERP system also support you in developing a fruitful customer-vendor relationship.

| Factor | Very Little Partnership | Complete Partnership |
|---|---|---|
| Vendor relationship | Mistrust, broad vendor base, frequent change of vendors | Complete trust, single sourcing, partnership, vendor support |
| Management | Focus on direct production costs, no commitment to partnerships, purchasing as a necessary evil | Focus on the supply chain, concentration on quality, costs, cycle times, early integration of vendors, sharing of the savings |
| Organization | Functional, decentralized purchasing | Horizontal, cross-sector teams, central corporate sourcing, and decentralized operative purchasing |
| Controlling | Price | Total costs (price, costs for insufficient quality, as well as poor vendor service) |
| Quality | No clear specification, incoming inspection, no SPC (Statistical Process Control) | Target quality, specified QM system, planned dynamic incoming inspection, SPC |
| Costs | The provider with the best offer receives today's contract, increasingly wider distribution spectrum | Target costing, reduction of the distribution spectrum, concentration of the business volume |
| Cycle times | High safety stocks, long lead times, no forecasts | Pull system (Kanban), just in time, short lead times, rolling forecasts |

**Table 5.2** Developing a Partnership in Supply Chain Management

## 5.3 Materials Management

The business processes of Materials Management (MM) are accompanied by activities of quality management that take place in the following areas:

- Procurement
- Production
- Sales and Distribution
- Services

### 5.3.1 Procurement

Let's first look at the release of vendor relations.

#### Release of Vendor Relations

The functionalities of the *quality info record* enable you to control the release of material and vendor relations. The release can occur on a time-related or quantity-related basis or by drawing on other criteria such as the existence of specific documents (recognition of technical vendor conditions, specifications, etc.). Depending on the weighting of the quality measures, the request, purchase order, or goods receipt is locked.

#### Vendor Selection

The activities of the vendor selection for new and existing products are organized across various specialist areas and culminate in the vendor evaluation under MM. In the vendor evaluation, you can assign scores to criteria that include delivery, price, and quality, and you can assess and summarize them as you wish. If you audit your vendor, the audit result is also included in the calculation of the quality score.

By comparing the requirements with the actual quality management system (ISO 9000 and those following, QS 9000, VDA, etc.), you can make sure that only companies with the corresponding certification are considered for vendor relationships.

#### Request and Purchase Order

QM agreements with the vendors are involved in the release of the vendor relationship. If these are not available at the time of the request or purchase order, the quality-control system can automatically warn the purchasing department against processing of the purchase order or, if necessary, call a halt to the request or purchase order.

#### Status of the Vendor Relationships

In the supplying of industrial products, a sampling procedure usually takes place before the actually supply occurs. Sampling involves inspection models, and, in cases where series of products are supplied, there will be models for preliminary series and for actual series. Different inspections are necessary for different supply stages. Depending on the supply status, the system is capable of providing the correct inspection plans.

#### Acceptance

Particularly in engineering and plant construction, the acceptance of products for supply on the vendor side is advisable. The QM component enables you to manage the acceptance dates and to create inspection lots that contain the acceptance criteria in a timely way.

#### Inventory Management with SAP QM

To document the properties of a delivered material, a material inspection certificate is often a direct component of the delivery. It is absolutely necessary that you determine the existence of such a certificate upon delivery. The system provides options to query the existence of a certificate immediately upon receipt of goods and to make sure a correct certificate is received. In critical cases, you can block the goods receipt or post the delivery in a blocked stock. If document management is provided in your project, you have the option of archiving the certificates through optical storage and assigning them to the deliveries.

At the MM level, you can post a delivery through the goods receipt to different stock categories, such as UNRESTRICTED-USE, USEABLE, LOCKED, or to the INSPECTION STOCK. In the case of a planned incoming inspection, the system places the goods in the QUALITY INSPECTION STOCK. The material is thus protected against an undesired posting in the unrestricted-use stock. From then on, quantity postings or stock transfers are only possible via the usage decision. Additional entries in the material master with regard to the entire duration of the goods receipt, and of the inspection duration, further support the materials resource planning (MRP). The functions of inventory management and of the SAP QM component are integrated in SAP ERP. In the supply status, the processes of QM stock postings and inspection-lot creation are activated and are available after the completion of a business-scenario modeling. For inspection-lot creation, you can select processes for inspecting only the first receipt of goods, an individual delivery, or one batch per purchase order.

To reduce the effort of inspection and maintain good supply quality, skip-lot procedures are available for a skipped inspection. In this context, the system generates inspection lots that automatically create an ACCEPTANCE usage decision during a skip level, which posts the goods to the free stock.

#### Inspection and Release of the Incoming Goods

The inspection lot, with the inspection plan provided through the task-list usage, contains all specifics on the document flow, the inspection instructions, and specifications — as well as the quantity and the sampling instructions. For inspection processing, the inspection lot is the core of all subsequent activities. You can navigate to the inspection processes via the inspection lot number or via the structure list in the WORKLIST FOR RESULTS RECORDING. For inspection, quantitative, and qualitative characteristics are provided in different recording types.

The USAGE DECISION is made on the basis of inspection results. You can record the quantities of the delivery according to acceptance and rejection criteria, determine the usage, and post directly to the desired stock.

Completing the usage decision with an evaluation code updates the quality score. The quality level for the next inspection can be updated after the usage decision or during the lot creation.

#### Manufacturer Inspection

If the supplier of the goods is not the actual manufacturer, but you want to evaluate the manufacturer, you can record the supply quality at the manufacturer level. Therefore, for most QM functions, it is possible to establish a reference to the manufacturer. For this reason, the reference is taken into account carefully in the areas of inspection planning, vendor approval, and evaluation and quality notifications.

#### Complaints About Deliveries

During the incoming inspection or in further processing of the products delivered, deficiencies can become obvious. To eliminate deficiencies, measures with regard to the vendor and the internal organization are necessary. An important activity in the case of complaints against vendors is to inform them and to demand a speedy elimination of deficiencies. In the complaint against the vendor, you can record the problem, the error analysis, and all measures related to this process. You can use the integrated form printouts to provide written information to the vendor. The complaint against the vendor allows you to establish a direct reference to the delivery, the purchase order, and the returns processing. The functions of the complaints against the vendors have a workflow character and can be processed by several departments.

#### Warehouse Management

Although the Warehouse Management System (WMS) is part of the Logistics Execution System (LES) component, it still represents an independent component within the SAP ERP logistics package. It is even possible to operate the WMS as an independent, decentralized warehouse-management system.

Through the WMS, the stocks are distributed to storage bins at the storage locations level. Often, the assignments to the storage bin must take place before the delivery has undergone the incoming inspection, or a skip posts the goods there directly. Due to the administration of QM, the goods also receive the stock identifier "Q" at the storage bin. The traceable document flow of the goods movements provides you with precise information on which goods are freely usable at the individual storage bins or are blocked for withdrawal.

During the inspection planning, you can already determine that the sampling portion of the inspection lot finds its way to the inspection point. The remaining quantity is moved immediately from the goods receiving area to the storage bin. It is also possible to postpone the delivery until release with the usage decision in the goods-receiving area and to manually post it to the storage bin at a later stage. For the lot quantities, the system generates transport orders based on the need for storage and qualifies the stocks at the storage bins according to the result of the usage decision.

#### Batches

The interoperation of the components MM and SAP QM enables you to implement a quality strategy that is based on batches. If batch management is active on the MM side, the inspection lot receives a batch reference for incoming inspections and recurring inspections. The usage decision defines the batch status at completion of the inspection lot. You can divide the different batches with recurring inspections in unrestricted use and blocked stocks. Another function within the recurring inspection is monitoring the durability of a batch. As soon as the expiration date is reached, the system converts the batch into the blocked status and changes the batch status to "restricted."

### 5.3.2 Production

With the Production Planning and Control component (PP), the SAP ERP system contains a complete system for production processes with different production strategies such as the following:

- Batch production in chemistry and food production (PP-PI)
- Single part and lot production in mechanical engineering
- Repetitive manufacturing, as in the automotive sector

With QM, SAP provides a standardized approach for all quality-relevant activities in different production forms.

#### Integrated Planning

The inspection processes that accompany production are also essentially value-creating activities, as are the other work processes required to manufacture a product. For this reason, inspection planning in production is completely integrated in the routing. Inspection planning and work scheduling are provided with a uniform design and the same user interface. The inspection characteristics and production resources and tools are each assigned to one or to several operations in the routing. Because the operation with inspection characteristics does not distinguish itself from other operations, capacity, and termination planning are also possible.

#### Inspections in Production

The automatic inspection-lot creation for inspections that accompany production is triggered by the release of the production order. Other forms of automatic inspection-lot creation also provide goods movements, for example, for goods issue or for withdrawal of goods from production on the basis of separate inspection plans. Batch-driven production is supported with inspections for individual batches or for the entire production order.

### Inspection Points

The alternative to inspection based on lots is sampling inspection at regular intervals or at fixed event times. This inspection control enables you to more precisely monitor production processes with repetitive or process manufacturing or extensive lot sizes. For SPC inspections, the inspection sequence must be controlled at fixed intervals. In the QM component, repetitive inspections during production for a specific production order are referred to as *inspection points*.

### Process Control

With the functions of SPC chart technology, QM provides a complete tool for statistical process control. The visual control chart in the form of graphical processes supports the plant operator inspection. The accompanying statistical methods that are based on the measured values entered, help in analyzing the process and determining optimal intervention limits.

To put it simply, SPC is a method that not only checks whether specification limits are being maintained within the process but optimizes the process by using distribution forms and statistical metrics. Such a procedure can free the process run of unnecessary fluctuations and influences, which cause losses in quality. In SPC-stabilized processes, the error rate is also considerably lower.

### Process Management

If you cannot use production processes with SPC, or if it is difficult to do so, then graphical representations of measured values can provide important information on the stability of the production. These illustrations of results are not even interrupted if attributes are adjusted during the running production. If changes to the inspection plan are necessary during the running process, you can create a new inspection lot for the same order, with the updated inspection plan after the inspection lot is completed.

### Batches

QM supports batch-driven production processes by connecting inspection results with the batch number and the batch evaluation.

#### Confirmations

The confirmation of a production order is normally executed through a function of the PP component. The confirmation contains the manufactured quantity, the scrap, and the portion of parts to be reworked. If inspection points are used, the confirmation is integrated in the results recording for the inspection point.

An operation that is exclusively selected for an inspection can be used to connect the confirmation with the quality notification. Via a simple enhancement, the confirmation directly triggers the quality notification, or the quality notification is generated during the results recording for the inspection. Thus, in later analyses, it is easy to establish a connection between the production orders and operations with the main error areas.

### 5.3.3 Sales

Initially, the quality documents are described.

#### Quality Documents on the Vendor Relationship

You can manage the technical terms of delivery and product specifications with info records in the same way as the operations in procurement. The system-integrated document management can also enable fast access to documents.

#### Goods-Issue Inspection

If a particular qualification is required for the products, events generate inspection lots during the shipping process. Controls can be set for when inspections are made and which usage-decision deliveries can be made, depending on the customer, the sales organization, and the material.

#### Inspections of Configuration Variants

Products with identical material numbers can be produced and sold in different versions. The system supports this procedure with its variant configuration. Characteristics that refer to variable attributes naturally must also be designed as variables. You can thus determine in the system that specifications defined in the customer order during inspections are also assigned the relevant characteristics.

### Batch Tracing

The system provides supporting functions for all processes for which you or your customers require batch management or tracing. In this context, knowledge of the interrelationship between the delivery and the batches used is of central importance. Batch tracing in the supply chain also enables you to identify which raw-material batches go into the final product. All inspection results, the usage decision, and the inspection lots contain the batch number as additional information and can be analyzed accordingly.

If different batches merge to form one product, you can inspect the product with regard to the batches it contains. You can use the same system functionality in reverse to learn which batches have been processed to form which products.

The where-used list provides the necessary information for a quality certificate with the inspection results from the preceding or used batches. All results can be compiled into one certificate and printed out as a form.

### Customer Complaints

The system supports extensive customer-complaint management with integrated functions. You can document the complaint process from the initial receipt of a complaint via the error analysis to the monitoring of measures. A customer complaint is a component of the SAP ERP notification system, with standardized and typical functional characteristics. Quality management can structure all notification-relevant business scenarios with the notification system and generate a workflow in the returns processing through the system.

### Certificates

The documentation of basic materials contained in the product and additional inspection results are often part of the delivery, and you must compile these as carefully as you do for the delivery itself. A complete documentation consists of plant-inspection certificates whose form is laid down in international standards, as well as freely definable certificates.

The creation of a certificate is determined by individual customer requirements regarding the form and content of the documents. The system provides the option of creating customer-oriented forms based on useful templates with SAPscript.

For deliveries, you can set the desired certificate up front. During the certificate creation the recipient, form, and content as well as the dispatch medium are taken into account. When compiling the certificate data, the program retrieves the specific master and transaction data relevant for the preparation of the report and consolidates this in the certificate printout. The report provides access to all relevant data from MM, QM, and SD, such as batch values, characteristic values, inspection results, and order information. The quality documents generated in this way can then be stored in the integrated document management by using SAP ArchiveLink.

#### Internet

Your customer can then retrieve information on the content of the quality certificates directly through the Internet. The advantage lies in the fact that you are able to access certificate data directly. Detailed dispatch processes and certificate creation in paper form are thus completely avoided. Before the actual delivery, the customer can evaluate the information contained in the certificate and make the necessary decisions.

### 5.3.4 Customer Service

Operations within Service Management (Service and Asset Management) frequently arise due to quality-related influences. Customer problems are recorded and documented in notifications that describe the problem situation and through which further processing is triggered until the problem is solved. In addition to further functions, the service notification as well as the customer complaint is a part of the SAP ERP notification system. In using these components, quality management and service work interact closely with each other.

Based on the notification recording, Service Management enables the processing of measures, service, and customer orders as well as the subsequent processes of confirmations, service entry and costs entry, delivery, and invoicing.

#### Returns

Returns processing is not a separate component. It is rather composed of numerous functions from MM, Production, and SD. The returns processing is then compiled with the selected system functions. The customer complaint in the form of a quality notification can also serve as a basis. The specialist areas involved operate on the basis of the notification and can, for instance, issue a rework order, execute stock postings, enter complaint costs, and initiate special inspections. The core processes of returns processing are stored in the system as reference models and thus serve as the basis for business-process modeling.

### Repairs Processing

As is the case for returns processing, a process is responsible that involves several components for repairs processing. The repair of a product runs through different organizational and technical phases, as shown in Figure 5.3. The most important object here is the repair order, which you can launch from both the quality notification and the service notification. In most cases, the material to be repaired is provided to you in a delivery. The movement of goods to the goods receipt can now create an inspection lot and thus initiate an immediate error analysis. At the same time, you prevent confusion of the material by carrying out the postings into the quality-inspection stock.

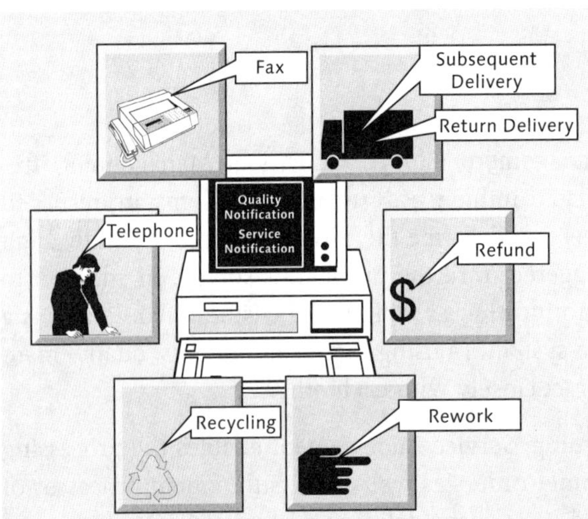


**Figure 5.3** Customer Service

The rework order created from the repair order is similar to the production order and contains the necessary processes for the elimination of deficiencies. After a repair has been completed, the inspection authority reaches a usage decision and can then release the stock for delivery. From the repair order, the process is completed with a goods delivery and an invoice to the customer.

### Plant Maintenance

Of fundamental importance in efficient quality management systems is *preventive maintenance*. This mainly involves internal and external maintenance tasks in production plants and production resources and tools. To support quality-relevant and general maintenance tasks, the system provides the Plant Maintenance (PM) module, which has been integrated with the components of SAP Enterprise Asset Management as of SAP ERP. All workflows of maintenance are connected with each other via data and functions without interfaces. As is the case with QM, the integration of PM in the supply chain involves nearly all application components of the SAP ERP system.

Test equipment management, including the maintenance of production resources and tools, is an integrated process based on the QM and PM components. Test equipment management, for instance, uses the objects "Equipment," "Functional locations," and "Maintenance task lists" from PM as well as "Inspection plans," "Characteristics," "Calibration regulations," and "Inspection lots" from QM. The calibration inspection is triggered by the maintenance order, which also contains the interval details for periodically recurring inspections.

## 5.4 Summary

Take note of the following during the QM implementation along the supply chain:

- Most of the QM functions can also be implemented individually. A general QM implementation is not necessarily required.
- The implementation of QM requires profound knowledge of logistics and business contexts.
- It is only through optimal process design before the implementation that the powerful functions of QM can be fully utilized.
- QM, unlike any other application component, is integrated in the business processes of logistics.
- The benefits of QM and the potential for savings through QM are considerable. The functions described here are mostly regarded as necessary in companies but are often not supported by the system.

*In this chapter, you will learn how to cope with the essential task of quality planning using SAP ERP, which is essential for all standard specifications for quality management: from the general business tasks point of view to the real-world details of inspection plans.*

# 6 Quality and Inspection Planning

This chapter not only describes the known inspection planning for procurement but also the quality planning in production up to delivery (quality planning in sales). At the end of this chapter, Section 6.9, FMEA and Control Plan, provides information about quality advance planning using FMEA and the control plan.

## 6.1 Basic Principles

Quality planning is a cross-disciplinary function, the aim of which is to improve the overall quality of products and processes while reducing total quality-related costs. The tasks of quality planning in terms of quality-related events and processes are as follows:

- To provide a channel for presenting the requirements of individual task areas to the QM department
- To create a quality-assurance system
- To develop quality-inspection methods
- To incorporate quality costs into the results-improvement strategy

Inspection planning is a component of quality planning, and the following chapters are chiefly concerned with the tasks and processes in this area. To plan the quality of products, a number of prerequisites have to be met:

- **Feasibility must be proven.**
  Using the specification of the customer (internal or external) as a basis, all of the technical departments involved create a concept for implementing the customer's requirements.

- **Failure Mode and Effects Analyses (FMEAs) must be created for both the construction phase and the process phase.**
  Identifying problems early on in the production process minimizes the risk of unexpected quality costs.
- **An inspection plan must be created.**
  An inspection plan that takes the realities of production into account, along with a careful selection of the characteristics to be inspected, is a prerequisite for effective problem prevention. Inspection characteristics and inspection frequencies are not cast in stone and do not determine the lifecycle of the product. Continually adapting the inspection factors is a very important task in managing inspection costs.
- **Vendors must be evaluated.**
  Selecting the right vendors is just as important for overall quality as the quality of internal activities.
- **The capability of machines and processes must be established.**
  Capability inspections of machines and processes play a very important role in problem prevention.
- **Model inspections must be carried out.**
  Along with the presentation to the customer and the documentation, the model inspection reflects the quality of the measures that have been put in place and of successful quality planning.

In enterprises today, quality planning is of equal status with production planning and controlling because it is the most important link to a customer-oriented process. In the ISO 9001 and QS 9000 quality-assurance systems, quality planning is one of the essential elements of an enterprise business plan.

Preparatory quality-control activities are another element of quality planning. Very precise definitions of catalogs are required for the purposes of problem description and error analysis, so that the results of later analyses are as meaningful and useful as possible.

#### Inspection Planning

You plan carefully to simplify the later job of inspection processing, so that the associated tasks can be processed as smoothly as possible. Also, a targeted approach to inspection planning usually significantly reduces the overall time and effort required for inspection purposes throughout the supply chain. Inspection planning itself is formally defined as *quality inspection planning* and is implemented as such in the SAP QM module. The term *inspection planning* refers to the planning of quality inspections throughout the whole production process, from GR to delivery. Inspection planning is used to implement quality-enhancing measures to products and procedures. This means adapting these measures to the specific conditions of each enterprise.

In inspection planning, inspection activities and operations are determined according to economic considerations and their type, location, frequency, time, and production cycle, as well as the type and scope of the quality inspection in question. To ensure that the quality-assurance process is as comprehensive as possible, all functions of the enterprise should be included in the planning process.

In an effective and successful inspection planning process, the approach taken should be targeted and methodical. From the economic point of view, the time and effort required for inspection planning and the inspections themselves should be minimized, whereas the resulting improvement in quality should be as great as possible. In light of these seemingly contradictory requirements, there will always be a potential for conflict. A carefully designed and sophisticated inspection procedure usually means that the product quality can be significantly improved, but the increased time and effort invested in quality planning cannot be allowed to put excessive pressure on the cost calculations.

#### Inspection Planning Terminology

In the remainder of this chapter, mainly SAP-specific inspection planning terminology is used. The meanings of these terms are usually the same as the generally accepted meanings. Even though in some cases the meaning may seem ambiguous, it is important that you be familiar with the industry-specific terms and those that are most commonly used in the specialist literature. This familiarity will help you achieve terminological consistency in your project work. The most important terms and definitions are as follows:

- **Attributive inspection**
  Quality inspection that uses qualitative characteristics. SAP ERP therefore correctly describes attributive characteristics as qualitative characteristics.
- **Goods receipt inspection (GR inspection)**
  Quality inspection of a received product.

- **Final inspection**
  The last quality inspection before hand-over to the customer.
- **Defect weighting**
  Classification of the possible defects in a unit into defect-weighting classes, in accordance with a defect valuation system, the aim of which is to place an economic value on the time and effort required for inspection purposes.
- **Inspection during production**
  Quality inspections that take place during the production process.
- **Characteristic**
  A property that makes it possible to differentiate a whole, both qualitatively (qualitative characteristic) and quantitatively (quantitative characteristic).
- **Process inspection**
  Quality inspection of a process that uses characteristics of the process itself or of its results.
- **Inspection schedule**
  Record of the sequence of quality inspections.
- **Inspection instruction**
  Instruction in carrying out a quality inspection.
- **Inspection setup**
  Information relating to the results of inspections: individual numerical results, measurement results, and the constraints data used to calculate the measurement result.
- **Inspection dimension**
  (In accordance with DIN 406, part 2) Dimensions that are particularly important in the process of deciding the scope of the inspection, for example, to establish the function of the object of the inspection. In drawings, a border around the dimension highlights the inspection dimension.
- **Inspection level**
  Predefined characteristic of a sampling scheme. It is based on samples and the lot size, and on the discrimination ratio (inspection severity) of the scheme.
- **Inspection plan**
  The inspection plan contains the following:
  - **Inspection specification**
    Specification containing the inspection characteristics and, if required, the inspection procedure for a quality inspection.

- **Statistical quality inspection**
  Quality inspection that uses statistical methods, especially samples.
- **Sampling plan**
  Plan specifying the size of the sample, the sample itself, and the criteria for accepting the inspection lot.
- **Sampling scheme**
  Collection of sampling instructions, structured under headings from the sampling system. For example, the acceptable quality limits and the inspection level are used as higher-order factors.
- **Sampling inspection**
  Quality inspection based on a sampling plan for evaluating an inspection lot.
- **Sampling system**
  Collection of sampling schemes with rules for use.

- **Variable inspection**
  Quality inspection that uses quantitative characteristics (quantitative inspection).

## 6.2 Overview of Quality and Inspection Planning

Quality planning in SAP ERP is an extensive modular system that consists of various master data and functions for all of the preparatory activities associated with inspection planning and inspection-lot processing. This chapter introduces the objects in quality planning and the relationships between them and then illustrates this with practical examples. This chapter covers the following topics:

- **Basic data (Section 6.3, Basic Quality- and Inspection-Planning Data)**
  - General master data
  - Basic inspection-planning data
- **SAP QM inspection plan (Section 6.4, SAP QM Inspection Plan)**
  - Administrating inspection plans
  - Structure of the inspection plan (plan structure)
  - Using multiple specifications in the inspection plan

- Using the inspection plan in procurement (Section 6.6, Quality Planning in Procurement)
- Using the inspection plan in production (Section 6.7, Quality Planning in Production)
- Using the inspection plan in sales (Section 6.8, Quality Planning in Sales and Distribution)
- FMEA and control plan

Before illustrating the implementation of the SAP ERP system, we want to make some general explanatory remarks on the subject of inspection planning. The main components of inspection planning in SAP ERP are the inspection plan or routing, and the inspection flow control. The following information must be specified in the *inspection plan*:

- Material reference
- Inspection characteristic with inspection instruction
- Inspection scope
- Inspection frequency (dynamic modification)
- Inspection data processing

The *inspection flow control* specifies the interaction with procurement and shop floor control activities, by means of the following information:

- Inspection necessity
- Inspection process
- Inspection method
- Test equipment
- Inspection-lot processing

Ideally, both the inspection plan and the inspection flow control should be preceded by an FMEA, the results of which are incorporated into the planning data used in quality assurance and production. Usually, you determine the inspection characteristics used in quality inspections in consultation with the other departments involved in the inspection: construction, production, and purchasing. From the process point of view, quality planning is therefore another important aspect of integration. Because the quality systems are integrated into the processes in question, the problems that can arise with interfaces between Computer Aided

Quality Assurance (CAQ) systems and master data and process data usually do not occur. Also, thanks to the availability of online access to all of the necessary data, there is no need to change systems and media, which make working out an inspection plan a simple matter.

## 6.3 Basic Data for Quality and Inspection Planning

The area of inspection planning uses a particularly large amount of cross-module master data from MM, Production, and other logistics components. Before accessing this data, it is highly advisable to discuss how you will use the data with the persons responsible. These discussions usually result in new ideas for system use and highlight other potential synergies in the area of QM integration. Table 6.1 provides an initial overview of the relevant master data. We will explain the most important points for quality management in detail.

| General Master Data | Module | Use in QM |
|---|---|---|
| Material master | MM | Inspection control |
| Change master record | MM | Material master, inspection plan, quality info record |
| Vendor master | MM | Inspection plan |
| Customer master | SD | Inspection plan |
| Batch master record | MM/PP | Results recording |
| Routing, reference operation set, rate routing, and master recipe | PP | Inspection plan, quality notification |
| Work center | PP | Inspection plan, quality notification |
| Production resources/tools (PRT) | MM/PP | Inspection plan, quality notification |
| User master record | BC | Inspection plan, quality notification |
| Quality documents | CA | Inspection plan, material specification |
| Basic Quality and Inspection Planning Data | Module | Use in QM |

**Table 6.1** Master Data in SAP ERP

| General Master Data | Module | Use in QM |
|---|---|---|
| Catalogs (defect, attribute, use, etc.) | QM | Inspection plan, quality notification |
| Sample control (sample plan, sample procedure, dynamic modification, SPC) | QM | Inspection plan, routing |
| Master inspection characteristic | QM | Inspection plan |
| Reference operation set (reference in inspection plan) | QM/PP | Inspection plan |
| Inspection plan/routing | QM/PP | Procurement, production, sales |
| Material specification | QM/MM | Material master record |
| Quality info record procurement | QM/MM | Procurement |
| Quality info record sales | QM/SD | Sales |

**Table 6.1** Master Data in SAP ERP (Cont.)

### 6.3.1 General Master Data

This section introduces you to the general master data. Let's first look at the material master record.

#### Material Master

The material master record in the SAP ERP system is a complex entity, the purpose of which is to control business and logistical processes. For the sake of clarity, the material master record is divided into different views. As of Release 4.5, these views are represented onscreen in the form of tabs. There is also an additional view, the quality management view (see Figure 6.1). If this view of the material is not available initially, the person responsible for the material master record can add it later at any time. This has no effect on any part of the logistics process (inventory management, for example). The functions for inspection-lot creation, stock posting, and — in particular — QM procurement control are activated later, when the quality management view is maintained further. For the purposes of mass maintenance of inspection data, there is a function for creating, activating, and deactivating inspection data under Material Master • Environment • QM Maintenance Functions (process inspection data).

An inspection type is used to set the *control mechanisms* for inspection-lot creation. Do not forget to activate the inspection type that you want to use later for inspection purposes as well; otherwise, the inspection lot cannot be created.

**Tip**

When you are maintaining the control indicator of the inspection data, we recommend that you use the predefined Customizing settings for each inspection type. This is important because different entries for the same inspection type cause different materials to be used or cause difficulties with the inspection-lot generation process. If a special inspection lot control process is required on the material level for the same inspection type, this must be carefully documented in each individual case.

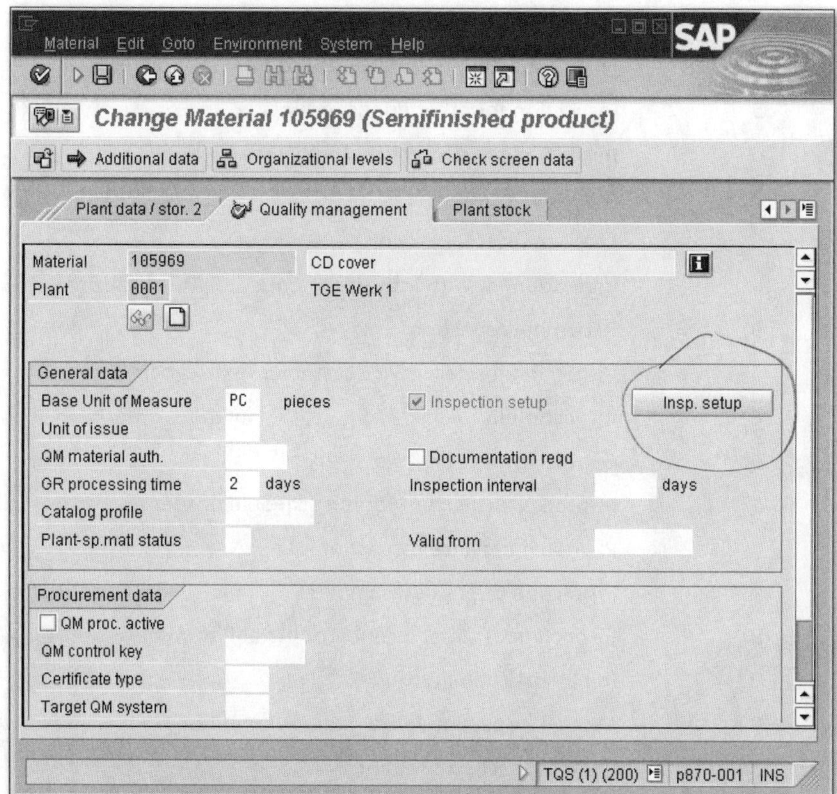


**Figure 6.1** Material Master Record, Quality Management View

Table 6.2 contains the various possible *inspection types* that you can assign in the material master record. The short text that goes with each type is self-explanatory.

| Inspection Type | Routing Reference | Short Text |
|---|---|---|
| 01 | 5 | Incoming inspection for goods receipt for purchase order |
| 0101 | 501 | Model inspection for goods receipt for purchase order |
| 0102 | 502 | GR inspection, pilot run |
| 0130 | 53 | GR inspection at goods receipt from external processing |
| 02 | 6 | Goods-issue inspection |
| 03 | 1 | In-process inspection for production order |
| 04 | 5 | Final inspection for goods receipt from production |
| 05 | 5 | Inspection for other goods receipts |
| 06 | 6 | Inspection for customer returns |
| 07 | 3 | Audit inspection |
| 08 | 5 | Stock-transfer inspection |
| 0800 | | Inspection lot with inspection stock at QM activation |
| 09 | 9 | Recurring inspection |
| 10 | 6 | Inspection for delivery to customer (with order) |
| 11 | 6 | Inspection for delivery to customer (without order) |
| 12 | 6 | General inspection for delivery |
| 13 | 1 | In-process inspection for run schedule header |
| 14 | | Plant maintenance inspection |
| 15 | 9 | Inspection of physical samples |
| 16 | 9 | Inspection of storage conditions (stability studies) |
| 1601 | 9 | Initial test (stability study) |
| 1602 | 9 | Manual inspection lot for storage conditions |
| 89 | 3 | Other inspection |

**Table 6.2** Inspection Types

These inspection types are provided with your SAP ERP installation in client 001 or 000 and are contained as listed in the preceding table in the test, consolidation, and production client (see Figure 6.2). The scope of each type and the short texts may vary, depending on the release. It is advisable in all cases to use the inspection types of the delivery client.

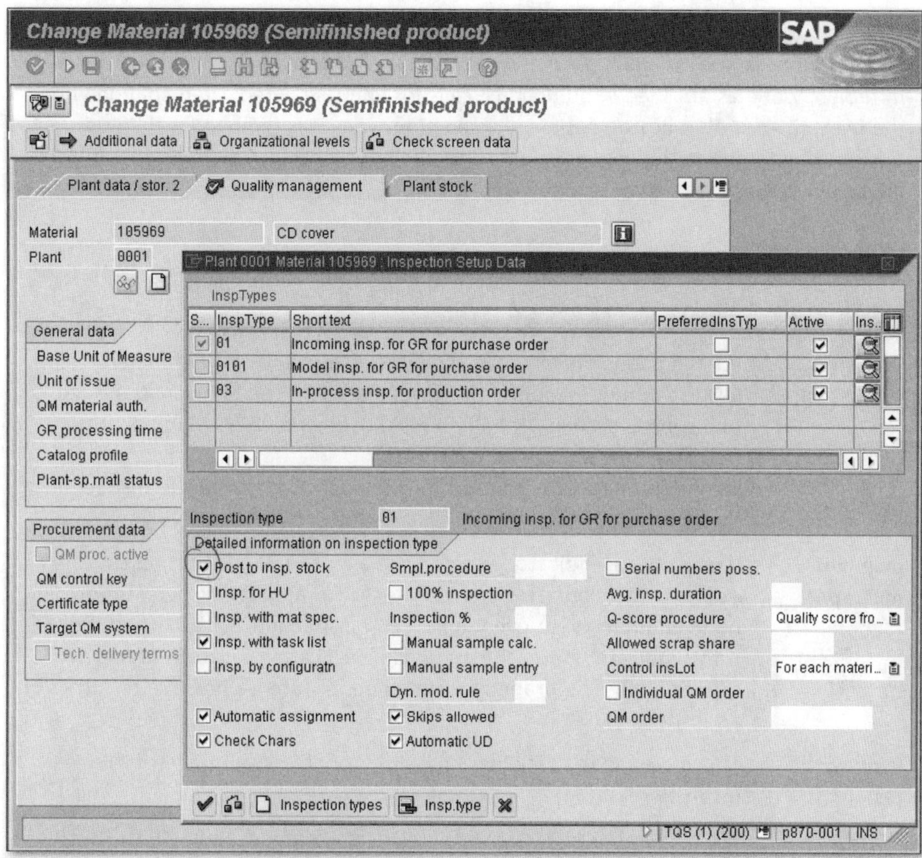


**Figure 6.2** Inspection Types in the Material Master Record

When delivered, every inspection type already has a different combination of control characters and a link to an inspection-lot origin. The link from the inspection type to the inspection-lot origin is set in Customizing. For specific inspection types, automatic inspection-lot creation is linked to the inspection lot origin (by means of goods movements or start of order, for example).

The control elements for each inspection type have a major influence on inspection processing; an incorrect interpretation can easily cause serious problems with process flows in implementation projects. Table 6.3 contains a list of control indicators and their effects. The descriptions of the effects are original SAP explanations taken from the context-sensitive help. However, you should be provided with an overview of all this information at this point so that you are in a position to make a correct decision regarding any one control indicator.

**Tip**

In project work, established good practice calls for entering a dedicated column with the relevant control indicators for every inspection type. This template is then used in Customizing to define the default values. This allows you to detect duplicate control indicators, at least within the same inspection type.

| Control Indicator | Effects |
|---|---|
| **Post to insp. stock** | Posts a goods movement to the inspection stock for the material. Only QM, within the scope of the usage decision, can book anything out of inspection stock. Not all goods movements in MM support this function. Therefore, if an exceptional case arises, the movement type itself determines whether or not the quantity is posted to inspection stock. |
| **Insp. with mat. spec.** | If you set this indicator, you can use a material specification to carry out an inspection. An inspection that uses a material specification can be in addition to, or even replace, an inspection that uses a routing. If this indicator is set, the material specification for the material in question must be properly maintained for it to be possible to carry out an inspection. |
| **Insp. with task list** | This means that a task list is required for an inspection with this inspection lot.<br>**Procedure:** If a task list is required, the system sets the indicator. The decision whether a routing is required is made when the inspection data is maintained in the material master record. The sample size can be determined only after a task list has been assigned to the inspection lot. |
| **Insp. by configuration** | If this indicator is set, configurations from the sales order or production order are taken into account in inspection-lot creation, with the result that the inspection specifications from the routing or the material specification are added to or modified. |
| **Automatic assignment** | This means that the system tries to automatically assign a routing or a material specification. |

**Table 6.3** Inspection Type Control Indicators

| Control Indicator | Effects |
|---|---|
| **Check Chars.** | Select this indicator if you want characteristic-based results recording to be carried out.<br>**Dependencies:** If you want characteristic-based results recording, you have to use a routing or a material specification for the inspection. Characteristic-based results recording is a prerequisite for characteristic-based dynamic modification. You can select a dynamic modification level in plans. |
| **Smpl. procedure** | A procedure that is used to determine the size of the sample in an inspection. The sampling procedure also defines the valuation type that is used for results recording (attributive, variable, manual, etc.).<br>**Use:** This field is of significance only in an inspection that does not use a routing or a material specification. If you enter a sampling procedure here, the total sample size is then calculated from the lot size. Select a sampling procedure that uses a valuation mode without valuation parameters.<br>**Note:** In the case of an inspection without a routing or a material specification, you have the following options for determining the inspection scope for a specific material:<br>▶ Select the indicator 100% INSPECTION.<br>▶ Specify a percentage.<br>▶ Specify a sampling procedure without valuation parameters. |
| **100% inspection** | There are two possible scenarios if you set this indicator:<br>**Inspect without routing or specification**<br>The whole sample size of the created lot is the same as the lot size.<br>**Inspect with routing or specification**<br>The whole sample size of the created lot is the same as the lot size. The sampling procedures set down in the inspection plan or specification are not taken into account in the sample determination process for the inspection characteristics. Instead, the system uses sample determination rules, which are preset in Customizing. The sample size of the created characteristics depends on whether the base unit of measure has decimal places. If the base unit of measure does have decimal places, the sample size of the characteristic is always 1; if the base unit of measure does not have decimal places, 100% of the lot size should be inspected in sample units of measure (rounded up) for the characteristic. |

**Table 6.3** Inspection Type Control Indicators (Cont.)

| Control Indicator | Effects |
|---|---|
| | **Dependencies:** If, in addition to either the 100% INSPECTION, INSPECT WITH ROUTING, or INSPECT BY CONFIGURATION INDICATORS, you also set the SKIPS ALLOWED characteristic, nothing changes in the sample calculation. However, the system does check whether the characteristic is to be inspected or not. The following criteria come into effect here:<br>▸ Current quality level (if available)<br>▸ The STAGE CHANGE characteristic is permitted in the sampling procedure. |
| **Inspection %** | As before, this field is of significance only in an inspection that does not use a routing or a specification. In this case, the overall sample size is calculated using this percentage value from the lot size. |
| **Manual sample calc.** | Means that the sample calculation in the inspection lot has to be triggered manually. The following two scenarios are possible.<br>In an inspection with a routing or specification, the sample is calculated using the sampling procedures specified in the routing or specification on the characteristic level.<br>In an inspection without a routing, either a 100% inspection is carried out, or the sample size is calculated using a percentage value. For these to be possible, you have to either set the 100% inspection characteristic or a percentage value in the QM inspection data. |
| **Manual sample entry** | If this characteristic is set, the sample size has to be entered manually for the inspection of this inspection lot. This characteristic is only taken into account in inspections that do not use a routing or a specification. |
| **Dyn. mod. rule** | Dynamic modification rule. Contains definitions of the inspection levels and the conditions that cause inspection levels to change.<br>**Use:** This field is significant only in an inspection that does not use a routing or a material specification. If you enter a dynamic modification rule here, a quality level for material, plant, and inspection type is set, and when the quality level is created automatically, the dynamic modification criteria for the inspection-lot origin are calculated.<br>**Dependencies:** If, in addition to the sample size, you control using a sampling procedure, the system checks whether the combination of dynamic modification rule and sampling procedure is permitted (permitted relationships). |
| **Skips allowed** | Means that inspection characteristics are allowed when the sample size is being calculated. |

**Table 6.3** Inspection Type Control Indicators (Cont.)

| Control Indicator | Effects |
|---|---|
| | **Dependencies:** The characteristic takes effect in the inspection lot if it is set in the QM inspection data of the material for the inspection type in question. If the characteristic is not set, in the dynamic modification process, the system selects the next nonskip inspection level instead of a skip level. If all of the characteristics to be inspected in an inspection lot have the "Skip" status, a skip lot is the result.<br>In the case of a skip lot, if both skips and automatic usage decision are allowed, inspection-lot processing is carried out without any user intervention. A time delay can be set for this in the Customizing. This triggers a "ship to stock" at the GR stage because the lot quantity is immediately posted to unrestricted-use stock.<br>**Note:** In the QM control function in Procurement (Q-info record), you can make a setting that skips the GR inspections. You can also specify in the inspection data for the material that an inspection is to be carried out only for the first GR per order or production order. To prevent individual characteristics from being skipped, proceed as follows:<br>▸ Assign characteristic weightings to the characteristics to prevent skips.<br>▸ Assign sampling procedures to the characteristics that do not permit stage changes. |
| **Automatic UD** | If this characteristic is set, the system can automatically make usage decisions for inspection lots. The inspection lots have to fulfill the following conditions:<br>▸ All characteristics are completed.<br>▸ No characteristic has been rejected.<br>▸ No defects have been recorded, and no quality notification has been created.<br>▸ The lead time set in Customizing must have expired. Inspection lots with the status "Skip lot" can also be taken into account here.<br>This characteristic takes effect in the inspection lot if it is set in the inspection data of the material for the inspection type in question. It is activated in the job administration functions. You can schedule and start jobs from the worklist in the quality inspection main menu. See the IMG for more information on planning automatic usage decisions.<br>**Note:** If an automatic usage decision cannot be made, you will have to make it manually. The system records an automatic usage decision in the long text that accompanies the usage decision. |

**Table 6.3** Inspection Type Control Indicators (Cont.)

| Control Indicator | Effects |
| --- | --- |
| **Avg. insp. duration** | Specifies the average duration, in days, of the inspection for every inspection type.<br>**Use:** If the start date of the inspection is entered during inspection-lot creation, the system calculates the end date using the average inspection time entered in this field. Conversely, if the end date of the inspection is entered during inspection-lot creation, the system calculates the start date using the average inspection time entered in this field. |
| **Q-score procedure** | Coded ID of the procedure that is used to calculate the quality score.<br>**Procedure:** One quality score procedure per inspection type can be stored in the material master record. This field is transferred to the inspection lot record when the inspection lot is created.<br>**Example:** In the simplest procedure, the quality score is taken from the code for the usage decision. In another procedure, the quality score is calculated on the basis of the scrap share in the inspected characteristics. The actual calculation procedure for the quality score takes place in a function module with a fixed interface. This function module is assigned to the quality score procedure in Table TQ06. Thus, the user can use function modules to define his own procedures. |
| **Allowed scrap share** | Some quality score procedures require an allowed scrap share to calculate the quality score.<br>**Procedure:** In normal cases, the scrap share is set to be half the acceptable quality level (AQL) value. |
| **Control insLot** | This characteristic applies to GRs and can be used for the following inspection lot origins: 01, 04, 05, 08. The following settings can be made:<br>**<Space>** One inspection lot per GR document item. In other words, one inspection lot is created for each GR document item.<br>**»X«:** One inspection lot per purchase order item or order item and batch. If you set this value, the system creates an inspection lot only for the first GR for each purchase-order item or production order, or, if the material is managed in batches, only for the first GR per purchase order item or production order and batch. This setting is restricted to the inspection lot origins "For purchase order (inspection lot origin 01)" and "For production order (inspection lot origin 04)." |

**Table 6.3** Inspection Type Control Indicators (Cont.)

| Control Indicator | Effects |
|---|---|
| | **»1«:** One inspection lot per material document, material, and batch. If you set this value, the system opens only one inspection lot per material and batch (in the case of batch management) for a material document (i.e., within a GR transaction). This can occur if several purchase orders or several partial deliveries of the same material are processed within one GR transaction.<br>**»2«:** One inspection lot per material and batch. If you set this value, the system opens only one inspection lot per material and batch (in the case of batch management). This setting is useful only for materials that require batch management.<br>In the case of X, 1, and 2, if the stock of the inspection lot that was created with the first GR is not completely discharged when further partial deliveries are received, these GR quantities are added to this stock. In the case of 1 and 2, if SKIP LOT is set, there is no direct change of the stock type from "In quality inspection" to "Unrestricted use." Instead, a transfer posting takes place as part of an automatic usage decision with a time delay. |
| **Individual QM order** | This characteristic specifies that an individual QM order with account assignment should be opened when the inspection lot for this inspection type is opened.<br>**Use:** If you set this characteristic, you are specifying that an individual QM order should be opened for this combination of material and inspection type.<br>**Dependencies:** If the field for the QM order is filled as well as the characteristic for individual QM orders being set, this field is only taken into account if an individual QM order cannot be created due to a missing account assignment in the inspection lot. A prerequisite for creating an individual QM order is that the inspection lot contains an allocation provision such as sales order, cost center, or plant. |
| **QM order** | A number that uniquely identifies the QM order to which the costs are to be charged. The QM order specified in the material master record in the inspection data is used as a template for inspection-lot creation, if an individual QM order has not been created for the inspection lot. |

**Table 6.3** Inspection Type Control Indicators (Cont.)

### Change Master Record

To manage the different versions of a drawing that belongs to a material master record, for example, it may be a good idea to also assign a version to every material. To this end, every version of the material master record is linked with a change master record (see Figure 6.3). You can access the menu for maintaining CHANGE MASTER RECORDS by choosing LOGISTICS • CENTRAL FUNCTIONS • ENGINEERING • ENGINEERING CHANGE MANAGEMENT. If you want to include inspection plans as well as the material master in Change Management, you also have to include the relevant OBJECTS (in this case, this means the inspection plan). A number of issues need to be considered in relation to working with the CHANGE MASTER RECORD in quality management.

**Example**

Let's assume that there are three versions of a material master record for a particular material in a manufacturing plant. According to materials planning, version two is valid until the end of 2009, and version three is then valid from January 1st, 2010 for production and outbound deliveries. The quality management process must then ensure that the relevant inspection plans are assigned to the versions or change master records for the material. This is described in detail in Section 6.4.2, Administrating Inspection Plans. If the material will be subject to an acceptance inspection, and if the supply relationship is controlled by the Q-info record, the version/change master record relationship has to be created in this case as well.

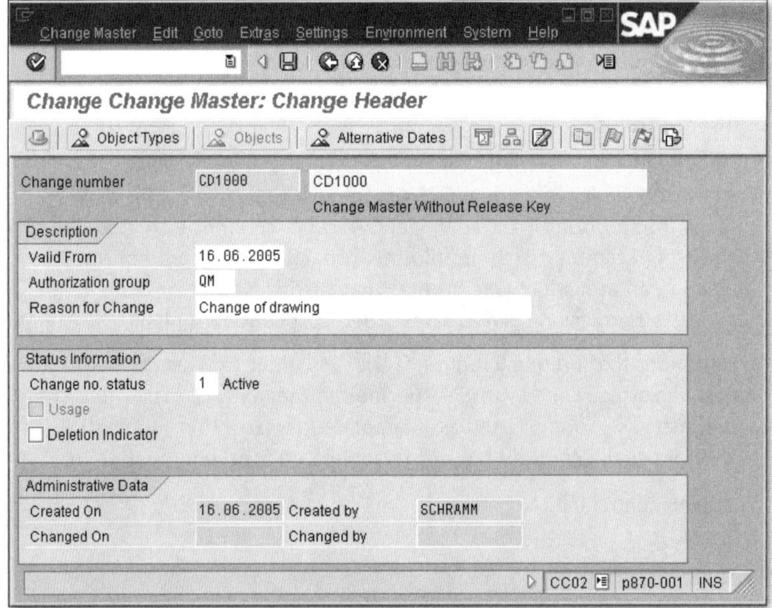


**Figure 6.3** Change Master Record

However, it is not possible to create a relationship with change master records in all areas of the QM component. This applies especially to inspection data in the material master record and to the quality level in inspection lot dynamic modification.

### Vendor Master

This master record contains all of the necessary information about a vendor from the purchasing and accounting point of view. Also, the buyer can set a lock under the LOCK DATA option, for quality reasons. This lock contains the same list entries as those in the quality info record for delivery control on the material vendor level. The details of the contact persons for purchasing and quality management are stored in the partner data.

### Customer Master

This master record contains all of the necessary information about a customer from the point of view of sales and accounting. The buyer can also set a lock, if this is necessary for quality reasons. This master record also contains partner data, such as the contact person in the customer's company. It can be very useful to also enter the details of a contact person for quality matters. This person is then named as the customer's contact person for customer complaints and also appears on the customer complaints form.

### Batch Master Record

If a delivered material or an in-house material is managed by batch management, a batch master record is created under LOGISTICS • MATERIALS MANAGEMENT • MATERIAL MASTER • BATCH (see Figure 6.4). The batch number can be assigned automatically or manually, for goods movements, production orders, or at any point in time. If batch management is active for a material, the system requests a batch number during inspections, and the inspection-lot data are assigned to the batches.

An important consideration for process industries is that the various batches of a material are separated according to their different properties. To this end, batches are divided into different classes, which are defined in advance in the batch characteristics. If, during the inspection, a batch fulfills the specification of a *batch characteristic*, it is assigned to the relevant *batch class*. If a material with the required properties is subsequently used for further processing or for a sales order, the *batch classification* finds the appropriate material. You also need the batch master record for order processing in the PP-PI module (Production Planning, Process Industries).

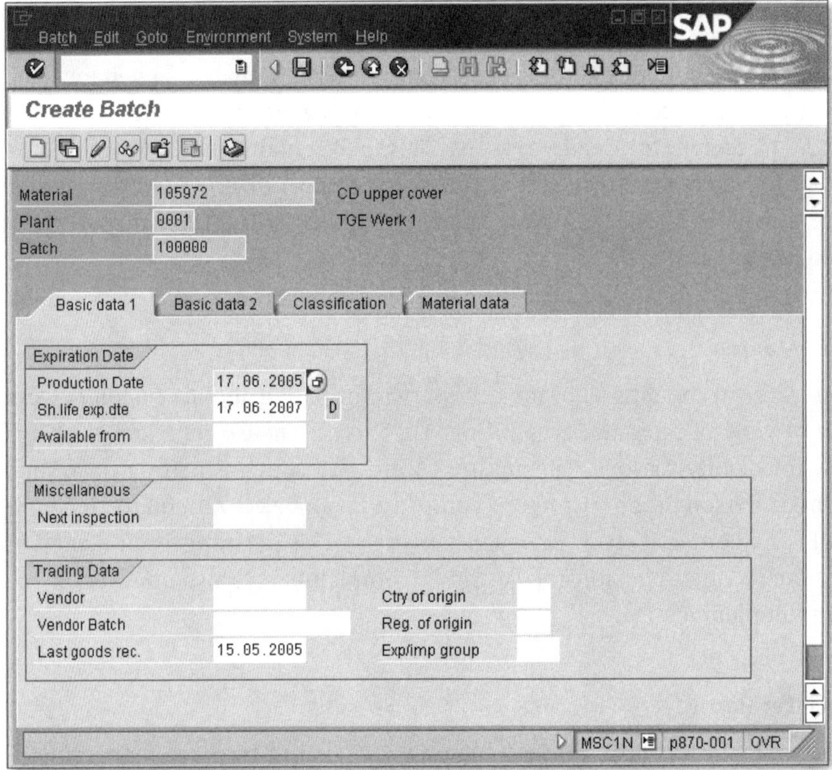


**Figure 6.4** Batch Master Record

It is because of batch management that stocks in MM that are assigned to a batch are managed separately and assigned individually to the bin inventories in Warehouse Management. Thus, batch selection makes it possible to trace inspection results. In the sales area, batch classification makes it possible to assign relevant batches to different customer requirements. For this purpose, batches contain *general characteristics* from the QM basic data. The products in the batch with the special properties of the general characteristics can then be made available to the delivery for the sales order.

### Routing

In this task list type, the work-scheduling function records all elements in the task planning area, and the quality-management function records all data for inspection planning. The production steps and capacities are linked to the work centers, and the required control functions for the production order are determined. The elements of inspection planning, inspection characteristics, sampling procedure, and so on, are fully integrated into the routing. For more information on this, see the paragraphs on task-list types in Section 6.4.1, General Remarks.

### Reference Operation Set

The reference operation set contains virtually all of the objects and functions of the routing. It is used mainly as a task-list template for variations of a production procedure or as a general template. The individual operations in the reference operation set are referenced for this purpose in the routing or in the inspection plan (a fixed reference; every change in the reference operation set affects the inspection plan and the routing). The reference operation set, routing, and inspection plan are the same in terms of their structure and essential functions. This makes navigating in the different task-list types quite simple for the inspection planner, who has to maintain the quality-relevant data in all task-list types. The topic of reference operation sets in inspection plans and routings is dealt with in more detail later on because this is an important component of effective inspection-plan creation.

### Work Center

The work center is a master record that is important mainly for PP and CO. It is likewise usually maintained by the Production Planning and Control department. In production, the work center is the central organizational element used to map the work-center hierarchy in the system. Because capacity planning and scheduling are also important in quality inspections, it is advisable, especially in special inspection procedures, to create specific work centers. Every work center is assigned to a cost center, so the accounting department can analyze quality costs. To this end, the system calculates the costs that arise from the work performed at the work center, on the basis of the allocation records for the individual cost centers.

### Production Resources and Tools

All of the resources required for production, such as documents, operating supplies, test equipment, tools, equipment, and so on, come under the heading of production resources/tools (PRTs). You need to assign the PRTs to the operations and inspection characteristics of a task list. Depending on the PRT type, the master record can be a material, a document, a PRT master record, or an equipment master record. The functions of test equipment management are described in Chapter 11, Test Equipment Management.

As of Version 4.0, the system features a wide range of extensions for this task. These include cross-elements from quality planning, repairs and maintenance (calibration test), and their master records (equipment). System-supported test equipment management has become such an important topic in quality management that it is treated in a separate chapter of this book (see Chapter 11, Test Equipment Management).

### User Master Record

A master record is created for every SAP ERP user. It contains several control functions and the authorization profile assigned to the user. In terms of quality management, the user is of significance in many parts of the system in terms of his input authorizations. Examples of this occur in change tracking in inspection plans and in defining the participants in workflow tasks based on the quality notification. You can always select worklists for inspection lot and complaints processing via the user. User authorizations are stored in *profiles*. It is advisable to discuss with the relevant system administrator the options for the standard QM component profile well before production starts to agree on any changes and extensions that may be necessary.

### Quality Documents

The document management system (CA module) of the SAP ERP system provides a wide range of document-management functions that can be used both inside (documents) and outside (e.g., Office documents) the SAP ERP system. Documents can be anything from drawings from external CAD systems to specification texts. However, displaying these documents requires special extensions known as *viewers*. For the purposes of quality planning, documents are defined as PRTs. Inspection instructions and work regulations are examples of this. However, the document-management functions are also ideally suited to managing a quality-management manual. With the help of the document-management functions, it is possible to make documents available right across the enterprise and to link them with SAP ERP objects from different areas of the enterprise, such as material master record, change master record, and the PRTs just discussed.

### 6.3.2 Basic Quality- and Inspection-Planning Data

This section describes the basic data of quality and inspection planning. First, the catalogs are taken into account.

#### Catalogs

Because of its central importance in inspection planning, you are now provided with a detailed description of the topic of catalogs, including the process of catalog creation as a whole. First this topic is considered from the general viewpoint and then from the SAP ERP viewpoint.

In the context of quality planning and quality inspection, the term *catalog* refers to a collection of unique keys that describe a subject, both in the positive and the negative sense. Catalogs contain defect descriptions, measures, and special characteristic attributes of an object or an activity.

In project work, designing the defect catalogs and other catalogs often takes up a lot of unplanned time because the existing catalog structures in the enterprise have to be migrated to a schema that suits SAP QM. Therefore, the most frequently occurring problem is not missing catalogs but rather the sheer number of catalogs and the fact that problem descriptions often overlap. The classic approach of classifying problem descriptions in catalogs according to defect location, defect type, and cause also often causes uncertainty with assigning the corresponding codes. Let's now use the example of a CD in its cover to illustrate the previously mentioned catalogs and their significance.

> **Tip**
>
> For the defect location, you can define the location at which the defect was caused, for example, a specific assembly or production area. However, it is not recommended that you use terms from both definition types in the same catalog type.

- **Defect type — what is wrong with the object?**
  There has to be an NOK ("not OK") definition for every OK definition. The NOK definition is the defect type, that is, the defect itself. This is a simple aid in the catalog creation process because it prevents the causes from being hidden in the defect types. For construction companies, grouping should be done according to function; for an individual material, it should be according to physical properties.

  Defect types for the CD example:

  - **Function:** OK — cover should close tightly; NOK — cover does not close.
  - **Physical properties:** OK — dots present; NOK — dots not present.

- **Defect cause — how did the defect occur?**
  In the context of problem description, identifying the cause of the defect is usually the stage that requires the greatest specialized knowledge of defect analysis. For this reason, always define the level of the cause structure first. The cause could be one of the following:

  - Prior or accompanying process step, for example, faulty tool
  - Error on the part of a vendor, for example, vendor XYZ
  - Environmental factors, for example, assembly temperature too high

From release 4.0, the catalogs under LOGISTICS • QUALITY MANAGEMENT • QUALITY PLANNING • BASIC DATA • CATALOG belong completely to user data and have clear maintenance functions. As many code groups as needed can be assigned to every catalog type, and as many codes as are needed can be assigned to every code group. Figure 6.5 contains an example. The short text fields of the eight-digit code groups and the four-digit codes contain explanatory texts that can facilitate multiple language versions, if required. Your SAP consultant can create new catalog types under the keys P-Z, but this is rarely necessary.

Function settings — such as create, maintain, and structure catalogs — are made directly by the user. Special settings, on the other hand, such as creating a new catalog type or a special catalog profile (here, assigning specific catalogs to an inspection type or a message type), are made in Customizing by your consultant. When an SAP ERP system is delivered, its catalog types are defined as follows:

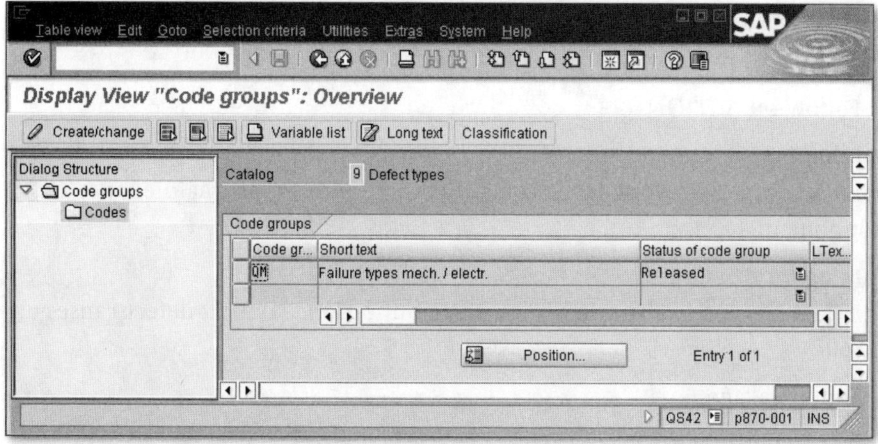


**Figure 6.5** Catalog Type "Defect Types" with Code Groups

- **Catalog type 1: Characteristic attributes**
  This catalog type is intended for results recording and for defining qualitative characteristics. It has special importance in the catalog system. One reason for this is that both OK and NOK definitions can be stored here; another is that the catalog entries can be accessed only via selected sets (see "Catalog Structure" in the following section). If you are using a rejecting-defect class for vendor valuation, you have to enter a defect class (major defect, minor defect, etc.). Rejecting defect classes are by nature the same as the defect types (defects) and are structured in the same way. If a qualitative characteristic has been created in the inspection plan, the valuation always uses a code from the selected set of the characteristic attributes.
- **Catalog type 2: Measures**
  You use this catalog to store the measures that are necessary in the context of quality notifications. The following are examples of typical measures:
  - Vendor visit
  - Test equipment calibration
  - Construction change
  - Process-capability test

  The automatic follow-up action functions can be activated here.
- **Catalog type 3: Usage decisions**
  This special catalog type is used only for inspection lot completions. It can be accessed only via special sets. Every code in the selected set has further control functions that can be used in the case of either acceptance or rejection:

  - Valuation (lot decision)
  - Quality score
  - Follow-on ACTION
- **Catalog type 4: Events**
  This catalog type contains events for the SAP Plant Maintenance (PM) component.
- **Catalog type 5: Causes**
  This catalog type is also used in quality notifications. Typical defect causes are as follows:
  - Tool breakage
  - Incorrect storage
  - Transport damage
  - Incorrect delivery specification
- **Catalog type 6: Consequences of defects (PM)**
  This catalog type contains the consequences of defects for the maintenance component (Enterprise Asset Management).
- **Catalog type 8: Actions**
  Here, you define the actions to be taken as a result of measures. Initially, it is recommended that you use only measures in the quality notifications because it is usually difficult to make a clear logical distinction between measures and actions.
- **Catalog type 9: Defect types**
  As with the characteristic attributes, you can assign defect classes to this catalog type. The structure of the catalog corresponds to the general definition.
- **Catalog type A: Activities**
  This catalog type contains the activities catalog for the maintenance component (Enterprise Asset Management).
- **Catalog type B: Object parts**
  This catalog type contains the object parts catalog for the maintenance component (Enterprise Asset Management).
- **Catalog type C: Damage (PM)**
  This catalog type contains the damage catalog for the maintenance component (Enterprise Asset Management).

- **Catalog type D: Codes**
  This catalog type contains the general description that is used as the title or subject of messages (error message, problem message, complaint, etc.). These entries are also the titles for the error-description text.
- **Catalog type E: Defect locations**
  The catalog structure is the same as the general definition from the previous section.

**Tip**

When the catalog entries are displayed in the results recording or the Q notifications, only the description of the code with its short text and key are displayed. If you also want the associated code group to be displayed, enter the symbol "&" in the code group text. The code text is then inserted into the code group text in place of the "&" symbol.

The *catalog hierarchy* usually has three levels, but in the case of catalogs with selected sets, it has four (see Figure 6.6).

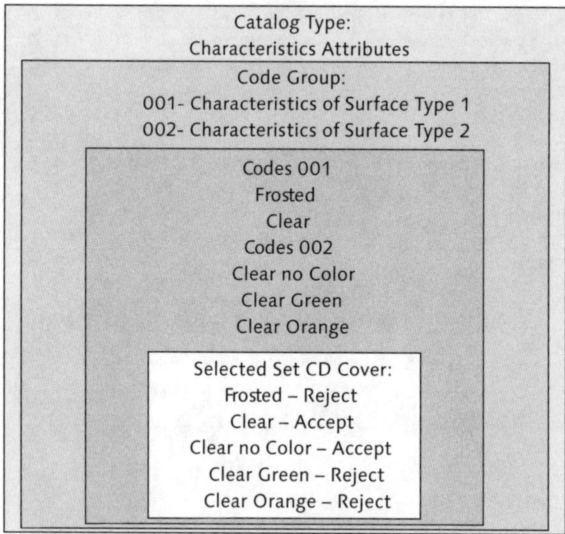


**Figure 6.6** Catalog Structure

Catalog types 1 (CHARACTERISTIC ATTRIBUTES) and 3 (USAGE DECISIONS) have an extra hierarchy level, called SELECTED SETS (see Figure 6.7). You can use this extra level to group subsets of a code group according to higher criteria. Also, an ACCEPT or REJECT valuation is assigned to every code in a selected set. You can also assign a follow-up action to the individual codes.

In the example of the CD cover, you would group together in a code group all of the characteristic attribute codes that belong to a subprocess. Regardless of the type of inspection – acceptance inspection, inspection during production, assembly inspection – the selected sets (see Table 6.4) contain only the codes that are appropriate to the test step.

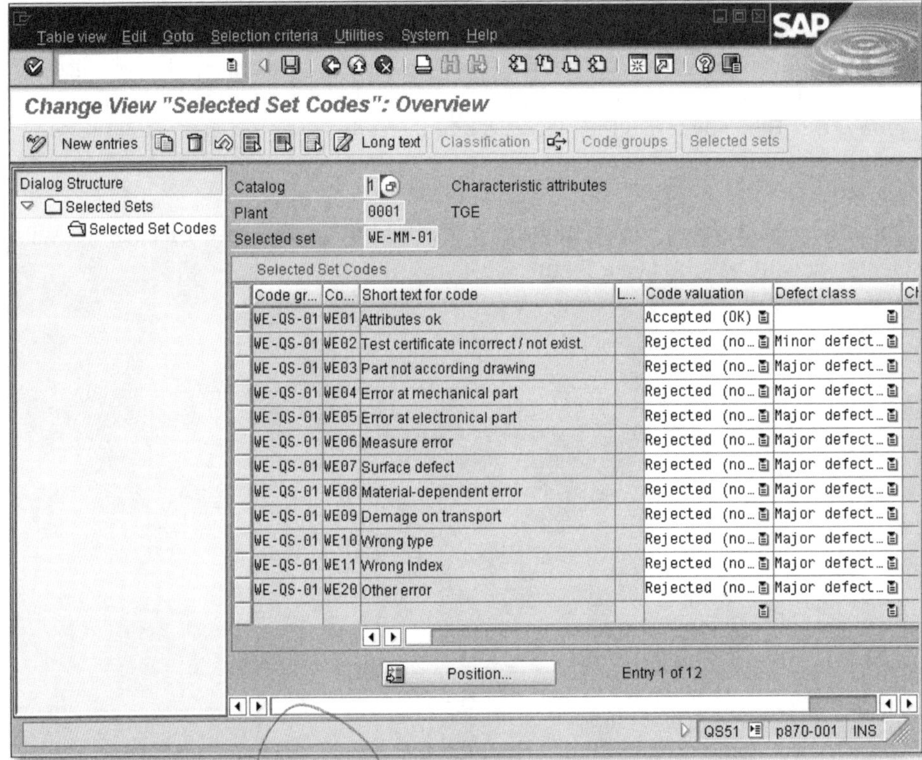


**Figure 6.7** Example of a Selected Set

**Example**

*Catalog type 1, characteristic attributes for injection molding parts*

You get the same part — that is, the CD cover — from a vendor, or alternatively, you produce it in-house.

Besides defect classes (catalog types 1 and 9) and acceptance codes (catalog 3), the following catalog types can also have default values for quality scores:

- 1: Characteristic attributes
- 3: Usage decisions
- 9: Defect types

You need these for the valuation procedures for vendor valuation in accordance with VDA (the German Automobile Industry Association).

At the time of the inspection, if a quality score valuation is to be carried out on the characteristic level with catalogs 1 and 9, or if a usage decision is to be carried out using catalog 3, the system determines the quality score from the defect classes. The quality score procedure to be used is specified in the material master record for the inspection type.

In the results recording, the quality score is calculated from the characteristics, as shown here:

- **Inspection characteristic with defect type**
  - Quality score from defect class
- **Inspection characteristic without defect type**
  - Inspection characteristic, quantitative — quality score from default values for acceptance or rejection on plant level
  - Inspection characteristic, qualitative — quality score from characteristic attribute

| Characteristic | Code Group | | Valuation | | | |
|---|---|---|---|---|---|---|
| | 100 | Attributes of CD covers | | Selected set for external delivery | Selected set for production | Selected set for assembly |
| Shape | 001 | Shape OK | Accepted | X | X | |
| | 002 | Shape not OK | Rejected | X | X | |
| Dimensions | 003 | Dimensions OK | Accepted | X | X | |
| | 004 | Dimensions not OK | Rejected | | | |
| Fit | 005 | Fit OK | Accepted | X | X | |
| | 006 | Fit not OK | Rejected | X | X | |
| Surface | 007 | Inclusions | Rejected | X | X | |
| | 008 | Scratches | Rejected | X | X | |
| | 009 | Ridges | Rejected | X | X | |
| | 010 | Color | Rejected | X | | |
| | 011 | Tears or cracks | Rejected | X | X | |
| | 012 | No defects | Accepted | X | X | X |
| Function | 013 | Mechanics/ function not OK | Rejected | X | X | X |
| | 014 | Incorrect component | Rejected | X | | X |

**Table 6.4** Selected Sets

During the results recording, the user can also decide whether he wants to accept the default values or change them manually. Table 6.5 shows a typical example of the defect classification for quality scores.

| Defect Class | Short Text | Quality Score |
|---|---|---|
| 01 | Critical defect | 1 |
| 02 | Major defect A | 20 |
| 03 | Major defect B | 40 |
| 04 | Minor defect A | 60 |
| 05 | Minor defect B | 80 |

**Table 6.5** Defect Classes

### Sample Control

This section introduces you to the following basic data elements:

- Sampling scheme
- Sampling procedure
- Dynamic modification rule
- Control charts and SPC

When delivered, client 000/001 contains the standard sample plans in accordance with ISO 2859-1 for attribute inspection and ISO 3951-1 for variable inspection. The most important international standards for sampling procedures (including sampling schemes, valuation rules, and dynamic modification rules) are as follows:

- ISO 3951, Part 1; variable inspection (SAP: quantitative)
- ISO 2859, Part 1; attribute inspection (SAP: qualitative): valuation according to number of defects or number of units with defects, without multiple samples and specification limit
- ISO 2859, Part 3, attribute inspection, skip lot. You can define every other sampling procedure yourself because this data is maintained in the user transactions. However, not every combination of sampling schemes and rules is permitted, and a system error message is displayed if your instructions contain a nonpermitted combination.

The IDs of the *sampling schemes* contain the keys shown in Table 6.6. Figure 6.8 shows a sampling scheme.

| A | | B | C |
|---|---|---|---|
| Standard ID | | Method ID | Level ID |
| 1 = ISO 3951, 2 = ISO 2859-1 | | 1 = S method | 1, 2, 3, 4, or S = 1, S = 2, etc. |
| **Example: 112—ISO 3951 / level II** | | | |
| 1 | | 1 | 2 |

**Table 6.6** IDs of Sampling Schemes

The inspection level is not defined as a function or as a table assignment inside the sampling scheme; instead, it has to be reflected in multiple sampling schemes. We recommend that you not change the existing levels and their assigned inspection severities. The relevant literature also points out that it is possible to specify that level II be used by default for normal cases.

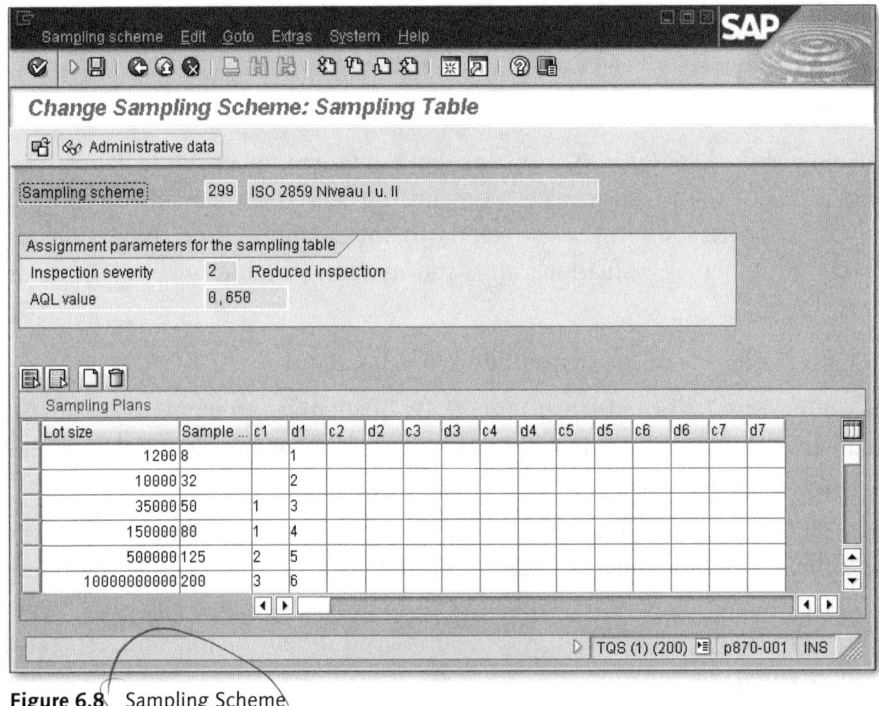


**Figure 6.8** Sampling Scheme

The inspection severity and the AQL are the initial values for the sampling scheme. It is possible to specify sampling plans for multiple inspection severities and AQLs for a sampling scheme master record.

The nature of the sample determination process depends on whether dynamic selection was selected:

- **With dynamic modification**
  Only the AQL is specified in the sampling procedure. The required inspection severity obtains the information about the sampling procedure from the current quality level.
- **Without dynamic modification**
  The inspection severity and the sampling scheme are stored in the sampling procedure.

Put simply, in a *sampling procedure*, you determine the sample size and the valuation rules for the inspection characteristics.

It is impossible to define generally valid rules for selecting sampling procedures. However, it is possible to state that sampling procedures based on AQL and ISO-2851/3951 sampling schemes are the preferred option for lot-based inspections, whereas fixed samples and SPC-type sampling procedures are the preferred option for production inspections. The sampling procedures that are selected should be those whose results are suitable for ongoing recording in the form of quality-control charts or quality histories. The sampling procedures that are delivered with your SAP ERP installation are usually adequate for this purpose and should not be modified. If necessary, however, you can create your own sampling procedures by combining the definition attributes in the upcoming list and use these for particular inspection tasks.

In particular, the industry-specific procedures in the automotive industry, such as Q101, QS 9000, and VDA, can be set using the sampling procedure functions in the SAP ERP system (see Figure 6.9).

The definitions of the sampling procedures that can be set in SAP ERP contain a combination of the following:

- Sampling scheme
- Valuation mode
- Inspection type
- Sample determination

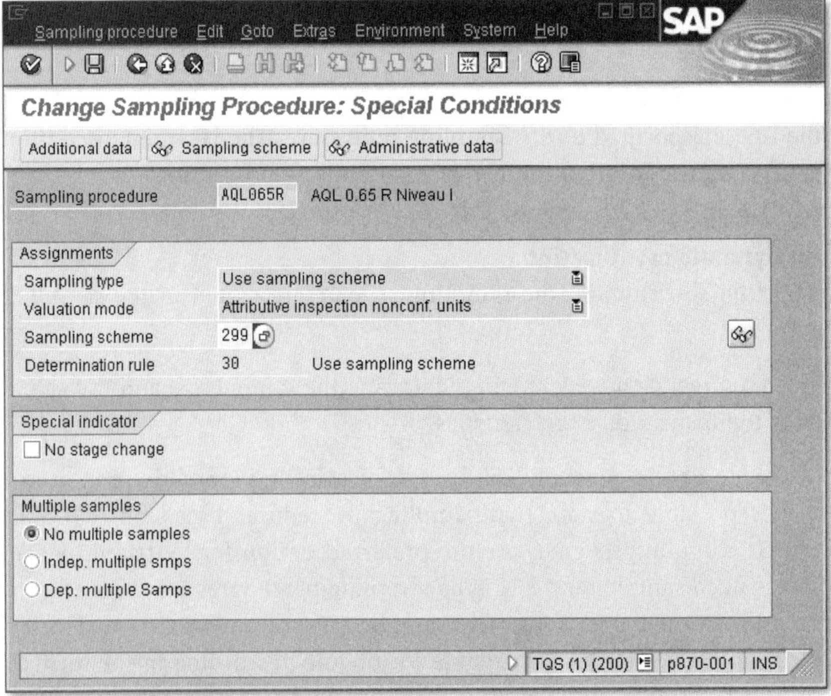


**Figure 6.9** Sampling Procedure

Other characteristics of the sampling procedure are the suppressible stage change for dynamic modification of the inspection scope, and the characteristic for an independent multiple sample.

The *independent multiple sample* should be used if multiple results for a characteristic of a part, or results from multiple samples for a characteristic, are to be recorded.

An example of an independent multiple sample is the repeated measuring of the diameter at different points of a wave. Note that the inspection results should be attributed to only one unit of inspection in this case. An arithmetical mean value of the measurements can then be calculated in a subsequent calculated characteristic. In a multiple sample, the characteristic is valuated as accepted or rejected by means of a function module, such as that used for the worst-case rule.

This function module, implemented as a small ABAP program, is assigned in Customizing and can be modified or extended as required. Documentation on the functioning of this function module is available only in the Customizing table.

In the context of evaluating inspection costs and rationalizing inspection outgoings, it can sometimes be desirable to increase or decrease the inspection scope or the inspection severity for a material that is obtained from a specific vendor, while taking the quality level into account. The quality level is mapped in its own screen, and you can change it retroactively.

The *dynamic modification rule* contains the instructions for inspection frequency and the findings of samples in the form of inspection stages. Conditions that apply after a stage change are assigned to every inspection stage. The criterion for a stage change is either OK or NOK. Figure 6.10 shows the process of dynamic modification.

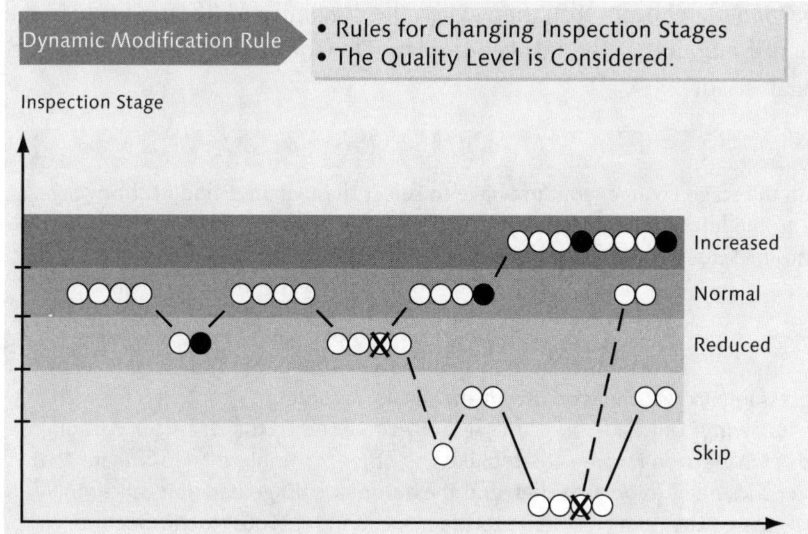


**Figure 6.10** Dynamic Modification Process

You access the screen for maintaining the dynamic modification rule via the menu path Logistics • Quality Management • Quality Planning • Basic Data • Sample • Dynamic Modification Rule. Here, you specify whether dynamic modification should run after the usage decision or when the lot is created. The inspection stages have a tabular structure.

Three different objects can be assigned to a dynamic modification rule:

- **Inspection type in material master record**
  With this option, the set characteristics are overridden by the inspection type settings in the material master record for the purposes of dynamic modification on the lot or characteristic level.
- **Inspection plan on header level**
  The decision whether dynamic modification references the lot or the characteristic is made on the basis of the selected control indicator in the inspection plan header.
- **Characteristic in inspection plan with characteristic-based dynamic modification**
  In this case, the indicator for characteristic-based dynamic modification is set in the inspection plan header. You then assign the dynamic modification rule in the maintenance function of the inspection plan (Dynamic Modification of Inspection Characteristic).

**Tip**

To maintain the stage change, you first have to select the dynamic modification stage in the box to the left of the table (see Figure 6.11). Then click on the STAGE CHANGE button, and the screen containing the detailed stage change settings opens.

**Tip**

Do not necessarily expect the worklist for the results recording to contain a lot with any of the following: SKIP, SKIP ON LOT LEVEL, or AUTOMATIC USAGE DECISION. Although these kinds of inspection lots are created like any other, a complete "skip" means that no characteristics need to be recorded, and the automatic usage decision can simply immediately assign the ACCEPTED value to the inspection lot. Thus, the inspection lot appears in the worklist only in the short period after it is created and before it is accepted by means of the automatic usage decision.

Another characteristic of an inspection level is the *inspection severity*, which is used to flexibly control the probability of acceptance and the inspection costs. ISO 2859 defines the following inspection severities:

- Normal
- Reduced
- Intensified

There clearly is no need to assign inspection severities to the skip levels.

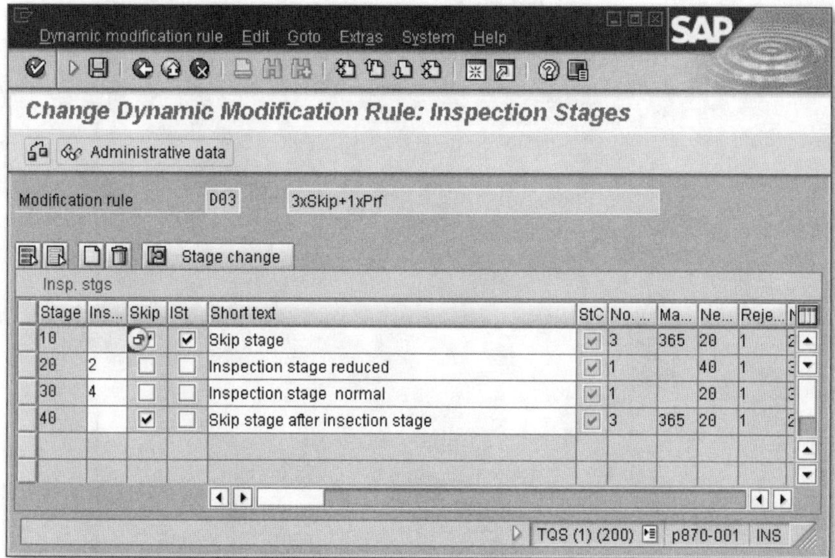


**Figure 6.11** Dynamic Modification Table for Basic Data

**Tip**

When you are maintaining dynamic modification rules, the system requires you to enter an inspection severity for all inspection levels that are not skip levels, even if you are actually working with sampling procedures without a sampling scheme. It makes sense to specify one or more inspection severities for this case (inspection without sampling scheme).

To view the current and future quality levels, an overview and maintenance function is available in the system under LOGISTICS • QUALITY MANAGEMENT • QUALITY INSPECTION • QUALITY LEVEL (see Figure 6.12). Here, you can also make a manual stage change, which is then retained in the system and documented. The quality level allows you to track each dynamic modification stage and to intervene manually, if necessary.

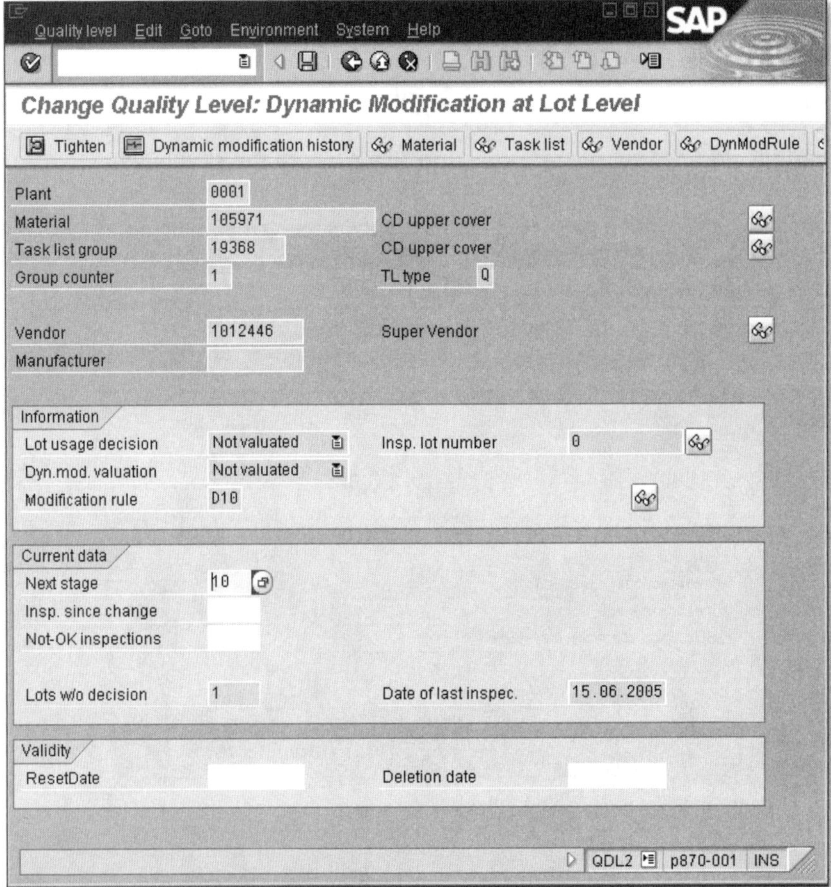


**Figure 6.12** Quality Level

**Tip**

See also Chapter 8, Quality Control and, in particular, Section 8.2, Usage Decision, for more detail. When an Accepted usage decision has been made, the process of changing the quality level is very likely to tend toward higher inspection costs. This happens when a single characteristic has been valuated as Rejected.

In this case, the worst-case rule applies (in Customizing under the Plant-Specific Settings). This rule uses a function module to describe the behavior of the quality level when lot defects occur. If you deactivate this function module, dynamic modification is carried out purely on the basis of the usage decision code.

### Control Charts and Statistical Process Control (SPC)

Control charts are most commonly used in the production area. Therefore, this section deals with only the basic settings parameters in the sampling procedure. Furthermore, this section considers the procedure model for the control-chart technique. Your system comes with a number of preset sampling procedures for SPC inspection planning (see Figure 6.13).

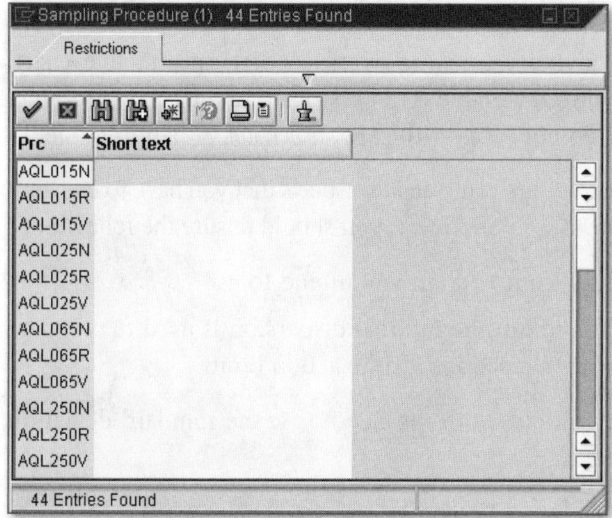


**Figure 6.13** Sampling Procedure for SPC

To define your own SPC sampling procedure in SAP ERP, proceed in exactly the same way as you would for the lot inspection. The sampling procedure input mask contains one extra attribute: the indicator for the inspection point. First and foremost, the inspection point control object allows you to set the inspection interval, that is, whether the inspection is to be container-based, time interval-based, or event-based.

Define the following first:

- **Sample type**
  Only a fixed sample is allowed.
- **Valuation mode**
  Select the special valuation mode, SPC inspection. With this setting, valuations of samples or characteristics use the action limits of the quality control chart. A rejection occurs if the action limits are violated. If there are not yet enough

measurement values to calculate an action limit, the procedure switches to manual calculation until the measurement values are sufficient.

- **Control chart type**
  You have to assign a control chart type for SPC sampling procedures. When you do so, the system checks whether the sampling procedure will use inspection points or independent multiple samples. With independent multiple samples, control chart types with samples are allowed; otherwise, control chart types without samples are allowed.

  In control charts with a memory (moving average chart, mean-value chart, moving-range chart), the control variable is not restricted to the current sample. These control chart tracks do not support the *SPC inspection* valuation mode.

When defining the *sample size*, there are some quality aspects that you have to take into account. If you want to use the sample size n = 1, you should ensure the following:

- That there is no S track in the control chart you intend to use
- That the overall dispersion and not the internal dispersion is used to calculate the process dispersion in the calculations for the action limits

The reason for this is that in samples with the size n = 1, the standard deviation is always 0.

In SPC inspections with measurement recording, samples sizes from 3 to 10 are normal. n = 5 is the most commonly-used value.

For quantitative characteristics, whose original values do not have a normal distribution, you can select a larger sample size to use the central specification limit set of the statistics, whereby the distribution of the mean values is almost normal. You can then use Shewhart charts for the mean value, even if the distribution of the population is not normal. The more the distribution deviates from the norm, the greater the sample size should be.

**Customizing Tip**

The SPC criteria determine the update process for the control chart and are controlled by function modules. Before a new control chart is created (during results recording), this function module checks whether a suitable chart already exists. The function modules are well documented and can be easily adapted to suit your own needs. It is also a simple matter to create a control chart for a characteristic or vendor only. This would result in the following kind of update: "The same characteristic via different vendors and different material numbers is written to the same track of a control chart." (This requirement arose in a project because basically identical materials with vendor-specific keys produced different material numbers in the material.)

The standard already contains the following function modules:

- QRKS_CHARACTERISTIC — control chart for characteristic
- QRKS_INSPECTION_LOT — control chart for characteristic or inspection lot
- QRKS_MATERIAL — control chart for characteristic or material
- QRKS_MATERIAL_CUSTOMER — control chart for characteristic, material, or customer
- QRKS_MATERIAL_MANUFACTURER — control chart for characteristic, material, or manufacturer
- QRKS_MATERIAL_SOLD_TO_PARTY — control chart for characteristic, material, or sold-to party
- QRKS_MATERIAL_VENDOR — control chart for characteristic, material, or vendor
- QRKS_MATERIAL_WORK_CENTER — control chart for characteristic, material, or work center
- QRKS_PURCHASING_DOCUMENT — control chart for characteristic or purchasing document

QRKS_SALES_ORDER — control chart for characteristic or sales order

For your *SAP QM implementation concept for sample control*, you should consider the fundamental issues in advance and perform your activities in the following order:

1. Make a list of the existing systems for sample determination, and describe the rules of your sample procedure in a matrix.
2. Which of the existing procedures do you want to keep? Assign a rule in the SAP ERP system to your enterprise's procedure.
3. Analyze your inspection procedures in terms of attributive (qualitative) or quantitative inspections.
4. Do you use sampling schemes according to ISO-Standards? If not, what are your own sampling schemes like? Define the procedure you will use in the future.
5. At what points in your inspection activities could dynamic modification be used to optimize the inspection scope? Make a list of all inspection types, and assign dynamic modification rules to them.

**Customizing Tip**

After you have made all your definitions, set your basic data in the order shown here:

- Sample types — Customizing
- Valuation modes — Customizing
- Sampling schemes — user data
- Dynamic modification rules — user data
- Allowed combinations of sample procedures and dynamic modification rules — user data

### Master Inspection Characteristic

You will use master inspection characteristics when creating task lists as copy templates, or you will reference (include) them in the inspection plan. The individual objects and control functions are the same as those of the characteristic in the inspection plan and are described there in detail. From the organizational point of view, the master inspection characteristics, like the inspection plans, are assigned to the plant.

If major changes are made to the master inspection characteristic, a new version of this master record is automatically created (see Figure 6.14). In the case of inspections that have already started and that have fixed tolerances, such as SPC inspections, you may not change the tolerance limits in an updated control chart. A reference is always made from the task list to a specific version of the master inspection characteristic. For this reason, it is important to carefully plan the material before it is referenced.

If the master inspection characteristic is used for quantitative inspections, it also makes sense to use the incomplete maintenance option. This means that the nominal value, the tolerance settings, and so on, do not have to be set when the master inspection characteristic is maintained. Complete settings only have to be made after the characteristic is used in an inspection plan. A fixed reference cannot be made to an incomplete characteristic. Incomplete characteristics are suitable only as copy templates.

You can also use master inspection characteristics for material specifications in which you cannot enter normal inspection characteristics. For their part, master inspection characteristics reference inspection methods and catalogs.

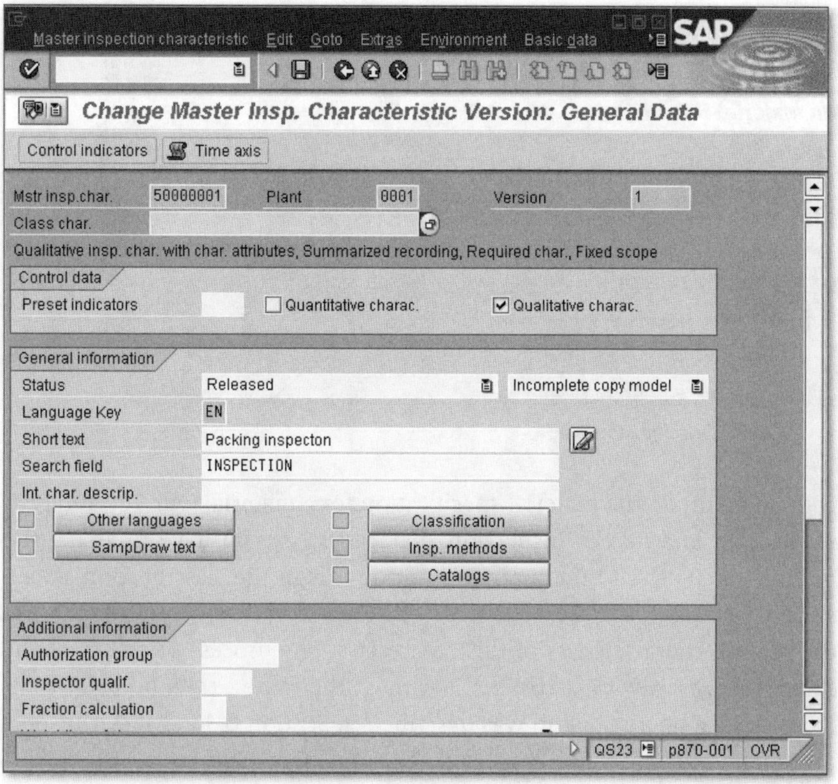

Figure 6.14 Master Inspection Characteristic

## Material Specification

The material specification is located under LOGISTICS • QUALITY MANAGEMENT • QUALITY PLANNING • INSPECTION PLANNING • MATERIAL SPECIFICATION (see Figure 6.15). This alternative to the general inspection plan (with operations and characteristics) in the SAP ERP system provides a simple variant of the inspection plan structuring process that does not contain any operations. More important is its use in batch classification. Simply put, a work regulation for quality inspections is prepared in the material specification, using completely maintained master inspection characteristics or general characteristics. The completed inspection characteristics then automatically transfer the inspection results to the batches.

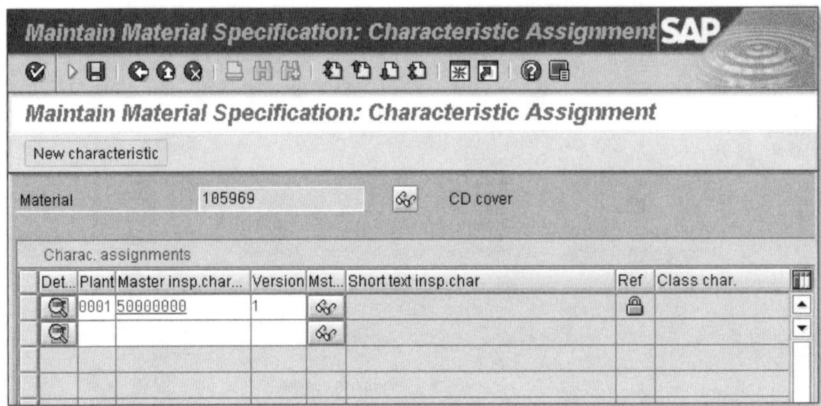


**Figure 6.15** Material Specification

Before you can maintain the material specification for a material with links to general characteristics and master inspection characteristics, you have to assign the corresponding batch class to the material. You do this in the classification screen of the material master data maintenance function. In this way, you create the link to the general characteristics of this batch class. The process of assigning the *referenced master inspection characteristics* is almost the same as the procedure for inspection-plan characteristics and was described in Section 6.3.2, Master Inspection Characteristic.

For a material without a batch class, you can use the material specification only on the basis of master inspection characteristics with a link to the general characteristics. Also, unlike the plant-based inspection plan, the material specification applies for all clients in the system.

### Quality Info Record: Procurement

This info record contains the information and control settings for the vendor in relation to the material supplied (see Figure 6.16). This info record provides lock and control mechanisms for deliveries for every vendor/material combination. These mechanisms relate to the delivery quantity, quality, audit result, time periods, and other agreements with the vendor.

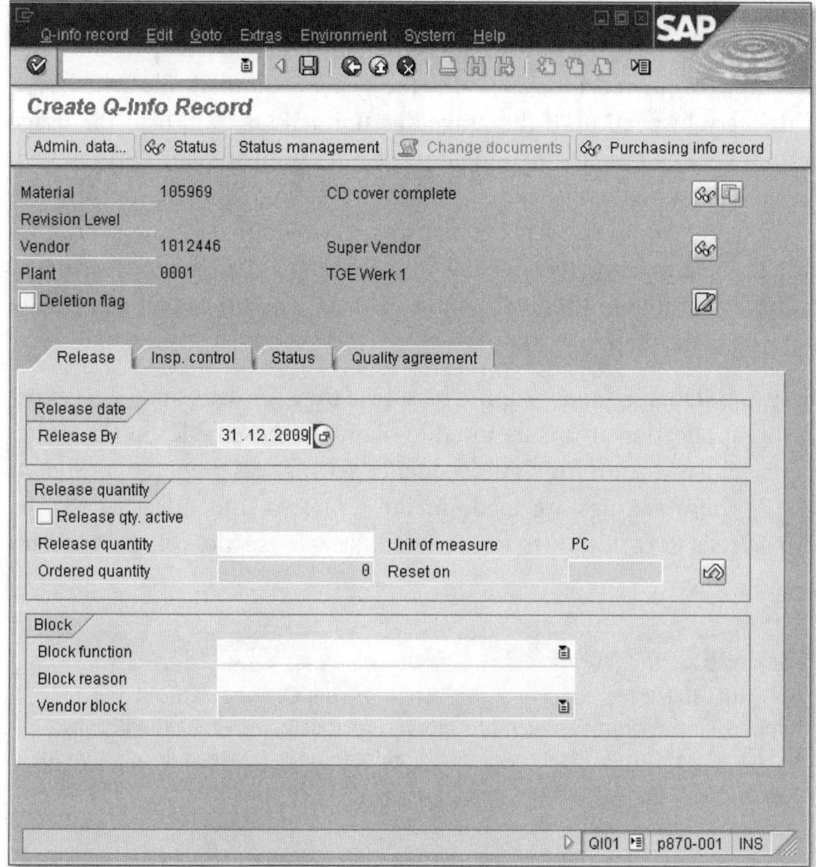


**Figure 6.16** Quality Info Record

The STATUS PROFILE plays a central role in quality planning. You can use this to control the sequence of the various inspection types (in a product rollout, for example). The status profile in the quality info record combines the quality- and inspection-planning elements in one control entity. A status profile can define a sequence for the following:

- Model inspection
- Regular delivery inspection
- Extra model inspection

One of the settings allows you to arrange the inspection types according to their usage decisions. In this case, the initial status would be the model inspection. After this is successfully completed and ACCEPTED, the system automatically switches to the regular delivery inspection. If the usage decision is REJECTED, or if the usage decision has not yet been made, the model inspection status remains unchanged. The switch to the extra model inspection is made manually when the specification is changed. After the inspection has been successfully completed, the procedure switches back to the regular delivery inspection. The status change and the current status situation are visible in the quality info record, and you can also manually set the status you want there.

Unfortunately, the status sequence cannot be set via the user data, and some experience with this application area is required to maintain these tables in Customizing. Therefore, a fully functioning status sequence setting was prepared, as shown in Figure 6.17. These settings are made in the QM area under DEFINE STATUS SEQUENCE OF SUPPLY RELATIONSHIPS in the PROCUREMENT section of the Customizing tables.

**Tip**

Note that the initial status has to have SUPPLY RELATIONSHIP OPENED without any inspection type assignment. In the example shown previously, the first GR will cause the status to change to MODEL INSPECTION and simultaneously create an inspection lot in accordance with the specified inspection type.

### Quality Info Record: Sales

The quality info record for sales controls the type and scope of the post-production inspections for every customer on the material level. Depending on the delivery status (series release, sample delivery, or subsequent delivery), other inspections may need to be carried out or specific customer requirements may need to be fulfilled. Documents (such as a customer specification) can be stored for every material.

The usage decision for the inspection lot determines whether the material is used in the goods-issue (GI) inspection, taking into account the customer requirements specified here.

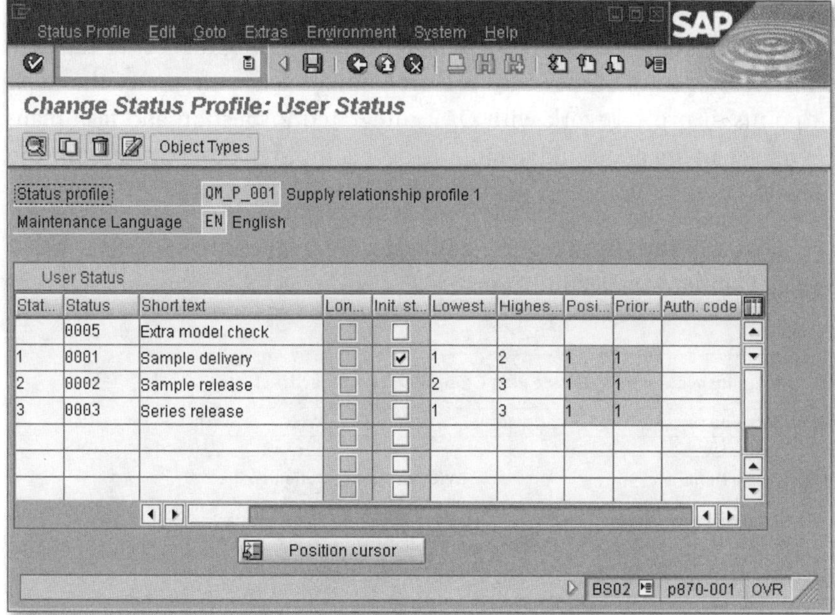


**Figure 6.17** Customizing Table Showing Status Sequence for Inspection Control

## 6.4 SAP QM Inspection Plan

This section deals with the inspection plan in SAP QM. You are first provided with general information on this topic, and then on the management of inspections plans, the task-list structure, and the engineering workbench.

### 6.4.1 General Remarks

As is also usually the case with other CAQ systems on the market, the actual SAP ERP inspection plan is similar to the structures of a computer-supported task-planning component. In the SAP ERP system, these production-based task list types are contained in the Production Planning (PP) and Production Planning for Process Industries (master recipe with PP-PI) areas. For QM purposes, this has the advantage that the inspection plan is structured in exactly the same way as the routing and thus already has useful and tried-and-tested planning instruments at its disposal. The basic structure, which consists of operations (work operations, inspection operations), is the same in all task-list types. In addition to this, every task-list type also has its own features, which arise from the way it is used.

The inspection plan is completely integrated into the supply chain of the SAP ERP system and also provides extended functions for task planning that cover capacity and costs. Therefore, in the following, you are familiarized with one of the most important points of project work with QM: integrated inspection and task planning. You will see that a good understanding of this topic is a prerequisite for the positive development of your QM plan.

Figure 6.18 illustrates the tasks to create and test a Reference Operation Set, which is also called a Standard Inspection Plan.

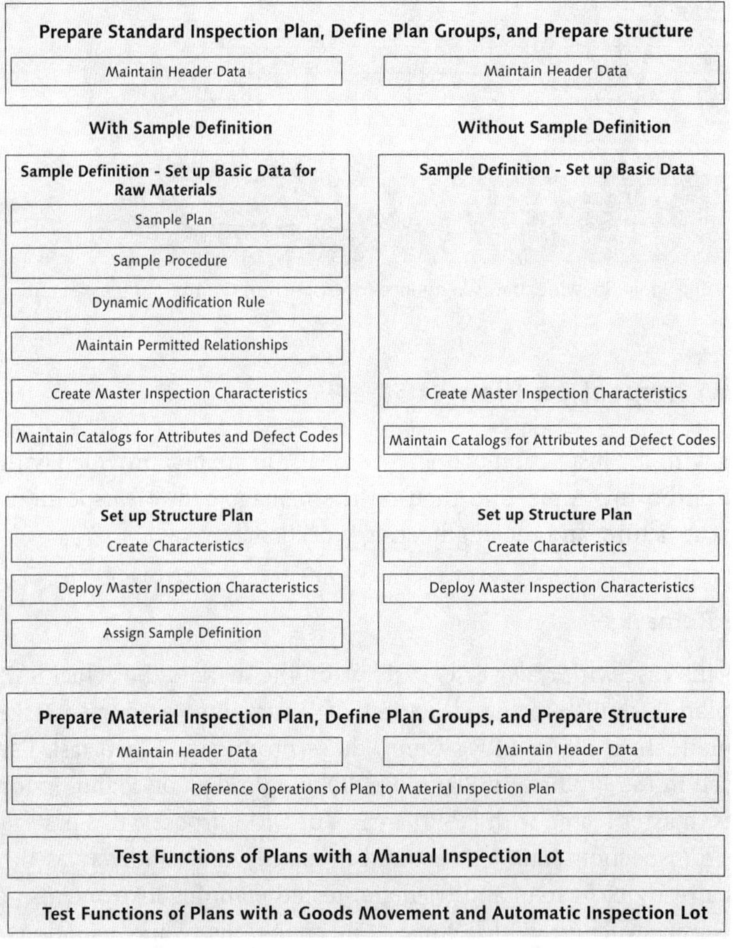


**Figure 6.18** Creating and Testing an Inspection Plan with Referenced Standard Plan

> **Tip**
>
> As part of your inspection planning, set up integration meetings with the Procurement, Production Planning, and Sales project groups early in the planning phase. In these meetings, introduce the participants to the whole area of inspection planning and explain how it is integrated with the various other technical departments. You should also use this opportunity to explain the organizational aspects and areas of responsibility that will be important when the team is working together on the inspection plan and the routing.

When delivered, the system has the following task-list types:

- Routing
- Master recipe (PP-PI)
- Inspection Plan
- Reference Operation Set

**Task-List Type: Routing**

Besides its basic functions, the routing (standard routing) also contains all of the functions of the inspection plan (see Figure 6.19). The ROUTING is described in detail here to illustrate the multiple benefits of the integrated task-list variant because all of the functions described here are also available to you in inspection planning.

In the routing, you use work operations to order the individual work steps in a sequence to plan a production run for your products. For this purpose, the routing contains the work centers at which the individual work steps will be carried out, as well as the required tools and PRTs.

The material is the main object of reference of the routing. The routing is thus initially independent of any order and is copied to the production order only when the order is released. Operations can be retroactively removed from or added to the production order.

Using the default values of the routing, you define the planned times at which the individual work operations will be executed. The default values, for their part, serve as the basis for lead-time scheduling, product cost planning, and capacity planning. They are plan values for the production order and can be retroactively modified there, just like the operations themselves.

The functional objects of a routing are as follows:

- Operations
- Material components (BOM)
- PRTs
- Inspection characteristics

In the SAP ERP system, routings are used in the following areas:

- In production orders
- In scheduling
- In capacity planning
- In costing

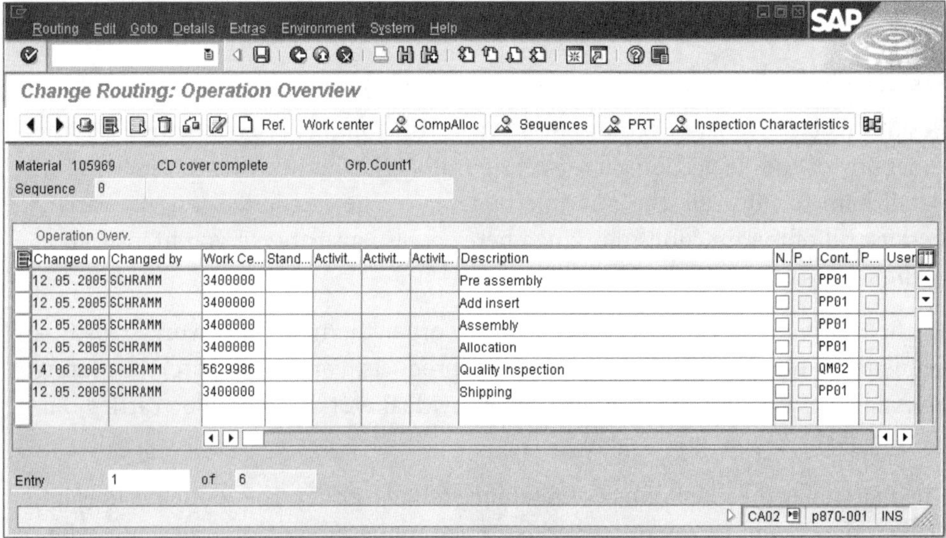


**Figure 6.19** Standard Routing with Quality Inspection Operation

As you can see from these functions, you are now operating fully in the areas of PP and CO. For example, the quality order in the QM quality notification uses the same billing system as the production order.

The rate routing is a variant of the routing and is mainly used in repetitive manufacturing. The main functions of this task-list type have already been described in connection with the standard routing.

### Task-List Type: Master Recipe (PP-PI)

Besides the functions and objects of the routing, the master recipe also contains other features arising from the requirements of process industries. The master recipe is particularly suitable for batch-managed production processes and is used in food production, the manufacturing of chemical and pharmaceutical products, and for special continuous processes such as those in the paper industry, to name a few. The master recipe is the task-list type of the independent SAP ERP component PP-PI. This component gathers together the attributes required for producing the product in question or to provide the service in question. As Figure 6.20 shows, the master recipe is located under LOGISTICS • PRODUCTION-PROCESS • MASTER DATA • MASTER RECIPES • RECIPE AND MATERIAL LIST • CHANGE.

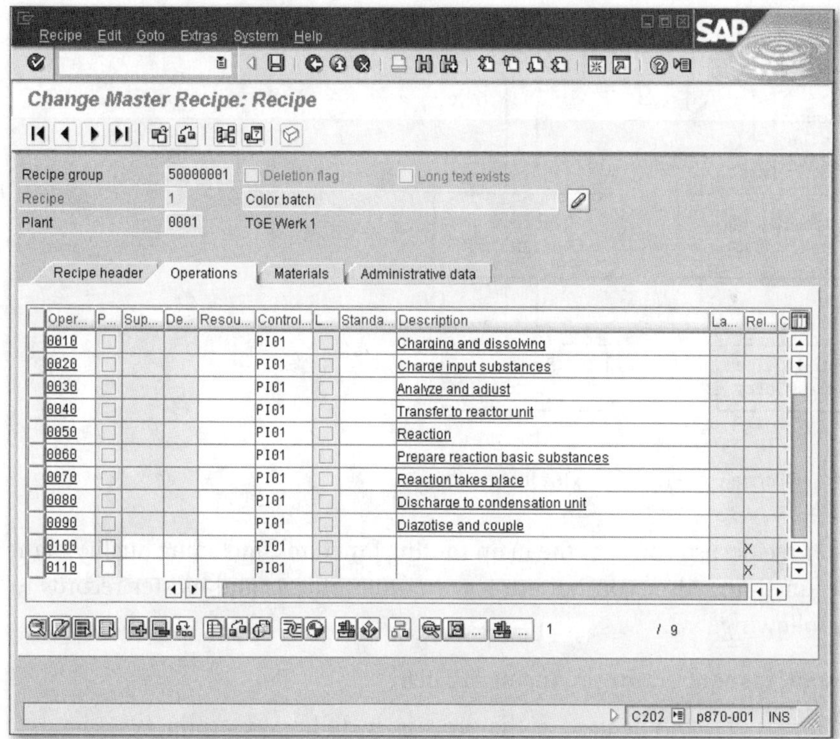


Figure 6.20 Master Recipe

Quality aspects and quality planning are particularly important in the PP-PI industry solution. Unlike those in discrete industries, many processes in PP-PI are completed very quickly, are not very error-tolerant, and retroactive corrections are rarely possible. For this reason, a targeted, integrated inspection planning process with inspection characteristics greatly contributes to the goal of enhancing effectiveness and quality. Figure 6.21 provides a clear overview of the various integration options in quality planning and quality control with the QM application component.

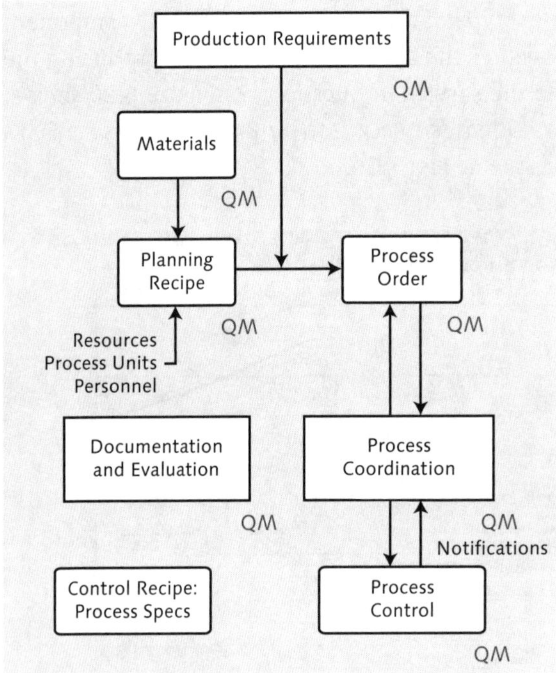


**Figure 6.21** Overview of PP-PI with QM Integration

The master recipe also contains the main routing functions, including quality management functions. Also, you can use it with other objects and master records to plan the following:

- All resources required for producing a batch
- All materials that will be used in the process, including by-products
- The operations and phases required for completing the process

From the process control point of view, you can define rules for procedures and control measures in the form of characteristic-based process instructions and warning messages, in accordance with health and safety regulations.

The PP-PI inspection planning functions do not differ greatly from those in PP, and so, for further information about this topic, see Section 6.6, Quality Planning in Procurement.

#### Task-List Type: Inspection Plan

You use the inspection plan task-list type in the QM module to process Procurement quality inspections. Its typical application areas are model inspections, GR inspections, GI inspections, and GRs from production. Its main functions are the same as those of the routing. Unlike the routing, however, the inspection plan only has a standard sequence of operations and no alternative sequences. Besides being assigned to the material, it is also assigned to the following:

- Material and vendor
- Material and customer

Both the routing and the inspection plan can include the reference operation set in their operations and thus use a modular system of operations and inspection characteristics. The inspection types that you assign via MATERIAL MASTER • QUALITY MANAGEMENT VIEW • INSPECTION SETUP and that use the INSPECTION PLAN task-list type are printed in the bold in the following list. The inspection types that are not in bold use the routing task-list type.

- **01 Incoming inspection for goods receipt**
- **02 Model incoming inspection for goods receipt**
- **03 Incoming inspection for goods receipt, pilot run**
- **04 Goods issue inspection**
- 05 In-process inspection for production order
- **06 Inspection for goods receipt from production**
- **07 Incoming inspection for goods receipt of initial series**
- **08 Inspection for other goods receipts**
- **09 Inspection for customer returns**
- **10 Audit inspection**
- **11 Stock transfer inspection**
- 12 Recurring inspection

- **13 Inspection for delivery to customer (with order)**
- **14 Inspection for delivery to customer (without order)**
- **15 General inspection for delivery**
- 16 Inspection for run-schedule headers
- 89 Other inspections

**Customizing Tip**

In project discussions, requests often are made for alternative inspection types; for example, inspection types that reflect different strategies for incoming inspections for fundamentally different materials. Unfortunately, this problem cannot be overcome, even if the system is customized to include extra inspection types. You therefore have no choice but to individually change the relevant control indicators under the INSPECTION DATA in the quality view of the material. In such a case, the only Customizing tasks are to customize the short name of the inspection type and the global control indicator for each existing inspection type. For this reason, it is not recommended that you create new inspection types in an attempt to solve the problem.

#### Task-List Type: Reference Operation Set

Reference operation sets are task-list types that are used indirectly for inspection planning and task planning. Because it is used indirectly, the reference operation set is not usually assigned to a material (although this is possible) and does not have its own ID number or name. It is best regarded as a component for other task-list types and is used (referenced) in PP and in QM. The reference operation set is where you describe frequently used sequences of operations and characteristics with the full inspection-planning functionality. The reference operation set has a continual link to the routing or inspection plan by means of referencing at the operation level. All modifications to the reference operation set are therefore immediately reflected in the task lists that contain associated references. You can find out what inspection plans contain the reference by means of a report displayed by the system. This report has both display and maintenance functions.

Note also that the dynamic modification rules on the header level cannot be maintained in the reference operation set. You therefore have to repeat these in the header data of the "real" task list. This is because only the operations for the reference are used, and an inspection plan can contain references from different reference operation sets.

### 6.4.2 Administrating Inspection Plans

First, let's consider the task-list usage.

#### Task-List Usage

In this section, we describe both the user data and the Customizing options. You are already familiar with the inspection type from the material master. If an inspection type is active, an inspection lot is created after a particular event, even if there is no inspection plan yet. This event could be a GR for the goods movement PURCHASE ORDER, for example. The link between the task-list usage and the inspection type is then created by means of the relevant Customizing settings for maintaining the inspection types and the task-list usage entry in the inspection plan. In other words, the inspection-lot creation function finds the right inspection plan by means of the task-list usage and the material. Figure 6.22 illustrates this set of circumstances.

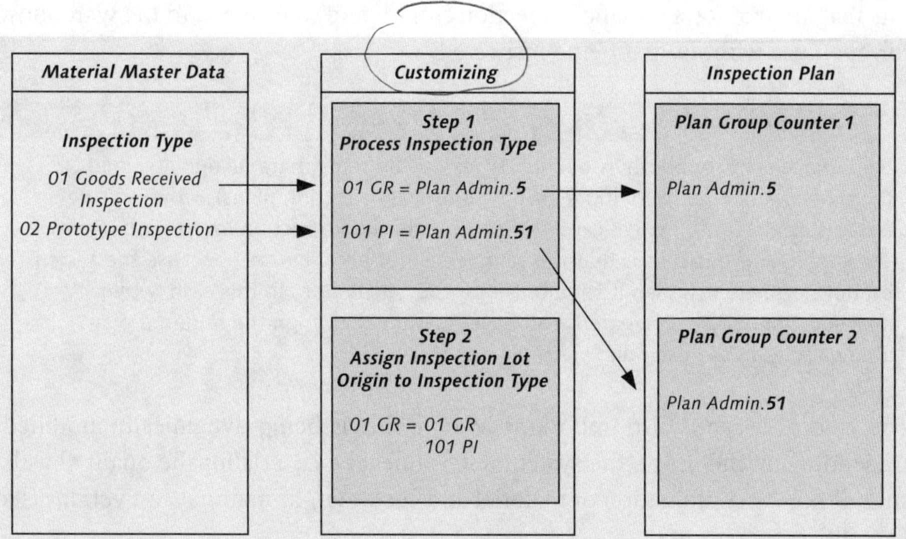


**Figure 6.22** Link from Inspection Type to Task-List Usage

**Example**

Here is an example of how to manually control consecutive inspection types. In an inspection plan for the same task-list group of a material, you want to create one inspection plan for the model inspection and one inspection plan for the incoming inspection. The model inspection is to be carried out first. For the purposes of inspection lot control, you create the inspection types 01 (INCOMING INSPECTION) and 02 (MODEL INCOMING INSPECTION FOR GOODS RECEIPT) in the material master but activate only inspection type 02 at first.

You assign related task-list usages to the task lists on the header level (in this case, incoming inspections). For the first goods delivery, the system creates only one inspection lot and provides you with the inspection plans defined by means of the task-list usage for selection. Select the appropriate inspection plan, depending on the inspection level you are at. If you are working without a status sequence, after the inspection has run successfully and assigned an "Accepted" valuation, you can simply deactivate the inspection type that will not be used for the next inspection (model inspection) and switch to regular delivery with inspection type 01.

However, the deactivation of an inspection type is subject to a restriction that makes sound business sense. If there are open orders for a material, the inspection type cannot be deactivated. All GRs must first be posted. This prevents delivery lots that are due for a specific inspection from being transferred to the warehouse for open use without first being inspected.

**Note**

If you have activated both inspection types for the same material and assigned the same plan usage to multiple group counters (inspection plans) without using a status schema, the system cannot then prepare the inspection lot for inspection. The problem in this case is that the sample cannot be calculated because the system cannot decide which plan it should use for the calculation. In this case, while an inspection lot is still created, you have to manually assign the required plan afterward, as in the example.

The kind of usage is also important when a role is being dynamically modified. Depending on the usage, the system determines the criteria for the quality levels, such as for the combination of material and customer, or material and vendor (see Figure 6.23).

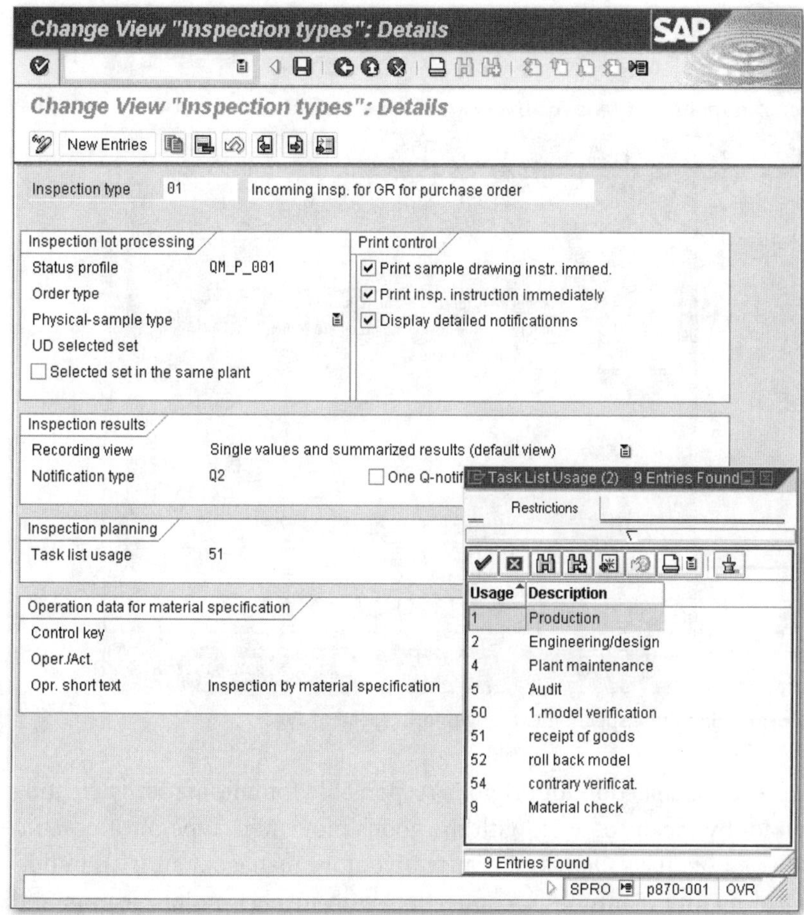


**Figure 6.23** Customizing the Inspection Type with Task-List Usage Entry

### Inspection Lot Origin

You can make other Customizing settings that ensure that the system knows the event (GR, production order, GI) to which the required inspection type and the correct task-list usage belong. Usually, however, the system's default settings should suffice. Figure 6.24 shows how the following inspection types are assigned to the inspection lot origin 01 (Goods Receipt):

- 01 Incoming Insp. for GR for Purchase Order
- 0101 Model Insp. for GR for Purchase Order
- 09 Recurring Inspection

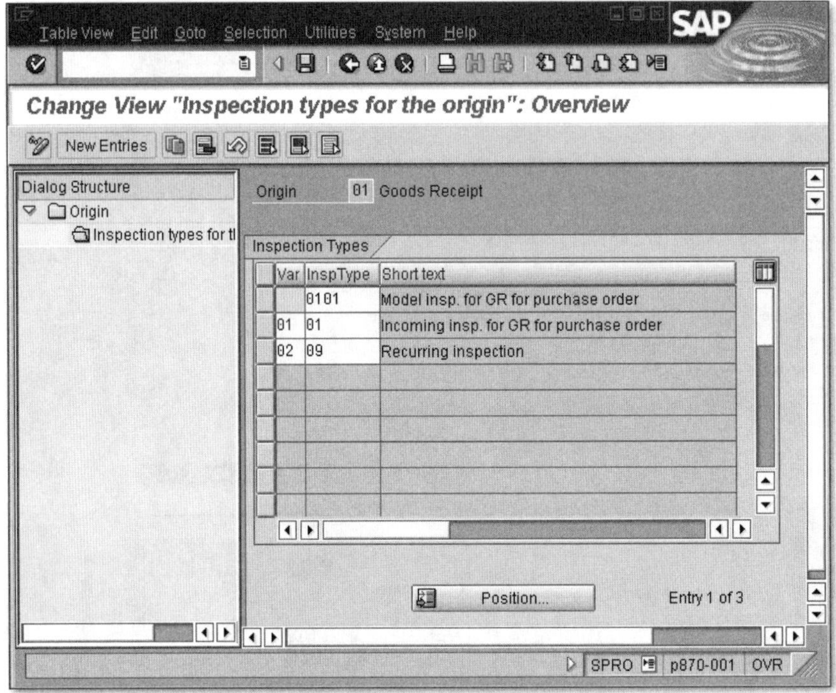


**Figure 6.24** Customizing the Inspection Lot Origin for Inspection Type

In this example, the inspection lot origin is responsible for automatically creating an inspection lot by means of a GR with the goods movement type 01 (INCOMING INSP. FOR GR FOR PURCHASE ORDER). Because inventory management is an important element of quality planning in connection with inspection-lot creation and inspection planning, this topic is illustrated in detail in Chapter 7, Quality Inspection. This chapter also contains important information on inspection stock.

Another important point in this context is that you can assign multiple inspection types to an inspection lot origin, but you cannot assign one inspection type to different inspection lot origins at the same time. The settings that govern which goods movements refer to a specific inspection-lot origin exist in Customizing under QUALITY MANAGEMENT • QUALITY INSPECTION • INSPECTION LOT CREATION • INSPECTION FOR GOODS MOVEMENTS. It is also important that no new inspection-lot origins can be added (unlike the situation with inspection types and plan usages) because these tables are located in the SAP ERP namespace.

### Task-List Assignment and Task-List Groups

To gain a better understanding of inspection plan management, let's now look at the structure of the inspection plan and its individual components. QUALITY MANAGEMENT • QUALITY PLANNING • INSPECTION PLANNING • INSPECTION PLAN • CREATE takes you straight to the second level of the administration structure: the material. You then specify the plant to which this inspection plan will apply. This is particularly important because by including the plant, the system is including a superordinate hierarchy level.

**Tip**

For the sake of clarity, it was assumed that the scenarios in the following hierarchy tables apply to a plant. Note, however, that if you run different inspections for the same material number in plants A and B, the material also has to be created for plants A and B for the purposes of quality management. If this is not the case, problems with inspection-plan assignment can arise.

If you do not make any entries in the GROUP and GROUP COUNTER fields, the system uses its internal number assignment function to enter a task-list group and group counter "1" here. However, the user may also manually assign a number to the task-list group. When you execute this function, you are specifying two things at the same time:

- The material is assigned to the task-list group.
- All other task-list group counters for this material (such as model inspection plan, incoming inspection plan, and extra model inspection plan) are assigned to this first task-list group with sequential task-list group counters (see Figure 6.25), even if they are re-initiated using CREATE INSPECTION PLAN. This creates the hierarchy shown in Table 6.7.

| Task-List Group 1000 | | |
|---|---|---|
| Material A | | |
| Task-list group counter 1 | Task-list group counter 2 | Task-list group counter 3 |
| Model inspection plan | Incoming inspection plan | Extra model inspection plan |

**Table 6.7** Task-List Structure 1 — All Vendors for a Material with the Same Inspection Plan

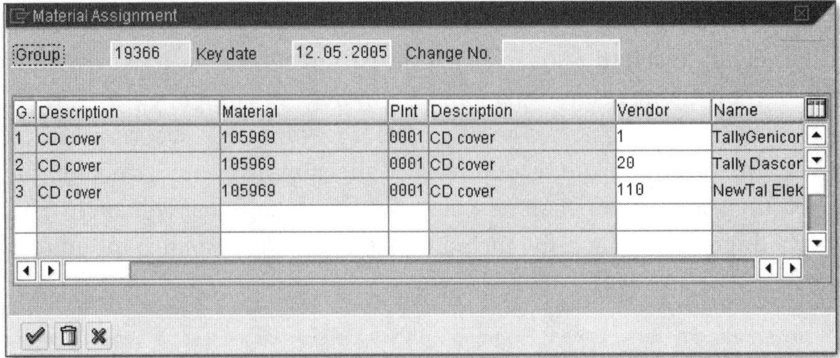


**Figure 6.25** Assigning a Material to a Task List

If inspection plans have the same material, but you want to assign different inspection plans to different vendors, this task-list assignment structure creates the hierarchy shown in Table 6.8.

| Task-List Group 1000 | | |
|---|---|---|
| **Material A** | | |
| Vendor A | Vendor A | Vendor A |
| Task-list group counter 1 | Task-list group counter 2 | Task-list group counter 3 |
| Model inspection plan | Incoming inspection plan | Extra model inspection plan |
| Vendor B | Vendor B | Vendor B |
| Task-list group counter 4 | Task-list group counter 5 | Task-list group counter 6 |
| Model inspection plan | Incoming inspection plan | Extra model inspection plan |

**Table 6.8** Task-List Structure 2 — Different Inspection Plans per Vendor, But Identical Material

However, you need this approach only if there are different inspection plans — which in this case are the same as the task-list group counters — for the different vendors. If the same inspection plan is used for all vendors, there is no need for any vendor assignment, and the hierarchy looks the same as in Table 6.7, Task-List Structure 1. The system automatically calculates the interconnections required for vendor evaluations and other analyses from the relationships between the order and the relevant goods movements.

In the next hierarchy, you see a variant in which the same inspection plan is used for different materials. Materials A, B, and C are located in the same task-list group.

Through the use of MATERIAL ASSIGNMENT, the existing task-list group counter remains in the list (see Table 6.9).

| Task-List Group 1000 | | |
|---|---|---|
| Material A | Material B | Material C |
| Task-list group counter 1 | Task-list group counter 1 | Task-list group counter 1 |

**Table 6.9** Identical Task List for Multiple Materials

It is not necessary here to assign the vendor, as described previously. Finally, you create an example that contains several of the alternatives already described. (Task-list group counter is abbreviated as TLGC here; see Table 6.10).

| Task-List Group 1000 | | | | | |
|---|---|---|---|---|---|
| Material A | Material B | | | Material C | |
| TLGC 1 | TLGC 2 | TLGC 3 | TLGC 4 | TLGC 5 | TLGC 6 |
| Vendor A | Vendor B | Vendor A | Vendor B | Vendor A | Vendor B |

**Table 6.10** Different Task Lists for Each Material, Depending on Vendor (or Customer)

Of course, the various examples do not include every possible combination. However, in general, note the following:

- The uppermost hierarchy is created by the task-list group, not by the material.
- A number of different materials can use the same inspection plan.
- A number of different vendors or customers can use the same inspection plan.
- A task-list group can contain different, alternative inspection plans for one material.
- Alternative inspection plans can also be linked to a vendor or customer, although this is not mandatory.
- The MATERIAL ASSIGNMENT function should actually be called the material/vendor/task list assignment function.

Figure 6.26 illustrates different task groups for different inspection types.

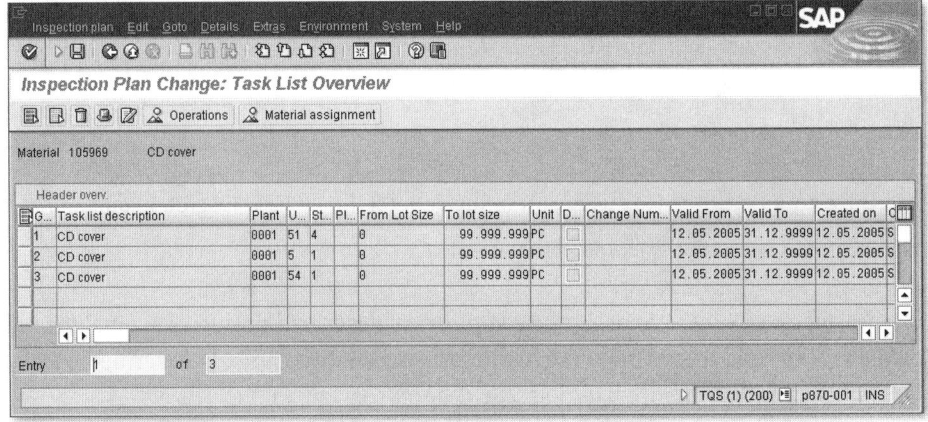

**Figure 6.26** Task-List Group Counters (Inspection Plans) of a Task-List Group for Different Inspection Types

**Tip**

Take the time to analyze your previous hierarchies and task-list assignments and to re-evaluate them in terms of a migration (data transfer) to the SAP ERP system. Then design a suitable model for task-list administration, based on the method illustrated here. You may be able to significantly reduce the number of your task lists and thus save yourself a lot of time and effort on task-list maintenance in the future.

### Creating an Inspection Plan for a Revision Level

You are already familiar with the change master record. One ongoing topic in inspection plan management is the need to track task-list changes in parallel with changes to specifications and drawings of the material. In response to this requirement, the system allows you to create different revision levels of an inspection plan as individual inspection plans within a task-list group, using the central Change Management function.

Making changes using the change master record is an option, but this is used only for major revisions, so you will probably make more minor changes without the use of the change master record. In this case, too, the change is documented in a change document and thus can be tracked. The KEY DATE field is used to set the time at which the change will take effect. To include inspection planning in Change Management, TASK LIST has to be added to the list of object types, as shown in Figure 6.27.

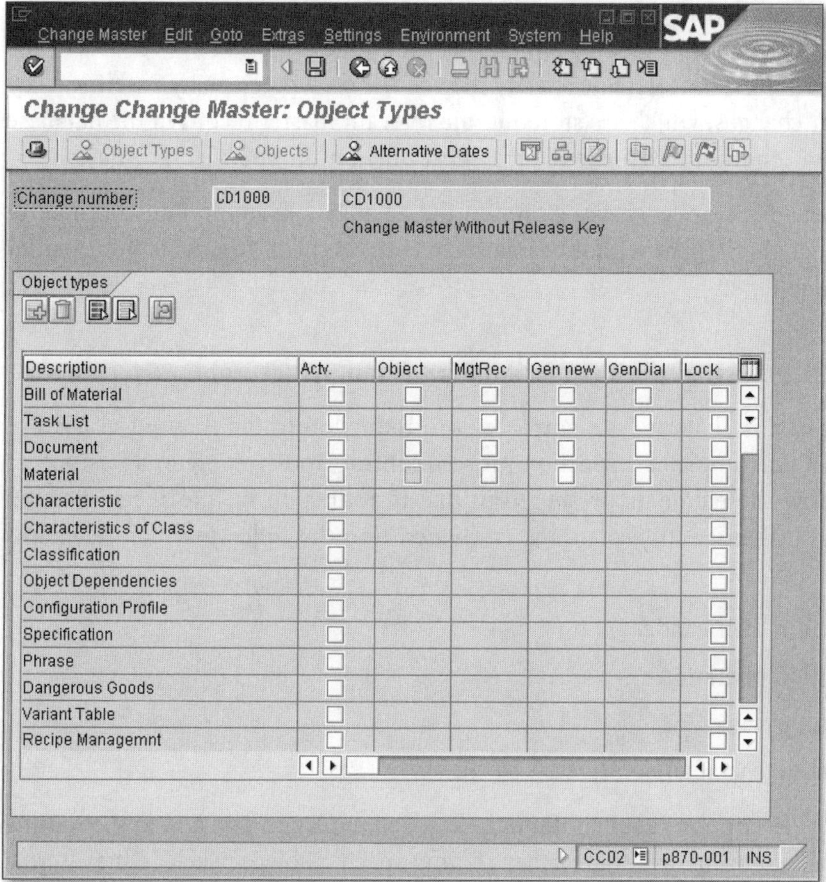


**Figure 6.27** Additions to the List of Object Types in the Change Master Record

> **Tip**
>
> If you assign revision levels to your inspection plans, and then set a reference to a reference operation set, you must ensure that the reference operation set has an allowed validity period. If the validity period of the reference operation set in question is outside the validity period of the inspection plan, the system outputs a corresponding error message. However, the text of the error message ("The plan has no original sequence") does not clearly explain the nature of the problem.

In business practice, you often come across the example of the new drawing index (SAP: version). As soon as inspection plan changes are planned, the index requires that the inspection plan be adjusted in line with the drawing index. Just as with the inspection plans, you can save these versions of the drawing index for the material as new master records and at the same time create a new version of the inspection plan. As before, you specify the validity of the version by entering a key date. Your changes, which are stored in the relevant master record in the database with a revision number, thus will take effect only on the specified key date.

All previous revision levels are stored in the database. Therefore, unlike the process of changing a plan without a master record, you can reactivate your earlier plans at any time.

### 6.4.3 Structure of the Inspection Plan (Plan Structure)

The start of this chapter gave you a brief introduction to the theoretical basis of inspection planning and inspection process control. You are now in a position to look at how the elements presented in that introduction fit into the inspection plan. SAP QM inspection planning is divided into the following main elements (see Figure 6.28):

- Inspection-plan header
- Inspection operation
- Test equipment
- Inspection characteristic

Again, the descriptions apply both to the inspection plan in QM and to the routing in PP. The latter only has some other routing-specific objects, such as the alternative operation sequence and the BOM function (material components).

Like most master data objects, the inspection plan also has the CREATE, CHANGE, COPY, and COPY MODEL functions, as well as several other resources. You can also use the relevant transaction code to access transactions that you use frequently (such as PP01 for creating an inspection plan). For the sake of clarity and structure, you are not provided a detailed description of all of the options of the task-list functions. The following sections provide explanations of all of the important elements from the QM viewpoint. The practical examples are described in Section 6.5, Multiple Specifications; Section 6.6, Quality Planning in Procurement; and in Section 6.7, Quality Planning in Production.

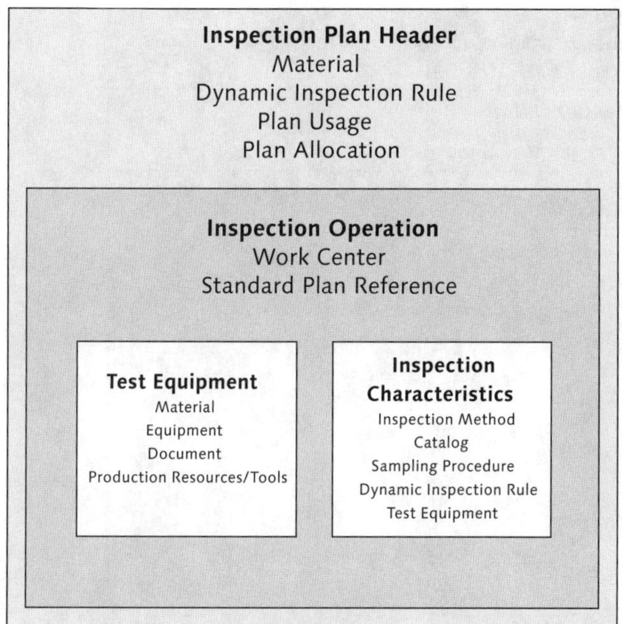


**Figure 6.28** Inspection Plan Structure

### Inspection-Plan Header

After you have made the required entries in CREATE or CHANGE mode, the screen shown in Figure 6.29 appears.

You can also use the CREATE-TASK-LIST-WITH-TEMPLATE function to create new inspection plans. The system then takes you through the individual task-list selection steps by means of a special dialog box. The contents of the selected task-list template are then copied to your new task list. Note one exception at this point: The copy function does not work if the template already contains references to the reference operation set.

The number of the task-list group is usually set by an internal numbering system (i.e., the system assigns a number itself). If you want to use an external numbering system, set the number range interval in Customizing accordingly. The options for assigning the material, task list, and vendor were described in Section 6.4.2 under Task-List Assignment and Task-List Groups.

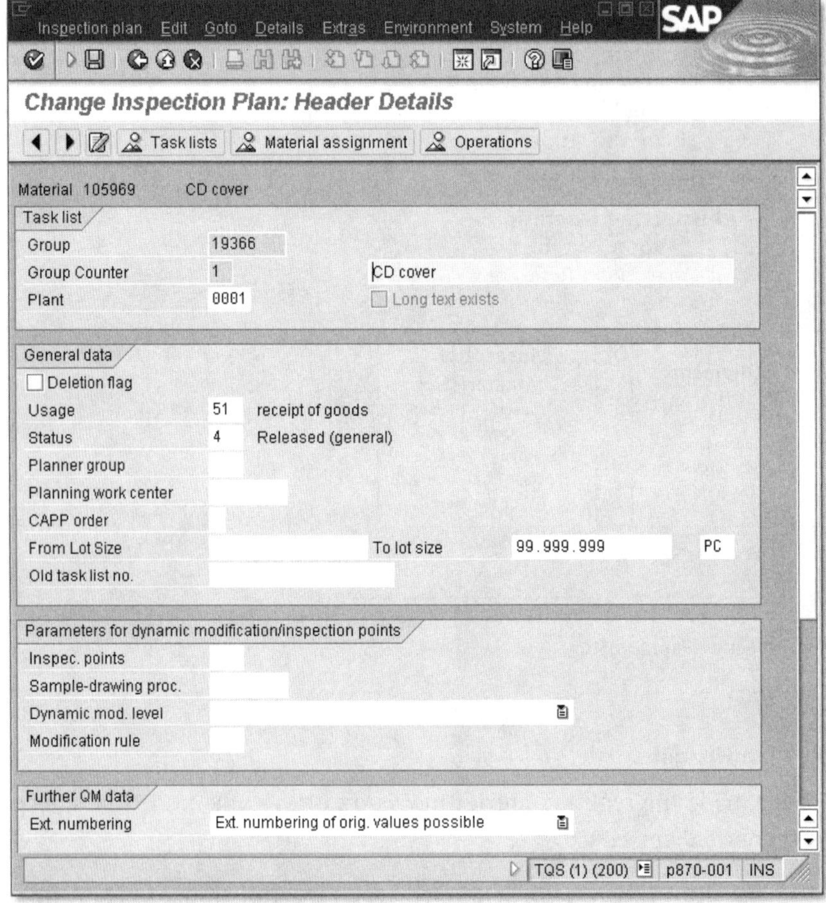


**Figure 6.29** Inspection-Plan Structure

### Task-List Group Counter

The task-list group counter is usually proposed automatically by the system. The task-list group counter can be manually assigned in the MATERIAL ASSIGNMENT or TASK-LIST ASSIGNMENT function.

### Deletion Flag

This indicator flags the task list for deletion. The inspection plan, along with all its change statuses and task-list objects, is deleted with the next reorganization run. A task list can also be deleted directly.

#### Planner Group

The planner group is not to be confused with the task-list group. The planner group is an independent ordering criterion. You can use the planner group when selecting task lists for selection.

#### Status

You use this to release the task list. The status can also be used to lock a task list that has not been released.

#### Unit of Measure

A unit of the material to be produced. This unit is used in the whole task list. It has to be converted to the base unit of measure of the material to be produced, as specified in the material master record. If the conversion is not maintained, an error message is output during the task-list inspection.

After the unit of measure is set in the first task list, the unit of measure for the whole task list is set and cannot be changed.

#### Lot Sizes

In this field, you specify the allowed lot size for this task-list group counter.

#### Legacy System

You enter the inspection plan number of the legacy system here.

#### Inspection Points

This function is described in greater detail in Section 6.6. For now, let us point out that the INSPECTION POINT is an SAP term for a sample taken during production for the purpose of statistical process regulation or more simply put to record continuous inspection data. You can therefore use inspection points only in the routing or in a master recipe. If this indicator is set, the DYNAMIC MODIFICATION function cannot be used because this kind of dynamic modification only makes sense for lot-based inspections. Dynamic modification of the inspection points is carried out on the basis of the sampling procedure, which was assigned on the characteristic level.

After you have set the Inspection Points indicator, the Field Combination and Partial-Lot (PL) Assignment fields appear.

### Field Combination

The user fields are used to specify the quantities assigned to the inspection points. If you have defined the inspection points as a quantity, for example, you can use key terms such as "container," "drum," or "pallet." If this task list is used to carry out an inspection, the selected field combination is displayed on the entry screen of the results recording function.

### PL Assignment

You indicate here whether the material quantities that are assigned to the inspection points also apply to partial lots. Depending on the requirements of the production process, you can do one of the following:

- Assign only inspection points to the produced quantities (no partial lots).
- Assign partial lots to the quantities for which one or more inspection points have been produced.
- Assign one or more partial lots to batches (provided that the material is produced in batches).

### Dynamic Modification Level

This is used to specify the level in the task list on which the dynamic modification rule is defined (e.g., the header level or the characteristic level of the inspection plan).

### Dynamic Modification Rule

Here, you enter the inspection levels and conditions that lead to stage changes. This procedure has already been detailed in Section 6.3.2, Basic Quality- and Inspection-Planning Data.

### Inspection Procedure

The Operations screen with the overview list contains the central control elements of the inspection plan. The information that is important for task planning, such as calculation and scheduling data, is assigned to the operation here.

In the case of the routing, you assign the inspection characteristics to the operations (production operation), just as in the inspection plan. If the Inspection plan task-list type is used, the operations divide up the inspection plan into individual inspection steps. The other assignments relate to the master data for the PRTs and work centers. When you are planning operations, do this first in the overview list. You then can double-click to see the detailed screen for the operation.

The procedure for the INSPECTION PLAN task-list type is very simple: You specify the control key and edit a short text. This completes all mandatory entries for the next step, which is to create the INSPECTION CHARACTERISTICS.

**Tip**

The control key with the control indicator INSPECTION CHARACTERISTICS (such as QM02 as in Figure 6.30, and the details in Figure 6.31) is not a mandatory entry. If a characteristic is missing here, only the INSPECTION-PLANNING function creates an error message. You therefore can use the production control indicators without any loss of functionality.

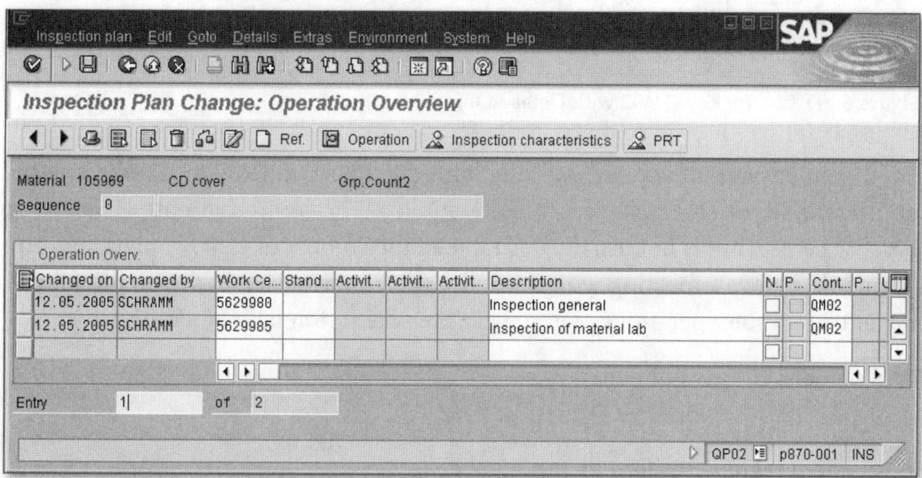


Figure 6.30 Operations Overview for an Inspection Plan for Incoming Inspections

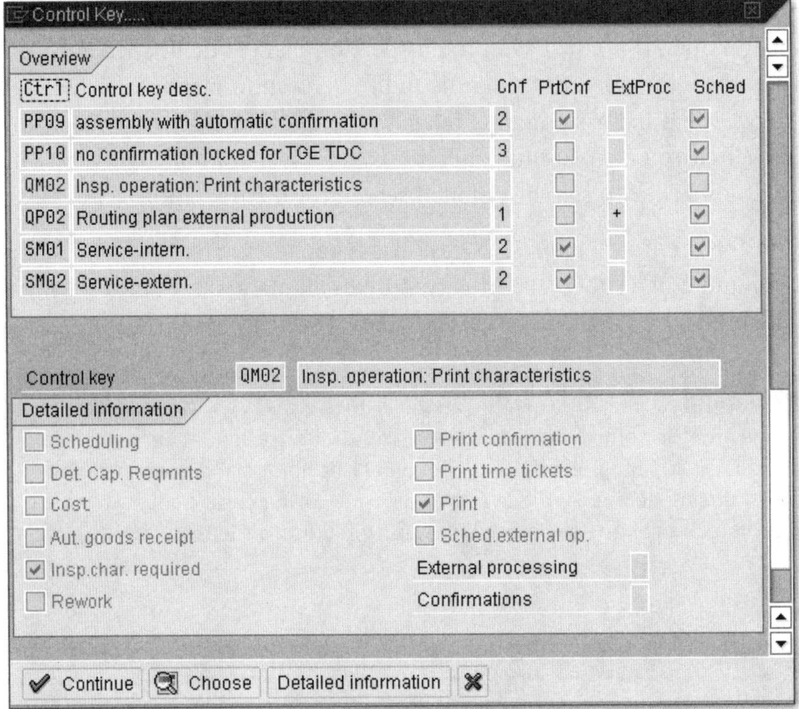


**Figure 6.31** Control Key QM02 with Detailed Information

On the other hand, if you are working with the STANDARD ROUTING task-list type, a different set of circumstances usually applies. The minimum entry is allowed here, as before, but is not usually desirable in the context of task-list planning. You should then have a meeting with the task-list planner to clearly define the following entries in the operations overview (which are not detailed individually):

- WORK CENTER assignment
- Assignment of plant number for the OPERATION
- Standard text-key assignment

You can also specify control elements in the DETAILED SCREEN FOR OPERATIONS ("puzzle" icon):

- Operation number
- Default values
- Calculation of standard values
- General data

- Required qualification
- External processing
- Quality management: General

**Tip**

One minor trouble spot is the simultaneous activation of all inspection operations of an inspection plan or a routing at the start of a production order. Only one inspection lot can be activated per production order at any one time. Problems arise if the order quantity decreases during production or if several independent inspections are to be processed in one production order.

SAP is already planning to develop a solution for this, although information about an implementation date was not available at the time this book went to press. However, you can create more inspection lots for a production order when you have fully completed the last inspection lot (status ICCO: "inspection close completed").

### Inspection Costs in Operation

A fully maintained operation with a work center is a prerequisite for acceptance of the inspection costs. The inspection costs can be calculated using the reported activity times, the cost center defined at the work center, and the activity type used for this. If you want to record and analyze inspection costs, it is essential that you arrange this in advance with the PP and CO teams. The reason is that most settings and analyses in this area require in-depth knowledge of the PP and CO application areas, and the Customizing settings need to be targeted and specific. For more information on the subject of inspection costs, see Chapter 8, Quality Control.

Next, you navigate from the operations overview to the INSPECTION CHARACTERISTIC or PRT to complete the inspection plan.

### Creating an Operation with a Reference Operation Set

If you have already created a reference operation set with all of the required entries, you can use the alternative method of creating an operation, which is to set a reference to a reference operation set. This function uses the modular principle in inspection planning, allowing you to create your individual inspection plan quickly and in a standardized manner. Simply place the cursor anywhere in the operations overview screen, select an operation, and click on the CREATE REFERENCE icon in the menu bar. The CREATE REFERENCE TO REFERENCE OPERATION SET dialog box opens. The system then asks you to make the following entries:

- The number of the operation that you want to create using a reference operation set
- The group of the reference operation set
- The group counter of the reference operation set

If you have selected a reference operation set, confirm this by pressing [Enter]. The system then creates a reference to the reference operation set and returns to the *operation-overview* screen. The new fields in the operations-overview screen have a gray background, which means that data for this operation can no longer be changed here. From now on, changes that are made in the referenced reference operation set (to all objects) directly affect all inspection plans and routings that have corresponding task-list references. The task-list reference is thus a useful instrument for the efficient mass maintenance of inspection plans, which relieves you of the time-consuming task of editing each individual plan.

### Test Equipment

You create the link to the test equipment in the operations overview, either by using the PRT icon in the toolbar or the detailed pull-down menu for PRTs (see Figure 6.32). It is possible to create several inspection resources and other resources for each operation by using the following categories:

- Material
- Equipment
- Document
- Production resources/tools

After you have created the first item, you can also insert the operation test equipment for each operation into an overview list and process it there. Because assignments for test equipment on the operation level are often too imprecise, the system allows you to continue using the individual PRT items on the characteristics level and to link them with the characteristic in a targeted manner. However, this assumes that the test equipment in question was previously assigned to the operation and that the relevant control indicator is set in the characteristic.

Because of its increasing importance in SAP ERP implementation projects, the topic of test equipment management is detailed in a separate chapter (Chapter 11, Test Equipment Management).

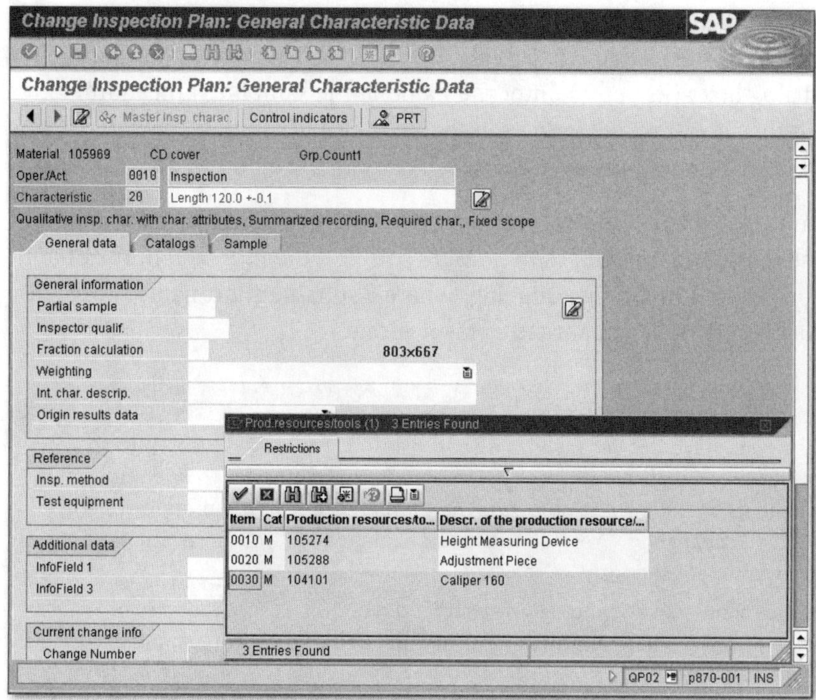


**Figure 6.32** Assigning Test Equipment to the Characteristic

### Inspection Characteristic

Navigate from the operations overview to the CHARACTERISTICS OVERVIEW by means of the relevant icon or menu option. You are now in the SAP QM area that is mainly maintained by the quality management department. In the areas of inspection planning that have been dealt with so far, there were always integration elements to be taken into account. The characteristics overview can be regarded as the heart of the inspection plan.

Before you start creating the *characteristic*, you have to make an important decision about the characteristic type. There are two different types:

- The quantitative characteristic (QN, for measurement inspections)
- The qualitative characteristic (QL, for attributive inspections)

The difference between these types concerns the data that you will enter in the system and not the equipment data that is measured or evaluated by means of other inspections. After you have selected QN or QL and made the other mandatory entries, another screen opens that contains the control indicators that are set in Customizing for the characteristic type. For characteristics with a sampling procedure, a dialog box asks you to enter the name of the sampling procedure. Enter the name in the short-text field. You can then either edit another characteristic or switch back to the operations overview.

If you have to re-edit the control indicators for the characteristic every time, it makes sense to use the *standard text key*. With this key, the individual control indicators are predefined in the Customizing, where a suitable short name is assigned to them, such as QN01 for quantitative inspections.

**Tip**

In both cases, you have not yet saved the characteristic. The data is written to the database only when you leave the inspection plan (this also applies to operations and all other elements of the inspection plan). Therefore, make sure to note the system dialog box ("Save changes?" "Yes") that appears at the end of your inspection plan activities and to take it seriously.

There have been many users who, after much hard work on an inspection plan, unintentionally click No here and then have to repeat all of their entries, much to their own frustration.

The *control indicators of a characteristic* are a source of much interaction with other planning elements from the inspection planning area and the material master settings. To list all of the possible combinations here would simply be confusing, so instead, we have compiled an overview of the control indicator functions in Table 6.11. For more practice-oriented combinations, taken from real-world business situations, see the sections on the application areas of quality planning (Sections 6.5, 6.6, and 6.7).

| | Meaning | Effects |
|---|---|---|
| LOWER SPEC. LIMIT | A lower specification limit in the inspection characteristic in the task list needs to be maintained. | |
| TARGET VALUE | You have to enter a target value for this characteristic. | If you set this indicator plus one or both tolerance indicators, the system checks whether the target value lies within the tolerance range. |

**Table 6.11** Meanings and Effects of the Control Indicators

<table>
<tr><th></th><th>Meaning</th><th>Effects</th></tr>
<tr><td>Upper Limit</td><td>An upper specification limit in the inspection characteristic in the task list needs to be maintained.</td><td></td></tr>
<tr><td>Characteristic Attribute</td><td>The characteristic is attributive in character and references a selected set of catalog type 1.</td><td></td></tr>
<tr><td>Sampling Procedure</td><td>A sampling procedure has to be assigned to this characteristic in the task list.</td><td>A procedure that is used to determine the size of the sample in an inspection. The sampling procedure also defines the valuation type that is used for results recording (attributive, variable, manual, etc.).</td></tr>
<tr><td>SPC Characteristic</td><td>If this indicator is set, a quality control chart is assigned to this characteristic.</td><td>If you set this indicator, you have to set the indicator for the sampling procedure. You then also have to enter an SPC criterion and a sampling procedure with a control chart type in the task list for the SPC characteristic.</td></tr>
<tr><td>Confirmation No. of Defects</td><td>You can confirm the number of errors in the results recording.</td><td>If you set this indicator, you can confirm the number of defective units in the results recording.</td></tr>
<tr><td>Additive Sample</td><td>The sample size is increased by the quantity that is required for this characteristic.</td><td>If a sample is used for multiple characteristics, the sample-drawing instruction contains only the total sample quantity to be drawn. This indicator can be set if the inspection for this characteristic destroys the samples. In this case, the indicator has the effect that the sample size is increased by the quantity that is required for the inspection of this characteristic.<br>Sample quantity:
<table>
<tr><th></th><th>I<br>Additive</th><th>II<br>Additive</th><th>III<br>Additive</th></tr>
<tr><td>Characteristic 2</td><td>30</td><td>X</td><td>X</td></tr>
<tr><td>Characteristic 3</td><td>20</td><td>X</td><td></td></tr>
<tr><td>Total</td><td>65</td><td>30</td><td>50</td></tr>
</table></td></tr>
</table>

**Table 6.11** Meanings and Effects of the Control Indicators (Cont.)

| | Meaning | Effects |
|---|---|---|
| Destructive Inspection | Flags characteristics whose samples are destroyed in the sampling process. In the usage decision, the system calculates the destroyed quantity and calculates a proposed inventory posting of the sample. The calculation includes all characteristics that are flagged as destructive and for which inspections have been carried out up to the time of calculation, in accordance with the actual sample size. | These can also be optional characteristics (skip), long-term characteristics, and unplanned characteristics. The sample calculation includes physical samples, alternative sample units of measure, partial samples, and the Additive Sample indicator. For the inventory posting, the system proposes only the part of the destroyed quantity that is over and above the quantity posted for the sample. |
| Summarized Recording | Only summarized values are reported for the inspection results of a characteristic after the inspection. | |
| Single Result | Individual values (measured values, codes, etc.) are recorded for the inspection results of a characteristic after the inspection. | |
| No Characteristic Recording | No results are recorded for a characteristic after the inspection. | |
| Classed Recording | The inspection results of a characteristic are recorded as classed values. | |
| Defects Recording | If this indicator is set, and a characteristic is rejected, defects recording for the characteristic is automatically called. | A prerequisite for background defect generation is that you define the defect codes in the task-list characteristic or in the master inspection characteristic. There are three defect codes for a quantitative characteristic: |

**Table 6.11** Meanings and Effects of the Control Indicators (Cont.)

| | Meaning | Effects |
|---|---|---|
| | | ▸ Defect code for general rejection<br>▸ Defect code for rejection at upper tolerance limit<br>▸ Defect code for rejection at lower tolerance limit<br>For a qualitative characteristic, define the defect code for general rejection. |
| Mandatory Characteristic | The inspection of a characteristic is closed by means of a confirmation. Inspection results for the characteristic must be confirmed before the usage decision can be made. | If you want dynamic modification to be characteristic-based, you have to flag all of the characteristics that are intended for dynamic modification as mandatory characteristics. |
| Optional Characteristic | The inspection of an optional characteristic can be closed without the need for confirmation. Inspection results for the characteristic do not have to be confirmed before the usage decision can be made. | If you want dynamic modification to be characteristic-based, you have to flag all of the characteristics that are intended for dynamic modification as mandatory characteristics. |
| After Acceptance | This conditional characteristic can be inspected only after the preceding mandatory characteristic in the same operation has been valuated as "A" (accepted). | |
| After Rejection | This conditional characteristic can be inspected only after the preceding mandatory characteristic in the same operation has been valuated as "R" (rejected). | |
| Scope Not Fixed | The inspection scope is not checked to make sure that it complies with the precalculated inspection scope in the results recording. | |

**Table 6.11** Meanings and Effects of the Control Indicators (Cont.)

| | Meaning | Effects |
|---|---|---|
| Fixed Scope | The inspection scope is checked to make sure that it complies with the precalculated inspection scope in the result recording. No deviations are allowed. | |
| Smaller Scope | The inspection scope can be smaller than the precalculated inspection scope in the results recording. | |
| Larger Scope | The inspection scope can be greater than the precalculated inspection scope in the results recording. | |
| No Documentation | No additional documentation needs to be created for this characteristic in the results recording. | |
| Documentation If Rejected | Additional documentation needs to be created for this characteristic in the results recording only if the characteristic is rejected. | |
| Documentation Required | Additional text, in the form of documentation of the inspection result, always needs to be created for this characteristic in results recording. | |
| Long-term Inspection | The inspection for this characteristic can run for a long period. | If you set this indicator for a characteristic, you can make a usage decision for the characteristic or set the status Short-Term Inspection Completion. During the long-term inspection, you can use material that has been inspected and thus reduce the stock of the inspection lot. This also means that you can also retroactively record results for the long-term inspection. |

**Table 6.11** Meanings and Effects of the Control Indicators (Cont.)

| | Meaning | Effects |
|---|---|---|
| SCRAPE SHARE / Q SCORE | The share of defective units for this characteristic are taken into account in the calculation of the scrap share in the inspection lot. | If the usage decision uses a quality score procedure that refers to the share of scrap in the inspection lot or the characteristic, the characteristic is used to calculate the quality score only if this indicator is set. |
| RR CHANGE DOCS. | If you set this indicator, change documents are written for this characteristic in the characteristics-based results recording. | The change documents are written only when characteristics have been fully processed (status 5), and the data is already in the database. |
| TEST EQUIPMENT ASSIGNMENT | If this indicator is set, you can assign an item of test equipment to the characteristic in the task list. If you do not assign anything, the system alerts you to this fact by means of a warning message. | |
| CONFIRM VALUES | Measurement values for this quantitative characteristic are inspected and confirmed. | |
| CALCULATED CHARACTERISTIC | The characteristic is a calculated characteristic. | The results for a calculated characteristic are not calculated by means of the characteristic inspection. Instead, they are calculated on the basis of the results of other characteristics within the same operation. |
| PRINT | If you set this indicator, the inspection characteristic is printed on the inspection instruction. | |
| DO NOT PRINT | If you set this indicator, the inspection characteristic is not printed on the inspection instruction. | |

**Table 6.11** Meanings and Effects of the Control Indicators (Cont.)

| | Meaning | Effects |
|---|---|---|
| Do Not Print with Skip | If you set this indicator, the inspection characteristic is printed on the inspection instruction only if there is no skip for the characteristic. | |

**Table 6.11** Meanings and Effects of the Control Indicators (Cont.)

You are already familiar with the definition of the sampling procedure. The system dialog box for entering sample rules is automatically displayed if you have selected SAMPLING PROCEDURES when determining the characteristic type in the control indicators. You can return to this screen later via the DYNAMIC MODIFICATION icon in the toolbar or by selecting from the pull-down menu.

**Tip**

Only the procedures that are allowed for this characteristic definition are displayed in the sampling-procedure selection screen. In the worst case, no selection options are available. The rules that you created for the sampling procedure then have to be checked. It can happen, for example, that you have selected SCOPE NOT FIXED in the control indicators and are trying to assign a sampling procedure for a control chart. This has the result that the sampling procedure does not appear in the selection because the sample size for a control chart has to be fixed. Therefore, you should set FIXED SCOPE.

To describe a *qualitative characteristic*, you can also assign more specific attributes with codes, as well as the more general view of a characteristic represented by acceptance (OK) or rejection (NOK). It is recommended in this case that you use the characteristic control indicator CHARACTERISTIC ATTRIBUTE because this allows you to access the selected sets.

**Tip**

Besides the NOK criteria of an inspection, the characteristic attributes also contain the OK criteria and are thus also suitable for describing positive (OK) characteristic results.

The CALCULATED CHARACTERISTIC is a tool that is necessary for *quantitative recordings* of measurement results (see Figure 6.33). This attribute is assigned by means of the control indicator of the characteristic. You can use the formula interpreter that comes with your system to make use of the standard mathematical functions for carrying out calculations with values from other characteristics, which are called calculation input characteristics. The calculated characteristic contains the following input functions:

- Numerical constants
- Calculated characteristics that take values and results of calculation-input characteristics (calculation input characteristics and calculated characteristics must be contained in the same operation)
- Calculated characteristics for external function modules

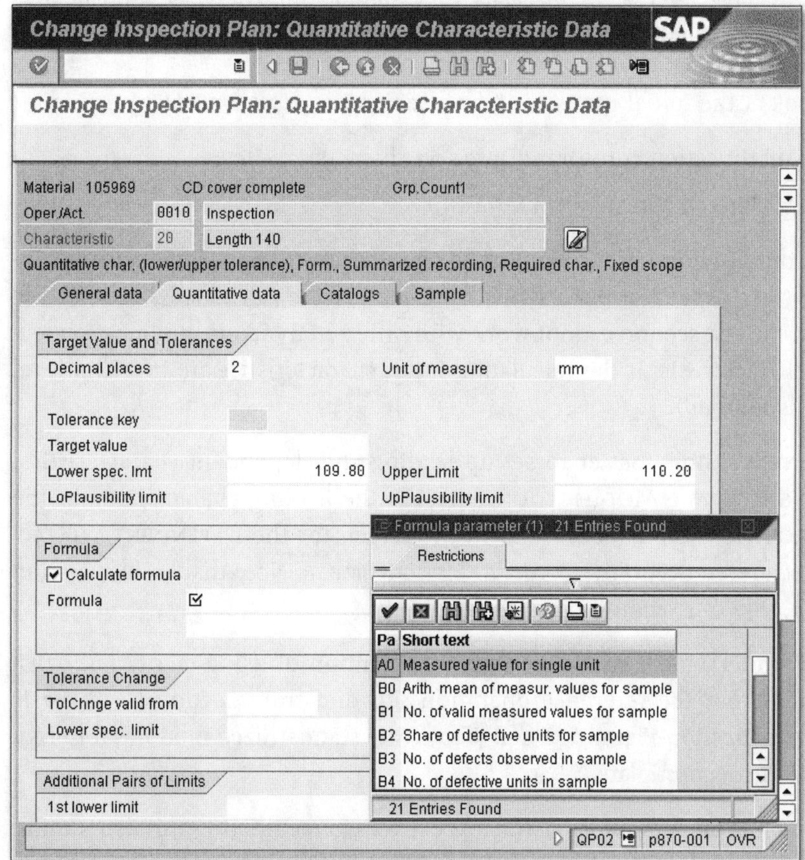


**Figure 6.33** Formula Parameter in Detailed View for Quantitative Data

**Tip**

If the existing calculated characteristics and operands are not sufficient, you can add extensions by means of Customizing. As with most extensions, in-depth knowledge of ABAP (the programming language of the SAP ERP system) is required. Again, make sure to discuss your system requirements in plenty of time in project meetings because programming resources become scarcer as the project progresses.

When compiling your calculation characteristic, make sure to take into account the LEADING AND DEPENDENT CHARACTERISTICS. The dynamic modification and the sampling procedure of the calculation input characteristics should be identical. To prevent errors, it is recommended that you use both leading and dependent characteristics. In the current example, the calculated characteristic is leading, and the calculation input characteristics are dependent.

Let's first look at the initial prerequisites of *leading and dependent characteristics:*

- Dynamic modification control indicator on characteristic level
- Mandatory characteristic control indicator

Using this combination in an operation for your characteristics can cause inconsistencies in the inspection process. This means that the calculated characteristic described in the last section cannot work with different dynamic modification levels for the characteristic, if the calculation input characteristics are in a skip level (inspection is skipped).

It is a relatively simple matter to set up leading and dependent characteristics. First, enter a DYNAMIC MODIFICATION RULE for the leading characteristic in the DYNAMIC MODIFICATION screen. Next, in the screen for the DEPENDENT CHARACTERISTICS, set a reference to the CHARACTERISTIC NUMBER. Note that each operation may contain only one leading characteristic.

You already understand that the underlying intention of using *master inspection characteristics* (from the reference operation sets and from Section 6.3.2, Basic Quality- and Inspection-Planning Data) is to create standardized modules for ergonomic use in inspection plans.

Reference operation sets and master inspection characteristics are also similar in the way they use referencing (permanent links). Thus, changes to the master inspection characteristic affect the inspection plans that contain this characteristic. There is one small exception: If you change essential attributes of the master inspection characteristic, the system forces you to create a new version. You then can activate this new version for all relevant inspection plans using a function specifically designed for this purpose.

There are two ways in which you can use the master inspection characteristic:

- The fully maintained master inspection characteristic with fixed reference
- The master inspection characteristic that is not fully maintained and that copies its attributes only to the selected characteristic

**Tip**

First test the functioning of the characteristic in the inspection plan as a simple copy template without any referencing. You can create manual or automatic inspection lots in your test system for this purpose. If you use the reference immediately, new versions of the *master inspection characteristic* may have to be created if changes are made. This procedure can easily cause the master data records to become unclear and confusing. If your characteristic is established enough, change the master inspection characteristic that has not yet been included in an inspection plan, and only then create the fixed reference.

You now have to perform another action, just as you would when referencing the reference-operation set. When using the SAMPLING PROCEDURE IN A MASTER INSPECTION-CHARACTERISTIC control indicator, the system opens the input window for the sampling procedure and the dynamic modification rule. These can be maintained only on the level of the inspection plan itself. If you use master inspection characteristics that are not fully maintained and to which other input, such as the formula or tolerance settings, needs to be added, the system prompts you to enter this by means of more input masks. You can assign a specific item of test equipment to the characteristic or select it from the list of test equipment in the operation (see Test Equipment in Section 6.4.3 and Chapter 11, Test Equipment Management).

Unlike the qualitative and quantitative attributes of inspection characteristics, the *inspection method* contains the description of the inspection process and other inspection-related information. You therefore use the inspection method chiefly for the textual representation of complex inspection processes, or if additional information is required for an inspection characteristic or an inspection plan. In this regard, the inspection method is a very good universal information medium. Also, the fact that it is master data makes it possible to centrally manage this module and maintain a good overview of it. The QM basic data menu bar for the inspection methods is used to navigate to the inspection method. You can then create, change, or delete inspection methods here. The main functions that can be accessed inside the inspection method are as follows:

- Long text processing
- Multilingual text creation
- Classification
- Management data
- Additional details

As soon as you have used a data record for an inspection plan or an inspection characteristic, the system sets a usage indicator. This indicator is used, among other things, to represent the relationships in the form of a report and thus to clarify them. There are also other prerequisites for deleting an inspection method: In the case of a usage indicator, all references must first be removed; and the status indicator has to be set to "4 — locked."

You can *assign defect codes to the characteristics*. In many cases, performing valuation of qualitative characteristic with OK/NOK or a quantitative characteristic with a measurement value is too general. For a more precise defect description in the case of a rejection, you can make available to the characteristic a special catalog with catalog type 9, DEFECT TYPES. This catalog is then automatically highlighted with a "Rejected" valuation in the results recording, and the system prompts you to enter a defect code.

Another important characteristic of this function is the automatic generation — during the results recording — of a defect record in the form of a quality notification. To activate this functionality, check the RESULTS RECORDING box in the control indicators of the characteristic. You can then continue to fully edit the messages with the message type Q2, INTERNAL QUALITY NOTIFICATIONS.

Maintaining other allocation values is relevant to you if you want additional or different criteria to apply in an inspection with regard to vendors, materials, or customers on the characteristics level. However, this does not apply to characteristics in reference operation sets and the master inspection characteristics. Because this function is hidden behind a term that is not very meaningful, see the following navigational aid and instructions:

1. Select the required characteristic.
2. Then, from the menu bar, select GOTO • SPECIAL INSPECTION CHARACTERISTICS TEMPLATES. The screen that opens shows the available allocation values.
3. You can now select EDIT • NEW ENTRIES • ENTER ALLOCATION VALUES TO ADD NEW VALUES. (Pay particular attention to the VENDOR, TOLERANCE, and TARGET VALUE columns.) See Figure 6.34.

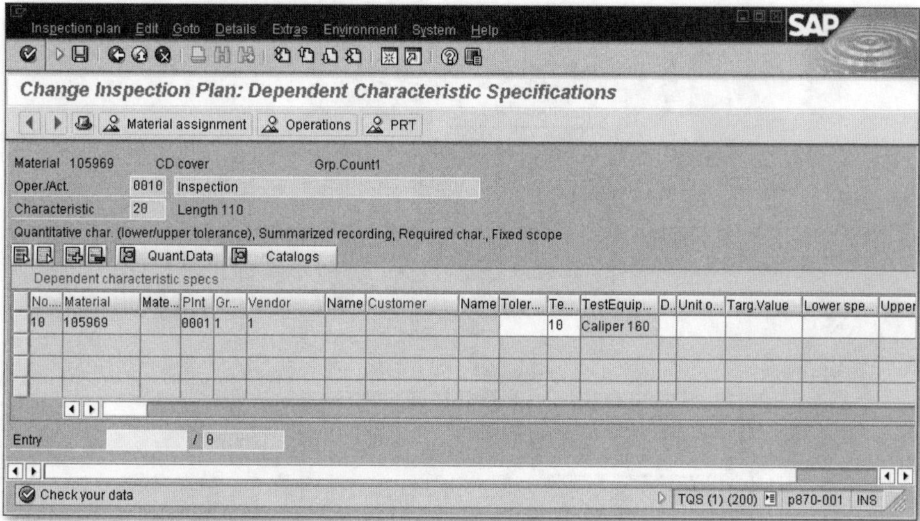


Figure 6.34 Allocation Values Screen

### 6.4.4 Engineering Workbench

This section provides details about the Engineering Workbench. Let's first look at the function of this tool.

#### Functions

The *Engineering Workbench* tool allows you to make mass changes to inspection plans and task lists in a straightforward manner. You can edit, exchange, change, and delete the operations of a task list from this starting point, just as you can the characteristics. Also integrated here are the maintenance functions for the material routing assignment and for the allocation of PRTs to support quality management.

### Work Area

The work-area settings make it possible for you to adapt your inspections to the special planning tasks in the QM area. A work area consists of a core and a working environment (see Figure 6.35). The core is the object type, based on which you make your selections. The object types that you want to display and edit make up the working environment. The content of the work area is defined in Customizing.

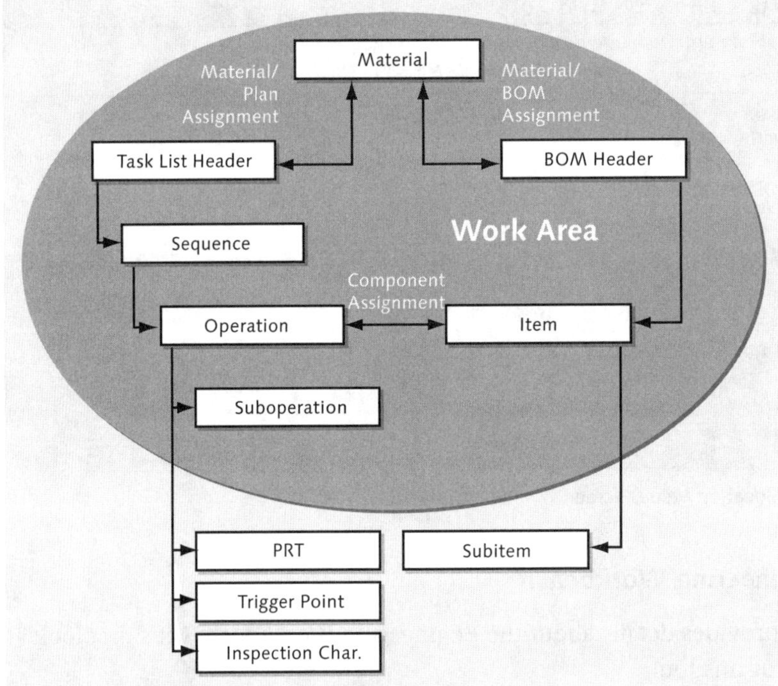


**Figure 6.35** Structure of the Work Area

### Example

Suppose you want to exchange the individual inspection characteristics of an inspection plan for unified master inspection characteristics. Choose LOGISTICS • QUALITY MANAGEMENT • QUALITY PLANNING • INSPECTION PLANNING • INSPECTION PLAN • WORKBENCH. Then select the standard work area Q_TSK_000000000010, and press [Enter]. You can obtain an overview of the task lists (see Figure

6.36) that are to be changed via the material selection and the LOAD TASK LISTS button.

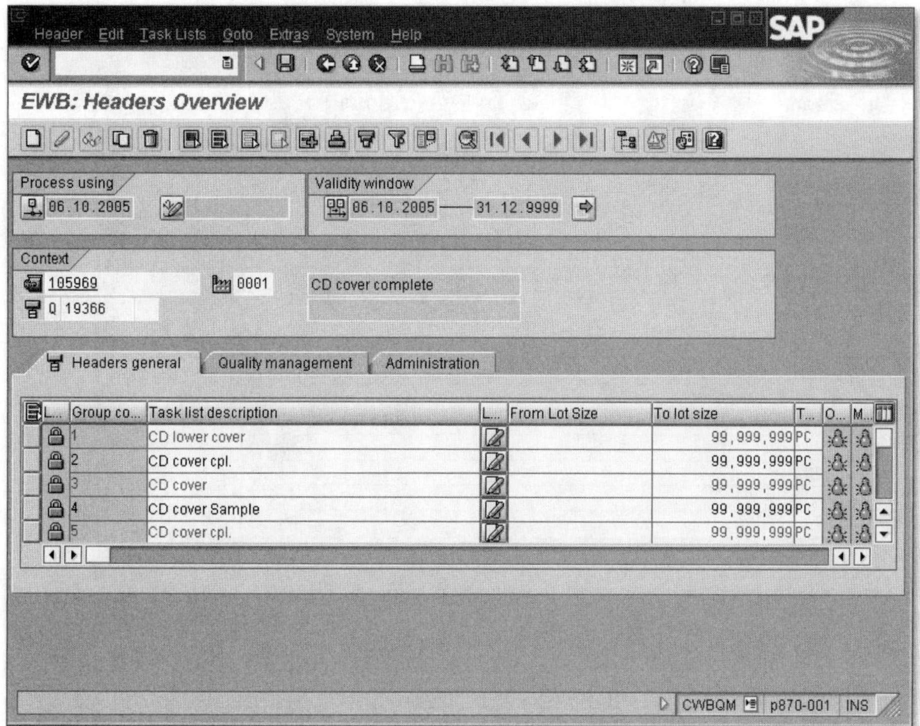


**Figure 6.36** Headers Overview

Now select TASK LISTS • INSPECTION CHARACTERISTICS. A list opens containing all of the inspection characteristics of the various task-list groups (see Figure 6.37). You can change the displayed characteristics in any way you like. To do this, simply select the one you want and use the INSPECTION CHARACTERISTICS • CHANGE/ LOCK function. In this case, you scroll the list as far as the field that is ready for input in the master inspection characteristics and use the required object there. After you choose SAVE, the following message appears in the information bar at the bottom of the screen: "Inspection plan characteristic 0010 [and possibly others] will be overwritten by the master inspection characteristic." This takes care of the exchange process, and there is no need to open the individual inspection plans.

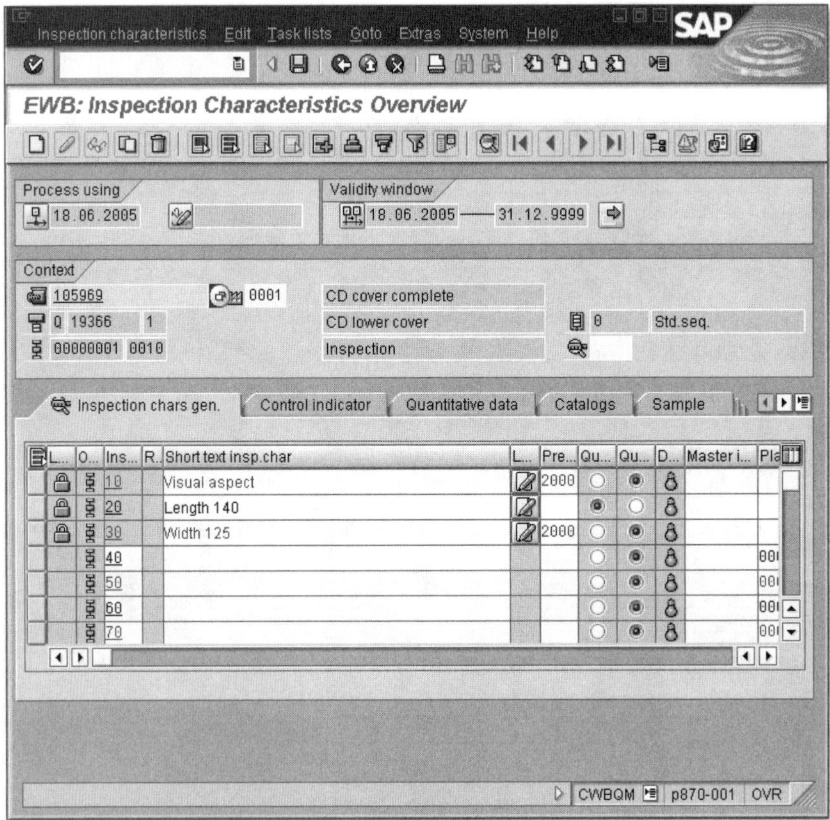

**Figure 6.37** Inspection Characteristics Overview

> **Tip**
>
> If you select the icon with the red arrow ("Copy as standard") when you first open the Engineering Workbench in the dialog window for the work area, your system remembers the selection criteria you used. Thus, if your session is interrupted for some reason, the worklist you selected is simply reactivated afterward.

## 6.5 Multiple Specifications

One of the more recent developments in the area of the QM module takes into account one of the elementary requirements of the process industry: to store specifications depending on freely selectable objects. This option has already been described briefly for the material-routing assignment in the context of specific characteristic specifications. There you can use different limits for various vendors or customers in the same inspection plan. Multiple specifications extend this topic by criteria that are dependent on the material, the vendors, and the customers. Questions on specification creation are usually very similar. For example: "Does the tolerance limit of the active substance content of a delivered substance meet the approval in a selected country (marketing authorization of pharmaceuticals for the countries)?"

The creation of such a multiple specification starts with the material master data and applies to the inspection characteristics, the usage decision, the hand-over to characteristics of the batch classification, and the certificate creation for the relevant batch.

Due to the scope and width of the application area of this powerful function, at this point, you are provided with a simple application example instead of the general options and settings. It is recommended and absolutely indispensable to carefully read the SAP documentation.

In the following application case, examine the initial question about the usage of a substance for a specific country.

For this purpose, you must first activate the multiple specifications in Customizing in IMG under Quality Management • Maintain Default Settings at Client Level • Activate Multiple Specification. Also, under Inspection Planning • General Data • Multiple Specification, the example requires the entries shown in Figure 6.38.

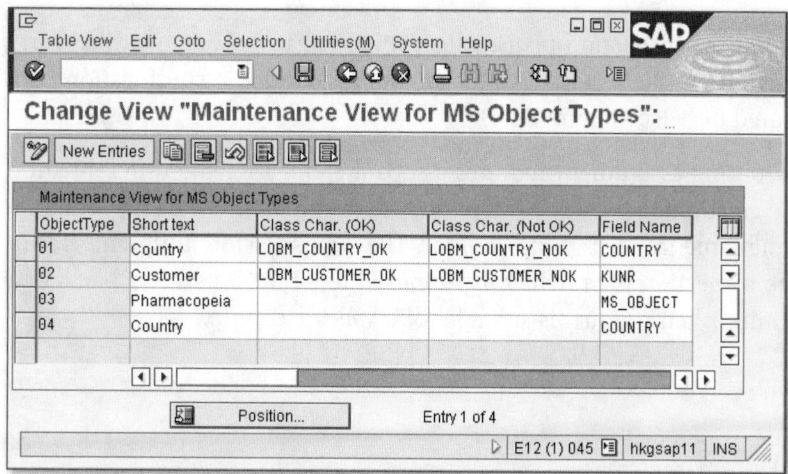


**Figure 6.38** Customizing Multiple Specifications — Object Types

Here, the LOBM characteristics are responsible for entering an evaluation criterion in the batch class later. Similar to the inspection characteristic value with associated batch characteristics, this is done automatically and requires no additional settings.

In the next Customizing step, additional differentiation criteria are added to the "country" object key, for example, "DE" and "GB" (see Figure 6.39). No additional settings have to be made for this application example.

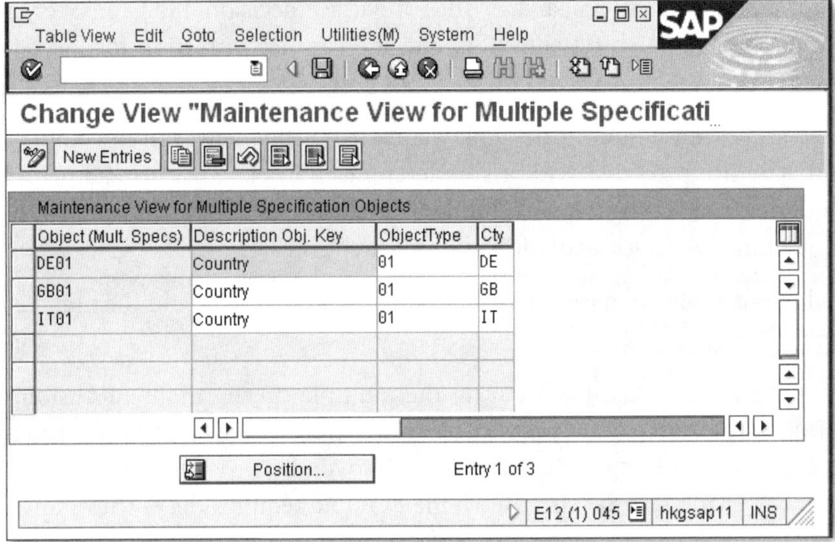


**Figure 6.39** Customizing Multiple Specifications — Objects

You then process the inspection plan exclusively by means of Engineering Workbench Transaction CWBQM because the functions of multiple specifications can only be executed here (see Figure 6.40).

The material-routing assignment requires a separate entry for the differentiation by county and an additional entry without object assignment for the task-list determination to the same task-list group counter. The aim is to store different specifications in one inspection plan, which is supposed to define whether a batch of a purchased semifinished product is suitable for a specific country.

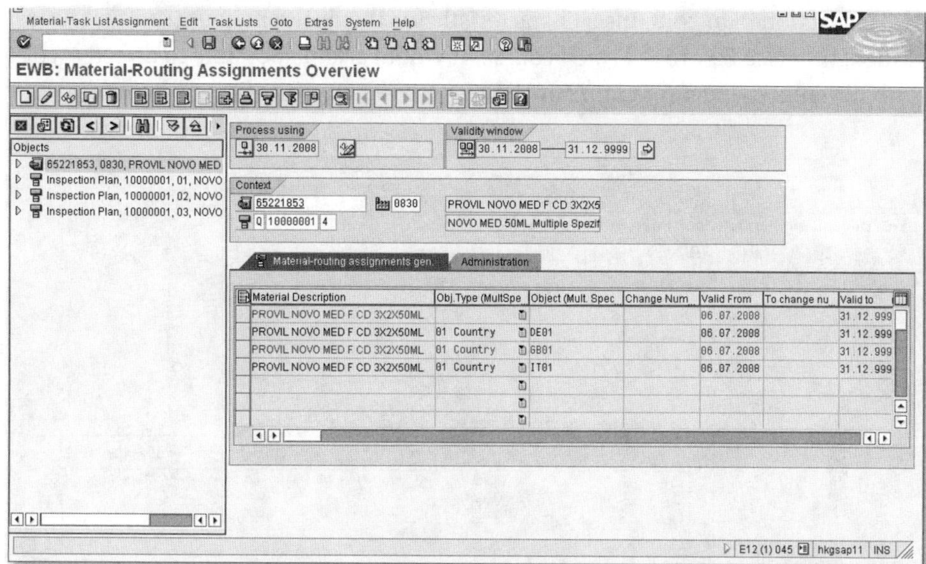

Figure 6.40 Material-Routing Assignment Using the Engineering Workbench

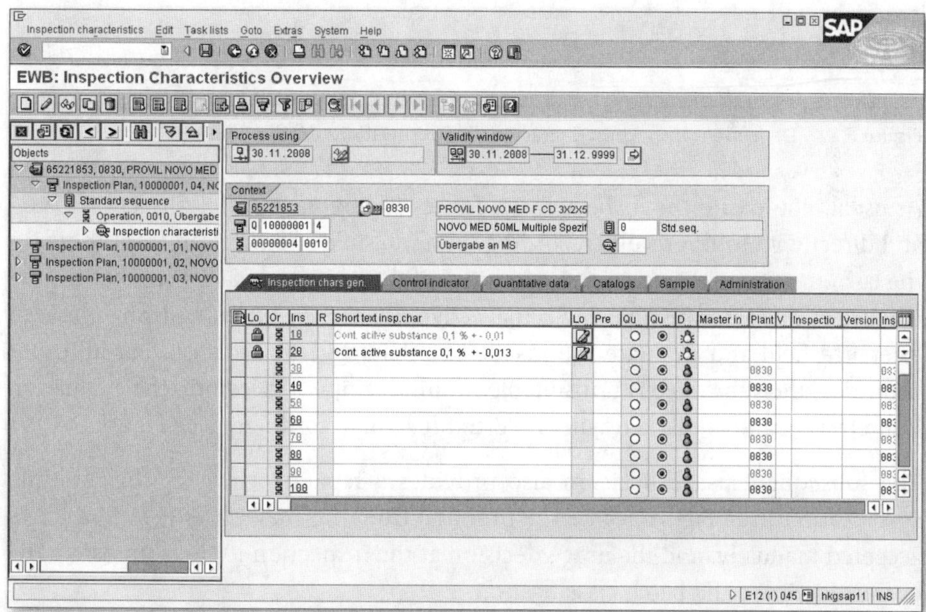

Figure 6.41 Inspection Plan with Country-Specific Characteristics

The inspection plan contains a characteristic for the different country suitabilities, respectively (see Figure 6.41). Of course, it would also be possible to directly work with different inspection plans for the respective countries (see Figure 6.42).

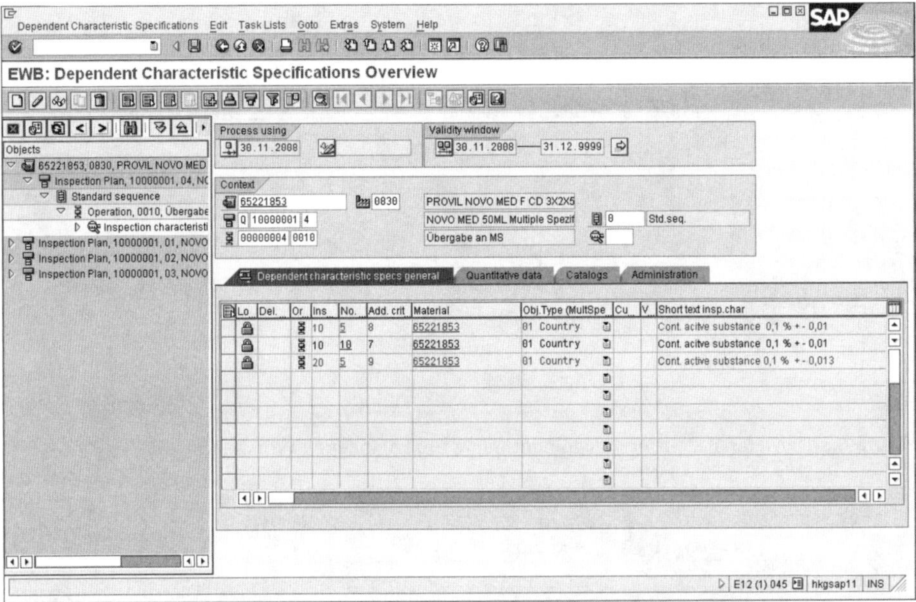

**Figure 6.42** Dependent Inspection Characteristic Specifications for the Country

As usual, you create the inspection lot for testing by means of Transaction QA01 and directly go to the results recording with multiple specification from there. In the current case, you assume the suitability of the active substance content for the country IT due a permissible and actual active substance content with an enhanced tolerance field and evaluate the inspection characteristic with OK. For all other countries, the substance is not suitable in this example. Therefore, the evaluation is a rejection and is marked with a red traffic light accordingly (see Figure 6.43).

The subsequent usage decision also provides a separate view for the multiple specifications (see Figure 6.44). The proposal from the characteristic evaluation is accepted manually, and the usage decision at the inspection-lot level transfers the characteristics to the batch classification.

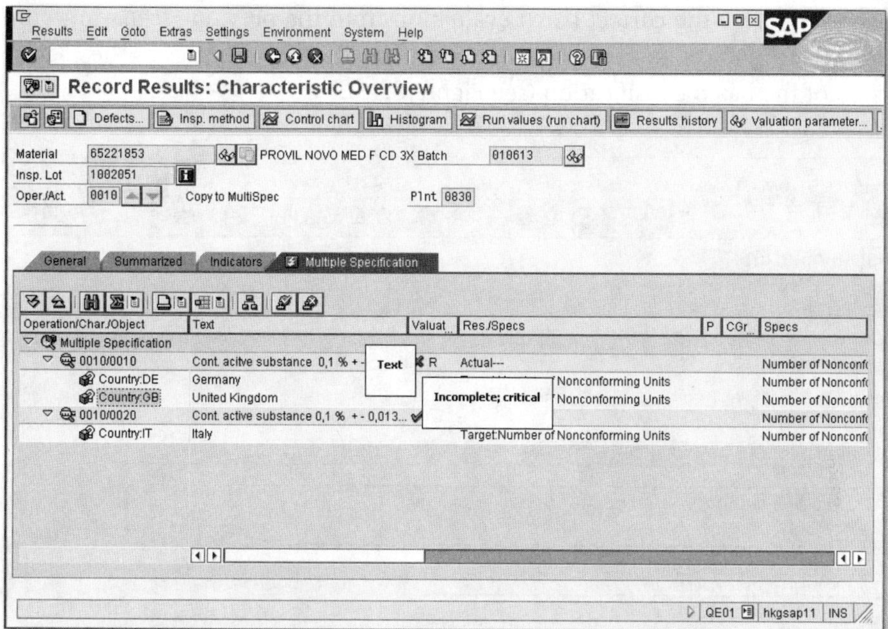

Figure 6.43 Characteristic Evaluation of Multiple Specifications

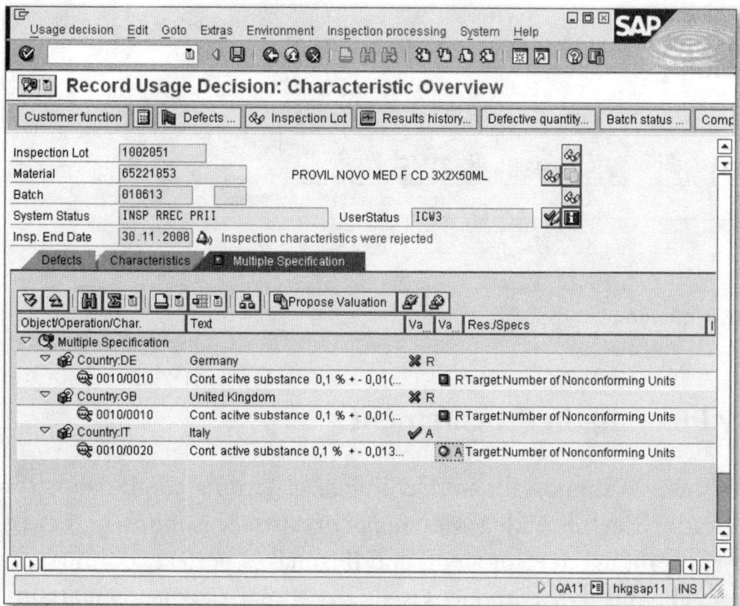

Figure 6.44 Usage Decision with Multiple Specifications

Finally, you check the correct batch evaluation from the previous scenario in the batch master; you can see the expected suitability for the countries as the characteristics of the batch classification (see Figure 6.45).

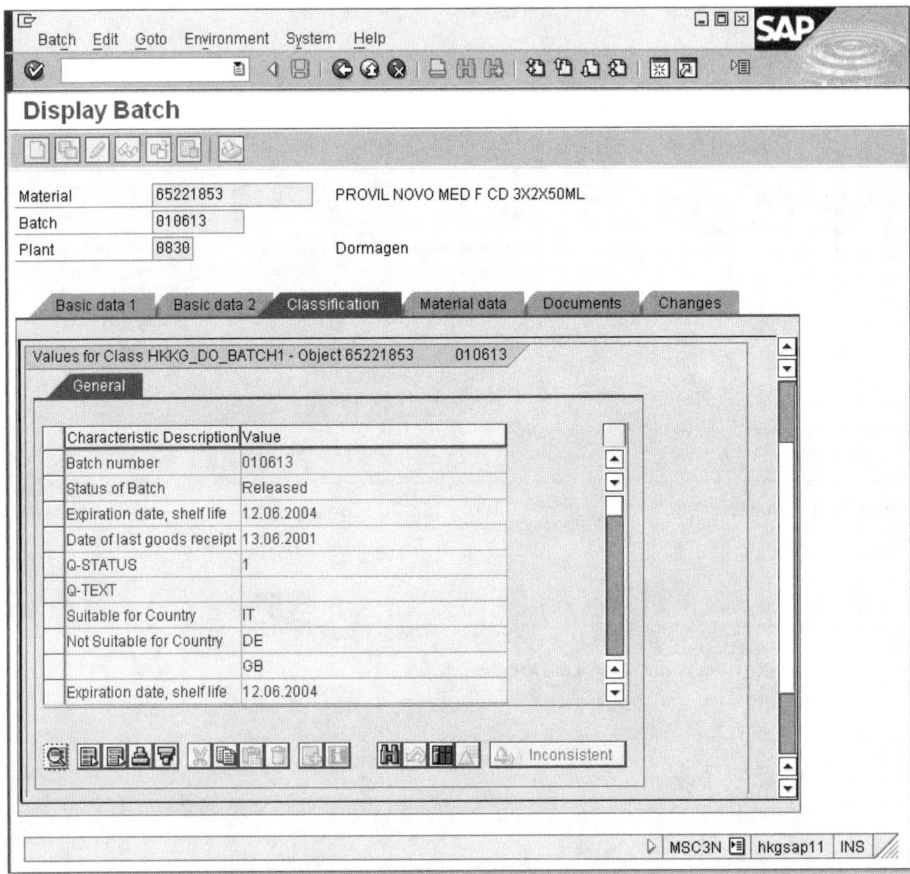


**Figure 6.45** Batch Classification

## 6.6 Quality Planning in Procurement

The example used here examines a manufacturer of electronic components for PCs and communication devices with a wide range of parts. This industry is characterized by very fast product development, and this makes perfect coordination between the vendors involved in a product essential. Let's look at quality planning for the procurement of a part that will take on more added value due to various production processes in the supply chain. The materials are obtained from various vendors, largely because no one manufacturer can provide sufficient production capacity for a single, complete delivery, and also because you prefer not to be dependent on one vendor. The product part in this example, as before, is the cover for the software CD for an ISDN card. The material is subject to a simple release procedure with a model sample and subsequent regular delivery. Any resamplings that have to be made as a result of changes made to the part are processed separately and lead to creation of new revision levels of the material. You therefore need to pay particular attention to design stability and the special attributive characteristics, which are regarded as critical.

Now we will track the quality planning procedure for a new vendor of the inner part of the CD cover. The previous vendor, Duff & Son Ltd., has a quality score of 35, so you no longer entirely trust them. Therefore, your sourcing team, with members from Purchasing and Quality Management, has decided to accept the tender of IQ Inc. for the same material. The important thing is that the material number in your system stays the same, no matter what vendor you use. After IQ Inc. has been entered into your system with a vendor master record, the procurement process itself can begin. However, the new vendor still has to fulfill the conditions of your release procedure up to the regular delivery stage. You now use the SAP QM system to make this process transparent and to manage it.

### 6.6.1 Material Master and Quality Info Record

This section describes the material master and the quality info record. Let's first look at the material master.

#### Material Master

In the material master, "Quality management in Procurement" is activated for the key "0001" (see Figure 6.46). This has the effect that IQ Inc. first has to be released for purchase orders and deliveries in the quality info record. To enable an inspection lot to be created for every received good by means of goods movement 01, GOODS RECEIPT FOR PURCHASE ORDER, you select and activate the following inspection types:

- 01 INCOMING INSP. FOR GR FOR PURCHASE ORDER
- 02 MODEL INSPECTION FOR GR FOR PURCHASE ORDER
- 03 INCOMING INSPECTIONS, RECURRING INSPECTION (DEPENDING ON DEMAND)

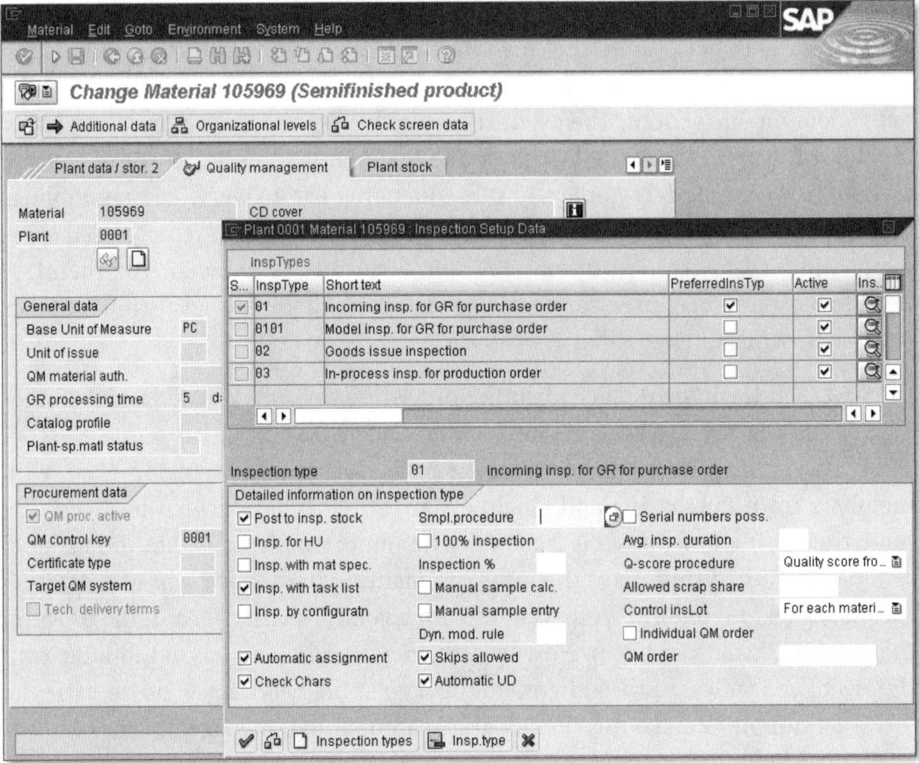


**Figure 6.46** Material Master for QM in Procurement

After the inspection type is activated, the QUALITY INSPECTION attribute disappears from the Q view. There is a particular reason for this. When an inspection type and the inspection type definition POST TO Q STOCK are set, the stock indicator "Q" is set for every delivery lot. The stock that was just posted is thus not released for further use. If you set the QUALITY INSPECTION attribute right at the start without using any inspection type, this has the same initial effect in terms of stock and posts the stock to QUALITY INSPECTION STOCK when goods are received. The difference is that you can manually repost the quality inspection stock created in this way as "Released," without the involvement of a usage decision.

**Tip**

Strangely, exactly the same QUALITY INSPECTION attribute is also contained in the PURCHASING view of the material master. You need to clarify this situation in an integration meeting with the relevant technical department and define who can activate this function.

### Quality Info Record

The required input for release control is made in the quality info record, which you have already created for the purposes of the new material/vendor combination (see Figure 6.47). Each vendor is released in accordance with specific in-house criteria. In line with this, you have created a *status schema* for the deliveries, using the Customizing variants, and selected this for the current quality info record. This is absolutely necessary because otherwise, no complete inspection lots can be created. After the required documents (such as evidence of QS-9000 certification) have been received, and you are happy with the vendor's first audit results, the *supply relationship status* takes effect, and the first delivery generates an inspection lot for model sampling.

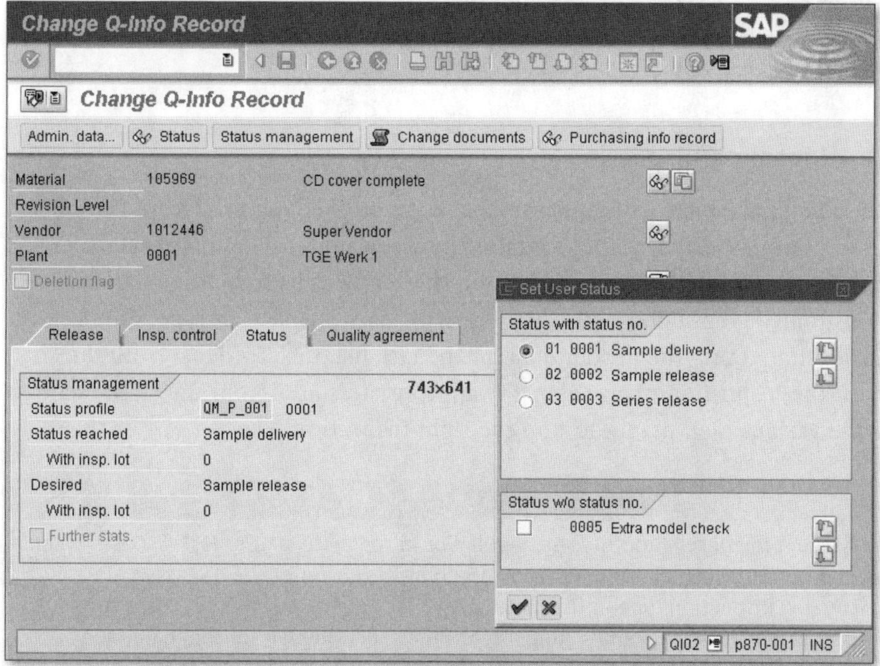


**Figure 6.47** Quality Info Record with Release Control and Status Information

> **Tip 1**
>
> You do not necessarily have to create a purchase order if you post model parts later. However, it is often not possible to monitor delivery dates in a targeted way for deliveries without orders. It is therefore always advisable to create orders, even for model sampling.

Only inspection type 01, GOODS RECEIPT FOR PURCHASE ORDER, is relevant for the vendor evaluation. Therefore, in the Q view of the material master, under the inspection type, you set the control indicator for quality score procedure 06, Quality Score from Usage Decision.

**Tip 2**

The system may require that you enter a quality score procedure for all inspection types. To prevent the model and the recurring sample from having an effect on the quality score, or to assign it a lower value, use one of the following three options:

- Create usage-decision codes in their own code group for model and recurring samples with alternative quality-score assignments.
- Assign values to the same usage codes in the usual way, and define the quality score manually.
- Define a special quality-score procedure in Customizing that does not have any effect on the updating of the quality score.

### 6.6.2 Incoming Inspection

Because you have been using the previously mentioned material from Duff & Son Ltd. for a long time, the system contains the associated inspection plans for model sampling, regular delivery, and resamplings, each with its own *task-list group counter*. Customizing contains a task-list usage for each inspection type. The task-list usage is entered into the header data for the task list, in accordance with the character of the inspection plan. Later, the appropriate status from the status schema uses the various plan usages to find the right inspection plan.

**Caution**

The system provides a good time-saving device in the *material and task-list assignment* function because you do not have to do anything at this point. As discussed already, an activated inspection type in the material master record activates the inspection type. Therefore, if there is an existing, identical inspection plan for the material, you do not have to define any further assignments for this vendor in the inspection plan. The vendor is then linked with the material in the inspection lot itself, by means of the goods movement. The calculations for the quality level, quality score, and status sequence are made automatically by the system using the data from the purchase order and the goods movement for this order.

### Model Inspection Plan

The actual model inspection plan consists of approximately 50 characteristics that are collected on the basis of the specification (see Figure 6.48). For the sake of simplicity, you create only 2 characteristics at this point: one for inspecting all quantitative characteristics, and one for inspecting all qualitative characteristics. The header data does not contain any entries for the dynamic modification level or the sampling procedure because the delivered quantities are not yet relevant, and dynamic modification is not appropriate for the model sampling.

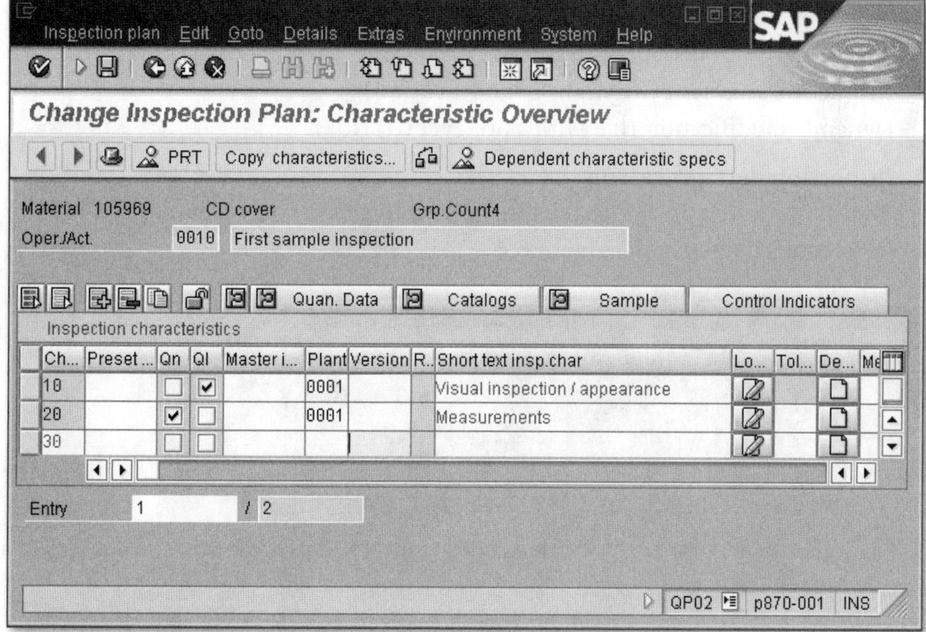


**Figure 6.48** Characteristics of the Model Inspection Plan

### Inspection Plan for Regular Delivery

In a way similar to the basics of inspection planning described at the beginning of this chapter, this inspection plan is structured as follows:

- **Material reference**
  A vendor assignment is not mandatory. The *material-routing assignment* is not enhanced.

- **Inspection characteristic overview with inspection instruction**
  Various quantitative and qualitative characteristics are assigned to the GOODS-RECEIPT, REGULAR-DELIVERY INSPECTION operation. The inspection characteristics are created in a reference operation set and referenced in an operation because this material is maintained in a number of variants, each with its own material number and task-list group. The qualitative characteristics can be maintained as master inspection characteristics and used in the reference operation set.
- **Inspection scope**
  One sampling procedure for the qualitative (QL01) and quantitative (QL02) characteristics. Sample size is calculated without sampling scheme for both types of inspection.
- **Inspection frequency (dynamic modification)**
  Dynamic modification rule with skip level (DYN01).
- **Inspection data processing**
  Results recording in the characteristic is active (see control indicators for the inspection characteristic, Figure 6.49).

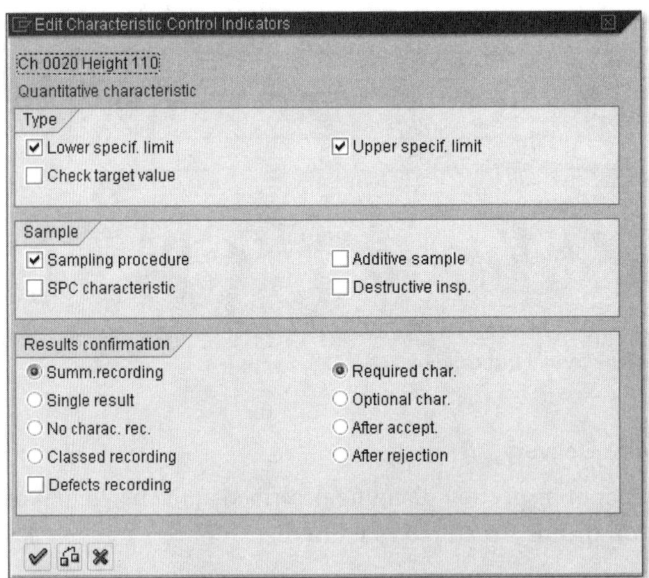


**Figure 6.49** Control Indicators for Quantitative Characteristic from Default

- **Inspection necessity**
  Set when the inspection type is activated in the material master

- **Inspection process**
  Inspect with task list in the inspection type is active, results recording in the characteristic is active, defects recording in the characteristic is active (creates quality notification with defects data record).
- **Inspection method**
  Inspection method assigned
- **Test equipment**
  Optional; can be assigned to the operation and the characteristic.
- **Process/create inspection lot**
  Controlled by means of the header data entered for the inspection plan (dynamic modification level 1, lot level):
  - Dynamic modification rule: D00, Dynamic modification XY
  - Task-list usage: 5, Goods receipt
  - Inspection type: 01, Incoming inspection in material master
  - The inspection lot itself is generated by goods movement 01, Goods Receipt for Purchase Order.

Figure 6.50 shows a characteristic overview of an inspection plan for an incoming inspection.

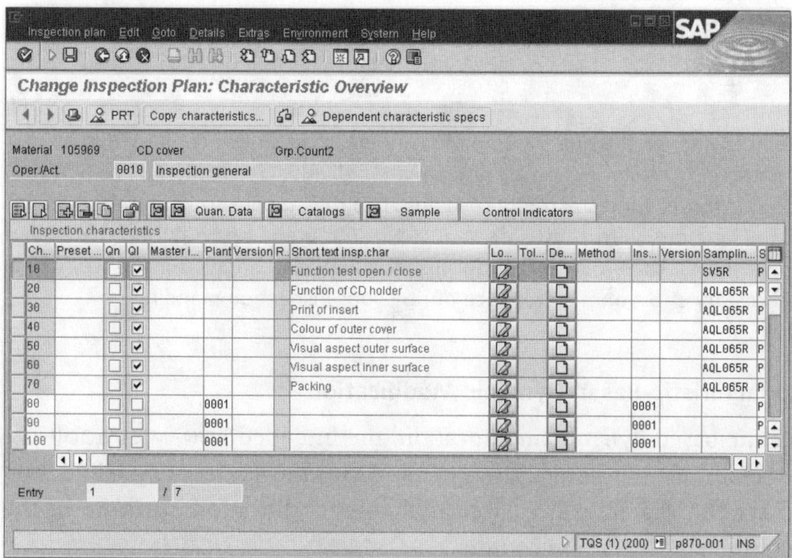


**Figure 6.50** Example of a Characteristic Overview for Incoming Inspection for Entire CD Cover

### Quality Planning for Inspection-Lot Processing with Quality Level

After the model inspection has been completed by means of the usage decision with the valuation "Accepted," the system switches to the inspection plan for regular deliveries. Taking a basis of approximately 20 deliveries of the material with delivery lots of approximately 1,000 units each, you have decided to use inspection dynamic modification on the lot level with the skip-lot function. You therefore selected the appropriate entry from the dynamic modification procedure you already created. Your dynamic modification rule includes an initial "inspect" stage; otherwise, it is the same as the example in Figure 6.12 earlier in this chapter. Chapter 8, Quality Control, contains more detailed information on this subject. As before, if this inspection plan is supposed to apply to different vendors, the entries in the header data and the characteristic data apply to all vendors who deliver the material and therefore have the same task-list group. If different characteristic attributes are still required, the *characteristic assignments* can be used here additionally with vendor-specific inspection plans.

For the sake of completeness, let's now examine the characteristics to establish the correct assignment for the sampling procedures and dynamic modification rules. (*Caution:* if the control indicator "sample task list" is set in the characteristic, this step must always be carried out on the characteristic level of the inspection plan.) The dynamic modification rule is entered on the characteristic level for characteristic-based dynamic modification, and on the header level of the inspection plan for lot-based dynamic modification.

> **Tip**
>
> Note that you can change the quality level of every material/vendor combination at any time. Therefore, it is seldom necessary to create individual inspection plans (with another task-list group counter). Strictly speaking, this rule applies to all inspection plan activities. Therefore, with a little forethought, you can end up with one "material inspection plan" rather than several "vendor inspection plans," and you may save yourself unnecessary effort on maintenance during your inspection planning.

### Planning Characteristic-Based Dynamic Modification

For characteristic-based dynamic modification, the intended DYNAMIC MODIFICATION RULE is added to the characteristic in the SAMPLING PROCEDURE menu. You also have to set the characteristic-based dynamic modification attribute in the header data of the task-list group counter.

**Tip**

Characteristic-based dynamic modification is not more time-consuming than lot-based dynamic modification. The functions are system-supported, which means that the costs and complexity of the inspection process are reduced. Not only must the connections between the leading and dependent characteristics be taken into account but also that inspections of serial parts (whose characteristics are reduced to the minimum in any case) are usually carried out in accordance with a certain schema.

With characteristic-based dynamic modification (see Figure 6.51), the inspector always has to answer the following question: "Which characteristics must I inspect and not inspect?" The process of answering this question may be more complicated for the employee in question than simply recording all of the characteristics of the inspection plan and documenting them in the system. The decision to use characteristic-based or lot-based dynamic modification is therefore ideally always preceded by analysis of the relative costs of both procedures.

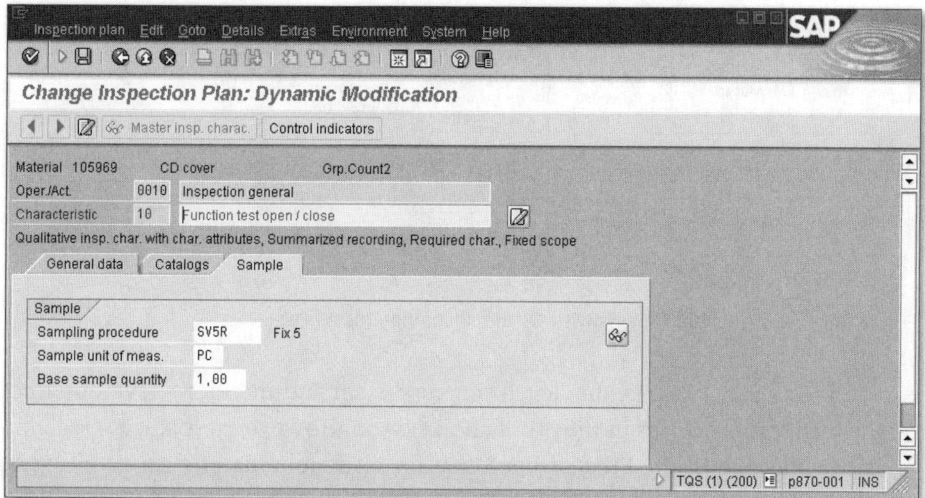


**Figure 6.51** Sampling Procedure and Dynamic Modification Rule in Characteristics Details with Characteristic-Based Dynamic Modification

### Inspection Plan for Repetitive Delivery and Subsequent Delivery

The inspection procedure for the repetitive model and the subsequent model is related to that of the model sampling, and you are using a separate inspection plan in any case. For these reasons, and for the sake of simplicity, the repetitive model inspection task list has been created by copying the model inspection plan. You have also assigned an inspection method to this inspection task list. This method describes the exact process of the inspection.

#### Procurement Process with Inspection-Lot Generation

Now that you have made all your inspection-planning preparations, you can run a complete procurement scenario. To do this, you naturally have to use the required transactions. In real-world implementations, it is usually the case that the people responsible for the individual modules in QM have mastered at least the basics of the ordering and goods-movements transactions so that they can test the different variants themselves. In this section, you will see the most important functions from these areas, with some screenshots and navigation aids from the example.

Figure 6.52 gives you an overview over the quality planning of a procurement process.

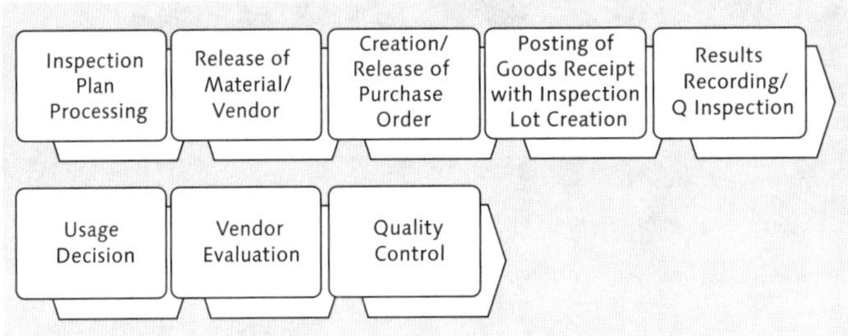


**Figure 6.52** Procurement Process with Quality Planning Process Paths

Also, all tests take place in the development system and therefore have no effect on the business processes in the production system. However, it is still a good idea to ask a colleague in the Procurement area for a suitable material that will work with the orders and goods movements you want to use. You should then tell the Procurement project engineers who are involved in the project and your consultants by email (as an express document in SAPoffice) about this "QM material."

#### Creating a Purchase Order

A prerequisite for ordering a material is fully maintaining the relevant views in the Purchasing material master. You have already created, and are using, material CD1000 and have assigned the Purchasing view to it.

First, you choose LOGISTICS • MATERIALS MANAGEMENT • PURCHASING, then PURCHASE ORDER • CREATE • VENDOR/SUPPLYING PLANT KNOWN, and enter the required elements by choosing CREATE PURCHASE ORDER. Next, you press [Enter] to switch to the header data of the order and then to the item overview (see Figure 6.53). Here, you specify the actual items in the order (see Figure 6.54).

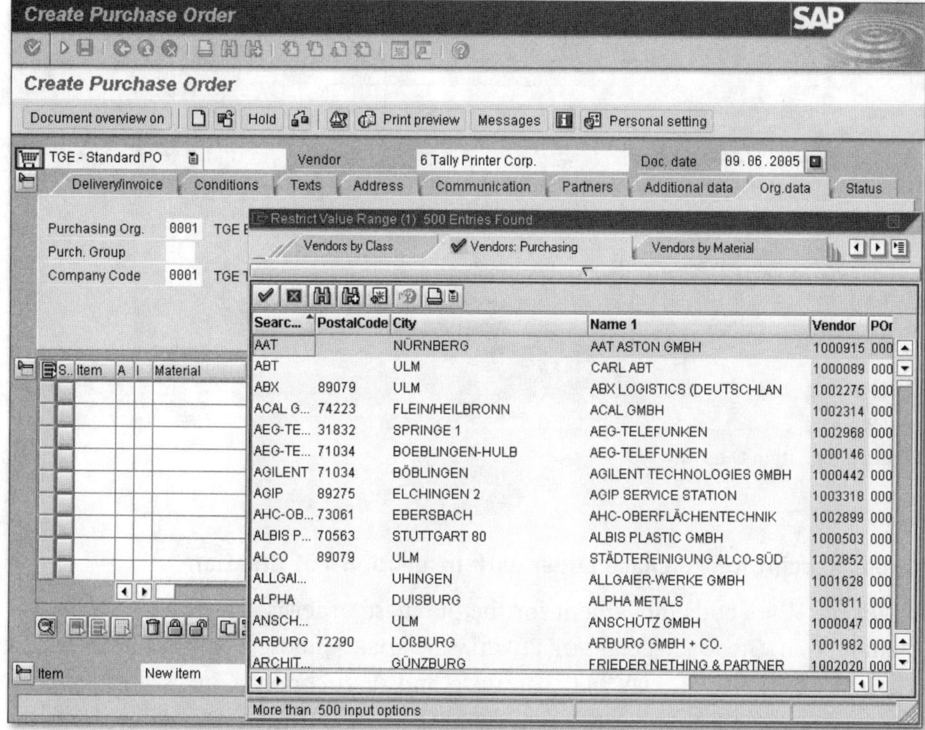


**Figure 6.53** Creating an Order

From the ITEM OVERVIEW, navigate back to the header data of the order, and release the order (the "green man/flag" menu icon). Now simply press [Enter], to save your entries, and the order posting can run. The order is now saved under a number, which, as usual, is shown in the lower part of the screen in the status bar. You can use this internally assigned number (purchasing document number) to identify and search for your inspection lot later on.

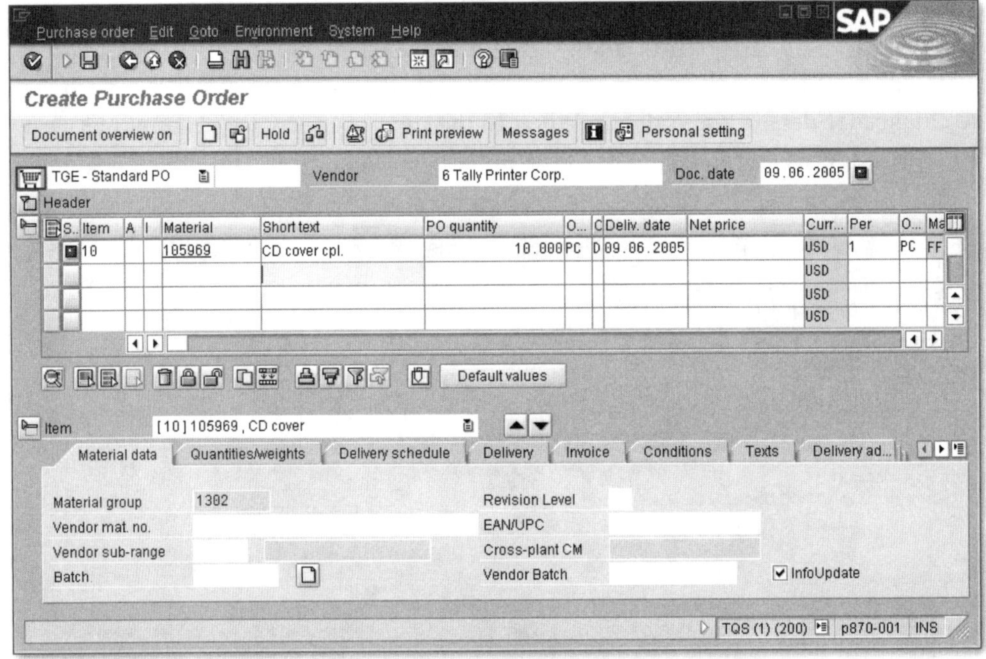

Figure 6.54 Item Overview

## Goods Receipt for Purchase Order with Inspection-Lot Creation

In general, the goods movement for the purchase order is linked with the movement type 01, GOODS RECEIPT FOR PURCHASE ORDER. Choose LOGISTICS • MATERIALS MANAGEMENT • INVENTORY MANAGEMENT, and then choose GOODS MOVEMENT • GOODS RECEIPT • FOR PURCHASE ORDER • PO NUMBER UNKNOWN. After the fields are filled with the appropriate data (see Figure 6.55), press Enter to go to the PURCHASING DOCUMENTS screen, where you select the appropriate document and the item.

Next, in the same screen, enter the delivered quantity for the relevant item, which can be different from the quantity ordered, and post this by pressing Enter. Assuming that you are working with activated QM in Procurement and certificate management, the system now opens a dialog window containing the question: "Has a certificate of the required type been received?" After you have answered "Yes" or "No" (in the latter case, the status ZNEG is set in the inspection lot, which prevents the final usage decision from being made) and confirmed by pressing Enter, the document is finally posted, and an inspection lot is created. The number that was internally assigned by the system is now retained as a material document (GR document number) and can be used to search for the inspection lot.

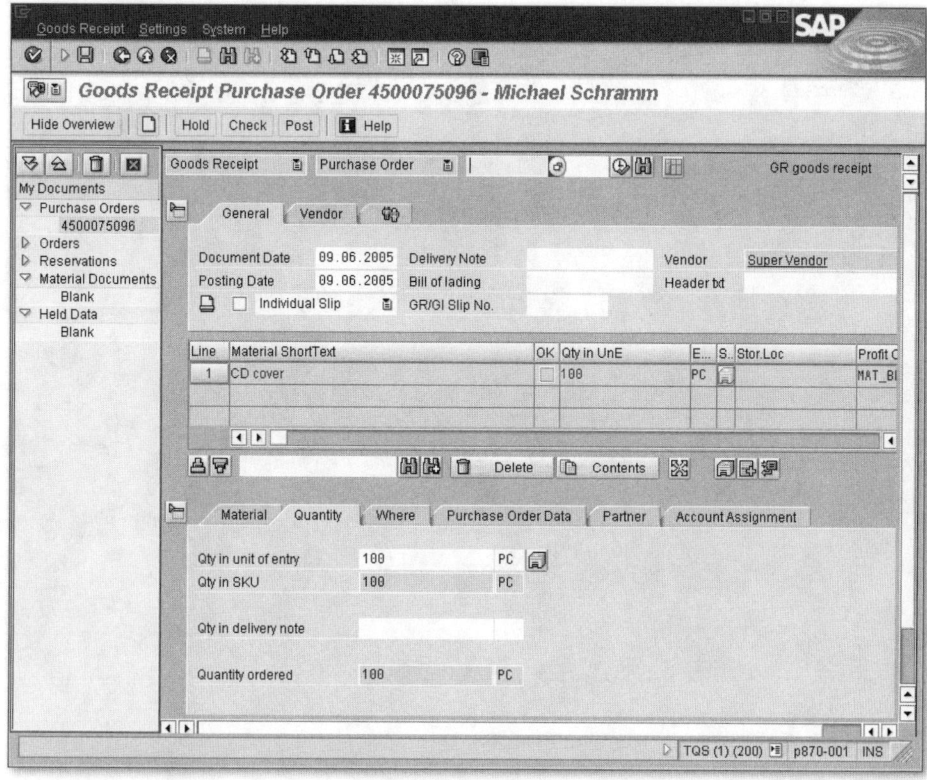


**Figure 6.55** Goods-Receipt Posting in Inspection Stock

**Tip**

In the initial tests, always closely observe the status bar at the bottom of the screen during the posting process. If the message "Quality inspection being prepared" does not appear during the GR posting, the worklist is sure not to contain an inspection lot for results recording. An incomplete inspection lot may still have been created, however. In this case, search for the inspection lot by choosing QUALITY INSPECTION • INSPECTION LOT • PROCESSING • DISPLAY. It is usually possible to find the inspection lot in this way. After you have identified the inspection lot, work step by step through the INSPECTION SPECIFICATIONS (see Figure 6.56) and INSPECTION-LOT-QUANTITY screens. Valid entries must be made in both screens before you can record results. If this is not the case, go back and check how you created the inspection plan and made your assignments, and also check the INSPECTION DATA in the Q VIEW for the material.

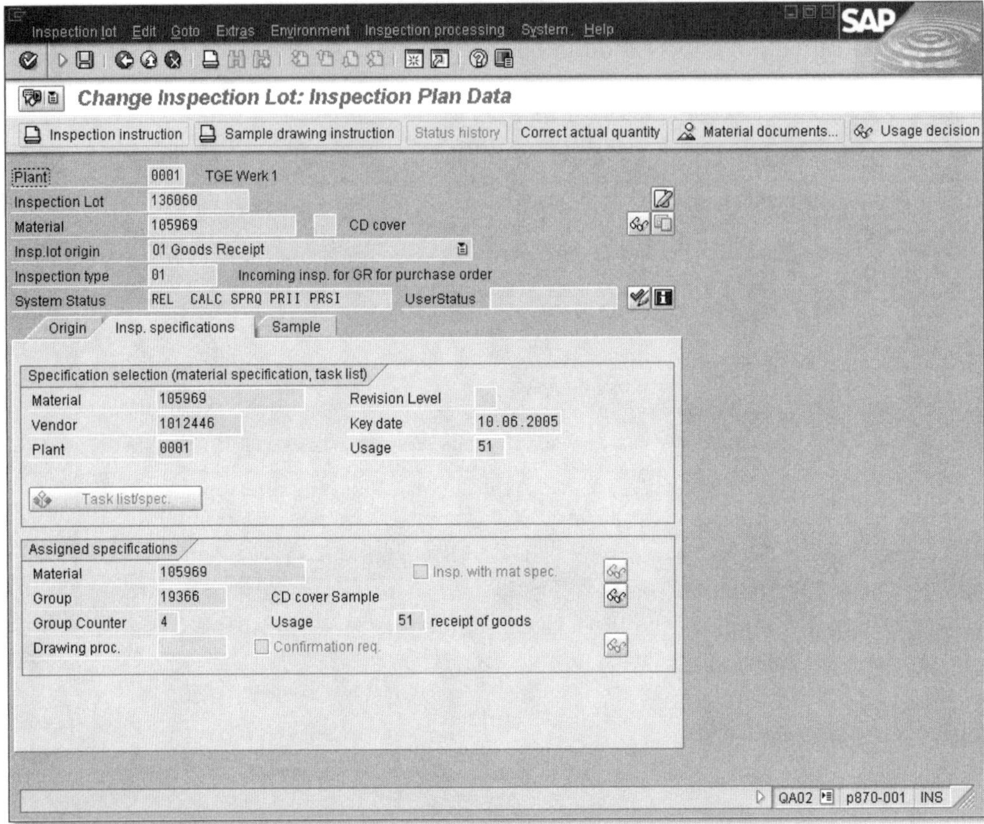


**Figure 6.56** Task-List Assignment for Inspection Lot

### Effects of Quality Planning on Inspection-Lot Processing

You now further process the inspection lot up to the usage decision (inspection- lot completion) and the quantity postings, as shown in Chapter 7, Quality Inspection, and Chapter 8, Quality Control.

After the usage decision is made, there are a number of process options for your planned status sequence:

- If the delivery was a model and if it was valuated with "Accepted" in the usage decision, the status sequence, in line with the Customizing settings, switches to "Regular delivery" with the next goods movement for this material/vendor combination.

- If the delivery was a model and if it was valuated with "Rejected" in the usage decision, the status sequence stays at "model." Another inspection lot with reference to the model inspection plan is then created with the next goods movement. This is then repeated until an "Accepted" usage decision is made.
- If the delivery was a regular delivery with an "Accepted" usage decision, the status sequence stays at "Regular delivery" unless it is being manually controlled.

If the situation requires, you can use the additional "Resampling" status sequence to create an interim status and to lock the orders/deliveries in the quality info record until the resampling yields a positive result, and the usage decision can thus be "Accepted." A prerequisite for this is, of course, that Customizing allows manual status changes.

**Tip**

Unfortunately, the status sequence has a little snag. It is not possible to use a definition in either the purchase order or the goods movement to create a reference to the status sequences so that a flag can be used to tell the system whether the goods in question constitute a model or to provide related information. The system simply assumes that the order of the GRs corresponds with the logic of the status sequence. In the case of multiple GRs of the same part, the preceding situation can cause problems because an individual delivery cannot be identified as a model, regular delivery, or a resampling. The only solution is an organizational one: The goods item is flagged accordingly and then received and inspected in the correct order.

## 6.7 Quality Planning in Production

Production planning and inspection planning tasks in the area of integrating the inspection plan into the task-list overlap in several ways. You will at first realize with surprise that there is no actual inspection plan for production. The inspection plan in this case is fully contained in the routing (the same applies to the rate routing and the master recipe). All of the functions contained in the inspection plan that were already discussed for procurement are available in the routing and inspection plan. You can thus also use sampling procedures and dynamic modification rules for inspection-lot processing here.

The "Release production order" event is used in most cases in production for inspection-lot generation. The only exceptions are production-based inspection types, such as "Goods receipt/issue for production" and so on, which create inspection lots with material movements. With these inspection types, a warehouse goods transfer to the production order creates the inspection lot.

In a quality-planning procedure with the goal of identifying a sample for the inspection lot, the procedure is the same as that for procurement. Therefore, we now take a practical example and look at SPC as a specialization of inspections during production. The main components in the SPC procedure are graphical run cards that should enable the inspector to document the process and to keep it within the *action limits* as much as possible. Despite criticism of this work method from some quarters, it must be said that, given the right conditions (relatively large series releases or recurring orders to the same machines), it can achieve results in process improvement. The prerequisites for a successful SPC process are listed in Figure 6.57.

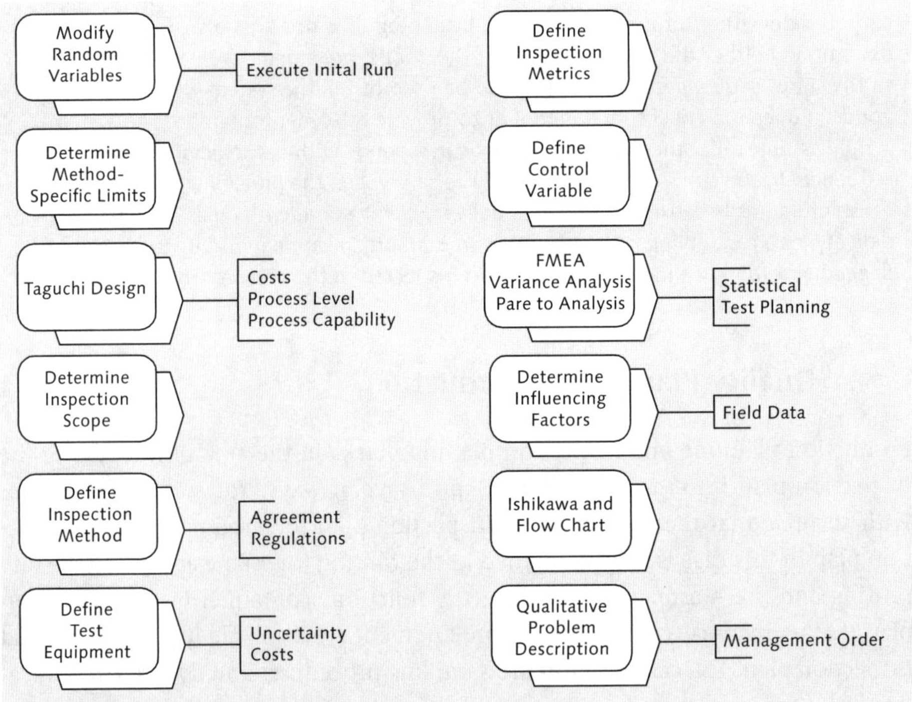


**Figure 6.57** Procedure Model for Quality Planning with Statistical Process Regulation

In SAP-speak, this is called inspection-lot processing with *inspection points*. Another difference to procurement inspection lots is the usage decision, which does not affect inventory management. Production stocks are managed using only the confirmation from the production order.

Based on the consideration of the incoming inspection of the CD cover, it is worthwhile analyzing the production quality planning for this part. The manufacturer's production process is now running, and the current process step is "injection molding," in which a linear measure of the diameter will create a control chart. The diameter of 10 mm ±0.1 is delimited on both sides and is inspected with a device into which the part is laid. A vernier caliper is then used to measure the required dimension at three positions, 120 degrees apart. The result should be one point on the control chart consisting of the arithmetical average of the three measurements at one part and a sample scope of three constant parts. It is also assumed that the distribution of the known process is normal. The aim of the temporary use of a control chart is to reduce the overall process distribution. The hypothesis is that, with a process regulation method that uses the action limits (unlike regulation within the tolerance limits), you can minimize scrap and improve the quality of the process.

You record the measurement values using an interface to the calipers, with the help of the keyboard wedge interface and a Steinwald interface box, for example. These measurement apparatuses are described in detail in Section 7.10, Interfaces to External Systems and Measurement Devices.

### Quality Planning for Production in the Material Master

Starting with the material master, as before, you now create the quality-management view for the material. The other views required for production, such as work scheduling, also have to be maintained. Theoretically, all views are relevant, but here you again restrict yourself to the quality view of the material.

**Tip**

Sometimes it is necessary to create a new material in your test system or client for testing purposes. You can implement this intuitively. In brief, choose MATERIAL • CREATE (GENERAL) IMMEDIATELY, select all views, and press [Enter] to make all mandatory entries from view to view. Then start the transaction you want to use, such as PRODUCTION CONTROL • ORDER • CREATE. If you forget some entries in your material master or do not create certain views, do not worry. When production orders are being executed, the system checks on a continuous basis whether the required data and views are available. If they are not, a message informing you of this is output in the status bar (at the bottom of the screen). Although the material master is a complex entity, users in your projects have never needed more than half an hour to provisionally prepare their material master records for a purchase order or production order.

Similar rules to inspection type 01 also apply to inspection types 05 and 03 (see Figure 6.58), but with the difference that it is not the goods movement, but the release of the production order that generates the inspection lot. The inspection lot is created regardless of whether an inspection plan is complete, not available at all, or available in several places. By the way, note that only one inspection lot can be assigned to each production order that has been released or not yet completed. It does not matter here whether the inspection lot in question was created manually or automatically.

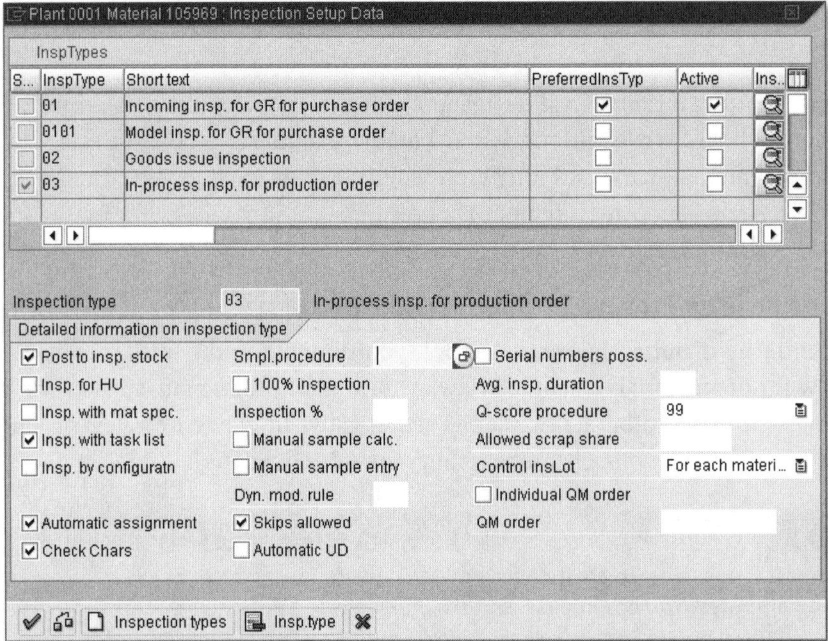


**Figure 6.58** Inspection Type 03 – In-Process Inspection for Production Order with Control Indicators

### Inspection Plan or Routing with Operations for SPC Planning

The basis of this example is a standard routing with various operations. It is assumed that the inspection plan for the SPC inspections of this material has previously been mapped to an external CAQ system. The technical departments in the enterprise sit down together to look at the available integrated routing and inspection plan, and work out the best position at which to place the SPC inspections.

> **Tip**
>
> This planning task is not always an easy one in an implementation project, and involves certain diplomatic challenges for the quality management team. In many cases, the routing structure has been in place for a long time, and it is often claimed that "the routing does not need any quality inspection," or the "let's-do-it-later" argument is used. In such cases, emphasize the benefits, and demonstrate the process to the technical departments to achieve the acceptance you need.

However, in the present case, the scheduling function is based on system ergonomics and lean management. The overall result looks like this: The inspection process gets its own operation number and is completely scheduled by QM as a reference operation set.

In the work-scheduling process, the reference operation set module that was created as the quality process only has to be used as a reference (see Section 6.4.3, Structure of the Inspection Plan [Plan Structure]) by the employee doing the scheduling. To prepare for this step, you have compiled the reference operation set under number "100, CD cover," as shown in Figure 6.59. The control indicator of the operation (PP01, QM01), the predefined work center, and the PRTs to be used are all agreed upon in the preparatory meetings with the persons responsible for work scheduling. The SPC inspection characteristic for the operation has already been created in the reference operation set.

> **Tip**
>
> Just one more comment about the *control key* in the operation. The control key does not cause the actual inspection process to change. Only the processes of inspection planning and printing the shop papers are different from the pure routing. Therefore, take a detailed look at the control options and the routing. It is quite easy to develop a control key for the routing process and the inspection process that is equally adequate for the requirements that will come from both directions.

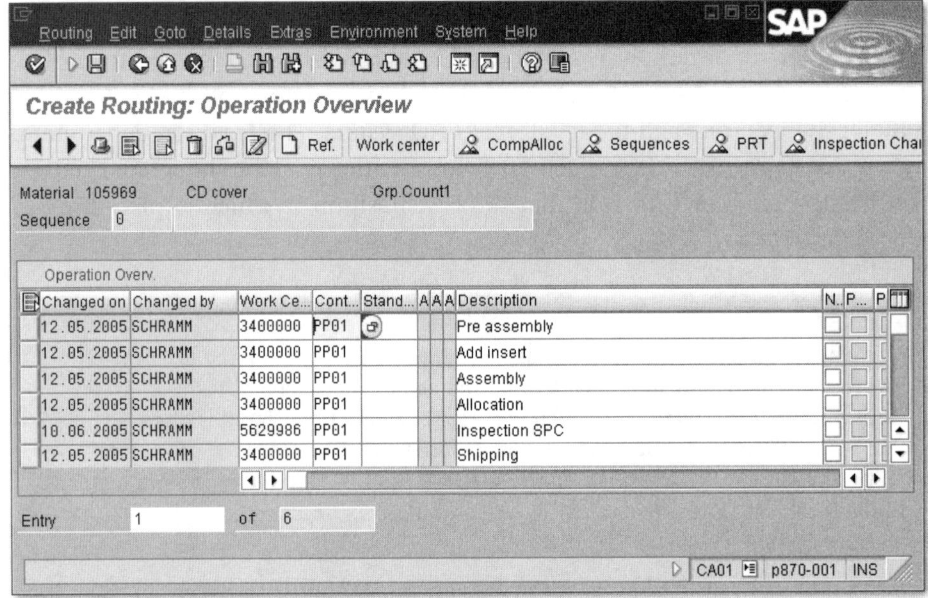


**Figure 6.59** Operation Overview with Referenced (Inspection) Reference Operation Set

### Planning Objects

As before, this inspection plan is structured similarly to the basics of quality planning and contains the following elements:

- **Material reference (in routing)**
  Usually, the person responsible for scheduling has already assigned the material. The *material-routing assignment* is only extended if a different routing is required for the material to be produced.
- **Inspection characteristic overview with inspection instruction**
  For the SPC inspection process, three results (i.e., the results of the three parts) are to be confirmed for each inspection point. These results are the arithmetical averages from the inspections carried out using the measurement devices.
- **Inspection scope (sample definition)**
  You select a sampling procedure SPC01 with a fixed sample scope of three units. You also define the following in the sampling procedure:
  - SAMPLE TYPE: fixed sample
  - VALUATION MODE: SPC inspection; the action limits of the quality control

chart are used to valuate the sample or the characteristic. A rejection is made if the action limits (not the tolerance limit) are violated.

  - *Control chart type*: Shewart, Xquer/s
  - SAMPLE SCOPE: 3, fixed

- **Inspection frequency**
  Prerequisites for this are that the SPC inspection indicator has to be entered in the control indicator for the characteristic, and the inspection points attribute has to be set in the header data in the characteristic overview. You set the following inspection frequency: ONE SAMPLE AFTER EVERY 100 PRODUCED PARTS. Note that despite this, only one inspection lot is created per production order.

**Tip**

If you want to inspect more than the sample size per inspection lot, in addition to the SPC inspection, you can do so using an INDEPENDENT MULTIPLE SAMPLE. This additional inspection is not included in the control chart update. You need to set the relevant attributes in the SAMPLING PROCEDURE and the CONTROL INDICATOR FOR THE CHARACTERISTIC.

- **Inspection data processing**
  Quantitative results recording is active in the characteristic (see the control indicator for the inspection characteristic in Figure 6.60) with the SPC inspection attribute.

  Select the FIXED SAMPLE setting for the SPC inspection (see Figure 6.61). SPC recording can be carried out only with this control indicator.

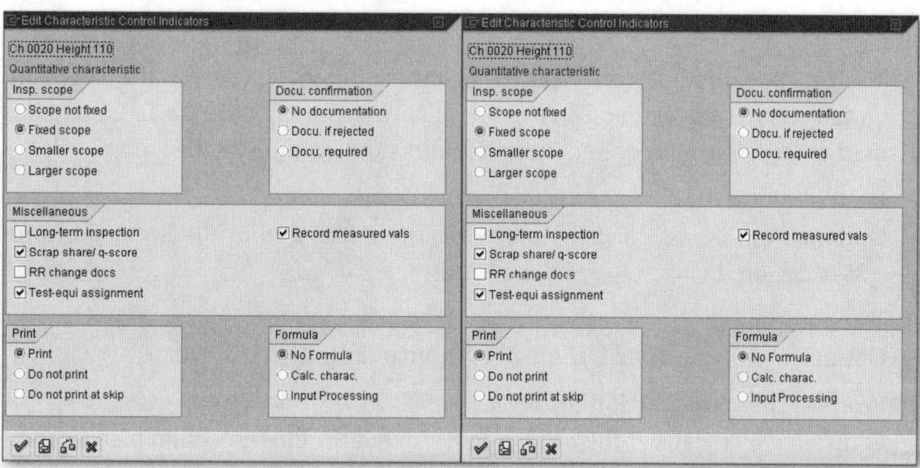


**Figure 6.60** SPC Inspection Characteristic Control Indicator

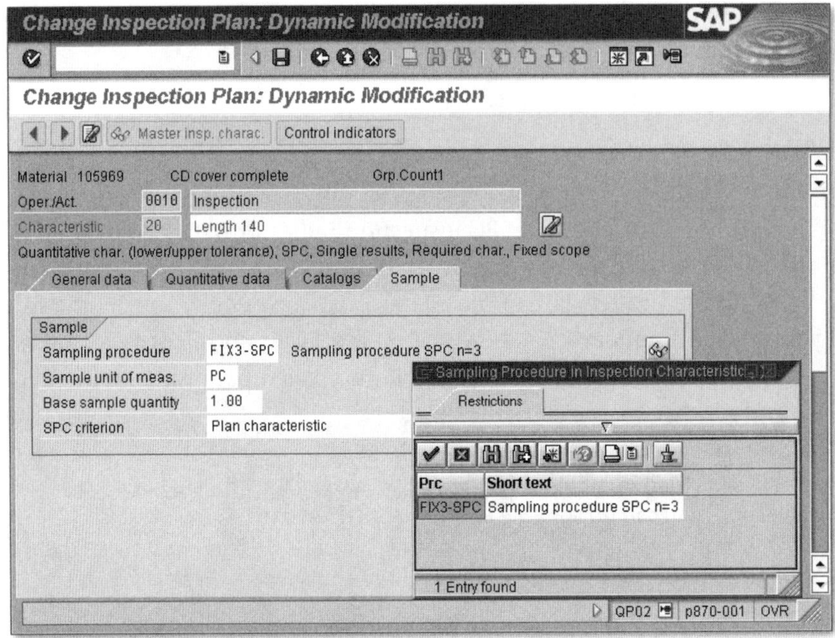


**Figure 6.61** Sampling Procedure for SPC

- **Inspection necessity**
  Set when the inspection type is activated in the material master.
- **Inspection process**
  - Inspect with task list in the task-list type is active.
  - Results recording in the characteristic is active.

  The function module for transferring measurement data from the keyboard wedge interface is active. After the results recording is called, a foot switch is used to transfer the required measurement value to the system.
- **Inspection method**
  Optional; can be assigned if a more precise description of the inspection process is required.
- **Test equipment**
  Optional; can be assigned to the operation and the characteristic.
- **Process/create inspection lot**
  Controlled by means of the header data entered for the inspection plan (inspection point processing, inspection lot origin 03) and the inspection type. The

inspection lot is generated by the production order release and by inspection type 03, IN-PROCESS INSPECTION FOR PRODUCTION ORDER.

### Valuation Mode

You can select any valuation mode you want. However, there is the special valuation mode SPC INSPECTION. With this mode, valuations of samples or characteristics use the action limits of the quality control chart. A rejection occurs if the action limits are violated. If no action limits have been calculated (initial run), the system automatically switches to manual valuation.

### Starting the Production Order

The routing or inspection plan is the basis of the "Production order with material," which you now create in a simplified but functioning form. Choose LOGISTICS • PRODUCTION • PRODUCTION CONTROL, and select ORDER • CREATE • WITH MATERIAL. Enter your data for the material, production plant, and planning plant, and then press [Enter]. The item data for the production order is then displayed. Now enter the quantity to be produced and the scheduling data, and press [Enter] again. If your routing has been correctly created and released and is more or less error-free, the system adds your previously created routing to this order in the routing-selection process.

To correctly understand this process, it is important to note that the production order copies the information or operations of the routing only as a template. You can therefore add and delete operations as much as you like.

### Releasing the Production Order

In this example, you are happy with the operations, and can release the order via the menu bar or by clicking the "green man" icon. Again, you keep a close eye on the status bar in the lower part of the screen. An inspection lot is generated by means of the interaction of inspection type, inspection plan, and production order, and this is briefly announced with the message "Quality inspection is being prepared" in the status bar. However, there are two other things that show that the process ran successfully: the extra status "PLOS" is assigned to the production order, which shows that an inspection lot was generated; and the inspection-lot number is displayed in the header data of the order.

#### Inspection-Lot Processing

For inspection-lot processing, see the process described in Chapter 7, Quality Inspection, and confirm the measurement results in that process. Every production order causes a new point to be entered in the control chart graphic.

#### "Outside Shop" Task-List Variant

The system contains a special function for situations where you execute certain operations of a routing outside your own enterprise and want to check the success of these operations when the delivery is made later. You use the EXTERNAL PROCESSING operation control and the subsequent settings to initialize this procedure.

- Create a control key for operations that use external processing.
- Enter an INSPECTION TYPE with origin 01, GOODS RECEIPT, in the detailed screen for external processing.
- Inspection type 01 is inserted and activated in the material master of the end product.
- You can assign a special task-list usage to every inspection type in Customizing.
- You thus have the option of creating special inspection plans for external processing and automatically assigning them to the inspection lot.

#### "Outside-Shop" Inspection-Lot Generation

- When a production order is *released*, a PURCHASE REQUISITION is created for external processing and is implemented in a purchase order.
- When the GR for this order is recorded, the system checks whether there is an inspection type in the operation for the order and whether this is active for the material. If this is the case, an inspection lot is generated for the end product of the order.
- After the GR posting, the inspection lot appears in the WORKLIST for results recording, just as it does for purchased parts.

## 6.8 Quality Planning in Sales and Distribution

Quality planning in SD is based not on a desire to inspect the delivered good all over again but to create a qualification process for special cases and, often, for the purposes of certificate documentation. The following example illustrates this kind of process.

### Delivery Certificate

Let us imagine a situation in which two customers have different quality and documentation requirements of the same product. The customer Megatech Inc. wants fixed dimension stability and certificate documentation of the characteristic Diameter 10 mm 0.01 for every delivery. Customer Cheap-o-Matic & Partners simply requires a standard certificate for the material used; in other words, a "works test certificate" (in accordance with DIN 50 049) without characteristics. This certificate without characteristics is also to be issued for all deliveries to Megatech Inc.

The GI inspection uses a standard inspection plan. It includes operation 0010, INSPECTION AS IN SPECIFICATION; the master inspection characteristics 020, QUALITATIVE ADDITIONAL INSPECTIONS, IN ACCORDANCE WITH CUSTOMER SPECIFICATION; and the extra quantitative characteristic specified by Megatech Inc., INSPECT DIAMETER 10MM 0.01.

Only when the inspection has been successfully completed does the delivery release take place using the usage decision from the inspection lot. A certificate is created in the delivery using the characteristics from the GI inspection (Megatech Inc.). The general works test certificate is issued for every material.

### Quality Planning for Sales and Distribution in the Material Master

The following inspection types are relevant to GI inspections:

- 13, INSPECTION FOR DELIVERY TO CUSTOMER (WITH ORDER)
- 14, INSPECTION FOR DELIVERY TO CUSTOMER (WITHOUT ORDER)
- 15, GENERAL INSPECTION FOR DELIVERY

Select inspection type 13, INSPECTION FOR DELIVERY TO CUSTOMER (WITH ORDER), because the sales order is the main object throughout the whole sales process.

### Processing Customer Info Records and Customer Specifications

As you have probably realized, customer info records are addenda to the quality info records from the procurement area. However, there is one important difference here: Customer info records control individual materials for a customer, whereas customer specifications apply to all materials of a customer. The example is based on a customer info record because this record provides better differentiation in terms of material assignment.

From the main menu, select LOGISTICS • QUALITY MANAGEMENT • QUALITY PLANNING • LOGISTICS MASTER DATA • QUALITY INFO RECORD: SD • CREATE (see Figure 6.62). Then fill in the CUSTOMER and the SALES ORGANIZATION, and choose CONTROL DATA. The screen for creating the QM control data in SD opens. Choose EDIT • NEW INFO RECORD to go to the dialog window for creating new data, and proceed as follows:

1. Enter the material.
2. Enter the delivery type.
3. Enter a short text for additional information (optional).
4. Set the quality inspection indicator.
5. Save the customer info record.

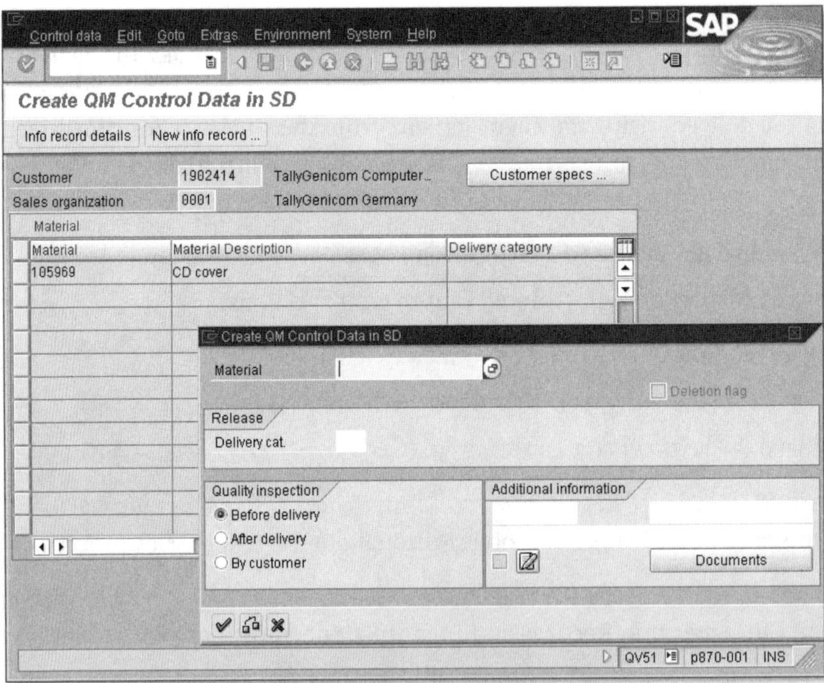


**Figure 6.62** Quality Info Record for Sales and Distribution

**Tip**

More work group objects are available if you are using SAP ERP's document-management system, or a document-management system that is linked to the SAP ERP system. When selecting DOCUMENTS, you also have the option of linking the quality info record with a quality document (e.g., quality assurance agreements or special specifications). In the dialog window for linking the QM info record to documents, use the input help to select the document you require.

### Planning Objects

Here you see some objects you need for your quality planning in SD:

- **Material reference**
  No customer assignment is necessary if all customers are inspected with the same task list. The *material-routing assignment* is not enhanced.
- **Inspection characteristic overview with inspection instruction**
  Various quantitative and qualitative characteristics are assigned to the "GR, regular delivery inspection" operation. The inspection characteristics are created in a reference operation set and referenced in an operation because this material is maintained in a number of variants, each with its own material number and task-list group. The qualitative characteristics can be maintained as master inspection characteristics and used in the reference operation set.
- **Inspection scope**
  One sampling procedure each for the qualitative (QL01) and quantitative (QL02) characteristics.

  Sample size is calculated with a sampling scheme for both types of inspection.
- **Inspection frequency (dynamic modification)**
  Every delivery should be inspected.
- **Inspection data processing**
  Results recording in the characteristic is active (see control indicators for the inspection characteristic).
- **Inspection necessity**
  Set when the inspection type is activated in the material master.
- **Inspection process**
  Inspect with task list in the inspection type is active, results recording in the characteristic is active, defects recording in the characteristic is active (creates quality notification with defects data record).

- **Inspection method**
  Inspection method is assigned.
- **Test equipment**
  Optional; can be assigned to the operation and the characteristic.
- **Process/create inspection lot**
  Controlled by means of the header data entered for the inspection plan (dynamic modification level "Lot level," inspection origin "Goods issue") and inspection type 13, GOODS ISSUE IN MATERIAL MASTER. The inspection lot itself is created as soon as the delivery is posted in the shipping process, and not later with the GI goods movement.

Figure 6.63 gives you an overview of the quality planning of the SD process.

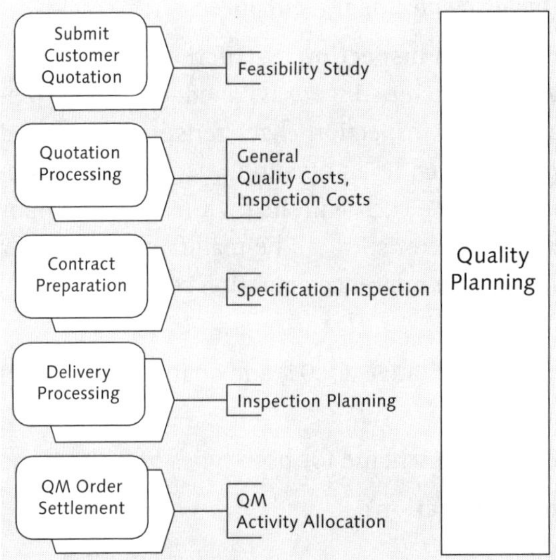


**Figure 6.63** QM Integration in the Sales and Distribution Processes

### Delivery Process for Sales Order with Inspection-Lot Generation

This process also depends on the integration skills of the Quality Management and the Technical departments, and requires the cooperation of the persons responsible for the sales project and their SAP consultants. We would now like to use an area of sales that has been simplified down to the core functions to present an example that you can simulate in your test system with your own data. The focus of this section is therefore inspection-lot generation triggered by the shipping process. The business case is as follows.

The customer has ordered 1,000 units of the "CD cover" material. This causes a sales order to be generated, and you are maintaining this order in the system. You can save this order with or without a delivery. Select "without delivery" for now; the shipping process will be described in more detail later. A delivery note, with a reference to a sales order, is created for this order. The sales order can then trigger a production order or the removal of material from stock.

The delivery can also be created directly in the SD area without a reference to a sales order. With the delivery, QM creates in the background an inspection lot for the inspection-relevant delivery items. Control over the goods is now transferred to QM, along with the inspection lot and usage decision functions, until the inspection has been completed. The delivery then can be released, depending on the usage decision for the GI posting.

#### Effect of Delivery Processing on Inspection Lots

If a delivery is created and processed in the shipping process, the SD actions in the delivery note also have an effect on the processing of the inspection lots in QM. The key events are as follows:

- **Create delivery note**
  If a delivery note is created in SD for an inspection-relevant material, QM automatically creates an inspection lot for the material as soon as the plant is identified. In the status bar, the system informs you that the quality inspection is being prepared.
- **Create delivery for order**
  You now deliver the order you just created with the exact quantity specified in the order. The data is transferred from the preceding document (purchasing document) to the delivery (see Figure 6.64).

To create an individual delivery, navigate as follows:

- In the shipping process, select SHIPMENT • CREATE.
- Create Shipment then opens.
- Enter the SHIPPING POINT.

Either you enter the SELECTION DATE, or the current date is automatically used.

If only one specific order item is to be delivered, enter the corresponding ITEM NUMBER RANGE. Press [Enter] to post the operation.

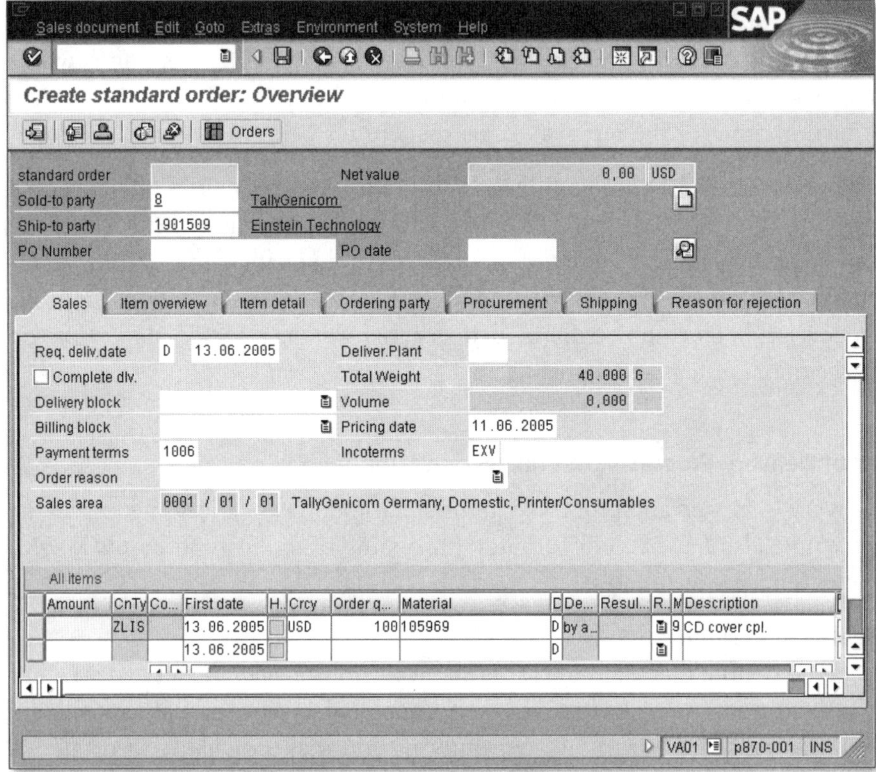

Figure 6.64 Creating a Sales Order

The system compiles the delivery using the basic data from the order, and the material, and so on. The delivery quantity is set in the delivery in accordance with availability. You can also enter additional information at this point; for example, you can provide more details about the goods transport or enter modified order data in the header data and item data fields. Choose DELIVERY • SAVE to save the delivery. The status bar in the lower part of the screen outputs the message "Quality inspection is being prepared." It also outputs the delivery number as soon as the document is saved.

**Tip**

When you create an individual delivery, you create only one delivery for an order. However, the delivery contains only the order items that are due. You now have the option of making changes based on materials resource planning (MRP) to the delivery (important for inspection-lot generation), if this is made necessary by the shipping situation.

**Inspection-Lot Processing**

You carry out any further inspection-lot processing tasks exactly as you did in the procurement or production areas, using results recording and the usage decision.

### 6.8.1 Certificate Processing

You might be wondering why this section is not contained in the quality control chapter. The answer is quite simple: Without a targeted quality planning process, it would be very difficult later on to generate a certificate with data from the inspection lot. The most important basis for transferring data from the inspection lot to the certificate profile is the use of *master inspection characteristics or general characteristics*. These characteristics first have to be created and assigned to the inspection plan.

A comprehensive description of all of the business cases that have to do with certificate creation is beyond the scope of this book. In any case, that discussion belongs to the more difficult topics of quality planning and quality control. Therefore, this example considers a relatively simple case of assigning a certificate to deliveries and sending the output to a printer.

Certificate profiles and SAPscript forms are used to define the form itself, complete with layout, formatting, and the content of the certificates. Processing this kind of form requires in-depth SAPscript knowledge, as with all forms, and is usually a job for your consultant or programmer. However, you should be aware of the following points:

- The certificate profile (e.g.,Q1001–01 with certificate type "works test certificate in accordance with DIN 50 049") controls the process of selecting inspection lots, partial lots, and characteristics.

- The form (e.g., QM_QCERT_01) controls the page layout and the format of the dates on the certificate.
- A form that is as general as possible can be linked with more certificate profiles than a specific one.
- In the certificate profiles, specify the range and order of the characteristics whose results will appear on the certificate. You can vary the origin and display of the data for every characteristic.

For this example, an uncomplicated certificate profile was created specifically for this material and with access to the characteristics data. In the following, the certificate profile is assigned to the material and then printed in the context of an inspection lot.

### Creating a Certificate Profile

To achieve the goal of listing a characteristic defined in the inspection plan on the certificate, choose the following from the main menu: LOGISTICS • QUALITY MANAGEMENT • QUALITY CERTIFICATES • OUTGOING • CERTIFICATE PROFILE • CREATE. Then enter the name of the form (QM_QCERT_01) in the ASSIGNED LAYOUT SET field. In the next step, select CHARACTERISTICS, and the overview screen for entering the master inspection characteristics opens (see Figure 6.65).

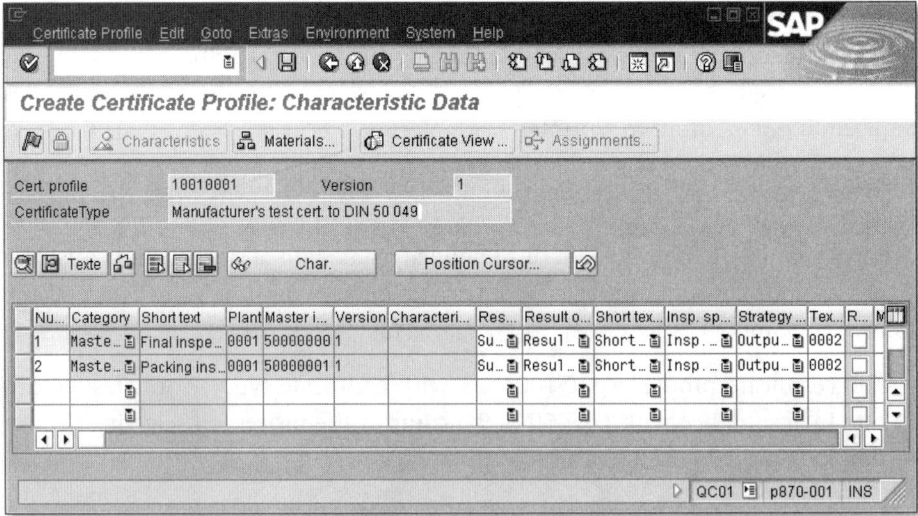


**Figure 6.65** Defining Characteristics for the Certificate Profile

After you select a characteristic, the following fields are filled automatically:

- Result origin
- Short text origin
- Inspection specifications origin
- Strategy for skip
- Text element

This is because otherwise, in the print process, the system outputs a short dump (an error message from the program) and shuts down. Now return to the header data of the certificate profile and save it.

### Assigning the "Works Test Certificate" Certificate Profile

To assign the certificate profile to a material, a material and a customer, or a customer, select LOGISTICS • QUALITY MANAGEMENT • QUALITY CERTIFICATES • OUTGOING • ASSIGNMENT • CREATE from the main menu.

The dialog window with the key combinations opens. You can see in the header bar that the ASSIGNMENT TYPE "QCA1" (condition type) is preset (see Figure 6.66). Select one of the KEY COMBINATIONS, and choose NEXT to open the overview for multiple assignments. The validity period specified here applies to all records that you enter here.

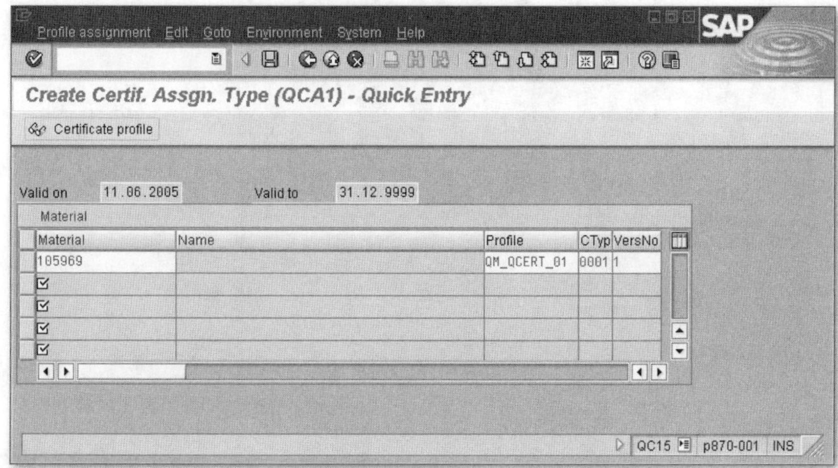


Figure 6.66 Assigning a Certificate Profile

Enter the name of the object (MATERIAL) for the assignment you want to make. Then specify the certificate profile, the certificate type, and the version.

Next, place the cursor in the VERSNO (version) column. A list of the possible certificate profiles opens when you call the input help. If you now select a profile, the system copies the complete settings for the profile to the entry-overview screen. Choose SAVE to complete the assignment.

### Printing a Certificate for the Inspection Lot

The quickest way to print a preliminary version of the certificate form is to choose the Test print option under QUALITY MANAGEMENT • QUALITY CERTIFICATES • OUTGOING • CERTIFICATION CREATION • FOR INSPECTION LOT (see Figure 6.67). One prerequisite is that the characteristics involved have been completed and valuated. Now select the INSPECTION-LOT CREATION variant because the whole delivery process does not have to be completed with this variant, and the certificate can be output and the goods provided directly after the inspection has been completed.

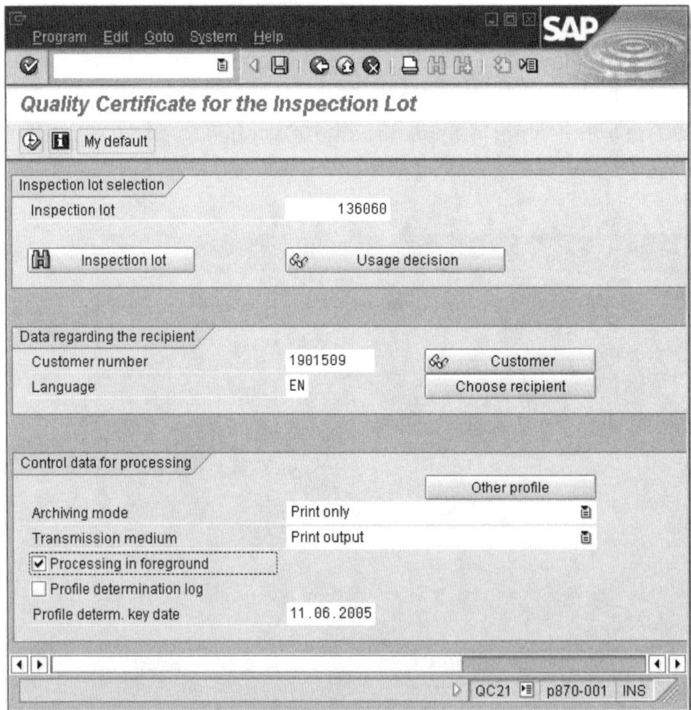


**Figure 6.67** Creating a Certificate for the Inspection Lot

Before the print request can be executed, the system prompts you to enter the relevant inspection lot. The form you just created is then completely filled out with the order data and customer data and is otherwise based on the assignment of the certificate profile.

The result is the printout of the certificate, complete with the data from the inspection lot, the order, and the delivery (see Figure 6.68).

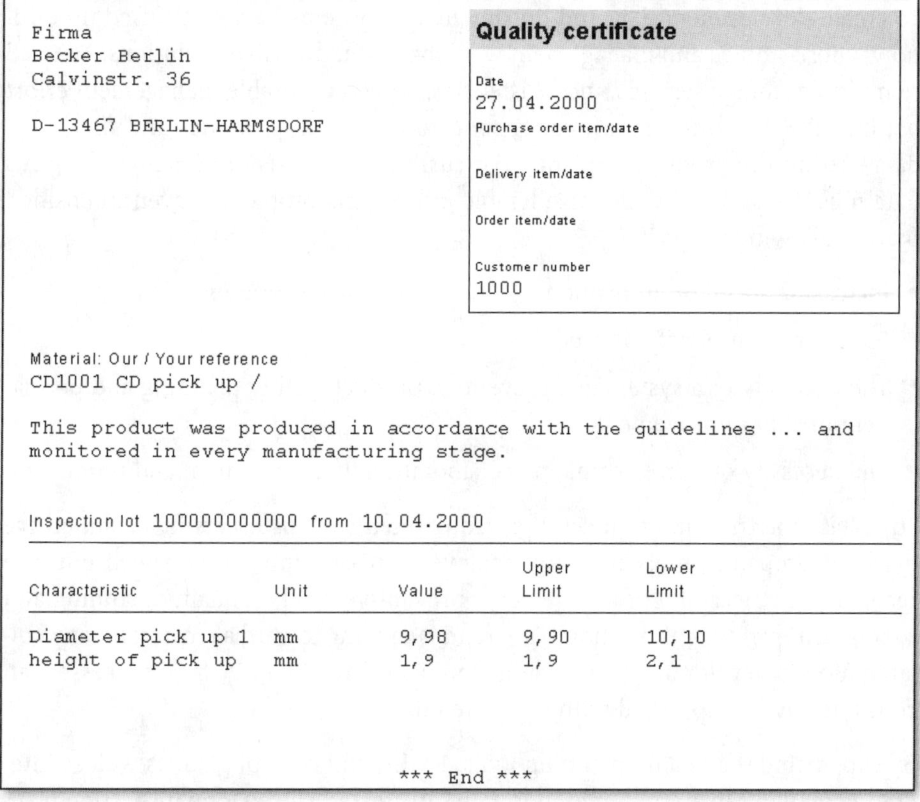
Firma
Becker Berlin
Calvinstr. 36

D-13467 BERLIN-HARMSDORF

**Quality certificate**

Date
27.04.2000
Purchase order item/date

Delivery item/date

Order item/date

Customer number
1000

Material: Our / Your reference
CD1001 CD pick up /

This product was produced in accordance with the guidelines ... and monitored in every manufacturing stage.

Inspection lot 100000000000 from 10.04.2000

| Characteristic | Unit | Value | Upper Limit | Lower Limit |
|---|---|---|---|---|
| Diameter pick up 1 | mm | 9,98 | 9,90 | 10,10 |
| height of pick up | mm | 1,9 | 1,9 | 2,1 |

*** End ***

**Figure 6.68** Certificate Printout

## 6.9 FMEA and Control Plan

In the industrial environment, the creation of a Failure Mode and Effects Analysis (FMEA) as well as the control plan belong to the important standard methods of quality planning. Customers and the standards and rules of QM demand the use of this tool. Because a large quantity of master data already exists in the SAP ERP system, it makes sense to also use the system for the creation of an FMEA, instead of reverting to a standalone solution. By default, the SAP ERP system with Enhancement Package 3 (EhP3) does not offer the functionality required to create an FMEA and a control plan, as it is required by QS 9000 and ISO/TS 16949, for example.

#### Prevention of Defects in Product Development and Improvement

To create development data and documents, IT systems have been used up until now whose storage and management were maintained as island solutions. That led to multiple storage systems, inconsistencies, and considerable management effort because the data often didn't correspond to the actual processes and the actual data used in the production plants. For customer requests or system audits, this data must be updated with considerable effort. This problem is even intensified by the following aspects:

- Increasing speed of innovation
- Increasing complexity of products
- The necessity of a systematic, preventive product quality planning and permanent quality improvement
- The necessity of a cross-company collaboration in development and production

To sustain the trust and to meet high requirements of customers in a competitive market, companies must not only achieve increased innovative speed but also recognize the necessity of a systematic, preventive product quality planning and permanent quality optimization. The trend is moving toward a cross-company collaboration in development and production. By using SAP ERP, these processes can continuously be supported with integrated data.

By supporting the quality planning tools, FMEA and control plan, as well as integrating previous inspection methods, you can create a closed loop inspection planning that results in continuous improvement of the production flow and the product quality (see Figure 6.69). This way, you fulfill another requirement that is part of every set of rules for quality management.

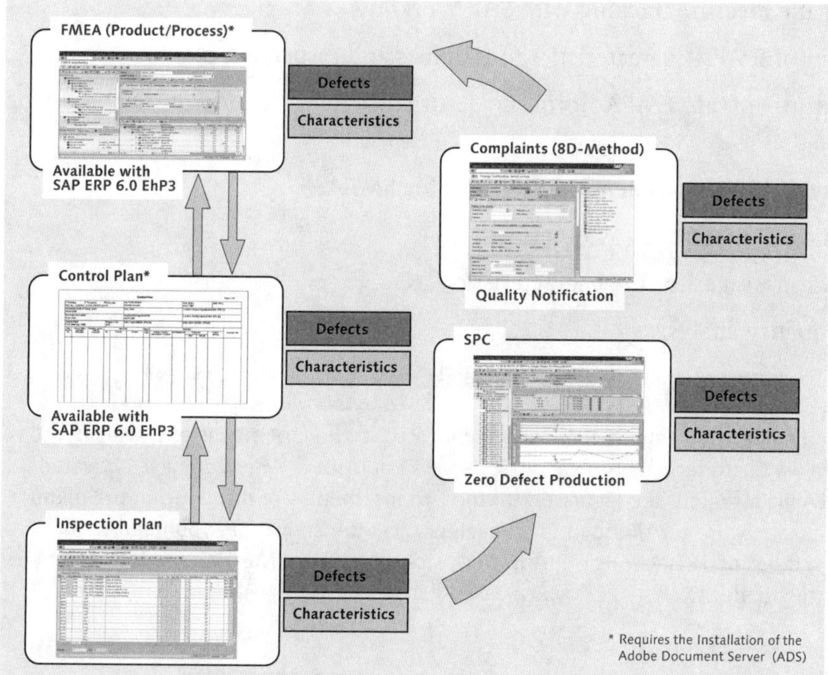


**Figure 6.69** Quality-Control Cycle

### Failure Mode and Effects Analysis(FMEA)

The FMEA records and analyzes potential errors in the development and production of a product and defines suitable measures for defect prevention and executes them in a controlled manner.

The following advantages emerge from the FMEA integrated with the SAP ERP system:

- Integration in work scheduling and inspection planning
- The use of standardized master and catalog data
- Integration in the internal and external complaints system (quality notifications)
- Conformity with the standards ISO/TS 16949, QS9000, VDA96
- Creation/adjustment of the FMEA process with regard to the Control Plan
- Management of the FMEA team with authorization
- Definition/adjustment of suitable corrective actions for defects using the SAP ERP solution database

- Automatic measure tracking with SAP Workflow
- Transfer of FMEA characteristics to task lists and inspection plans
- Formatting of an FMEA form in accordance with standards QS 9000 or VDA96
- Display of similar problem notifications for FMEA
- FMEA evaluations such as
  - Error messages for the characteristic
  - Frequency analysis

**Customizing Tip**

The functional enhancements for FMEA are located in the QM extensions, which you can open via Customizing and Activate Business Functions. After you have activated the FMEA via a switch (see Figure 6.70), the enhancements are displayed in the menu structure (see Figure 6.71) and in Customizing. After the activation, you need to make various settings and selections of BAdIs in Customizing. The FMEA can be found in Customizing under Quality Planning.

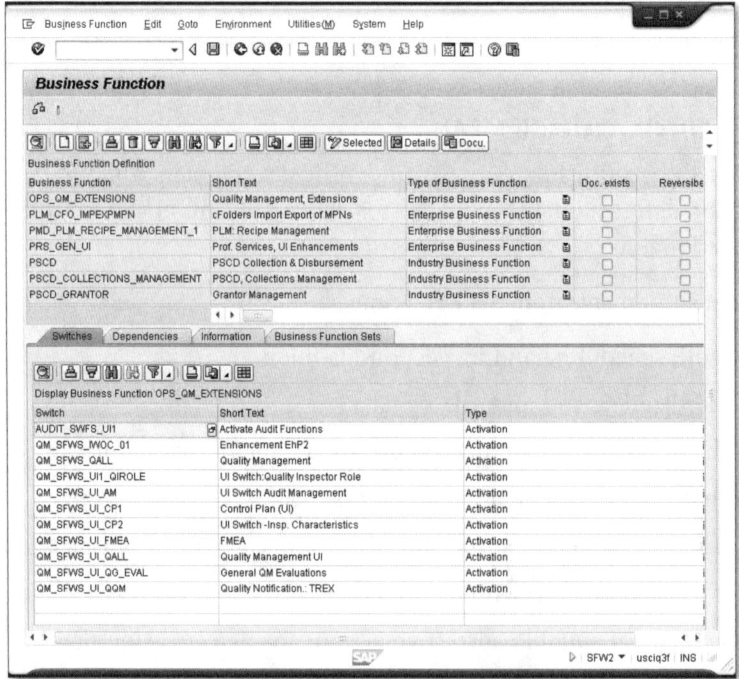


**Figure 6.70** Activation Switch of FMEA in Customizing

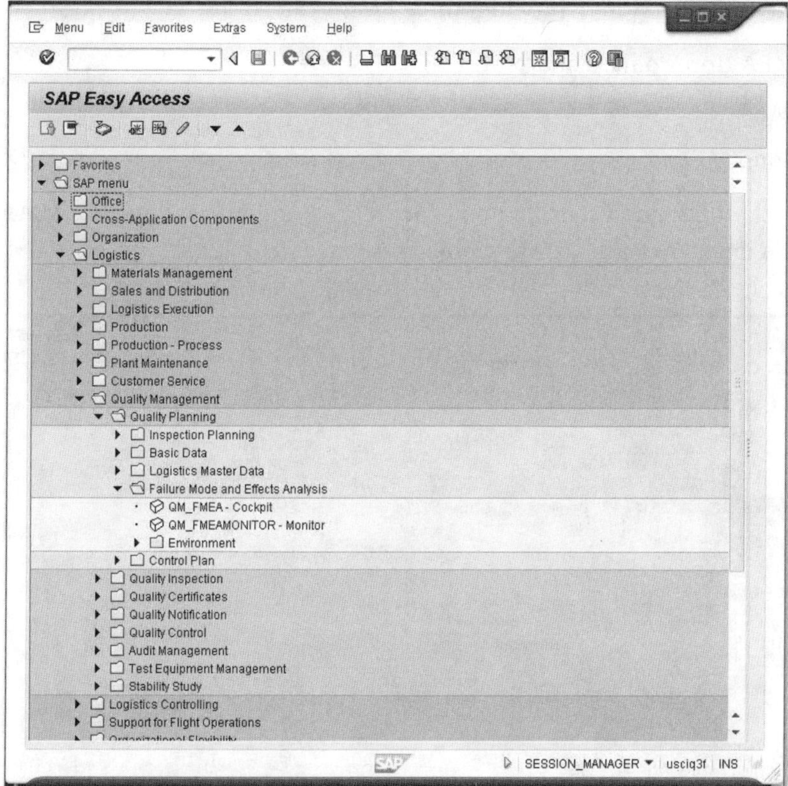


**Figure 6.71** Menu Tree with Path to FMEA

## Typical Process Steps for Creating an FMEA

- Create a new FMEA for a process or a product.
- Assign the necessary objects (material, process, etc.).
- Assign a team and the relevant documents.
- Set up the structure:
  Product, functions, possible defect, and so on.
- Evaluate the characteristics with high risk.
- Specify preventive and detection measures.
- Define or calculate the risk priority figures.
- Print the results of your FMEA in VDA96 or QS9000 format.

By default, the SAP ERP system provides three FMEA categories:

- System FMEA (for products and processes)
- Process FMEA
- Construction FMEA

The FMEA cockpit is a good starting point for creating and processing an FMEA. There, you can enter the basic data and objects (see Figure 6.72).

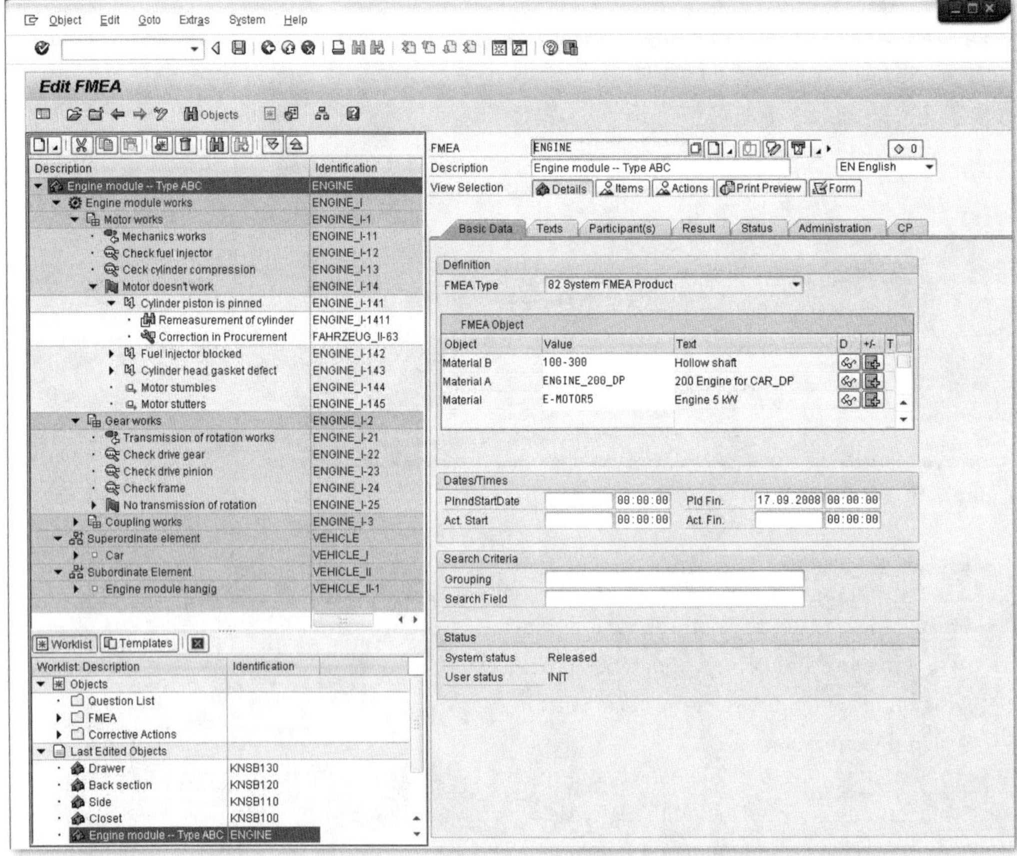


**Figure 6.72** FMEA Cockpit

Then, you set up your FMEA step by step (see Figure 6.73).

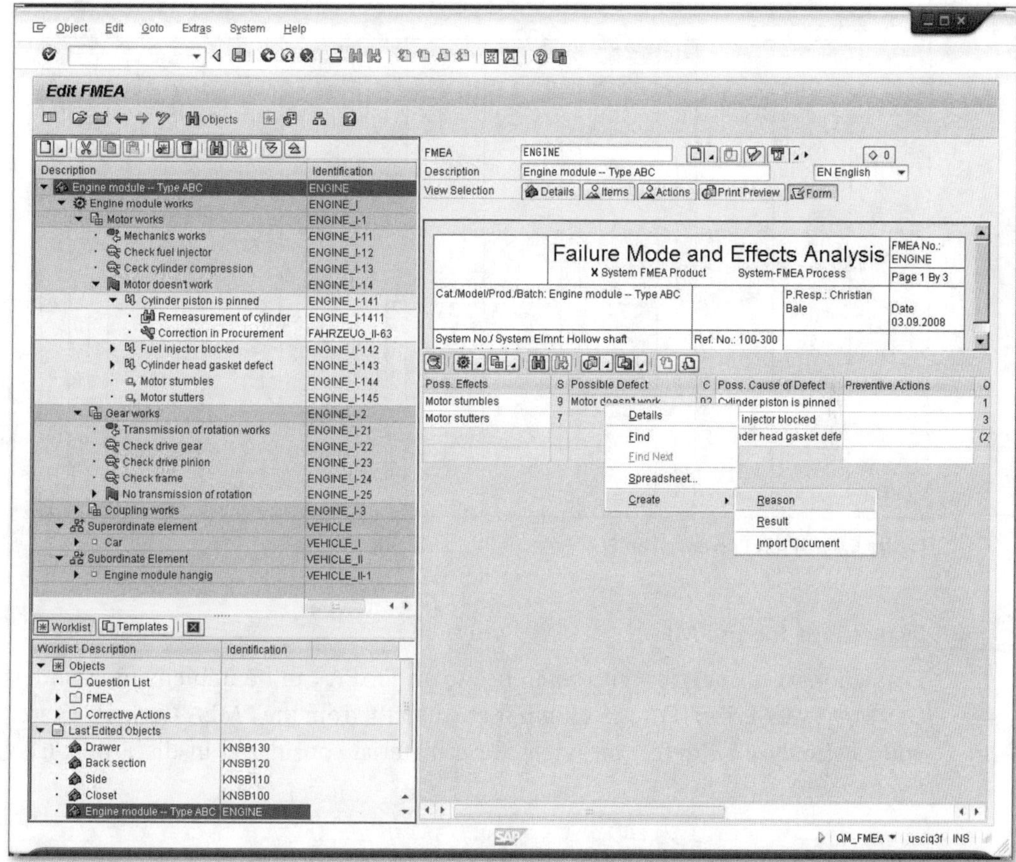


**Figure 6.73** Input of Defect Causes

After you've processed an FMEA, you can print the analysis; here, you can select whether you want to use the QS9000 or VDA96 form (see Figure 6.74).

**Failure Mode and Effects Analysis**
Design FMEA

FMEA Number: ENGINE
Page 1 of 1

Part: Hollow shaft
Model Year(s)/Vehicle(s):
Team: Mr. Jürgen Kniephof;Christian Bale

Design Responsibility: Christian Bale
Planned Closing Date: Sep 17, 2008

Prepared by: MATZS
Created:Feb 6, 2008 Processed:Sep 3, 2008

| Function | Defect Type | Effect | S | C | Cause of Defect | O | Preventive Action | Detection Action | D | RPN | Recommended Action | R/D | Improved Condition | | | | |
|---|---|---|---|---|---|---|---|---|---|---|---|---|---|---|---|---|---|
| | | | | | | | | | | | | | Action Taken | S | O | D | RPN |
| Motor works | Motor doesn't work | Motor stumbles | 9 | 02 | Cylinder piston is pinned | 1 | | | 10 | 90 | | | Remeasurement of cylinder [D] | 9 | 1 | 2 | 18 |
| | | Motor stutters | 7 | | | | | | | | | | Correction in Procurement [A] | 9 | 1 | 2 | 18 |
| | | | | | Fuel injector blocked | 3 | | | 10 | 270 | | | Miscellaneous [A] | 9 | 3 | 10 | 270 |
| | | | | | | | | | | | | | Other Task [D] | 9 | 3 | 5 | 135 |
| | | | | | Cylinder head gasket defect | 2 | | | 10 | 180 | | | [D] | 9 | 2 | 4 | 72 |
| | | | | | | | [Rejected] | | | | | | | | | | |
| Gear works | No transmission of rotation | Gear doesn't work | 7 | 01 | Drive gears not adjsuted | 5 | | | 10 | 400 | Test drive gears [D] | Mr. Jürgen Kniephof / 25.04.2008 | | | | | |
| | | Drive gears cant | 8 | | | | | | | | Order drive gears acc. to specification [A] | Mr. Jürgen Kniephof / 13.03.2008 | | | | | |
| | | | | | Deformation of frame | 4 | Order frame acc. to specification | Check frame for cohesiveness [Rejected] | 10 | 320 | | | | | | | |
| Coupling works | Changing of gears difficult | Can't change gear | 9 | CC | Connecting component deformed | 4 | Order connecting part acc. to spec. | Measure connecting part | 5 | 180 | Measure connecting part with devices [D] | Mr. Jürgen Kniephof / - | | | | | |
| | | Can only drive in 1st gear | 7 | | | | | | | | Produce connecting part [A] | Mr. Jürgen Kniephof / - | | | | | |
| | | | | | Mechanism of disconnecting doesn't work | 4 | | | 10 | 360 | Use lubricant acc. to specification [A] | Mr. Jürgen Kniephof / 23.05.2008 | | | | | |
| | | | | | | | | | | | Test lubricant [D] | Mr. Jürgen Kniephof / 26.02.2008 | | | | | |

**Figure 6.74** Print Preview of an FMEA According to QS9000

## Evaluations for an FMEA

Evaluations and analyses with reference to an FMEA can be implemented under GENERAL EVALUATIONS. You can jump there directly from the FMEA Cockpit. There, you can analyze all defect messages for a material considered in the FMEA (see Figure 6.75).

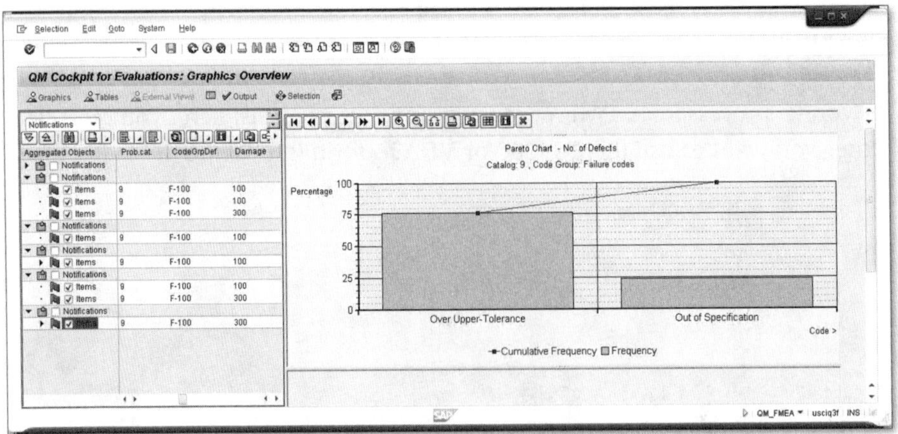


**Figure 6.75** Evaluating a Defect of a Material

### Control Plan

The creation of a control plan for prototypes, pilot runs, and series production is a requirement of the already mentioned set of rules. The control plan enables you to plan, monitor, and document all quality assurance measures in the value chain. Here, you are supposed to consider the previously created FMEAs. From the defect possibilities or detection measures, you can derive control plan checks and implement them in inspection characteristics that are processed based on inspection plans and task lists.

The creation of control plans within the SAP ERP system provide similar benefits as already mentioned for FMEA (in contrast to a standalone solution):

- Direct access to master data, material, and so on
- Connection to the existing FMEAs
- Access to the respective inspection plans and task lists and their characteristics
- Integration of quality notifications (e.g., customer complaints)
- Conformity with the standards ISO/TS 16949, QS9000, VDA96

**Customizing Tip**

The function enhancements of control plans must be activated using a switch, just like for FMEA (refer to Figure 6.70). Then, the enhancements are displayed in the menu structure (refer to Figure 6.71) and in Customizing. After the activation, you need to make various settings and selections of BAdIs in Customizing. The control plan can be found in Customizing under QUALITY PLANNING.

**Typical Process Steps for Creating a Control Plan**

- Create a control plan for a new product.
- Assign the necessary objects (material, BOM, etc.).
- Assign a team and the relevant documents.
- Assign existing FMEAs.
- Integrate existing quality notifications (e.g., complaints).
- Accept the characteristics from the FMEAs.
- Transfer the relevant characteristics to task lists and inspection plans.
- Print the control plan in QS 9000 format.

By default, the SAP ERP system provides three control plan categories:

- For prototypes
- For the pilot run
- For the series production

The Control Plan cockpit is a good starting point for creating and processing a control plan. There, you can enter the basic data and objects (see Figure 6.76).

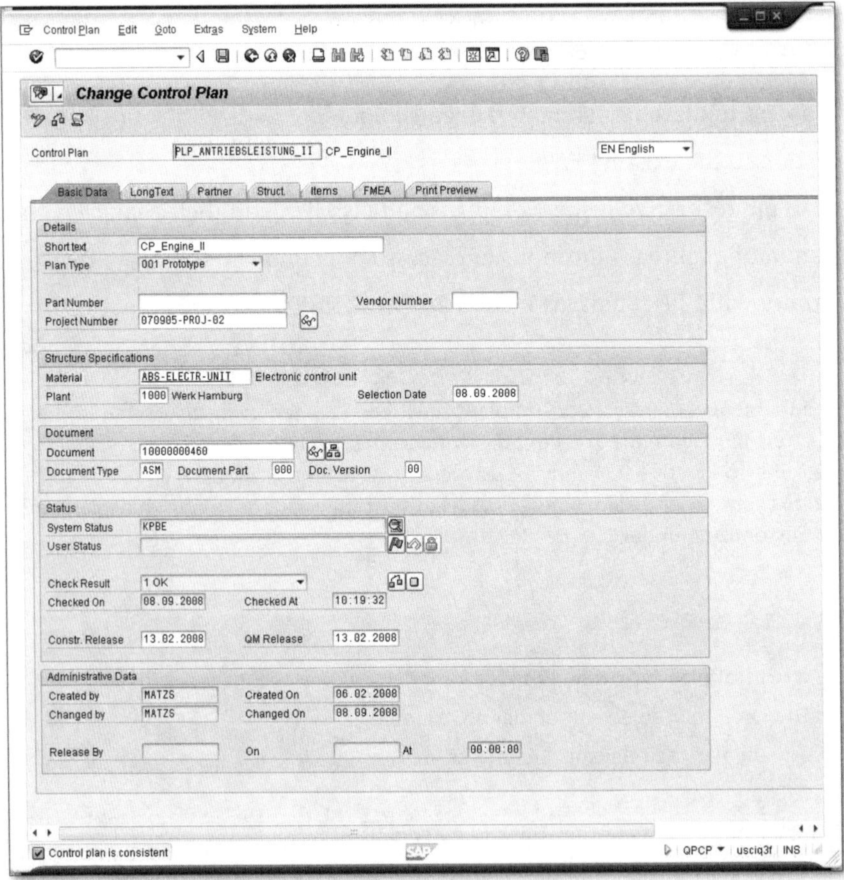


**Figure 6.76** Cockpit for the Control Plan

Connect the existing FMEAs with the control plan (see Figure 6.77).

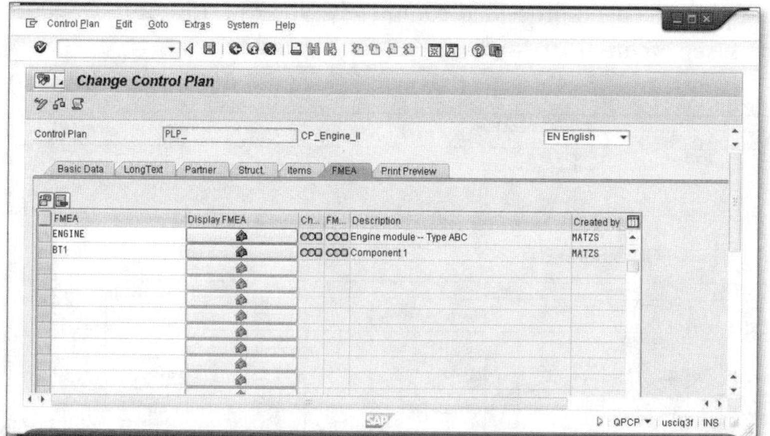

**Figure 6.77** Integrating FMEAs with the Control Plan

Transfer the check characteristic from the FMEAs or add new characteristics using the corresponding inspection plans and task lists to which you can jump from the control plan (see Figure 6.78).

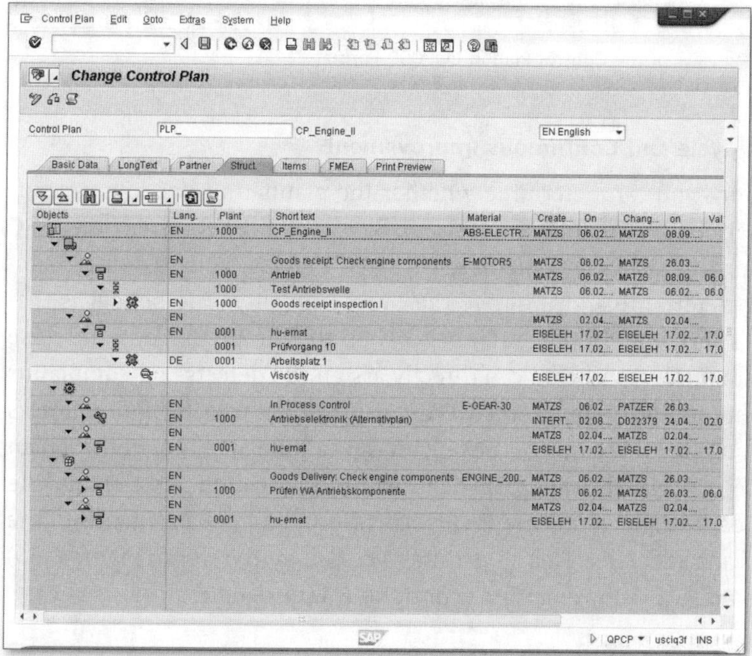

**Figure 6.78** Control Plan Structure

After the control plan has been processed completely, you can print it in QS9000 or VDA96 format (see Figure 6.79).

**Control Plan** Page 4 of 8

| ☒Prototype ☐Pre-launch ☐Production<br>Plan No.: PLP_ANTRIEBSLEISTUNG_II | | Key Contact/Phone<br>Ms. Stephanie Jameson | Date (Orig.)<br>Feb 6, 2008 | Date (Rev.)<br>Sep 8, 2008 |
|---|---|---|---|---|
| Part Number/Latest Change Level<br>ABS-ELECTR-UNIT | | Core Team | Customer Engineering Approval/Date (If Req'd)<br>Feb 13, 2008 | |
| Part Name/Description<br>Electronic control unit | | Supplier/Plant Approval/Date | Customer Quality Approval/Date (If Req'd)<br>Feb 13, 2008 | |
| Supplier/Plant<br>Werk Hamburg / 1000 | Supplier Code<br>4445 | Other Approval/Date (If Req'd) | Other Approval/Date (If Req'd) | |

| Part/ Process No. | Process Step / Operation Description | Machine, Device, Tools for Production | Merkmale | | | Spec. Char. Class | Methoden | | | | | Response Plan |
|---|---|---|---|---|---|---|---|---|---|---|---|---|
| | | | No. | Product | Process | | Product / Process/ Specification/ Tolerance | Test Equipment | Stichprobe | | Control Method | |
| | | | | | | | | | Size | Interval | | |
| N-500 00009-10 | Materialbereitstellung | Assembly IV | 10 | Check frame | | 01 | | | Fixed sample of 1 | | Visual inspection | |
| N-500 00009-20 | Platine einsetzen | Assembly IV | 10 | Check frame | | 01 | 95 /94 /96 | | fixed 5 | | Measuring inspection | |
| | | Assembly IV | 20 | Check drive pinion | | 02 | 100 /95 /105 MM | | fixed 5 | | Function inspection | |
| | | Assembly IV | 30 | Check drive gear | | 02 | 70,00 /69,60 /70,40 MM | | fixed 5 | | Measuring inspection | |
| N-500 00009-30 | Netzteil einbauen | Assembly IV | 10 | Check frame | | 01 | 100 /95 /105 | | Fixed sample 5-1 | | Function inspection | |
| | | Assembly IV | 20 | Check drive pinion | | 02 | 200 /190 /210 MM | | Fixed sample of 1 | | Function inspection | |
| | | Assembly IV | 100 | Prüfen des Schutzes vor Vibration | | 02 | 100 /90 /110 NAM | | Fixed sample of 1 | | Measuring inspection | Response plan 3 |
| | | Assembly IV | 110 | Zapfenlänge | | 02 | 100 /90 /110 MET | | | | | |
| N-500 00009-40 | Kabelbaum montieren | Assembly IV | 10 | Check protection against vibration | | 02 | 100 /95 /105 | | Fixed sample of 1 | | Function inspection | |
| | | Assembly IV | 20 | Ceck cylinder compression | | 02 | 90 /88 /92 % | | fixed 5 | | Measuring inspection | |
| | | Assembly IV | 30 | Check fuel injector | | 02 | 70,00 /69,60 /70,40 MM | | Fixed sample 5-0 | | Measuring inspection | |
| N-500 00009-50 | Display einsetzen | Assembly IV | 10 | Check fuel injector | | 02 | 70,00 /69,60 /70,40 MM | | fixed 5 | | Measuring inspection | |

**Figure 6.79** Print Preview of the Control Plan in QS9000 Format

### Quality-Control Cycle and Continuous Improvement

During production, you can determine whether the planned inspections are sufficient or whether improvements are necessary. By evaluating GR inspections, SPC characteristics, process capability figures, occurred defects, and customer complaints, you can determine and improve the process quality. The benefit is that all information is provided in the system and is up to date if you constantly use the SAP ERP system. This way, you can directly assign the defects and complaints recorded in quality notifications to an FMEA to supplement possibly ignored risks and preventive measures. For this purpose, you can call the FMEA or control plan belonging to the material directly from the quality notification. As a result, the control plan is adapted and supplemented by corresponding enhancements of the inspection plans and task lists. This constitutes a closed loop (refer to Figure 6.69) and fulfills the standard requirement for continuous improvement.

*Planning laid the foundations for creating inspection lots and record inspection results. Even though more and more inspections are outsourced to the vendor, the in-house inspection results constitute a data basis from which you can often derive improvements. This chapter details the options available for quality inspection from the results recording, to cost entry and sample management, to connection of external measurement systems.*

# 7 Quality Inspection

Quality inspection plays a central role in quality management. If solid foundations were laid in quality planning, quality inspection can begin. *Inspection lots* are generated by material movements, production orders, or deliveries, or they are created manually. Inspection lots then undergo quality inspections based on predefined properties. Along with the inspection-lot completion, important information is transferred to the quality info system and is then available for quality control.

Quality inspection is basically divided into *inspection-lot creation*, *results recording*, *inspection-lot completion*, and *appraisal-costs processing*. Figure 7.1 shows an overview of the quality inspection process.

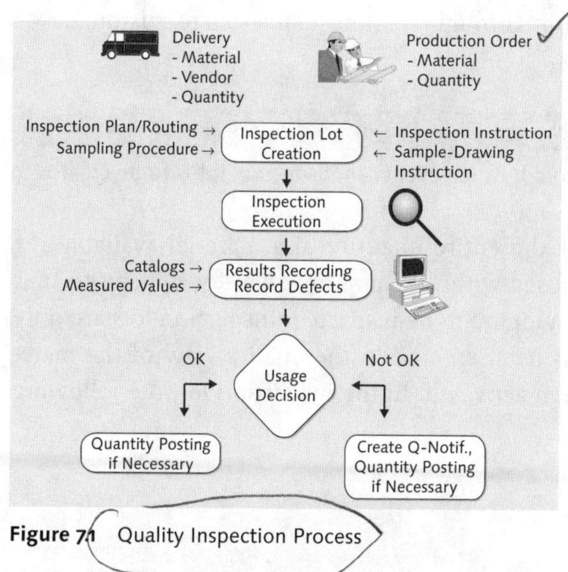


**Figure 7.1** Quality Inspection Process

## 7.1 Basic Principles

First, we explain a few terms and contexts that are important for understanding the following sections.

### Inspection Lot

Inspection lots represent a request to inspect a specific quantity of a material. Inspection lots can be created automatically or manually.

In MM, inspection lots can be generated through goods movements such as the following:

- GR inspection
- Goods issue
- Stock transfer

In production, inspection lots can be generated through recurring batch inspections or through the release of the following:

- Production orders
- Process orders
- Run schedule headers
- Goods issues from production

In SD, inspection lots come about through creating deliveries to customers or receiving returns from customers.

> **Customizing Tip**
>
> In Customizing, you determine through which events an inspection lot is to be created.

The size of the inspection lot is the entire quantity of a material available for inspection. This is not to be confused with the sampling quantity, which specifies how many parts of the inspection lot are to be inspected. Inspection lots are only created if an inspection type has been entered in the quality view of the material (material master) and has been activated. In the inspection lot, the following important data is stored:

- Inspection specifications
- Inspection results
- Inspection costs
- Usage decision

**Stock Types**

The stocks can be assigned to three stock types:

- **Unrestricted-use stock**
  Freely available material that either has already been released or doesn't undergo any quality inspection — identifier: blank or F
- **Inspection stock**
  Material that is currently undergoing a quality inspection — identifier: X or 2
- **Blocked stock**
  Material that is currently blocked — identifier: S or 3

An inspection lot may or may not be stock-relevant. This depends on the inspection lot generation and on the inspection-lot origin. Manually generated inspection lots and the inspection lots with the following origins are not stock-relevant:

- 02 Goods issue
- 03 Inspection during production
- 06 Customer returns
- 07 Audit inspection
- 10 Delivery of the customer order
- 11 Delivery without customer order
- 12 General delivery
- 13 Production order for run schedule header
- 14 Maintenance

If a goods movement is a stock-relevant transaction type such as the inspection-lot origin 01 (Goods receipt for purchase order), the inspection lot quantity goes into the inspection stock. Through the *inspection lot stock* in the usage decision, you can transfer the material from the inspection stock to an unrestricted-use or blocked status or also return it to the vendor.

### Ship to Stock

Depending on the quality capability of your vendor, you possibly want to partly or completely skip acceptance inspection. Skipping individual inspections is called ship to stock (direct delivery into the warehouse), inspection skip, or — in SAP terminology — skip. You can control this via dynamic modification rules. If a vendor of a material is located in skip, this means no acceptance inspection is required. The inspection lot is automatically released after a predefined period of time, and the quantity is posted from inspection stock to unrestricted-use stock.

### Delivery Certificate

The QM module supports the management of the receipt of certificates which must be part of the delivery. Such certificates can, for instance, include works-test certificates, material certificates, model inspection reports, or inspection confirmations. The certificate receipt is confirmed during goods receipt (see Figure 7.2). If the certificate is missing, you cannot make any usage decision at this stage.

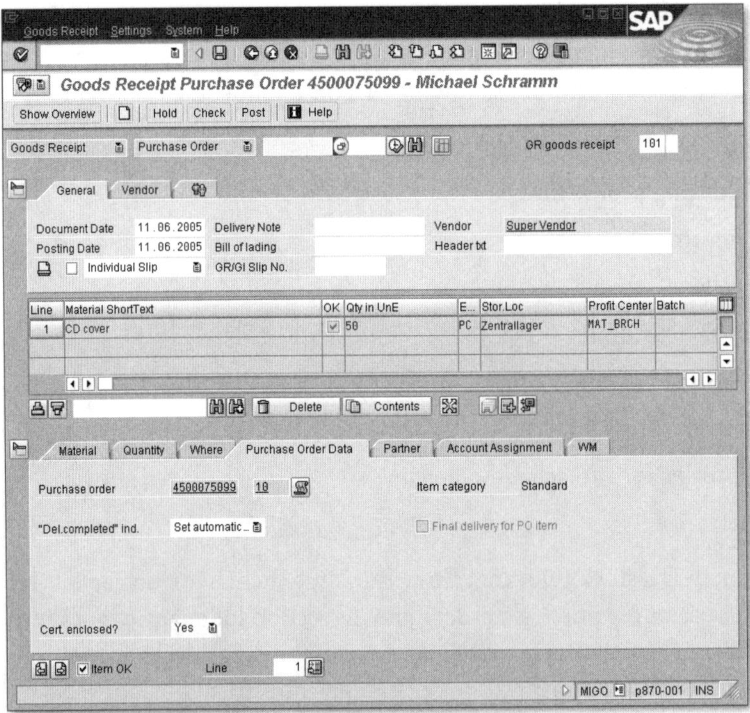


**Figure 7.2** Certificate Query at Goods Receipt

During the usage decision at the latest, the receipt of the certificate must be confirmed so that the material can be posted to the unrestricted-use stock.

**System Status**

If you closely examine the display of an inspection lot, you notice the SYSTEM STATUS field, which displays the inspection-lot status with different four-letter abbreviations. It makes sense to monitor this status because it reveals important details. It is particularly useful in the search for defects, when the system does not behave as you expect it. You can often find out the reason quickly by monitoring the status. Table 7.1 shows the long text of the status notifications. You can display the long texts of the status by choosing EXTRAS • INSPECTION LOT STATUS, or clicking on the corresponding icon.

| Abbreviation | Meaning | Abbreviation | Meaning |
|---|---|---|---|
| CALC | Sample calculated | PREQ | Plan/specification required |
| CCTD | Inspection characteristics created | PRII | Inspection instruction printed |
| CHCR | Characteristic must be created | PRSI | Sample-drawing instruction printed |
| CROK | Certificate receipt confirmed | QLCH | Quality level relevant |
| CRTD | Created | REL | Released |
| CTCM | Certificate confirmation missing | RREC | Results confirmed |
| DEF | Defects were recorded | SKIP | Skip lot |
| DU | Usage decision has been made | SPCO | Stock posting completed |
| FLEX | Specifications assigned | SPRQ | Quantity posting required |
| ICCO | All inspections completed | STIC | Short-term inspection completed |
| INSP | Inspection active | STUP | Statistics updated |
| PASG | Plan/specification assigned | | |

**Table 7.1** System Status of the Inspection Lots

For an inspection lot to receive the status "REL," that is, to be released for inspection, the following steps usually must be completed (although there are exceptions):

- The inspection lot has been created (inspection-lot number has been assigned).
- An inspection plan or a material specification has been assigned.
- The sample has been determined.

The inspection lot status tells you which steps have been taken. If not all of the steps could be performed, the inspection lot does not appear in the results recording worklist. If that happens, refer to Section 7.3, No Inspection Lot in the Worklist, which explains what you have to do then.

#### User Status

You can, for instance, display information on whether a supplied material has the status MODEL, SERIES, or CHANGE SAMPLE. The user can also change the status manually.

#### Status Profile

In addition to the user status, you can enter a status profile in the quality info record (or Q info record). A corresponding status profile enables you to control the inspection type and also the use of a specific inspection plan, depending on the status of a vendor relationship (model, series, etc.).

## 7.2 Inspection-Lot Creation

To create an inspection lot, the basic data for the material must be maintained. For this reason, the quality view of the material master must have been created, and at least one inspection type must have been entered in the inspection data and activated. According to the properties of the inspection type, a valid inspection plan or a material specification must exist. Whether and to which degree a sample is to be drawn depends on the details in the quality view of the material, the quality level, and the details in the inspection plan or routing. Inspection lots can be created *manually* or *automatically*.

### Manual Inspection-Lot Creation

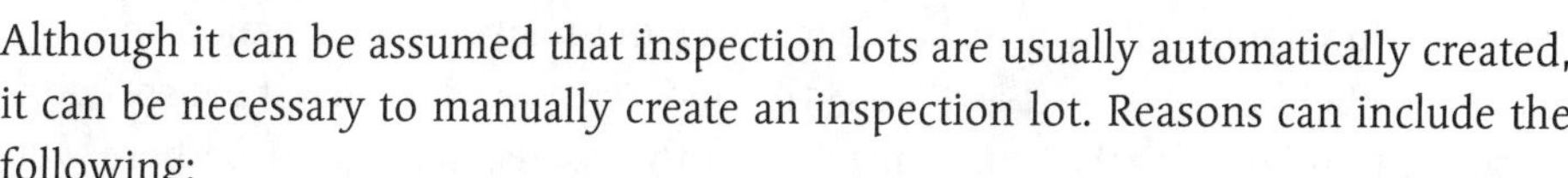

Although it can be assumed that inspection lots are usually automatically created, it can be necessary to manually create an inspection lot. Reasons can include the following:

- Subsequent inspection of a released material because of a suspicion of defect
- Inspection of a material whose GR inspection was skipped
- Inspection of a material because of a complaint by production or a customer

The process of the manual inspection-lot creation, which you can view by using a simple example from MM, begins with the selection of the corresponding menu.

Make the following selection from the main menu: LOGISTICS • QUALITY MANAGEMENT • QUALITY INSPECTION AND INSPECTION LOT • PROCESSING • CREATE.

In the initial screen, enter the MATERIAL (here, 105969), the PLANT (here, 0001), and the INSPECTION-LOT ORIGIN (here, 01 = goods receipt). Pressing [Enter] brings you to the CREATE INSPECTION LOT MANUALLY screen (see Figure 7.3).

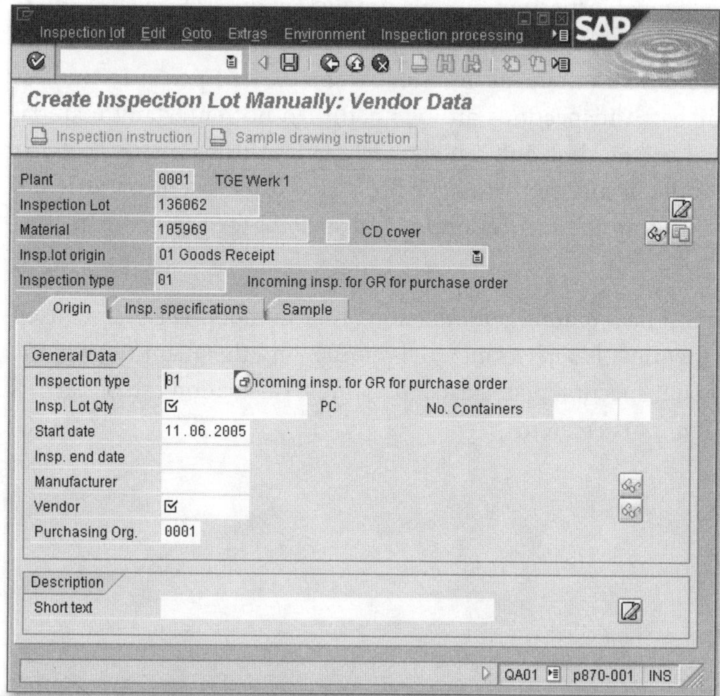


**Figure 7.3** Manually Creating an Inspection Lot for Goods Receipt

The system has already assigned the internal inspection-lot number. This means the only thing you still need to do is to enter the relevant information into the mandatory fields, INSPECTION-LOT QUANTITY and VENDOR. Note that the inspection-lot quantity represents the entire quantity of the goods, and that from here, you determine the size of the sample according to the sampling plan rules that you have defined in the inspection plan or the inspection percentage record.

After you have filled out the required entry fields and confirmed this by pressing [Enter], the inspection lot is created, and the sample is determined, provided that a valid inspection plan exists. If no inspection plan exists, the error message "No plan could be assigned" is displayed. As soon as you SAVE the inspection lot, it is available for further processing.

Note that the manual inspection lot for the goods receipt does not change the stock type. If the material is already in the unrestricted-use stock, it remains in this stock type as long as it is not specifically reposted. Here, the manual inspection lot differs essentially from the automatically generated inspection lot of the goods receipt.

You can also create a manual inspection lot for a production order. However, this is only possible if no inspection lot has already been created for the same production order because no more than one inspection lot can be created per order (unless inspection points or batch inspections are planned). Do not enter any material number in the initial screen, but only enter the PLANT and the INSPECTION-LOT ORIGIN (e.g., 03 = Production). After you have pressed [Enter], a screen created in a different way than during the inspection lot is displayed for the goods receipt (see Figure 7.4).

Under ORDER, you must now enter the production order number. The system itself then retrieves the other details such as material number and the quantity from the production order. If an inspection plan exists, the sample calculation can be carried out, and an inspection lot is created.

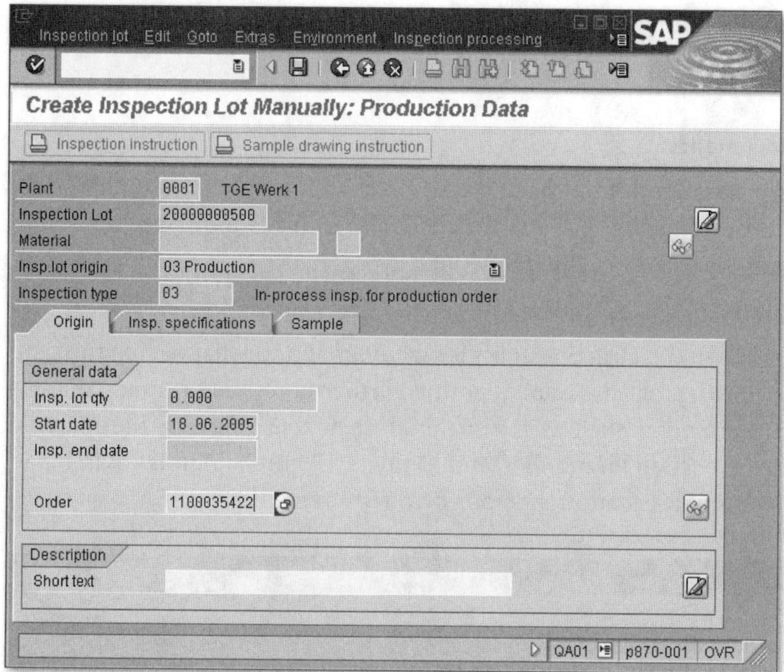


Figure 7.4 Manually Creating an Inspection Lot for Production

### Automatic Inspection-Lot Creation

It may be advantageous for most companies to configure the QM module in such a way that a goods receipt for a purchase order automatically creates an inspection lot. You can notice this during the goods-receipt posting because there, in the status bar, the notification "Quality inspection in preparation" is displayed briefly. After you save the goods receipt posting, the inspection lot is created, and the inspection documents are printed out.

If the inspection type is configured correspondingly, the goods also can be posted to the inspection stock when the inspection lot is created. In this respect, the automatically generated inspection lot differs from the manually created inspection lot, for which the stock type of the goods does not change.

In production, the inspection lots can also be automatically generated. The system can, for instance, be configured in such a way that the inspection lot is created upon the release of the production order or upon issue of goods from production. In SD, an inspection lot would typically be created for a goods issue. If inspection lots are created for serialized materials, the serial numbers can be transferred to the inspection lot.

### Inspection Documents

As soon as an inspection lot has been created, the relevant shop floor papers are printed out (in Customizing, you can define whether this is to happen automatically). These papers consist of the following:

- **Sample-drawing instruction**
  The sample-drawing instruction specifies whether and to what degree the sample is to be drawn from the total quantity. Furthermore, the printout contains additional information such as the material document number, the material number, the inspection lot number, and so on (see Figure 7.5). It is advisable to customize the report according to your own requirements.

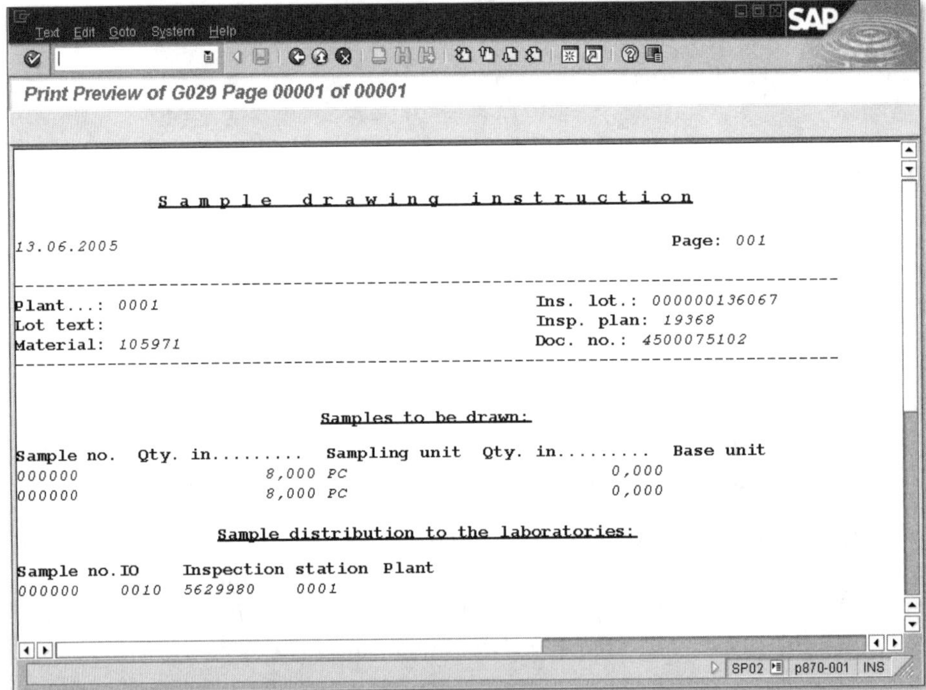


**Figure 7.5** Example of a Sample-Drawing Instruction

- **Inspection instruction**
  For an inspection with an inspection plan, the inspection instruction contains the inspection operations, characteristics, and the test equipment as well as other additional information. Figure 7.6 contains an example. If the shop floor paper has been designed appropriately, the inspector can note results on the inspection instruction.

If your system is configured in such a way that the inspection instruction is not printed automatically, or if you want to print out one of the inspection documents again, go to QUALITY INSPECTION, and choose INSPECTION LOT • PROCESSING • DISPLAY.

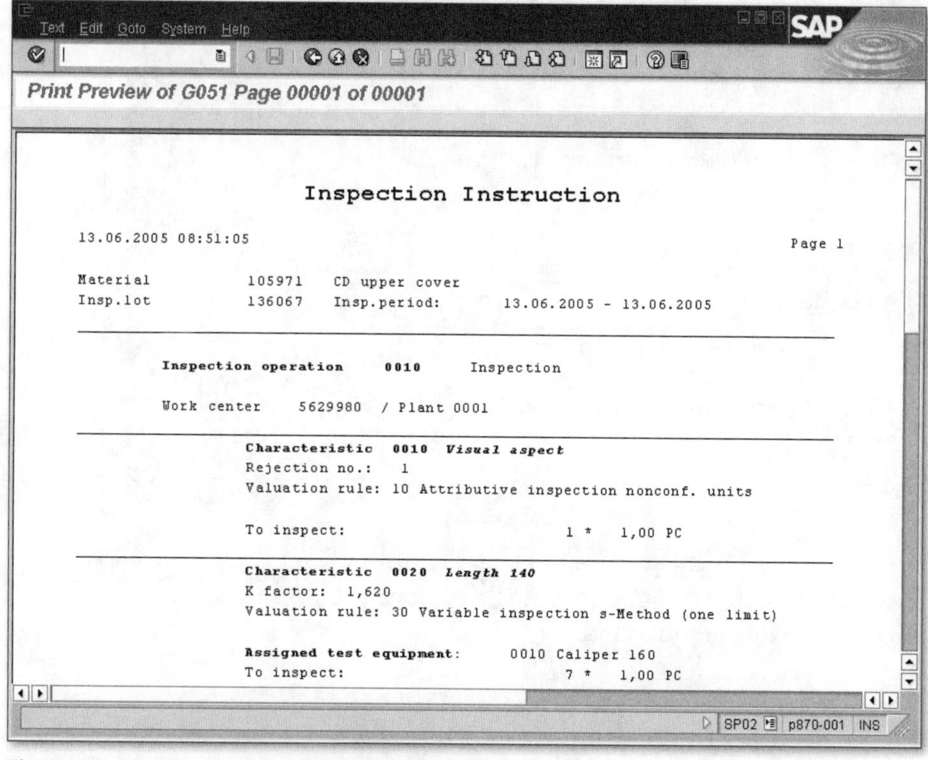


**Figure 7.6** Example of an Inspection Instruction

After entering the required inspection lot number (if necessary, via SELECT INSPECTION LOTS), the inspection lot is displayed as shown in Figure 7.7.

Through the menu path EXTRAS • PRINT, you can now specify whether you want to print the SAMPLE-DRAWING INSTRUCTION or the INSPECTION INSTRUCTION.

By using the sample-drawing instruction, you can draw the sample in the goods receipt and send it to the quality assurance department. There, the inspection is executed on the basis of the inspection instruction.

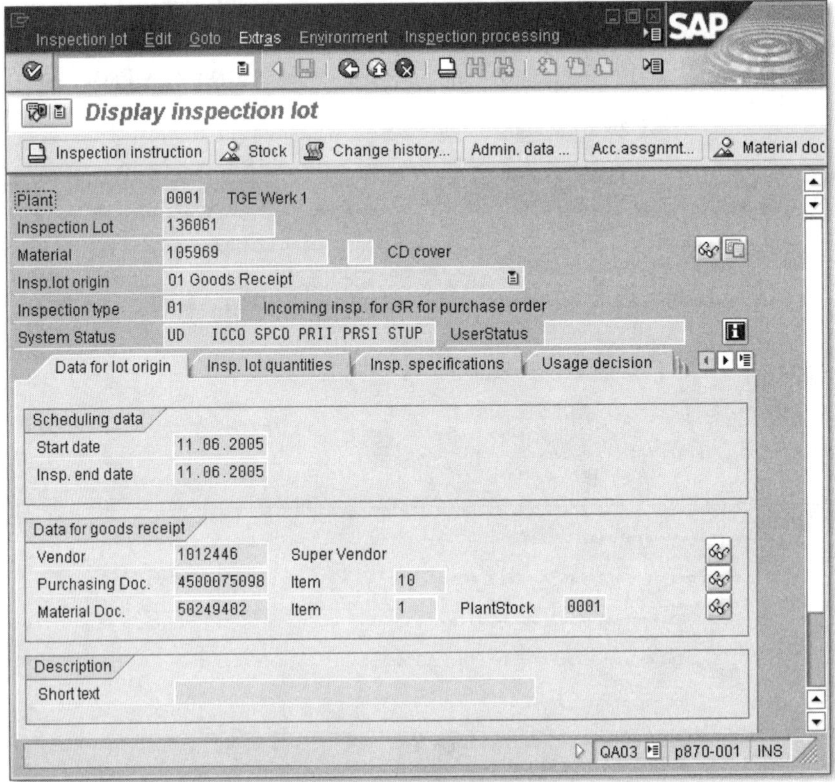


**Figure 7.7** Selecting Inspection Lots

## 7.3 Results Recording

Results recording is carried out to document your inspection. If you want to execute a results recording according to characteristics, you must be able to assign an inspection plan or a material specification to the inspection lot. In this book, we assume that you inspect according to inspection plans and that there is at least one inspection operation with one or several inspection characteristics.

### Worklist

As is the case with many applications of the SAP ERP system, there is also a worklist for inspection-lot processing. Before you can begin the results recording, the corresponding inspection lot must be located in the worklist.

As of Release 4.6, the SAP Easy Access design introduced a few new transactions that can be easily recognized from the "N" placed at the end of the transaction code. The display of the worklist for results recording with Transaction QE51N is one of the changes to the QM module. The advantage of this newly designed view is the combination of the worklist in list form with the screen for results recording in one screen. As an option, you can also use a screen segment for help display during the learning phase. The size of each screen window can be set individually and depends on the hardware used such as a monitor and a graphics card. Figure 7.8 shows an example of a worklist for results recording with this new type of display.

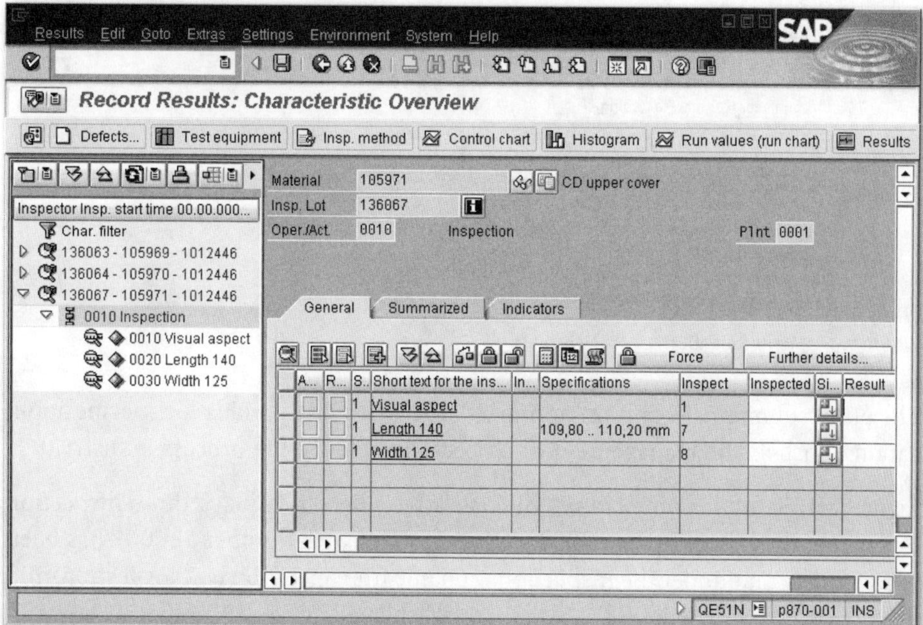


Figure 7.8 Transaction QE51 with Worklist and Results Recording

The familiar results recording transactions from Releases 3.1, 4.0, and 4.5 can now be found under the menu item VARIANTS FOR RESULTS RECORDING. The following selection options are available there:

- USING LIST
- FOR PHYSICAL SAMPLES
- FOR ALL INSPECTION LOTS
- FOR INSPECTION POINTS
- FOR MASTER INSPECTION CHARACTERISTIC

Select Transaction QE51, which is common to all releases, through the menu tree with WORKLIST • VARIANTS FOR RESULTS RECORDING • USING LIST (see Figure 7.9), and only enter the PROCESSING MODE CHAR. FILTER "1" (for "All Characteristics"). You then obtain a list of all inspection lots in the worklist. You can use this structure list to enter your individual selection criteria, which allows you to limit the selection by date, material number, vendor number, or work center, for example.

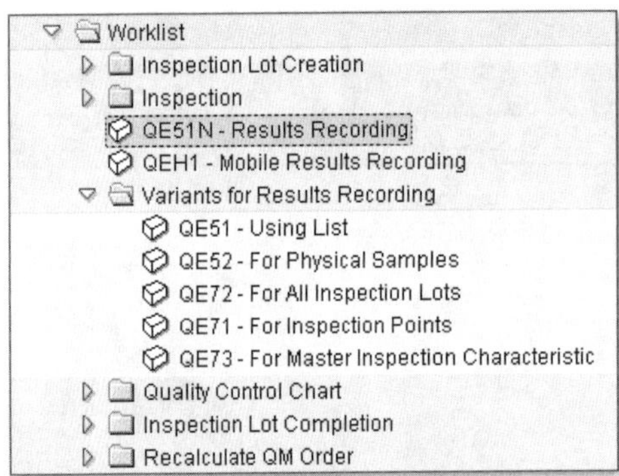


**Figure 7.9** Menu Selection for the Worklist

The other submenus enable an optimized display of the worklist for specific applications, such as the management of physical samples in the process industry.

Figure 7.10 contains an example of such a worklist. It displays three inspection lots where the hierarchy tree for the inspection lot with number 136067 has been expanded so that under the inspection lot name, the operation (GR inspection) and inspection characteristics (0010–0030) are displayed as well.

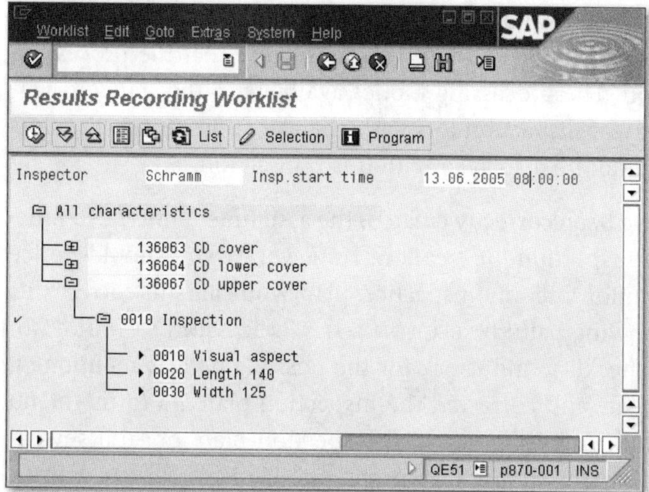


**Figure 7.10** Menu Selection for the Worklist

### No Inspection Lot in the Worklist

Sometimes it can happen that although an inspection lot is created (Status CRTD), it does not contain the status RELEASED. This means that it cannot be seen in the worklist but rather only via the following menu: INSPECTION LOT • PROCESSING • DISPLAY. If the inspection lot hasn't been released, no plan can be assigned in most cases. This can occur for several reasons:

- The identifier for the automatic specifications assignment is not set in the material master record.
- No valid inspection plan/material specification is available.
- The inspection plan/material specification is not released.
- The inspection plan is not yet valid at the key date or is no longer valid.
- The revision of the material and the inspection plan are different.
- The plan usage and the inspection type in the material master don't match.
- In the material-routing assignment, the inspection plan is assigned to a vendor other than the one that actually supplied the material.
- Several inspection plans exist, and thus a clear assignment is not possible.

Looking at this list — and it is not even a complete one — you realize that it can be difficult to learn why a task-list assignment is missing. You will find it informative to look at Chapter 6, Quality and Inspection Planning, on this matter. When displaying the worklist for results recording, you must note that the processing mode performs a selection. The processing modes available in the standard version only allow the display of inspection lots with characteristics. Inspection lots without characteristics cannot be displayed with this transaction.

If the inspection plans have been correctly created, the assignment must also function properly during the inspection-lot creation. However, if you should notice that the inspection lot cannot find any inspection plan, you can still correct this problem through the following path: INSPECTION LOT • PROCESSING • CHANGE. To do this, use the list as a checklist, and check for the possible defects mentioned. If you have found the defect and corrected the inspection plan, go to the menu PROCESSING • CHANGE, and assign the changed inspection plan, or — if several inspection plans are involved — choose the correct one via INSP. SPECIFICATIONS. After you have pressed the Enter key, the status changes from CRTD (created) to REL (released).

After SAVING, the inspection lot is displayed in the worklist, and the inspection documents are printed out.

**Tip**

To avoid having to execute this inspection-lot change too often, you can — as soon as an order has been created — check whether the system finds a valid inspection plan for the material ordered.

To perform this check, go to QUALITY PLANNING • INSPECTION PLANNING • INSPECTION PLAN • MISSING OR UNUSABLE INSPECTION PLANS IN PROCUREMENT. In the selection screen, you can enter a range of relevant material numbers. After starting the selection by clicking the EXECUTE icon, the system displays a list of the procurement orders for which either no inspection plan or an incorrect inspection plan exists (see Figure 7.11). If in the status bar the message "No entries found" is displayed, then there's no current problem, and all inspection lots that are created for the current procurement orders also appear in the worklist.

The good thing about this list is that you can go directly to the material view to check the entries there. Unfortunately, there is no corresponding function that enables you to view the corresponding inspection plan as well.

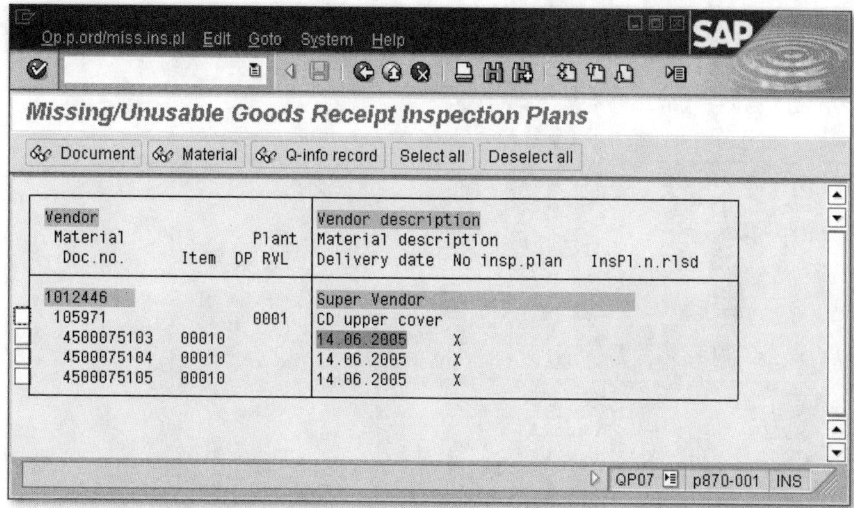


**Figure 7.11** Missing Inspection Plans

The MISSING OR UNUSABLE INSPECTION PLANS evaluation works in the same way. The only difference is that all selected material numbers are checked there whether or not a procurement order has been created.

It is advisable to carry out this check regularly (e.g., weekly) or — better still — to plan a job that automatically runs every Sunday and provides you with the results list through SAPoffice.

## 7.3.1 Characteristic Results

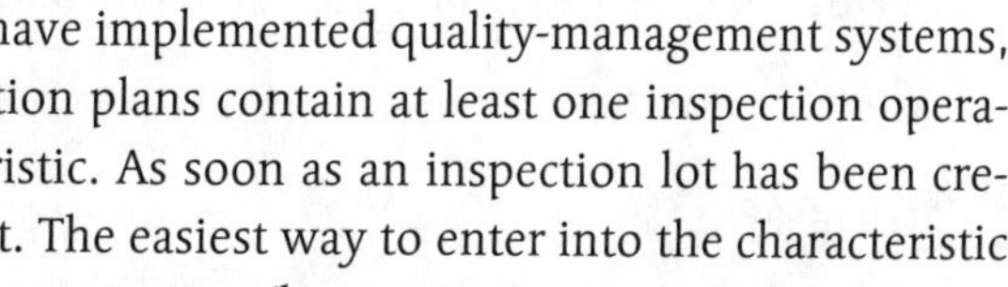

If your company, like others that have implemented quality-management systems, does plan inspections, the inspection plans contain at least one inspection operation and one inspection characteristic. As soon as an inspection lot has been created, it is displayed in the worklist. The easiest way to enter into the characteristic results is by double-clicking on the operation (here, GR INSPECTION). For this reason, the hierarchy tree of the inspection lot must previously have been expanded as can be seen for inspection lot number 136067 in Figure 7.10, shown earlier.

If you go to the RECORD RESULTS: CHARACTERISTIC OVERVIEW screen (see Figure 7.12), all characteristics are displayed that should be inspected.

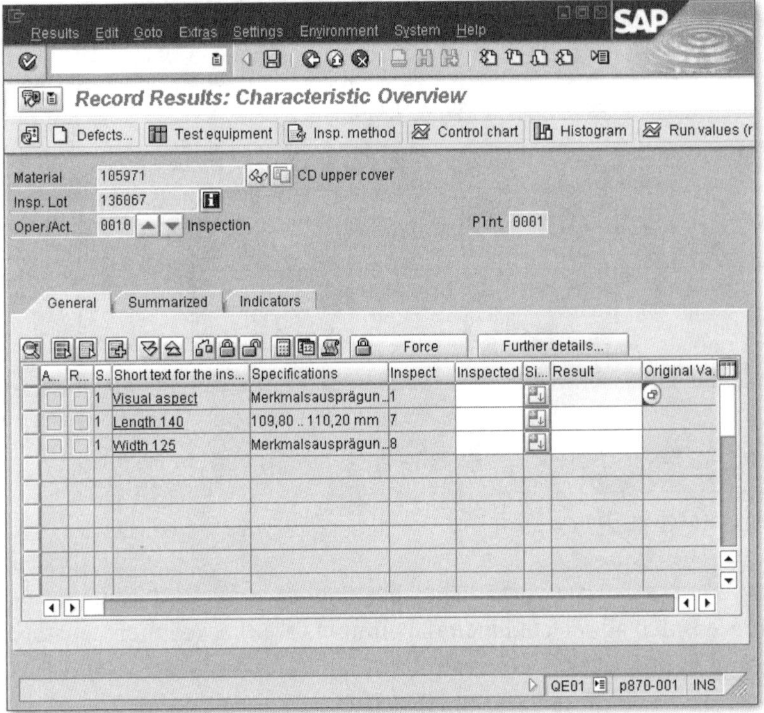


**Figure 7.12** Screen for Recording Characteristic Results

In Chapter 6, Quality and Inspection Planning, we described that it is possible to plan variable and attributive characteristics for the inspection. This means the confirmation of the inspection results is also different. In this example (see Figure 7.12), you must record results for three attributive characteristics.

The CHARACTERISTIC OVERVIEW screen contains the following three tabs:

- GENERAL
- SUMMARIZED
- INDICATORS

Instead of the summarized recording, inspection planning can also provide for the recording of classed values (i.e., the number of events within value classes) or of individual values (if necessary, by entering the number of the unit to be inspected). The name of the tab changes accordingly. A separate screen is available for recording individual values, in which you can enter the characteristic values per individual item or serial number.

If independent multiple samples were provided for by inspection planning, you can record results for several samples per inspection characteristic. It is even possible to enter a higher number than the number of pieces specified in the sample procedure.

Other planning variants for attributive inspection are double and multiple samples. For inspections according to AQL (ISO 2859), the result of a sample can lie between the acceptance number and the rejection number. Consequently, the sample will be increased. A new evaluation takes place after recording the results for the new sample.

The inspection characteristic changes its status during the individual processing steps (see Figure 7.13). Possible statuses include the following:

- The characteristic must be/can be processed
- Skip
- Processed
- Evaluated
- Completed

9 Blocked for evaluations
0 Can be processed
7 Fixed (cannot be processed)
1 Must be processed
2 Processed
5 Processing is completed
A Rqd char.when controlling char.accepted
B Rqd.char.when controlling char.rejected
4 Skip
6 Transfer Characteristic to Subsystem

**Figure 7.13** Characteristic Status

When you call the RECORD RESULTS screen, the GENERAL tab is activated, and the RESULT column is ready for entries. You can begin recording the characteristic results.

### Attributive Characteristic Results

This example provides for the confirmation of attributive (qualitative) characteristic results. If you want to record qualitative results, you can only record the evaluation "Acceptance"/"Rejection" or the more differentiated evaluation by using the catalog for characteristic attributes. Figure 7.14 contains an example of a simplified characteristic catalog.

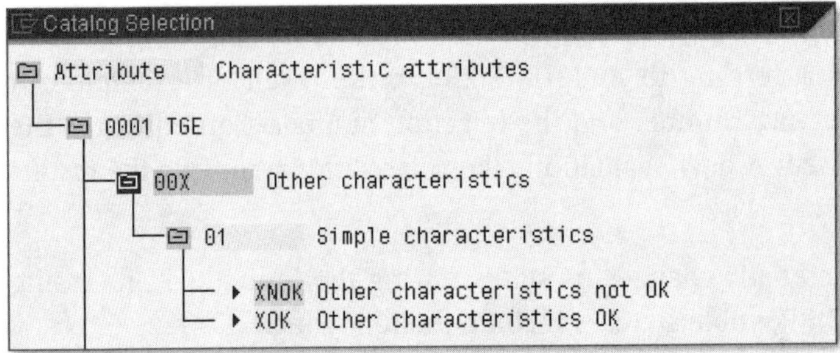


**Figure 7.14** Simple Catalog for Characteristic Attributes

However, in case of failure, the information "Other characteristics not OK" is not very informative. Therefore, a more meaningful catalog should be used. Figure 7.15 shows an example of this.

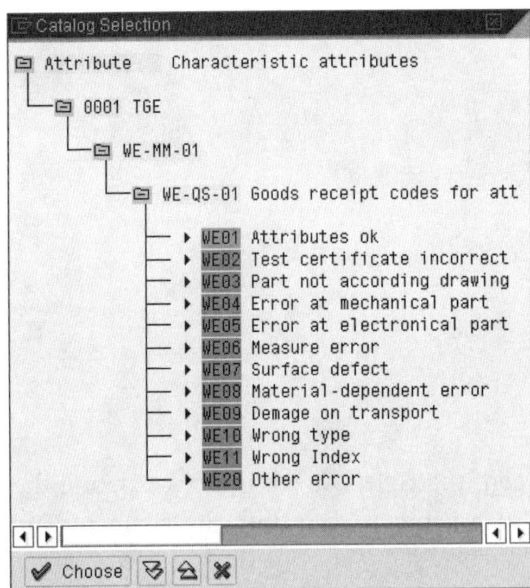


**Figure 7.15** Catalog for Characteristic Attributes with Error Type Specification

You can save an inspection description for each characteristic as additional information.

When making entries in the CHARACTERISTIC OVERVIEW screen, the specification of the quantity to be inspected is also used as the inspected quantity. However, especially for units with nonconforming characteristics, it is worth knowing the number of samples that contain the defect. To record this information, you need to select the characteristic by highlighting it and following the menu path EDIT • CHARACTERISTIC • CHOOSE or by double-clicking on it. This selection brings you to the CHARACTERISTIC SINGLE SCREEN screen, and you can enter the exact quantity for INSPECTED and NON-CONFORMING.

An example of the CD lid characteristic "width" is shown in Figure 7.16. In this example, instead of the required eight pieces, only seven pieces were inspected. This means that upon completion, the message "The inspected sample scope does not match the planned scope" is triggered. However, this warning can be skipped by using the FORCE function. This message is triggered by the control indicator for the inspection characteristic FIXED INSPECTION SCOPE.

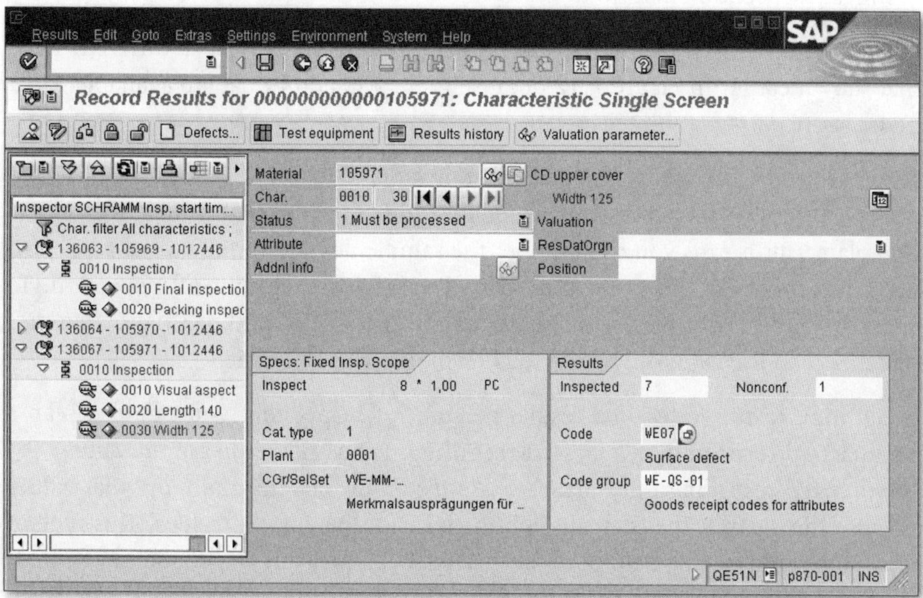


Figure 7.16 Characteristic Single Screen

Processing of the characteristics must be completed at the end of the results recording. This task can be carried out for each individual characteristic or for all characteristics together. First select all characteristics, and then select the menu EDIT • CHARACTERISTIC • CLOSE.

If not all characteristics have been confirmed, or if the quantity inspected is different from the specification (as in Figure 7.16), you will obtain a notification. You can skip this message and force the completion. If no error code has been specified for a characteristic, and you force the completion, the system requires you to decide whether the characteristic is to be saved as accepted or rejected. This entry is important in enabling the system to make specific suggestions for the usage decision, as you will see.

#### Quantitative Characteristic Results

In contrast to the attributive (qualitative) characteristic results for quantitative (variable) characteristics, you can also confirm specific measured values. In this context, it is also possible to include both qualitative and quantitative characteristics in an inspection operation.

For quantitative characteristics, the CHARACTERISTIC OVERVIEW is different from that shown earlier in Figure 7.12 because there's an additional tab available: UNIT OF INSPECTION.

The reason for this is that the control indicator INDIVIDUAL RESULT was selected under RESULT CONFIRMATION during the creation of the characteristic in the inspection plan. This means you can number the sample devices serially (or use an existing serial number) and enter a measured value for each unit of inspection. To enter the measured values, you should use the SINGLE VALUES FOR CHARACTERISTICS screen. To do this, you only need to click on the characteristic.

In addition to the individual results per unit of inspection, you can also plan a summarized recording or a classed recording. For variable measured values, the summarized recording only makes sense if you do not need any original values because the mean value is created on the basis of the entered values. This type of recording could also be helpful if, for instance, you measure the diameter of a shaft at several points, but only the mean value is to be documented. A classed recording can be useful if you plan an evaluation with the histogram because the planned measured-value classes are also used to display the histogram.

Let us take the example of the CD cover, described in previous chapters, in which the characteristic "0010 length" is created as a quantitative characteristic, Figure 7.17 shows entry values for a sample of seven units. By closing the variable characteristic, a few evaluations take place, which you can also see in Figure 7.17. First, the result is evaluated with regard to acceptance/rejection. As all measured values were located within the required tolerances, the evaluation was completed with ACCEPTANCE (indicated on your screen by a green checkmark). In addition, the fields were correspondingly set with INSPECTED and NON-CONFORMING, and the mean value and standard deviation were calculated. In addition, the HISTOGRAM function was called to display the standard distribution according to the measured values. In addition, you can also calculate and display the process capability indices cp and cpk.

For Figure 7.17, the SAP Easy Access display was selected. In this display, all information is displayed in one screen. Of course, this requires a correspondingly large monitor and a higher resolution. However, the options from older releases are also still available, in which the information is displayed in several overlapping windows on the screen. You can thus select your preferred display form by specifying the type of access in the menu tree.

Another way to display quantitatively recorded individual values is the *run chart*, which displays the run of the measured values of a characteristic as a curve. There, you can identify trends and the situation in relation to tolerance limits, although no action limits are displayed.

In many cases, these evaluation and display options should be sufficient and eliminate the need for an external statistical program. In those cases where the requirements for statistical evaluation are higher, the SAP statistical interface (QM STI) provides the option of further processing the data with an external statistical software.

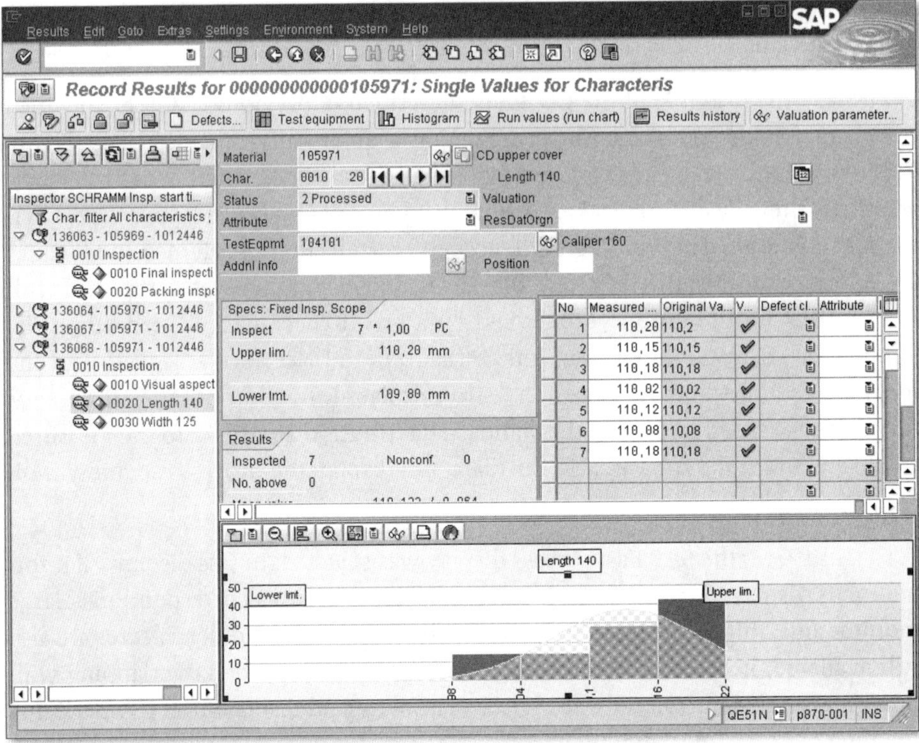


**Figure 7.17** Recording Screen for Individual Characteristic Values

> **Tip**
>
> If you must record the measured values as quantitative inspection results only occasionally, you can make the entries manually via the keyboard. However, if this occurs frequently, a keyboard wedge is advisable. You can directly connect test equipment to it and transfer measured values directly in the input screen. For further information, refer to Section 7.10, Interfaces to External Systems and Measurement Devices.
>
> As is the case with the attributive characteristics, you also can force completion for quantitative characteristics without having entered any measured values. The system then displays a warning message and asks if the characteristic should be accepted or rejected.

### Required and Optional Characteristics

In inspection planning, you can use the control indicators of the inspection characteristics to determine whether results recording is mandatory (required characteristic) or optional (optional characteristic). In the results-recording screen, this is indicated by the status of the characteristic (0 = optional characteristic). The processing doesn't need to be completed; completion is absolutely necessary only for required characteristics.

In an enhanced hierarchy tree of the results-recording worklist, you can recognize on your screen the status of the characteristics also from the color. Required characteristics are displayed in yellow, and optional characteristics are displayed in light blue (Transaction QE51).

### Unplanned Characteristics

You might want sometimes to record results for a characteristic that was not provided for in the inspection plan. To do this, you enter a new characteristic in the results recording. However, there is a little snag to it: You can only enter master characteristics.

**Tip**

You can simply create a master inspection characteristic called "Other characteristic" and enter this as required as an additional characteristic.

Provided you have already created this master characteristic, from the EDIT menu of the RECORD RESULTS: CHARACTERISTIC OVERVIEW screen, call the CREATE ADDITIONAL CHARACTERISTIC item. Enter the source code for the master-inspection characteristic. The system then requests the sample procedure for this new characteristic, and you can then use it for results recording.

### Results Recording Using Control Charts 

In the QM module, you can use the following types of control charts (see Figure 7.18):

- Mean-value chart considering tolerance values (acceptance chart)
- Shewhart chart for the mean value
- Shewhart chart for the standard deviation

The type of control chart used is established during the inspection planning of the characteristics and the sampling procedures used. You can specify whether a separate control chart is to be used for each inspection lot or whether you want to use a control chart for several inspection lots.

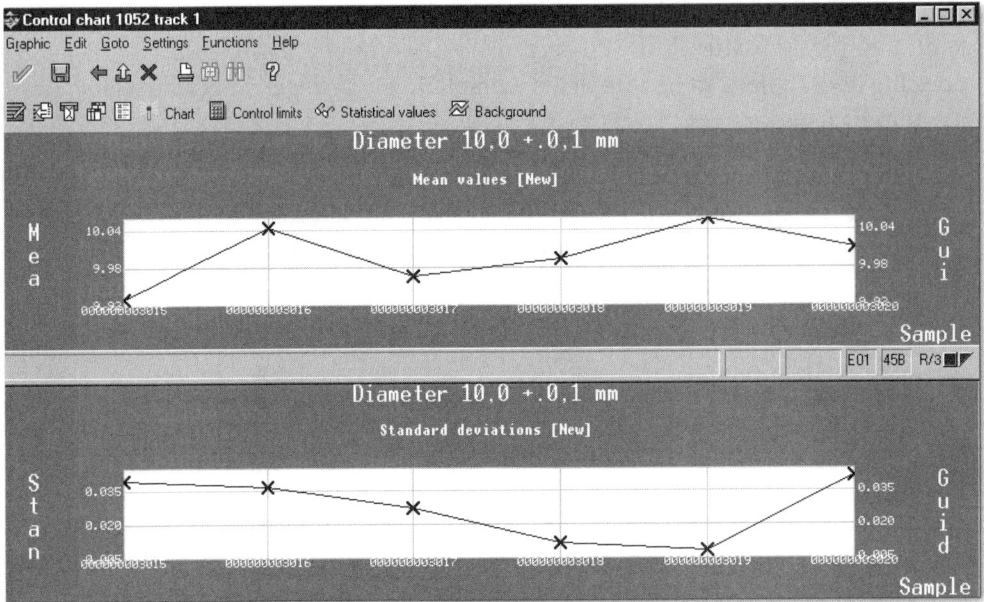


**Figure 7.18** Example of an Acceptance Chart for Mean Values and Standard Deviation

When the inspection lots are created, the control chart numbers are created automatically for the characteristics for which a control chart has been provided. In results recording, you can then enter measured values for these control charts, whereby for each track of the chart, a specific graphic window is opened. These windows display the results already recorded from the previous inspection lots and the newly entered ones. Depending on the settings, either the system calculates the action and warning limits from the initial run or from the measured results, or you specify these.

The evaluation of the results recording can take place automatically. If, for instance, the action limits are exceeded or not reached, the characteristic is rejected. You can also manually run the evaluation.

If you want to complete a control chart, this can be done in almost the same way as the completion of an inspection characteristic. In the next inspection lot, a new control chart is opened with a new number. You should not complete the control chart if it is to be used again for the next lots.

### Inspecting Without a Plan

Until now, the descriptions were based on the assumption that the inspections are carried out on the basis of an inspection plan. However, this is not absolutely necessary. In the inspection data for the material concerned (in the material master), you can also omit the checkmark for INSPECT WITH PLAN, and then an inspection without a plan is also possible. While sampling procedure per characteristic is specified for inspections with a plan, this procedure must be entered in the inspection data for inspections without a plan.

With these settings, for instance, you can create an inspection lot at goods receipt. Unfortunately, this inspection lot is not contained in the results-recording worklist because only inspection lots with characteristics are displayed there. However, because no plan exists, there are no characteristics for which a result should be recorded.

For such an inspection lot, you must go directly to INSPECTION LOTS WITHOUT USAGE DECISION without confirming inspection results. Therefore, in the input screen for the usage decision, only the two tabs, DEFECTS and INSPECTION LOT STOCK, are available. Of course, you can record defects for the usage decision (inspection lot), as described in Section 7.3.2, Defects. However, these can only be defects in the inspection lot and not on the operation or characteristic because these are only possible during an inspection with a plan.

### Evaluations

After you have completed a characteristic, it is evaluated, and a decision is made on its acceptance or rejection. The evaluation is indicated on your screen with a green checkmark (acceptance) or a red X (rejection). You can set different types of evaluation:

- Manual evaluation
- Evaluation based on codes from the catalog of characteristic attributes
- Evaluation based on nonconforming units or the number of defects
- Evaluation based on the tolerance range of variable characteristics
- Evaluation based on the violation of action limits for quality control charts

If an automatic evaluation is provided for but cannot be executed — if, for example, no characteristics or too few characteristic results were confirmed — an input window appears with the request to carry out a manual evaluation.

### 7.3.2 Defects

The recording of characteristic results as measured values, or via the attribute code of the characteristic catalog, is also referred to as planned characteristic results. In contrast to this, unplanned characteristic results represent the creation of a defect-data record. This is not to be confused with the negative characteristic results reflected in the characteristic catalog. The entry of defects represents an independent process that opens further options. It is, for instance, ideally suited to meet the standard requirements of ISO 9000 with regard to carrying out corrective and preventive measures.

Defects can be created at different stages of results recording for the inspection lot. Thus, a distinction is made among the following defects:

- Defect for characteristic
- Defect for operation
- Defect for inspection lot

Let's now run through the creation of a defect-data record in the case of "Defect for characteristic" to describe the options of this instrument.

In the RECORD RESULTS: CHARACTERISTIC OVERVIEW screen for each characteristic, you can see a paper symbol in the DEFECT FOR CHARACTERISTIC column. As soon as you click on this symbol, the input screen for the defect recording is called. You can also call the screen via the menu structure. Select the EDIT menu, and under DEFECT you find the three listed defect input options.

Before entering a defect, you will first be prompted to select a defect code from Catalog 9, DEFECT TYPES. This is a different catalog than Catalog 1, CHARACTERISTIC ATTRIBUTES, which you know already from recording the characteristic results. The advantage of this type of defect recording is obvious: for each characteristic, you can enter several DEFECTS, the respective NUMBER OF DEFECTS, and a descriptive TEXT. You can see an example in Figure 7.19.

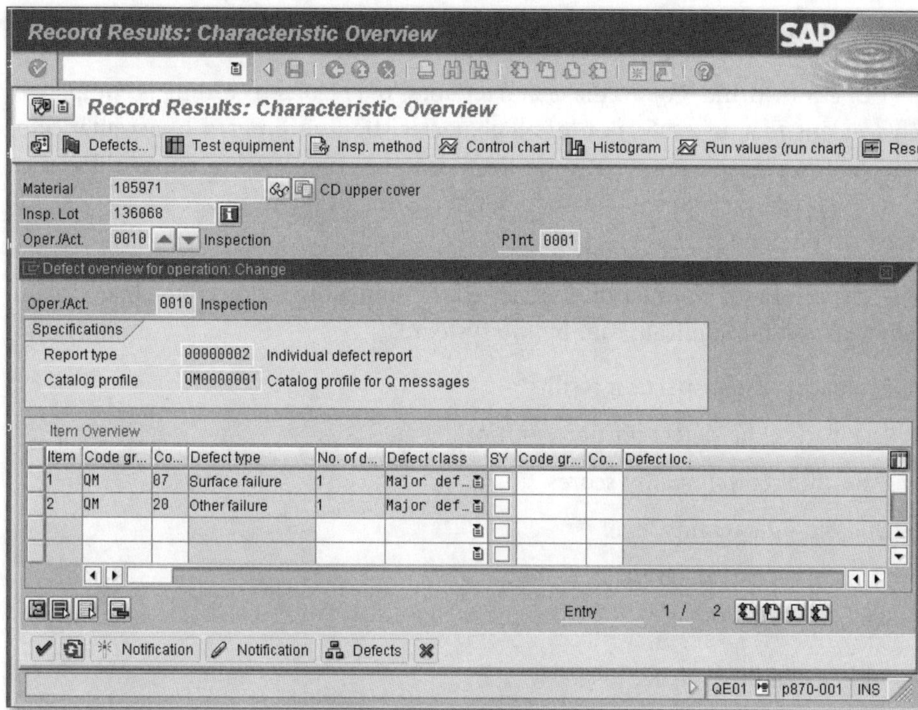


**Figure 7.19** Defect Recording for the Characteristic

**Tip**

It has been proven in practice that you can design defect catalogs for the characteristic attributes and the defect types in the same way because each characteristic that is not okay also can be assigned a defect type.

Finally, at every level of the defect creation, you can activate a quality notification manually as well as automatically. This means you can inform an internal or external partner quickly about defects that have emerged. If several defects were recorded, for instance for different characteristics and for the operation, the quality notification contains a list of these defects. The automatic creation of a quality notification should be used with caution because it is through this setting that a large quantity of created notifications emerges in the system, which must be systematically processed. In real life, the manual creation of the quality notification for a defect has proven to be the most reliable option. Additional details on the subject can be found in Chapter 9, Quality Notification.

## 7.4 Inspection-Lot Completion

By COMPLETING and SAVING the characteristics, the results recording is completed. This means that an evaluation of all characteristics with regard to acceptance or rejection is available. For the inspection lot to be completed, the usage decision, and, for stock-relevant inspection lots, the posting of the inspection lot stock, still needs to be done.

The inspection-lot completion is assigned the following actions, which are manually taken or automatically run by the system:

- Evaluating the inspection results
- Calculating the defect portions per lot
- Determining the quality scores
- Updating the quality level
- Making a usage decision
- Posting the stock
- Calculating the inspection costs
- Updating the key figures in the QM information system

Because some of the actions mentioned in the preceding list are directly related to the tasks of quality control, these will be described in detail in Chapter 8, Quality Control.

#### Inspection Results

To reach an informed usage decision with regard to an inspection lot, you must know the inspection results. The RECORD USAGE DECISION screen provides all of the information needed to make the decision in the following tabs:

- CHARACTERISTIC (see Figure 7.20)
- DEFECTS
- INSPECTION LOT STOCK (insofar as the lot is relevant to the stock)
- INSPECTION POINTS (provided that inspection points have been planned)

By double-clicking on individual characteristics, you can display additional details of the characteristic results, and you can read inspection descriptions.

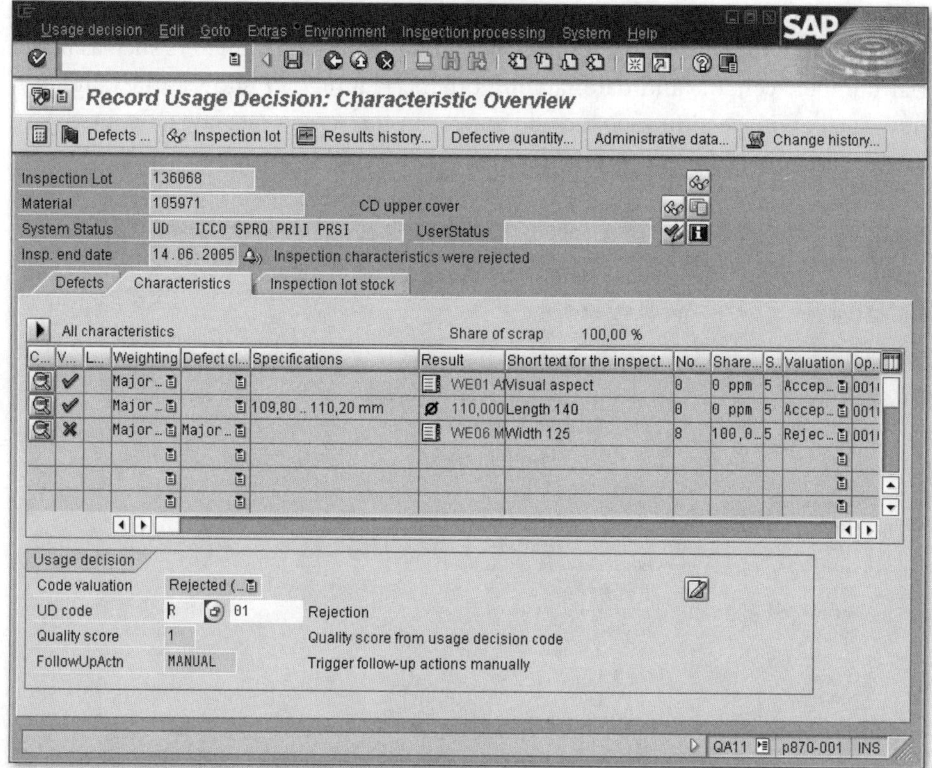

Figure 7.20 Usage Decision Screen with Characteristic Results

## Inspection Report

The inspection report displays the inspection results and comments on every characteristic on the screen or in the form of a printout. This means it can also be used to provide an overview of the inspection carried out, or it can be referred to as a basis for the usage decision. It can also serve as an attachment to a quality notification to the vendor or to internal departments to describe in detail the deviations of individual characteristics according to type and scope in the case of defects.

To display the inspection report, select the following path from the menu tree: QUALITY INSPECTION • INFO SYSTEM • INSPECTION RESULT • PRINT. Then the RESULTS PRINT selection screen is shown.

If the inspection lot number is known, you can enter it directly. Otherwise, the selection allows you to make limitations through known parameters such as material number, vendor, and date, among others. Figure 7.21 shows an example of how such an inspection report could appear in the screen display. Of course, you can also print out this inspection report.

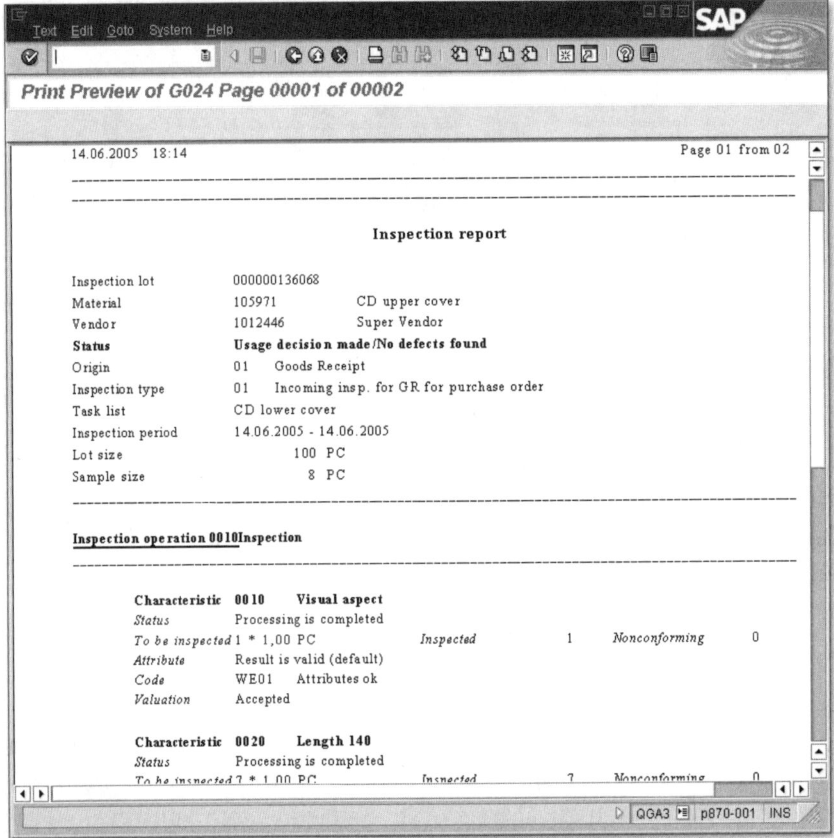


Figure 7.21 Inspection Report

## 7.5 Inspection Costs

The consideration of quality-related costs also belongs to the tasks of quality management. In many companies, these costs can form an essential part of the expenses. By recording and evaluating quality-related costs, a company can initiate improvements that increase efficiency and profitability.

Quality-related costs are usually divided into the following categories:

- Inspection costs
- Prevention costs
- Nonconformity costs

The collection and evaluation of costs in companies is carried out in the Controlling module (CO). In that module, the quality-related costs that were recorded in the QM module as inspection and nonconformity costs are merged and can be formatted for quality evaluation. There are different order categories to record costs from the different applications in CO. For example, to record costs from QM, the QM order with order category 06 is provided. The QM orders are then once again divided into the following types (see Figure 7.22):

- General QM order for inspection costs (one order for several materials/inspection lots)
- Individual QM order for inspection costs (one order for a specific inspection lot)
- QM order for nonconformity costs (one order for a quality notification)

The inspection costs cannot be directly specified in monetary amounts. They are instead calculated on the basis of confirmed performance times achieved for the inspection operation in the CO module from the scales set. As in work scheduling, the performance times are compiled from time and labor data, set-up times, and machine times. The confirmation of performance occurs with the results recording or the usage decision. In production, it is carried out together with the confirmations of the production order.

The nonconformity costs are recorded with the processing of the quality notification. For this reason, the QM order must be created manually as a cost collector in the quality notification. In this order, which is assigned to the notification header, you can record the costs such as rework costs, sorting costs, or warranty costs. This way, you can determine all types of nonconformity costs related to the quality notification and, if necessary, charge the person responsible and analyze the costs in CO.

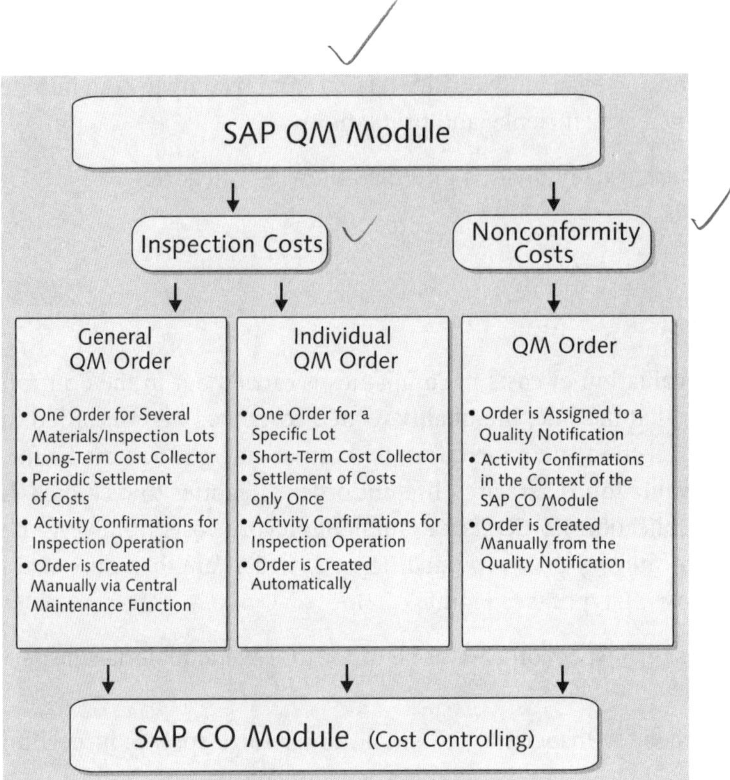


**Figure 7.22** Recording Quality-Related Costs

The prevention costs, which mainly include training measures, are recorded through the Human Resource (HR) component.

## 7.6 Sample Management

In the process industries (e.g., chemical, pharmaceutical, and food industries), the withdrawal and management of physical samples is very important. The generation of physical samples can be necessary at goods receipt or during production. The requirements of Good Manufacturing Practice (GMP) in the process industries are met with sample management.

The system supports the following types of sample generation:

- Automatic generation of physical samples during inspection-lot creation

- Manual generation of physical samples (if needed, with reference to an inspection lot)
- Manual generation of inspection lots for existing physical samples

### Sample Data Record

For each physical sample, a physical-sample record is created, which contains the following essential information:

- Sample number
- Sample type (from GR, from production, from customer complaints)
- Physical-sample category (primary sample, pooled sample, reserve sample)
- Sample origin (material, batch, order)
- Detail data

### Planned Physical Samples

If the physical samples are planned in a sample-drawing procedure, they are automatically generated during inspection-lot creation. The sample-drawing procedure determines how many samples are to be drawn, the scope of the samples, whether the sample drawing is to be confirmed, and what physical-sample category is to be used. This procedure is logically assigned to the inspection plan or routing. When the physical sample is generated, a sample-drawing instruction can also be printed out with the inspection-lot creation, which contains detailed information on how the sample is to be drawn.

The following physical-sample categories are available for selection:

- **Primary sample**
  The primary sample is drawn directly from a material/batch stock. You can inspect these samples or create pooled samples from them.
- **Pooled sample**
  This sample is created by mixing other physical samples from the same material/batch.
- **Reserve sample**
  The reserve sample is drawn from a material/batch stock and stored for other inspections.

If the material is supplied in different physical-sample containers, you can store corresponding instructions depending on the physical-sample container.

### Unplanned Physical Samples

In the context of sample management, it can also be necessary to draw physical samples that were not planned. This can be done in two different ways:

- You can manually generate an entirely new physical sample.
- You can manually generate a physical sample for an existing physical-sample record.

### Manual Inspection Lots

For each existing physical sample, you can also create manual inspection lots. These can, for instance, perform additional inspections for reserve samples or for samples that were not accepted by the customer. As already described in Section 7.2, Inspection-Lot Creation, no stocks can be managed with manual inspection lots.

### Confirmation

In the sample-drawing procedure, you can determine whether automatically created physical samples are to be released automatically or manually (confirmed). Upon confirmation of a physical-sample drawing, all corresponding physical samples are released. Under the security aspects of GMP, a manual confirmation can be required. In addition, there is the option of entering a digital signature, which ensures that only authorized employees can execute certain activities (e.g., the confirmation). Manually created physical samples must always be confirmed manually.

### Label Printing

For automatically created physical samples, you can print out labels for the samples. You can create these labels according to your requirements and ideas, and you can print details, such as name, date, time, batch, sample number, and inspection-lot number, and even add a barcode. Of course, you can also manually trigger label printing for the sample data record.

### Results Entry and Usage Decision

The results recording for the physical sample is done in the same way as the inspection lot results recording. The physical samples are located in a specific results recording worklist (related to the work center or the user) and can be processed from there. One or several physical samples can exist per inspection lot. Only when all physical samples for an inspection lot have been processed and evaluated can you make a usage decision for the inspection lot. Unplanned (manually created) physical samples must first be manually released (confirmed) before you can record results.

## 7.7 Quality Inspection in Sales and Distribution

Inspection-lot generation and results recording in SD is only slightly different from the procedures in MM. Instead of generating the inspection lot for goods receipt, the inspection lots are generated at goods issue, for specific goods movements (e.g., for a return), or for a customer complaint. There is also the option here to manually create inspection lots.

The inspection-lot generation can also be connected to the material or customer so that the agreed inspections are only executed for specific customers or materials. Results recording in SD corresponds to the process already described.

### Certificates

Different customers require specific certificates, for example, on properties warranted, material quality, works test certificates, or inspection proof. You can configure the system so that these certificates are automatically generated for the respective customers and deliveries, and are automatically printed out or faxed.

## 7.8 Quality Inspection in Production

Regarding the essential processes, quality inspection in production basically corresponds to that in MM. There are, however, a few important differences.

Inspection in production is based on the idea that inspections executed during the production process are your own responsibility (operator inspection). Therefore, quality inspection in production is integrated in production planning and execution. As we already described in Chapter 6, Quality and Inspection Planning, the operations of quality inspection in production are contained in the routing. The inspection operations are not basically different from other production processes in the routing. It is only at the next level, at which the inspection operations are also assigned inspection characteristics, sampling procedures, and characteristic catalogs, that the additional functionality of the QM module opens up. You can see an example of a routing with an inspection operation in Figure 7.23.

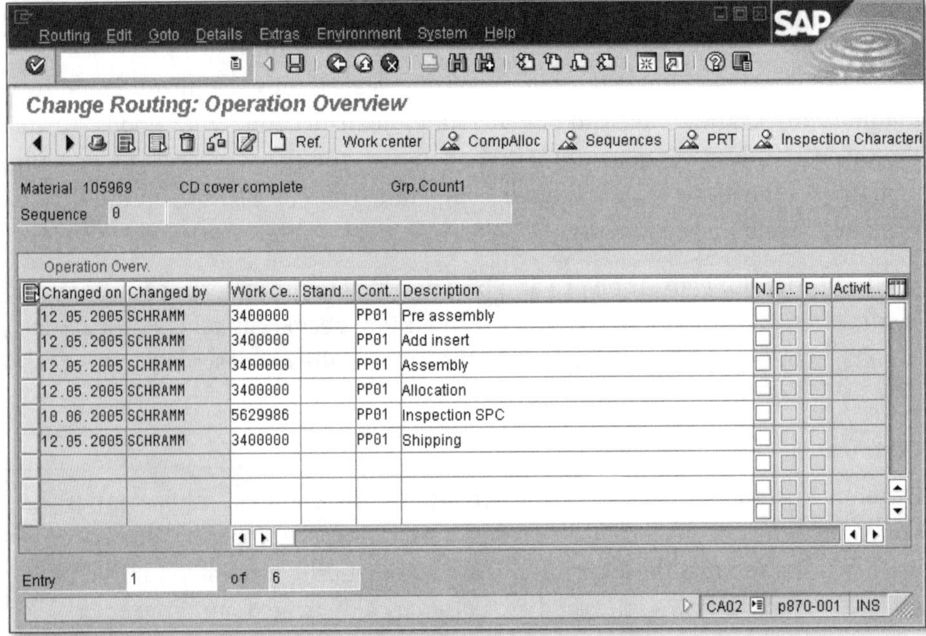


**Figure 7.23** Routing with Inspection Operation

The release of a production order generates the inspection lots for the inspection operations. The entire quantity can also be split into partial lots. The inspection documents (sample-drawing instructions and inspection instructions) are printed out together with the shop floor papers. Due to the sequence of inspection steps in the routing, you can map both in-process inspections and final inspections.

Inspection lots for production can be created manually, as well as through goods movements or a GR from production.

The integration of inspections in the routings requires a close collaboration between inspection planning and work scheduling, provided this is not done by a central authority or a responsible person. In the production operation "Inspection," the test equipment is displayed as a production/resource tool. Separate inspection plans are not required.

The inspection results are confirmed in the same way for each inspection lot and inspection characteristic as already described. Here, inspection in production is the same as inspection in the other applications.

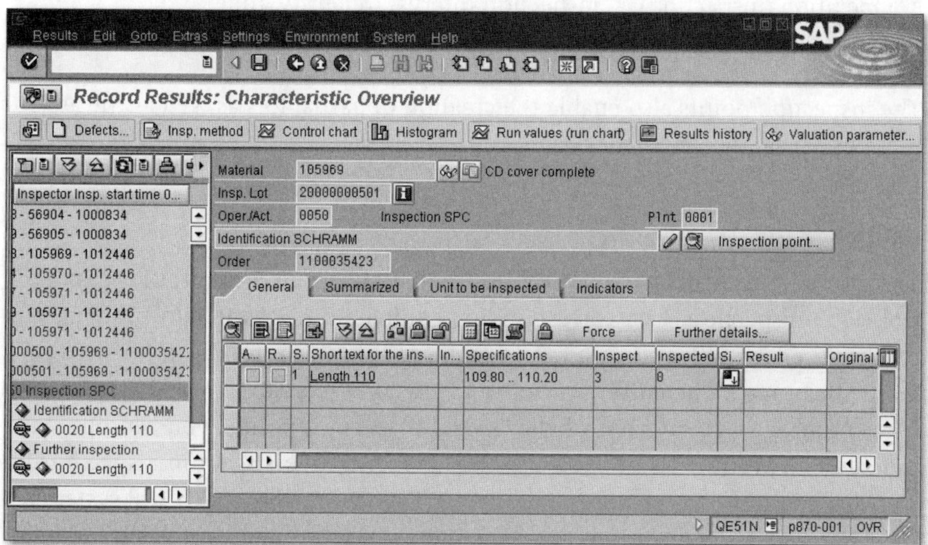


**Figure 7.24** Results Recording for a Production Order

The inspection completion is also accompanied by a usage decision (see also Chapter 8, Quality Control); although the quantity confirmation does not occur in the usage decision but rather in the production order for the respective operation. You enter the relevant quantities To Unrestricted, To Rework or To Scrap. You have the options of partial confirmation, final confirmation, and automatic final confirmation. Thus, you can first inspect a part of the production lot and confirm this, and at later time, inspect and confirm the rest (final confirmation).

### Inspection Points

If you want to perform inspections at specific time intervals, at specific points in time, after the production of specific production quantities, or in response to specific events, you need inspection points. Such events can, for instance, include a change of containers for finished goods or a shift change. A typical reason for the implementation of inspection points would be the hourly inspection of a sample from running production.

For the implementation, at least the following entries are required in the routing:

- Planning header — parameters for inspection points
- Operation (inspection) — inspection interval (quantity, time)
- Characteristic — sample size (fixed size)

The inspection points also enable the creation of partial lots as well as the assignment of partial lots to batches.

### Control Charts

Typically, the control chart is used in production in the Statistical Process Control (SPC) inspection. In a corresponding configuration of the QM module, you can use the SAP ERP system as an instrument for SPC in production. By using a direct measured value entry (see Section 7.10, Interfaces to External Systems and Measurement Devices), control charts, and inspection points, you can optimally monitor the production process without having to invest again in a specific SPC software solution. You can use the existing IT structure of the SAP ERP system for the measured-value recording in production, which will help you keep the hardware costs within reasonable limits.

Section 7.3.1, Characteristic Results, contains more information on control charts. You will find a detailed section on the subject of SPC in Chapter 8, Quality Control.

### Batches

If you intend to implement batch management for your materials, you can assign batches to the partial lots or summarize several partial lots to a batch. The inspection results of the partial lots can be directly forwarded to the batch and used for the batch classification and for direct creation of quality certificates.

**Tip**

To transfer inspection results to the batch classification, a material specification must also be maintained for the material that is subject to batch management requirements.

### Inspection in the QA Department

If your company's independent inspections are planned in a quality assurance department (QA), this can be mapped without any problem. Inspection lots can also be created in production via goods movements. This means a goods movement leads directly to an inspection lot, or you can manually create such a lot, provided you have customized it correspondingly.

As inspection in this case is separated from production planning, you must set an inspection type and a relevant plan usage in the system. In addition, an inspection plan must be created with this plan usage. For instance, Inspection Type 04, which is available in the standard version, is suitable (GR from production).

This scenario is more or less similar to GR for purchase orders. As previously described, the results are recorded for the planned characteristics.

**Example**

The process of an operator inspection is illustrated using an example from the company's own plastics-molding plant. The following assumptions are made here:

- A plastic part is molded in your own production (production by lot size).
- The quality inspection is active for the material.
- Attributive characteristics for an inspection operation exist in the context of a plant operator inspection.
- The release of the production order automatically creates an inspection lot.

Consequently, this inspection lot must be available in the worklist. Therefore, you select the selection screen for RESULTS RECORDING, as it was described in Section 7.3, Results Recording. To restrict the inspection list to the data that originate from production, it is useful to first enter the inspection lot origin in the selection screen (03, PRODUCTION).

If you compare Figure 7.25 with the worklist from MM (refer to Figure 7.10), you will see that there is essentially no difference between the two apart from the number range of the inspection lot numbers. Further inspection and results confirmation are also quite similar in both worklists. Therefore, refer to the corresponding process in Section 7.3.1, Characteristic Results.

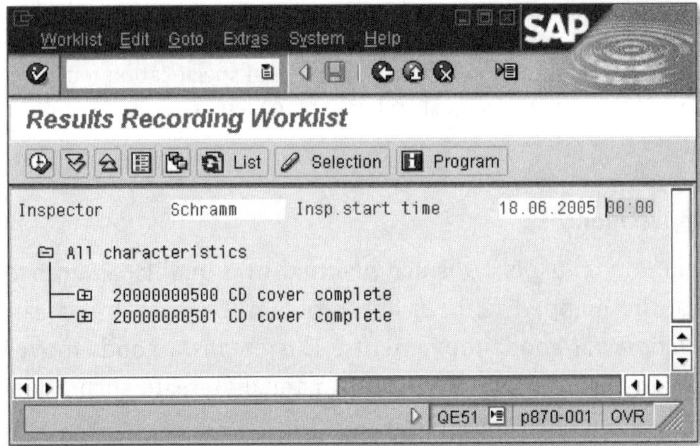


**Figure 7.25** Example of a Worklist of Inspection Lots from Production

## 7.9 Quality Inspection in Procurement

Now that we have covered the processes in MM, we describe in more detail two specific scenarios that can occur on a daily basis.

> **Scenario**
>
> Changing the status of a material upon goods receipt from "subject to quality inspection" to "not subject to quality inspection."

Let's look at the following situation: An eager colleague maintained some materials as "subject to quality inspection" in the SAP ERP system, although they are not to be inspected. This defect is not noticed at first. The purchaser can create its purchase order without a problem and send it out. One day, there is a delivery of material, such as a pallet of toilet paper, and immediately upon the GR posting, the goods are in the inspection stock. Depending on the configuration of the system, an inspection lot is generated directly. At the latest, when someone wants to take the toilet paper from the warehouse stock, they will notice that it is located in the inspection stock and was incorrectly provided for a GR inspection.

To salvage the situation, a usage decision is made for the current inspection lot, and the goods are posted from the inspection stock into "unrestricted stock." This means the goods are available and can be withdrawn. To ensure that this unwanted inspection lot does not cause incorrect key figures, the inspection lot is canceled, which can be easily done via INSPECTION LOT • USAGE DECISION • CHANGE WITH OR W/O HISTORY and USAGE DECISION • FUNCTIONS • CANCEL LOT.

To correct this defect for subsequent deliveries, it is sufficient to set the inspection type as inactive in the quality management view of the material by unchecking the ACTIVE field. If the inspection type is no longer active, the material is no longer subject to quality inspection. Because it does not make sense to keep the inspection type in the quality management view of such a material master, it is even better to delete the inspection type entirely.

In some circumstances, this may not be sufficient. If a larger quantity was ordered by purchasing, and only a partial quantity is delivered due to a scheduling agreement schedule, this means that the same problem will occur again at the next GR, and it will happen even if the inspection type was deleted in the meantime! The explanation for this is that the respective time validity periods must be taken into account. The purchase order is based on whether the material is subject to quality inspection at the time of the purchase order. If the material, as in this case, is later changed to "not subject to quality inspection," this does not in turn affect the current purchase order but rather affects purchase orders that are newly created.

The reverse scenario is also not unusual. Let's assume that after the posting of a GR, you find out that this material should actually always undergo a GR inspection. To ensure that the following scenario of a catch-up GR inspection also makes sense, it is assumed that the goods are still available, so that on the one hand a sample can still be drawn, and on the other hand, the goods can be blocked due to a negative inspection result.

**Tip**

If a material that was planned for quality inspection is changed so that it is no longer subject to quality inspection, you should check whether open purchase orders exist for this material. If this is the case, the change only affects new purchase orders. However, if you want this change to take effect immediately, the current purchase order must be changed. To do this, you must uncheck the QUALITY INSPECTION field in the CHANGE PURCHASE ORDER menu and save the purchase order. Before you do this, the inspection type in the quality view of the material master must be set to inactive.

**Scenario**

Changing the status of a material upon goods receipt from "not subject to quality inspection" to "subject to quality inspection."

The solution to this scenario is quite simple: You perform the required actions for inspection planning for this material afterwards, then cancel the GR and carry a new GR posting. The change from "not subject to quality inspection" to "subject to quality inspection" takes immediate effect here. In other words, the new GR posting now generates an inspection lot, and the goods are posted to the inspection stock. This also applies to all other purchase orders and GRs, as long as you do not undo the inspection planning settings.

## 7.10 Interfaces to External Systems and Measurement Devices

Entering measured values via the keyboard is probably the simplest method but certainly not the most economic solution. This depends on a company's internal prerequisites and the conditions on site.

SAP ERP provides interfaces for specific tasks for quality inspection and control, through which additional, external systems can be connected to the QM module. To determine if such a connection is required, you should clarify the following issues:

- How frequently do you have to record measured values?
- Is digital measurement equipment already being used?
- Which statistical evaluations are required?
- Does the measurement data entry take place in a rough environment (production hall, processing center) or in a laboratory?
- Are there already systems for measurement data entry or evaluation in use, for example, Computer Aided Quality Assurance (CAQ), SPC, or Laboratory Information and Management (LIM)?

After you have clarified these issues, analyzed the operational prerequisites, and defined the resulting requirements, one of the following solution options can be of use:

- Measured value processing in the SAP ERP system
- Inspection processing in an external CAQ or LIM system
- Online measurement data entry
- External statistics program

### Measured Value Processing in the SAP ERP System

With regard to system integration, the complete results recording and further processing in the SAP ERP system is the optimal solution. Provided that the numerous evaluation options in the QM module meet their requirements, you must make sure that the measurement results are transferred to the system. For attributive characteristic results for an inspection plan, codes from a characteristic catalog must be entered. The simplest way of doing this is to use the keyboard. The variable measurement results can be transferred by using a direct connection to a piece of digital test equipment. The simplest solution here is an interface box (keyboard wedge), which is available on the supplies market for this reason. This box is interposed between the keyboard and the computer, and it is connected with the test equipment. This means you can enter a measured value via your keyboard, or you can transfer it directly from the digital-testing device to the computer. Such test equipment can include digital calipers, indicating calipers, barcode readers, or electrical multimeters with interfaces. An advantage of this low-priced solution is that it neither makes changes to the system nor requires additional software because the keyboard entry is only simulated (see Figure 7.26).

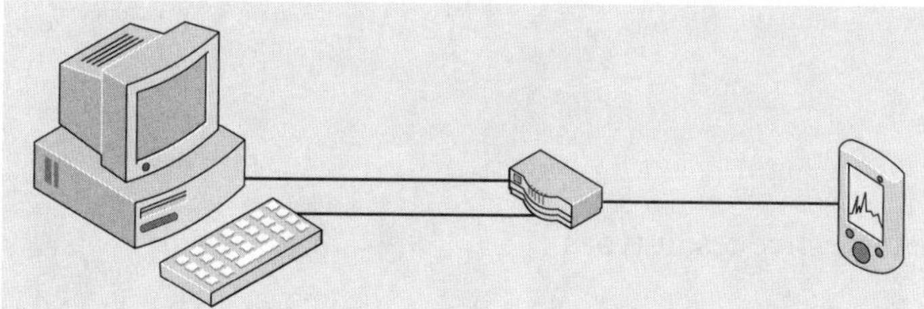

**Figure 7.26** Test Equipment Connection Using a Keyboard Wedge

### Inspection Processing with the QM IDI Interface

If you want to continue using an existing external CAQ system, this is also possible. These systems are connected through the QM IDI (Inspection Data Interface) provided in the SAP ERP system. Physically, this can be done via a local area network (LAN) or through the serial interface of a client PC. Corresponding drivers are installed in the SAP ERP system (host) and in the client computer.

The task sharing between the SAP ERP system and the CAQ system might appear as follows:

- The integrated functions are processed in the SAP ERP system (e.g., inspection costs, usage decisions, quantity postings, stock types).
- The inspection operations and measured values are processed in the subsystem.

By using an RFC (Remote Function Call), the data can be exchanged with the subsystem in both directions. If data is transferred to the external system, this process is referred to as a *download*. The following information is relevant for the download:

- Worklist (open inspection lots for a work center)
- Catalogs (characteristic attributes, defect types)
- Inspection plan data (operations, characteristics, inspection severity)

The following data can be relevant for the *upload*, that is, the transfer from the subsystem to the SAP ERP system:

- Individual results
- Characteristic results
- Sample results
- Inspection points
- Usage decisions
- Error codes for the respective result types

During processing in the CAQ system, the operation is locked in SAP QM. After the inspection has been processed in the subsystem, the results are confirmed in the SAP ERP system. The interface programs also check the data for consistency.

An external system can also be required, for instance, if very large quantities of measurement data accumulate. If measurements need to be carried out in a matter of seconds or fractions of seconds, this can only be done in the subsystem. There, the data is evaluated, and the results of the evaluation can trigger immediate actions (e.g., drop head halt). The aggregated data is then transferred at regular intervals (inspection points) to the SAP ERP system (e.g., mean value, minimum value, maximum value).

## 7.11 Connecting Complex External Measurement Systems

From a technical viewpoint, there are four different possible solutions for the connection of external measurement and analysis systems. These are described in more detail in the following sections.

### 7.11.1 Overview

The following solutions are available:

- Keyboard wedge
- Test equipment connection to the SAP GUI interface
- Subsystems with separate user interfaces
- Direct integration of inspection and analysis systems

Some of these solutions provide additional benefits in addition to the pure transfer of result values, for instance, the control of measurement processes based on SAP inspection planning guidelines, the integration of production control systems, the documentation of inspection processes and raw data in the Document Management System (DMS), or the connection of existing statistical databases.

In deciding if one of the solutions provided is selected or if measured values are manually entered in the SAP ERP screens, a costs-benefits analysis is generally carried out. The basis of this analysis is the subject of inspection frequency. The additional effort of manually entering data generates additional costs. A further decision criterion is the acceptance by the user. Most often, a legacy system is to be replaced whose user friendliness is the yardstick for the acceptance of the new solution. A third criterion is the probability of incorrect result values to be expected for a manual entry.

Among the solutions, there is a choice between standard products and individual developments. Both solutions enable an exact adjustment to production and laboratory conditions. Standard products generally offer a more extensive functionality and a higher degree of investment protection for the future.

### 7.11.2 Keyboard Wedge

When using the keyboard wedge, the user works with the SAP GUI entry screens. A measured value is imported into the entry screen field by pressing a key (e.g., by pressing a foot switch). Due to the keyboard wedge, the user doesn't need to enter the values manually.

A keyboard wedge is an interface box that is switched between the keyboard and the PC. The measurement devices and the foot switch, too, are connected to the interface box. Keyboard wedges are used for simple test equipment such as calipers or scales.

Using a keyboard wedge is a purely hardware-based solution for which only standard components are used. This guarantees future viability.

### 7.11.3 Test Equipment Drivers for SAP GUI

The user works with the SAP GUI entry screens. A measured value is requested by clicking a button in the screen. The measurement is performed, and the result is imported into the screen field. In this simple form, its use is comparable with that of a keyboard wedge. The advantage of this solution, however, is that it can be enhanced.

Some providers have expanded the functionality: For instance, there is a solution for gas chromatography and coordinate-measurement machines, which can also process extensive analysis results. When you click the button in the inspection unit view of the entry screen, the result values of all characteristics of the analysis of a unit to be inspected are imported in the screen fields. Another solution contains enhancements for controlling measurement devices, transferring analysis documents, and for enhanced traceability in the regulated environment.

The implementation in terms of software consists of two modules, a user exit inside the SAP software and a test equipment driver outside the SAP software. Both modules communicate with each other via RFCs. The data definitions of the interface between the two modules are not standardized and are not certifiable.

SAP consulting provides drivers for the interface boxes of two manufacturers. An individual solution can be created on this basis by SAP consulting. Some providers enable you to conclude standard maintenance agreements for this solution.

### 7.11.4 Subsystems with Separate User Interfaces

Many scenarios require a user interface that a worker, inspector, or laboratory assistant can use to execute an inspection by pressing just a few keys, often even without a mouse. In this case, you should use a subsystem with functions that are geared to and optimized for the inspection process. The operational processes of a subsystem can be flexibly adapted to different requirements.

When using a subsystem, a distribution of tasks between SAP ERP and the subsystem takes place in such a way that all planning functions are carried out with SAP GUI, whereas all executing functions are carried out with the subsystem. The results are generally stored in the SAP ERP database and are available there for an evaluation. Subsystems also contain evaluation options (e.g., SPC) and reporting functions.

Subsystems provide connections to all measurement devices and analysis systems. They contain a wide range of useful additional functions.

A subsystem works outside the SAP ERP software. SAP has defined the QM IDI for connecting subsystems and established it as a standard. The important providers have had their subsystems certified by SAP with regard to the QM IDI. In addition to this purely technical certification, SAP Germany has appointed a few providers as software partners. Standard maintenance contracts can be set up for subsystems.

### 7.11.5 Direct Integration of Inspection and Analysis Systems

Analysis systems and complex measurement devices are frequently controlled via a PC. Usually the PC is used to run the software of the analysis device manufacturer. These systems can also be directly connected to SAP ERP systems. The user then works exclusively with the familiar software and uses SAP without taking any notice of this fact.

The same functionality is used in automatic production lines. The subsystem then also performs tasks to coordinate the material flow in the line. Apart from communicating with QM, it also communicates with line controls and machine controls.

The direct connection to SAP is established via a variant of the subsystem. The functions of the subsystem work as already described but without the user interface.

### 7.11.6 Importing a Plan

The results logs of the analysis systems and inspection devices also contain information on the characteristics to be inspected, based on which routings and inspection plans can be generated in SAP ERP. Different subsystems contain an option with this functionality.

A results log can be used to create an inspection plan, and then to confirm results in the inspection lot generated from the plan. This process is used in many companies, where a programmer of the measurement program of a coordinate-measurement machine or the developer of the methods of an analysis device fixes the inspection characteristics.

Documents of the development department such as CAD models, inspection regulations, or control plans (according to ISO/TS 16949) can also serve as a basis for the inspection plans. A legacy system, a LIM system, or a CAQ system can also be used as a basis. Several thousand plans can be automatically imported very quickly.

## 7.12 Example

The following sections illustrate the usage options and the procedure on the basis of a sample company. They describe several implementation options that have been proven in practice.

### 7.12.1 Sample Company

The sample company is a manufacturer of fastening technology with two product areas: the manufacture of power tools (e.g., hand drills and accessories) and the production of adhesives.

The production processes in both areas are very different:

- The power tools area is a device production with mechanical and electrical components.
- The adhesive area corresponds to a chemical company in its analysis technology.

### 7.12.2 Quality Assurance in the Power Tools Area

A subarea produces mechanical and electrical components for power tools. Dimension inspections are executed on metal and plastic parts. The electrical components are inspected for their electrical parameters.

A final inspection of the completed devices completes the production process. The final inspection also contains criteria for the electrical security of the devices.

The in-process inspection is designed as an operator inspection. Several inspection islands are set up in the production hall, which are each responsible for several production lines. Test equipment (calipers, micrometers, measuring rods) and multiple point measuring fixtures are available in the inspection islands.

A subsystem is used as software. The operators execute the inspections in a simple dialog box on the PC. The characteristics to be inspected are displayed in workpiece drawings.

A typical inspection dialog box is displayed in Figure 7.27.

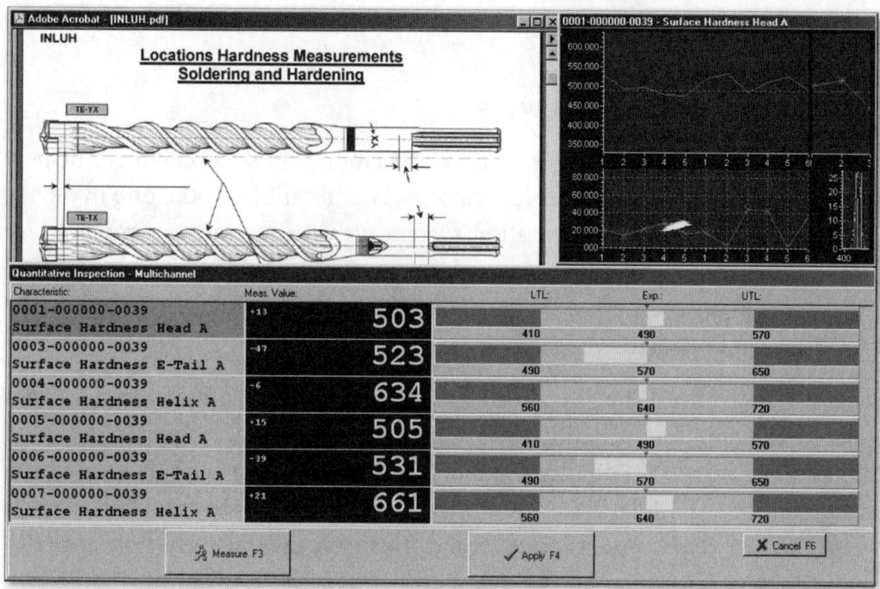


**Figure 7.27** Work Center at the Subsystem EiQMI for Operator Inspection (Source: Hilti GmbH, Kaufering, Germany)

For complex parts, the manual inspections performed by the operators are supported by coordinate-measurement devices. For this purpose, all of these parts are brought to the measurement lab where they are inspected by technicians. The results of the coordinate-measurement devices are evaluated and automatically transferred to QM via the subsystem. At the same time, the measured values are evaluated according to the SPC methods. If the results of the statistical criteria are not sufficient, the operator is automatically notified. The critical results, including the inspection logs, are displayed on the operator's screen. The operator decides which corrective measures are to be taken and documents these in the subsystem. The corrective measures are transferred to the QM as a quality notification. Based on the quality notifications, you can later carry out a verification of the measures actually taken.

In the final inspection, the devices are entirely inspected at an automated work center. The required values and inspection parameters that are important for the inspection are defined as planned values for inspection characteristics in the inspection plans and as class characteristics in the material classification. The inspection device receives the SAP ERP specifications from the subsystem. It performs the inspections on the basis of the inspection parameters and makes a decision for each unit to be inspected, based on the tolerance values from QM, as to whether the device can be delivered or not. Finally, the inspection device notifies the subsystem of the inspection results and the evaluation. The subsystem carries out the return transport to the QM inspection lot.

### 7.12.3 Analyses in the Adhesives Area

The adhesives area operates several analytical laboratories for chemical inspections. The situation in the analysis laboratories is different from the one in device production. The laboratory information system previously used was replaced by SAP QM years ago. The employees in the laboratories are trained in the use of SAP software and use it to enter analysis results. Some scales were connected to the SAP software via keyboard wedges.

Until now, the results of the gas chromatography and other complex analysis systems have been entered manually into SAP ERP screens, and the company decided to change this situation. For this reason, the subsystem was enhanced with an additional option. The final results are now directly transferred from the analysis device to the SAP entry screens and further processed there. In addition, for critical analyses, the protocols of the GC (gas chromatography) are transferred via raw values, analysis processes, and results into the SAP DMS, where they are archived together with the analysis results.

A typical screen design when connecting gas chromatography devices to the SAP GUI, including the display of the chromatogram, is shown in Figure 7.28.

### 7.12.4 External Statistics Program

The SAP ERP system already provides you with some statistical evaluation options such as the mean value, standard deviation, and process capability indices. However, if you have additional requirements, you can also use an external statistics program. The necessary data is transferred from the SAP ERP system to the subsystem via the QM STI (statistical interface) with the RFC. There you can execute additional evaluations. You can transfer the following data:

- Inspection results (measured values)
- Specifications for the statistical evaluation (tolerance limits, action limits, etc.)
- Reference data (sample number, inspection lot number, material number, etc.)
- Additional data (names, units, etc.)

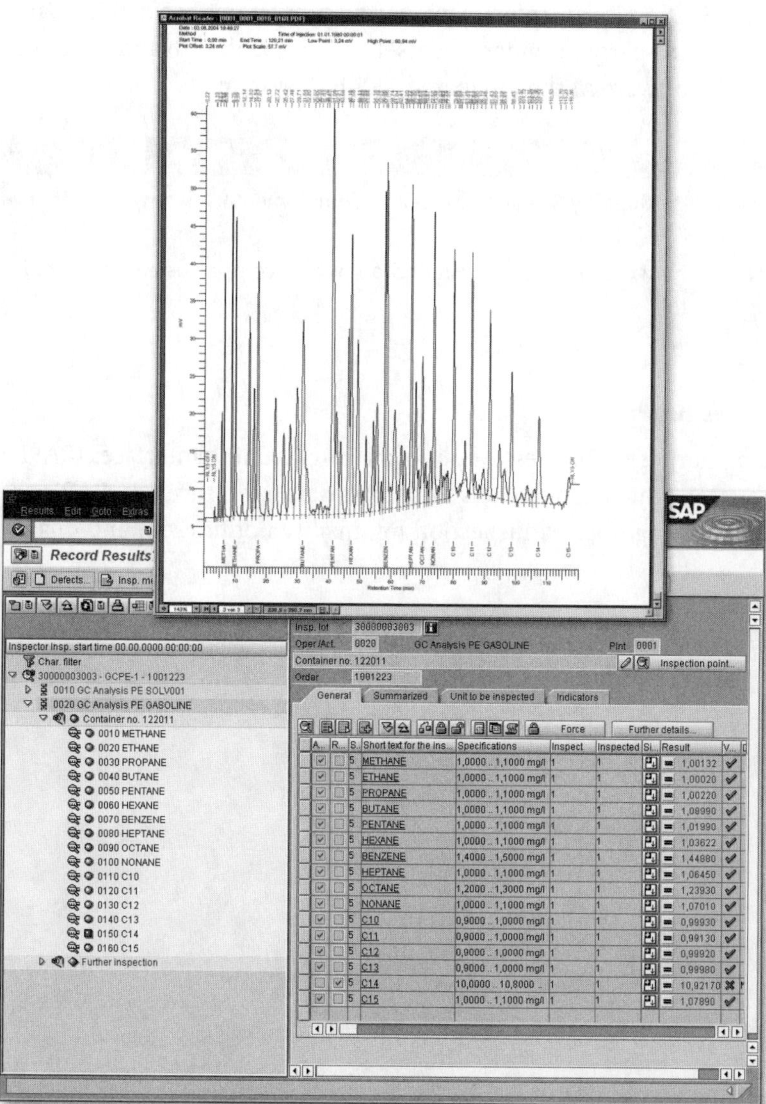


**Figure 7.28** Connecting the Gas Chromatography Device to SAP GUI; Transferring Result Values and Analysis Reports (Source: Dr. Eilebrecht SSE, Leonberg, Germany)

### Certified Interfaces

Third-party providers and their products can be certified by SAP. This ensures that the interface of the SAP ERP application functions with the interface of the external application. The certification of the interfaces is advantageous for the users, SAP, and the third-party providers. The user can rely on the fact that the interfaces were checked by SAP. SAP can refer to powerful subsystems from third-party providers, and the third-party providers themselves can use the advantages of the connection of their software in the integrated SAP ERP system.

**Tip**

Third-party providers certified by SAP are also called Complementary Software Partners (CSP).

On the Internet under *www.sap.com*, you can find out which companies are registered as CSPs.

### Program Interfaces (BAPI)

For programming purposes, Business Application Programming Interfaces (BAPIs) are provided through which applications can access data and processes. BAPIs are defined for the following objects: inspection lot, quality notification, and quality certificate.

*The tools of quality control are used to monitor and control your processes. This chapter introduces the available tools to help you learn which may be beneficial for your company.*

# 8 Quality Control

In accordance with ISO 9000, quality control encompasses working techniques and activities that seek to monitor processes and to remove the causes for unsatisfactory results. To remove these causes, corrective and quality-promoting measures are required that prevent a defects recurrence.

## 8.1 Basic Principles

The SAP ERP system provides a wide range of tools for quality control:

- Usage decision (UD)
- Quality level
- Quality notification
- Vendor evaluation
- Statistical Process Control (SPC)
- Dynamic modification of inspection frequency and severity
- Batch record
- Quality costs
- Quality Management Information System (QMIS)

Because the topics quality notification and quality management information systems and evaluations are very extensive, they are discussed in separate chapters (Chapter 9, Quality Notification, and Chapter 10, Information Systems and Evaluations).

## 8.2 Usage Decision

Typically, the usage decision (UD) is the last step in the inspection of an inspection lot and is therefore often referred to as the *inspection-lot completion* even though the inspection is already completed with confirmation and completion of all characteristic results. However, the inspection lot disappears from the worklist only if the UD for the inspection lot has been made.

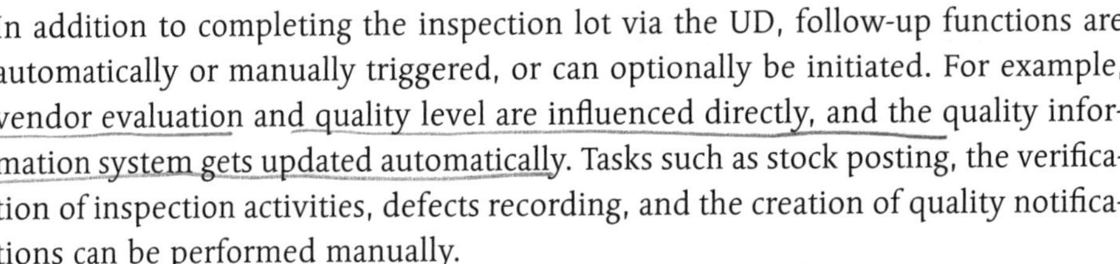

In addition to completing the inspection lot via the UD, follow-up functions are automatically or manually triggered, or can optionally be initiated. For example, vendor evaluation and quality level are influenced directly, and the quality information system gets updated automatically. Tasks such as stock posting, the verification of inspection activities, defects recording, and the creation of quality notifications can be performed manually.

As stock postings, defects recording for UD and the creation of quality notifications are all corrective measures geared toward increasing the quality of products and procedures. Therefore, the UD is discussed in this chapter instead of Chapter 7, Quality Inspection.

### Possible Usage Decisions

After the inspection of all characteristics of an inspection lot has been completed, you can determine the usability of the inspection lot. You must decide whether the inspection lot can be used (acceptance) or should be rejected (rejection). Other decision levels are available in the UD that are established in the basic data of Catalog 3, USAGE DECISIONS. A typical catalog for UD is shown in Figure 8.1.

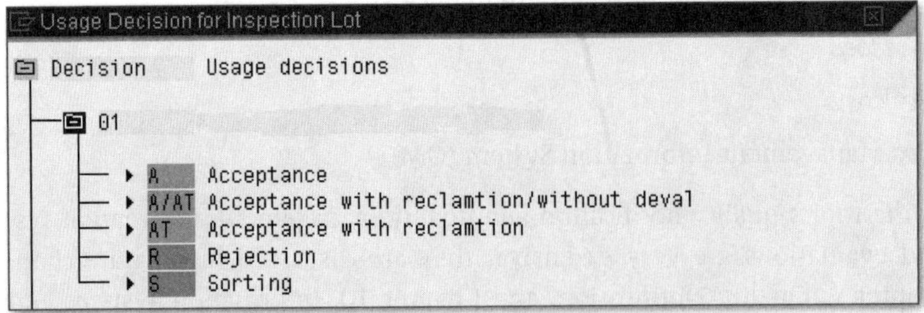


**Figure 8.1** Catalog for Usage Decision

### Quantity Posting

An additional function for stock-relevant inspection lots (e.g., goods receipt from vendors) is the quantity posting. Some of the tasks in quantity posting belong to quality control. For example, the decision REJECTION with quantity posting RETURN DELIVERY or TO SCRAP ensures that no goods of low quality are circulated.

During inspection, the goods are in the inspection stock. The UD provides the following transfer postings relevant for MM:

- **To unrestricted use**
  You post a quantity of the quality stock into the stock for unrestricted use.
- **To scrap**
  Unusable material can be posted directly to scrap.
- **To sample usage**
  This is an option for planned destroyed samples, but you can also post unplanned destroyed quantities here.
- **To new material**
- **To reserves**
  If you want to reserve a demonstration sample, you can choose this option.
- **Return Delivery**
  In the event of returns due to poor quality, enter the quantity here.

You can perform quantity postings before, during, and after making the UD. Partial quantities can also be posted. However, for manually created inspection lots and inspection lots for production orders (see Usage Decision in Production in Section 8.2), there are no postings required.

The material documents are critical, especially for quantity postings. You can view the material documents for an inspection lot directly from the current menu via EXTRAS • MATERIAL DOCUMENTS.

Other pertinent information for quantity posting is the stock overview that can be called from the current menu via ENVIRONMENT • STOCK OVERVIEW. The overview is structured according to plant, storage bin, and batch, and indicates whether the material quantities are usable without restrictions, contained in the inspection stock, or blocked.

### Defects to Usage Decision

Defects recording and tracing are valuable tools for quality control. Evaluations can be targeted to defect location, type, and cause as user-defined catalogs can be created for these categories. The existence of an inspection plan or a material specification is not a requirement for defects recording.

Defects can be recorded to inspection characteristic, inspection process, and UD. If during an inspection, serious defects are revealed that might require the creation of a quality notification, we recommend that you record such defects in the UD because a quality notification can be created in the UD if necessary. If the quality notification for the inspection lot is created through the UD, it is ensured that all relevant data of the inspection lot, such as inspection lot number, GR number, vendor and material number, are automatically inserted into the quality notification. This makes evaluation with the QMIS more effective because there is a relationship between inspection lot and relevant quality notification.

As already mentioned in Chapter 7, Quality Inspection, we recommend that you structure Catalog 9, Defect Types (see Figure 8.2), and Catalog 1, Characteristic Attributes, in the same way because these catalogs are closely interlocked. Prior to defects recording, the type of defect needs to be specified. If a quality notification is created for the defect, this input can be extended with Defect Locations (see Figure 8.3), and with defect cause during further processing of the quality notification.

**Tip**

The term defect location can be understood in different ways. It can be viewed as a position on a part or assembly on which the defect was discovered (e.g., a scratch on the front); or, it can be understood as the place where the defect was revealed (e.g., at GR, during the assembly process, or at the customer). The latter interpretation of defect location permits a more reasonable evaluation than the first one.

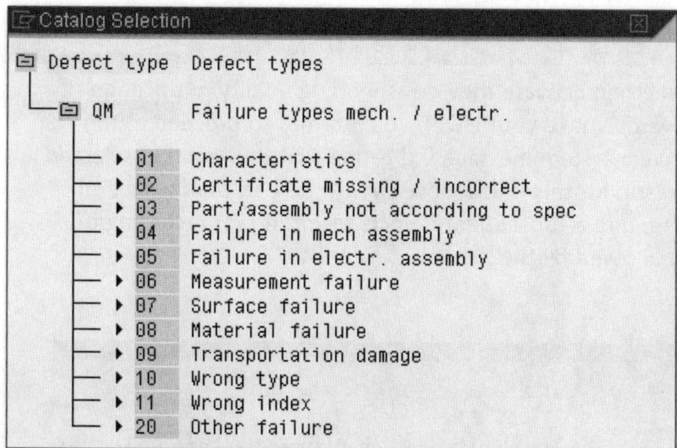


**Figure 8.2** Catalog 9, Defect Types

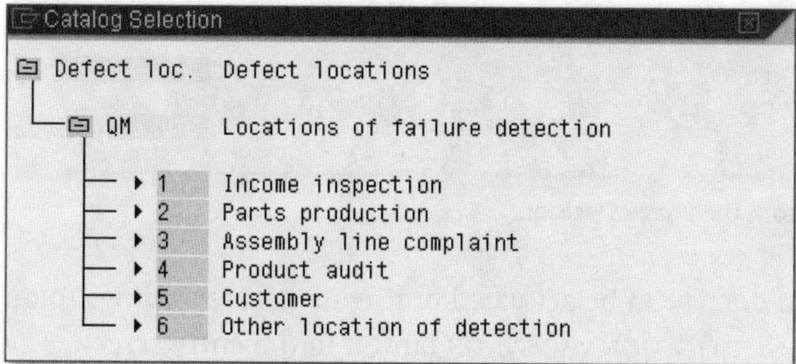


**Figure 8.3** Catalog E, Defect Locations

It gets interesting if a quality notification is created for the defect(s). In Customizing, you can specify the types of available quality notifications. In general, you create an INTERNAL PROBLEM NOTIFICATION (notification type Q1) for an inspection lot from production and a COMPLAINT TO VENDOR (notification type Q2) for an inspection lot from the GR.

With the quality notification, you can give a more precise description of the defect together with defect location and defect cause as well as various supplementary texts. In addition, measures and actions can be traced. For more detailed information, see Chapter 9, Quality Notification. Figure 8.4 shows a defect overview for a specific inspection lot.

**Tip**

Always enter the defect first, then activate the corresponding quality notification (if applicable), and only afterwards, make your UD. If you attempt to proceed in the reverse order, you will receive a system message indicating that the function selected cannot be executed. The reason for this is as follows: With the UD, the inspection is considered to be complete, and a subsequent defects recording (or recording of characteristic results) is not allowed by the system.

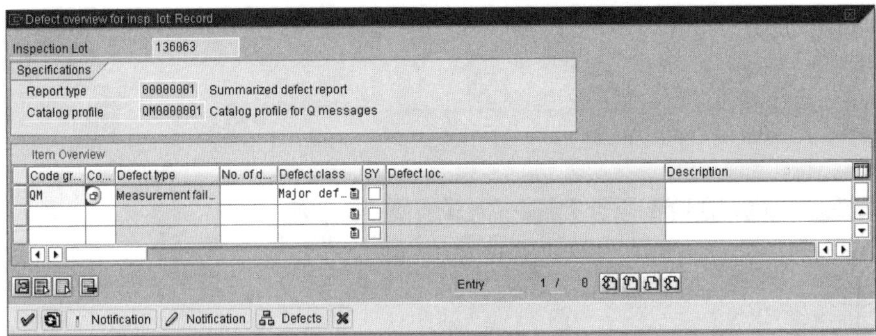


**Figure 8.4** Creating Defects from the Usage Decision

A quality notification for a defect can be activated during defects recording. To do so, simply click on the Q-NOTIFICATION (ACTIVATE) button in the entry screen. The quality notification should then be supplemented with a few additional entries (defect location, defect cause, transactional user, comments, etc.).

### Views in the Usage Decision Screen

The UD screen contains various tabs, the number and appearance of which can vary according to whether you perform an inspection planning or results recording.

- **Characteristics**
  Initial view with relevant inspection characteristics and inspection results.
- **Inspection lot stock**
  Only for inspection lots that are relevant for the stock.
- **Defects**
  In Release 4.0, this view only appears if defects were recorded.
- **Inspection points**
  Only if inspection points or physical samples are planned.

In the characteristics view, initially, only the required characteristics are displayed. Optional characteristics or skipped characteristics are suppressed but can be displayed by clicking on the ALL CHARACTERISTICS button. If characteristic results have previously been confirmed and completed, the evaluation of the characteristics is also shown. Accepted characteristics are identified with a green checkmark; rejected characteristics are identified with a red cross.

By double-clicking or clicking once on the magnifier icon, you can display detail information on the current view. Additional information can be retrieved via the function keys and the ENVIRONMENT menu:

- Inspection lot data
- Results history
- Defective quantity
- Batch status, batch, and batch where-used list
- Management data
- Inspection specifications
- Material data
- Quality level
- Stock overview
- Production order or sales order
- Master data of the vendor, manufacturer, or customer
- Vendor evaluation or cost report

This wealth of information and data can be called quickly for UD and considered for decision finding.

#### Influence of the Usage Decision on the Quality Score

After the UD has been made, the quality score (QS) for the material and vendor, and thus the vendor evaluation gets updated. Whether or how the individual UD influences the QS is defined in Customizing and within the USAGE DECISIONS catalog. For more information, see Section 8.4, Vendor Evaluation. After you enter the UD in the input field and confirm your input by pressing the Enter key, the system calculates the QS for the inspection lot according to the set procedures and displays the QS in the QUALITY SCORE field (see Figure 8.6 later in this chapter).

### Influence of the Usage Decision on the Quality Level

The UD updates the quality level (Q level) of material and vendor. This is critical if you defined dynamic modification rules that, for example, enforce intensified inspection for rejected characteristics or allow inspections to be skipped after multiple inspections with positive results. It is only with the UD made that the Q level is updated; that is, the changed Q level can affect the creation of new inspection lots. Already existing inspection lots remain unaffected by a changed Q level, even if the inspection lots were created at a later time. For more information, see Section 8.3, Quality Level.

### Influence of the Usage Decision on Quality-Related Costs

Within the QM module, the quality-related costs can be recorded in different ways. You can, for example, confirm the expenses for setup and HR at the work center during results recording and UD and calculate the costs in CO. Prior to entering confirmations for action types, however, you need to create a QM order. If this is the case, you can confirm the individual activities through the menu EDIT • CONFIRMATIONS and RECORD • CONFIRMATION. Any costs that were previously recorded for a QM order can be displayed through EXTRAS • QM ORDER COST REPORT.

### Certificate Receipt

If you have provided for the receipt of certificates (e.g., a plant inspection certificate) for specific GRs in the materials master (Q view), the certificate receipt must be confirmed prior to making a UD. This makes sense because you can only make a UD after receipt of the certificate. If you try to make a UD without confirmation of certificate receipt, you will receive an error message. Figure 8.5 shows an overview of possible certificate types.

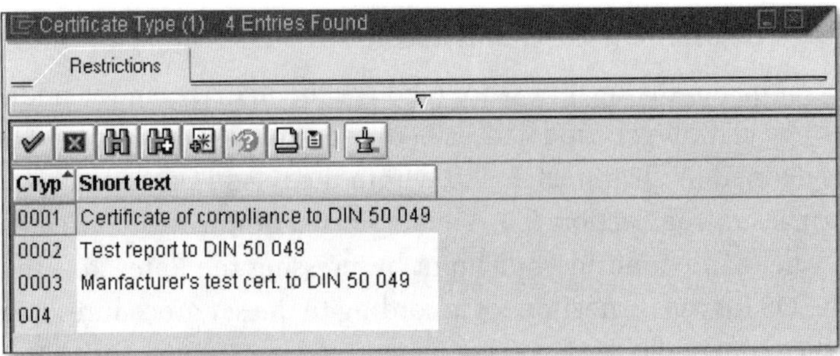


**Figure 8.5** Possible Certificate Types

### Batch Management

The UD can be used to perform various actions for batch management, including the following:

- Changing the batch status
- Displaying the batch list
- Displaying the where-used list of batches
- Displaying batch values
- Posting batches as new material

For stock-relevant inspection lots, you can change the batch status from RELEASED to NOT RELEASED if the UD is negative. To do so, select GOTO • BATCH STATUS. You can define a default value for posting the batch status using catalog USAGE DECISIONS (Catalog type 3).

You can display the list of batches with GOTO • BATCH LIST.

If you need information about the composition of charges or the use of raw materials in completed batches, you can examine the batch where-used list. The menu path for this evaluation is EXTRAS • BATCHES • BATCH WHERE-USED LIST • TOP-DOWN or BOTTOM-UP.

To compare the characteristic values of a batch with the inspection results, you can display the names of the characteristic, the characteristic value in the batch, and the inspection result. To do so, select EXTRAS • BATCHES • BATCH VALUES.

If a batch is posted as a new material, select the menu GOTO • OTHER MATERIAL. The system generates a new batch number automatically that can be overwritten if necessary.

### Automatic Usage Decision

If the inspections are to be skipped using dynamic modification rules, the automatic UD can be used. Automatic UDs can be activated if the inspection has been skipped, or if the inspection was completed and no characteristic was rejected. An additional prerequisite is that the receipt of any required certificates was confirmed.

The automatic UD is performed if all of these requirements are met, the AUTOMATIC USAGE DECISION flag of the affected materials in the material master (Q view – inspection type) is enabled, and a job for it has been scheduled. In this way, you can process all inspection lots with the automatic UD at night, assuming that the mentioned requirements are met.

You plan a job for the automatic UD via the menu LOGISTICS • QUALITY MANAGEMENT • QUALITY INSPECTION and WORKLIST • INSPECTION LOT COMPLETION • AUTOMATIC USAGE DECISION (GENERAL) • JOB PLANNING or AUTOMATIC USAGE DECISION (ORDERS) • AUTOMATIC USAGE DECISION (GENERAL) • JOB PLANNING. In the menu path, "GENERAL" refers to inspection lots from procurement; "ORDERS" are inspection lots from production.

After the job has been completed, a print output is generated informing you which inspection lots were processed and where errors occurred (e.g., because of a missing certificate receipt).

#### Usage Decision for Manually Created Inspection Lots

The manual creation of an inspection lot does not involve a goods movement or rebooking. This means that the stock type of the goods does not change. Generally, the goods are and remain in the released stock and are not posted in the quality stock. Therefore, no quantity postings in the released stock are necessary after the inspection was completed.

If the inspection reveals that a special action (e.g., rework or return to vendor) is required, the resulting goods movements are controlled through special transaction types that have to be set up (outside of the QM module) in Customizing and must be handled through MM.

#### Usage Decision Without Previous Inspection

Usually, the UD is performed after completion of results recording. This includes the confirmation of characteristic results, for example, via an attribute code and the completion of the characteristic. If all required characteristics are completed, the inspection is finished. Whether characteristics are completed is indicated by the characteristic status and the color of the inspection lot in the worklist. If the inspection lot is highlighted in yellow, for example, more characteristic results are expected.

You can, however, make a UD without all characteristics having been completed. In this case, you receive the warning "Requested inspection still open!" You can decide to first complete the inspection, or you can ignore the warning and make a UD. If you make a positive UD, no negative effects occur. If you make a negative decision, however, a potential dynamic modification does not take effect because it is based on the characteristic results. For negative inspection results, to ensure that the dynamic modification rule leads to an inspection intensification for the next inspection lot, you must confirm at least one rejected characteristic with the negative inspection result.

#### Documentation Required

When a material is said to require documentation, you must always comment on the UD if no previous inspection took place, the inspection was performed only in part, or a positive UD (acceptance) was made although characteristics have been rejected. A UD can only be changed subsequently "with history"; that is, if a modification document is attached.

#### Processing a Usage Decision

After all this theory, the following practical example describes how a UD is processed. In this example, a UD is made for a GOODS RECEIPT FOR PURCHASE ORDER. The typical entry screen is the worklist for results recording, which can be opened by choosing LOGISTICS • QUALITY INSPECTION • WORKLIST • VARIANTS FOR RESULT RECORDING • USING LIST.

If you enter a "1" (for "all characteristics") in the PROCESSING MODE field and select EXECUTE in the selection screen, the entire worklist is displayed. The inspection lots for which you can make a UD without additional details are highlighted in light blue. Inspection lots containing required characteristics that are still to be inspected are highlighted in yellow. If you double-click on a light blue inspection lot number, the input screen for the corresponding UD opens (see Figure 8.6).

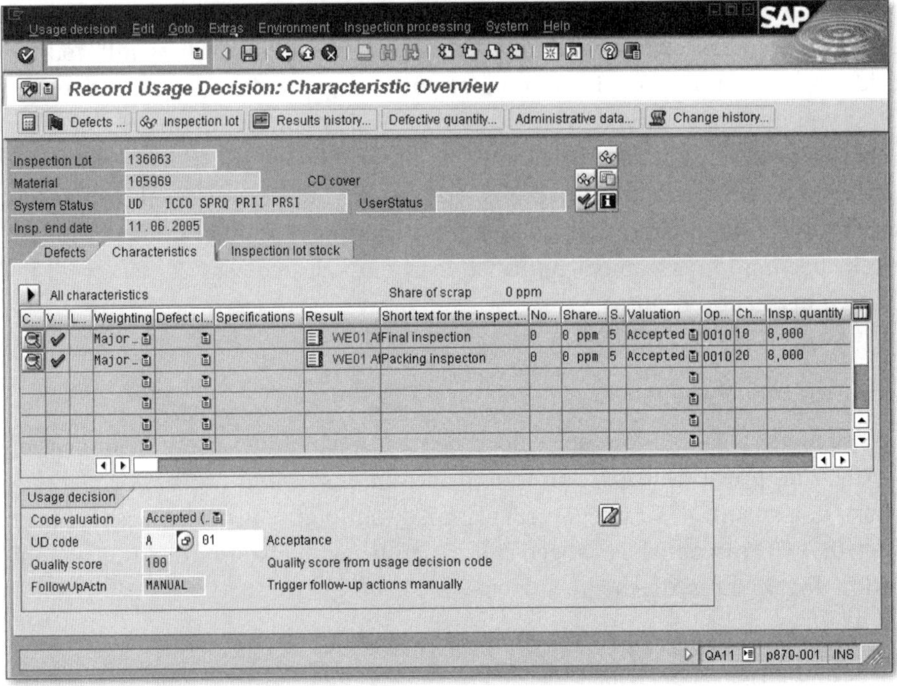


**Figure 8.6** Record Usage Decision: Characteristic Overview

**Tip**

If you have several inspection lots, the display can become crowded quickly. Therefore, we recommend that you specify additional selection criteria such as lot origin, material number, or work center to help you find the appropriate inspection lot quickly.

For the inspection lot shown in Figure 8.6, a manual UD is to be made. At the opening of the screen, the cursor is already in the UD CODE field. You can directly enter a code from Catalog 3, USAGE DECISIONS (refer to Figure 8.1) or make your selection in the selection screen. After you confirm your selection by pressing [Enter], the associated QS is displayed. If you click SAVE now, you are automatically redirected to the next view, RECORD USAGE DECISION: STOCK (see Figure 8.7).

If no defects were revealed during inspection, you post the entire inspection lot quantity TO UNRESTRICTED USE in this view. If you click on SAVE again, the UD and the quantity posting are saved, and you return to your worklist. After you update the view, you will recognize that the inspection lot has disappeared from the worklist.

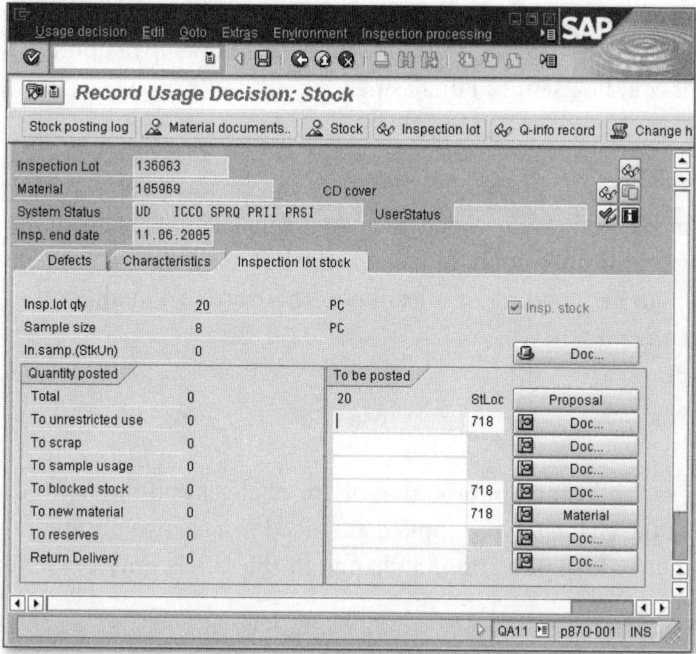


**Figure 8.7** Record Usage Decision: Stock

> **Tip 1**
>
> If you have to make many UDs on a daily basis and don't want to select each inspection lot individually, you can create a list of inspection lots and make UDs for the lots contained for a specific time period.

> **Tip 2**
>
> When processing Catalog 3, USAGE DECISIONS, you can assign fixed posting instructions to individual decisions for the inspection lot stock. It would be useful, for instance, to assign the decision ACCEPTANCE the posting TO UNRESTRICTED USE. In this way, UD and quantity posting are performed simultaneously, and an additional entry in the INSPECTION LOT STOCK view is not necessary. This preassigned posting of instructions is not recommended for other UDs because you need to perform different postings according to each material in stock.

### Follow-Up Actions for Usage Decision

Given that a corresponding Customizing exists, the RECORD USAGE DECISION input screen allows you to trigger follow-on actions for a UD. If, however, the MANUAL display is open, and no automatic follow-up actions were defined, you must trigger the desired action manually. For example, as an automatic follow-up action for a negative UD, an email could be sent to Purchasing.

#### Changing a Usage Decision

After a UD has been made, you can no longer change the inspection results of the inspection lot. However, this does not hold true for the UD itself. You can change a UD subsequently due to new findings, for example. There are two methods that allow a subsequent change:

- With history
- Without history

When making changes with history, information on the changes and the status of the information before the changes were applied are saved in a change document. For materials that require documentation, a change to the UD is only possible with history.

#### Usage Decision in Sales and Distribution

With a UD in SD, you determine whether goods can be shipped to the customers. Consequently, the catalog used is different from the one used in GR; for example, DELIVERY RELEASE replaces ACCEPTANCE.

#### Usage Decision in Production

The UD in Production refers to inspections during or after the production process.

This UD is different from others in that the stock view is missing. All stock postings are performed in the Production Planning (PP) module by using the confirmation for production order. In the QM module, you only decide on the "Acceptance" or the "Rejection" of an inspection lot.

#### Usage Decision in Materials Management

The UDs made in MM generally refer to inspection lots that emerge through GR from a vendor. In GR, the goods can be posted to the inspection stock (stock indicator Q). Goods of acceptable quality are posted to the released stock using the stock posting options in the UD; defective goods are usually returned to the vendor.

The UD in MM has a direct impact on the vendor evaluation (provided that the respective settings in the material master and in Customizing exist).

## 8.3 Quality Level

The quality level (Q level) is a data record containing information on inspection levels for characteristics, inspection lots, material and – for purchased parts – information on the vendor. The Q level is relevant only if you are using dynamic modification rules that determine how you can control a change to the severity of the inspection or in fact skip an inspection. In short, the Q level is a kind of reminder on how the next inspection is to be handled.

For a scheduled dynamic modification, the system automatically creates a Q level with the next inspection lot. For the first inspection lot, the inspection severity is derived from the start level of the dynamic modification rule. A difference is made between dynamic modification by characteristic and dynamic modification by lot, which you can specify in the inspection plan header.

### Updating the Quality Level During Inspection-Lot Creation

If no quality level was created, it will be done automatically during inspection-lot creation. Initially, the evaluation is set to ACCEPTANCE, and the relevant counters are increased. Results recording by characteristic has no initial effect on the evaluation. The evaluation might change with the UD. Even if only one characteristic was rejected (worst-case rule), this leads to a "Not OK" (NOK) evaluation for a lot-based dynamic modification. Therefore, it is not the UD (e.g., REJECTION) that influences the dynamic modification but the rejection of the characteristic. For dynamic modification by characteristic, the only determining factor is the evaluation of the particular characteristic.

### Updating the Quality Level on Usage Decision

Here, too, the quality level is automatically created (assuming that it wasn't created earlier) as soon as a dynamic modification rule is used. The UD updates the Q level according to the characteristic evaluations. In the event of a lot-based dynamic modification, the lot is rejected if even one characteristic is rejected (worst-case rule). For dynamic modification by characteristic, the only determining factor is the evaluation of the particular characteristic.

**Tip**

This worst-case rule also makes the following tip easy to understand: If you make a UD without confirming any characteristic results (which is possible), the dynamic modification cannot work in the event of a characteristic rejection. The dynamic modification can only work as intended if at least one characteristic is confirmed and completed with a negative result.

### Manual Creation of the Quality Level

As already mentioned, the quality level is created automatically as soon as it is required for dynamic modification. However, we suggest that you create the quality level manually in advance; because of certain material, you'll need to specify a different start level than the one preset in the dynamic modification rule. A Q level can only be created for lot-based dynamic modification.

Creation of the Q level is done via the menu path LOGISTICS • QUALITY MANAGEMENT • QUALITY INSPECTION and QUALITY LEVEL • CREATE. Enter the necessary details in the respective fields (see Figure 8.8).

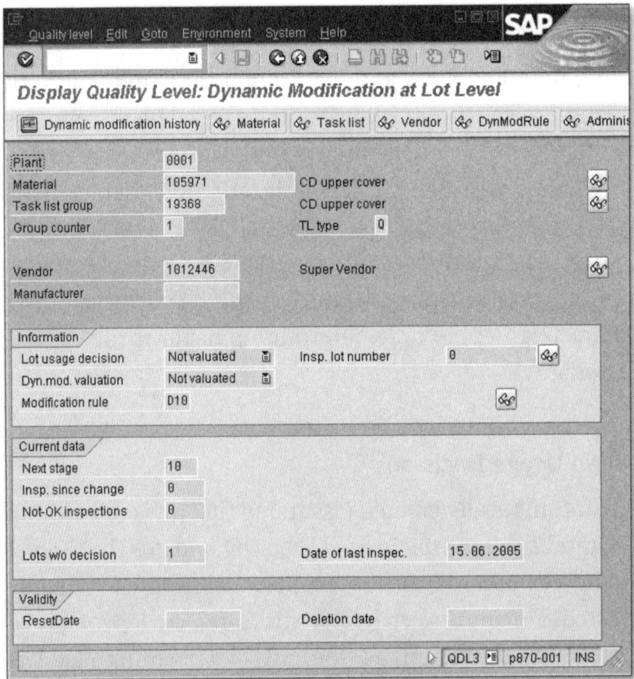


**Figure 8.8** Quality Level

## 8.4 Vendor Evaluation

The vendor evaluation makes it easier for Procurement and Quality Management to pursue their objectives by providing clear and comprehensible key figures. These objectives include the following:

- Determine the current status of a supply relationship.
- Show the vendor to what extent the requirements of the purchaser are met.
- Create a basis for vendor selection or vendor reduction.
- Determine support after the request of quotation and extend the supply relationship.
- Determine support for higher weighting of the GR inspection and inspection planning.
- Provide background information to conclude a quality assurance agreement.

In the vendor evaluation, subcriteria and main criteria are used to establish key figures that allow an evaluation of individual criteria and the creation of a ranking (hitlist) regarding the overall score. Based on these key figures, corrective measures and improvements can be initiated in a targeted manner. Therefore, a meaningful vendor evaluation is not restricted to determining the current status; instead, it forms the starting point for future quality improvements.

### 8.4.1 Basic Principles

The vendor evaluation is an essential element of quality control. In Section 6, Procurement, of the quality management standard ISO 9001, it says:

*The organization must judge vendors based on their ability ... Criteria must be set for selection and regular evaluation. The results of evaluations ... must be recorded.*

The SAP ERP system provides you with flexible tools to evaluate your vendors. All of these tools meet the standards requirements and can easily be adapted to meet the needs of your company. Because quality is the main focus of this book, our descriptions will focus on the quality criterion.

Vendor evaluation takes an intermediate position between Purchasing and Quality Management because it incorporates the information and criteria from both a commercial and quality-related point of view. In the SAP ERP system, you find in the vendor evaluation in MM, as holds true with the majority of cases, that the criteria is evaluated from a commercial point of view, and the vendor evaluation is assigned to Procurement in the ISO 9001 standard. In addition, master and transaction data are extracted from MM, such as material and master vendor records. Vendors are evaluated on the purchasing organization level. The purchasing organization is assigned to one or more plants.

The vendor evaluation makes it possible to evaluate each vendor by using a quality score (QS). This QS is a combination of all criteria, so that a hitlist (a ranking) of vendors can be created. Each criterion, however, can also be considered to be isolated. In addition, the QS can also be created based on a certain material or different vendors of a material.

The vendor evaluation does not only cover vendors of materials, but also vendors of services, such as maintenance service, cleaning service, and crafts, and can be evaluated.

### 8.4.2 Master Data

For vendor evaluation, existing master data in the system is accessed. This includes in particular:

- The vendor master record
- Material master record
- Purchasing info record

In addition to name, address, and contact information, the vendor master record contains the terms of payment and the currency applicable to the vendor.

The material master record with its different views provides all necessary information on a material. For the vendor evaluation, the quantity unit, the procurement quantity unit, the buyer group, the overdelivery, and the underdelivery tolerance — as well as the inspection types — are relevant.

The relationship between vendor and material is established in the purchasing information record (also referred to as the information record). Not only can you find details on which materials were offered or delivered by which vendor; you can also determine the relevant prices and conditions, delivery times, and other data on offers and purchase orders.

### 8.4.3 Evaluation Criteria

To evaluate vendors, the standard SAP ERP system provides five main criteria and additional subcriteria. These are the main criteria:

- Quality
- Price
- Delivery
- External service provision
- Service

The main criterion "Quality" has the following subcriteria:

- **Goods receipt inspection (GR inspection)**
  Determination of the QS from the quality of the inspection lot of the individual GRs.
- **Audit (quality audit)**
  Determination of the QS from one or several audits.
- **Shop floor complaint**
  Determination of the QS from complaints to vendors.

**Customizing Tip**

This standard setting can be tailored to meet the needs of your company. Main criteria or subcriteria can be supplemented or removed. In total, up to 99 main criteria and 20 subcriteria are possible per main criterion. You can also set the weighting of the different criteria. Furthermore, you can set different weightings (EQUAL WEIGHTING, DIFFERENT WEIGHTING) that can be selected later through the WEIGHTING field. You will find the settings for weighting in Customizing (TOOLS • CUSTOMIZING • IMG • EDIT PROJECT) in the SAP reference IMG under MATERIALS MANAGEMENT • PURCHASING • VENDOR EVALUATION • DEFINE PURCHASING ORGANIZATION DATA FOR VENDOR EVALUATION. Below the WEIGHTING navigation point, you can enter the corresponding weighting factors.

If all main criteria or subcriteria are to be weighted equally, you must enter "1" for each criterion and in this way define the weighting as 1:1:1:1. If a main criterion is not to be weighted, select "0" instead of "1". See the example in Figure 8.9.

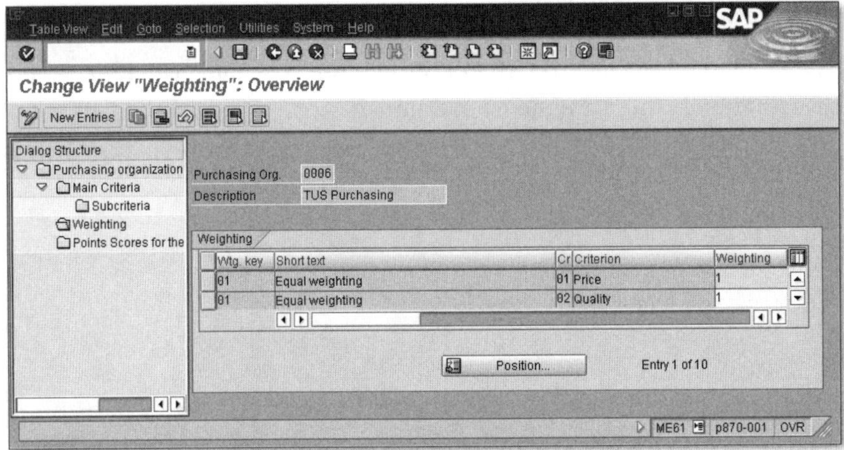


**Figure 8.9** Setting the Main Criteria for Equal Weighting

Figure 8.10 shows how the subcriteria must be set to achieve the weighting defined in Table 8.1. For an *audit*, the checkmark in the MANUAL MAINTENANCE column enables you to manually enter the QS from the vendor audit.

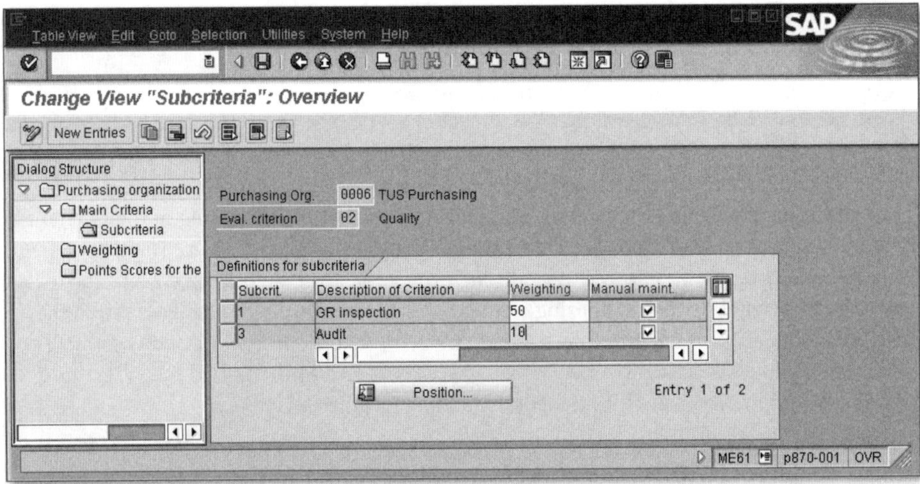


**Figure 8.10** Setting the Subcriteria According to the Example from Table 8.1

The QS is established bottom-up, which means that you evaluate the subcriteria first. You determine the QS of the corresponding main criterion by combining the subcriteria according to the weighting key. Lastly, the main criteria in the corresponding weighting are reflected in the overall score.

The QS of the subcriteria can be determined automatically, semi-automatically, or manually. For GRs or complaints, the QS is usually calculated automatically. For the quality audit, a manual entry can be useful as well because you can transfer the QS from the audit result. A semi-automatic calculation is integral to the subcriteria of "Service" and "External service provision" where an automatic calculation is not possible.

### Scoring

We explain the scoring by using some examples. Table 8.1 shows some typical settings. Note that you can adapt these examples to reflect your company's needs via Customizing.

| Main Criteria | Weighting | Subcriteria | Weighting |
|---|---|---|---|
| Quality | 60% | GR inspection | 50% |
| | | Audit | 10% |
| | | Shop floor complaint | 40% |
| Delivery | 40% | On-time delivery | 50% |
| | | Quantity reliability | 50% |

**Table 8.1** Main and Subcriteria with Sample Weighting Factors

### Subcriteria "Goods Receipt Inspection"

The UD for an inspection lot is important for scoring the subcriteria for GR. You can define a weighting factor for every UD (Acceptance, Rejection, Sorting) in a catalog. The UD "Acceptance" is assigned 100 points; the UD "Rejection" is assigned 1 point. The QS is calculated by factoring the weighting factors of all UDs for GR inspection lots in the analysis time frame.

**Example**

If five inspection lots for GR inspection were evaluated in the analysis time frame, of which four were accepted and one was rejected, the QS for the subcriterion GR inspection is (100 + 100 + 100 + 100 + 1) divided by 5 = 80.2 points (see Figure 8.11).

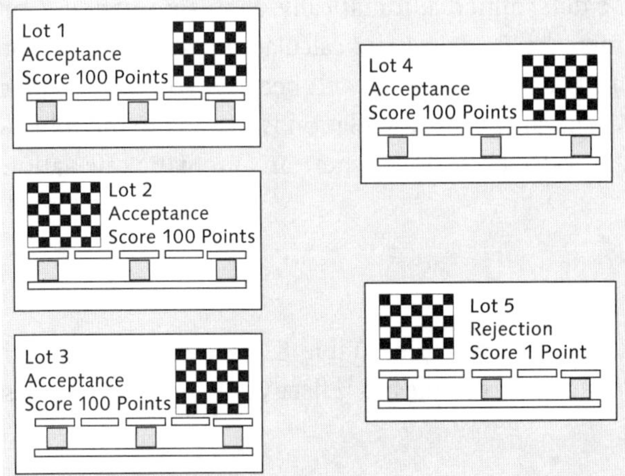


**Figure 8.11** Goods Receipts Lots with the Valuation from the Usage Decision

### Subcriterion "Audit"

The subcriterion "Audit" can be automatically calculated, provided that in Customizing the system was configured to generate audit inspection lots for each audit. The QS for audits is calculated from the UDs for audit inspection lots using the scores in the catalog. The advantage of this method is that several audits can be combined to equal one QS.

The simpler method is the manual entry of the QS to the last vendor quality audit. Instead of a quality audit, you can use a process or product audit or create a specific subcriterion for each audit type. After summarizing several subcriteria, you can only obtain figures that make sense if you standardize the key figures to the maximum value (typically 100 points).

**Tip**

If you do not perform any quality or process audits yourself, you can document the information of a vendor self-disclosure, a VDA 6.1 audit, or other audit evaluations under this subcriterion.

### Subcriterion "Shop Floor Complaint"

As soon as a quality defect caused by a vendor is discovered, whether it be at GR inspection, during production, in the end product, or even by the end user (the customer), a quality notification is created as a COMPLAINT TO VENDOR. By using this subcriterion, the number or value of the complaints (quality notifications) can be included in the vendor evaluation.

In general, this subcriterion is used to display shop floor complaints separately. A shop floor complaint is a defect in the goods delivered that is only discovered during processing in Production, not at GR.

**Tip**

Remember that a simultaneous use of subcriteria "Goods Receipt Inspection" and "Shop floor Complaint" might reduce the QS twice. The negative UD and the quality notification created influence the vendor evaluation. Therefore, we recommend that you use only one of these subcriteria for vendor evaluation. The specific needs of your company determine which subcriterion is more suitable.

### Main Criterion "Quality"

The QS of the main criterion "Quality" is calculated from the mentioned subcriteria. To do so, each subcriterion is weighted according to the factor set. A requirement is that the weighting factors have been selected in a way that they total 100% (otherwise, the system standardizes to 100). Each subscore is multiplied by the predefined factor; the subtotals are added to the total.

**Example**

In Table 8.2, you find accepted scores and a weighting factor for the three subcriteria. The subtotals are calculated by multiplying the weighting with the scores of the subcriteria. The QS is the sum of the subtotals for the subcriteria.

| Subcriteria | Score (QS) | Weighting | Subtotal |
|---|---|---|---|
| GR inspection | 80 | 50% | 40 |
| Audit | 95 | 10% | 9, 5 |
| Shop floor complaint | 90 | 40% | 36 |

**Table 8.2** Example for the Weighting of the Subcriteria to the Main Criterion "Quality"

In this example, the subtotals of 40 + 9.5 + 36 = 85.5 points for the main criterion "Quality."

**Tip**

It has proven effective to weight the most important subcriterion with a factor of 100% and all other subcriteria with 0%. By using this method, all subcriteria are recorded, but only the important subcriterion determines how the main criterion is calculated from the subcriteria and can be used in the hitlist as a sorting criterion.

### Main Criterion "Delivery"

The main criterion "Delivery" from Table 8.1 is comprised of the subcriteria "On-time delivery" and "Quantity reliability" that were equally weighted in the example (but can also be weighted differently). For each delivery, you determine to which extent the guidelines for adherence to delivery dates and the correct delivery quantity were met. In the same way that you determined the score for the main criterion "Quality," the score for the main criterion "Delivery" is calculated from the evaluation scores of the related subcriteria.

Another criterion from the standard setting of the SAP ERP system is the shipping instruction. You can evaluate the degree to which your vendor meets the instructions for shipping type and packaging. For example, often a returnable packaging, an ESD compatible packaging, or a maximum weight per pallet is prescribed.

### Main Criterion "Price"

The main criterion "Price" can be used to evaluate the price level of the vendor in relation to the average market price. The lower the price, the better the evaluation. If the price is higher than the market price, this results in a poorer evaluation.

A prerequisite for a price evaluation is that comparative data of competitors exists for the same materials that were recorded in the system.

### Main Criterion "Service"

The main criterion "Service" refers to material delivery. Typical subcriteria are the following:

- Reliability
- Innovation
- Flexibility

Apparently these subcriteria cannot be determined by the system because they include subjective estimations that depend on industry sector and several other factors. For such subcriteria, a semiautomatic determination of the QS is provided. Deliveries are evaluated by the responsible specialist department, taking into account the subcriteria defined; the result is supplied manually. The system automatically consolidates the individual evaluations so that they equal one figure when updating the vendor evaluation.

### Main Criterion "External Service Provision"

The main criterion "External service provision" is used for assessment of services. The quality of service provision is evaluated. Because this evaluation cannot be done automatically by the system, it is performed during acceptance of services or at completion of tasks and manually entered into the system. Examples of services are the maintenance of machines or vehicles by a subcontractor, janitorial services, and maintenance of grounds.

An increase in the outsourcing of services means that an evaluation and an evaluation comparison become ever more important.

### Overall Score

Finally, the overall score (overall QS) is calculated from the individual main criteria (see Figure 8.12). For calculation, the same methods are used as for calculating the main criteria from the subcriteria.

In real-life situations, it's apparent that the calculation of an overall score for the main criteria is not critical. Although this particular calculation does allow for a ranking (hitlist) of the vendors, it raises the question of the need for a negative rating, which, in turn, prompts you to ask which main or subcriteria led to the negative valuation. In our daily work and our need to constantly improve the quality of our work, the monitoring of subcriteria is of far greater interest.

**Tip**

Do not select too many main criteria and subcriteria! A small number of criteria will increase the level of acceptance and comprehensibility. Start with a simple approach; that is, use only the criterion "Quality" with subcriterion "GR inspection," and the UD as the basis of the QS.

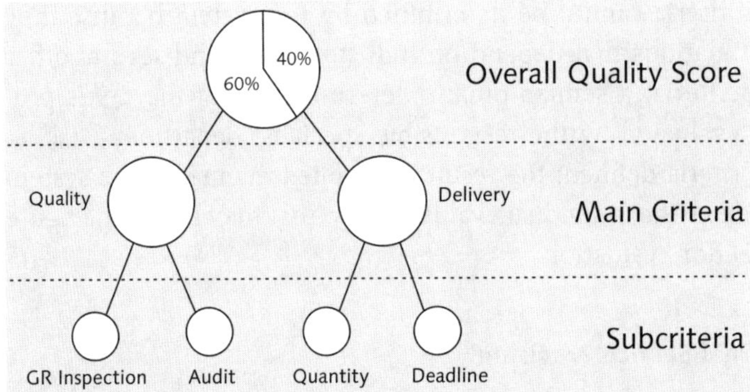


**Figure 8.12** Example for an Overall QS Calculated from Main Criteria and Subcriteria

### 8.4.4 Vendor Evaluation

The practical performance of vendor evaluation in the system can be shown easily with an example. The starting point for the vendor evaluation is the PURCHASING screen. To open this screen, use the menu path LOGISTICS • MATERIALS MANAGEMENT • PURCHASING.

The MASTER DATA submenu contains the VENDOR EVALUATION menu with several selection options.

Prior to evaluating a vendor, you must open the menu VENDOR EVALUATION • MAINTAIN (see Figure 8.13).

#### Maintain Vendor Evaluation

In the initial screen, specify the number of the purchasing organization and vendor for which you want to create a vendor evaluation.

Initially, for a vendor who has not yet been evaluated, the fields for the main criteria are not populated, indicating that no QS has yet been determined. First, you must select a weighting key (here 01, EQUAL WEIGHTING) and click on EDIT AUTO. NEW EVALUATION (see Figure 8.14). The system will recalculate all subcriteria and all main criteria, as well as the overall score for the current data.

After the AUTOMATIC REEVALUATION has been performed, the fields for the overall score, as well as the main criteria and subcriteria, are populated with the current QS.

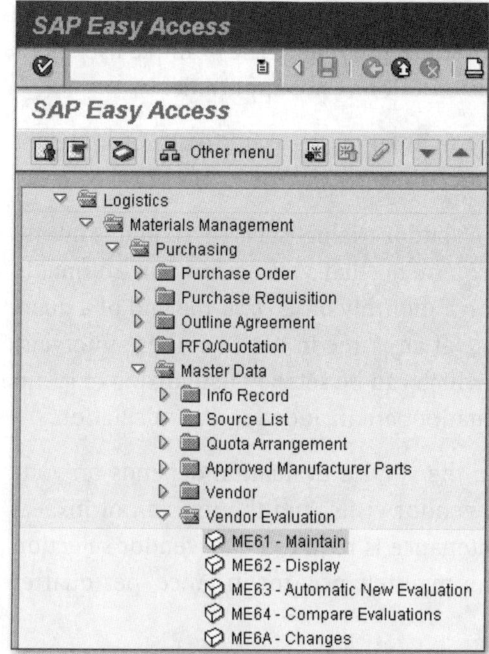


**Figure 8.13** Opening the Maintain Vendor Evaluation Menu

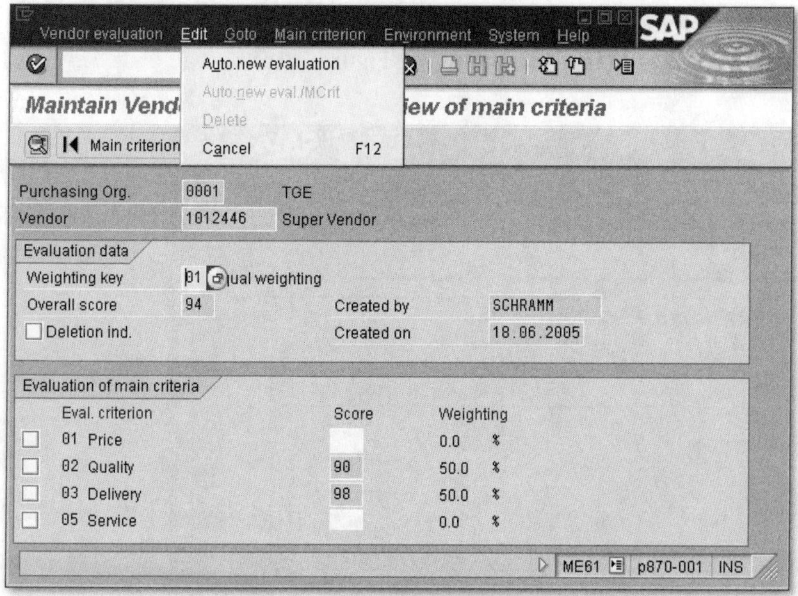


**Figure 8.14** Maintain Vendor Evaluation Screen with Evaluated Main Criteria

If the External Service Provision main criteria appears, it will be grayed out because this criterion is only relevant for service providers. The example used here involves a material vendor for which this criterion is not applicable.

The Service criterion could be manually maintained here but will not be taken into account in this example.

When you click on Save, the status of the vendor evaluation is saved and is immediately available upon next call. We recommend that you perform an automatic new evaluation regularly, for example, on a monthly basis or at the end of a quarter. However, you can perform an update at any time in between these intervals. All relevant events for a certain period, which can be set via Customizing (e.g., up to 1 year) up to the day of the new evaluation, are included in the calculation.

The frequency with which you maintain the vendor evaluation depends on your requirements. For vendor negotiations, vendor visits, and the revision of inspection plans, a short-term (monthly) maintenance is required. For vendor selection or for vendor reduction, a medium-term maintenance, for instance, per quarter or per term, makes sense.

### Display Vendor Evaluation

Via the menu Vendor Evaluation • Display, you can display the vendor evaluation that was saved in the Maintain menu (see Figure 8.15).

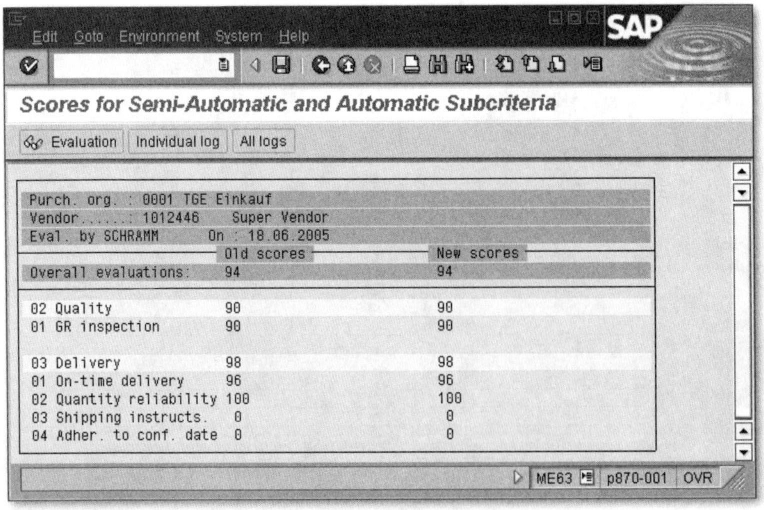

**Figure 8.15** Log After an Automatic New Evaluation

**Vendor Evaluation—Automatic New Evaluation**

In the AUTO.NEW EVALUATION submenu of the VENDOR EVALUATION menu, you can trigger the reevaluation of all main criteria. In the initial screen, you must enter the VENDOR and the PURCHASING ORGANIZATION of your operation. Optionally, you can specify that only vendors who have not been evaluated since a specific date (NOT EVALUATED SINCE ...) are reevaluated. You can trigger the evaluation of all criteria by pressing [Enter].

In Figure 8.16, the results of the automatic new evaluation are shown. This log supplies a comparison of the scores between the last evaluation and the current evaluation with regard to the overall score, as well as the main criteria and subcriteria.

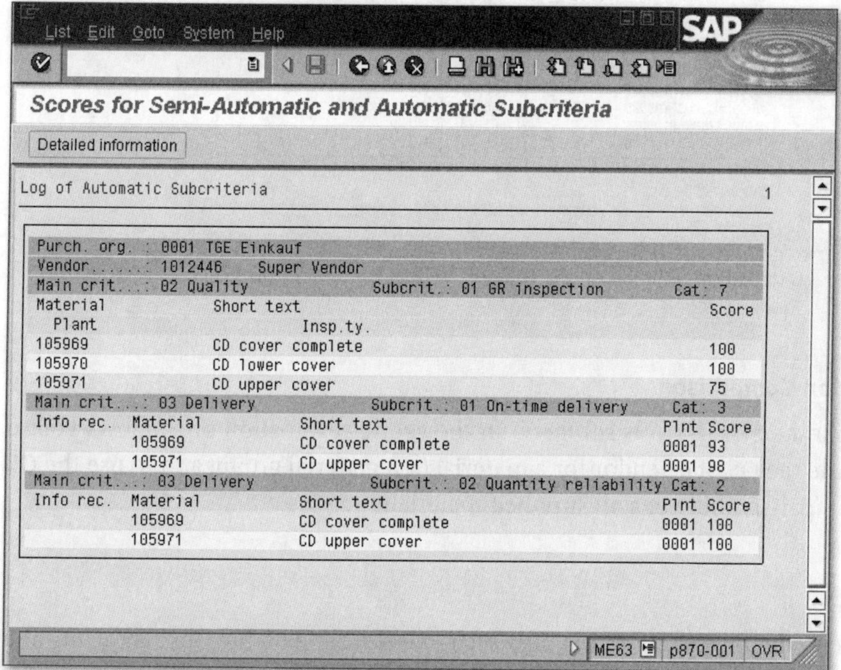


**Figure 8.16** Display of All Logs

For an analysis of the reasons leading to an evaluation, additional details can be interesting. By clicking on the ALL LOGS button, you receive a listing of the scores per material number.

If you select the material number, click on DETAILED INFORMATION, select the material number again, and then click on the DISPLAY INSP. LOTS button, a list of the relevant inspection lots showing the date of the UD and the relevant QS will be displayed for the particular material (see Figure 8.17).

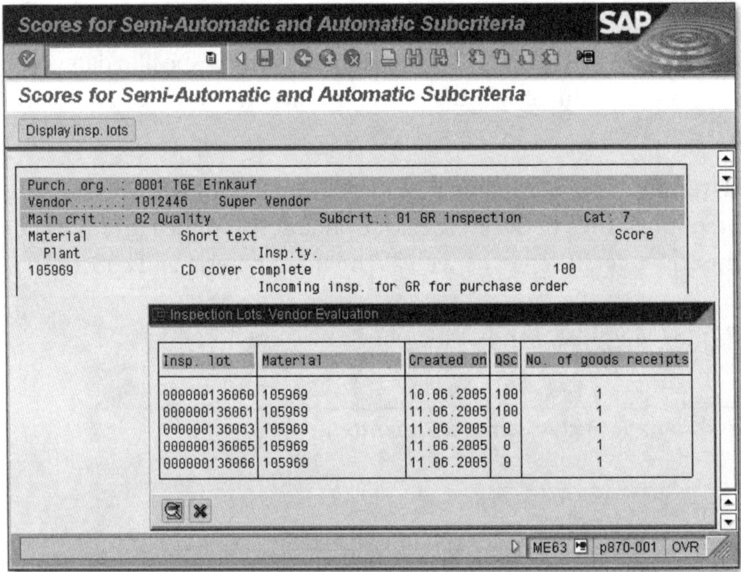


**Figure 8.17** Detailed Information on the Material with Additional Inspection Lots Screen

### Evaluation Comparison

The Compare Evaluations submenu in the vendor evaluation only allows you to determine the QS of a vendor for a material or a material group, and to use the QS for a comparison between all supplied materials.

### Changes

Each new vendor evaluation is also a change to the existing one. By using the Changes submenu, you can determine by whom and when a new vendor evaluation was created and therefore display the previous as well as the current values.

### Follow-On Functions

The Follow-On Functions submenu provides three submenus with additional functions (see Figure 8.18).

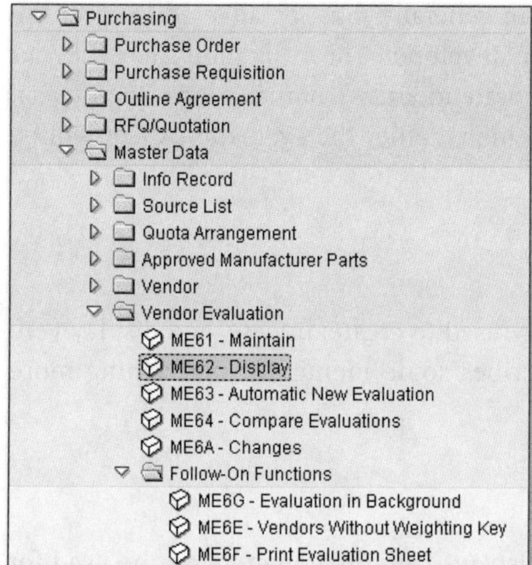


**Figure 8.18** Follow-On Functions Menu with Submenus

### Evaluation in Background

With this submenu option, you can maintain a job that regularly runs in the background and, for example, performs a reevaluation of the vendors on a monthly basis. You can specify when a background evaluation is to be run and at what intervals it is to be repeated. For information on the creation and maintenance of jobs, contact your system administrator.

### Vendors Without Weighting Key

If you access the automatic evaluation in the background, the weighting key assignment might be missing. An assignment of weighting keys is necessary if you have evaluated vendors with different weighting keys in the background evaluation or have not specified a weighting key. You can use this submenu option to maintain the background evaluation with the weighting key.

### Print Evaluation Sheet

To document the current evaluation of a vendor with the overall score, main criteria, and subcriteria, the evaluation can be printed out via this menu option. Often the printed out evaluation sheet is sent to the vendor to inform him of the current status. Prior to this, the default form generally must be adapted to meet the company's requirements by an SAPscript developer. The evaluation sheet's layout is usually adjusted so it reflects the corporate identity (company logo, logotypes). In this context, you also need to determine whether the evaluation sheet will be printed on company or generic paper.

### 8.4.5 Evaluations

The menus described so far are primarily used to create, update, and display vendor evaluations. The next section describes some menus for performing more detailed evaluations.

#### List Displays

The common denominator for all list displays is that parameters can be used for selection; however, this allows you to display only specific vendors. The listing operation is always triggered with RUN. You can display more detailed information for the resulting lists (glasses icon, see, for example, Figure 8.20 later in this chapter). You can select different types of list displays in the menu tree (see Figure 8.19), each of which will be explained next.

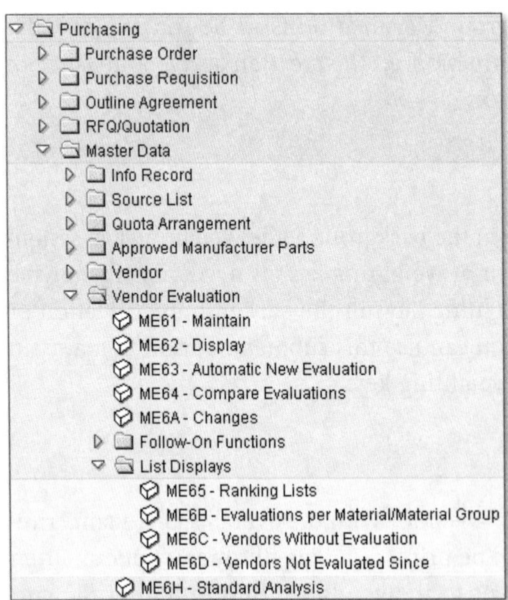


**Figure 8.19** Submenus of the List Displays Menu

### Ranking List of Vendors

Starting from an initial SAP ERP screen, the RANKING LISTS submenu allows you to display a list of vendors with the corresponding overall scores and the scores for the main criteria (see Figure 8.20). You can select the vendors to be displayed in the initial screen. To do so, you can, for example, restrict the number range of the vendors or the vendor class (see Figure 8.20).

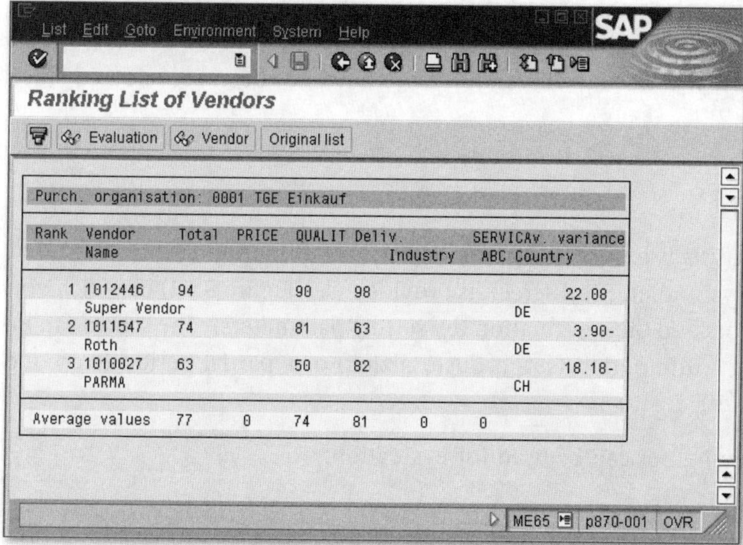


**Figure 8.20** Ranking List of Vendors

You can sort the hitlist to display the vendors in descending order, not only in terms of the overall score but also in terms of the main criteria. If you select a vendor and click on the EVALUATION button, you will receive a detailed evaluation of these vendors for the specified main criteria and subcriteria. In addition, you can display the vendor master record by clicking on the VENDOR button. To return to the initial display, click on the ORIGINAL LIST button.

### Evaluations per Material/Material Group

This submenu generates a hitlist of the vendors for a specific material or material group. Such a list can be especially interesting if the same material is supplied by different vendors.

### Vendors Without Evaluation

This submenu allows you to display a list of vendors, for whom no vendor evaluation has been performed yet.

### Vendors Not Evaluated Since

This submenu generates a list of vendors for whom no vendor evaluation has been performed for a specific period. To create such a list, you need to enter the purchasing organization, the number range of the vendors to be evaluated, and a key date. The list will display all vendors who have not been reevaluated since this key date.

### Standard Analysis

The standard analysis is embedded in the Logistics Information System (LIS). For the standard analysis, a selection screen is provided (see Figure 8.21) in which you can display vendors and their evaluation (by setting parameters). The scores can be evaluated for the entire period (set in Customizing) or a partial period (e.g., one month or a quarter).

The following key figures can be used for evaluation:

- Quantity reliability
- On-time delivery
- Adherence to confirmation date (deviation from shipping notification)
- Shipping notification (is not updated in version 4.0B)
- Shipping instruction
- Quality audit (is not updated in version 4.0B)
- Quality of external service provision
- Timeliness of service provision

Unfortunately, the often-required evaluation according to the criterion "Quality" is not provided in this standard analysis. To provide this option, either a developer must adapt the report, or a new report must be created according to your requirements. Another option is to create a flexible analysis, as described in Chapter 10, Information Systems and Evaluations.

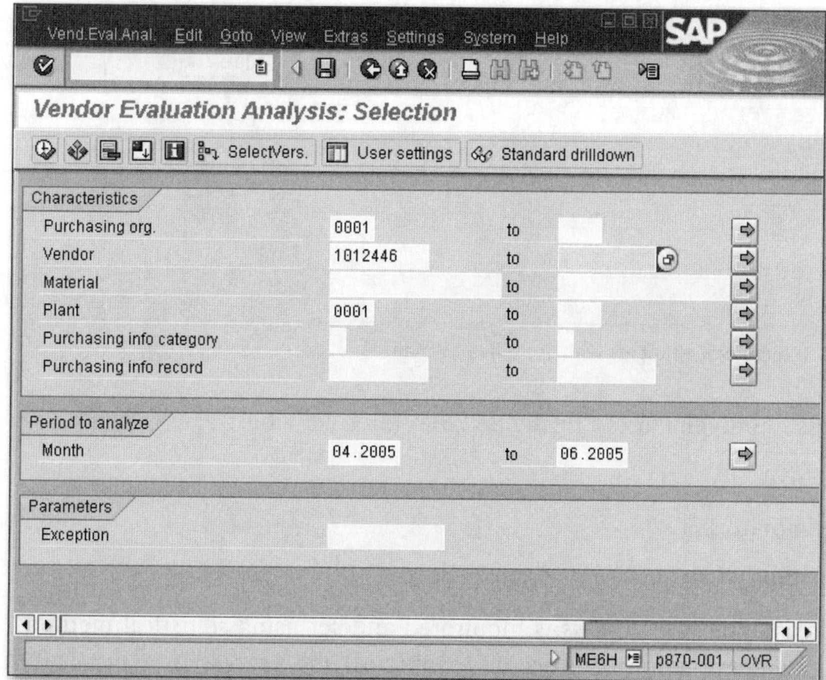


**Figure 8.21** Standard Analysis for Vendor Evaluation

## 8.5 Statistical Process Control (SPC)

Each process is subject to dispersion. In this context, a distinction is made between random dispersion and systematic dispersion. With random dispersion, small deviations occur constantly, depending on the respective process parameters, such as tools, operators, and materials. Systematic dispersion, on the other hand, occurs irregularly and can often be traced to specific influences, such as temperature or tool wear-and-tear. A process under control is only influenced by random dispersion. The systematic influences have been eliminated during the development of processes toward a controlled process. Figure 8.22 illustrates a process with a systematic variance showing an accumulation at the upper tolerance limit.

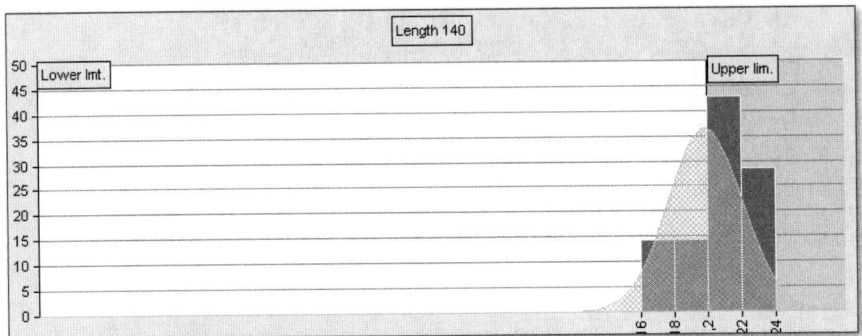


**Figure 8.22** Example of a Process with Systematic Variance

The process improvement can be divided into three activities:

- Process analysis
- Process monitoring
- Process improvement

In process analysis, the process is monitored and set using statistical methods, including an examination of process capability. If the process is stable, it will be monitored with the methods of Statistical Process Control (SPC), and possibly existing systematic variances will be eliminated. Finally, an attempt is made to optimize the process. To achieve this, statistical process monitoring methods are used to determine where random deviations occur and how these deviations can be eliminated. These three activities are iterated several times to continually improve and manage the process.

For process monitoring and improvement, several methods and tools are provided:

- Control charts
- Histogram
- Standard distribution
- Run chart
- Ishikawa diagram (cause-effect diagram)
- Pareto chart
- Distribution chart
- Process capability examinations

The QM module of the SAP ERP system provides solid support for some of these tools.

### Control Charts

The use of quality control charts forms the basis of statistical process control. SPC allows you to analyze, monitor, control, and improve processes.

Quality control charts date back to a technique that was developed by Walter A. Shewhart (1891-1967) in 1924. His "control chart" enabled the Western Electric Company to reduce their inspection effort greatly.

In general, a control chart is used to monitor the production process. You can soon determine whether a process is under control or how changes influence the process. Control charts can also be used in the procurement process, for example, for several GR inspections according to the scheduling agreement with regular releases. In this case, the control chart can indicate whether the production process was under control. In actuality, the critical measurement items are set, a sample of the same size is taken at regular intervals, the control variable is determined by measurement and calculation, and the control variable is entered graphically into the control chart. The typical control variables include the following:

- Mean value x
- Standard deviations
- Range R
- Median
- Original value
- Number of defective parts
- Number of defects

Each control variable can be selected as a track for a control chart. If two control variables are selected, you get a dual-track control chart. A typical example of a dual-track control chart is the x/s control chart (mean value and standard deviation). Depending on the control chart type, a center line, tolerance, warning, and action limits can be entered. The warning and action limits are calculated during a preliminary phase under real process conditions and entered in the control chart.

The classic types of control charts for quantitative (variable) characteristics include the following:

- **Accept chart** (e.g., mean-value chart with tolerance)
  This is focused on tolerance and gives you upper and lower control and warning limits.
- **Shewhart chart** (e.g., standard deviation chart)
  This uses internal process parameters without considering the tolerance limits.

The following are typical control chart types for attributive (countable) characteristics:

- **For defective units:**
  - p chart (fraction)
  - np chart (number — for constant sample size)
- **For defects per unit:**
  - u chart (fraction)
  - np chart (number — for constant sample size)

Figure 8.23 shows a few types of quality control charts already set up in the standard system. In addition to these chart types, other quality control charts are used in industry, such as the pre-control chart.

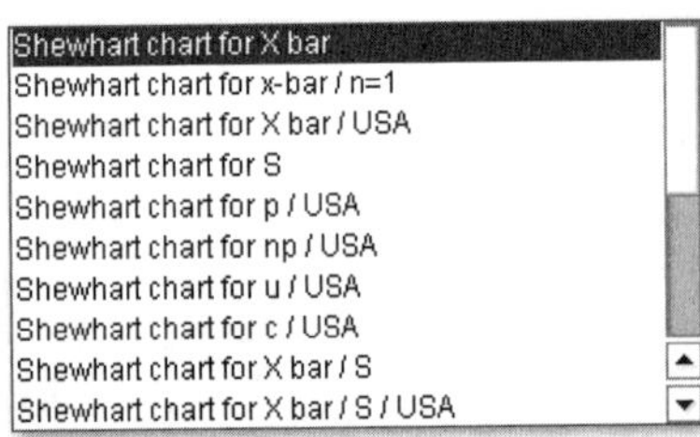


**Figure 8.23** Types of Quality Control Charts

The control chart enables you to monitor and analyze your processes and plan corrective measures according to the principles of quality control. For analysis purposes, it is necessary to evaluate the control charts by answering the following questions:

- Is it a natural process?
- Is there a trend recognizable (increasing or decreasing tendency)?

- Are there systematic or periodic fluctuations?
- Are there jumps in the process?
- Does the process situation change over time?
- Do strong, short-term deviations occur in the control variables?
- Is the process stable (no exceptionally strong fluctuations)?

If analysis or other quality information shows that the process does not yield the desired results, the process must be changed, or suitable actions must be taken to achieve a stable and controlled process. The success of these changes can be checked with a quality control chart.

#### Histogram and Standard Distribution

A clear and useful tool (which is available in the standard system without any special settings) is the graphic display of variable measurement values in the form of a histogram. Additionally, you can insert the standard distribution by using the context menu (right-click). An example is shown in Figure 8.24.

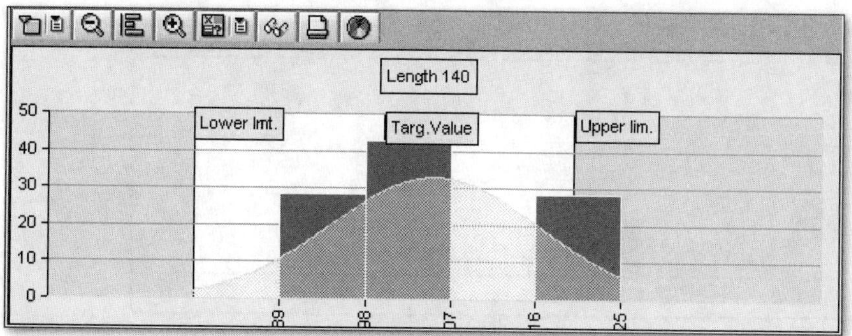


**Figure 8.24** Histogram with Standard Distribution

Using the glasses icon in the SAP graphic, you can also calculate and display the process capability. In addition to the mean value and the standard deviation, the cp and cpk value will be determined, provided that the planned value and the tolerance limits for the characteristic are maintained. These values are the process capability indices. The first value is a measure for the process dispersion (is the process controlled?), whereas the other value describes the position of the mean value in relation to the tolerance limits and therefore indicates whether or not the process is capable. For a controlled and capable process, both of these values should be higher than 1.33. In many industries, the minimum requirement for a process capability index is now 2.0 and higher!

Prerequisites for the use of the histogram are the variable recording of characteristic results as individual or classed values, as well as the maintenance of tolerance limits and planned values. Managing a control chart is not required for using the histogram. The histogram classification for individual values is calculated through an internal algorithm. If the inspection results have already been recorded as classed inspection results, this classification will be used as the histogram basis.

### Run Chart

The run chart is a simple method to show time-related trends. This makes it possible to display the measurement results of one or several samples (see Figure 8.25).

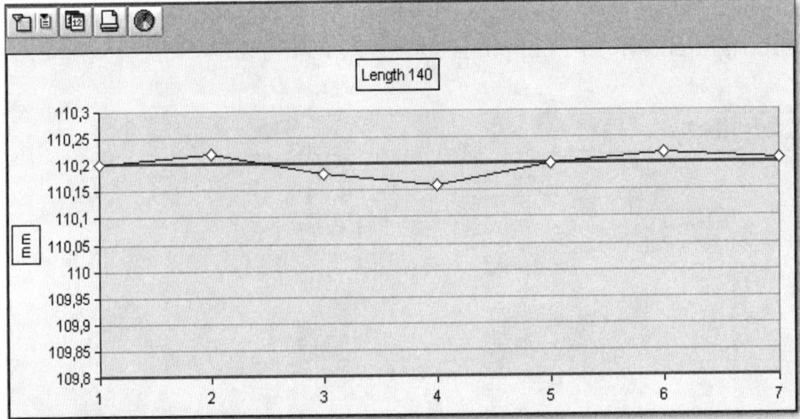


**Figure 8.25** Run Chart

In the SAP graphic, the planned values as well as the upper- and lower tolerance limits are displayed as colored lines. If you right-click in the graphic, a context menu appears that allows you to further process the display.

A prerequisite for this evaluation is that variable measurement results have been recorded as individual values.

## 8.6 Dynamic Modification of Inspection Severity and Inspection Frequency

The dynamic modification of inspection severity and inspection frequency is a very useful instrument of quality control. By reviewing the last or the most recent inspection results, you can establish a rule as to how intensive the next inspections should be. The basic principle here is quite simple: The better the quality, the lower the level of inspection effort; that is, the inspection severity and the inspection frequency are reduced to the point whereby skipping inspections is possible. If the quality is lower or has deteriorated, the inspection severity and inspection frequency are increased.

For changes in the inspection intensity, you can define so-called dynamic modification rules that automatically adjust the inspection severity and inspection frequency.

ISO 2859-1 classifies the following levels of inspection severity:

- Reduced
- Normal
- Intensified

With the dynamic modification rule, not only can you establish the dynamic relation between the inspection severities — depending on the inspection results — you can also determine whether GR inspections or inspection characteristics can be skipped completely. The definition of these rules is quite complex but can be performed with little effort by an experienced inspection planner.

If inspection plans are used, the dynamic modification rules can be set in the inspection plan header. Here you can determine whether you want to perform the dynamic modification at the lot or characteristic level. At the lot level, all characteristics of the lot will undergo a tightened inspection, even if a defect for only one characteristic was revealed. At the characteristic level, the inspection severity of each characteristic can change individually and independently of the respective result. If no inspection plan is provided, the dynamic modification can also be recorded in the quality view of the material master.

Depending on the capability index of a vendor, you can use different dynamic modification rules. For a vendor with good quality audit results, for example, you could assign a dynamic modification rule that permits a reduced inspection severity and frequent skipping of the GR inspection. For a suboptimal vendor, inspections are performed with normal or increased inspection severity, and no inspections are skipped until delivery quality has improved.

The change of inspection severities in the dynamic modification rule is called a level switch. The level of a supply relationship is shown in the quality level. By changing the quality level, you can manually change the level of a dynamic modification rule. If, for example, the skip level has been reached, the next inspection lot does not need to be inspected. You could, however, manually change the inspection level in the quality level to have the next inspection lot inspected.

Remember that although the quality level is updated with the UD, this does not have a direct impact on the dynamic modification. For dynamic modification, only the characteristic results are relevant. If you reject an inspection lot by a UD without confirming any defects, the dynamic modification rule works in accordance with an OK evaluation. Only if at least one characteristic has been rejected does the dynamic modification rule work in accordance with a Not OK evaluation.

**Tip**

For inspections without an inspection plan, the dynamic modification rule can be recorded in the inspection type of the material master. If an inspection plan exists, however, the definition of the dynamic modification rule in the inspection header is the more flexible method. Each change to the plan due to quality control has a direct impact on the next GR. Changes in the material master, however, only take effect on the next procurement of material.

## 8.7 Batch Logs

A central requirement of Good Manufacturing Practice for Pharmaceutical Products (GMP) is the creation of a processing log for each manufactured batch.

The GMP guidelines originate in the United States where they were issued by the Food and Drug Administration (FDA) and are legally binding for the pharmaceutical industry. Over the years, these guidelines have developed into an internationally accepted standard that must be adhered to in many countries.

In the SAP ERP system, these GMP guidelines are taken into account by the fulfillment of the requirements of a processing log. This was implemented in the Production Planning Process Industry (PP-PI) module by providing the batch log.

The origin of the batch log is the process order and the corresponding quality-related data. The essential requirements of the GMP guidelines are met in the associated print list. These include the identification of each printed page with the batch number, material number, charge quantity, page numbering, and a special identification of the last page.

The batch log is only created after the production and inspection of the batch has been completed. After creation, the batch log can be transferred to an archive with SAP ArchiveLink. The archived logs are approved via a digital signature. The system can be configured in such a way that only after approval of the batch log can the UD be made for a GR inspection lot of the batch, and the batch status can be changed to "released."

| Data of the Batch Log | Assignment in the SAP ERP System |
|---|---|
| Relevant parts of the manufacturing and process instructions | Process order and material list |
| In-process and postprocess controls, the inspector cipher, and the inspection results | Inspection lot for in-process inspection and for GR inspection |
| Actual data for the process | Process notifications and manufacturing instructions |

**Table 8.3** Data in the Batch Log

## 8.8 Quality-Related Costs

This section describes the quality-related costs. First, some basic information is provided.

### 8.8.1 Basic Principles

There are several important reasons for exploring the subject of quality-related costs in the context of quality management:

- The quality-related costs, resulting from the costs of inspection costs, additional costs caused by defective products, and the costs for quality planning and control amount to a considerable part of the manufacturing costs.

- Quality costs are an important indicator of quality-related and thus financial weaknesses in a company. Analyzing these costs helps to reveal starting-points for improvement in the quality of products and the efficiency of the company.
- Top management is far more willing to appreciate the need for projects and measures for quality improvement and quality promotion if the arguments for these projects and processes aimed at quality improvement can be supported with business data such as costs and profitability.

The quality-related costs (QC) are usually split into three categories:

- Inspection costs
- Nonconformity costs
- Prevention costs

*Inspection costs* refer to costs for production inspections in the area of quality assurance. This includes inspection personnel, costs for accommodation and infrastructure, as well as costs for measuring devices and equipment. Inspection costs can include the following:

- GR inspection
- Quality inspection in production
- In-process and final inspections
- Audit inspections and product audits
- Laboratory examinations
- Source inspections for models, prototypes, and pilot series

*Nonconformity costs* arise because products do not comply with the quality requirements set. A distinction is made between internal and external nonconformity costs:

- **Internal nonconformity costs**
  - Scrap
  - Rework
  - Decrease in value due to quality deficiencies
  - Nonconformity costs due to missing quantities
  - Nonconformity costs through screening and recurring inspections
- **External nonconformity costs**
  - Processing of complaints to the vendors

- Settling warranty claims
- Consequential costs due to reconstruction, delay, and shutdown
- Product liability costs

*Prevention costs* are costs that arise through proactive actions in the name of quality assurance. Some examples of prevention costs include the following:

- Personnel for quality control and quality management
- Quality planning, inspection planning
- Quality audits, vendor audits
- Quality capability examinations
- Quality reporting and quality analysis for quality control
- Quality promotion and quality training
- Vendor evaluation
- Vendor development and promotion

The modern approach provides only for a dichotomy of the quality-related costs, a classification that has also been established in standardization. ISO 8402 classifies the costs into the following:

- Costs to ensure a satisfactory quality
- Losses due to nonachievement of a satisfactory quality

### 8.8.2 Cost and Performance Accounting

The data for quality-related costs comes from the company accounting department, in particular, from cost and performance accounting, described in more detail in the following sections.

Costs are quantities of production factors (output, operating facilities, and basic materials) evaluated on a monetary basis, as well as third-party services, taxes, and duties that are used to generate the company output.

#### Cost Types

In a first step, Cost Accounting records the production factors consumed in a company as cost element accounting and evaluates and classifies them according to their origin. The following are the most important groups of cost types:

- Personnel costs (wages, salaries, social fees)
- Material costs (raw materials and supplies)
- Investment costs (depreciation, interest)
- Costs for utility services (electricity, water, cleaning, etc.)

**Cost Center Accounting**

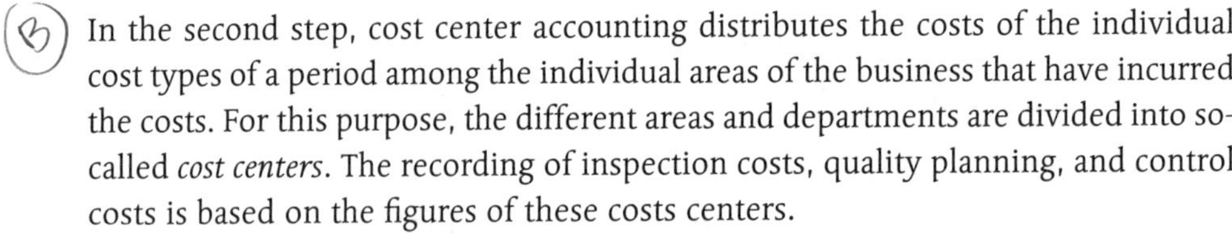

In the second step, cost center accounting distributes the costs of the individual cost types of a period among the individual areas of the business that have incurred the costs. For this purpose, the different areas and departments are divided into so-called *cost centers*. The recording of inspection costs, quality planning, and control costs is based on the figures of these costs centers.

**Cost Object Controlling**

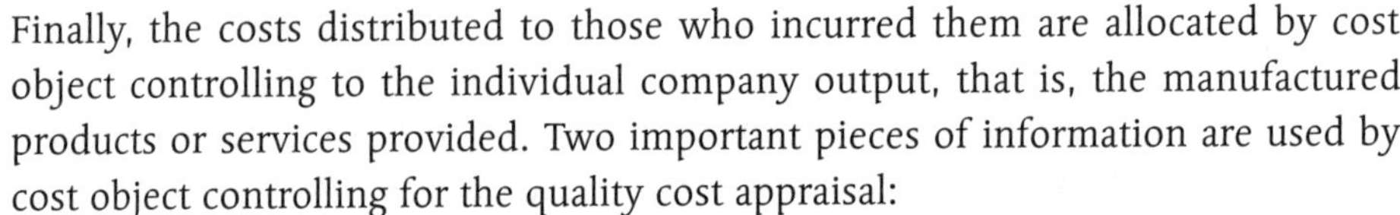

Finally, the costs distributed to those who incurred them are allocated by cost object controlling to the individual company output, that is, the manufactured products or services provided. Two important pieces of information are used by cost object controlling for the quality cost appraisal:

- To determine the nonconformity costs of scrap parts and rework parts, the manufacturing costs determined by cost object controlling for the different processing steps of the part are used.
- By determining the manufacturing costs per item, the evaluation of the output of a production area per accounting period is possible. These figures are required as reference values to analyze the quality costs.

With these three partial accounts, the company cost and performance accounting provides the essential data for quality cost elements.

### 8.8.3 Recording Quality-Related Costs

For cost center accounting, separate cost centers for the different types of quality-related costs must have been established. By having separate cost centers, allocating the inspection costs for procurement to a GR inspection department or inspection area becomes quite feasible. This clear assignment is falsified by nonrelated activities that normally occur in these departments, for example, sorting work, which should actually be assigned to the nonconformity costs. It becomes more difficult when allocating planning activities for the recording of costs for quality planning. Because planning tasks belong to the management tasks for employees in Development, Construction/Engineering, Quality Assurance and Production, an allocation to cost centers is not possible. Frequently, the costs of cost center quality assurance and GR inspection are roughly apportioned on a pro-rata basis to quality inspection and quality planning.

Cost accounting is of little use for the recording of nonconformity costs because the costs are incurred either as additional costs in the different cost types and cost centers, or as a decrease in earnings. Reduction in earnings means that the production costs incurred for a product have no corresponding proceeds in the market and therefore no corresponding performance credit.

To record the various nonconformity cost types, a supplementary system must be established. The system must be able to record the causes of defects and to distinguish between the different nonconformity cost types. Cost object controlling represents one option in that the costs that arise from manufacturing are reported as nonconformity costs. Another option is the recording of nonconformity costs via separate orders that will be grouped and allocated accordingly at a later time.

### 8.8.4 Evaluation of Quality-Related Costs

To record the quality-related costs for the maintenance and continued improvement of quality control, meaningful evaluations are required. These evaluations should indicate quality-related and commercial weaknesses and should provide support in locating these weaknesses. This is why quality cost reports should be clearly laid out and presented with informative and appealing graphics.

Comparisons are a frequently used method of analyzing weaknesses, for example:

- Comparisons between different areas/companies (internal/external)
- Comparisons of different time periods over time
- Comparisons between planned and actual costs
- Comparisons between different products

Evaluation tools such as the ABC analysis or the Pareto chart allow you to determine the main causes of weaknesses and to reduce weaknesses using targeted measures.

The evaluation of quality-related costs should be up to date (weekly/monthly), sent to a fixed distribution list, and have a uniform structure to ensure a quick orientation and good comparability over a certain period.

### 8.8.5 Implementation Options with SAP ERP

The integrated SAP ERP system supports the mentioned business requirements or goals in a wide variety with the close interaction of its QM and Cost Accounting components.

Cost center accounting can be performed using the CO component without involving the QM component.

However, when using the SAP ERP component, QM, you can implement a much more precise recording of inspection costs through inspection planning and the assigned work centers. In precisely the same way as is done for inspection equipment in work planning, implementation and inspection times for personnel can be planned and recorded via confirmations. This means that the inspection costs can be recorded material or order-related and are therefore also available for detailed evaluations.

For the recording of nonconformity costs, the QM order tool is available. In conjunction with the quality notification, you can create QM orders and confirm the same expenditures in the form of personnel (times) and material (costs). By allocating the QM orders, you can distinguish between internal and external nonconformity costs, and group and evaluate the costs according to different criteria such as material, vendor, and customer. The cost report for a QM order can be displayed from the USAGE DECISION screen.

*The quality notification is a very powerful and versatile function of the SAP ERP system. In addition to supporting the processes of defect and complaint processing, it also provides a wide range of options that will be detailed in this chapter.*

# 9 Quality Notification

The notification system in SAP ERP provides benefits not only to the quality managers. The use of existing master data enables you to simply create notifications irrespective of the reason for recording. The qualification notification is used most frequently for incoming complaints (customer complaints) and for complaints to vendors. The notification creation is only the initial step of a comprehensive process that you can design according to your requirements.

## 9.1 Basic Principles

The communication of quality-related complaints is one of the touchstones of every customer-vendor relationship, whether it is internal or external. Initially, such events are usually accompanied by more or less unpleasant circumstances, which means people are unwilling to go into detail on the subject of "complaints processing." Even standard works on the topic of quality assurance tend to omit this topic. In the development of customer-oriented processes, experts approached the subject from a sales and marketing point of view, which led to flashy slogans such as: "Use a complaint to improve your business relationships!" Practical methods primarily emerged in the automotive industry. For example, the 8D report method developed by Ford (1995) is a milestone in the standardization of complaints processing.

However, the will to reengineer the complaints processes does not suffice. Anyone who examines the overall business context will discover how a complaints process places demands on the areas of Materials Management (MM), Production Planning and Control (PP), Sales and Distribution (SD), and, of course, Quality Management (QM). This primarily results in the need for smooth organization, supported by suitable tools such as computerized notification systems. In addition, there are not only external customer complaints but also a similar amount of internal problem notifications as well as complaints aimed at the vendors (see Figure 9.1). From a business point of view in the area of PP, it is crucial to reveal and resolve problems in the production chain as early as possible. As a rule of thumb, you can reckon with a high increase in costs with each operation. A suitable notification system in the production environment supports production, detects process weaknesses, and supplies the necessary transparency with regard to the emergence of errors and defects.

**Figure 9.1** Notification Types for Quality Management

In general, several company areas and employees are involved in processing a complaint. In the case of a customer complaint, the process moves from a company-external starting point through the processing by the addressee and returns to the external starting point. This requires a cross-company communication with suitable communication paths.

At the outset, a complaint is assigned a number to ensure its clear identification, supplemented with a reference object, such as the customer order, the customer number, the delivery note number, and additional reference data. Ideally, the organizational responsibilities for further processing are clearly defined. One person should be appointed as the person in charge, and the others involved should be assigned with clearly defined tasks within a case of complaint. Basically, complaints processing is similar to a small project with a defined starting point and, hopefully, a successful end.

The internal process depends on fast and effective information distribution and an immediate execution of corrective actions. The basis for correct decisions is formed by both experience and access to the knowledge acquired from complaint cases that have already been processed. The measures taken and the time necessary for performing these actions are the pieces of information that need to be transferred rapidly and, most importantly, in the correct form to the person making the complaint. Subsequently, the evaluation of a complaint that has emerged provides important information on the weaknesses of the product affected and the performance of the company. The requirement to fulfill all the conditions detailed gives you an idea of the complexity of the task. In larger companies, complaints management and processing without using high-performance software wouldn't be feasible.

With regard to an improved customer orientation, the use of computer-supported complaint management in service companies, energy providers, banks, and insurance companies, for example, should be of particular interest. The following examples are based on logistic core processes and can be transferred without great difficulty to all commercial implementation areas, whether it is trade, production, or services.

## 9.2 Quality Notifications in SAP ERP

The official allocation of the quality notification to the QM application component leads to the impression that it is a separate QM application within the logistics processes. In fact, however, the notification system within the SAP ERP system is a cross-modular system. The default version of the SAP ERP system contains the notification types listed in Table 9.1. The quality notifications are highlighted in dark gray; all other notification types are highlighted in a light gray.

| | | |
|---|---|---|
| F1 | Customer failure | Quality notification |
| F2 | Vendor failure | Quality notification |
| F3 | Material failure | Quality notification |
| M1 | Maintenance request | Plant maintenance |
| M2 | Malfunction report | Plant maintenance |
| M3 | Activity report | Plant maintenance |
| MQ | Malfunction report from QM | Plant maintenance |

**Table 9.1** Notification Types

| | | |
|---|---|---|
| Q1 | Customer complaint | Quality notification |
| Q2 | Vendor fault list | Quality notification |
| Q3 | Internal problem notification | Quality notification |
| QS | StabilStudy with material | Quality notification |
| QR | StabilStudy without material | Quality notification |
| S1 | Service notification | Service notification |
| S2 | Activity report | Service notification |
| S3 | Service request | Service notification |
| S4 | Service: material/service notification | Service notification |
| S5 | Maintenance service request | Service notification |
| Z3 | Generally in problem notification | Quality notification |

**Table 9.1** Notification Types (Cont.)

The notification system provides a valuable integration potential in the area of logistics. In contrast to business cases, which are often processed by only one organizational unit and where a change in the organization does not improve the process, the goal of problem notification must be to form a workflow process across several specialist departments. The main task of the notification system is to handle external and internal complaints in connection with vendors and customers, and to trace problems in the production environment.

As the use of quality notifications is generally seen in the context of "nonquality," a few more aspects of active quality control with the SAP ERP notification system are listed here:

- Organization of the company notification system
- Coordination with the customers in the automotive area in terms of the QS 9000 requirements,
- Support of processes that were initialized by the FMEA (Failure Mode and Effects Analysis) team

For the aforementioned areas, you can add your own notification types to those of the shipped system to enable an individual notification structure. There are many ways of tailoring each notification type so it meets the requirements of the user, and since Release 4.5, there are ways to communicate in a simple way with applications outside the SAP ERP system, for example, by email applications. In terms of performance, the notification system compares favorably with similar external systems specifically developed for this purpose. The advantage of an integrated application is particularly strong with regard to the quality notification. Virtually all data from logistics that needs to get processed can be loaded into the application with just one click, and you can navigate easily to the logistical objects involved by simply selecting them (see Figure 9.2).

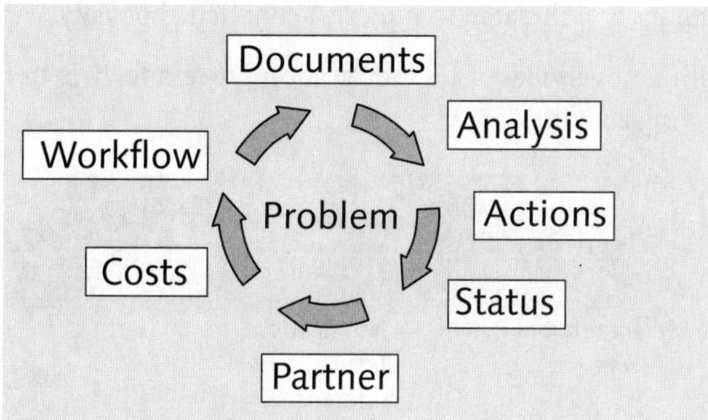


**Figure 9.2** The Interplay of Components and Objects of a Quality Notification Allow the Processing of a Quality Problem

In addition, the notification system also spans the SAP ERP application components Maintenance and Service Management (Service and Asset Management). For the processing of service and customer service tasks, specific notification forms have been developed that are based on the same systematics as quality notifications.

As described in Chapter 1, Implementing Management Systems with SAP, the notification system can be used to implement the requirements of corrective actions and prevention measures of ISO 9000 and those that follow.

### 9.2.1 Scenario: Complaint Management with Quality Notification

Let's now trace the processing of a customer complaint using a typical case. In this example, it will soon become apparent to you that the company, Duff & Sons Ltd., has once again delivered parts that do not exactly meet the required specification.

The business scenario deals with the notification type Q1, Customer Complaint, from a delivery of 10,000 assemblies of the CD casings that you already know from

Chapter 6, Quality and Inspection Planning. In the assemblies, it is the CD plastic hub in the CD case that is causing problems. The plastic hub does not provide enough grip, and the CDs fall out of the casing when opened. You have already processed a part of the material in delivery units for a customer order and delivered them to your customers. The customer is extremely annoyed. In this case, the customer lodging the complaint notifies your Sales and Distribution department and demands an immediate subsequent delivery. If you do not take action, you must assume that this customer will threaten to impose a contractual penalty.

Table 9.2 provides you with an overview of the notification process for a better understanding of the following activities.

| Individual Step | Contents of Activities | Navigation in the Notification | Workflow |
|---|---|---|---|
| **Receipt of the Complaint** | | | |
| Start of relationship | Select reference objects | Notification header, reference objects | Start |
| | Select reference documents | | |
| | Select organizational unit | | |
| | Select partner | | |
| **Transfer of Descriptions into the Notification** | | | |
| Document the subject | Select type of notification | Subject | Transfer |
| | Describe subject | | |
| | Enter quantities affected | | |
| **Record and Analyze Defects** | | | |
| Problem analysis | Select defect type | Items | Transfer |
| | Select defect location | | |
| | Select defect cause | | |

**Table 9.2** Schematic Flow of a Quality Notification

| Individual Step | Contents of Activities | Navigation in the Notification | Workflow |
|---|---|---|---|
| **Task Management** | | | |
| Initiate and monitor tasks | Create immediate task | Tasks, item tasks | Transfer |
| | Schedule immediate task | | |
| | Create additional tasks | | |
| | Schedule additional tasks | | |
| **Action Management** | | | |
| Define additional actions | Create actions | Actions | Transfer |
| | Schedule actions | | |
| **Conclusion of Complaint and Archiving** | | | |
| Conclude complaint | Perform completion inspection | All areas | End |
| | Perform efficiency review | | |
| | Determine costs | | |
| | Set completion flag | | |

**Table 9.2** Schematic Flow of a Quality Notification (Cont.)

You use a standard installation of the SAP ERP notification system to trace the case and perform a complete documentation and defects analysis in the notification system. This will be done under the following aspects:

- Defect type
- Defect location
- Defect cause
- Measures

The goal is to satisfy the customer as quickly as possible and to eliminate a recurrence of the defect via a proactive quality assurance. The processing flow used (every other sequence could be mapped similarly) dictates that an incoming customer complaint with reference to a sales document is first processed by Sales and Distribution. Because complaints usually arrive at Sales and Distribution, the notification header and the subject of the complaint are filled out by Sales and Distribution.

In the processing flow of this example, it was also agreed that the Quality department will be responsible for all subsequent data inputs and for the completion of the notification. In this case, the responsibility for the tracing of tasks in the area of QM lies within the Quality Management department and that the Sales and Distribution department is thus relieved of additional notification administration. In your company, the processing of complaints can of course be organized in a completely different way. Therefore, it is strongly recommended that you model the business processes with all parties involved and do so thoroughly to ensure quality assurance.

After you have obtained a description of the situation from your customer by phone, ask the customer to send a short written note by fax or email that you can use as a reference in the quality notification.

### Creating a Notification

A notification is created during the first telephone call. You create a notification using menu path LOGISTICS • QUALITY MANAGEMENT • QUALITY NOTIFICATION • CREATE. Select notification type Q1, Customer Complaint. A dialog box opens (see Figure 9.3) where you can enter the requested document numbers from customer order or delivery. You must also enter the item numbers here; otherwise, the system cannot find the contents of the document (such as the material ordered) and cannot transfer this data into the notification. If you press Enter, the system transfers the most important document data for the quality notification into the notification header (see Figure 9.4).

> **Note**
>
> As of Release 4.5, the user interface of the quality notification in the QM application component has been changed to allow the use of a tab view. The term *Reference Objects* refers to the area above the tabs and the SUBJECT tab (see Figure 9.4).

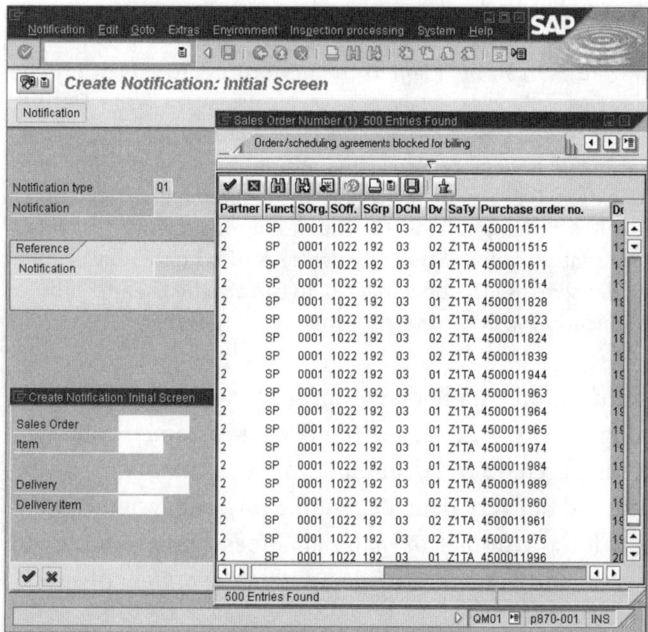


**Figure 9.3** Initial Screen for Notification Type Q1, Customer Complaint

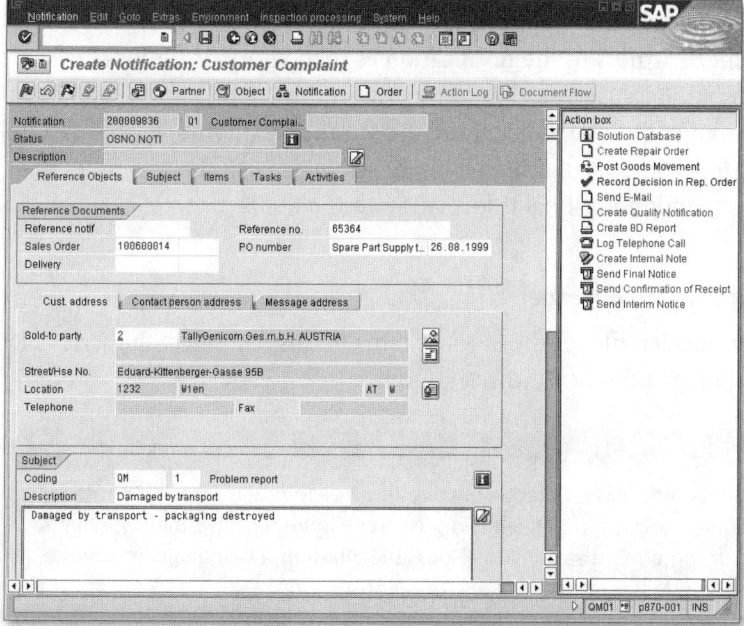


**Figure 9.4** Notification Header with Reference Objects of Sales and Distribution

**Customizing Tip**

The dialog box shown in Figure 9.3 can be adapted to your process to a high extent using the Customizing tables DEFINE SCREEN TEMPLATES FOR NOTIFICATION TYPE • DEFINE INITIAL SCREENS. In the example, initial screen 130, SALES DOCUMENT was selected. There are a total of eight different initial screens available that are described in detail in the context help. For the notification types with reference to Procurement, Production, and SD, there are specific initial screens for the corresponding documents available. However, it is not mandatory that you fill out the initial screens. If no data is available, you can skip over the particular screens. The document data can also be used to subsequently complement the notification with targeted information.

The system assigns the notification number in accordance with the settings of the number range interval internally. By entering the related customer order, you obtain relevant data, such as purchase order number, material number, production date, delivery quantity, and delivery date, depending on your system setting. If notifications already exist for a customer or material, a message informing you of their existence is displayed, and you are provided with an overview of similar complaints with the same reference.

All that is required as the mandatory partner (see Partner Data of the Notification in Section 9.2.2) of the customer complaint is the name of the customer who is already assigned a master data record in the SAP ERP system. Of course, it is also possible to set other partners of the notification as mandatory or optional in Customizing beforehand. Because you don't know where the defect is located at this time, you must take additional steps and conduct a more thorough analysis. To achieve this, the department handling the initial activities — in this example, Sales and Distribution — adds additional information to the SUBJECT tab.

### Filling Out the Notification Header

In the notification header, fill out the SUBJECT tab. On this tab, select the ASSEMBLY LINE COMPLAINT entry in the CODING selection list.

**Tip**

For the sake of clarity, you should place only two or three logically separate entries in the basic data catalog CODING in the selection list (see Figure 9.5). Ultimately, what's important here is to determine as quickly as possible whether a case really involves a complaint or simply entails a normal request or a note.

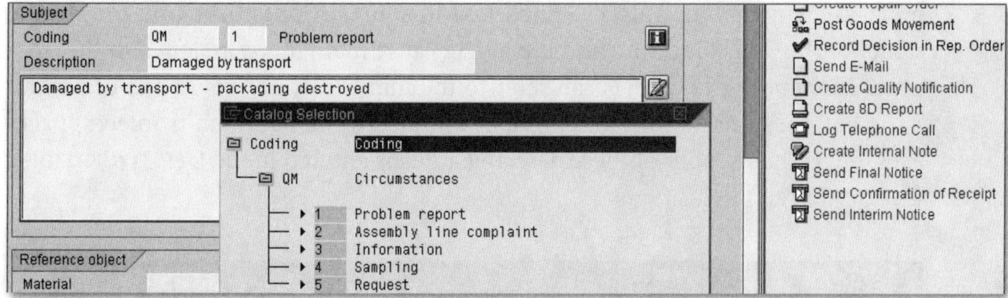


**Figure 9.5** Subject of the Notification

In the DESCRIPTION field, enter the following: "Damaged by transport—packaging destroyed." The long text could be: "Defect causes not yet known, but Duff & Sons delivered material with this defect twice last year. However, as the last five deliveries were without defects, the inspections are in skip mode, and therefore no inspection was performed."

In this example, the entry concludes the notification processing for the Sales and Distribution department. It is assumed that actions will be initiated and monitored in QM. It is, without doubt, important to agree on how complaints can be processed as quickly as possible, but now, the focus is on the QM department and the performance of a defect analysis. Perhaps a more detailed analysis will reveal the defect quickly, and under certain circumstances, an appropriate task performed quickly can prevent even further damage.

### Problem Analysis

You now begin immediately with an initial defect analysis to rule out a recurrence of the same defect in current deliveries. In the processing of the quality notification, it is also possible to first implement an immediate task (e.g., "Deliver new parts immediately" or "Delivery stop") and then continue with a defect analysis.

Navigate to the ITEMS tab where you can perform a defect analysis (see Figure 9.6). You create a defect item by selecting an entry from the selection list of defects. You can display the detail view by double-clicking on a list entry. The structure of the quality notification provides for one defect item for each defect in a complaint. From now on, "items" or "notification items" are also used. The defect analysis relies on a well-prepared defect catalog structure and therefore requires the selection of a defect code for each item. However, you can supplement each entry with a user-defined text in short or long form. You can do the same for the defect location and the defect cause that will be assigned to the item next. The number of defects can refer to the number of defects in one or several parts but does not indicate the number of defective delivery units (pieces, packages, etc.). The number of these defective units is entered in the DEFQTY(INTERN.)/ DEFQTY(EXTER.) fields.

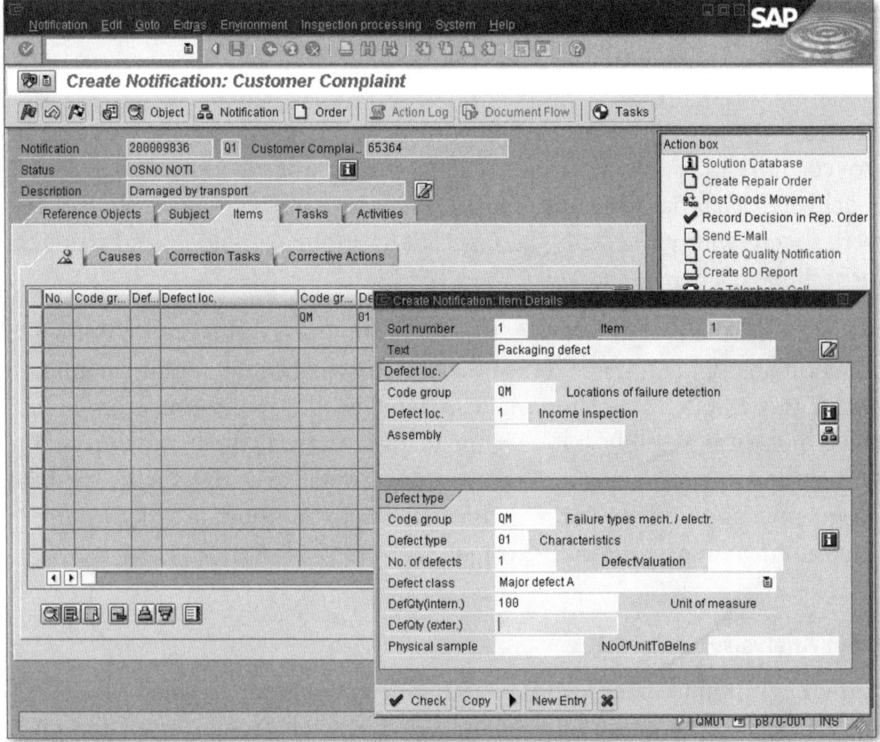


**Figure 9.6** Item Details

A detailed examination of the sample sent by the customer has shown that the CD plastic hub does not perform its intended function because the circumference of the hub is too small. Create one or more defect items by selecting the individual coding from the catalogs already created, for example:

- Defect loc.: Inner case with CD plastic hub
- Defect type: Function CD hold
- Defect cause: Material vendor

### Displaying Assemblies

If a material defect in an assembly is involved, you can enter the material number of the defective part of an assembly as additional information by selecting DEFECT ITEM • DETAIL • ASSEMBLY ICON. The assembly refers to the bill of material (BOM) for the material (105969). The graphic display of the relevant BOM is shown. For more complex assemblies, this function enables you to display the defect location in the form of a hierarchy. On the first level, a part of the assembly is specified as the defect location; on the second level, the selection of an entry from the catalog DEFECT LOCATION shows the occurrence of the defect in more detail.

**Customizing Tip**

Unfortunately, the catalog types used do not provide the SELECTION SETS function. This means that the selection of a code must always be performed from the entire pool of code groups. However, particularly in larger companies, a separation between different business areas is useful for defect analysis; here, a selection from all existing error codes would soon become confusing.

The solution lies in using a catalog profile. In Customizing, you must first assign specific code groups to a defined catalog profile. In this example, you can design specific notification types for domestic and foreign sales units based on the standard notification Q1. In the next step, you create a specific catalog profile for each notification type and assign it to the corresponding notification type (see Table 9.3). Populating fields for defective quantities or recording summarized defects will enable you to evaluate the extent of the damages later.

| | Notification Type Short Text | Catalog Profile | Catalog Profile Short Text | Catalog Type | Code Groups |
|---|---|---|---|---|---|
| KI | Domestic customer complaint | CUSDOM | Domestic customer complaint | 5 | 1–2 |
| | 9 | 1–2 | | | |
| | E | 1–2 | | | |
| KA | Customer complaint, foreign | CUSFOR | Customer complaint, foreign | 5 | 3–4 |
| | 9 | 3–4 | | | |
| | E | 3–4 | | | |

**Table 9.3** Allocation of Notification Types to Catalog Profile

### Informing Customers Using the 8D Report

One of the most important tasks of customer-oriented notification processing is sending a report to the complaining party regarding the general situation, the processing status, and the reference number that can be used to obtain additional information about their complaint. The generally accepted 8D report from the automotive industry can be of service here. As of Release 4.5, the standard system provides a specific form supporting the 8D process. If you are planning a later release change, the 8D report can be mapped using form programming in SAP-script. The example in Figure 9.7 can serve as a sample for this report. All values of the fields are derived from the quality notification and are processed through SAPscript programming.

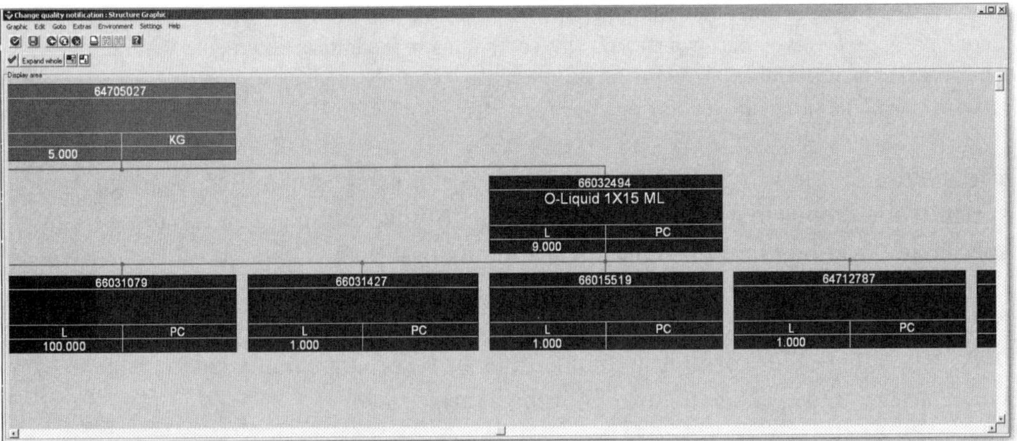


**Figure 9.7** Error Item with Reference to Bill of Material

### Problem Description

The solution for operational problems or the implementation of proposed improvements, for example, in the scope of a continuous improvement process, frequently fails due to a lack of systematic processes and a lack of consistent documentation and review of the individual solution steps. In this instance, the 8D methodology and the 8D report can prove very useful. The application of the 8D report has already proven to be effective in many companies and industries, namely, the automotive industry.

### What Is the 8D Method?

The 8D problem solution methodology (also referred to as the *eight-step plan*) is a series of eight steps (disciplines) that should be run through as soon as a problem emerges. If handled correctly, this method helps in finding a timely and complete solution for the problem in question. It's essentially fact-oriented approach makes certain that solutions, decisions, and planning are based on hard data, ensuring that the core problem is solved instead of merely addressing the symptoms. Furthermore, the 8D report that should accompany the process serves as a progress control and catalyst, which ensures that all steps of the 8D process are adhered to and implemented.

### Creating the 8D Report

The 8D report is updated and populated with the relevant attachments by a single person after the conclusion of each step. This report reflects the current status of the problem solution and is a dynamic document. Because the 8D Report is stored in a generally accessible archive system, it is available to teams and individuals who may encounter similar problems and thus benefit from the information already outlined.

### The Basic Principle

The 8D process is a problem management tool supported by a specific report form, thus specifying and ensuring a uniform standard for companies and vendors.

### Reasons for Ineffective Problem Solving

The 8D process has been developed to increase the efficiency of problem solving in the areas of production and development. Ineffective problem solving is caused by any of the following factors:

- **Incorrect description of the problem**
  A clear, detailed description of the problem is necessary. A clear description and strict definition needs to be provided before a team can effectively process a problem.
- **Rushing the problem solution process**
  In the problem-solving process, steps are skipped inappropriately in an attempt to find a solution quickly.

- **Poor cooperation among team members**
  Not all members of the team are actively cooperating, which means that the team cannot record all causes of the problem.
- **No logical process flow**
  There is no systematic approach for setting priorities, performing analyses, and investigating the problem.
- **Lack of technical skills**
  The persons involved lack the technical skills and know-how required to use the tools and implement the working techniques that support the problem solution process.
- **Impatience of management**
  Due to a lack of knowledge of the problem solution process and an underestimation of the required work, management sets unrealistic deadlines. This pressure on the employees leads to insufficient analyses.
- **Errors in identifying the basic cause**
  Sometimes a possible cause of the problem is accepted too readily as the basic cause, and the investigation of the problem ends. However, later, the problem comes up again because the actual cause was not properly clarified.
- **No introduction of permanent improvement tasks**
  Though the basic cause of the problem may have been identified, insufficient or even temporary improvement tasks were initiated. For permanent improvement tasks to be effective, support on the part of management for approving costs and implementing tasks is required.
- **Lack of documented information**
  There is not enough information available on the current problem or on similar problems that might have previously occurred.

#### The Eight Disciplines (Steps)

The eight steps are described here:

1. **Tackle the problem!**
   Enter the name of the person who starts the 8D report and supplement the header data (problem, ref. no., start date, status on [date], part description).
2. **Describe the problem!**
   Define the problem of the internal or external customer as precisely as possible.

Work out the root cause of the problem, and quantify it. Collect and analyze statistical data.

3. **Initiate temporary tasks to limit the damage and check their effect!**
   Initiate tasks that, where possible, keep the effects of problems of internal or external customers at bay until a permanent solution is found. Constantly check the effectiveness of these temporary tasks and, if necessary, implement additional tasks.
4. **Identify the root cause or causes of the problem and determine whether these are really the basic cause(s)!**
   Determine whether the problem can be solved. Search for all possible causes that could explain the occurrence of the problem. Determine the possible cause(s) and check via comparisons with the problem description and the existing data whether a likely cause is a basic cause. Prove your assumption with tests and experiments.
5. **Determine improvement tasks and check their effectiveness!**
   Search for all possible tasks that could eliminate the cause(s) and solve the problem. Choose the optimum permanent improvement task(s), and prove by means of appropriate tests that the selected permanent improvement tasks really solve the problem and do not have any undesirable side effects. If necessary, determine tasks for possible scenarios, based on risk analysis.
6. **Implement improvement tasks and examine their effect!**
   Create an action plan to implement the selected improvement task(s) and determine which controls will ensure that the cause of the problem is really eliminated. Implement the action plan, observe the effects, and, if necessary, execute the tasks provided for possible scenarios.
7. **Determine tasks that prevent a recurrence of the problem!**
   Change the management and control systems, instructions, and usual processes to avoid a recurrence of the same or similar problems. Identify improvement possibilities, and initiate process improvement tasks.
8. **Conclusion of the 8D report!**
   The QM department head (date, name) acknowledges the completion of the 8D report.

**Tip**

The 8D report can be used at any time within the notification flow for customer information. In this instance, it is not important whether all relevant information is already available in this report.

You can indicate the current processing status of the complaint on the form. This signifies that the 8D report is a dynamic form that you can use for various communication purposes without having to deviate from a certain standard in form and flow (see Figure 9.8).

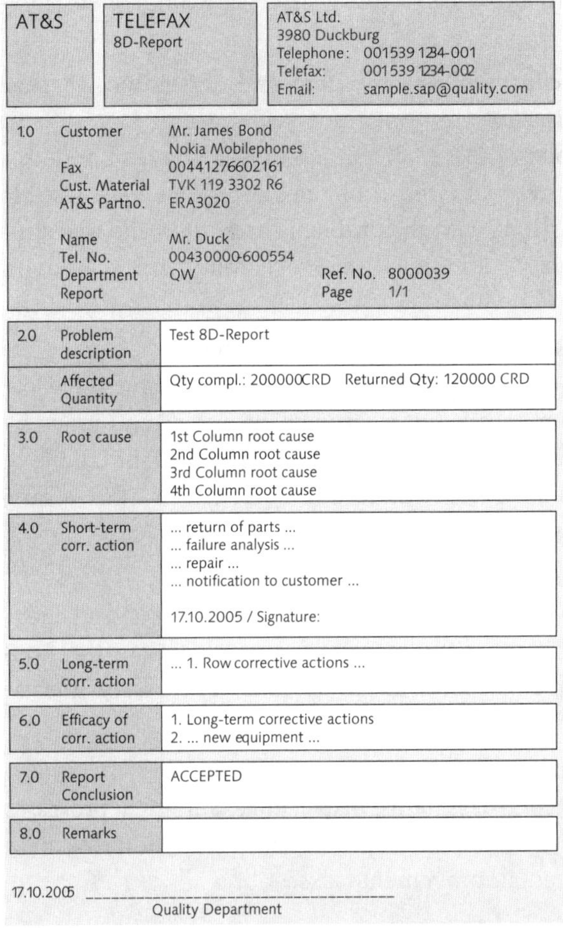

| AT&S | TELEFAX<br>8D-Report | AT&S Ltd.<br>3980 Duckburg<br>Telephone: 001539 1234-001<br>Telefax: 001539 1234-002<br>Email: sample.sap@quality.com |
|---|---|---|

| | | |
|---|---|---|
| 1.0 | Customer | Mr. James Bond<br>Nokia Mobilephones |
| | Fax | 00441276602161 |
| | Cust. Material | TVK 119 3302 R6 |
| | AT&S Partno. | ERA3020 |
| | Name | Mr. Duck |
| | Tel. No. | 00430000-600554 |
| | Department | QW — Ref. No. 8000039 |
| | Report | Page 1/1 |

| | | |
|---|---|---|
| 2.0 | Problem description | Test 8D-Report |
| | Affected Quantity | Qty compl.: 200000CRD Returned Qty: 120000 CRD |
| 3.0 | Root cause | 1st Column root cause<br>2nd Column root cause<br>3rd Column root cause<br>4th Column root cause |
| 4.0 | Short-term corr. action | ... return of parts ...<br>... failure analysis ...<br>... repair ...<br>... notification to customer ...<br><br>17.10.2005 / Signature: |
| 5.0 | Long-term corr. action | ... 1. Row corrective actions ... |
| 6.0 | Efficacy of corr. action | 1. Long-term corrective actions<br>2. ... new equipment ... |
| 7.0 | Report Conclusion | ACCEPTED |
| 8.0 | Remarks | |

17.10.2005 ____________________
Quality Department

**Figure 9.8** Example of an 8D Report in the SAP ERP System

### Immediate Task

In the next step, you record an *immediate task* through which — depending on the cause of damage and a precise defect analysis — you can expand the notification. To do so, select TASKS from the tab in the notification header.

What is the difference between an immediate task and an item task? In this case, additional tasks from defect analysis are not to be implemented; instead, tasks involving an immediate distribution of information, submission of a complaint number to the customer, or creation of a response plan should be performed. You can use this process to implement a two-level program of tasks if it does not appear useful for your complaints processing.

### Control of Tasks Using the Worklist

The system automatically places all tasks created within the notification in a special notification list, the *worklist* (see Figure 9.9). This assumes that the employee responsible performs his assigned task within the predefined framework and views the worklist. In this case "traffic light" functions signal the status of the individual tasks of the notification and inform about the completion period. You can immediately switch from the list to the notification with a click of the mouse.

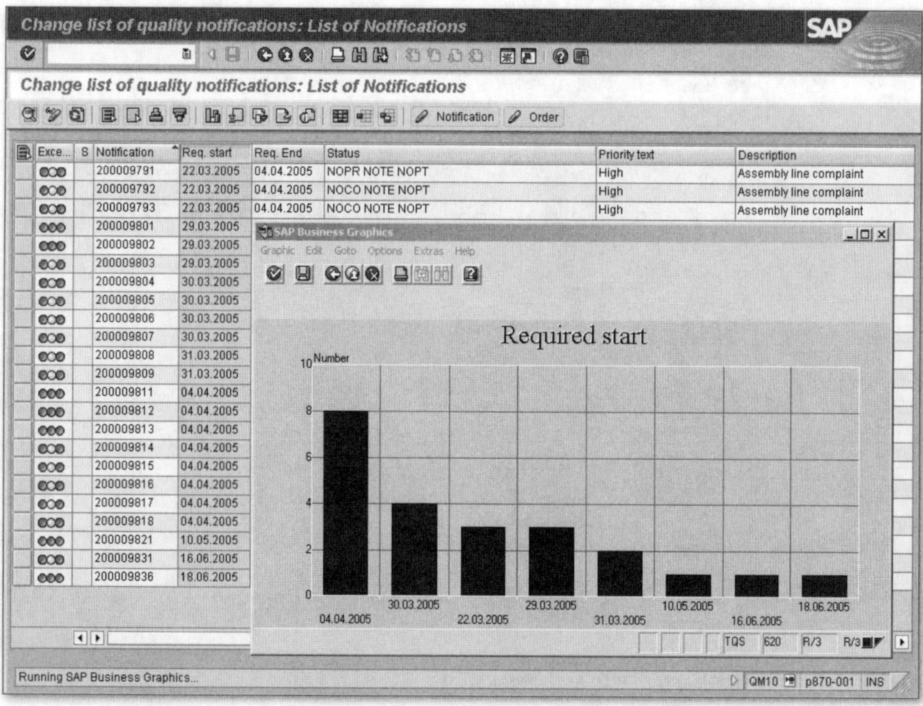


**Figure 9.9** Worklist

The worklist is a report that can be individually parameterized in many areas to be tailored to meet user requirements. In addition, you can create simple graphics from the overview that can, for example, provide information on the focal point of the task list.

In addition to the listing, the immediate task initiated contains detailed information that can be retrieved by double-clicking on an item. The detailed view is opened in a separate window. Here, as is the case for all list functions, whether you work with the detail view or with the configurable table control list is purely a matter of taste. After the planned start and planned finish fields of the task have been entered, and the user responsible for the task has been identified, you must save the tasks by returning to the notification header (see Figure 9.10).

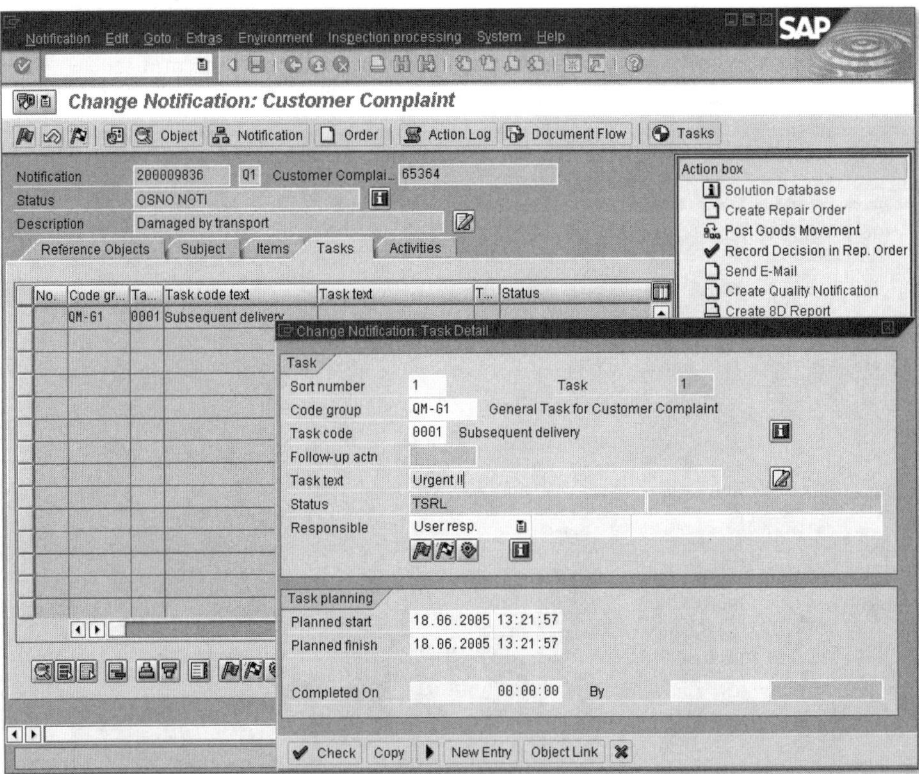


**Figure 9.10** Overview Screen of the Immediate Task

Because QM has extended the notification in this example to an immediate task, the various specialist departments must now process the case. At this point, you start an internal workflow process in connection with the quality notification as an alternative to the process control via the worklist described earlier. You can run the workflow process with or without the SAP Module Business Workflow in SAP ERP and display it in simplified form with three variations:

1. **SAP Business Workflow already in productive use**
   In this case, the SAP Business Information Warehouse (SAP BW) module is started according to predefined rules. The employee responsible receives specific workflow information via SAPoffice, for instance, "New notification with open tasks." Later in this chapter, you get more detailed information on this topic.
2. **SAP NetWeaver BI module is not in productive use**
   The employee responsible is informed about new quality notifications via conventional communication techniques and fetches the information from the relevant worklist.
3. **One of the components located in the action box is used**
   This communication component contained in the notification header is used to provide information for those who process the notification afterwards, for example, via email.

In this case, the third variation is used. QM sends an urgent email to SD, asking for immediate processing and an instant response. The notification is then saved and closed.

After the email has arrived, the processing Quality Assurance (QA) office opens the notification from the worklist, a selection list, or directly by entering the number specified internally (from the system) or externally (from the processor). In addition, QM creates an additional task via the TASKS tab. The TASK CODE is: "Retrieve parts." The TASK TEXT provides the following description: "Necessary to send a sample part with the relevant defect per express." However, you now adhere to the task that you first entered and perform a precise defect analysis by entering an additional defect item on the ITEMS tab to locate the defect more accurately.

#### Correction Task

The correction task contains the same elements as the immediate task and only differs regarding the selection of a certain group of task codes. You reach the task code via the ITEMS • TASKS tab in the menu bar of the item list.

You now deal with a targeted correction task for the notification item. Unlike the immediate task that we described earlier, this targeted correction task is not assigned to the notification header but directly to the defect item. The item tasks contain the next steps for defect removal. In this example, this means that because the CD inlets cannot be reprinted quickly enough, all delivered CD casings must be fitted with a new CD pick up (assuming that you have an appropriate assembly machine; etc.). You then create a task plan with the following content (see Figure 9.11):

- QM-G1—0001: Subsequent delivery
- QM-G1—0004: Price reduction
- QM-G1—0006: Rework

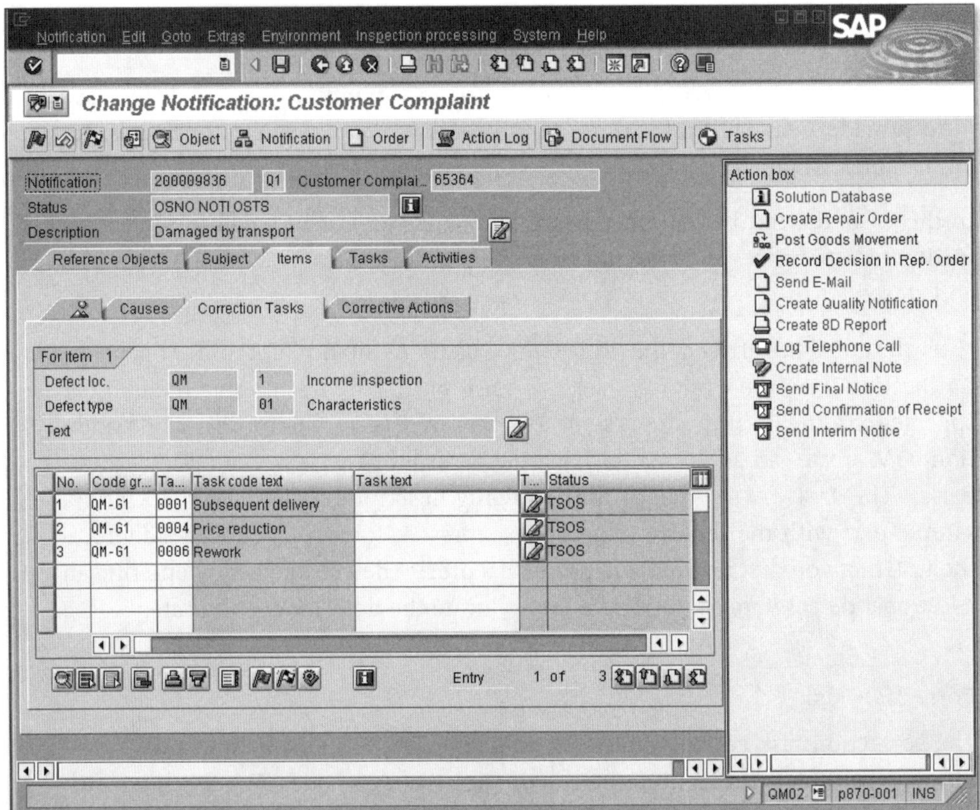


**Figure 9.11** Task List on Item Level

When all tasks have been defined, the first measures for defect removal are distributed, and from the point of view of QM, you can file a temporary customer complaint until the next events occur. As you have specified in the vendor fault list, you must initiate the notification type Q2, VENDOR FAULT LIST (select via QM01 • LOGISTICS • QUALITY MANAGEMENT • QUALITY NOTIFICATION • CREATE) in the next step.

You open the detail screen of the task by double-clicking it. In the TASK PLANNING area, you schedule the planned start and finish of each task and can therefore trace the current processing status throughout the process (see Figure 9.12).

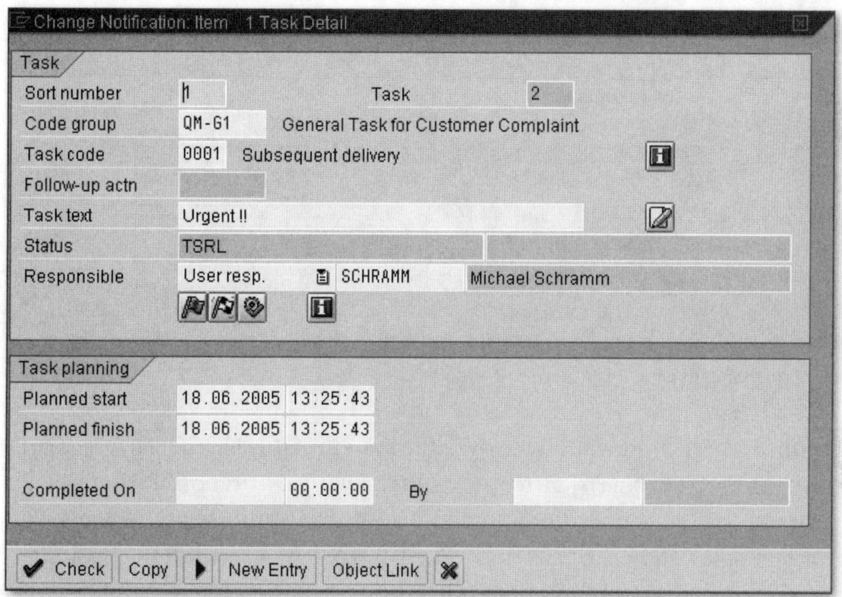


**Figure 9.12** Task Detail

### Changing the Activities Status and Completing the Notification

When the replacement delivery is received, an assembly order is started for the parts to be exchanged. After successfully performing this activity, you process the status of immediate and item tasks in the notification:

By double-clicking on a task in the task overview, you receive the detail view where the status can be changed (RELEASED, COMPLETED, SUCCESSFUL). You first select COMPLETED, and then directly after that, SUCCESSFUL. The completion date is entered by the system based on the notification priority from the notification header (refer to Figure 9.12). The relevant processing times for task planning are assigned an appropriate priority in Customizing.

After all immediate tasks have been performed, you can select additional notification items and the related tasks, for example, correction tasks, from the list (see Figure 9.13) and mark these as completed in the detail screen. A notification completion is only possible with completed tasks. For this reason, you make a selection in the menu from the quality notification: NOTIFICATION • FUNCTIONS • COMPLETE... • EXTERNAL ORIGIN.

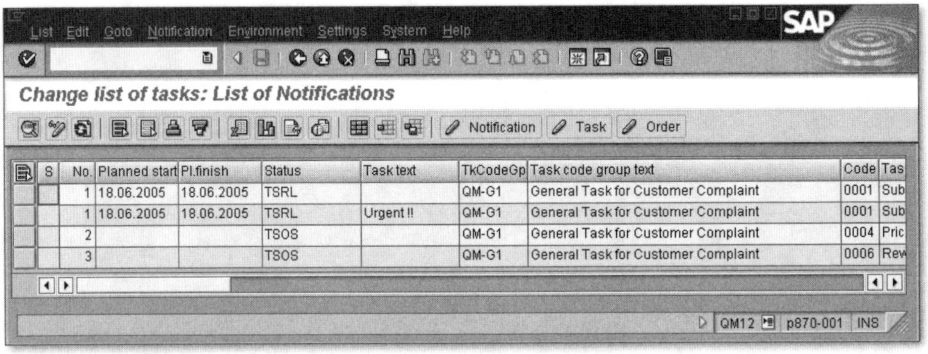

List Edit Goto Notification Environment Settings System Help

Change list of tasks: List of Notifications

Notification Task Order

| S | No. | Planned start | Pl.finish | Status | Task text | TkCodeGp | Task code group text | Code | Tas |
|---|---|---|---|---|---|---|---|---|---|
| | 1 | 18.06.2005 | 18.06.2005 | TSRL | | QM-G1 | General Task for Customer Complaint | 0001 | Sub |
| | 1 | 18.06.2005 | 18.06.2005 | TSRL | Urgent !! | QM-G1 | General Task for Customer Complaint | 0001 | Sub |
| | 2 | | | TSOS | | QM-G1 | General Task for Customer Complaint | 0004 | Pric |
| | 3 | | | TSOS | | QM-G1 | General Task for Customer Complaint | 0006 | Rev |

QM12 p870-001 INS

**Figure 9.13** Processing Status of the Tasks

With this function, the notification receives the system status NOCO, NOTIFICATION COMPLETED, and NOTE, NOTIFICATION EXTERNAL ORIGIN. The notification header then appears in gray and does not allow any additional processing. However, in the same menu path, there is a back door, PUT IN PROCESS, an option that is limited to a few users with a corresponding authorization profile.

The example shown only contains the basic functions of notification processing, but makes it clear that a careful modeling of the business scenario is essential for a meaningful use of the notification system. In the next sections, the most important additional functions are outlined along with the quality notification.

### 9.2.2 Functions and Elements of the Quality Notification

Figure 9.14 illustrates once more the general structure of the quality notification. In the following section, we will explore some of the functions of the quality notification that we have not yet dealt with.

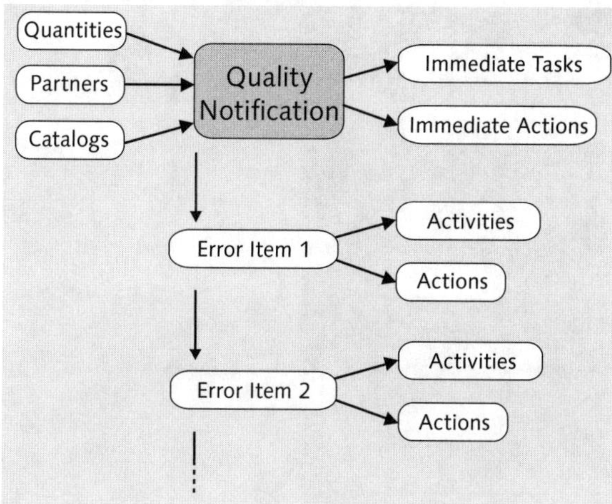


**Figure 9.14** Structure of the Quality Notification

### Quantity Details of the Quality Notification

During transfer of order, document, or supplier data, the system enters the specified quantities of the respective order items in the notification. The quantity details are then listed in the QUANTITIES section of the SUBJECT tab. A further division of the defect quantity into "internal" and "external origin" enables you to perform an informative analysis of the occurrence of defects.

### System Status and User Status

For the quality notification, you can use two status forms: the system status with its standard profile already defined in the shipped version, and the user status, which can also be set (see Figure 9.15). The user status can be configured so that it can be used to override the system status manually. In Customizing, the status profile is assigned to and set up in the structure of the quality notifications. The status profile functions precisely as described in the Quality Info Record section of Chapter 6, Quality and Inspection Planning.

You can display an overview of the status forms of your notification type by clicking on the information button to the left of the status bar in the notification header and then selecting EXTRAS • OVERVIEW (see Figure 9.16).

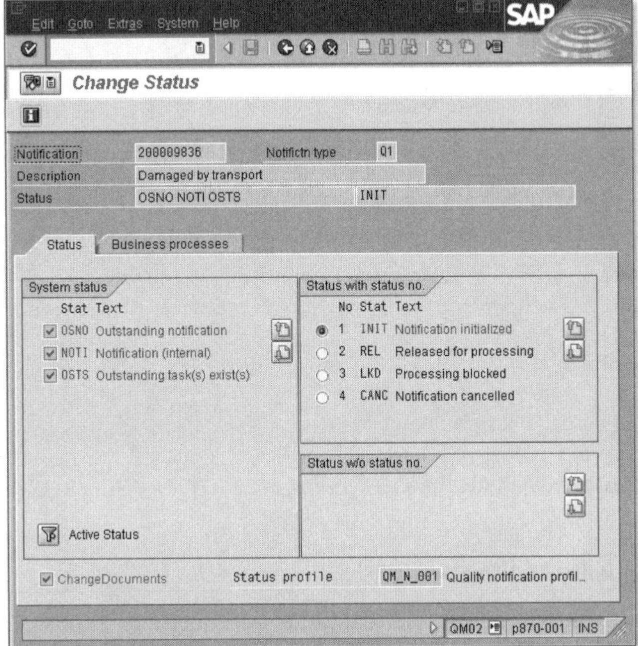


Figure 9.15 System Status and User Status

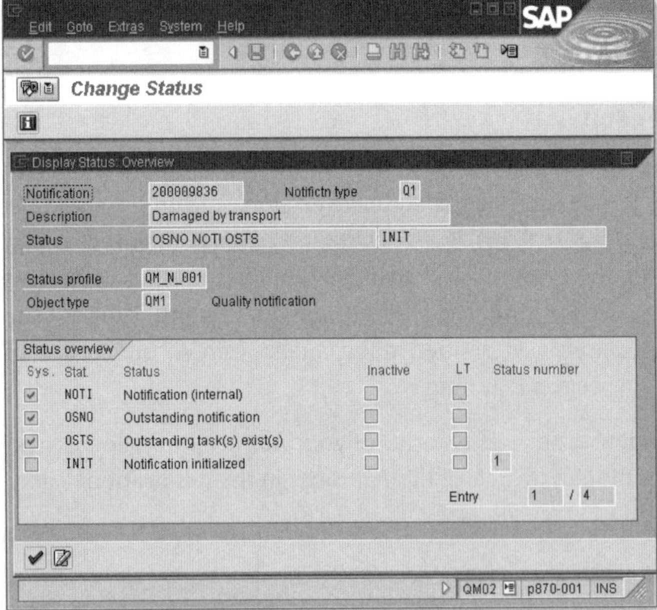


Figure 9.16 Status Overview

### Action

These functions in the menu bar of the notification header help to provide a more precise distinction between the task and other activities to be performed. The action refers to an additional catalog and describes activities that are performed in parallel to the tasks.

### Follow-on Action

With the follow-on action, you can automatically trigger system functions such as extended quality inspections, changes to the vendor relationship, openings of an additional notification, and other logistic processes. The function is selected in the task detail from a catalog and is activated when saving the task. Basically, the follow-on action is the start of a function module. The system provides a template for this in the corresponding Customizing table. Based on the template, a suitable function module will be programmed for you that can essentially call all system transactions. From Release 4.5 on, a collective function can be used to group different follow-on actions in an action box (see Figure 9.17). These follow-on actions can then be run consecutively in the system.

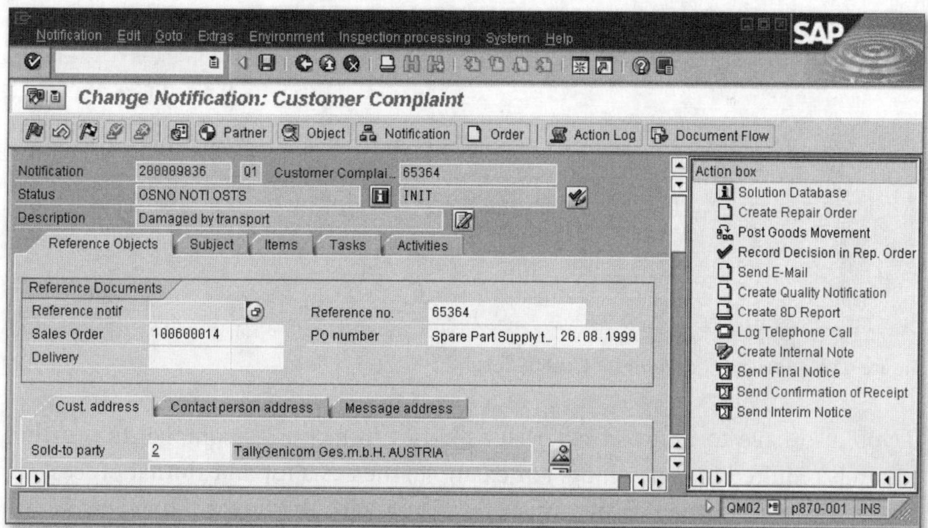


**Figure 9.17** Action Box

### QM Order in Controlling/Quality Costs

The individual activities and costs related to the complaints process enable you to draw important conclusions on the non-conformity costs within the company. A dedicated assignment of quality-related costs allows you to differentiate quality costs of external origin from those of internal origin. However, this type of cost allocation is possible only if the activities are cleared and assigned to accounts according to standard accounting principles. The main components of an order are the clearing accounts and the activity types. Activity types can be machine hours, labor hours of quality management, laboratory inspections, and additional quality inspections. The sending cost center usually specifies the quality management cost center (see Figure 9.18). Table 9.4 illustrates a simple assignment to an order.

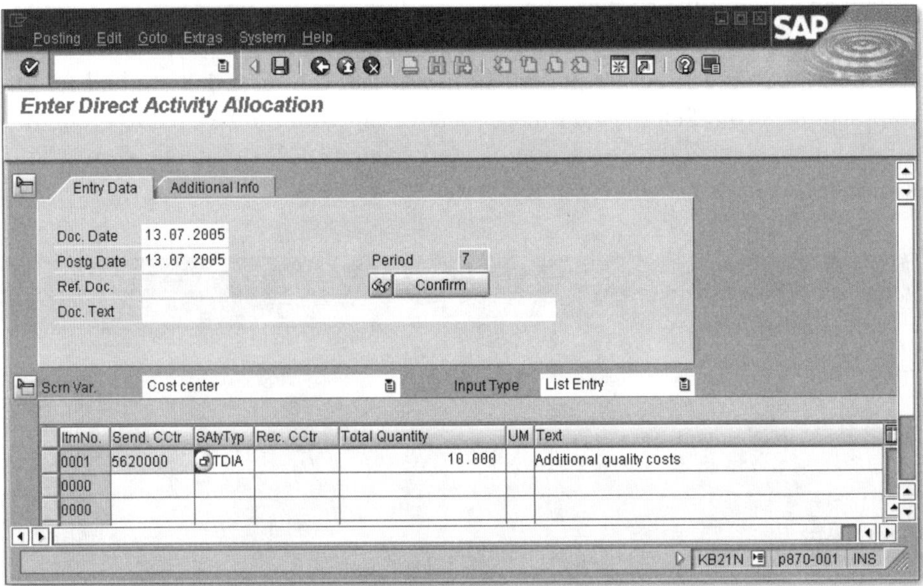


**Figure 9.18** Activity Allocation for Quality Costs

If you also have to draw on external activities to process a complaint, a further action is required in controlling. For example, the costs for an external processing are then posted to the quality order and, along with the internal business activities, form the overall costs of the quality order in a business order completion. The quality order is a fully fledged order that can be invoiced in the CO module with the special order type QN01, QUALITY ORDER. In the SAP ERP system, the ORDER function in the notification header creates such an order, generates an order number, and creates the basic data for the order. Activity allocations, that is, actual costs, must then be recorded for this order.

For reasons of clarity, the subject of "quality-related costs" is discussed separately in this book. Chapter 7, Quality Inspection, describes inspection costs in greater detail. Chapter 8, Quality Control, contains an overview of the quality-related costs. This chapter deals with quality-related costs that are closely linked with quality notification.

You can access the screen for activity allocation via the menu path LOGISTICS • QUALITY MANAGEMENT • QUALITY NOTIFICATION • COSTS • ACTUAL POSTINGS • ACTIVITY ALLOCATION • RECORD. The document items are filled out as shown in Table 9.4.

| Field Contents | Meaning | Entry in the Example |
|---|---|---|
| **Send CCtr** | Cost center (of quality management) | 5620000 — quality management |
| **SAtyTyp** (Enter activity type) | For instance, an activity type specially set up for notification processing | TDIA — notification processing |
| **Activity consumption** | Time unit | 10 h |
| **Receiving cost center** | Either enter a receiving cost center or name the receiving order in the next field | As required |
| **Rec. CCtr** (Receiving order) | Here, in general, the order number of the quality order from the Q notification is entered. | |

**Table 9.4** Activity Allocation

The order can immediately be analyzed in terms of costs after the activity allocation is completed. To do this, use the INDIVIDUAL SETTLEMENT function from the menu path LOGISTICS • QUALITY MANAGEMENT • QUALITY NOTIFICATION • COSTS • ACTUAL POSTINGS.

However, to use the *QM order*, it can be treated as a preliminary neutral cost collector. For this purpose, the CO must only create cost centers and clearing types that are exclusively used by quality management. It is advisable, upon agreement with the Controlling department, to create a manageable number of accounts and activity types that enable a simple internal activity allocation. Such an allocation enables you to calculate assigned costs of quality notifications from operating profit and regards them as statistical costs.

**Tip**

In many quality notifications, the accrued costs represent the actual focus of later analysis and are therefore an important component of company management from the beginning of the SAP ERP project. However, from the point of view of Controlling, this has proven to be problematic. The costs of quality assurance are generally allocated as overhead costs. If additional quality costs are entered, this results in a duplicate entry of quality costs in profitability analysis. This means that a systematic allocation of activities from the quality order type cannot take place until the accounting period has ended, at which time the quality costs have been recorded in detail. Consequently, a conversion from overhead cost accounting to direct cost accounting for quality management is not possible without additional effort, which is seldom provided for, especially in implementation projects.

### Shop Floor Papers

The individual forms and lists that belong to a quality notification can be printed, faxed, or forwarded by email (from Release 4.5 from the action box). In particular, documents for external use must be adjusted to reflect the corporate design and must meet the requirements regarding their information content. The desired changes must then be implemented via an ABAP List Viewer (ALV) and SAPscript programming. You should allow for two to four days of extra work per form – for form changes that aren't simply cosmetic – and include this additional effort in your schedule. In general, the programming resources for implementation projects are tightly budgeted. The documents contained in the standard SAP ERP version should only be regarded as suggestions:

- **Notification overview form**
  The notification overview is a printout of all information of a quality notification (see Figure 9.19).
- **Item list form**
  The item list either displays a part or all of the defect items contained in the quality notification. This means you can include or exclude individual defect items in the printout.

- **Vendor fault list form**
  This form should be used for all vendors who supply defective or incorrect goods. The shop floor paper is only relevant for the quality notification type Q2, VENDOR FAULT LIST. In addition, you can also define other shop floor papers according to the specific requirements in your company. The control tables for the print functions are defined centrally in your company so that you can display and select the relevant shop floor papers using the following online help functions:
  - Processing note to the customer
  - 8D report (as of Release 4.6)
  - Interim report
  - Final report

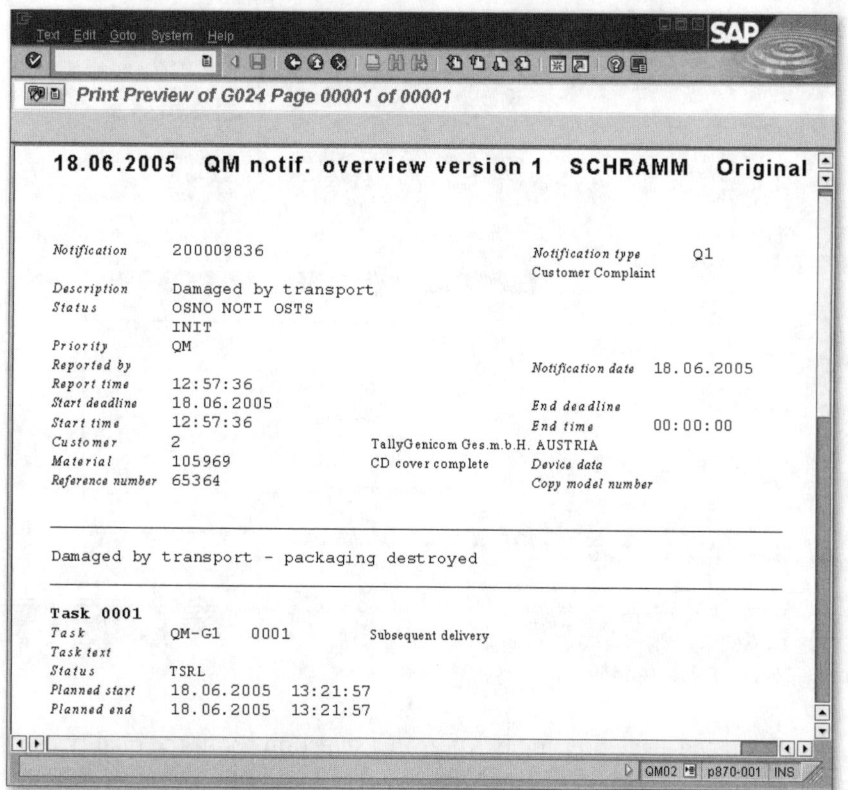


18.06.2005 QM notif. overview version 1 SCHRAMM Original

| | | | | |
|---|---|---|---|---|
| *Notification* | 200009836 | | *Notification type* | Q1 |
| | | | Customer Complaint | |
| *Description* | Damaged by transport | | | |
| *Status* | OSNO NOTI OSTS INIT | | | |
| *Priority* | QM | | | |
| *Reported by* | | | *Notification date* | 18.06.2005 |
| *Report time* | 12:57:36 | | | |
| *Start deadline* | 18.06.2005 | | *End deadline* | |
| *Start time* | 12:57:36 | | *End time* | 00:00:00 |
| *Customer* | 2 | TallyGenicom Ges.m.b.H. AUSTRIA | | |
| *Material* | 105969 | CD cover complete | *Device data* | |
| *Reference number* | 65364 | | *Copy model number* | |

Damaged by transport - packaging destroyed

**Task 0001**

| | | | |
|---|---|---|---|
| *Task* | QM-G1 | 0001 | Subsequent delivery |
| *Task text* | | | |
| *Status* | TSRL | | |
| *Planned start* | 18.06.2005 | 13:21:57 | |
| *Planned end* | 18.06.2005 | 13:21:57 | |

**Figure 9.19** Notification Overview

### Partner Data of the Notification

Partners are companies or individual persons who are involved in the context of the notification. For example, vendors and responsible processors are the mandatory partners set for the notification type Q2, VENDOR FAULT LIST, without which a notification cannot be saved. In the case of customer complaints, the customer and the responsible employee are the mandatory partners. The mandatory partners of the notification are entered on the CONTACT PERSON ADDRESS tab (until Release 4.0, the NOTIFICATION HEADER section) (see Figure 9.20).

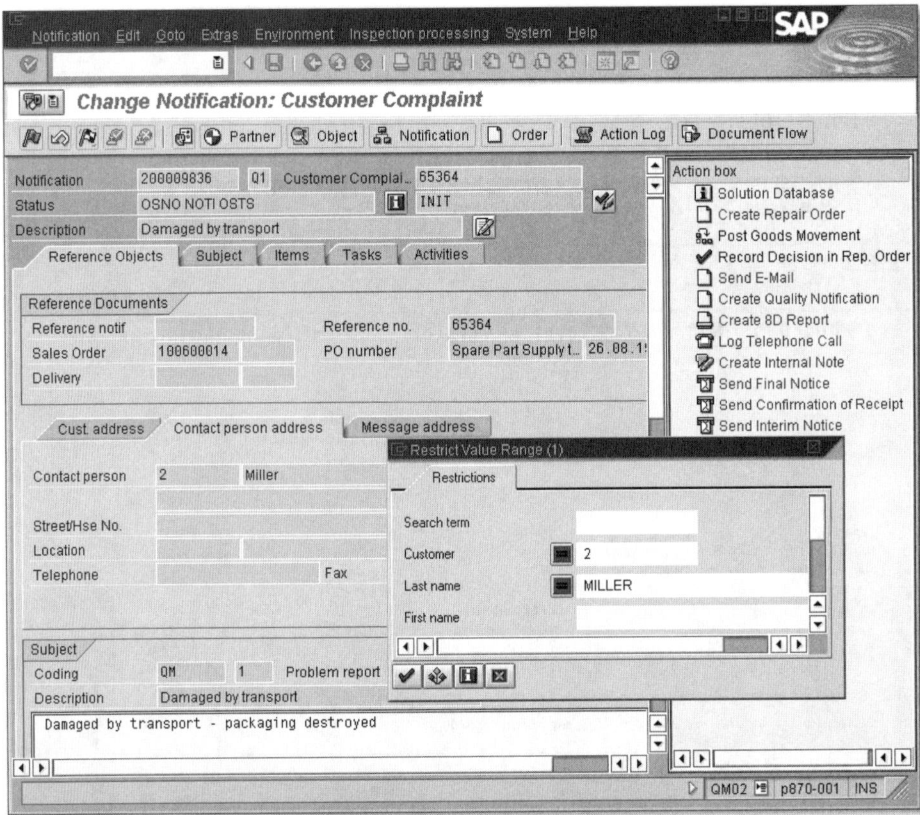


**Figure 9.20** Contact Person Address Tab

Alternatively, you can also enter the partners in a selection list in the quality notification menu bar via GOTO • PARTNER. You can also specify info partners via the PARTNER DATA menu item, provided these partners are assigned to the partner profile of this notification type in Customizing. Through the partner selection, you can then create useful analyses.

#### Reference Objects

Reference objects are data that are related to the notification in terms of accounting. Examples of reference objects include the customer order for notification type Q1, CUSTOMER COMPLAINT, or the material document from GR for notification type Q2, VENDOR FAULT LIST. The predefined reference objects are described in detail in this chapter in Section 9.3, Quality Notification with Integrated Document Management; Section 9.4, Quality Notification in Sales and Distribution; and Section 9.5, Quality Notification in Production. You can subsequently change these reference objects of a quality notification by entering the header data.

#### Response Profile

If the function to automatically determine tasks is active, the system can suggest tasks that should be executed first, on the basis of the predefined parameters in the response profile or service profile. The response and service profiles define the times and the period during which tasks are to be performed in a specific manner to react to a notification.

> **Example**
>
> You create a notification at 10 a.m. In the response profile, a period of two hours is defined for the measure code, RETURN CALL TO CUSTOMER, and a period of four hours for the code, CHECK IF TECHNICIAN IS WITH THE CUSTOMER. The times defined in the service profile are from 8 to 12 a.m. and from 2 to 6 p.m. In this case, you must call the customers back by noon to discuss or clarify the problem. If the customer requires technical help, a technician must arrive on-site by 4 p.m. You can use the automatic determination of tasks to define a range of standard tasks for immediate reaction (such a task can necessitate that a customer with priority 2 is called back within two hours).

#### Catalog Profile in General

In larger company structures, it is often necessary to make a separation between the catalog group's defect type, defect location, defect cause, and task of the same notification type. For this purpose, you can add additional notification types with an identical character to the basic settings of the delivery system in Customizing and assign a catalog profile to them.

**Example**

"Internal problem notification plant 1" and "Internal problem notification plant 2" are assigned to a relevant code group from DEFECT LOCATIONS and contain correspondingly tailored selection of defect codes after the relevant notification type has been selected.

The catalog profiles can also be assigned to materials in the same way. For an existing catalog profile at the notification and material levels, the catalog profile of the material is prioritized.

### Workflow

By using the SAP Business Workflow module as part of SAP NetWeaver, the system performs the predefined tasks for distributing notification data information. Depending on the status of notifications or tasks, it places *workitems* in the SAPoffice mailboxes of the responsible partners and thus immediately provides users with the required functions and the individual work steps. From then on, the processing status is transparent for those involved in the notification, and uncompleted tasks are immediately visible and can be traced further. From the workitem displayed, you can use the EXECUTE icon in the menu bar to go directly into notification processing.

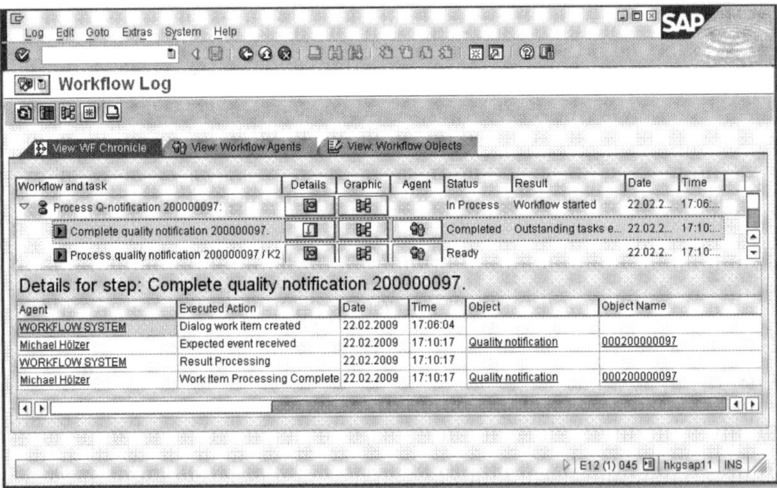


**Figure 9.21** Workflow Log for a Quality Notification

Although the workflow component of the SAP ERP system is contained in the standard version, it requires extensive Customizing as well as numerous settings if you want to use it to its full extent, and it should be configured by an experienced consultant. SAP ERP has already prepared a few scenarios for quality management, which you can view and activate in Customizing under BUSINESS MANAGEMENT • SAP BUSINESS • TASK-SPECIFIC CUSTOMIZING (see Figure 9.21 and 9.22).

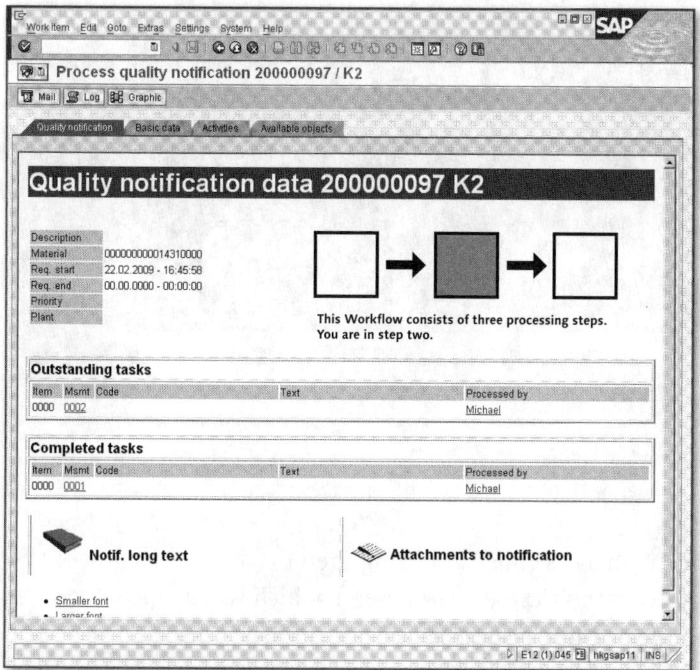


**Figure 9.22** Workflow with Process Steps for a Quality Notification

With the SAP Business Workflow module, you can use all external mail and workgroup programs such as Lotus Notes or Microsoft Outlook, which you can't do directly from the SAP QM application. From SAP R/3 Release 4.5 on, there are extensive enhancements available for these activities in the *action box*.

### Lists and Evaluations

By using the menu path QUALITY NOTIFICATION • INFO SYSTEM • NOTIFICATION, you can navigate to configurable reports about key figures and selection lists for the further processing of notifications. A time series analysis, which can also be found there, enables a graphical display of the number of notifications in a specific period, depending on different selection parameters (see Figure 9.23).

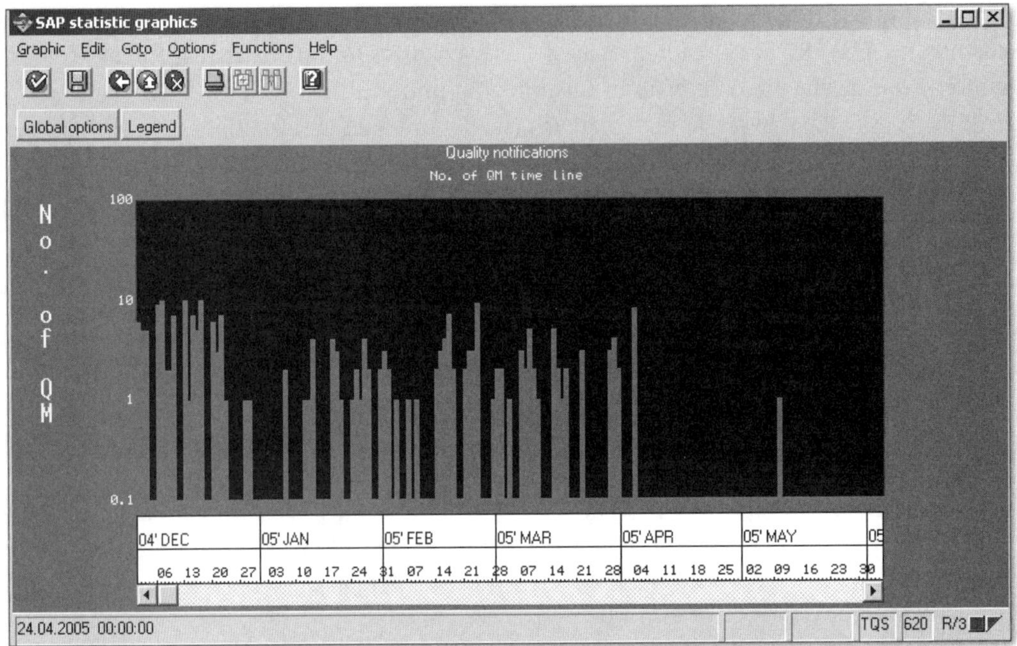


**Figure 9.23** Overview: Number of Notifications as Time Series Diagram

You can reach additional analysis functions using the QUALITY INFORMATION SYSTEM function from the LOGISTICS CONTROLLING menu, which is described in greater detail in Chapter 10, Information Systems and Evaluations.

### Archiving and Deleting Quality Notifications

To ensure data security, a notification that has been created once cannot be easily archived or deleted at the click of a button. If you want to archive or delete a notification, first set a new notification status via the following menu path: DELETION FLAG • SET. Objects with a set deletion flag are usually archived and deleted in the basis administration according to enterprise-specific rules.

### Internal Number Assignment

For each quality notification, the system generates a specific number under which the notification is stored. The basic settings provide for an internal number assignment (i.e., the system defines sequential numbers) with a predefined number range.

**Customizing Tip**

A frequently occurring problem when tracking quality notifications is the system-internal number assignment via *buffering*. So that system performance is not affected, there is always a quantity of numbers available in a buffer. The notification itself then uses the numbers from the buffer. This is useful if many documents are to be generated within a very short period. Without the buffer, the system would have had to generate single numbers in a separate process. The negative effect in buffering, however, is an undefined skip of the number sequence; that is, 101 does not follow 100 but rather 105 or 111.

To eliminate this effect, you must slightly change the settings of the production system. Transaction SNRO brings you directly to the input screen of the number range object. Here, you enter the object "QMEL_NR," select CHANGE NUMBER RANGE, and then EDIT • SET BUFFERING • NO BUFFERING. The notification number is then continuously updated without a skip.

### Processing Overview with the Action Log

The action log provides a detailed overview of all user actions in a quality notification via EXTRAS • NOTIFICATION DOCUMENTS • ACTION LOG (see Figure 9.24)

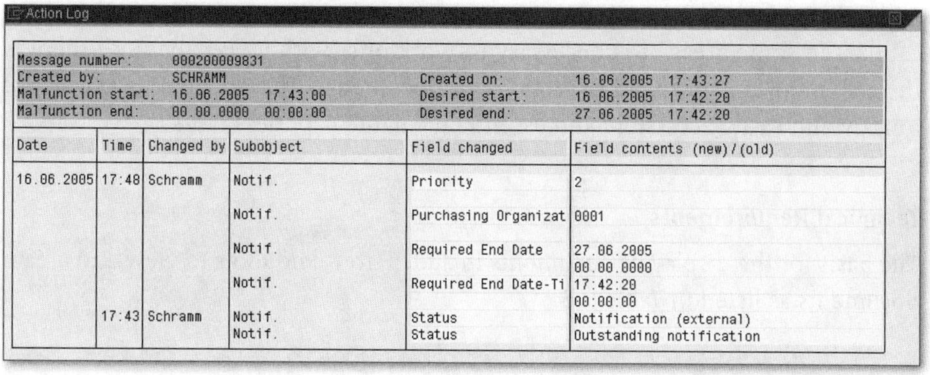

Action Log

Message number: 000200009831
Created by: SCHRAMM — Created on: 16.06.2005 17:43:27
Malfunction start: 16.06.2005 17:43:00 — Desired start: 16.06.2005 17:42:20
Malfunction end: 00.00.0000 00:00:00 — Desired end: 27.06.2005 17:42:20

| Date | Time | Changed by | Subobject | Field changed | Field contents (new)/(old) |
|---|---|---|---|---|---|
| 16.06.2005 | 17:48 | Schramm | Notif. | Priority | 2 |
| | | | Notif. | Purchasing Organizat | 0001 |
| | | | Notif. | Required End Date | 27.06.2005<br>00.00.0000 |
| | | | Notif. | Required End Date-Ti | 17:42:20<br>00:00:00 |
| | 17:43 | Schramm | Notif. | Status | Notification (external) |
| | | | Notif. | Status | Outstanding notification |

**Figure 9.24** Action Log

## 9.3 Quality Notification with Integrated Document Management

(QM) manages large quantities of documents that are important for the production and inspection of products. Speedy access to these files cannot always be guaranteed due to the traditional storage of documents. Important QA processes take place in SAP ERP. Therefore, it makes sense to view SAP document management along with the SAP QM transactions. SAP ERP provides corresponding functions for SAP QM transactions in the form of a module-integrated document management system.

The use of this module has no influence on nearby logistics modules because specific document types can be generated for use in QM. Initially, the documents are only managed; that is, the individual files are still located on the office servers and increase the data volume of the SAP ERP database to only a small degree.

#### Goals

The main task is the assignment of documents to the following QM objects:

- Q-info record
- Inspection plan/routing
- Quality notification
- Results recording

It should be possible to view the relevant document directly from the QM applications. In some areas, it is necessary to work only with *viewers* because there is the risk of an uncontrolled processing of documents. The documents should be quickly and easily accessible and essentially enable paperless work.

#### Technical Requirements

The basis for the display of documents includes front-end tools to view and create documents as listed in Table 9.5.

| Viewers | | | |
|---|---|---|---|
| ACD | AutoCAD | A2 | |
| ACR | Acrobat Reader | *.pdf | Software free of charge |
| LIM | Large image | *.jpg *.gif | |
| SIM | Small image | *.jpg *.gif | |
| SND | Sound | *.wav | |

**Table 9.5** File Formats

| | | | |
|---|---|---|---|
| WRD | Word | *.doc | |
| WWI | WinWord 6.0 | *.doc | |
| XLS | Excel | *.xls | |
| **For File Creation** | | | |
| ACD | AutoCAD | A2 | |
| ACR | Acrobat Distiller | *.pdf | License required |
| LIM | Large image | *.jpg *.gif | |
| SIM | Small image | *.jpg *.gif | |
| SND | Sound | *.wav | |
| WRD | Word | *.doc | |
| WWI | WinWord 6.0 | *.doc | |
| XLS | Excel | *.xls | |

**Table 9.5** File Formats (Cont.)

It is advisable to use only one viewing tool for documents of the same work environment. Acrobat Reader is the best solution for this because it neither uses many system resources nor does it burden the budget. Acrobat Distiller converts different file formats (Microsoft Word, Excel, graphics files) into a uniform *.pdf format. The respective server is acceptable as the physical storage location for the files. You should keep in mind that access to this server is also possible from the front end where the document is to be displayed.

### Organizational Prerequisites

The success and acceptance of a document management system is dependent on the following factors:

- Fast access
- Clarity
- Completeness

You can meet these criteria relatively easily with the following measures:

- Appoint an administrator for the maintenance of individual document types in SAP ERP.

- The employees master and use the application in defined areas of SAP ERP.
- The storage locations outside SAP ERP are protected and have a fixed structure.
- The processing of original documents is subject to a certain policy with regard to creating, changing, and viewing them.

## 9.3.1 Creating a Document

Initially, let's outline the creation of a document without a template.

### Creation Without a Template

Select LOGISTICS • CENTRAL FUNCTIONS • DOCUMENT MANAGEMENT • CREATE DOCUMENT WITH PERMISSIBLE DOCUMENT TYPE (see Figure 9.25). Continue with ENTER DESCRIPTION; here you can store important information on selecting the document.

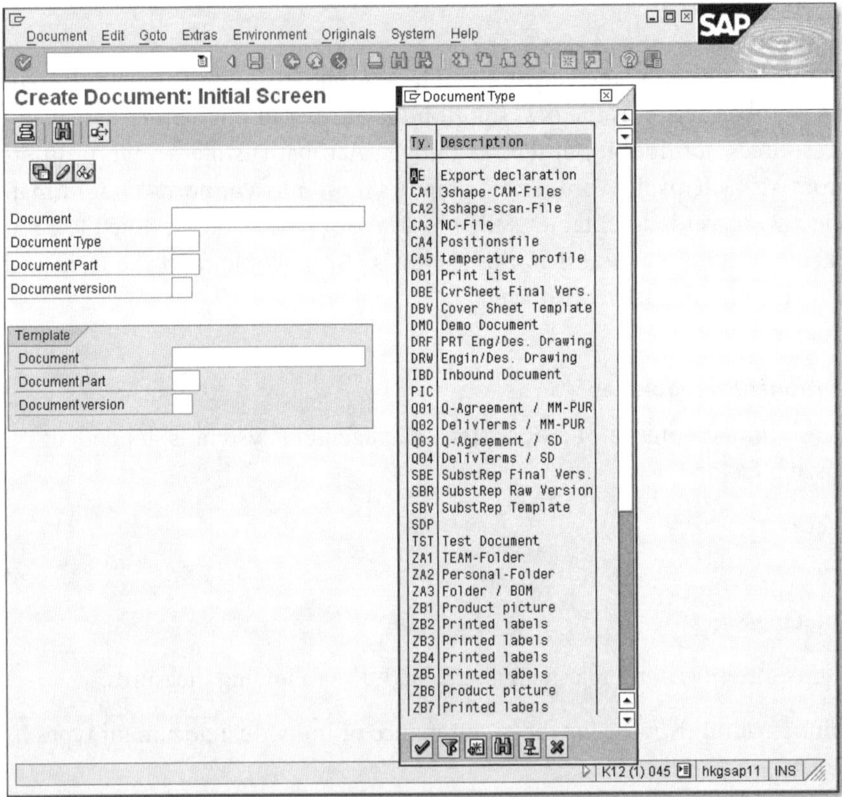


**Figure 9.25** Creating a Document

### Creation with Template

Select the document that is to be used as a template, and confirm by pressing Enter. If an object link existed in the template of the document, this will also be transferred to the new document.

> **Example**
>
> The document that serves as a template was linked with a quality notification. The new document contains the same link and is also assigned as a document in the quality notification.

Then the system asks you if the originals are also to be transferred from the template. The original files are suggested through a dialog box of the application.

### Assigning Original Documents

You can assign two originals (files) to each document, which can later be directly displayed in the linked object (inspection plan, quality info record, quality notification, etc.). The assignment of several "additional files" is possible for each file. However, you cannot display these files directly. The use of such additional files is primarily conceived for subordinate documents or graphics that are not saved in the original files but are supposed to be displayed there.

The original files can be linked both locally or through the network. However, the latter is only useful for test purposes. The two originals that you store can have different file formats and different storage locations. However, you should always consider using the same original and change only the file formats.

### Status of the Document

In the status IC, IN CREATION, you can still perform changes, for example, you can still reassign original documents. In the status REL, RELEASED, it is almost impossible to make any changes.

### Document Structure

You should use the BOM function if a document is to consist of different items. All documents must previously be created as SAP ERP documents. You reach the bill of material through LOGISTICS • CENTRAL FUNCTIONS • DOCUMENT MANAGEMENT •

Environment • Bills of Material • Bill of Material • Document Structure • Create (Change, Display) (see Figure 9.26).

The document structure can then be displayed via Environment • Product Structure (see Figure 9.27).

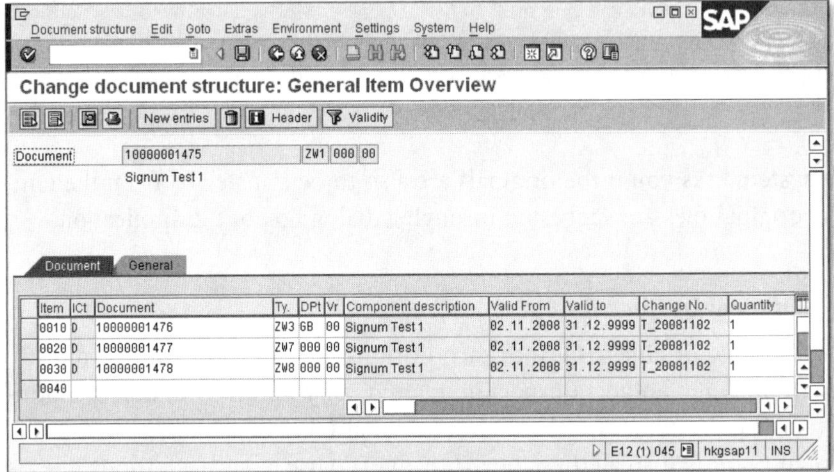


**Figure 9.26** Document Structure

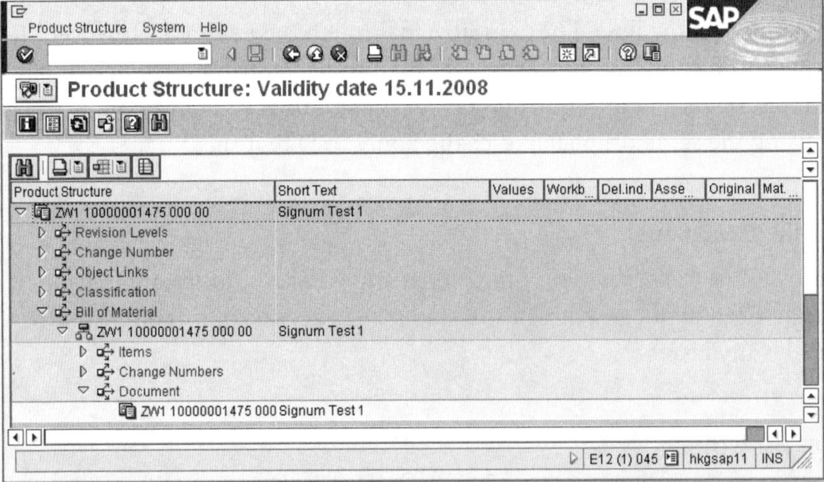


**Figure 9.27** Document Structure

#### Changing Original Documents

Changes to an original file don't affect document management. If, for instance, you make changes to a Word file with the same file name and save it again, you can see the latest version of your *.doc file when you call it from SAP ERP. The following section shows you how to manage several "real" versions.

#### Assigning a New Original Document to an SAP ERP Document (Creating a Version)

Extensive changes to an original document ideally lead to a new version status of the original file and the SAP ERP document. The original file is saved with a new file name. In SAP ERP document management, you assign the new file to the previous document. Changing the original file is no longer possible, if the document status is set to RELEASED. For this reason, another version of the document is generated. The versions are identified by sequential numbers in relation to the document number. For example, the object relationship to the inspection plan must also be maintained so that the current original document can be displayed.

#### Assigning Documents to an Object

You can assign several documents to an object. The originals can be displayed from the respective module. In front-end applications that permit changes, you can change the originals immediately.

### 9.3.2 Documents in the Quality Notification

In the quality notification, select ENVIRONMENT • DOCUMENTS.

Navigate to the glasses icon to view the original. Due to the object link defined in Customizing, you can determine in the document with which quality notification the document is linked (see Figure 9.28).

### 9.3.3 Documents in the Quality Info Record

Select LOGISTICS • QUALITY MANAGEMENT • QUALITY PLANNING • LOGISTICS MASTER DATA • QUALITY INFO RECORD: PROCUREMENT • CHANGE AND THEN QUALITY AGREEMENT IN THE INFO RECORD. Then, click on the glasses icon to view the original. Due to the object link defined in Customizing, you can determine in the document with which quality notification the document is linked.

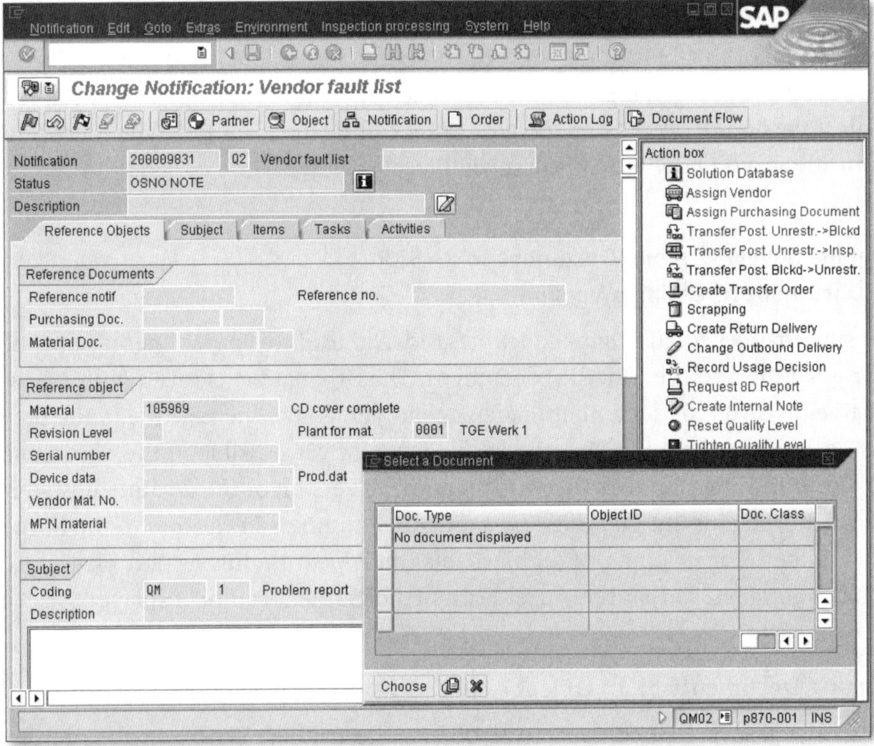


Figure 9.28 Linking a Document

### 9.3.4 Documents in the Inspection Plan/Routing

Select Inspection Plan Change • Operations and PRT • (Production Resources/Tools).

The assignment is carried out by creating PRTs. The document displays one of four different PRT types. At the operation level, you can assign any amount of documents. At the inspection characteristic level, however, only one PRT (document) is allowed. Via Environment • Production Resources/Tools • Original PRT Docs, you can view the document.

## 9.4 Quality Notification in Sales and Distribution

The functionality and operation of the different quality notifications are basically identical. The major differences can be found in the reference objects of the header data and in the individual processing profile of the company that uses them. You have already seen an example of this in the previous scenario of the customer complaint. In addition, the partner schema contains separate partner roles for each notification type. We recommend that you keep the mandatory partners as provided in the standard version as well as the customers and the responsible processors.

#### Notification Type Q1/F1, Customer Complaint

The following are the reference objects of the CUSTOMER COMPLAINT notification type:

- Customer (mandatory partner)
- Enter the material
- Sales order
- Sales organization
- Division
- Distribution channel
- Delivery

When you select specific reference objects through the initial screen displayed in the example, the system transfers additional data from a document (sales order, delivery) to the notification. In other words, little effort is required when making entries to create the notification.

#### Triggering the Customer Complaint

Select LOGISTICS • QUALITY MANAGEMENT • QUALITY NOTIFICATION • CREATE and then notification type Q1, CUSTOMER COMPLAINT. Once again, follow the path LOGISTICS • QUALITY MANAGEMENT • QUALITY NOTIFICATION • CREATE, and select notification type Q3, VENDOR FAULT LIST. When you confirm by pressing [Enter], a dialog box opens (see Figure 9.29) to enter the document data (Customizing is required through the initial screen: QUALITY MANAGEMENT • QUALITY NOTIFICATION • NOTIFICATION CREATION • NOTIFICATION TYPES • DEFINE SCREEN TEMPLATES, choose DEFINE INITIAL SCREENS, and insert 0130 as INITIAL SCREEN), or the notification processing opens directly at the header level.

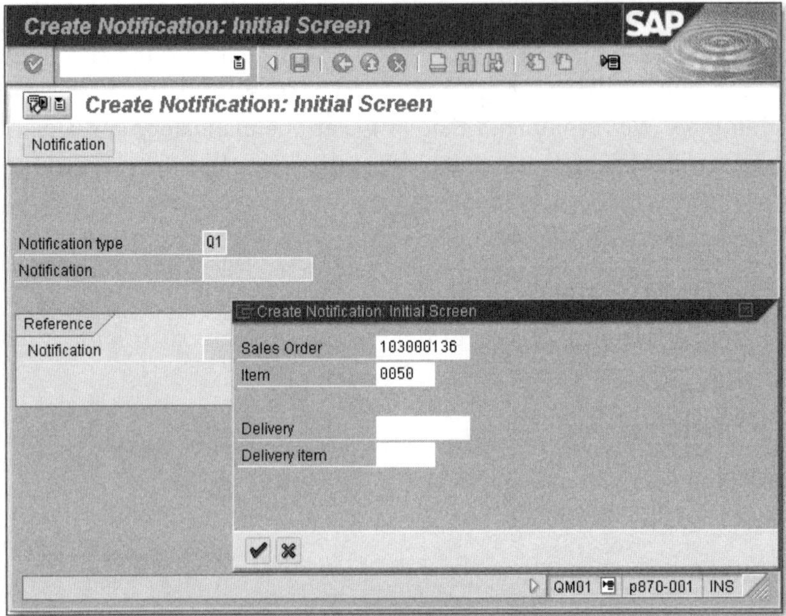


**Figure 9.29** Creating a Notification via Initial Screen 130, Delivery

In most cases, this notification type is created manually, after a telephone or written complaint by the customer. It is also possible to create this notification type via an SAP Business Workflow function. The most important step in implementing this notification type is a straightforward design of the business process. Figure 9.30 contains a simplified example of this design.

### Sales Summary

Another interesting function in the customer complaint is the display of the sales summary, which you can reach via ENVIRONMENT • SALES SUMMARY. There you can find comprehensive information from the customer transaction data combined with the current specifications on the complaint process and the last notifications. Because the sales summary is an interactive report, you can double-click on the notification number to see the quality notification (see Figure 9.31).

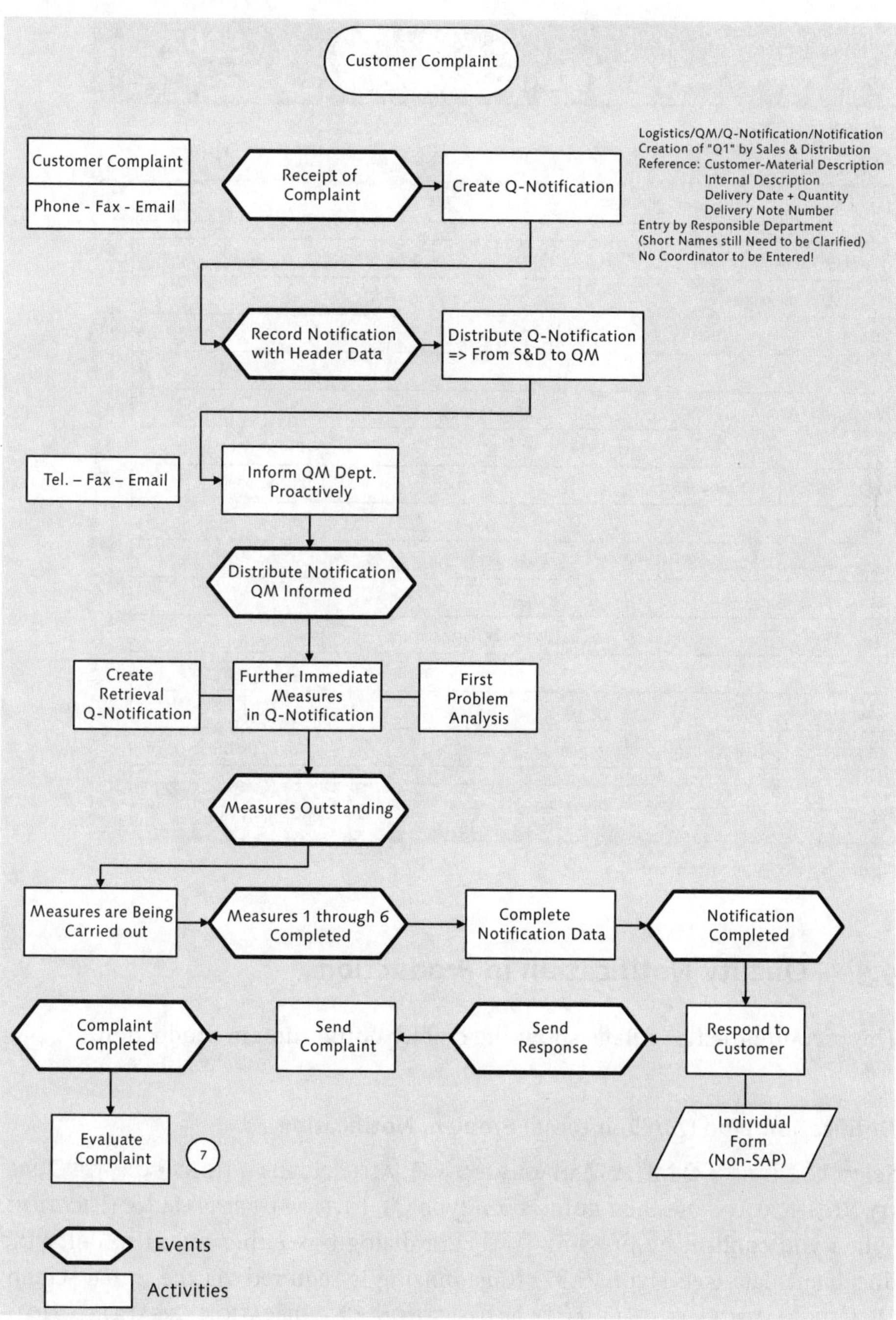


**Figure 9.30** Flowchart of a Customer Complaint (Simplified)

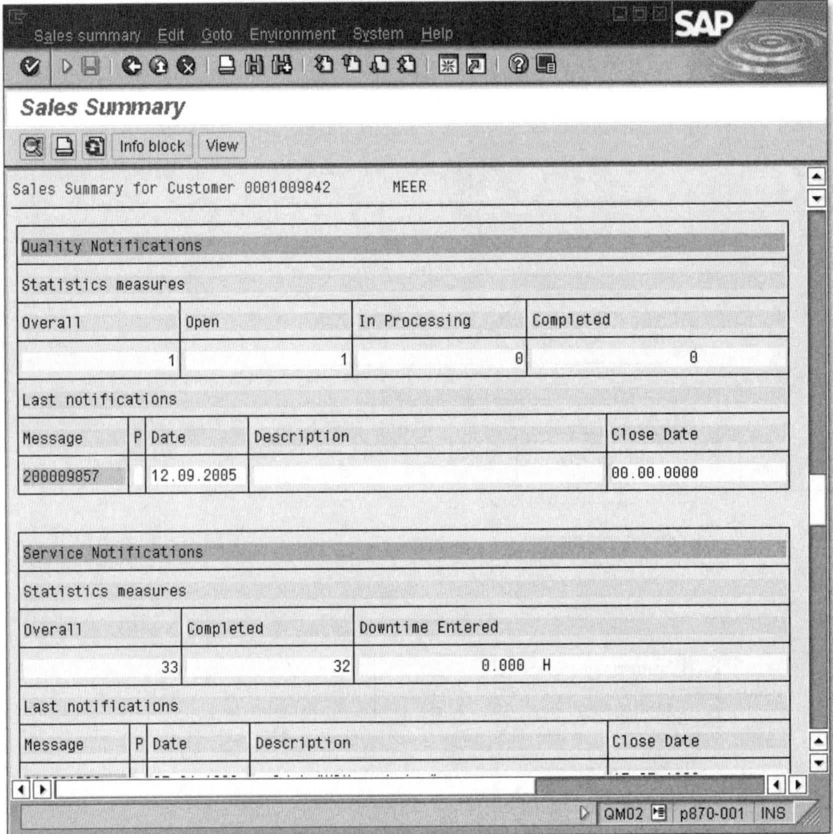


Figure 9.31 Sales Summary

## 9.5 Quality Notification in Production

This section provides details about the quality notification in production.

### Notification Type Q3/F3, Internal Problem Notification

Select Logistics • Quality Management • Quality Notifications • Create Quality Notification and then notification type Q3, Internal Problem Notification. When you confirm by pressing Enter, a dialog box either opens to enter the document data (see Figure 9.32) (Customizing is required via the initial screen: Quality Management • Quality Notification • Notification Creation • Notification Types • Define Screen Templates, choose Define Initial Screens, and insert 0140 as INITIAL SCREEN), or the notification processing opens directly at the header level (see Figure 9.33).

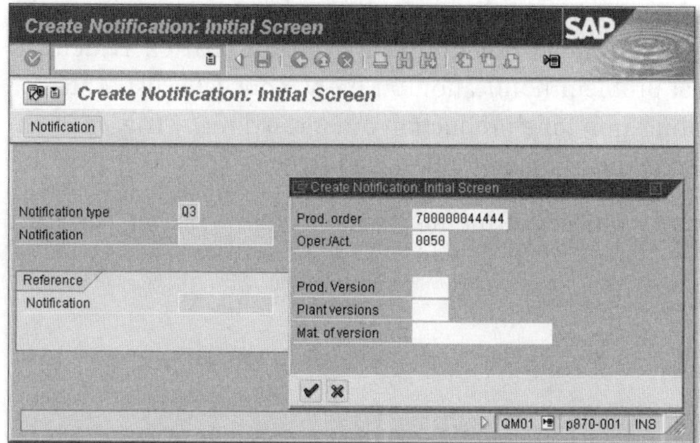


Figure 9.32 Creating a Notification via Initial Screen 140, Production Order

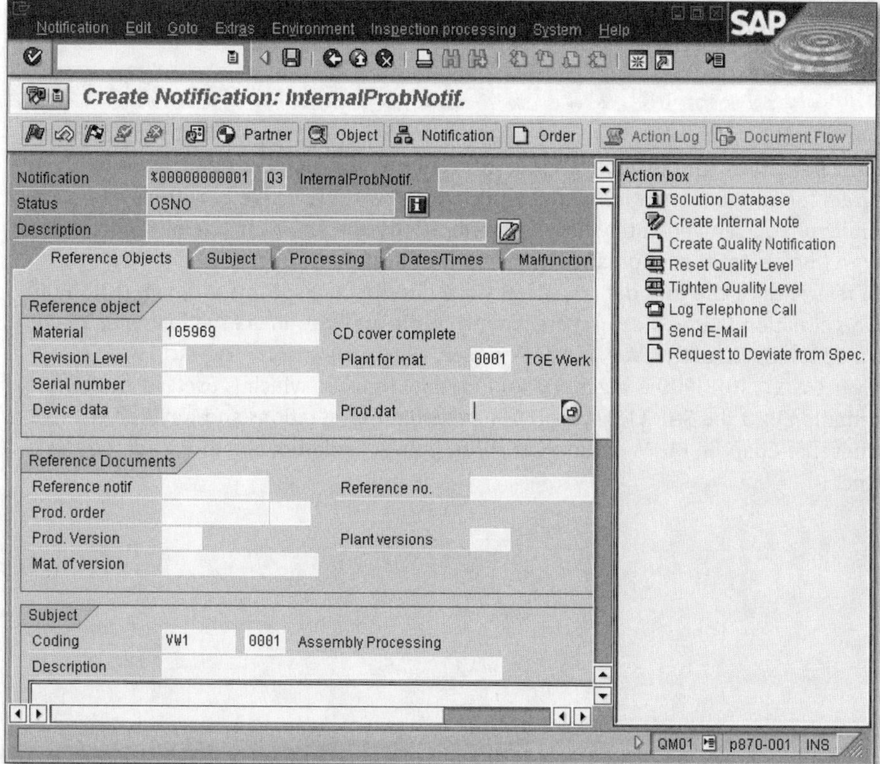


Figure 9.33 Notification Header of the Internal Problem Notification

An internal problem notification refers to problems that emerge within your own company (e.g., defects that are notified for a material or an operation during the production process). Additional areas of use are all events that take place in the company, which are to be traced immediately and for which actions need to be taken. Since Release 4.5, additional functions are available that exert defined influences of the internal problem notification on the vendor fault list. Thus for instance, the internal notification for a production order can directly trigger a vendor fault list and change the quality score of the vendor.

Following are the reference objects of the notification type INTERNAL PROBLEM NOTIFICATION:

- Internal partner
- Material, batch (mandatory partner)
- Production order or run schedule header
- Work center
- Inspection lot
- Author (mandatory partner)

**Customizing Tip**

Generate notifications automatically using a batch input (a program that simulates a manual entry through the application). This way, you can create a small ABAP help program for each confirmation of the work process with defective quantities in the PP module, or you can generate your own notification from an external application. It's easy to implement the automatically created notification through a partner schema with reference to the user data. SAP has since developed a specific program (RIIBIP00) for this situation that you can access directly in the application via the following menu path: LOGISTICS • QUALITY MANAGEMENT • QUALITY NOTIFICATIONS • ENVIRONMENT • DATA TRANSFER. RIIBIP00 is a general tool for data transfer, which is used to enter information into the SAP ERP system using standard transactions and function modules. In Chapter 14, Migration Concepts, you find additional information on this subject.

### Triggering the Internal Problem Notification

You can create notifications from production through manual and automatic functions and through initialization from other QM components, for example, via the usage decision or the inspection lot in the event of a defect.

## 9.5.1 Scenario with Notification Type Q3/F3, Internal Problem Notification

The INTERNAL PROBLEM NOTIFICATION (see Figure 9.34) refers to occurrences of nonconformity in your own company. The two most important reference objects are the production order and the inspection order. The processing logic is the same here as with the other notification types in QM. In this scenario, a quality inspection in production has automatically generated an enhanced defect data record in the form of a quality notification.

**20.10.2005 QM notif. overview version 3 SCHRAMM Copy**

| | | | | |
|---|---|---|---|---|
| *Notification* | 200009843 | | *Notification type* InternalProbNotif. | Q3 |
| *Description* | First sampling | | | |
| *Status* | OSNO NOPT | | | |
| *Priority* | QM | | | |
| *Reported by* | | | *Notification date* | 06.07.2005 |
| *Report time* | 18:08:43 | | | |
| *Start deadline* | 06.07.2005 | | *End deadline* | |
| *Start time* | 18:08:43 | | *End time* | 00:00:00 |
| *User* | SCHRAMM | Schramm | | |
| *Material* | 105969 | CD cover complete | *Device data* | |
| *Reference number* | | | *Coppy modelnumber* | |
| *Production order* | | | | |
| *Run schedule header* | | | | |

First sample report is missing.
Measure 7.25 +-0.05 needs correction.

**Detail item** 0001

| | | |
|---|---|---|
| *Problem* | QM 06 | Measurement failure |
| *Object part* | QM 2 | Parts production |
| *Text* | | |
| *Cause* | | |
| *Cause text* | | |

**Figure 9.34** Sample Print of an Internal Problem Notification

During the inspection, the employee is supposed to roughly classify the defect when it is discovered. You can do this classification by having the inspection task prompt you to enter a predefined defect code, if the evaluation result is DEFECT. Then the inspector simply selects an applicable defect code and completes the inspection step. This step can be repeated for several inspection characteristics. The system was configured in such a way that each defect evaluation during the quality inspection generates a defect data record and also a quality notification.

The quality notification already contains the header data and the necessary reference objects for the subsequent processing. In this case scenario, you can trace the number of Q3 notifications from the quality management side. For this reason, the worklist is regularly viewed, which is one of the duties of the responsible employees in the quality department. You can tailor the list individually to reflect the tasks of a specific person, whereby the overview contains only those items that are to be processed at a specific time. Figure 9.34 shows a sample printout of an internal problem notification. Later in the process, the notification receives the required information for defect removal and analysis from the QM transactional user or other involved persons.

Often the discovered defect is not caused during production but rather by an insufficient delivery of an external vendor or a previous production step. If this occurs, the notification system enables you to transfer the data from the previous notification into a new notification (vendor fault list or additional internal problem notification). This procedure ensures the monitoring of a notification back to the origin of the defect.

## 9.6 Quality Notification in Procurement

Let's take a look at the quality notification in procurement.

### Notification Type Q2/F2, Vendor Fault List

Select LOGISTICS • QUALITY MANAGEMENT • QUALITY NOTIFICATIONS • CREATE QUALITY NOTIFICATION and then the notification type Q2, VENDOR FAULT LIST. When you confirm by pressing [Enter] a dialog box opens prompting you to enter the document data (see Figure 9.35). (Customizing is required via the following screen:

QUALITY MANAGEMENT • QUALITY NOTIFICATION • NOTIFICATION CREATION • NOTIFICATION TYPES • DEFINE SCREEN TEMPLATES, choose DEFINE INITIAL SCREENS, and insert 0100 as INITIAL SCREEN), or the notification processing opens directly at the header level (see Figure 9.36).

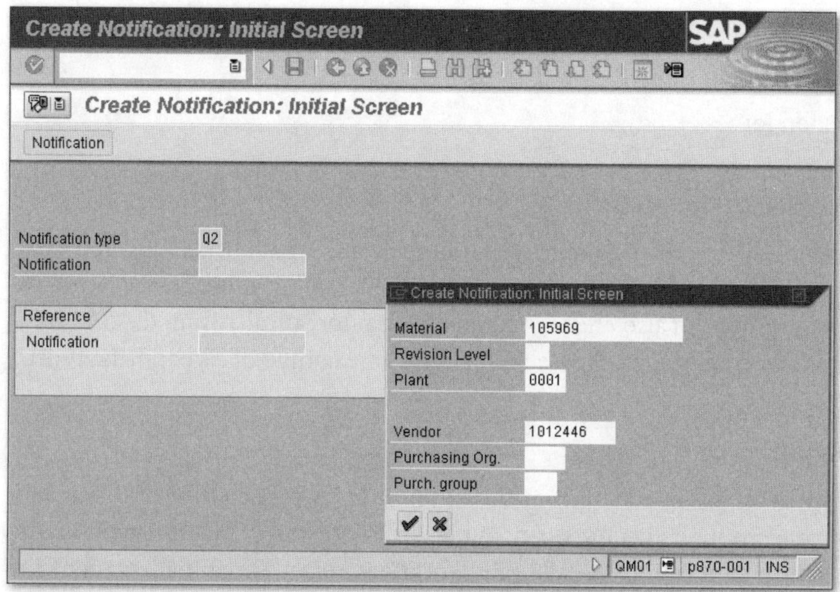


**Figure 9.35** Creating a Notification Through Initial Screen 100, Purchasing Document

In the notification types Q2/F2, the complaints against vendors or other external partners are processed and managed. In this context, we also speak of the vendor fault list. With the vendor fault list, QM provides a comprehensive tool for quality control in MM.

In addition to the standard functions, the created notifications can also influence the vendor evaluation and record cost analyses for expenses related to the vendor fault lists. For this notification type, there are also specific forms available that can be used for communication with the vendors (in a raw version). Figure 9.37, later in this chapter, shows an example of a customized form.

The reference objects for the notification types Q2/F2, VENDOR FAULT LIST, are as follows:

- GR document
- Material, batch
- Vendor (mandatory partner)
- Purchasing organization
- Inspection lot

### Triggering the Vendor Fault List

In the previously described sample scenario, the vendor fault list is triggered by an action item in the troubleshooting process and generated via the CREATE NOTIFICATION function. You can also create it manually or automatically from the SAP Business Workflow component. Figure 9.36 shows an example of a vendor fault list.

### Cost Control

If a quality order is generated from the notification, a cost control of the quality problem concerning its vendors is possible. To create vendor fault lists, it is useful to establish connections to SAP ERP workflow items. The initialization of the notification from the inspection lot or the usage decision is also provided for this notification type.

### Effects of the Vendor Fault List on the Quality Score

In Customizing the vendor evaluation (see Section 8.4, Vendor Evaluation), you can manipulate the quality score  of the vendors when each vendor fault list submitted.

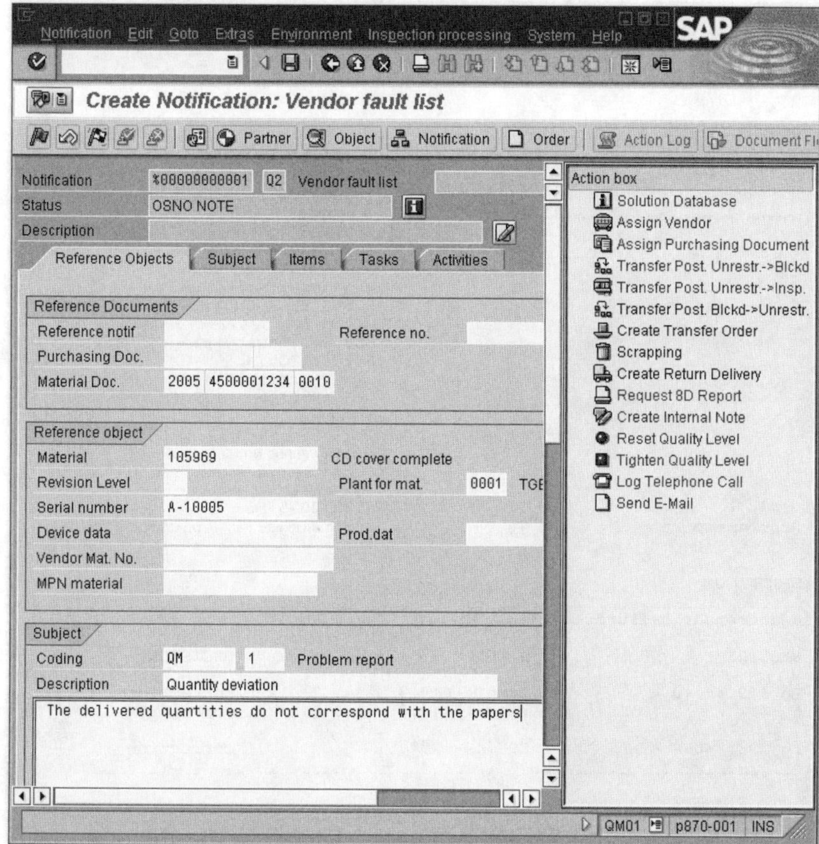


**Figure 9.36** Notification Header of the Vendor Fault List

## Buyer's Negotiation Sheet

The buyer's negotiation sheet is the counterpart to the sales summary SD and is available both in Procurement and in QM. Via LOGISTICS • QUALITY MANAGEMENT • QUALITY NOTIFICATIONS • ENVIRONMENT • BUYER'S NEGOTIATION SHEET, you will obtain the view of the named report (see Figure 9.37).

There you will find extensive information from the transaction data and master data of the vendor, combined with the current specifications on the complaint processes and the latest notifications. Because the buyer's negotiation sheet is an interactive report, you can double-click on the notification number to see the quality notification immediately. All functions associated with the notification are also available to purchasing.

TallyGenicom®

**QUALITY-REPORT**

TallyGenicom Computerdrucker GmbH · Postfach 29 69 · D-89019 Ulm

NO./DATE
200009820 / 05.04.2005
DELIVERY-NO.
2005133
PURCHASE VOUCHER / POSITIONS NO:
4500071946 / 00020
MATERIAL VOUCHER / POSITIONS NO:
50248485 / 0001
MATERIAL NO.: **62423**
**Housing lower, prep. Roll Holder T3010**
QUANTITY / RETURN TO VENDOR
49 PC 0 PC
SUPPLY NO.
1011366
AUTHOR / PHONE NO.
Schramm / 0731/2075-299
FAX NO./E-mail
0731/2075-553
mschramm@tallygenicom.de

Problemreport

DESCRIPTION

**Measurement failure**

| REQUIREMENT: | ACTUAL: | DECISION: |
|---|---|---|
| Lg 449.4 +0.4 | front: 447.3 - 447.7 | correction |
| | rear : 448.3 - 448.5 | correction |
| Lg 298 +0.4 | 297.4 - 297.5 | correction |

REMARK
See also our Quality-Report 200007177-62119 from Sept 03, 2003.
The delivery is conditionally accepted.

With best regards

TallyGenicom Computerdrucker GmbH

i.V. Schramm i.A.

TallyGenicom Computerdrucker GmbH
Geschäftsführer: Jan Sundelin, Vorsitzender
Bengt Stahlschmidt
Dr. Matthias Ullrich
Kevin Wright
Sitz der Gesellschaft: Ulm
Eintragung im Handelsregister:
Amtsgericht Ulm HRB 4804

Postanschrift:
Postfach 2969, D-89019 Ulm
Firmenanschrift:
Heuweg 3, D-89079 Ulm

Ust.-IdNr.:DE811209773

Telefon (0731) 2075-0
Telefax (0731) 2075-100

HypoVereinsbank Ulm
Kto.-Nr.2 510 251 (BLZ 630 200 86)
SWIFT-Code: HYVE DE MM 461

DQS-zertifiziert nach
ISO 9001:2000
Reg.-Nr 3905

**Figure 9.37** Sample Printout for a Customized Vendor Fault List (Quality Report)

## 9.7 Solution Database

The solution database (SDB) is an application that you can use to save, connect, and call problem symptoms, solutions, and internal know-how.

The solutions search is integrated in the following processes: problem management in Customer Service (CS), Plant Maintenance (PM), Quality Management (QM), and the agent front office of the Customer Interaction Center (CIC). The solutions database contains symptoms, solutions, and references through which solutions and symptoms are connected to each other.

### Symptom

A change in a product or a system that represents a malfunction is called a *symptom*. Symptoms can be described with plain text, attributes of code catalogs for problem code, problem cause and problem location, configured attributes, and priorities and status. Symptoms can be connected with any business objects such as products, equipment parts, or an installation.

### Solution

An action or a process that eliminates the symptom and problem communicated by the symptom is referred to as a *solution*. Solutions can be described with plain text, tasks to be performed, and attachments that support the problem resolution and the solution.

### Managing the Content of the Solution Database

Symptoms, solutions, and references are maintained and linked to each other in the management environment. If you want to maintain the content of the solution database, use Transaction IS01 or the following menu path: LOGISTICS • QUALITY MANAGEMENT • QUALITY NOTIFICATION • SOLUTION DATABASE • EDIT. With the reference function, the integration in the notification system provides additional links to use the knowledge stored in SAP ERP synergistically. Figures 9.38 to 9.40 contain the entry screens to create, change, and manage symptoms and solutions.

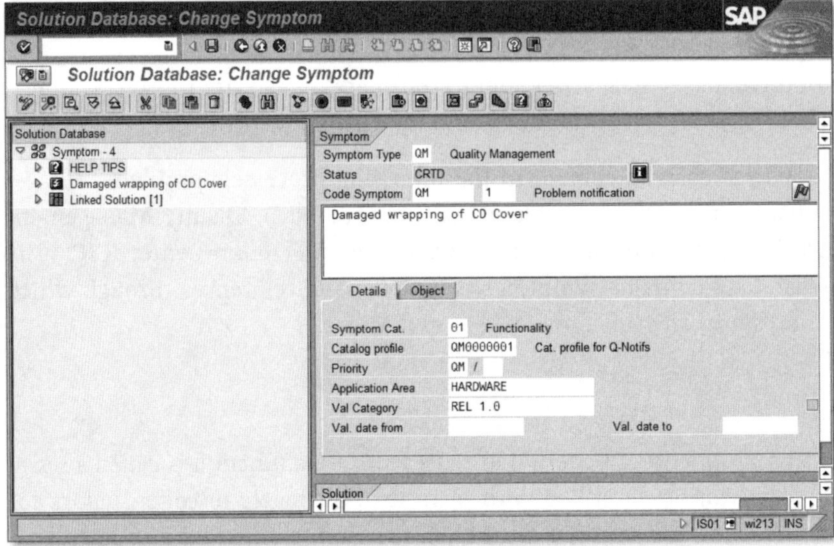


Figure 9.38 Create/Change a Symptom in the Solution Database

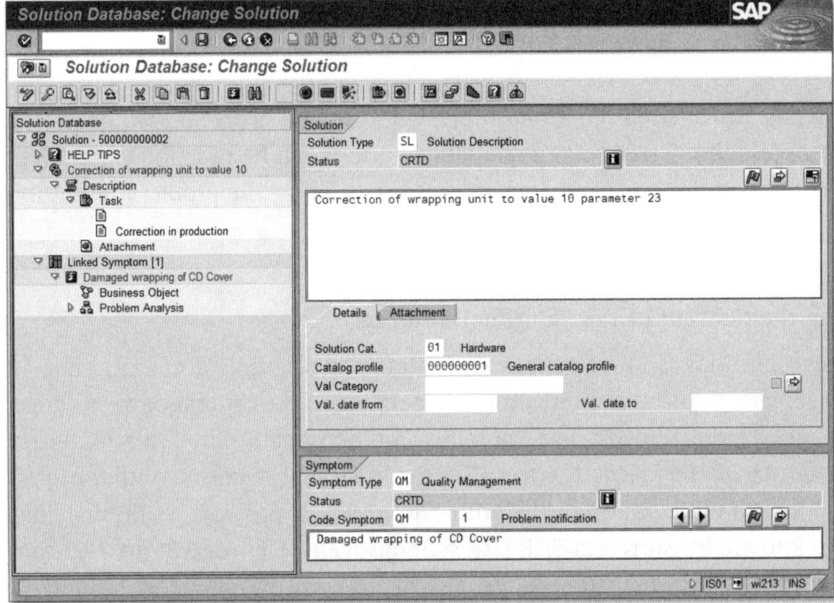


Figure 9.39 Changing the Solution and Adding Tasks

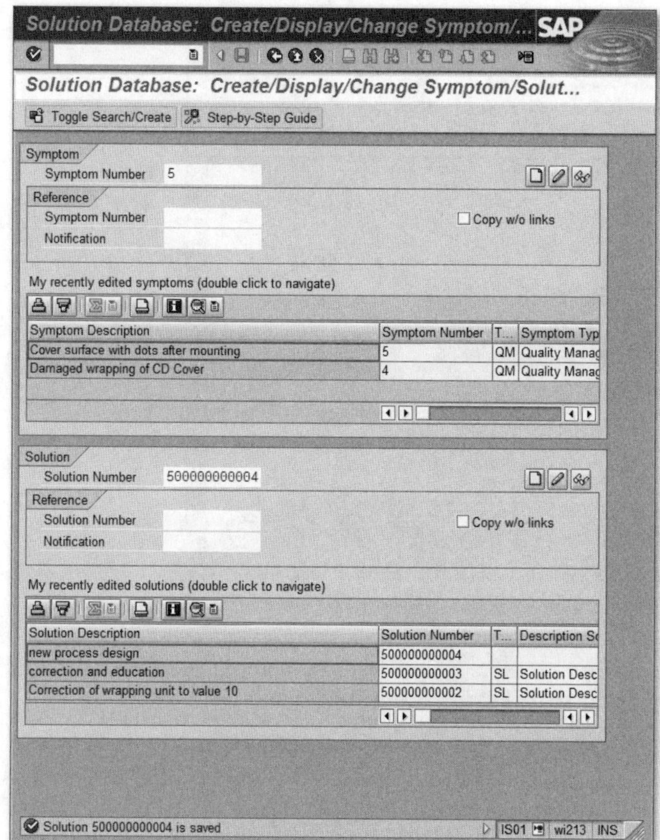


**Figure 9.40** Managing Symptoms and Solutions

### Searches in the Solution Database

The search is supported by a search engine via QUALITY MANAGEMENT • QUALITY NOTIFICATIONS • SOLUTION DATABASE • INDEX and provides a generic solution that enables you to use a text string to search precisely and quickly for documents (see Figure 9.41). The following are the most important characteristics of the search engine:

1. An index system is created for existing documents.
2. During the search, the text that is searched for is compared to the index system.
3. A group of weighted hits with clearly identifiable documents is returned.

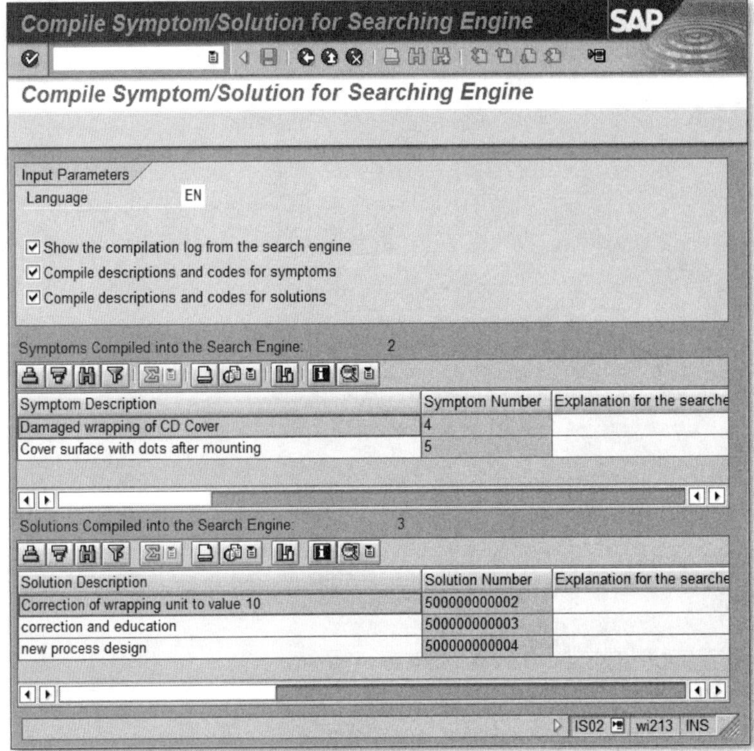


**Figure 9.41** Solution Search Engine

## 9.8 Stability Study

Stability studies examine the behavior of products under different conditions such as temperature, humidity, and brightness over certain periods of time. They are frequently carried out in the process industries such as the pharmaceutical, chemical, cosmetics, and food industries.

There are regulations in place for the implementation of stability studies, for example, by the Food and Drug Administration (FDA), or international guidelines such as Good Manufacturing Practice (GMP).

### 9.8.1 Description

To implement stability studies:

- Physical samples are taken from the product.
- These samples are stored under controlled conditions.
- They are drawn again at specific times.
- They are inspected in adherence to defined or flexible inspection specifications.

The stability study is completely integrated in SAP QM. In addition to quality notifications, this study also employs sample management, inspection planning, inspection processing, and the maintenance plan from Plant Maintenance (PM) for time-scheduling purposes. This study is displayed in the system as a separate menu item in the QUALITY MANAGEMENT branch.

**Customizing Tip**

The functional enhancements for the stability study are located in the Enterprise Extension Set, which you can open via Customizing and ACTIVATE BUSINESS FUNCTIONS. After you have activated the PLM extension via a switch (see Figure 9.42), the enhancements are displayed in the menu structure (see Figure 9.43) and in Customizing. After activation, different settings are required in Customizing — such as defining the number range — before the stability study can be used.

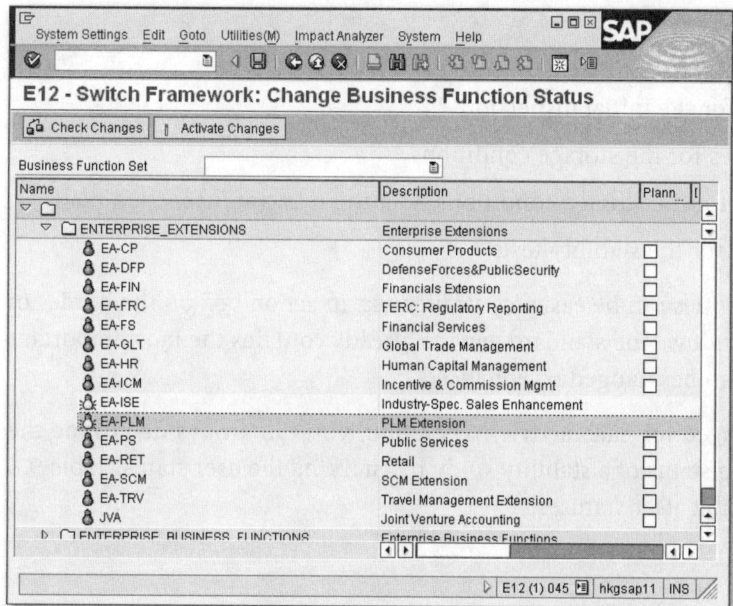


Figure 9.42 Activation Switch in Customizing

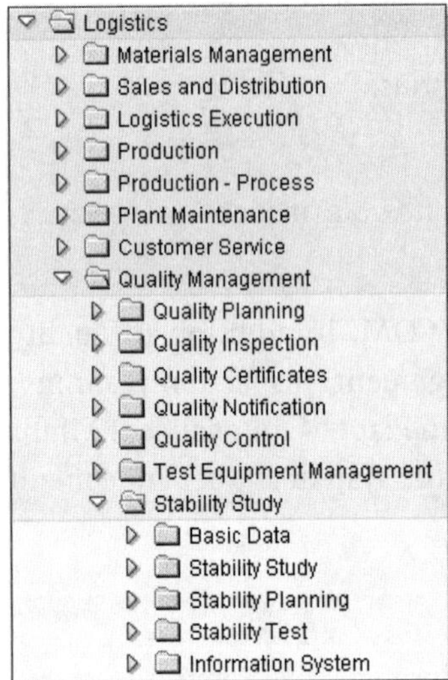


**Figure 9.43** Menu Tree with Path to the Stability Study

The stability study is assigned the objects that are generated during the course of the study. These objects include the following:

- Initial samples
- Stability BOM
- Documents
- Inspection lot for the initial inspection
- Physical samples for the storage conditions
- Time schedule for the storage conditions with the relevant inspection plans
- Inspection lots for the stability tests

The different activities can be easily controlled via an action box on the border of the processing window. The standard version already contains the most important activities, but it can be changed or enhanced.

The status is changed for each activity. Therefore, you can always determine the current processing status of a stability study by checking the user status. Table 9.6 shows a few possible user statuses.

| User Status | Meaning | User Status | Meaning |
|---|---|---|---|
| ACTV | Stability Study Active | SCDF | Storage Condition Defined |
| CRIS | Create Initial Sample | STOR | Stability Sample Stored |
| BOMA | Bill of Material Assigned | CRTS | Create Testing Schedule |
| ISCR | Initial Sample Created | TSCR | Testing Schedule Created |
| ISRL | Initial Sample Released | TSCO | Testing Schedule Completed |
| CRIL | Create Initial Test | STRT | Start of the Study |
| ILCR | Initial Test Created | COMP | Study Completed |
| COIL | Initial Test Completed | CANC | Study Canceled |
| DFSC | Define Storage Condition | INAC | Study Inactive |

**Table 9.6** The User Status of the Stability Study

The stability study process is divided into the following phases (see Figure 9.44):

- Start of a stability study with the initial test
- Stability planning (planning the inspections)
- Stability tests
- Completing the Stability Study

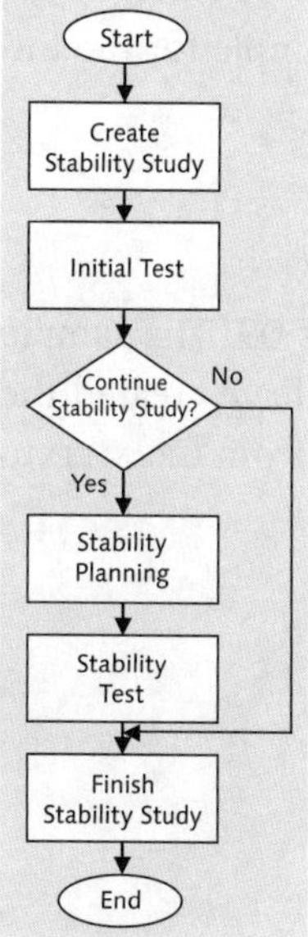


**Figure 9.44** Workflow of a Stability Study

The following scenario describes the individual steps in the phases.

## 9.8.2 Scenario for the Stability Study

The following scenario is used and implemented to describe the stability study in greater detail: After an initial test, an ink print head is stored for six months, after which time certain characteristics are examined.

### Creating a Stability Study

First you must create the stability study. The following two notification types are provided in the standard version:

- Notification type QS (stability study *with* reference to the material)
- Notification type QR (stability study *without* reference to the material)

Because the ink head is a material that has already been created, select the type QS with reference to the material number.

After you have entered the material and plant, you have already completed the first step. We recommend that you supplement this study with a coding from the catalog and a description (see Figure 9.45). The stability study has been created and can be saved. On the right-hand side of the window, you see the action box, which is helpful in processing the stability study. From here, you can trigger the next activity — creating the initial sample, that is, the physical sample for the initial sample.

### Creating an Initial Sample

The recommended physical sample type for the stability study is 09. The sample category 5 indicates that it is the initial sample. As soon as you have created the initial sample, the stability study is active and the status changes from CREATED to IN PROCESS (see Figure 9.46).

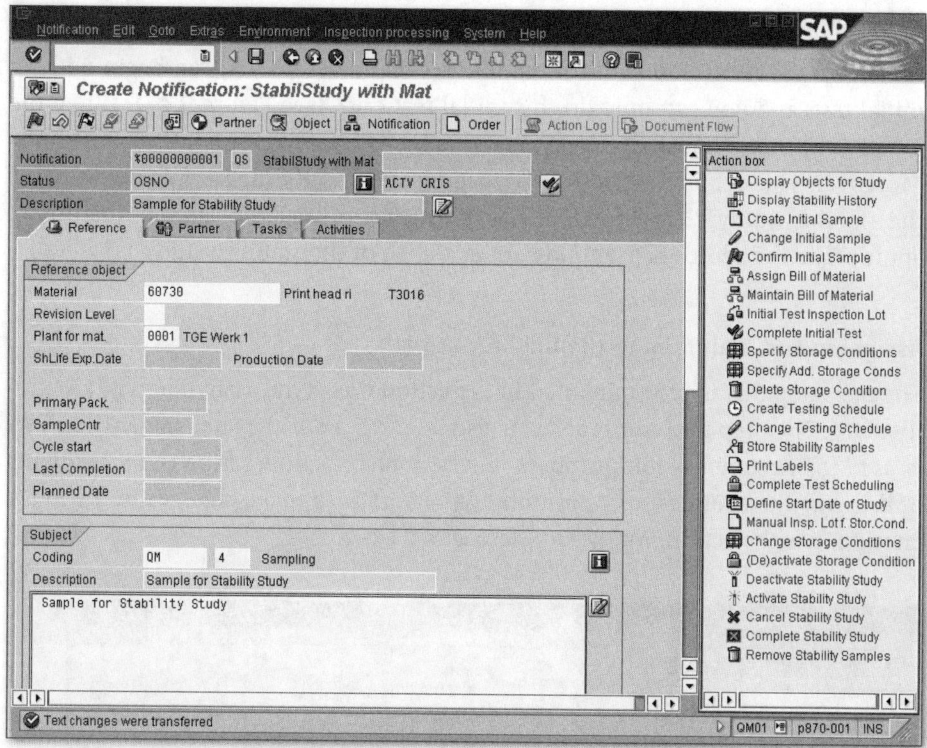


**Figure 9.45** Creating a Stability Study with Reference to the Material

**Create Initial Sample**

**Data for Physical-Sample Drawing**

| | | |
|---|---|---|
| Material | 60730 | Print head ri T3016 |
| Plant | 0001 | TGE Werk 1 |
| Notification | %00000000001 | |

**Detail Data for Physical Sample**

| | | |
|---|---|---|
| Phys.-Samp.Type | 09 | Sample for stability study |
| PhysSampCategory | 5 | Initial Sample |
| PrimaryPackaging | FOIL | Clear PVC Film, Airtight |
| Sample Container | | |
| Sample Quantity | 100 | PC |
| StorageCondition | 00000001 | |
| Sample location | Temp. box | |
| Short Text | | |

And Change Notification

**Figure 9.46** Creating an Initial Sample for the Stability Study

### Confirming an Initial Sample

It is imperative that you confirm the initial sample before you can begin with an initial test, and you can only do this initial test once (see Figure 9.47). When the initial sample is confirmed, the laboratory acknowledges the receipt of the sample. Moreover, you define the primary packaging and specify the sample quantity for the stability study. Consequently, you must ensure that the sample quantity is appropriate for additional samples in the course of the stability study.

### Assigning and Maintaining the Bill of Material

The next step that is recommended in the action box is the assignment of a stability BOM. This step is optional and can also be carried out at a later stage. The BOM is used for documentation purposes, for example, it can describe the ingredients of drugs or the chemical composition of a material. To make changes to the BOM later on, use the action, MAINTAIN BILL OF MATERIAL.

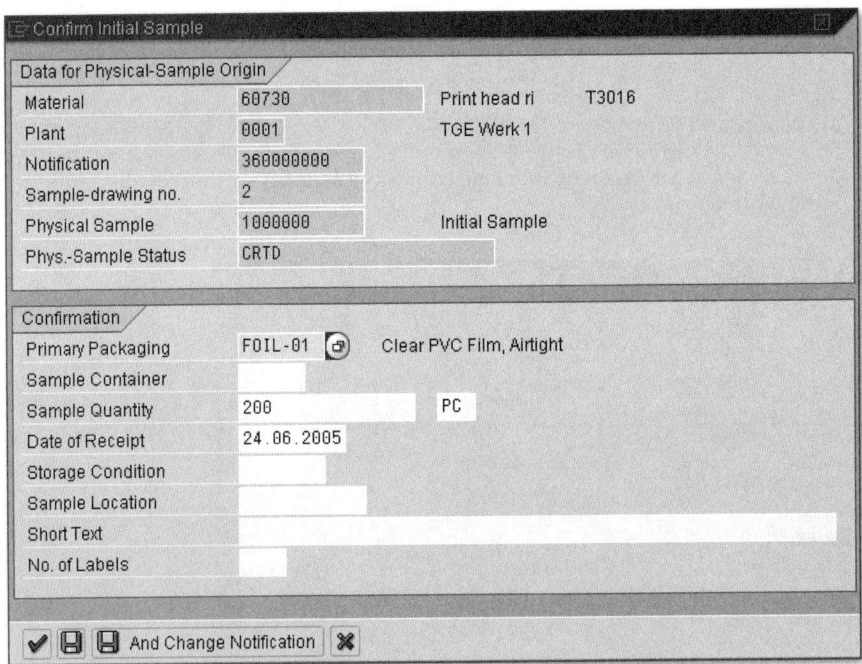


**Figure 9.47** Confirming the Initial Sample

### Initial Test Inspection Lot

An inspection lot is required when conducting the initial test on the initial sample. You can trigger it by clicking on the INITIAL TEST INSPECTION LOT action in the action box (see Figure 9.48).

Because the inspection type is already suggested by the system (here 1601), you must only enter the task list type group and the group counter of the inspection plan to be used. If you click on the INSPECTION LOT button, the window FLEXIBLE SELECTION AND CHANGING OF SPECIFICATIONS is displayed.

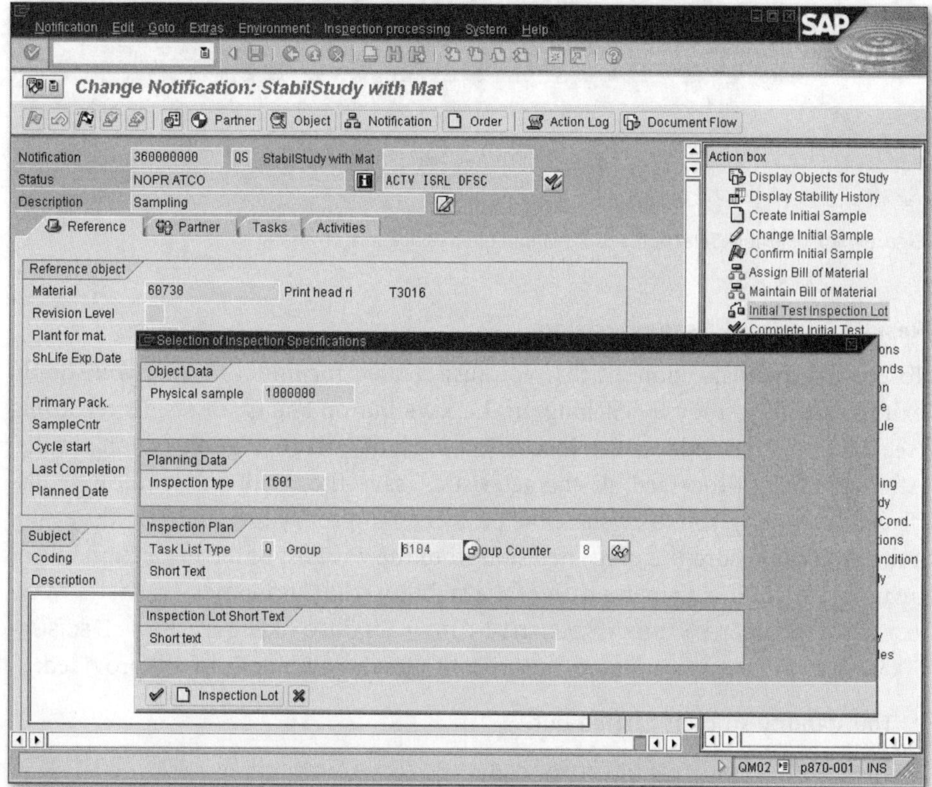


Figure 9.48 Generating an Inspection Lot for the Initial Test

This is a function that is available in SAP R/3 from Release 4.7 on. This function enables you to transfer all or some of the inspection characteristics from an overall inspection plan. For the present scenario, three characteristics (see Figure 9.49) were selected and transferred by setting the green checkmark. An example of a change to the specifications would be the modification of the tolerance limits, which is also possible at this point.

Flexible Selection and Changing of Specifications

InspCharact.

| Op... | Operation short text | Ch... | SText insp.char | T.. | Q.. | R.. | Target value | Lower spec. lmt | Upper Limit | D.. | Unit o... | CodeGr... | Plant | Smpl.pr... | Ins |
|---|---|---|---|---|---|---|---|---|---|---|---|---|---|---|---|
| 0010 | Inspection Index -... | 10 | Visual aspect | | | ✔ | | | | | | WE-MM-01 | 0001 | SV5R | |
| 0010 | Inspection Index -... | 20 | Test rack | | | ✔ | | | | | | WE-MM-01 | 0001 | SV5R | |
| 0010 | Inspection Index -... | 30 | Length 0.075 +0.07... | | ✔ | ✔ | 0.075 | 0.075 | 0.150 | 3 | mm | | | SV5R | |
| 0010 | Inspection Index -... | 40 | Short circuit test | | | ✔ | | | | | | WE-MM-01 | 0001 | SV5R | |
| 0010 | Inspection Index -... | 50 | Glue rim density | | | ✔ | | | | | | WE-MM-01 | 0001 | SV5R | |
| 0010 | Inspection Index -... | 60 | Identification | | | ✔ | | | | | | WE-MM-01 | 0001 | SV5R | |

Copy All

**Figure 9.49** Flexible Selection and Changing of Specifications

### Results Entry and Usage Decision

To process the inspection lot that you just created for initial testing, you should exit the stability study by clicking on the Save button and go to results recording (see Section 7.3). Process the inspection lot, and record the inspection results. After you have processed all characteristics, save the results. A window is displayed prompting you to evaluate the physical sample. Confirm and save the evaluation. You can record the usage decision from the worklist of the inspection lots or by using the following menu path of the stability study: Logistics • Quality Management • Stability Study • Stability Study • Change • Record Usage Decision (Transaction QA11) (see Figure 9.50). The following two options are provided:

- The stability study is carried out.
- The stability study is not carried out.

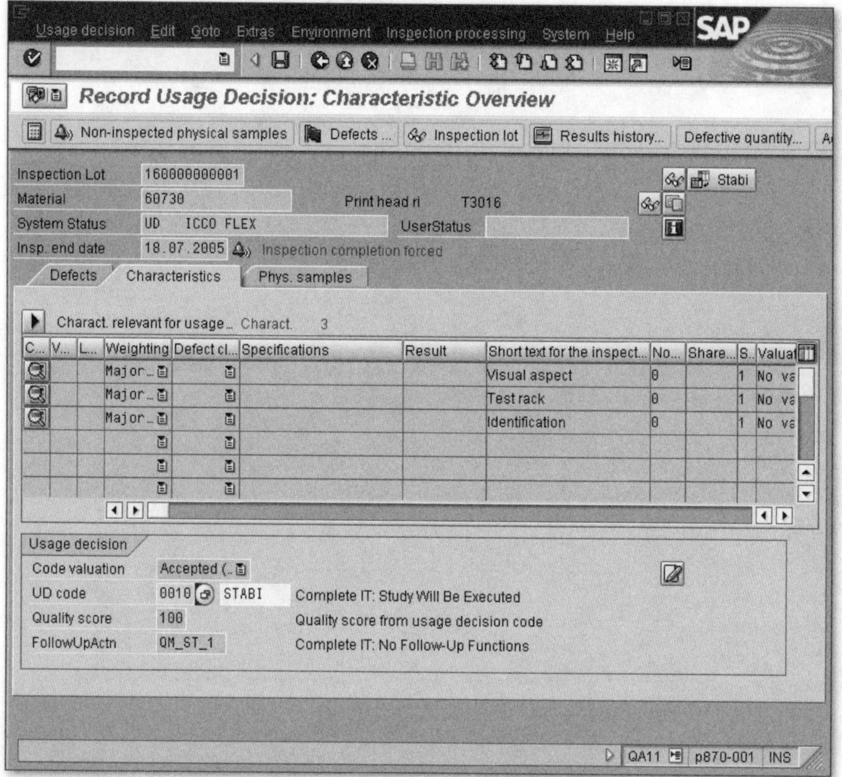


**Figure 9.50** Usage Decision for the Initial Test

In this scenario, you select UD code 0010, "The stability study is carried out." This concludes the initial test.

### Defining Storage Conditions

Now the phase begins in which you plan the stability test for the period of the study. The first step in this phase is the assignment of storage conditions. The definition of storage conditions that you can assign must be carried out upfront in Customizing. To do this, open the stability study again to change it (Logistics • Quality Management • Stability Study • Change Stability Study), and from the action box, select Define Storage Conditions (see Figure 9.51).

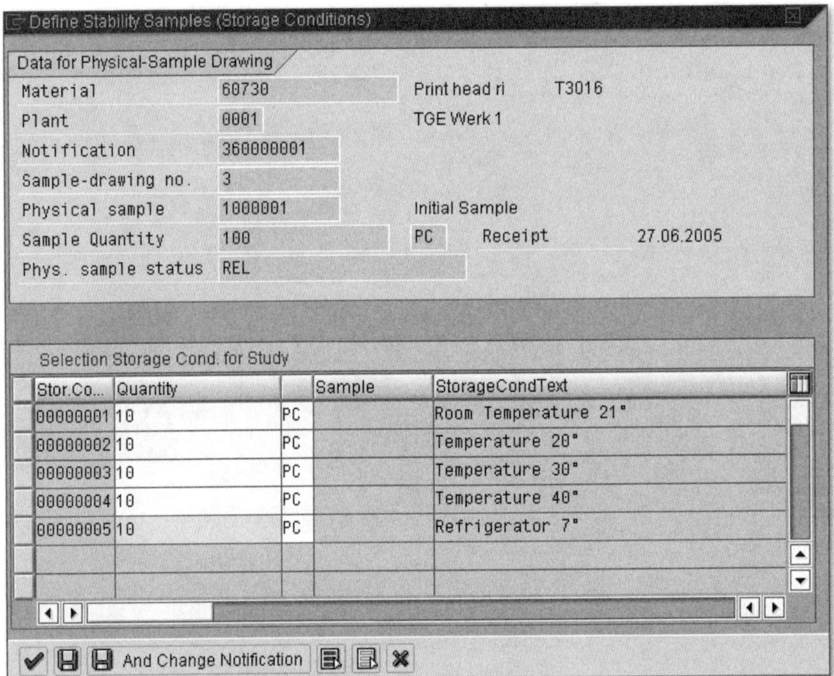


**Figure 9.51** Defining Storage Conditions

From the storage conditions provided, select those conditions for which you want to use your stability study and save them. Additionally, you have defined samples and specified the sample quantity for each storage condition. This means that you have now defined in planning exactly how many samples are to be stored. When these samples are to be drawn again and how they are to be inspected is planned in the next two steps.

### Creating a Testing Schedule

The step CREATE TESTING SCHEDULE is also carried out via the action box (see Figure 9.52). The testing schedule is a special form of the maintenance plan; that is, you also find it in Section 11.10.2, Maintenance Plan. It defines what is to be inspected and when and how. However, a prerequisite is that a maintenance strategy has been determined beforehand. In this scenario, you revert back to the sample maintenance strategy QSTABI that is available in the standard version.

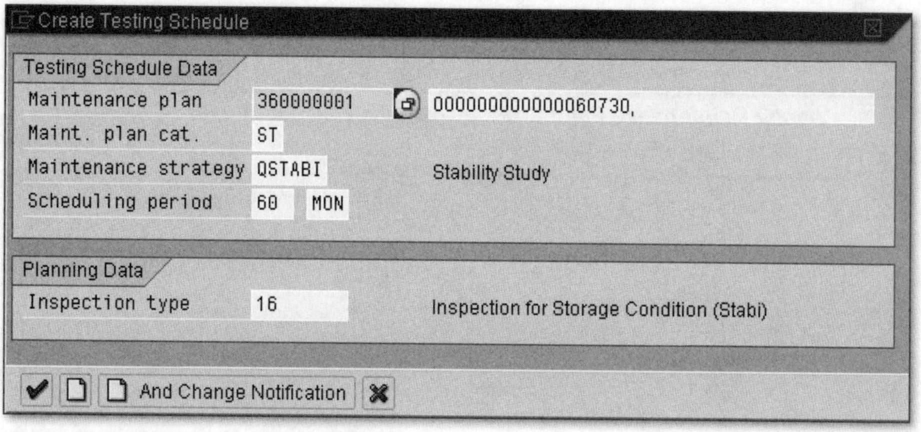

**Figure 9.52** Creating a Testing Schedule

In addition to the maintenance strategy, specify the scheduling period that determines over what period of time the stability study is to run. Upon saving, a physical sample is created for each storage condition. The quantity of the physical sample has already been previously defined via the QUANTITY field under DEFINE STORAGE CONDITIONS. However, this still doesn't answer the "how" for the inspection. This is done in the next step.

### Changing and Completing the Testing Schedule

After you have selected the CHANGE TESTING SCHEDULE action from the list of actions, you must assign an inspection plan to each item and storage condition. Furthermore, you must ensure that the inspection plan refers to the same strategy (in this case, QSTABI) as the testing schedule (see Figure 9.53). In addition, you must have assigned a maintenance package to the inspection operations in the inspection plan.

After you have assigned an inspection plan to each item (each storage condition) and have stored these changes in the testing schedule, complete the time scheduling via the corresponding action. This completes the stability planning phase.

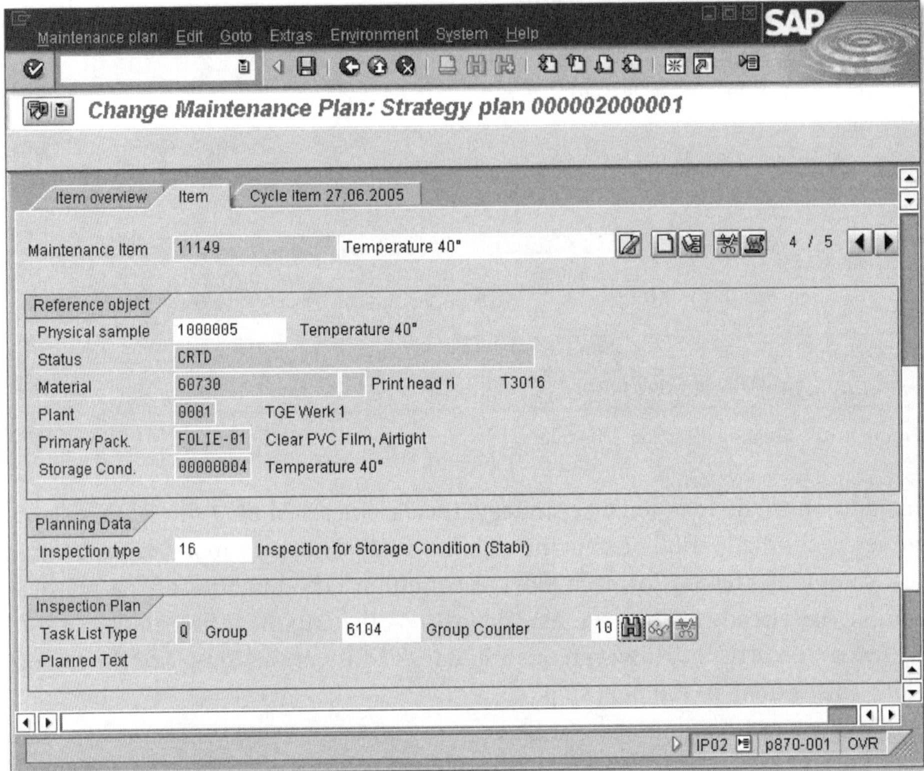


**Figure 9.53** Changing the Testing Schedule (Maintenance Plan)

### Storing Stability Samples/Printing Labels

The storage of stability samples is also documented by an action. At this point, you can still correct quantities or the storage data, if this data differs from the suggested data (see Figure 9.54).

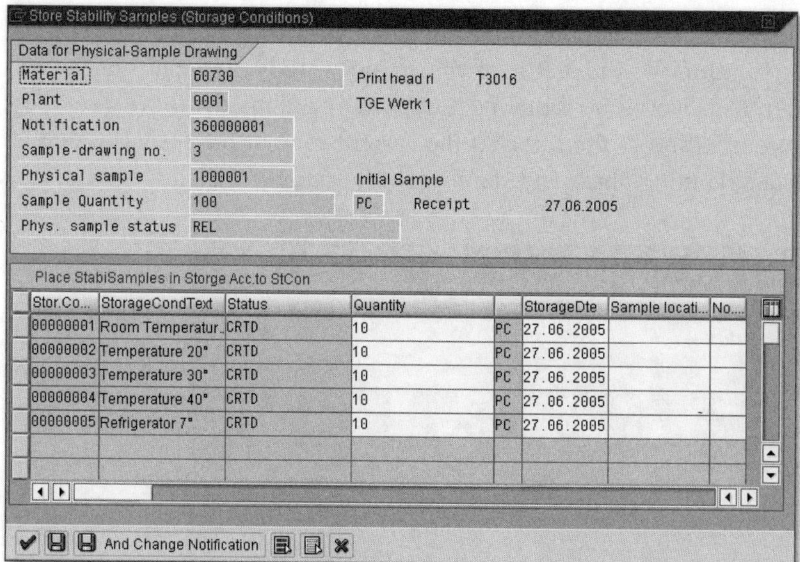


**Figure 9.54** Storing Stability Samples

If you are in Transaction Change Stability Study, you can print out a storage list through the menu item Notification • Print • Notification. The storage list contains the description of the storage conditions, the sample quantity, and the number of inspections per storage condition. After this, the notification is automatically saved. You can also trigger the printing of labels via the action box.

### Defining the Start of the Study

The end of the planning phase is followed by the start of the stability study. Upon starting, the test dates of the stability tests are calculated for the entire runtime of the study. To start the study, you must select the corresponding action from the list and accept or change the suggested start date (cycle start) (see Figure 9.55).

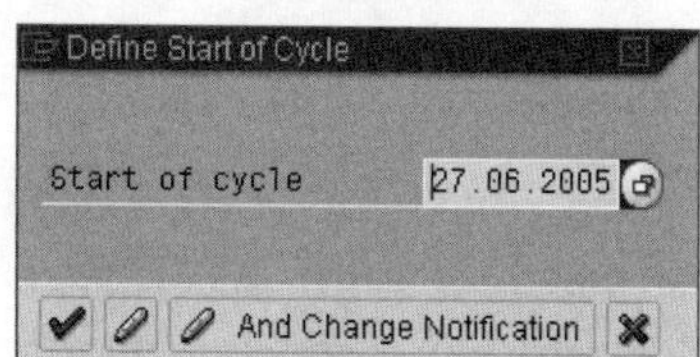


**Figure 9.55** Setting the Start Date for the Stability Study

### Status of the Stability Study

Click on the I button for the status of the stability study, and the system will display a plain text overview of the most important actions that have been performed. Figure 9.56 shows the status at the current time of the scenario, that is, with completed planning phase and stability study started.

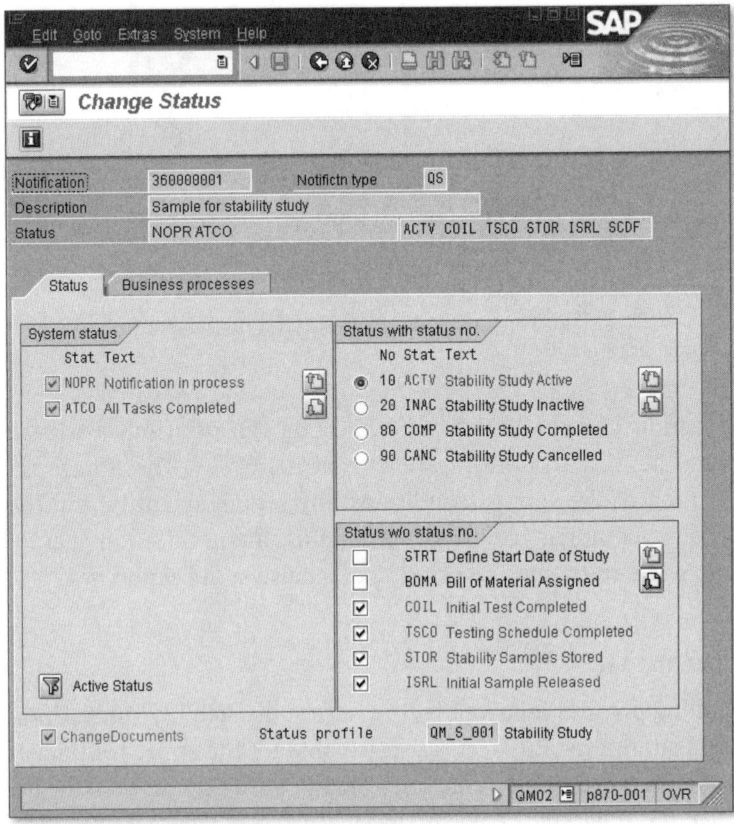


**Figure 9.56** Status Display for the Stability Study

### Objects for Study

An interesting item in the action box is the entry, OBJECTS FOR STUDY. If you select this item, the *document flow* is displayed, as shown in Figure 9.57. In accordance with the scenario at the current time, the inspection lot, which was concluded with the initial test, and the physical samples that were created for the storage conditions are displayed there. The inspection lots for the physical samples are created only when the planned interval has ended (after six months in this scenario).

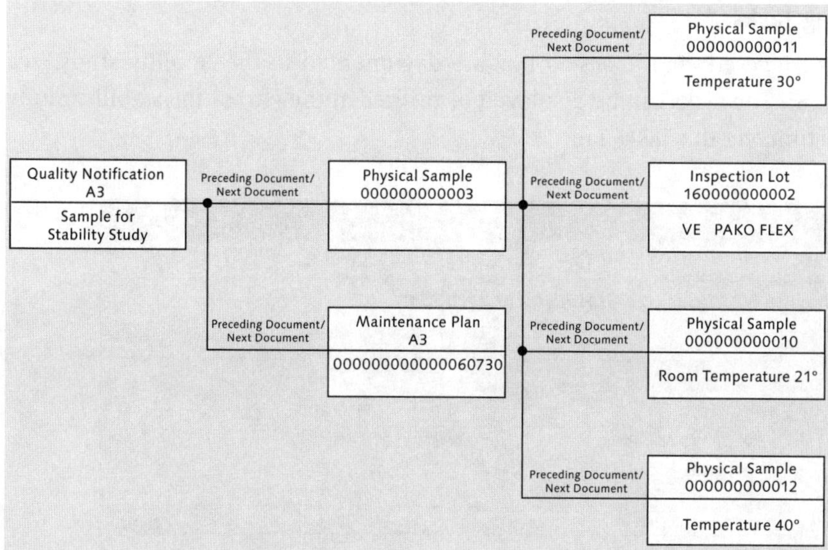


**Figure 9.57** Displaying Objects for the Stability Study

### Performing Stability Tests

In this phase, you carry out the stability tests at the scheduled dates over the entire course of the study. In general, a background job ensures that an inspection lot is created at the relevant inspection date, which is then displayed in your worklist.

The inspection lots are processed, results are confirmed, and usage decisions are made, as already described in the context of the initial test.

### Completing the Stability Study

After all stability tests have been carried out over the runtime of the study, the stability study is completed in the last phase.

Again you are in Transaction STABILITY STUDY CHANGE. Select COMPLETE STABILITY STUDY from the action box. You will be notified if all inspections have not been completed.

A premature cancellation of the stability study is also possible. To do this, you can use the action CANCEL STABILITY STUDY.

## Displaying Tasks

The tasks triggered via the action box are documented in the stability study (see Figure 9.58). The tasks can be displayed or printed at the end of the stability study or at any time via the TASKS tab.

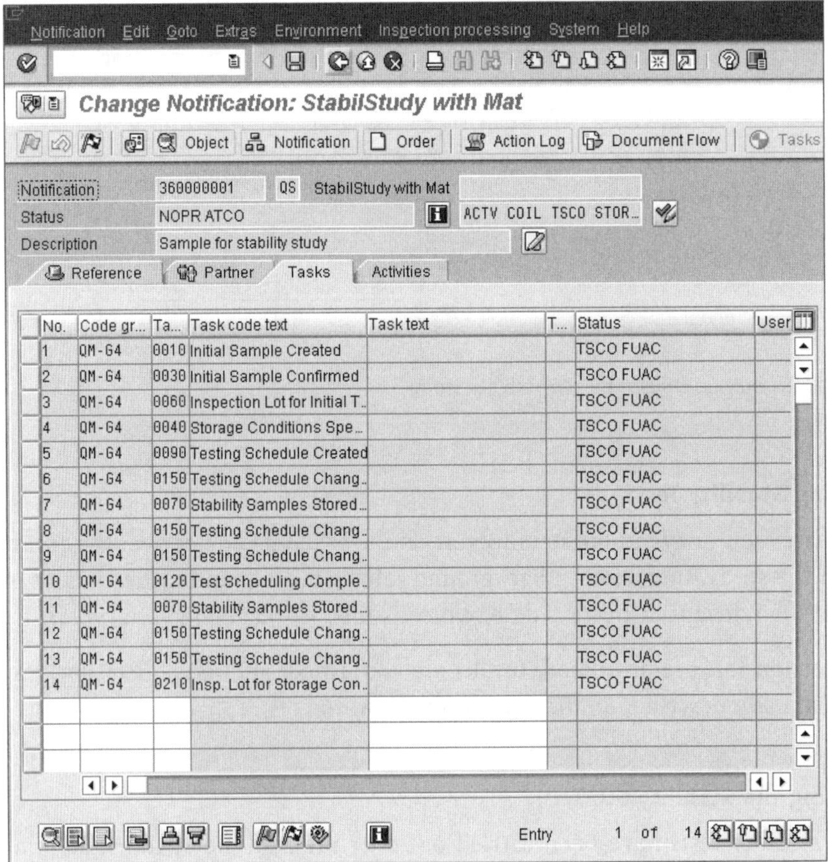


**Figure 9.58** Tasks for the Stability Study

*A lot of data are managed in the SAP ERP system. This data basis enables comprehensive evaluations that can contribute to improving processes and consequently the operating profit. This chapter outlines the available information systems and how you can use them for evaluations.*

# 10 Information Systems and Evaluations

In many processes and quality elements of the ISO 9000 series of standards, the recording and documentation of inspections and inspection results is required. Everything that you enter or confirm in the SAP ERP system must meet these requirements. To find and analyze the appropriate data further to ensure that the data meets ISO 9000 standards, SAP ERP provides different information systems, reporting techniques, and ways in which to present the information.

## 10.1 Basic Principles

In general, the evaluation options in the SAP ERP system can be divided into two groups:

- Evaluation of original documents
  - Evaluation of the results history with integrated trend analysis
  - List of inspection lots or notifications
  - General QM evaluations
- **Information systems**
  - Standard analyses
  - Flexible analyses
  - Report lists that can be created without any programming effort using Report Writer
  - Lists that are programmed in ABAP or using a query
  - Transfer to SAP NetWeaver Business Intelligence (SAP NetWeaver BI)

All tables created using these tools can be transferred to Microsoft Excel, where they can be further processed. By means of individually defined Excel macros, you can easily create regular monthly reports including meaningful graphics based on the SAP data.

## 10.2 Evaluation from Original Documents

First, the evaluation of inspection results is taken into account.

### 10.2.1 Evaluation of Inspection Results

Measured values can be evaluated material-specific using the history of task-list characteristics or across all materials based on master inspection characteristics (see Figure 10.1). You can create a graphical trendline for these results.

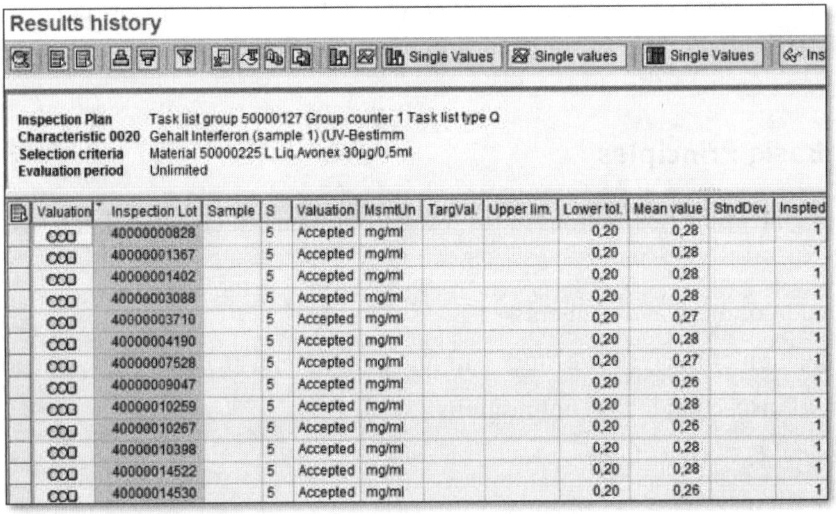

Results history

Single Values | Single values | Single Values | Ins

| | |
|---|---|
| Inspection Plan | Task list group 50000127 Group counter 1 Task list type Q |
| Characteristic 0020 | Gehalt Interferon (sample 1) (UV-Bestimm |
| Selection criteria | Material 50000225 L Liq.Avonex 30µg/0,5ml |
| Evaluation period | Unlimited |

| Valuation | Inspection Lot | Sample | S | Valuation | MsmtUn | TargVal. | Upper lim. | Lower tol. | Mean value | StndDev | Inspted |
|---|---|---|---|---|---|---|---|---|---|---|---|
| OOO | 40000000828 | | 5 | Accepted | mg/ml | | | 0,20 | 0,28 | | 1 |
| OOO | 40000001367 | | 5 | Accepted | mg/ml | | | 0,20 | 0,28 | | 1 |
| OOO | 40000001402 | | 5 | Accepted | mg/ml | | | 0,20 | 0,28 | | 1 |
| OOO | 40000003088 | | 5 | Accepted | mg/ml | | | 0,20 | 0,28 | | 1 |
| OOO | 40000003710 | | 5 | Accepted | mg/ml | | | 0,20 | 0,27 | | 1 |
| OOO | 40000004190 | | 5 | Accepted | mg/ml | | | 0,20 | 0,28 | | 1 |
| OOO | 40000007528 | | 5 | Accepted | mg/ml | | | 0,20 | 0,27 | | 1 |
| OOO | 40000009047 | | 5 | Accepted | mg/ml | | | 0,20 | 0,26 | | 1 |
| OOO | 40000010259 | | 5 | Accepted | mg/ml | | | 0,20 | 0,28 | | 1 |
| OOO | 40000010267 | | 5 | Accepted | mg/ml | | | 0,20 | 0,26 | | 1 |
| OOO | 40000010398 | | 5 | Accepted | mg/ml | | | 0,20 | 0,28 | | 1 |
| OOO | 40000014522 | | 5 | Accepted | mg/ml | | | 0,20 | 0,28 | | 1 |
| OOO | 40000014530 | | 5 | Accepted | mg/ml | | | 0,20 | 0,26 | | 1 |

**Figure 10.1** Results History

### 10.2.2 List of Inspection Lots or Notifications

To quickly obtain information about deliveries or complaints, you can also use the worklists for evaluation. The layout of the evaluations can be adapted and managed individually; for the sake of clarity, you can also calculate subtotals.

**Scenario**

In the following example, a list of defects for customer complaints is to be created (see Figure 10.2).

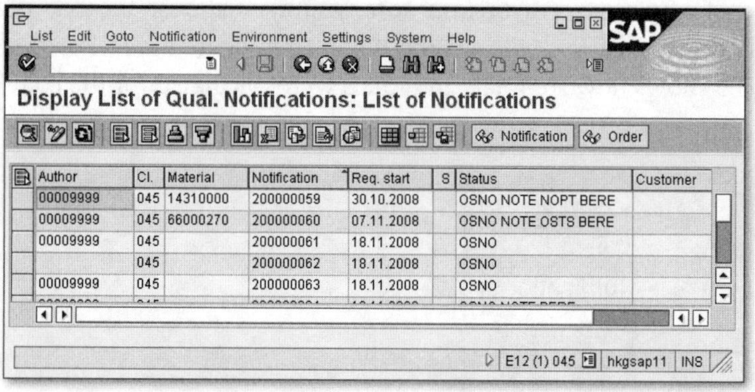

List Edit Goto Notification Environment Settings System Help
SAP
Display List of Qual. Notifications: List of Notifications
Notification
Order
Author
Cl.
Material
Notification
Req. start
S
Status
Customer
00009999 045 14310000 200000059 30.10.2008 OSNO NOTE NOPT BERE
00009999 045 66000270 200000060 07.11.2008 OSNO NOTE OSTS BERE
00009999 045 200000061 18.11.2008 OSNO
045 200000062 18.11.2008 OSNO
00009999 045 200000063 18.11.2008 OSNO
E12 (1) 045
hkgsap11
INS

**Figure 10.2** List of Notifications

First, you change the layout for which you can select the corresponding columns and information in accordance with the respective report requirements (see Figure 10.3).

Change Layout
Displayed Colu
Sort Order
Filter
View
Display
Displayed Columns
Column Name
Selected line
Notification
Required Start
Required End
Status
Priority text
Description
Material
Customer
Vendor
Manufacturer
Column Set
Column Name
Client
Notification type
Priority type
Priority
Created by
Created on
Changed by
Changed on
Notification time
Notification date
Reported by

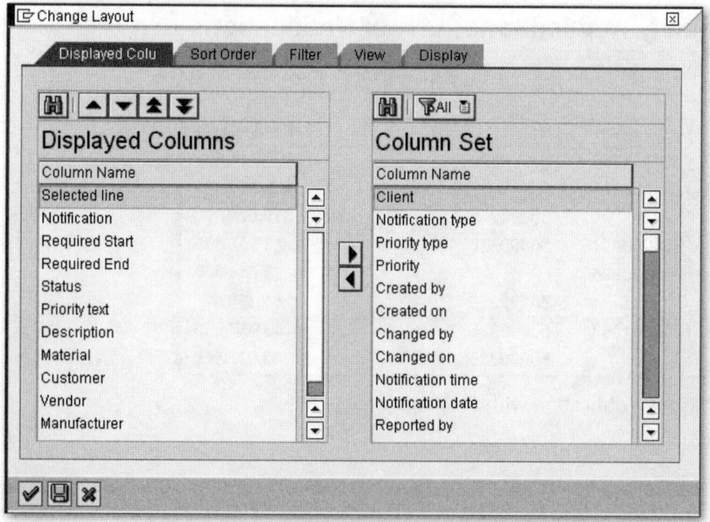

**Figure 10.3** Changing the Layout

The columns to be displayed are selected by clicking. By double-clicking a field, it is moved to the respective other table (left – column selection = displayed columns; right – column set = additional columns). If numeric fields (quantity fields) exist, you can use them for calculations. This way, you can generate totals, mean value, minimum, and maximum. For this purpose, you must choose the desired columns and select the calculation type via the menu (see Figure 10.4). For this example, Figure 10.5 shows how subtotals and totals were calculated for the complaint quantity.

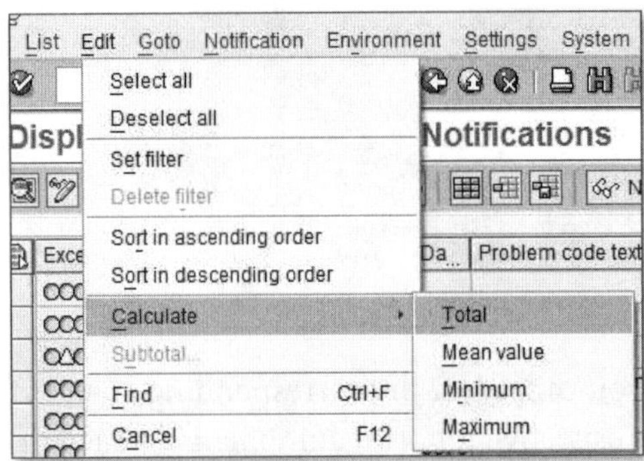


**Figure 10.4** Layout Column Selection

Change list of quality notifications: List of Notifications

| Exce... | S | Notif.date | Notification | Material | Σ Complaint quantity |
|---|---|---|---|---|---|
| OOO | | 02.09.2008 | 200001004 | 50000320 | 155.314,000 |
| OOO | | 08.09.2008 | 200001071 | | 155.314,000 |
| | | | | 50000320 | **310.628,000** |
| OOO | | 01.09.2008 | 200000994 | 50000326 | 25.552,000 |
| OOO | | 01.09.2008 | 200000996 | | 25.744,000 |
| | | | | 50000326 | **51.296,000** |
| OOO | | 12.09.2008 | 200001093 | 50000335 | 43.937,950 |
| | | | | 50000335 | **43.937,950** |

**Figure 10.5** Result – List of Notification with Totaling

### 10.2.3 Control Charts

To display the process capability, the most common types of quality control charts are available. The key figures and action limits are calculated automatically. A graphical display ensures the information value of the control chart.

### 10.2.4 General QM Evaluations

Using the QM cockpit, you can create evaluations of quality inspections with meaningful graphics. You can adapt the graphics to your specific requirements. It is possible to evaluate both current and archived data.

The following evaluations are available:

- **Evaluations of inspection lots**
  Comparison of inspection results for multiple characteristics. For this purpose, both tables (see Figure 10.6) and graphics (trend analyses or control charts) are available.
- **Evaluation of defects for an inspection lot or as notification items, together with their causes**
  You are provided with the Pareto chart graphics type to document defects or cause frequencies.
- **Evaluation of quality-related data for components or semifinished products of a material (using the where-used list of batches)**
  For components, you can evaluate both inspection lots and notifications or defects from the production chain. For inspection characteristics, the correlation chart enables the examination of causal interrelations of the individual characteristics.

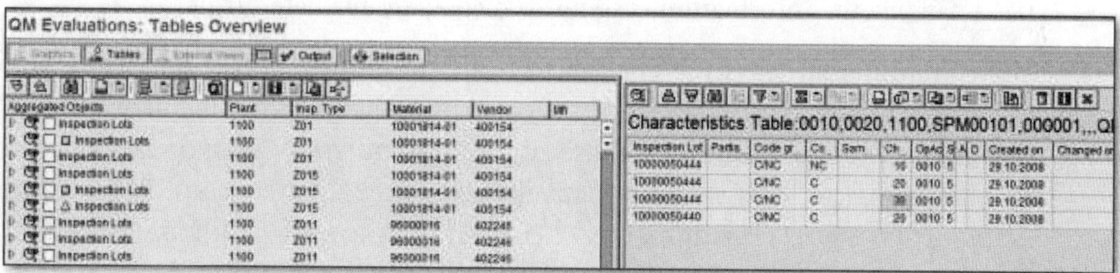


**Figure 10.6** General QM Evaluations

## 10.3 Key Figures in the Information System

The following are the most important information systems in the SAP ERP system:

- EIS (Executive Information System)
- LIS (Logistics Information System)

- AIS (Accounting Information System)
- HIS (Human Resources Information System)

The information systems can be called from the respective applications.

### 10.3.1 Logistics Controlling

For quality management, logistics controlling, a submenu of the LOGISTICS menu, is particularly efficient. It consists of different information systems:

- Logistics Information System (LIS)
- Inventory Controlling
- Purchasing Information System
- Sales Information System
- Shop Floor Information System
- Shipment Information System
- PM Information System
- QM Information System (QMIS)

Essential data from business scenarios and events is summarized and saved in information structures. Different types of analyses allow you to call this summarized data via the information systems to display or evaluate further.

There are different ways in which to navigate to the LIS. On the one hand, you can do it centrally via LOGISTICS CONTROLLING from the LOGISTICS menu or through the respective application. You choose LOGISTICS • LOGISTICS CONTROLLING • LOGISTICS INFORMATION SYSTEM or alternatively INVENTORY CONTROLLING, PURCHASING INFORMATION SYSTEM, SALES INFORMATION SYSTEM, SHOP FLOOR INFORMATION SYSTEM, SHIPMENT INFORMATION SYSTEM, PLANT MAINTENANCE INFORMATION SYSTEM, QUALITY INFORMATION SYSTEM.

### 10.3.2 Quality Management Information System (QMIS)

In QMIS, all key figures are displayed in an accumulated manner for each month. You can get to the QMIS by choosing LOGISTICS • LOGISTICS CONTROLLING • QM INFORMATION SYSTEM. Figure 10.7 shows the different submenus that will be described in the following sections.

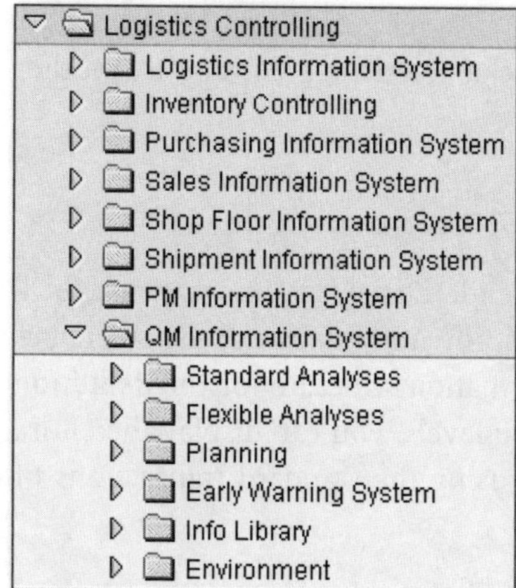


**Figure 10.7** Menu Structure of the QM Information System

### 10.3.3 Standard Analyses

Here, you can perform standard analyses that are predefined in SAP ERP; their layout and drilldown can be customized.

By using the standard analyses of the QMIS , you can evaluate the data from inspection-lot processing and quality notifications. In terms of material, vendor, or customer, the following analyses are provided:

- Lots (rejection rates, quality key figures, lead times, quantity overview of postings from the inspection lot)
- Notifications (vendor, customer, and material statistics: number and quantities of complaints)
- Defects (indication of problem frequencies, including their evaluations)

After you've performed a standard analysis, a basic list is displayed (see Figure 10.8). Based on this initial standard analysis, the system provides three navigation options.

- **Standard drilldown**
  Double-clicking a characteristic takes you to the next level of a predefined standard drilldown.

- **Drilldown according to**
  A drilldown can be implemented for each characteristic according to another characteristic.
- **Switch drilldown**
  The entire drilldown can be displayed for another characteristic.

A separate standard drilldown exists for each standard analysis. This standard drill-down can be set for all users and set user-specifically. You can use all characteristics and the periodicity of the corresponding information structure for the definition of this drilldown. From the different expansion levels, you can display the entire master data record or document information using the standard transactions of the application.

Various special functions are available for the individual business examination of key figures and characteristic attributes, on which an analysis is based. All functions are supported by graphics for statistic evaluation. For example, from the list displays of the analyses, you can call further functions in the EDIT menu such as CUMULATIVE FREQUENCY CURVE, CORRELATION, ABC ANALYSIS, CLASSIFICATION, SEGMENTATION, or even hitlists.

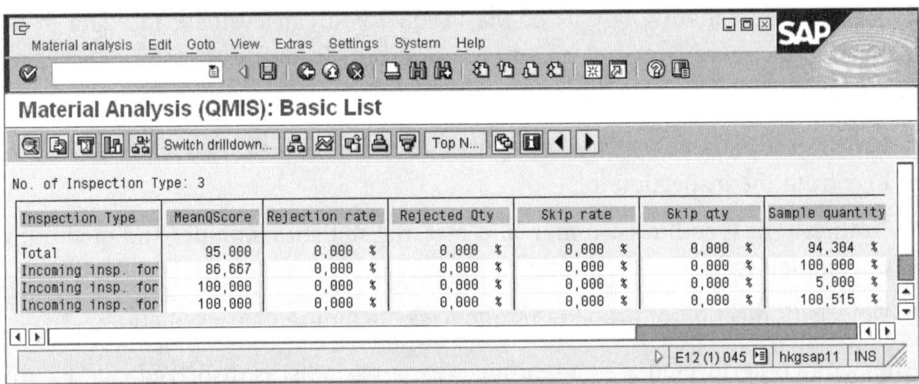


**Figure 10.8** Example of a Standard Analysis for Material

**Scenario**

You want to find out when vendor 1000 received a quality notification within a specific period (e.g., in Q4 2008).

To do this, select the information system using the following menu path: Logistics • Logistics Controlling • QM Information System. In the Standard Analyses menu item, select Vendor • Notification Overview. After entering the vendor number and the analysis period, you will obtain an overview of all created notifications to this vendor, where these are subdivided according to the processing status (Outstanding, In Process, Completed). The submenu Extras • Q-Notifications provides you with a list of the relevant quality notifications, including date and inspection lot number in an additional display window (see Figure 10.9).

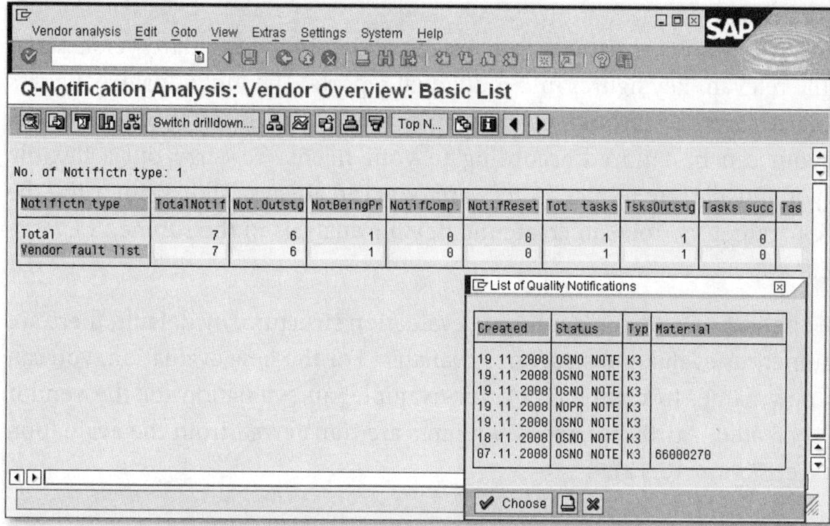


**Figure 10.9** Notification Analysis for a Vendor, Including the List of Q-Notifications

### Time Series

Based on the drilldown list of a characteristic, you can create a time series for any key figure (see Figure 10.10). The period corresponds to the predefined analysis period, which you determine in the initial screen of the standard analysis.

Time series

Key figure TotalNotif

| Notifictn type | 01.2006 | 02.2006 | 03.2006 | 04.2006 | 05.2006 | 06.2006 | 07.2006 | 08.2006 | 09.2006 | 10.2006 | 11.2006 |
|---|---|---|---|---|---|---|---|---|---|---|---|
| Total | 0 | 2 | 17 | 16 | 6 | 6 | 12 | 6 | 32 | 1 | 0 |
| Complaint ag. Vend | | 2 | 17 | 16 | 6 | 6 | 12 | 6 | 32 | 1 | |

**Figure 10.10** Time Series

### 10.3.4 Flexible Analyses

Here you can define and execute analyses. *Flexible analyses* enable an easy entry to the Report Writer, which is a utility that can be used to create individual reports for different applications. A part of this functionality is used within flexible analyses.

You can evaluate the information structures provided in the standard version and compile the relevant key figures into individual reports. The individual key figures can be linked together through calculation formulas and inserted into a report whose layout can be tailored according to your needs. To carry out a flexible analysis, you must create it once. Afterward, you can always call it again using the respective parameters. You can create the flexible analysis in the submenu EVALUATION • CREATE.

Select the application and an appropriate evaluation structure. By default, there are already numerous evaluation structures available. For the new evaluation, you can choose a new name. In Figure 10.11, for example, an evaluation for the vendor statistics is created. Attributes and key figures are transferred from the evaluation structure (see Figure 10.12).

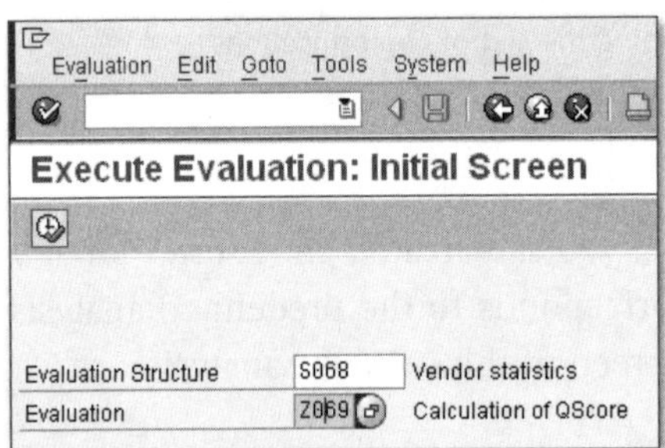


**Figure 10.11** Performing a Flexible Analysis

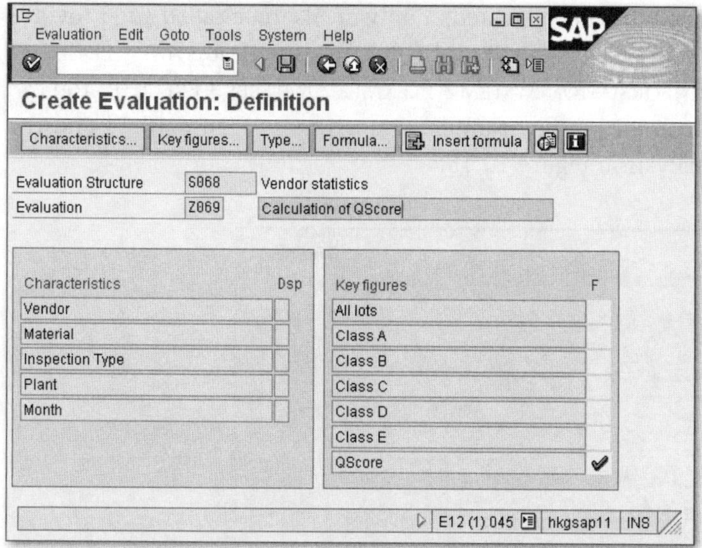


**Figure 10.12** Customizing the Evaluation

In the evaluation, key figures can also be processed by using formulas. An example of a formula to calculate a quality score is shown in Figure 10.13.

Insert Formula

Key figures

| Label | Technical Name |
|---|---|
| All lots | S068-ZHLSELECT |
| Class A | S068-KLASSE_A |
| Class B | S068-KLASSE_B |
| Class C | S068-KLASSE_C |
| Class D | S068-KLASSE_D |
| Class E | S068-KLASSE_E |
| Total QScore | S068-SUMQKZ |

Formula

Name QScore

(100*'S068-KLASSE_A'+50*'S068-KLASSE_C'+'S068-KLASSE_E')/'S068-ZHSELECT'

**Figure 10.13** Editing a Formula in Flexible Analysis

After the flexible analysis has been created, it only needs to be called and provided with the required parameters. You can call it by choosing LOGISTICS • LOGISTICS CONTROLLING • QM INFORMATION SYSTEM • FLEXIBLE ANALYSES • EXECUTE. You can see the selection screen with a few sample parameters in Figure 10.14 and the result of a flexible analysis in Figure 10.15.

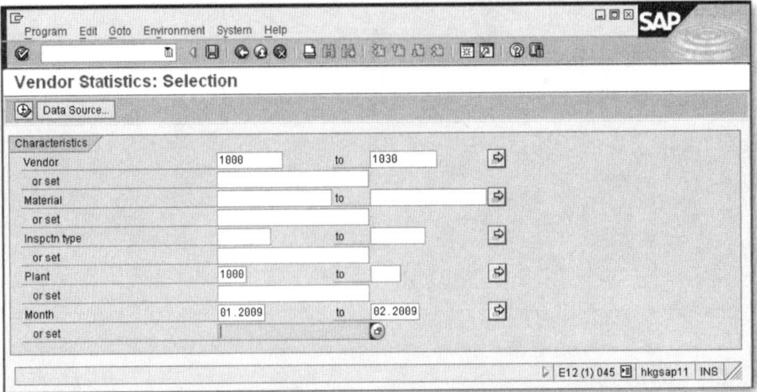


**Figure 10.14** Selection Screen for a Flexible Analysis

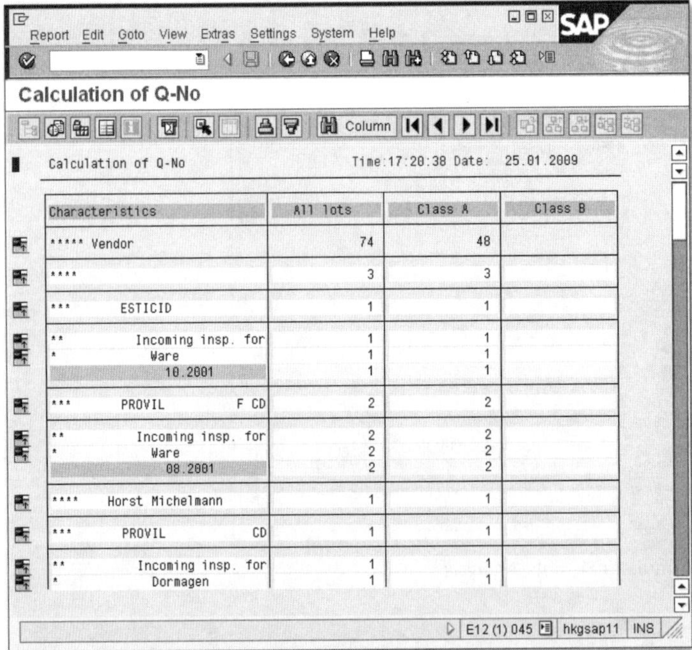


**Figure 10.15** Selection Result of a Flexible Analysis

### Planning

Here you can enter planning data and create forecasts. In the context of standard analyses, you can then contrast actual data and planning data. Planning in information systems is based on the information structures already described for flexible analyses, which are provided in the standard version, or you can also define them yourself.

### Early Warning System

The Early Warning System enables you to search for weak points and exception situations in logistics and can be used for all logistics applications.

The exception situation, also referred to simply as an *exception*, consists of the definition of attributes or attribute values (e.g., material, vendor) and conditions. The following can be defined as conditions:

- Threshold value
- Trend
- Plan/actual comparison

There are three options available in searching for exception situations:

- Standard analysis
- Exception analysis
- Periodic analysis

In the standard analysis, the exception situation is highlighted in color in the display. The exception analysis filters out the standard cases, and therefore shows only the exception situations that are highlighted in color. The periodic analysis automatically executes an analysis of the exception situations in previously defined intervals (hourly, weekly, monthly) and informs you of their emergence via email, fax, or workflow.

### Info Library

You can record, classify, or select key figures with the *Logistics Information Library* (LIB), which is a part of the LIS. You cannot generate new key figures with the LIB; however, you can use existing information in the system.

The logistics info library provides the following advantages:

- Access to all key figures
- Simple availability of information
- Convenient search
- Simple user guidance
- Possibility of grouping information into InfoSets

Similar to a search engine on the Internet, you can search and display a key figure in the INFO LIBRARY by choosing INFO LIBRARY • KEY FIGURE RETRIEVAL • USING TEXT STRINGS. The search for VENDOR and EVALUATION generates a list of the relevant key figures. Selecting VENDOR EVALUATION OF VENDORS FROM PURCHASING brings you directly to the display of the vendor evaluation.

### 10.3.5 Report Lists

For your reports, you can use those reports provided in the standard version, or, if these are not sufficient, you can create your own reports. You can find the reports that are used most frequently under INFORMATION SYSTEMS in the standard menu tree, and also in the respective applications under INFORMATION SYSTEM (see Figure 10.16).

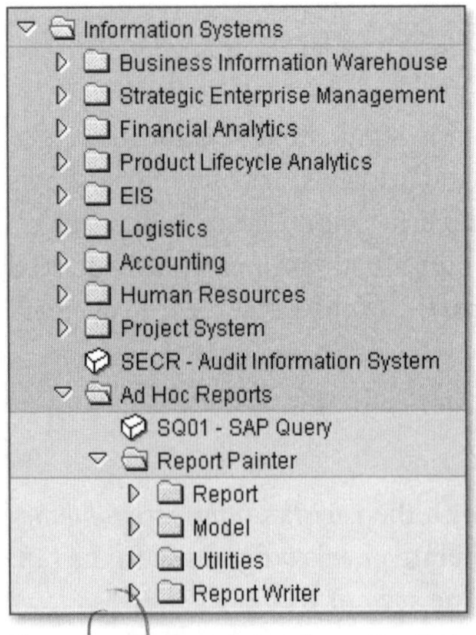


**Figure 10.16** Reports in Information Systems

### Report Writer

If the functionality of the standard analyses is not sufficient, you can use the Report Writer to create special reports by selecting, evaluating, and formatting specific data to meet your own individual requirements. Here are some of the options that are provided by the Report Writer:

- Calculating key figures, percentages, and variances
- Grouping reports in different categories
- Comparing data (e.g., plan/actual or previous year/current year)
- Downloading report data to the PC (for further processing)
- Sending reports by email

### Report Painter

The Report Painter is a downsized version of the Report Writer with limited functionality. By giving up a few functions of the Report Writer (e.g., the sets), the graphical report structure is used as a basis of the report definition; the Report Painter is easier to understand and use.

### Quick Viewer

The *Quick Viewer* is a tool for creating ad-hoc reports. Its operation roughly includes the following three steps: define the data basis, create the list/selection screen, and execute the list/selection screen.

You are provided with different types of data sources. In the simplest case, you just access a table. You can also connect multiple tables in a table join especially for your *QuickView*. To implement the QuickView, you only have to define it; saving, in particular, is not required.

### ABAP Query

With an ABAP Query, you can create reports without having to program in ABAP. Here, the term *query* is synonymous with database request. The entire process is called an ABAP Query because the system generates an ABAP report internally, responding to the database request. There are three report types available:

- Basic lists
- Statistics
- Ranked lists

These report types can also be combined with each other.

**Scenario Complaints Statistic**

You want to obtain absolute and percentaged information about complaints of a vendor within a specific month.

For this purpose, you create an InfoSet with a join that links the Information Structures S098 (QM vendor statistics) and S012 (Purchasing vendor statistics) via the vendor and the material. The complaint rate is inserted as a calculation field in the query. This way, you can quickly generate complaints statistics relating both to the vendor and the material. Figure 10.17 shows that a threshold value has been exceeded.

complaint quantity

| Month | POrg | Plnt | Vendor | Vendor Account Number | Material | Qty of goods recvd | BUn | Complaint quantity | BUn | Quote |
|---|---|---|---|---|---|---|---|---|---|---|
| 05.2007 | 1000 | 1100 | 6295 | REHAU GmbH | R92264-000 | 200,000 | KG | 100,000 | KG | 50,00 |
| 10.2007 | 1000 | 1100 | 6295 | REHAU GmbH | R80012-000 | 0,000 | KG | 5,000 | KG | 0,00 |
| 12.2007 | 1000 | 1100 | 6295 | REHAU GmbH | R92264-000 | 400,000 | KG | 550,000 | KG | 137,50 |

**Figure 10.17** Query Vendor Analysis

### ABAP Reports

By programming evaluation programs in ABAP/4, the programming language for the SAP ERP system, you have the greatest flexibility and range for creating and evaluating a report. The price for these almost unlimited options is that a profound knowledge of the system and the programming language is required to program such a report. If this knowledge is available in your IT department or can be brought in from the outside, you can create customized reports to meet the specific needs of your company.

## 10.4 SAP NetWeaver BI

With SAP NetWeaver Business Intelligence (SAP NetWeaver BI, previously SAP BI and SAP BW) is based on the idea of a cross-functional information system in the context of a data warehouse to ensure competitiveness, optimize processes, and operate quickly and in line with the market. As a core component of SAP NetWeaver, BI provides a data warehousing functionality, a business intelligence platform, and a suite of business intelligence tools to enable enterprises to achieve their goals. The result is the merging of data from the SAP ERP system and external systems, and the processing of this data. Consequently, an external, relational database is created in which you collect all of the data to be analyzed for the entire company. This database is installed on a separate SAP ERP system and consists of several previously prepared SAP and Office tools. Similar to the info systems described in this chapter, evaluations of the data of the different SAP ERP and controlling processes are preconfigured.

The aim of SAP NetWeaver BI is to display evaluations and reports in collaborative environments, in the company portal, or just in the web browser. The use of a common reporting tool provides benefits in terms of availability, maintenance, and use on the system side, as well as transparency, flexibility, and usability on the user side.

#### Business Content

SAP NetWeaver BI provides preconfigured objects that are referred to as *SAP Business Content*. These objects shorten the implementation of the SAP NetWeaver BI because they supply ready-to-use solutions for business information requirements. The following objects are already preconfigured:

- DataSources
- Process chains
- InfoObjects
- InfoSources
- Data targets (InfoCubes and ODS [operational data store] objects)
- Variables
- Data mining models
- Queries
- Workbooks
- Crystal reports
- Web templates
- Roles

## SAP NetWeaver BI and Quality Management

The quality-relevant reports are provided as *InfoCubes* and queries in compliance with the general lingo used in data warehouse systems. For quality management, the InfoCubes are formatted similarly to the QMIS — they contain a comprehensive collection of frequently used reports (see Figure 10.18).

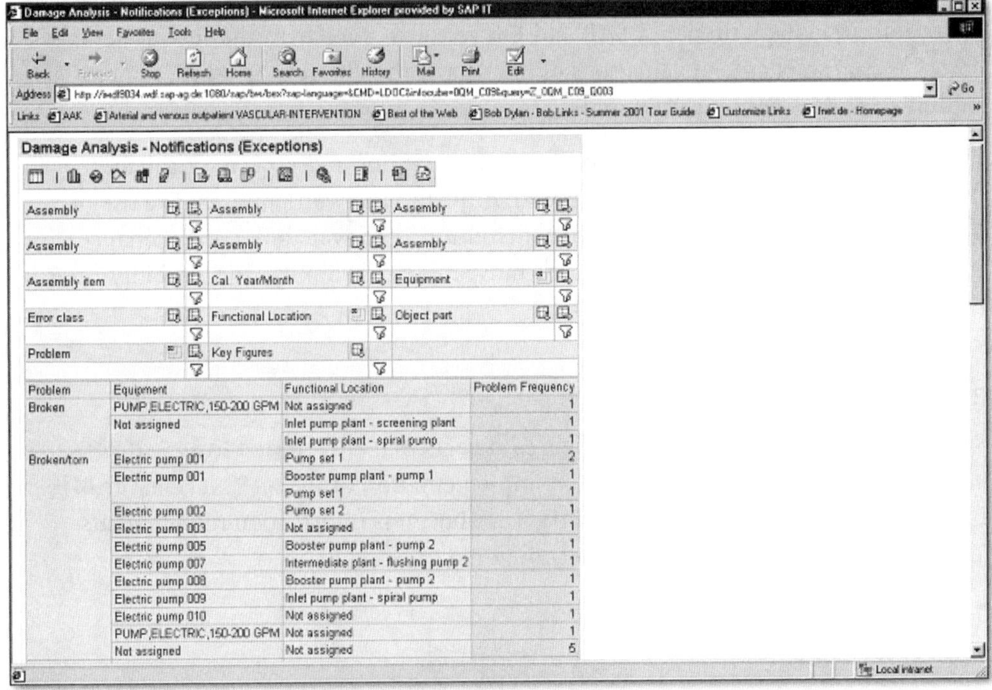


**Figure 10.18** Quality Notifications Query in SAP NetWeaver BI

The following are the most important queries in quality management:

- Process capability (Cpk values) — Top 10
- Model analysis
- Problem analysis: Problem analysis notifications
- Problem analysis: Material — defect evaluation
- Vendor analysis: Inspection lots
- Vendor analysis: ppm (leaders)
- Vendor analysis inspection lots (Top 10)

- Vendor evaluation: Problem frequency
- Vendor evaluation: Notifications
- Vendor evaluation: Quality score
- Vendor evaluation: Skip rate
- Vendor evaluation: Skip rate general
- Vendor evaluation: Number of accepted lots
- Vendor evaluation: Number of lots not accepted
- Vendor evaluation: Problem frequency
- Material analysis: Inspection lots
- Notification analysis: Customer problems
- Notification — actions (QM): Selected actions
- Notification — measures (QM): Selected measures
- Notification — cause analysis (QM): Selected causes
- MiniApp: Problem analysis
- MiniApp: Notification analysis
- Inspection results: Rejection quota for inspection results
- Inspection results: Tolerance observance
- Inspection results: Stability study
- Inspection results: Quantitative data
- Usage decisions

#### Examples of QM Content in SAP

As described, roles are already preconfigured in SAP NetWeaver BI, for instance, for the quality manager or the quality planner. For these roles, some evaluations are compiled in the form of workbooks that have a typical meaning for their owners. In the following examples, you are provided with some examples of the workbooks of the roles:

- Quality manager (SAP_BWC_0ROLE_0071) (see Figure 10.19)
- Quality planner (SAP_BWC_0ROLE_0004)

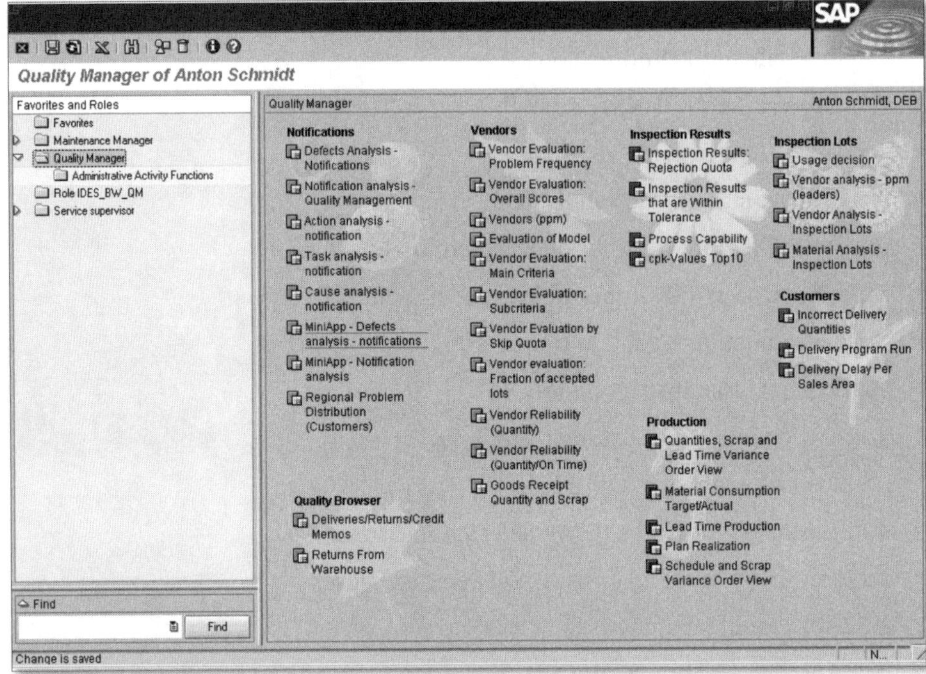


**Figure 10.19** Starting the SAP NetWeaver BI Front End (BEx Browser) — Example of the Quality Browser of the Quality Manager

## Example 1: Problem Analysis in Goods Receipt

In the first example, an analysis of the error types and frequency is to be created by the SAP NetWeaver BI in the GR inspection. For this purpose, the quality manager begins a routine execution of a notification analysis that shows the frequency of the error emergence during the goods receipt inspection in consolidated form.

After the initial access in the query, the data must first be updated. This occurs via the symbol REFRESH, whereby no filter values should be set. Figure 10.20 shows a possible result. By right-clicking on a column (e.g., PROBLEM FREQUENCY), you can sort the table.

Now you can still make changes to the existing query. If, for instance, you want to see the "Top 10" problems, you must create a condition. To do this, select the

CHANGE QUERY function by clicking on the symbol (global definition). The result can also be displayed as a graphic.

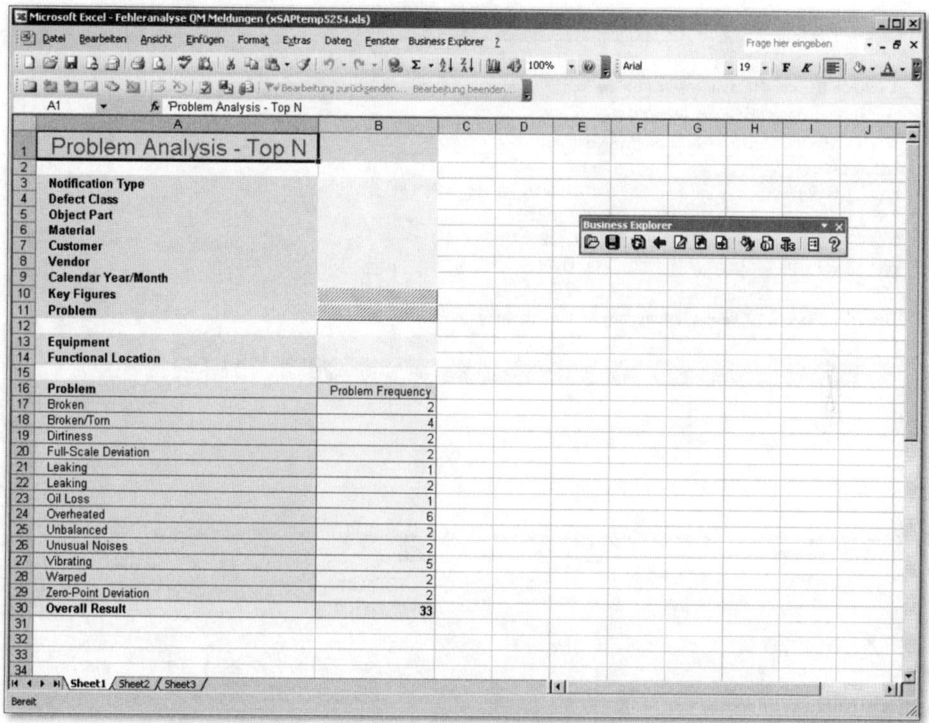


**Figure 10.20** Workbook Problem Analysis — Notifications

If you click on CONDITION, you can create a condition for the "Top 10" (see Figure 10.21).

**Figure 10.21** New Condition — Top 10 Problems

The following steps are necessary to define the settings of a new condition (see Figure 10.22):

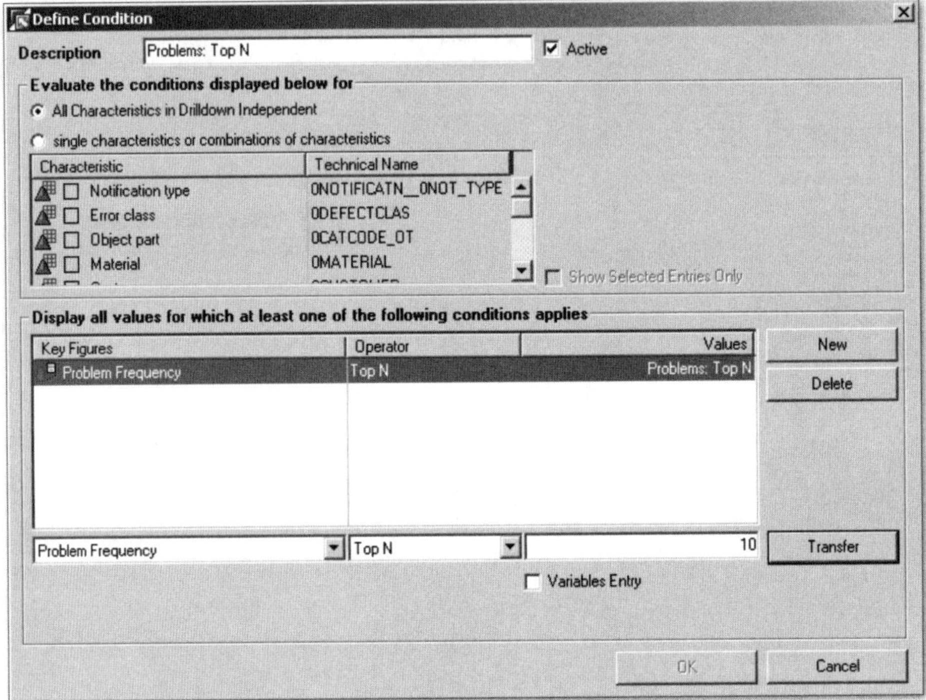


**Figure 10.22** Defining Details of the Condition

Save the query with or under a new name with .

After refreshing the query again by clicking on the symbol , the new settings are activated.

To integrate a graphic for the results, select the LAYOUT function. The following steps are then necessary (see Figure 10.23):

- Select the type of graphic (e.g., bar chart)
- Adjust the graphic according to the content of the required size
- Scale the y-axis (by right-clicking)

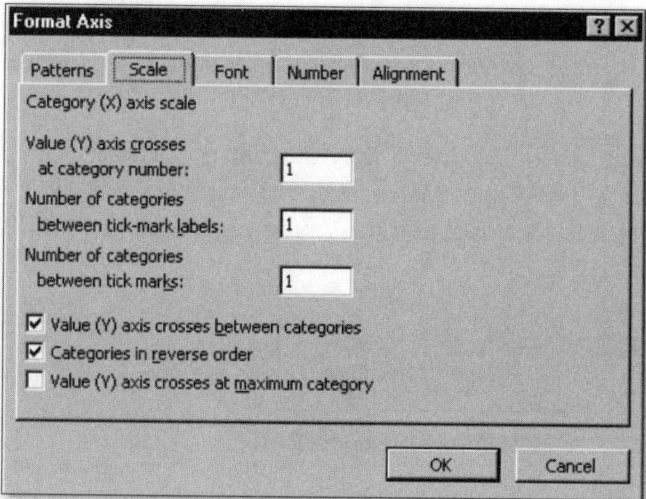


**Figure 10.23** Formatting the Integrated Graphic

Figure 10.24 shows the result.

You can save a modified workbook via [save icon] in the favorites. In addition, you can also store the Excel sheet locally via [save icon].

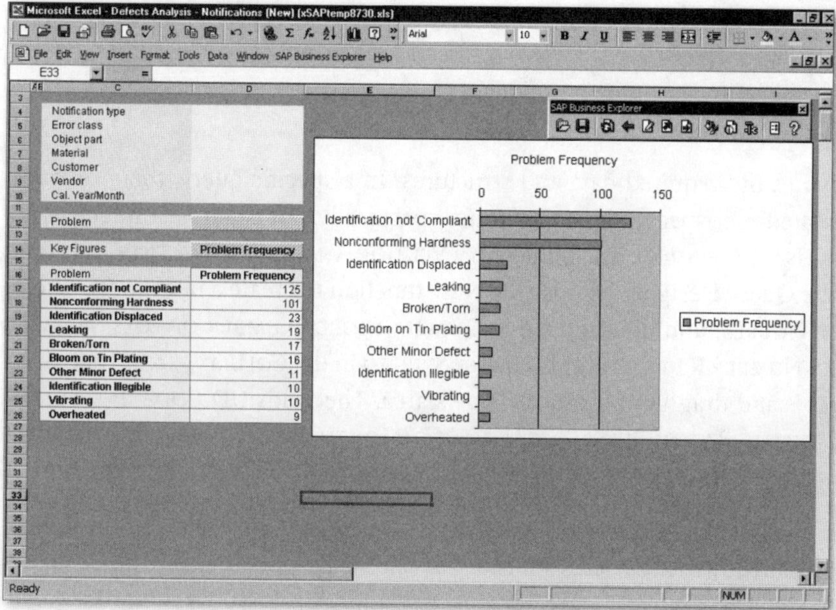


**Figure 10.24** Excel Worksheet Created from SAP NetWeaver BI

### Example 2: Creating a New Vendor Analysis

In the second example, a vendor analysis is to be created for specific key figures in SAP NetWeaver BI.

Open the *BEx Analyzer* and then the query with the function OPEN QUERY: . Under INFOAREAS and SUPPLY CHAIN MANAGEMENT/QUALITY MANAGEMENT • INSPECTION LOT/USAGE DECISION, you will find the VENDOR ANALYSIS: INSPECTION LOTS menu item (see Figure 10.25).

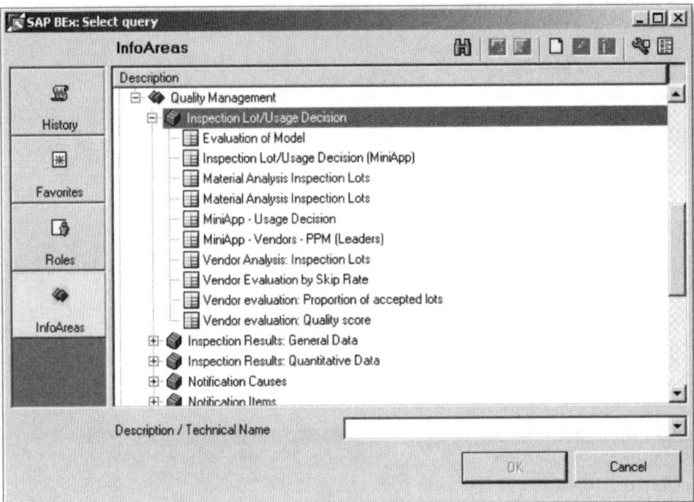


**Figure 10.25** Selecting a Query

This provides the required data and structures. In a specific query, the evaluation can be created user-specifically or customer-specifically. For example, under INSPECTION LOT/USAGE DECISION, select the entry VENDOR ANALYSIS: INSPECTION LOTS, and then in the Query Designer, choose the NEW function to create a new query. There, open KEY FIGURES, and drag the fields QUALITY SCORE, NUMBER OF LOTS, NUMBER ACCEPTED, NUMBER REJECTED, and NUMBER SKIPPED in the COLUMNS area. Then open DIMENSIONS and drag VENDOR to the ROWS area. The fields UD CODE, INSPECTION TYPE, MATERIAL, BATCH, PLANT, and CAL.YEAR/MONTH (period) serve as free attributes. Figure 10.26 shows how the request now appears in the Query Designer.

Save the newly created query. The query can be executed by clicking on the symbol. As already mentioned, you can save the workbook as a favorite or save it locally as an Excel file (see Figure 10.27).

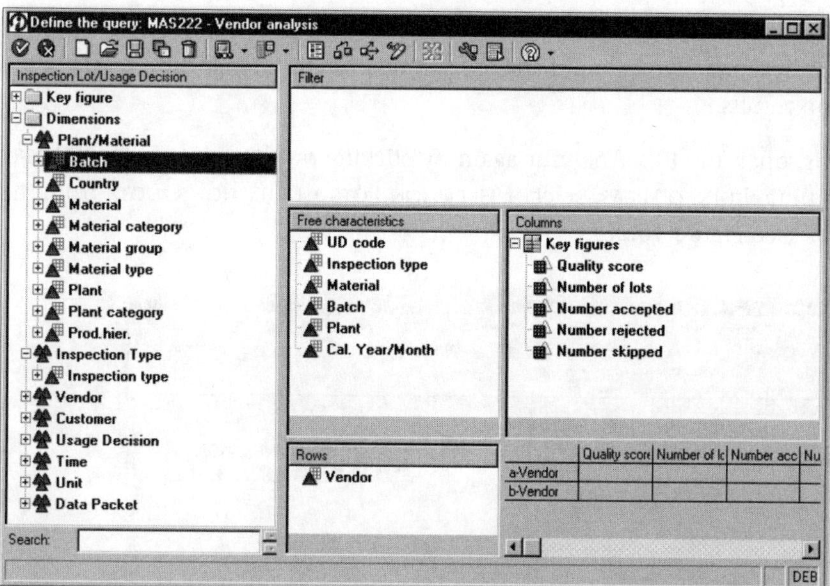

Figure 10.26 Created Query in the Query Designer

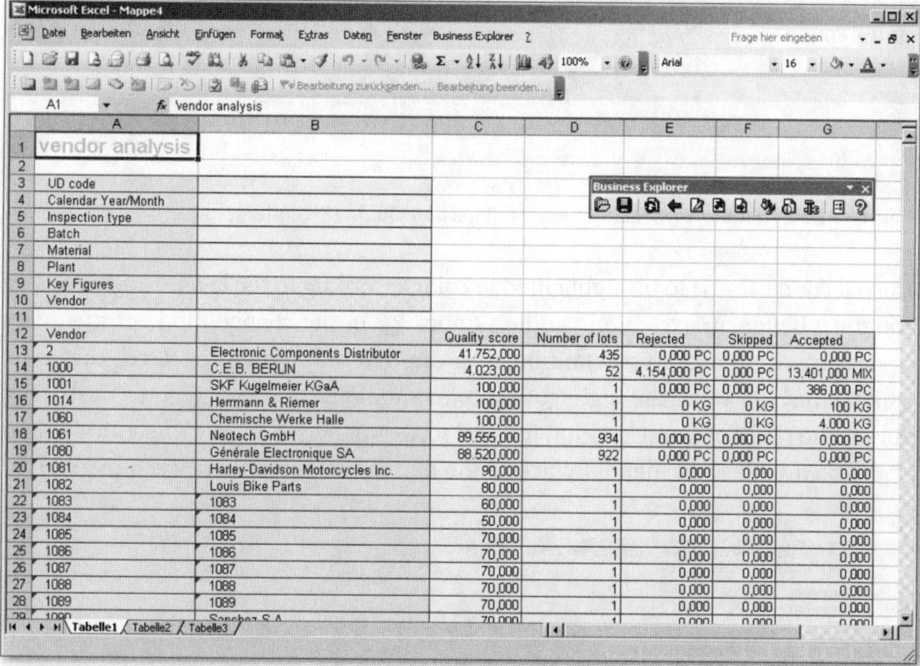

Figure 10.27 Complete Vendor Analysis as an Excel Worksheet

### Example 3: Inspection Results

In the third example, you should create an evaluation of the rejection quota in the inspection results.

To do this, open the BEx Analyzer again by clicking on the symbol OPEN QUERY . This time, in INFOAREAS, select INSPECTION LOTS • REJECTION QUOTA from the workbook (see Figure 10.28).

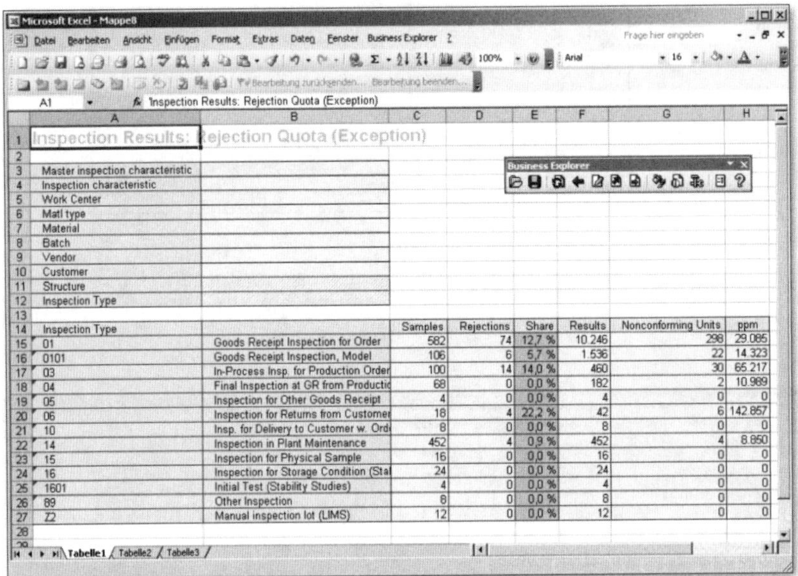


| Inspection Type | | Samples | Rejections | Share | Results | Nonconforming Units | ppm |
|---|---|---|---|---|---|---|---|
| 01 | Goods Receipt Inspection for Order | 582 | 74 | 12,7 % | 10.246 | 298 | 29.085 |
| 0101 | Goods Receipt Inspection, Model | 106 | 6 | 5,7 % | 1.536 | 22 | 14.323 |
| 03 | In-Process Insp. for Production Order | 100 | 14 | 14,0 % | 460 | 30 | 65.217 |
| 04 | Final Inspection at GR from Productic | 68 | 0 | 0,0 % | 182 | 2 | 10.989 |
| 05 | Inspection for Other Goods Receipt | 4 | 0 | 0,0 % | 4 | 0 | 0 |
| 06 | Inspection for Returns from Customer | 18 | 4 | 22,2 % | 42 | 6 | 142.857 |
| 10 | Insp. for Delivery to Customer w. Ord | 8 | 0 | 0,0 % | 8 | 0 | 0 |
| 14 | Inspection in Plant Maintenance | 452 | 4 | 0,9 % | 452 | 4 | 8.850 |
| 15 | Inspection for Physical Sample | 16 | 0 | 0,0 % | 16 | 0 | 0 |
| 16 | Inspection for Storage Condition (Stal | 24 | 0 | 0,0 % | 24 | 0 | 0 |
| 1601 | Initial Test (Stability Studies) | 4 | 0 | 0,0 % | 4 | 0 | 0 |
| 89 | Other Inspection | 8 | 0 | 0,0 % | 8 | 0 | 0 |
| Z2 | Manual inspection lot (LIMS) | 12 | 0 | 0,0 % | 12 | 0 | 0 |

**Figure 10.28** Workbook Inspection Results: Rejection Quota (Exception)

The rejection value is to be highlighted in color according to the level. To achieve this, you must define an exception via the symbol  in the change mode of the query (see Figure 10.29). In this definition, you can determine the *Alert Level*, that is, at which threshold value the highlighting color should change (see Figure 10.30). You can see the result of the evaluation in Excel format in Figure 10.31. The critical values are marked with a red square (which in the illustration can only be seen in gray).

**Figure 10.29** Defining the Start of the Exception for the Rejection Quota

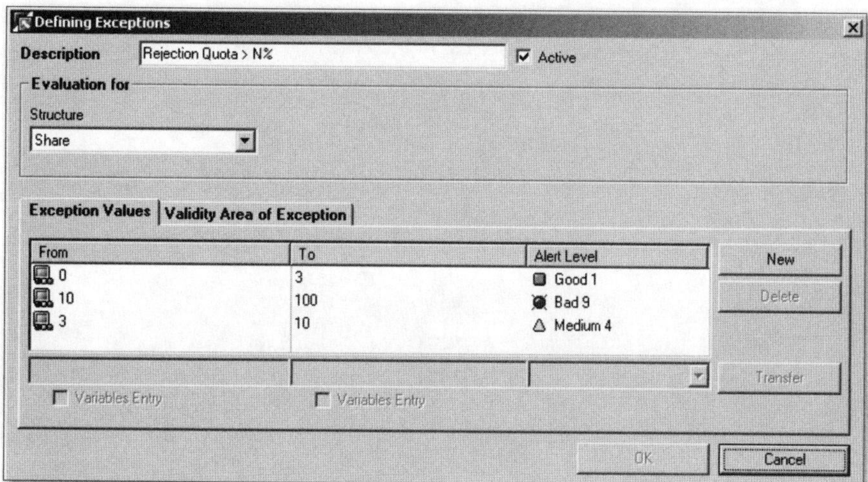


Figure 10.30 Determining Exception Values

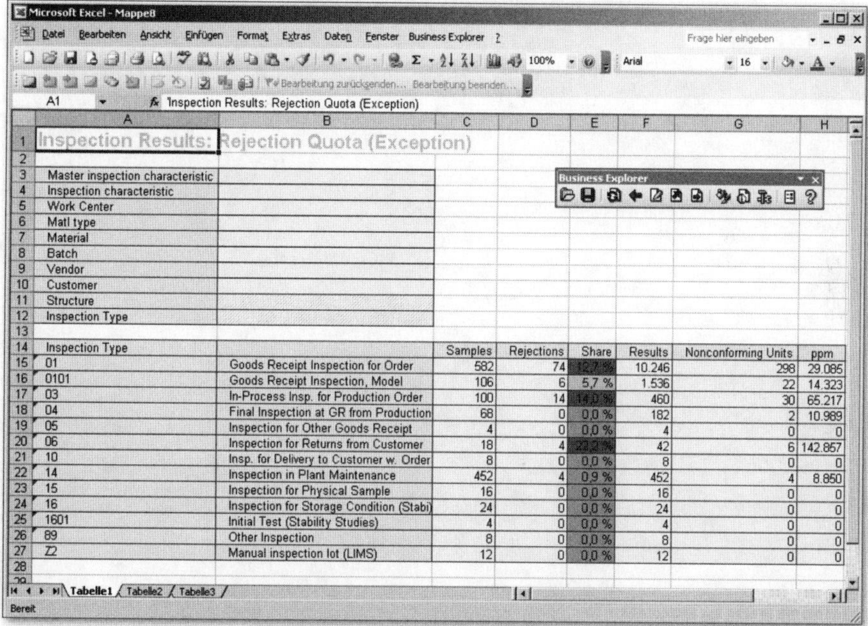


Figure 10.31 Excel Worksheet with the Rejection Quota from the Inspection Results

*The management of monitoring and test equipment is an essential element of the quality management standards, for instance, ISO 9001. This chapter outlines how you can meet the requirements of those standards using SAP test equipment management.*

# 11 Test Equipment Management

For a quality management system, it is essential that all inspections be implemented using reliable and capable test equipment and measuring devices. For this reason, test equipment management is of high significance.

## 11.1 Basic Principles

The importance of test equipment management for quality management is also reflected in the SAP ERP system. The menu structure allows you to branch directly from quality management to test equipment management (see Figure 11.1).

Building on the functions of the modules Plant Maintenance (PM) and Quality Management (QM), the SAP ERP system provides integrated test equipment management that combines the important planning and processing functions of both modules. Therefore, this combination of the planning and processing functions should not be viewed as a separate module but rather as an operating interface that combines the appropriate functions of the different modules for test equipment management and monitoring, providing them to the user in a compact form.

An integrated software system such as SAP ERP provides the core functions of the different modules, but with its broad operating distribution and wide-ranging integration, it also provides the following advantages for test equipment management:

- Cross-module information and evaluations
- Standardized use of the company's basic data
- Constant access to information via every SAP ERP workstation

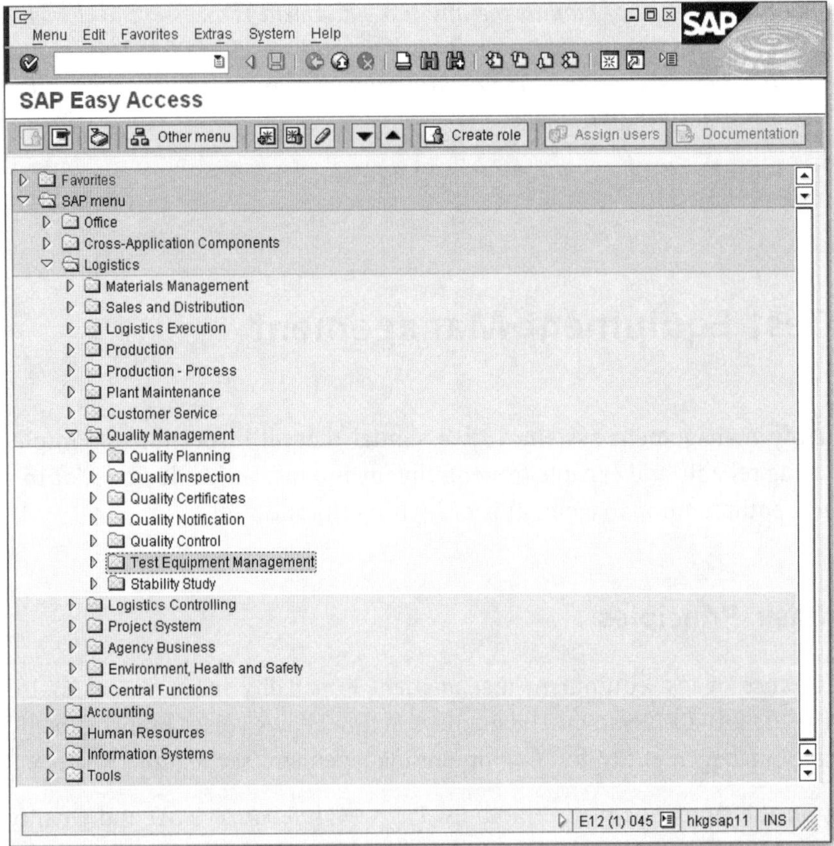


**Figure 11.1** Menu Structure with Integration of Test Equipment Management in Quality Management

The PM module, which has been integrated with the components of SAP Enterprise Asset Management (EAM) as of SAP ERP, is referred to as maintenance in the following section because this concept is frequently used in the application and still common in practice.

This chapter describes the functionality of the PM module in sufficient detail for the purposes of test equipment management; however, it cannot describe every possible variant. The descriptions restrict to typical applications that have already been implemented in routine scenarios. In the appropriate places, you are provided with notes and tips on how you can optimize the SAP ERP system to meet your specific test equipment management requirements.

## 11.2 Business Tasks

The following section describes management of test equipment and measuring devices using the PM module. Because there are different options for every implementation made using SAP ERP, you are first introduced to a business task for which a practical solution is provided.

Here, you want to meet the requirements of the "management of monitoring and test equipment" element of ISO 9001. To do this, the monitoring and test equipment (referred to as test equipment in the following) must be entered with detailed data on device type, unique ID, usage site, inspection frequency, inspection method, and acceptance criteria, as well as measures to be performed in the event of unsatisfactory results. Also, the inspection results for the test equipment must be listed, evaluated, and saved.

For the operational environment, it is assumed that an external calibration system or calibration devices are being used, but they are not connected directly to the SAP ERP system. The inspection specifications are either available in external systems or on paper in the form of inspection instructions or calibration regulations. After calibration is performed, the calibration results should also be saved externally in electronic or paper format. These assumptions apply to companies that previously used a PC system to perform their own test equipment monitoring or that commissioned an external service provider to perform the calibration.

The SAP ERP system should be used to meet the standard requirements for entry, identification, usage site, inspection frequency, next calibration date, inspection status, measures to be taken, and the listing/saving of inspection results (although only "good"/"bad").

This task does not exhaust all SAP ERP system options, but it does make it possible to achieve productive status relatively quickly, which can be expanded on later for operational requirements at any time. This task is unique because it is based on a scenario that has actually been implemented, rather than on mere assumptions.

## 11.3 SAP Module Configuration

The implementation options for test equipment management are closely connected to the productively applied or applicable modules of the company in question (see Figure 11.2). If priority is given to realizing a comprehensive test equipment management concept, then this can create increased requirements when using the required modules.

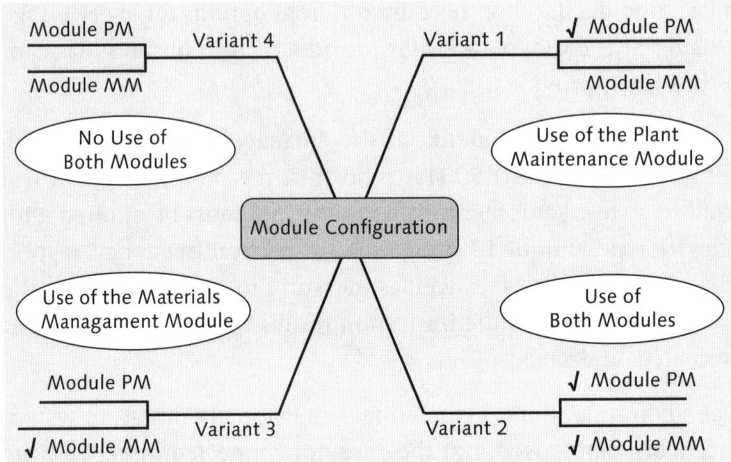


**Figure 11.2** Mind Map for Possible Module Configurations for Test Equipment Management

### 11.3.1 Variant 1: Plant Maintenance Module without Materials Management Module

In PM , you can enter test equipment as PM "pieces of equipment," hierarchically structured, and assigned to a detailed maintenance plan. This makes it possible to monitor inspection dates and to create and process maintenance plan orders (e.g., for calibration). You can control the entire inspection laboratory using the functions for capacity planning.

Pieces of equipment can be created and managed independently of material master data. Special functionalities in Materials Management (MM), such as purchase order, GR, and storage, are not used in this variant.

#### Variant 2: Plant Maintenance Module with Materials Management Module

This is the most workload-intensive but also the most performant variant. The implementation example is based on this variant. If both modules are implemented, the functions of both modules can be combined and used. Test equipment can be ordered as a material and posted in GR. Moreover, it can also be serialized and managed as a piece of equipment.

#### Variant 3: Materials Management Module without Plant Maintenance Module

This is an attractive variant that allows test equipment management with restricted functionality.

In MM, you can create test equipment as material masters and process all management of purchase requisitions, purchase orders, and GRs. Furthermore, the materials created can be integrated with the different task list types in the same way as the production resources/tools.

This variant does not include any of the PM special functions, such as calibration monitoring and their documentation.

#### Variant 4: Neither Materials Management Module nor Plant Maintenance Module

This variant enables only a restricted management of test equipment as production resources/tools or a document master record, and, ultimately, it is important only for the where-used list in QM. In this variant, calibrations are not planned, executed, or documented in the SAP ERP system.

## 11.4 Master Data

In SAP ERP, test equipment is used in different places within the QM module. For example, test equipment can be specified in task lists or inspection plans for planning or documentation purposes.

In quality planning, test equipment is managed as *production resources/tools* (PRT), which can be defined in the SAP ERP system by using different types of master records:

- PRT master record
- Document master record
- Material master record
- Equipment master record

Due to the variability of PRT, there are different starting points for representing test equipment in SAP ERP. Depending on the required functionality, the test equipment data can be represented in one or more of the types of PRT listed. Also, functions specific to the PRT used are available for the test equipment.

### Test Equipment as Production Resource/Tool

When you create test equipment as a PRT, you can store information on status and location, as well as the standard SAP ERP system management data. You can also group the test equipment (e.g., measurement equipment, inspection equipment, etc.) or classify it using the central classification system.

The master record for PRT does not contain a great deal of data, which seriously restricts the related functionality in the SAP ERP system. In most cases, when test equipment is represented as a PRT, only rough master data is entered. Other logistical functions are not supported.

For this reason, representing test equipment as a PRT is the simplest option and does not allow any additional functionality beyond providing a where-used list. Test equipment is not usually entered individually but according to its characteristics (e.g., caliper gauge 0-150 mm).

### Test Equipment as Document

The PRT master record can be used to refer to document data, or the document master records are used directly in task lists and inspection plans as PRT. The interfaces and functions in document management enable direct access to drawings and other documents.

The representation of test equipment in document records or the inclusion of document records in the other types of PRT makes it possible to use test equipment in terms of documents (e.g., drawings, descriptions, etc.).

This method is also primarily used for planning and documentation of test equipment usage. It is characterized by special document management functions.

### Test Equipment as Material

If you need general, logistical functions such as procurement, or storage or quality inspection, then it makes sense to represent test equipment in material master records. This provides all of the views of the material master record, as seen in Figure 11.3.

**Figure 11.3** Possible Views in a Material Master Record

The material merely defines the type of test equipment. This is sufficient for processing Purchasing and planning operations (task lists, inspection plans, etc.) because the individual pieces of test equipment of a given type usually have the same properties and are therefore interchangeable. For inventory management too, the individual pieces of test equipment are not relevant; rather, it is the number of pieces of test equipment that is important.

With the option for serializing materials, SAP ERP also provides the option to represent individual pieces of test equipment. In this case, the material itself corresponds to a particular configuration for test equipment, and the serial number represents the individual test equipment.

When representing the test equipment as a material, you can use a wide range of SAP ERP logistics functions such as procurement, GR inspection, and inventory management for the test equipment.

#### Test Equipment as PM Equipment

The greatest range of functionality is provided by representing the test equipment as equipment in PM. Equipment master records are maintained in the PM module and allow you to define individual devices and structure them hierarchically. This means that you can represent both individual test equipment and combined test equipment or more complex measuring tools.

The PM module provides comprehensive functions for managing, monitoring, maintaining, and calibrating the test equipment. When pieces of equipment are included in task lists, you can check whether all of the relevant test equipment is available when production lots are issued.

When material numbers are serialized, SAP ERP provides an elegant option for defining and linking both master records in one process. First, you enter the material number or select an existing number. Then, you generate a new serial number using the SERIALIZATION function. In the subsequent dialog box, you can then switch to the equipment view, activate the equipment master record, and add device-specific data.

You can generate reports such as results history, graphical trend analyses, and usage lists.

### Summary

Due to the many alternatives for representing test equipment in the SAP ERP system, you should first check very carefully which requirements test equipment management should satisfy. This is the only way that can you can weigh the different variants properly and find the optimum solution for the corresponding area.

Table 11.1 gives you a brief overview of the advantages and disadvantages of the previously described alternatives.

| Variant | Advantages | Disadvantages |
|---|---|---|
| Production resources/ tools | ▸ Simple data entry. | ▸ Generally low functionality.<br>▸ Very little system support for management of individual test equipment. |
| Documents | ▸ Document storage.<br>▸ Document management functions (display, archiving, etc.). | ▸ Not much test equipment-specific functionality. |

**Table 11.1** Advantages and Disadvantages of Alternatives for Managing Production Resource/ Tools

| | | |
|---|---|---|
| **Enter the material** | ▸ High functionality in the areas of logistics, procurement, quality management.<br>▸ Representation of individual test equipment via serialization. | ▸ Requires careful master data creation and maintenance. |
| **Equipment** | ▸ Wide-ranging functionality that is well suited to test equipment. | ▸ The work-intensive data model is complex to use.<br>▸ PM structures must be defined in the system (plant, workstation, etc.).<br>▸ PM orders and inspection processes must be processed. |

**Table 11.1** Advantages and Disadvantages of Alternatives for Managing Production Resource/Tools (Cont.)

## 11.5 Scenario for Test Equipment Management

In the following scenario, test equipment management has been successfully implemented in a company already since R/3 Release 4.0B, which can also be modeled with SAP ERP. You should keep in mind that the individual steps described have been tailored for this scenario because it is not possible for us to examine all of the possible variants and settings that can be used. Some points have been set up in Customizing for this scenario so that you will not always find completely identical screen views in your system.

The scenario describes the following processes:

- Creating the test equipment master data
- Procuring the test equipment
- Planning test equipment monitoring
- Performing test equipment monitoring

The *material and equipment combination* variant is used in this scenario. After creating the material master, you can use serialization to create several pieces of test equipment with different individual serial numbers under one material number. These are then added to the equipment view. The following example demonstrates the advantages of this variant.

A company has 30 dial gauges of type 0-10 mm. This type of dial gauge should have 1 standard material number but 30 different serial numbers. This enables you to enter dial gauge data in the material master, while entering individual data such as the location of a particular dial gauge in the serial number. This procedure must also be used when referring to test equipment in an inspection plan (see Chapter 6, Quality and Inspection Planning) because you do not want to refer to an individual test gauge for "Mr. Smith" but to a dial gauge of type 0-10 mm.

## 11.6 Editing the Material Master

Editing the material master forms the basis for test equipment management. Editing the material master includes creating new material master data, as well as changing existing material master data. Figure 11.4 shows these editing options as an event-driven process change (EPC; see also Section 2.3, Event-Driven Process Chain [EPC]).

First, you create the material master for the measuring equipment. You then choose the menu path LOGISTICS • QUALITY MANAGEMENT • TEST EQUIPMENT MANAGEMENT and then TEST EQUIPMENT • MATERIAL • CREATE.

Provided that the system is configured for external number assignment (which is recommended if you want to continue using an existing test equipment numbering system), you can enter the MATERIAL (test equipment number) and the MATERIAL TYPE (in this case, PRT). After pressing `Enter`, the system displays the view selection (see Figure 11.5).

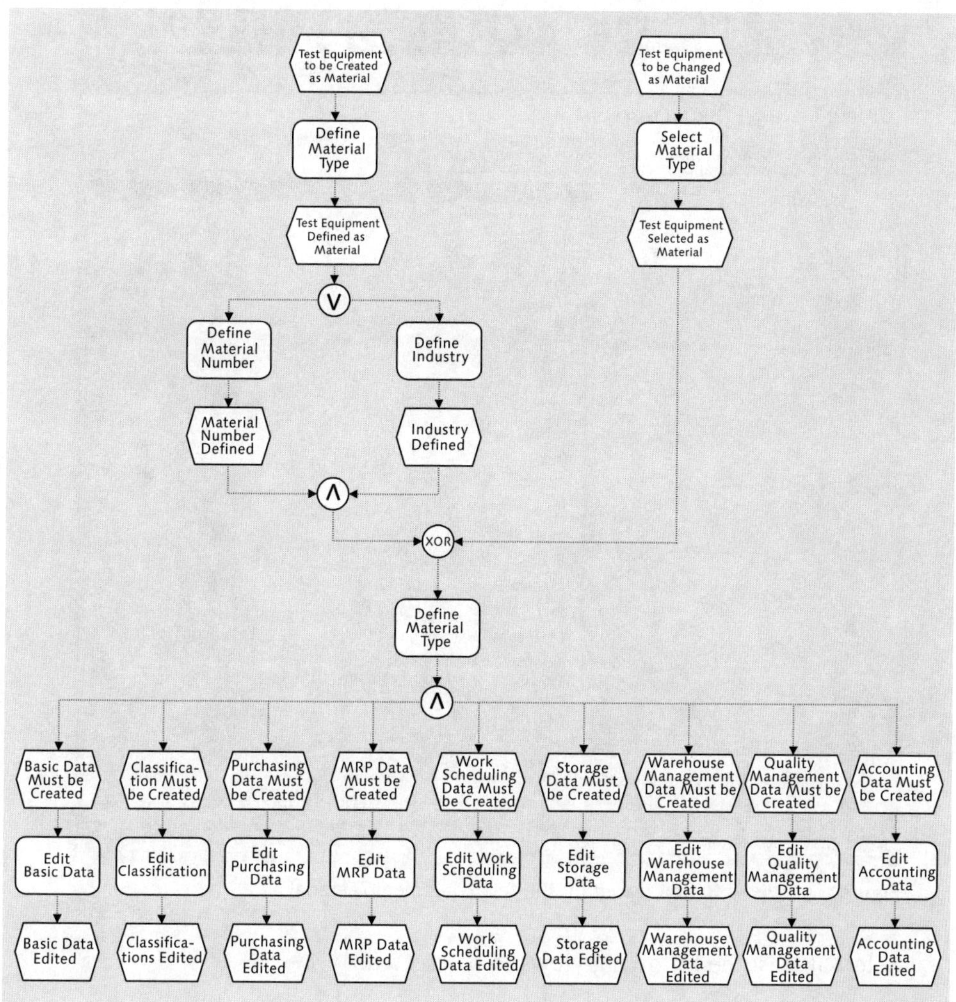


**Figure 11.4** EPC for Editing the Material Master in SAP Material Management

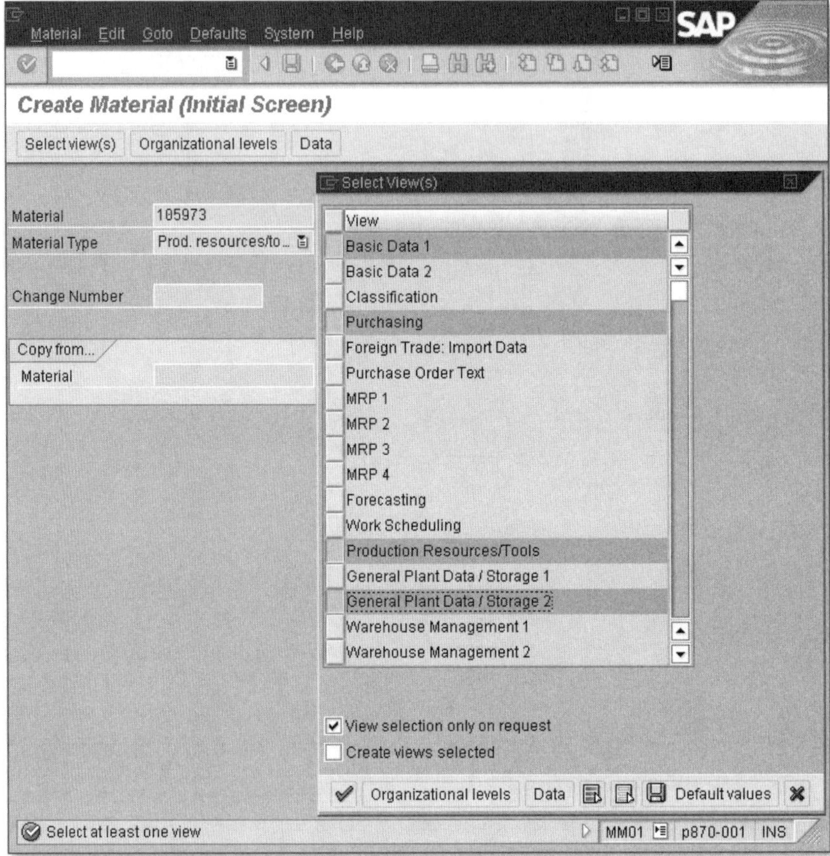


**Figure 11.5** Views to be Created for the Test Equipment Material

Select at least the following views to be created:

- Basic Data 1
- Purchasing
- Production Resources/Tools
- General Plant Data/Storage 2

If you want to use the option for test equipment procurement and inventory management, you must include additional views.

In the BASIC DATA view, you maintain the NAME (here "Dial gauge 010 mm"), the BASE UNIT OF MEASURE (usually "unit"), and the MATERIAL GROUP (see Figure 11.6).

**Tip**

For the material group, we recommend that you group test equipment with mechanical and electronic test equipment, for example, and then include even more equipment (into plug gauges, caliper gauges, dial gauges, etc., or into multimeter, three-digit oscilloscopes, etc.). This division into material groups simplifies searching for materials later on.

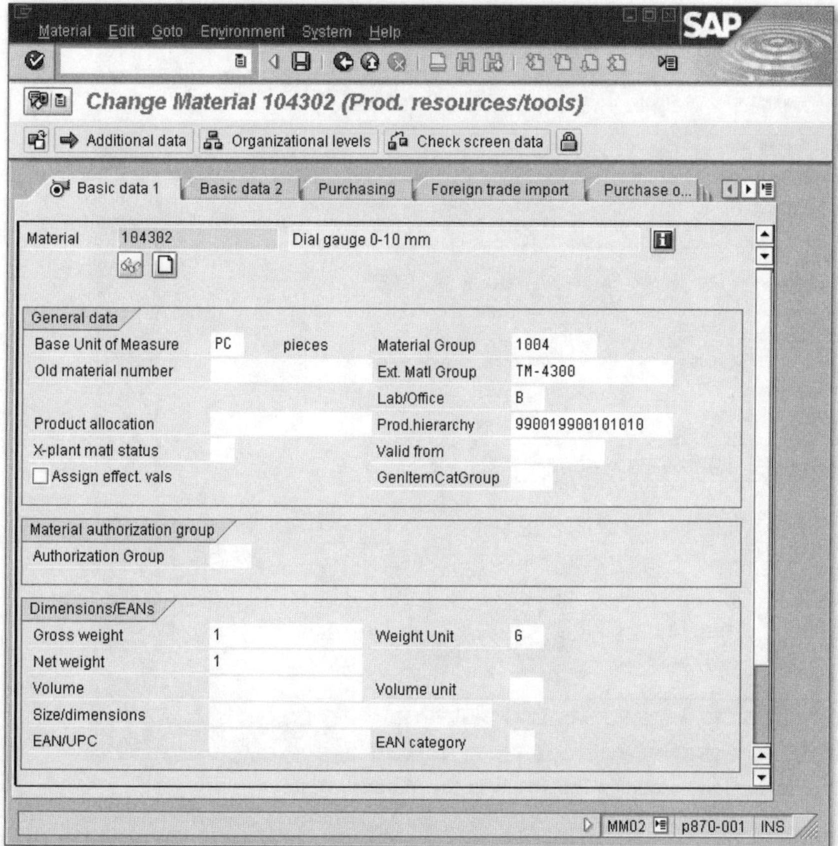


**Figure 11.6** Basic Data View in the Material Master

Enter the appropriate PURCHASING GROUP in the PURCHASING view. By maintaining the Purchasing view, you enable the purchasing application to copy master data automatically when you purchase more test equipment of this type.

Finally, the PRODUCTION RESOURCES/TOOLS view is displayed (see Figure 11.7). This is where you enter the PLANNED USAGE (009 = all task list types) because you want to include the test equipment in your inspection plans and task lists. Choose CONTROL KEY: PRINT (2).

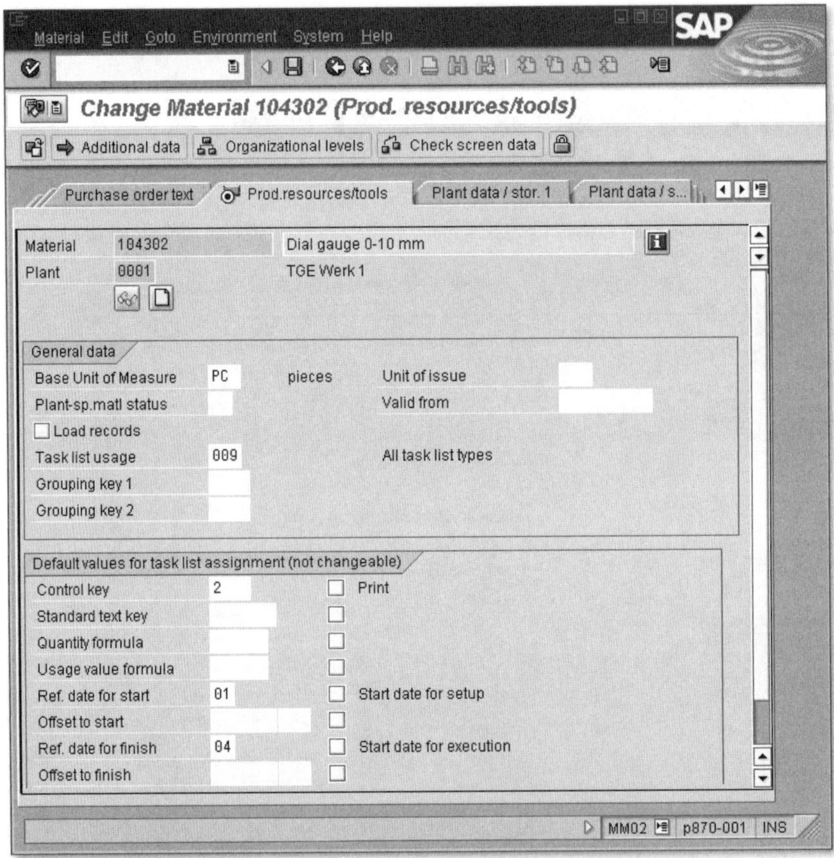


Figure 11.7 Production Resources/Tools View in the Material Master

Then, in the STORAGE 2 view, you must enter the SERIAL NUMBER PROFILE (here ZPMV) to enable subsequent serialization. In Customizing, you can use the profile to define the different business operations, whether serial numbers or a stock check is required, or whether an equipment master record needs to be created. This makes it possible to use serial number assignment differently in the various SAP ERP components (e.g., for finished products and test equipment). The serial number profile used here was especially set for test equipment monitoring.

Now that you have created these views, the setup for the material master for test equipment is completed.

## 11.7 Procuring Test Equipment

When material master data has been maintained for the test equipment, this test equipment material can be procured. Figure 11.8 displays the basic procurement flow.

The business process shown in this figure assumes that the test equipment is procured as warehouse material. Procurement processes usually start with a purchase requisition, which can be triggered by the department requesting the test equipment. The purchase requisition is a two-part process that consists of editing and releasing the purchase requisition.

The purchase requisition is then forwarded to purchasing. This is where the purchase order is processed (vendor selection, price negotiation, etc.), released, and finally transferred to the vendor. After the delivery deadline, the ordered goods are delivered to the company, and GR is processed with reference to the generated purchase order. After posting to GR, three different subprocesses are triggered:

- **Subcriterion**
  - Inspection-lot opening
  - Inspection-lot processing
  - Inspection-lot completion
- **Warehouse management**
  - Placement in storage
- **Invoice processing**
  - Invoice processing with reference to GR

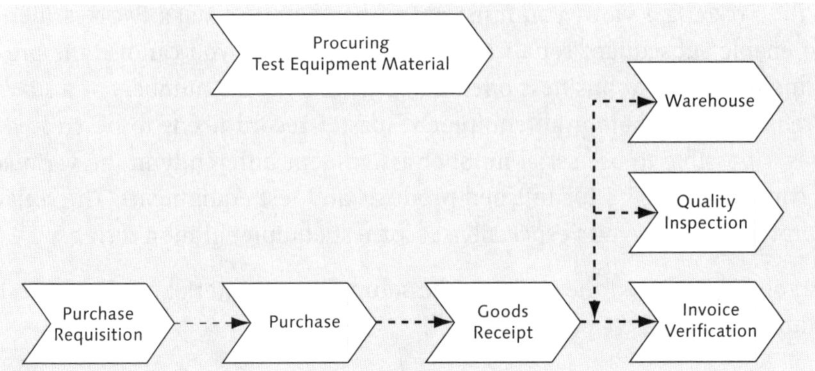


**Figure 11.8** Procurement Process for Test Equipment

When the test equipment has been procured, serialization between the existing or new serial numbers creates a fixed reference between the test equipment and the management system.

## 11.8 Serializing the Material

You can use the path LOGISTICS • QUALITY MANAGEMENT • TEST EQUIPMENT MANAGEMENT and TEST EQUIPMENT • MATERIAL • CREATE to create the test equipment as a material, but you cannot serialize it here. You get to serialization either via LOGISTICS • QUALITY MANAGEMENT • QUALITY PLANNING • LOGISTICS MASTER DATA and then SERIAL NUMBERS • CREATE, or via the MATERIALS MANAGEMENT menu (i.e., LOGISTICS • MATERIALS MANAGEMENT • MATERIAL MASTER). In the ENVIRONMENT menu, you then follow the submenu ENVIRONMENT • SERIAL NUMBERS • CREATE, CHANGE OR DISPLAY.

Enter the material number (in this example, 104302) in the MATERIAL field. If you want to assign a specific SERIAL NUMBER to the material because the test equipment already has a serial number, enter it in the appropriate field. If you leave this field empty, the system assigns the next highest number automatically. Finally, you must also make an entry in the TYPE field (in this case, "P" = PRT).

After pressing [Enter], the system displays the detail view for the serial number, as displayed in Figure 11.9. Later, GR posting will provide the PLANT and STORAGE LOCATION fields with data.

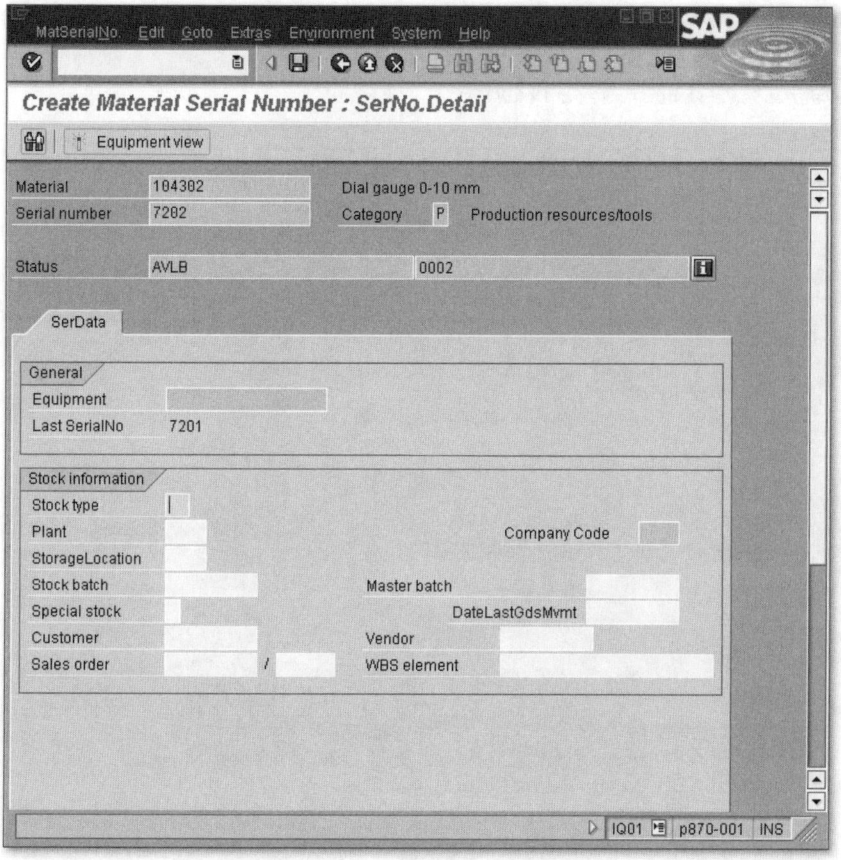

Figure 11.9 Serial Data When Creating a Material

## 11.9 Creating a Material as Equipment

Click on the EQUIPMENT VIEW button to assign the test equipment with material and serial numbers for a fixed equipment number. Note that the other tabs, GENERAL, LOCATION, ORGANIZATION, STRUCTURE, and SERDATA, are displayed on the screen when you activate this view. This starts the enhancement of the material master record with the equipment master record.

You finish creating the test equipment by filling out the required fields on the tabs (see Figure 11.10). You fill the OBJECT TYPE field (equipment type) on the GENERAL tab.

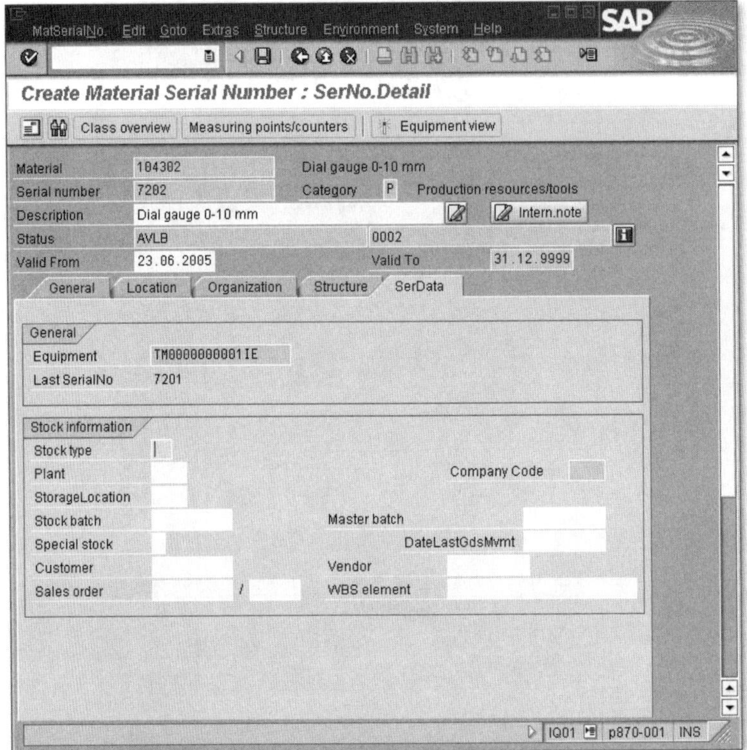


**Figure 11.10** Tabs in the Equipment Master Record

**Tip**

For greater clarity, the same structure for the equipment type was selected as for the material group when creating the material. Like the material group, this field is primarily intended to facilitate searching and grouping. Therefore, it's advisable to define the same structures for this scenario.

You then click on the Class Overview button in the application toolbar. To access the Values for Class screen, select the Class Type (002 = Equipment class), the Class Description TEM (Test Equipment Management), and the Edit • Evaluation menu. The fields for this screen were created using the class system so that input data will meet the business requirements.

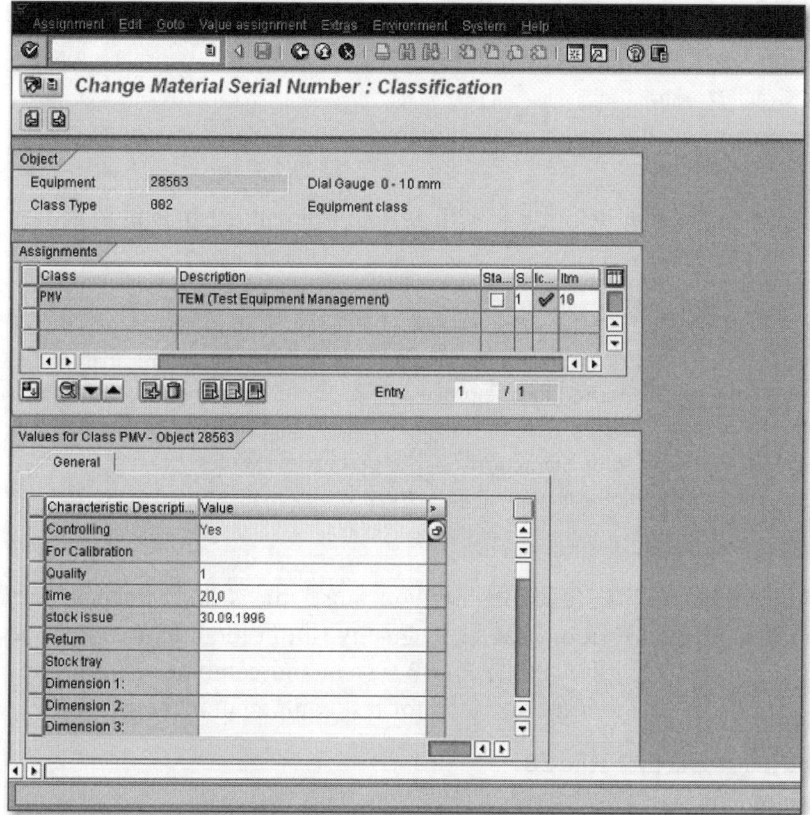


**Figure 11.11** Classification Screen with Input Fields for Characteristics

The CLASSIFICATION screen (see Figure 11.11) provides the following input fields, which you can add to or remove, according to your requirements:

- REQUIRES MONITORING
  Where you enter whether the test equipment also needs to be monitored regularly after entry.
- GRADE
  Input option for the grade (e.g., for measuring instruments).
- TIME REQUIRED
  For calibration.
- ISSUE DATE
  From test equipment warehouse to user.

- RETURN DATE
  From user to test equipment warehouse.
- STORAGE SHELF NUMBER
  Classification aid for the test equipment warehouse.
- VALUE FIELDS
  Classification and search help for specific test equipment, such as plug gauges or minor caliper gauges.

**Tip**

Using the class system, you can supplement master data, such as equipment, material, and so on, with any fields required for the process flow. These fields are then available in numerous standard evaluations.

Note that during the creation of characteristics, the permissible values, the input format, and the type of field, for example, mandatory or optional entry field, are controlled.

The next application toolbar function that you must edit is the PARTNER function. As you have already seen in Chapter 9, Quality Notification, partners can be defined for specific tasks within the SAP ERP system and combined into groups (*Roles*). Two groups of partners are provided for test equipment management:

- **User internal – partner role ZB**
  A test equipment user.
- **Processor – partner role ZM**
  Persons responsible for calibrating the test equipment.

In this example, the corresponding employees are selected with their personnel numbers for both roles. The master data for the employees is drawn from the Personnel Management module (HR). For data security reasons, only the name of the employee can be accessed here, and this must be done only by the restricted group of users with access to test equipment management functions.

**Tip**

Through Customizing of partners, you can also set other underlying master data for partner roles, for instance, customer, vendor, work center, user master record, and so on.

The LOCATION tab contains the LOCATION DATA group. This is where you fill out the fields, MAINTPLANT (here, 0001) and WORK CENTER (here, 5629983). WORK CENTER is the same field as the one you already know from inspection plans and task lists. In practice, managing this field makes it easier to find a piece of test equipment when it is required for an inspection.

You get to the STATUS submenu by clicking on the I button. The system displays the permitted USER STATUS values on the right-hand side of the selection menu (see Figure 11.12). The status was tailored to the requirements of the example in Customizing.

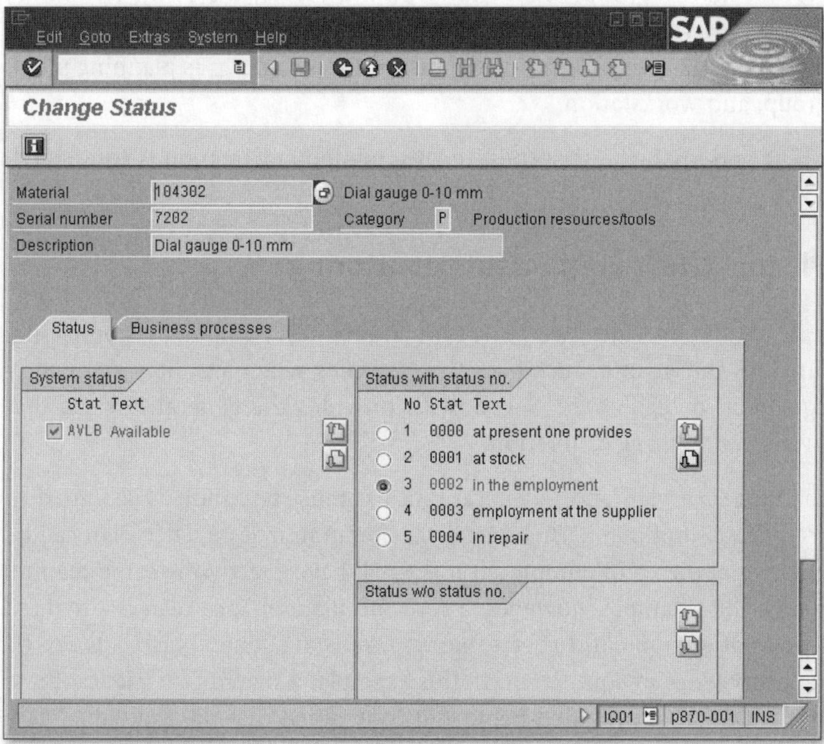


Figure 11.12 User Status

Some possible status values are listed here:

- 0001 – the test equipment is in storage
- 0002 – the test equipment is being used
- 0004 – in repair

You must then fill out the ORGANIZATION tab. In the ACCOUNT ASSIGNMENT group, enter the cost center calculated for internal activity allocation for the test equipment. With the appropriate Customizing settings, the time taken to calibrate the test equipment can be billed to this cost center via PM Order Management.

In the RESPONSIBILITIES group, enter the PLANNING PLANT, the PLANNER GROUP, and the responsible workstation. These entries correspond to the entries that you already know from Chapter 6, Quality and Inspection Planning, as planning plant, planner group, and workstation.

After finishing and saving your entries, the test equipment creation is completed.

## 11.10 Planning Test Equipment Monitoring

The SAP ERP system provides two tools for planning test equipment monitoring. First, it provides the maintenance plan that specifies when and how frequently something should be calibrated. Secondly, it provides the general task list that specifies what to do during calibration.

Then, a maintenance plan and a general task list must be uniquely assigned to every piece of test equipment. Theoretically, a common maintenance plan can be assigned to several pieces of equipment if they all have exactly the same maintenance date. In this example, however, a separate maintenance plan is provided for every piece of equipment. In the same way, separate general task lists can be assigned to every piece of equipment. In this example, a shared task list "calibrate according to task list" is provided because it is assumed that the individual calibration instructions are available in printed format. For other scenarios, detailed individual general task lists can be created. Figure 11.13 displays the relationship between equipment, maintenance plan, and general task list.

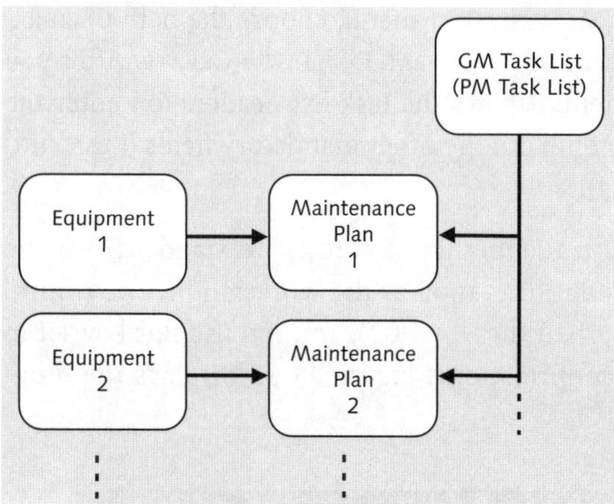


**Figure 11.13** Planning Test Equipment Monitoring

### 11.10.1 General Task List

You must first create a general task list. This is a type of routing for the maintenance and calibration tasks to be performed. In some places in the SAP ERP system, therefore, the term *task list* or *PM task list* is used.

This means that the corresponding sections from Chapter 6 apply to the general task list. Therefore, in this section, we only provide you with a short description of the required entries. You can create operations for the individual work steps, assign workstations and PRT to the operations, schedule set-up times and work times, and enter corresponding costs.

In this example, it is assumed that one general task list suffices for all of the equipment because the detailed calibration instructions are kept outside the SAP ERP system. The advantage here is that you use only one task list (general task list) that can be assigned to all maintenance plans from the very beginning. At a later point in time, the printed calibration instructions can be entered and assigned gradually as individual task lists in the SAP ERP system. Moreover, it is assumed that there is only one central calibration point with one workstation. Costs are entered at a flat rate via cost center accounting and are not dependent on calibration duration. This configuration provides you with a relatively easy-to-implement scenario, which can still be enhanced and adapted to changing requirements at any time after a productive start.

Starting from the TEST EQUIPMENT MANAGEMENT menu, choose the path CALIBRATION PLANNING • MAINTENANCE TASK LIST • GENERAL TASK LIST • CREATE. After you enter task list group PMV, the system displays the task list header. You enter the task list name "Calibration Task," and fill out the other mandatory fields (PLANNING PLANT and STATUS; see Figure 11.14).

Then, you create the operation. Use "Calibration according to standard" for the operation name, and enter the calibration station as the workstation. The control key set in Customizing is also important (here, PM01). You can use this key set to control special functions such as confirmations. Figure 11.15 displays the input screen filled out.

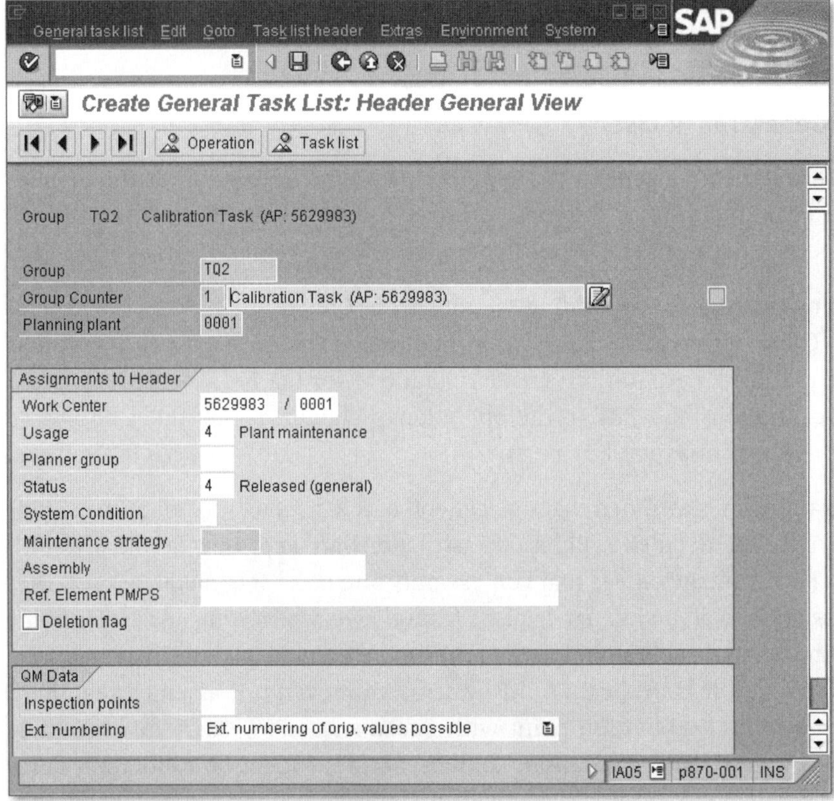


**Figure 11.14** Example of a General Task List

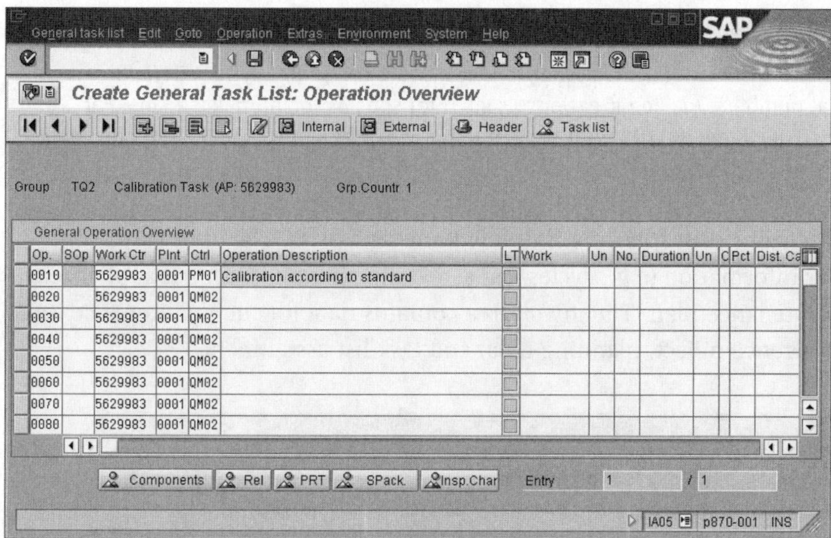


**Figure 11.15** Operation for a General Task List

After you have saved your general task list, you can create the maintenance plans for the individual pieces of test equipment.

### 11.10.2 Maintenance Plan

The maintenance plan is used for planning deadlines and cycles for calibration. Here, you're using only time-dependent planning. However, the system also supports activity-specific planning (e.g., calibration after 500 uses), or a combination of both (e.g., check after 1 year or 500 uses). In addition, order specifications or maintenance strategies can be assigned. The type of activity is defined using a reference in the maintenance plan to the corresponding task list.

A prerequisite for creating the maintenance plan is that you have created the test equipment that you want to calibrate with this plan, as well as the corresponding general task list.

In the TEST EQUIPMENT MANAGEMENT menu, you select the path CALIBRATION PLANNING • MAINTENANCE PLANNING • MAINTENANCE PLAN • CREATE SINGLE CYCLE PLAN. Only the MAINTENANCE PLAN CATEGORY (here, maintenance order) needs to be entered in the initial screen. You start with the maintenance plan name.

**Tip**

When choosing names for maintenance plans, use a combination of material numbers and serial numbers, making it easier to search for specific maintenance plans. For example, dial gauge 104101 with serial number 7261 would receive maintenance plan name "10410107261 calibration plan" (see Figure 11.16).

The maintenance plan structure is divided into two parts. The upper area contains the header information (e.g., cycles and scheduling parameters) that applies to the entire maintenance plan. The lower area contains data for the maintenance item, such as reference object, planning data, and task list assignment.

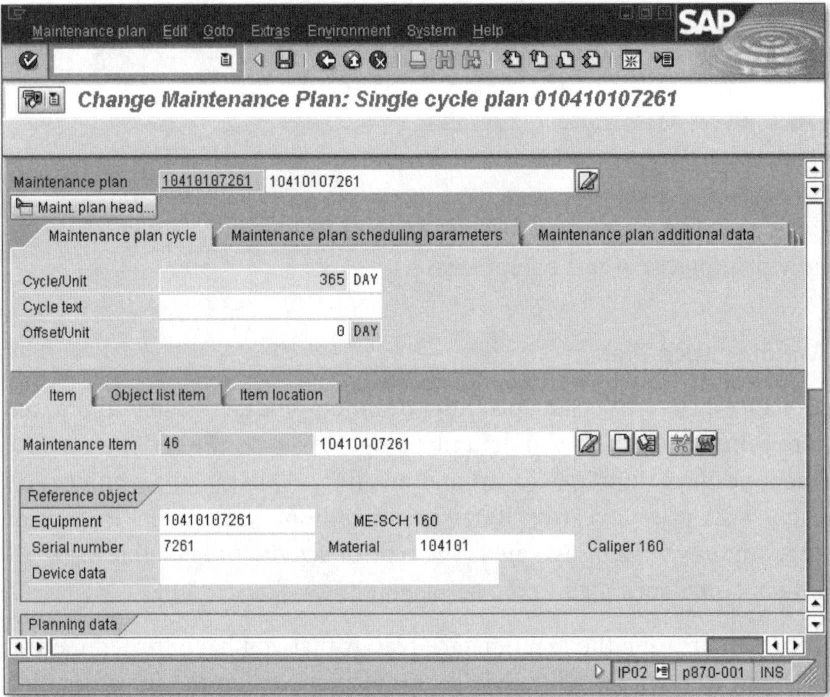


**Figure 11.16** Example of a Maintenance Plan

In the MAINTENANCE PLAN CYCLE tab, you enter the cycle (frequency) of the calibration interval. This value defines after how much time the next calibration should be performed. Typical values are three months, six months, or one year. In Figure 11.16, 365 days are entered.

You then enter the name in the ITEM tab (see Figure 11.17).

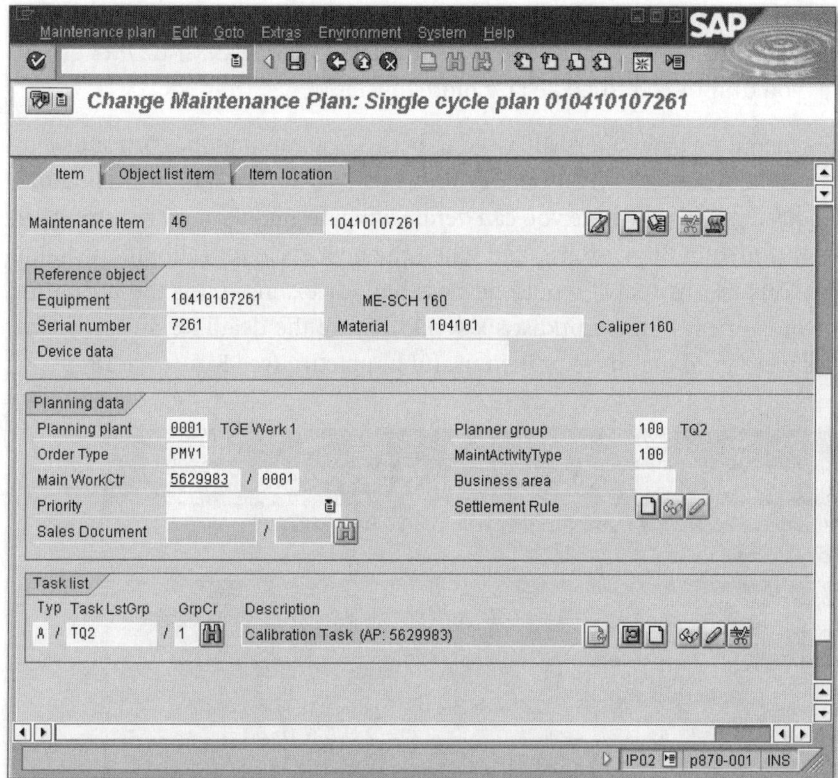


**Figure 11.17** Item Data for a Maintenance Plan

> **Tip**
>
> The item name is used in the order text when creating calibration orders. Choose a formulation that provides as much relevant information as possible because PM may create a large number of PM orders. This makes searching and monitoring the worklist much easier.

In the REFERENCE OBJECT group, enter the serial and material numbers for your test equipment in the respective fields. Then, you fill out the TASK LIST group. This is where you create the link between this maintenance plan and your general task list. If you know the task list type, the plan group number, and the plan group counter for your general task list, then you can enter them directly in the respective fields. Otherwise, you can also search for the general task list using the binoculars icon in the application toolbar and copy the data. In this case, take a look at task list type A (task list). You have already encountered task list type P (inspection plans) and N (normal task list) in Chapter 6.

If you entered the data correctly in the equipment and in the Customizing settings, the system will automatically copy the available data to the PLANNING DATA group. Therefore, you don't need to make any more entries.

Lastly, the scheduling parameters still need to be set. You can find the corresponding submenu via the MAINTENANCE PLAN SCHEDULING PARAMETERS tab in the maintenance plan header. This is where you can define when test equipment requiring calibration is included in the worklist, and when the next cycle for calibration should start again. This means that it would be possible, for example, for the upcoming calibrations to appear in the worklist six weeks before the deadline. In this example, entries were used that have proven useful in practice (see Figure 11.18).

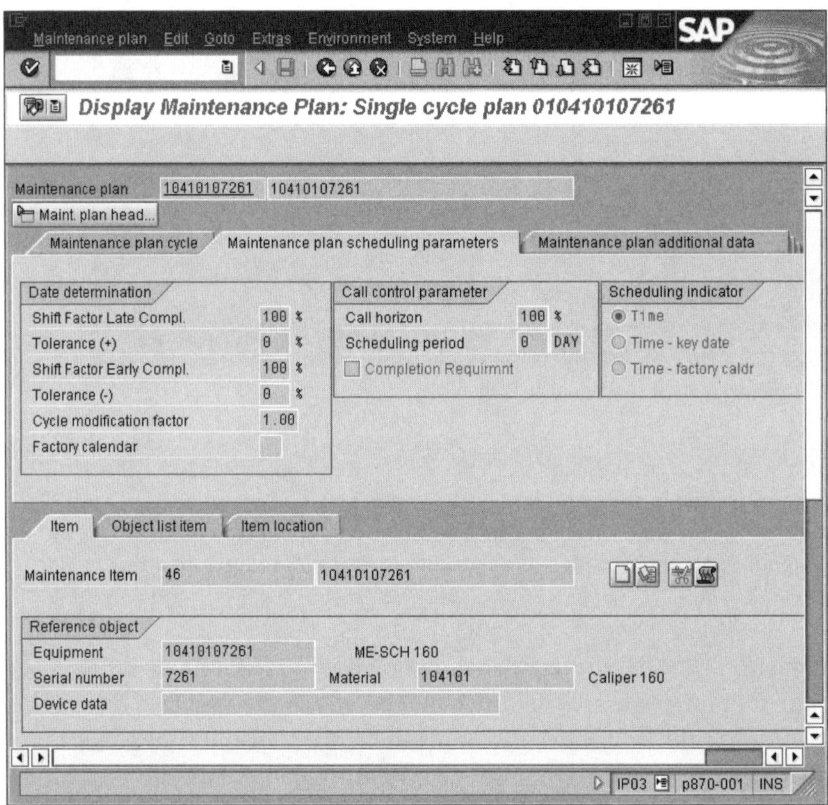


Figure 11.18 Scheduling Parameters

When you have confirmed your entries by pressing [Enter] and clicking SAVE, the maintenance plan is complete.

### 11.10.3 Scheduling

To start automatic monitoring of calibration deadlines, scheduling must begin after a piece of test equipment and its maintenance plan have been created. This is done via the menu CALIBRATION PLANNING • MAINTENANCE PLANNING • MAINTENANCE PLAN • SCHEDULING.

For scheduling, you must enter the internal maintenance plan number. Because you probably don't know this number, you must open the selection window to search for it. This is where you reap the benefits of using the combined material/serial number for the material plan number. Enter this number in the MAINTENANCE PLAN TEXT field of the search window, and click on EXECUTE. The system will then display the maintenance plan that you are looking for.

After you have clicked on the START button, you can enter the start date for the cycle and activate it by pressing SAVE.

### 11.10.4 Scheduling Monitoring

To receive calibration orders, you must manually trigger scheduling monitoring of the system in the TEST EQUIPMENT MANAGEMENT screen via menu CALIBRATION PLANNING • MAINTENANCE PLANNING • MAINTENANCE PLAN • DEADLINE MONITORING (see Figure 11.19). In practice, however, it has proven beneficial to schedule a periodic batch program that can start scheduling monitoring once a week, for example, and can generate the maintenance orders for the test equipment to be calibrated.

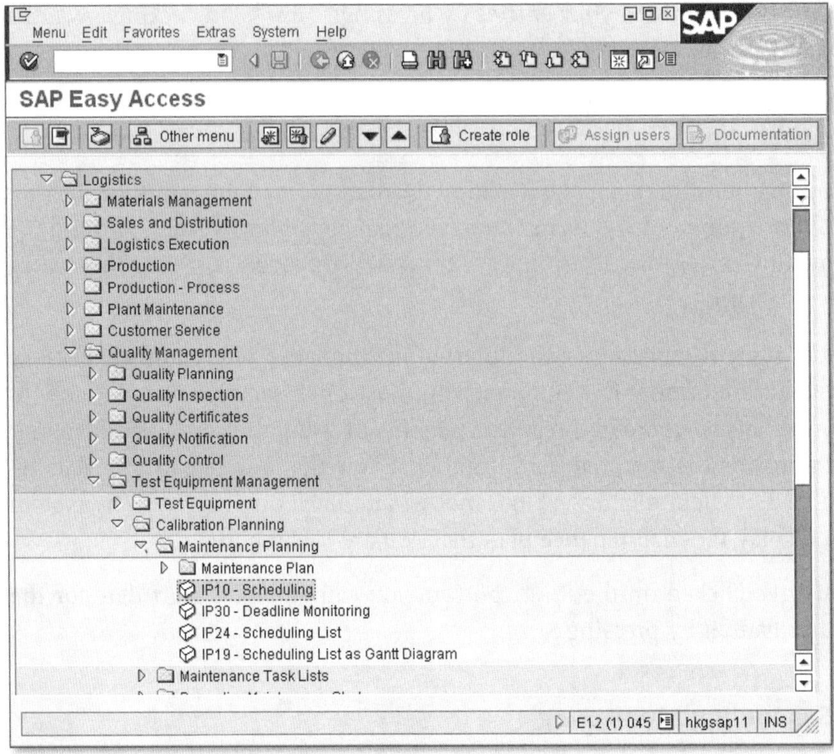


**Figure 11.19** Menu for Scheduling

## 11.11 Calibrating and Checking Test Equipment

Processing test equipment calibration consists of the following activities:

- Releasing calibration orders
- Performing calibration
- Entering inspection results
- Making inspection-based decisions
- Completing the order (inspection completed)

### 11.11.1 Calibration Orders

The order list contains all of the test equipment used for calibration. The list is filled automatically by the periodic batch program for scheduling monitoring. The list is processed manually.

You start from the Test Equipment Management screen and choose Calibration Inspection • Order • Order List • Change Data. Of course, you can also choose Display Data, but you want to start work directly.

The system displays one of the selection screens for list display (see Figure 11.20).

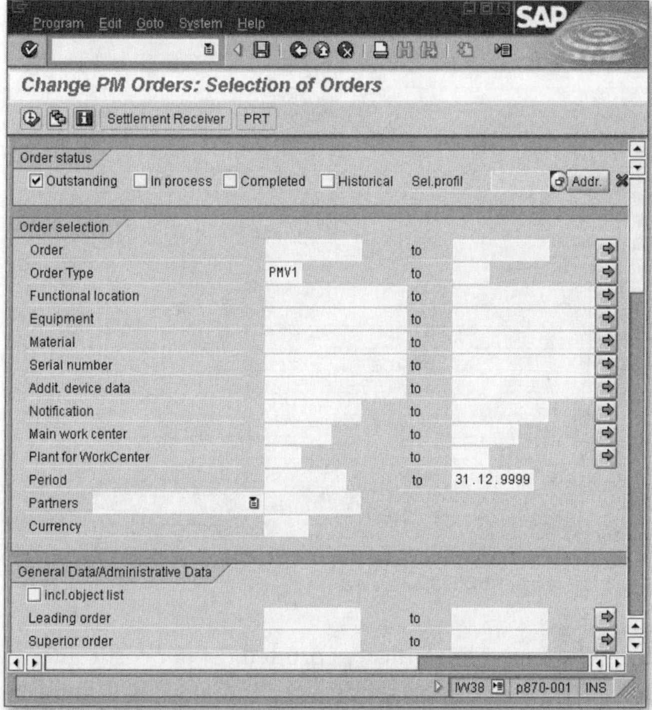


Figure 11.20 Selection for Open Calibration Requests

It is important to select the Order Status Outstanding checkbox because all new inspection orders start with the Outstanding Status. In the Order Type field, you enter "PMV1" (for "calibration orders") because you only want to select orders that are due for calibration.

Upon EXECUTION, the system provides you with a list of orders of test equipment that are due for calibration (see Figure 11.21).

To start calibrating the test equipment, you must first select the required line and release the order using the RELEASE ORDER function.

This creates an inspection lot with all of the data required for calibration inspection. At the same time, the status of the order is changed to IN PROCESS. This manual release can also be performed automatically if the correct settings are made in Customizing.

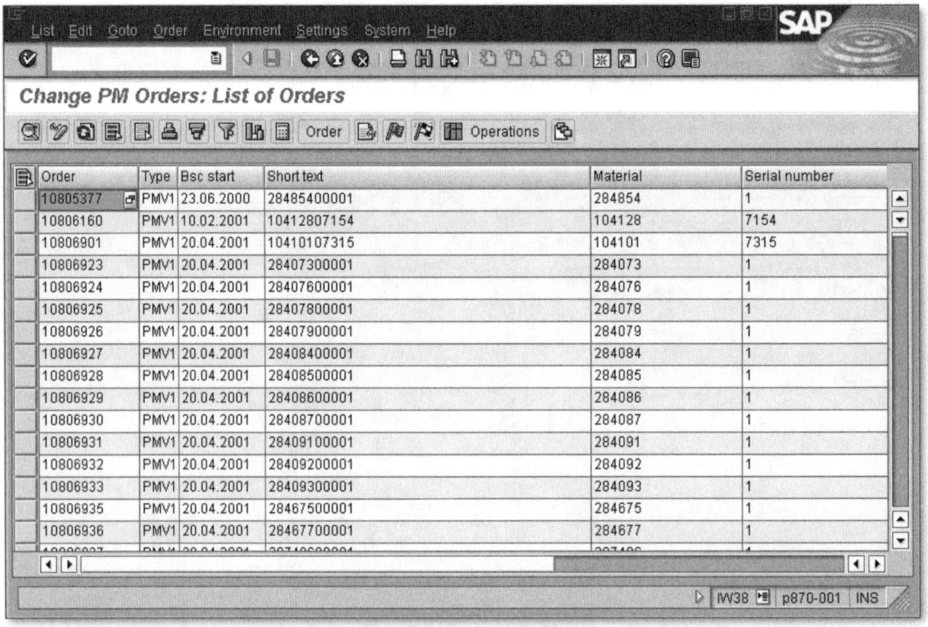

List Edit Goto Order Environment Settings System Help

**Change PM Orders: List of Orders**

| Order | Type | Bsc start | Short text | Material | Serial number |
|---|---|---|---|---|---|
| 10805377 | PMV1 | 23.06.2000 | 28485400001 | 284854 | 1 |
| 10806160 | PMV1 | 10.02.2001 | 10412807154 | 104128 | 7154 |
| 10806901 | PMV1 | 20.04.2001 | 10410107315 | 104101 | 7315 |
| 10806923 | PMV1 | 20.04.2001 | 28407300001 | 284073 | 1 |
| 10806924 | PMV1 | 20.04.2001 | 28407600001 | 284076 | 1 |
| 10806925 | PMV1 | 20.04.2001 | 28407800001 | 284078 | 1 |
| 10806926 | PMV1 | 20.04.2001 | 28407900001 | 284079 | 1 |
| 10806927 | PMV1 | 20.04.2001 | 28408400001 | 284084 | 1 |
| 10806928 | PMV1 | 20.04.2001 | 28408500001 | 284085 | 1 |
| 10806929 | PMV1 | 20.04.2001 | 28408600001 | 284086 | 1 |
| 10806930 | PMV1 | 20.04.2001 | 28408700001 | 284087 | 1 |
| 10806931 | PMV1 | 20.04.2001 | 28409100001 | 284091 | 1 |
| 10806932 | PMV1 | 20.04.2001 | 28409200001 | 284092 | 1 |
| 10806933 | PMV1 | 20.04.2001 | 28409300001 | 284093 | 1 |
| 10806935 | PMV1 | 20.04.2001 | 28467500001 | 284675 | 1 |
| 10806936 | PMV1 | 20.04.2001 | 28467700001 | 284677 | 1 |

IW38 p870-001 INS

**Figure 11.21** List of Orders of Test Equipment to be Calibrated

Despite the goal of achieving the "paperless office," a printed list per cost center is the best medium for this task. This list can be sent via the in-house mail, informing the recipient of which test equipment needs to be calibrated. In this scenario, an ABAP/4 program has been created to print all test equipment to be calibrated by each cost center with number and name. This program can also be run weekly as a batch program or called via the menu path SYSTEM • SERVICES • REPORTING. It will then print a monitoring list (in Figure 11.22, users have been grayed out in the list).

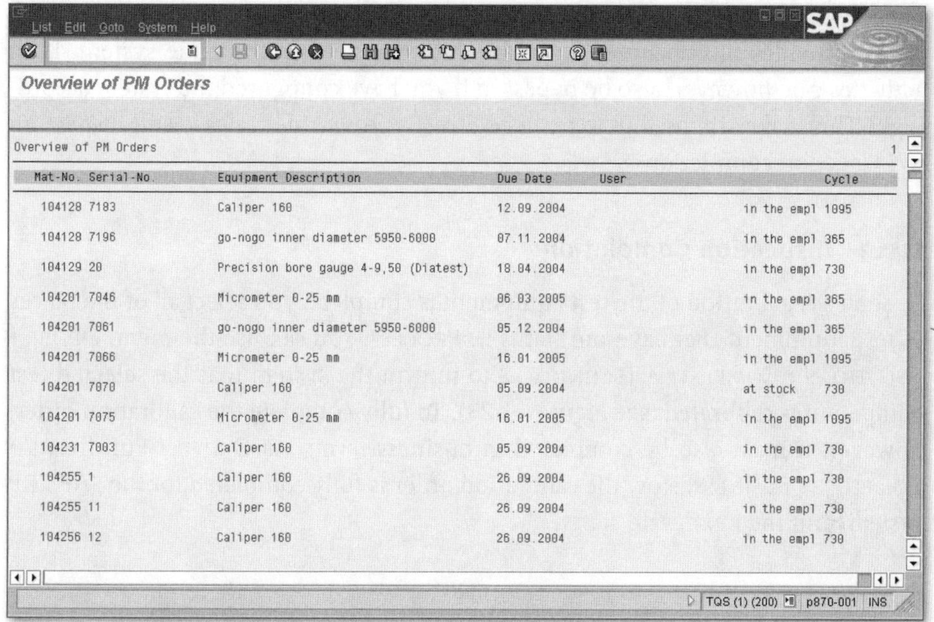

List Edit Goto System Help

Overview of PM Orders

Overview of PM Orders

| Mat-No. | Serial-No. | Equipment Description | Due Date | User | | Cycle |
|---|---|---|---|---|---|---|
| 104128 | 7183 | Caliper 160 | 12.09.2004 | | in the empl | 1095 |
| 104128 | 7196 | go-nogo inner diameter 5950-6000 | 07.11.2004 | | in the empl | 365 |
| 104129 | 20 | Precision bore gauge 4-9,50 (Diatest) | 18.04.2004 | | in the empl | 730 |
| 104201 | 7046 | Micrometer 0-25 mm | 06.03.2005 | | in the empl | 365 |
| 104201 | 7061 | go-nogo inner diameter 5950-6000 | 05.12.2004 | | in the empl | 365 |
| 104201 | 7066 | Micrometer 0-25 mm | 16.01.2005 | | in the empl | 1095 |
| 104201 | 7070 | Caliper 160 | 05.09.2004 | | at stock | 730 |
| 104201 | 7075 | Micrometer 0-25 mm | 16.01.2005 | | in the empl | 1095 |
| 104231 | 7003 | Caliper 160 | 05.09.2004 | | in the empl | 730 |
| 104255 | 1 | Caliper 160 | 26.09.2004 | | in the empl | 730 |
| 104255 | 11 | Caliper 160 | 26.09.2004 | | in the empl | 730 |
| 104256 | 12 | Caliper 160 | 26.09.2004 | | in the empl | 730 |

TQS (1) (200) p870-001 INS

**Figure 11.22** Calibration List per Cost Center

The list of calibration orders is suitable for the calibration station in the company, but not every employee has the opportunity to constantly check the system to determine whether the test equipment that he uses is included in the list and needs to be calibrated.

### 11.11.2 Results Entry and Usage Decision

You can use the worklist for the equipment to enter results for the individual inspection lots and pieces of test equipment. In this simplified scenario, the inspection results are documented in the external system, so results entry is not necessary in SAP ERP.

In addition, the SAP ERP system allows you to define a usage decision for every inspection lot. Consequently, this involves the same procedure that is used in the GR inspection (see Chapter 7, Quality Inspection). In the usage decision, you determine whether the test equipment can be used again, or whether it needs to be serviced.

The advantage of entering results and a usage decision in the SAP ERP system is that it provides full documentation for the inspection in the same system. Both activities can, however, also be bypassed if you have configured the system accordingly. This makes it possible to proceed directly from order release and inspection to inspection completion.

### 11.11.3 Inspection Completion

As soon as calibration of the test equipment is complete, you select all of the pieces of test equipment that have the status IN PROCESS. You can use the menu ORDER • FUNCTIONS • COMPLETE • TECHNICALLY to inform the system that the selected test equipment is calibrated (see Figure 11.23). To fully complete the calibration order, however, it must also be completed in business terms via ORDER • FUNCTIONS • COMPLETE • BUSINESS. Now the calibration order is fully completed for the SAP ERP system, and the next cycle starts.

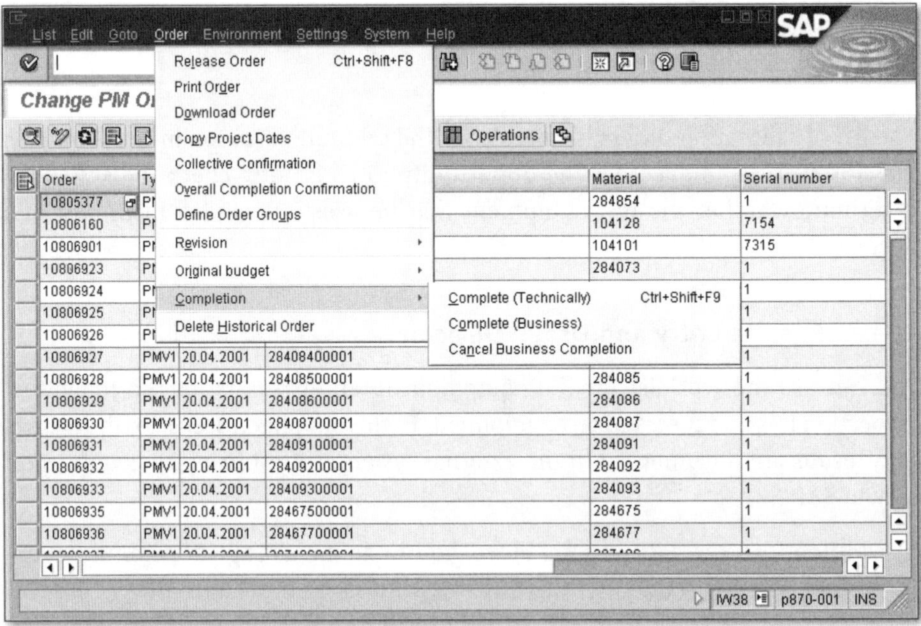


Figure 11.23 Order Completion

**Tip**

If the calibration operation takes a longer amount of time (e.g., after being sent to an external calibration station), you must remember to also set the user status accordingly in the equipment view of the serialized material (refer to Figure 11.12). The status of the PM order should not be confused with the user status of the equipment.

## 11.12 Evaluations

As in all applications, mandatory and optional reports are also available for test equipment management. There can be any number of required evaluations, for example, total number of pieces of test equipment, where-used lists for test equipment in specific departments, individuals or warehouses, calibration costs, number of calibration orders, and reported errors. With the results history, you can display changes to specific characteristics of a piece of test equipment across defined periods. You can also display these changes in a run chart. After a thorough analysis, you can use these evaluations to forecast when a plug gauge will have been so heavily used that it will no longer fall within the tolerance limit.

With the appropriate Customizing settings, you can use the PM InfoSystem or the connection to SAP NetWeaver Business Intelligence (SAP NetWeaver BI) with very flexible options. The statements in Chapter 10, Information Systems and Evaluations, apply to the PM InfoSystem.

The evaluation options for the standard configuration of the SAP ERP system can be used to cover most requirements, which are enhanced successively in new SAP releases (e.g., test equipment tracing). Consider the cost center-specific usage list. This is interesting for managers who want to identify test equipment in certain locations within their own cost centers.

If you want to identify the location of specific test equipment within your own center, you would start with the menu path LOGISTICS • MATERIALS MANAGEMENT • MATERIAL MASTER, and then ENVIRONMENT • SERIAL NUMBERS • LIST EDITING • DISPLAY. A list selection screen for serial number selection (the same as in other applications) is displayed, in which you can make a selection according to many criteria. In this example, you want to select test equipment within the cost center, so you fill out the fields, PLANT, MAINTENANCE PLANT, and COST CENTER, with the required values. While PLANT and MAINTENANCE PLANT are not mandatory fields, restricting the search scope (in this case, to plant), when dealing with large data stocks and several locations, can significantly reduce the search time. Figure 11.24 displays the completed selection screen. After performing the selection, the system displays the list of test equipment in the cost center.

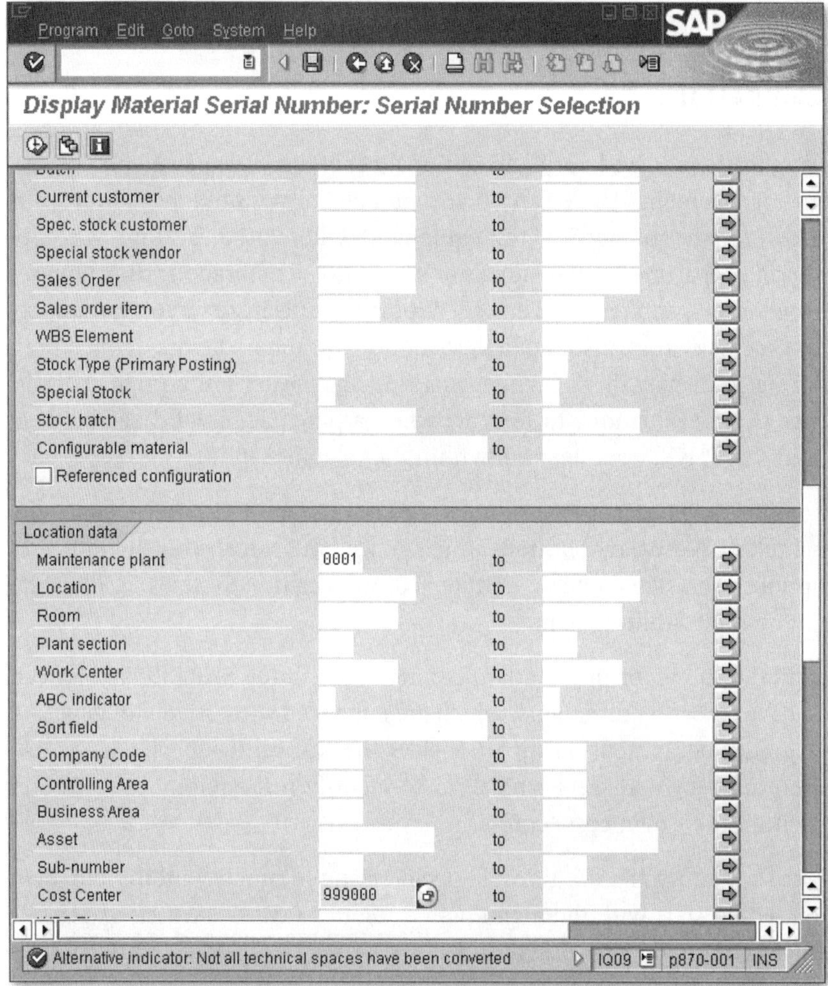


Figure 11.24 Test Equipment Search via Serial Number Selection

## 11.13 Using Subsystems

Due to system integration, the exclusive use of the SAP ERP system for test equipment monitoring has many advantages. At the very least, however, you should be running the MM module as well as the PM module to enable calibration planning. This would make any previously used external calibration system superfluous.

If you are not using the PM module, for example, or you want to continue using a tried-and-tested calibration system, you could connect to a new or existing calibration system as a subsystem.

The tasks of test equipment management and calibration (i.e., master data maintenance, calibration planning, and calibration inspection) must therefore be divided between the SAP ERP system and the subsystem, while ensuring data exchange. There are two possible variants:

- Variant 1: Material Master in SAP ERP — Calibration Planning and Inspection in the Subsystem
- Variant 2: Master Data and Calibration Planning in SAP ERP — Inspection in the Subsystem

### Variant 1: Material Master in SAP ERP — Calibration Planning and Inspection in the Subsystem

Master data is created in the SAP ERP system in MM. This is required so that test equipment can be ordered, received, and scheduled in task lists and inspection plans within SAP ERP.

The subsystem is used to serialize material numbers for individual pieces of test equipment and to manage locations and users. It is also used for inspection planning and results entry.

Data exchange is required for reconciling the material master data. For this reason, the subsystem must be linked to the SAP ERP system via a defined interface. For example, the data reconciliation can be run once a night because the inspection results remain in the subsystem. In some circumstances, evaluations can also be performed in the subsystem. Figure 11.25 displays this variant. It is also suited to representing the process with an external calibration station. In this case, the external calibration station is the external subsystem. Master data can be reconciled either on list printouts or online.

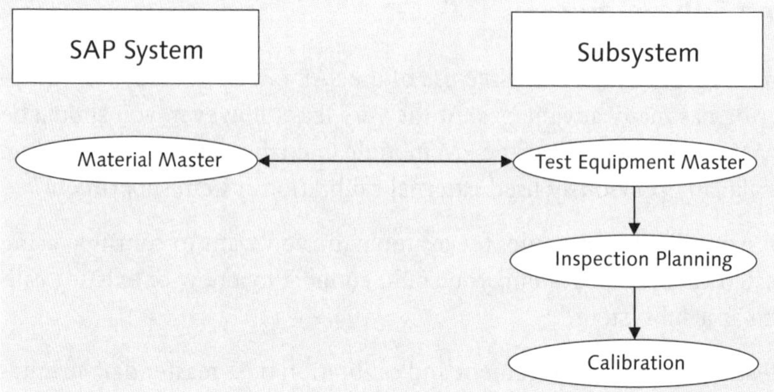


**Figure 11.25** Test Equipment Master Data Management in SAP ERP — Inspection Planning and Inspection in the Subsystem

#### Variant 2: Master Data and Calibration Planning in SAP ERP — Inspection in the Subsystem

If you are running both the MM module and the PM module, then you can use the advantages of both modules. The MM functions enable you to process procurement, whereas the PM functions deal with test equipment management and monitoring. Inspections are then performed in the subsystem.

This variant requires more intensive data exchange between SAP ERP and the subsystem because the material master data, the equipment data of the serialized material, and the pending calibration orders must be transferred to the subsystem, whereas the calibration results must be transferred from the subsystem to the SAP ERP system. Here too, it is sufficient to perform the data reconciliation once a night.

This variant (displayed in Figure 11.26) is suitable if you are using an existing calibration system with an SAP ERP system, thus enabling you to retain the accustomed work environment. The subsystem connection can be implemented at different levels. The scenario described, for example, assumes a manual entry of inspection completion, making implementation of the interface superfluous. It is risky, however, not to reconcile the master data; otherwise, the data in the SAP ERP system and the subsystem could start to diverge.

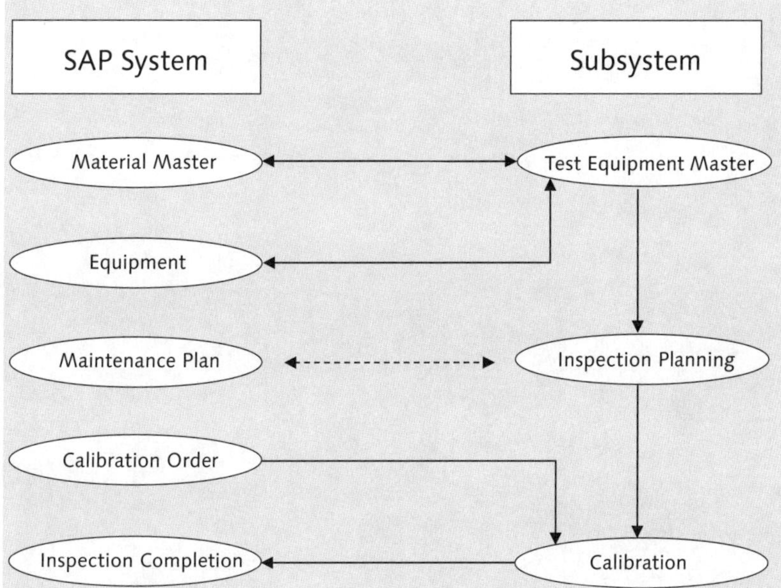


**Figure 11.26** Test Equipment Management in SAP ERP — Inspection in the Subsystem

SAP provides various options for technical connection of subsystems. The SAP ERP standard provides the following options:

- Entry of measurement data via keyboard
- Copying of inspection results via a PC interface
- Open QM-IDI interface (Inspection Data Interface)
- Mobile results entry with palm and handheld devices
- BAPI (Business Application Programming Interface)

You should choose the subsystem connection and its technical implementation in close coordination with the IT department of your company to ensure integration in the existing system landscape. For further information, refer to Section 7.10, Interfaces to External Systems and Measurement Devices.

*The implementation of internal audits and vendor audits is mandatory for the use of management systems. This chapter describes how you can plan, implement, and evaluate different audit types using SAP ERP.*

# 12 Audit Management Using SAP ERP

Most data that you require for preparing and implementing audits is already contained in your SAP ERP system. For vendors, for example, you can use master data, delivery data, and quality data from the GR inspection and the complaints processing. So, it is obvious to handle audit management in the SAP ERP system.

## 12.1 Functions of SAP Audit Management

Audit management is an Internet-enabled independent application within SAP Product Lifecycle Management (SAP PLM). All activities can be summarized according to a uniform audit management (see Figure 12.1).

- Support of all audit types
- Companywide availability of information
- Online reports
- Avoidance of unintended multiple auditing
- Efficient monitoring of outstanding actions
- Benchmarking and best practices
- Support of a continuous improvement process in companies
- Meeting legal or company-specific requirements
- Fast implementation

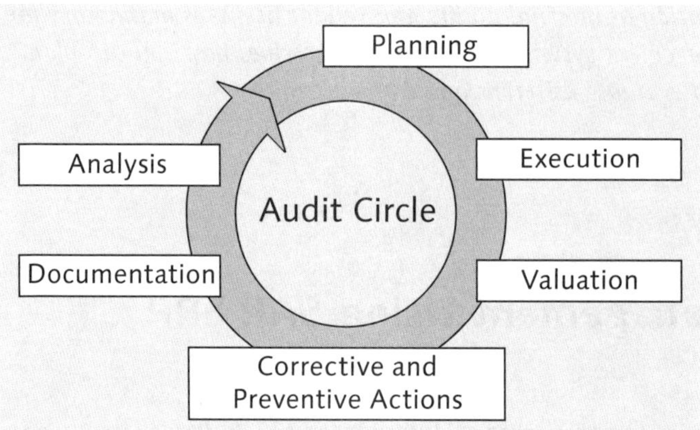


**Figure 12.1** Audit Circle

Audit management uses a few familiar tools from SAP QM so that experienced QM users should be able to use this application quickly.

## 12.2 System Requirements

As of SAP ERP Release 6.0, you can use audit management as an integral part of the SAP ERP system. It can be found in the menu under Cross-Application Components.

## 12.3 Definition of Audits from the Quality Management View

In general, audits are executed by the sold-to party to ensure that defined requirements of products, processes, services, or organizational units are met in accordance with defined quality standards. Legal regulations or provisions, such as Good Manufacturing Practice (GMP), ISO 9001, ISO/TS 16949, or QS 9000, support the execution of audits in many areas.

Following are the supported audit categories:

- **Quality assurance**
  - Internal audits
  - System, process, product audit (ISO/QS 9000)

  - Support of the audit process according to ISO 19011
  - From planning to evaluation
- **Purchasing department**
  - Vendor qualification and classification
  - Vendor release in accordance with general audit guidelines
  - Vendor audit
- **Environmental protection and safety at work**
  - Environmental audits (ISO 14001)
  - Plant security/building management
  - Internal occupational health (e.g., checklist for ergonomic offices) and hygiene audits

Auditing can refer to a specific process, to a product, or to a quality management system. SAP's original goal was to develop an application in collaboration with several customers, which could be implemented across different industries for all audit types and comprised the entire workflow of an audit — from planning via execution to evaluation and monitoring of corrective actions. This audit workflow also includes the documentation of audit plans, audit reports, and corrective actions.

## 12.4 Time Scheduling and Resource Planning

Audit management supports all phases of auditing — from audit planning through the actual auditing to the audit report — and, if necessary, the monitoring of improvement and preventive actions (see Figure 12.2). An audit is subject to certain planning rules that are similar to those used in project management. Each audit is stored in the system as a data object. You are already familiar with data objects such as inspection plans or quality notifications. The header of such a data object generally contains the audit type and the audit trigger, as well as the audit object.

The following phases and tasks are part of an audit planning:

- Planning the audit program (e.g., in the form of annual planning regarding the type, object, and time of the audit)

- Preparing the individual audits
- Determining the partners involved in the audit and the role allocation
- Providing data (rules, documents)
- Scheduling the audit

After scheduling and resource allocation, the "audit project" is ready for processing. The system offers configurable worklists. If a participant is to be proactively informed, a notification function with email connection is possible.

Import and export functions to Microsoft Project enable a convenient exchange of schedules and facilitate the integration into the non-SAP world.

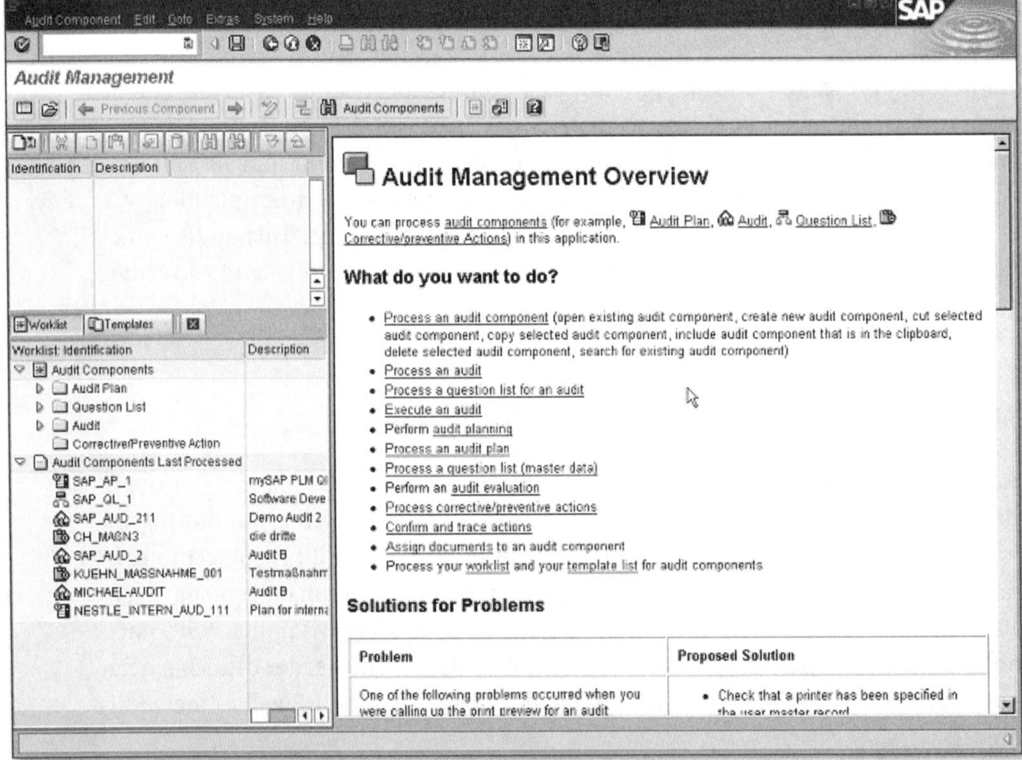


**Figure 12.2** Audit Management Overview

## 12.5 Planning the Question Lists

Questions that are hierarchically structured in question lists make up a central component of audits. Some standards stipulate standard questions or elements. You can copy or change these question lists if you have the corresponding authorization. You can maintain the texts of the questions in multiple languages, which is essential for the global use of a solution in an international company. Question lists are used to store recurring audit questions or criteria according to which the audit object is evaluated. These lists are treated like master data. The planning of general question lists (general criteria) depends on the relevant standards, regulations, or rules of the application area. The standard package does not contain any default question lists. The transfer of the lists can be done by using a macro that enables you to load correspondingly formatted Excel files via an XML interface (see Figure 12.3).

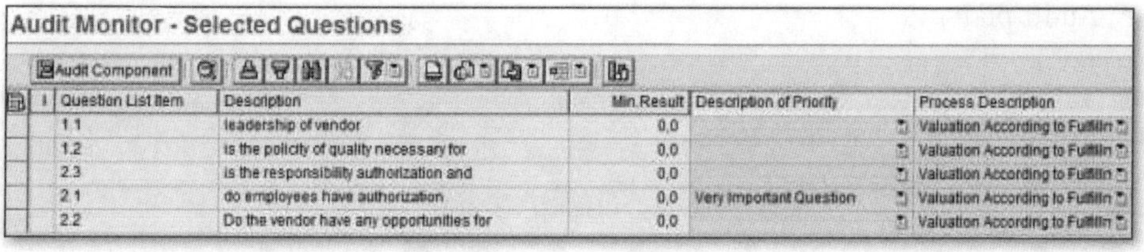

Audit Monitor - Selected Questions

Audit Component

| Question List Item | Description | Min.Result | Description of Priority | Process Description |
|---|---|---|---|---|
| 1.1 | leadership of vendor | 0,0 | | Valuation According to Fulfilln |
| 1.2 | is the policity of quality necessary for | 0,0 | | Valuation According to Fulfilln |
| 2.3 | is the responsibility authorization and | 0,0 | | Valuation According to Fulfilln |
| 2.1 | do employees have authorization | 0,0 | Very Important Question | Valuation According to Fulfilln |
| 2.2 | Do the vendor have any opportunities for | 0,0 | | Valuation According to Fulfilln |

**Figure 12.3** A Loaded Audit Question List

## 12.6 Execution

SAP Audit Management contains a status management that provides information on the respective processing status. Upon release of the audit, the participants can be notified by email. Usually the question lists are sent as a document along with the notification. The next step consists of recording the results (statements, documents). The audit execution is supported by numerous upload and download functions (see Section 12.10, Mobile Audit).

## 12.7 Reports and Evaluations

The audit report documents the audit result (see Figure 12.4). The system creates the report in tabular form or with diagrams on the screen. It can also be printed as a form based on freely definable templates (smart forms). After completing the questions and re-audit, and after the results have been transferred from the work papers of the auditor or from the mobile device into the system, the audit object is evaluated. Based on the evaluations of all question list items that can be and have been evaluated, the overall assessment for the audit is determined. To consolidate the evaluations across several hierarchy levels of the question list, the average degrees of fulfillment or deviation that have been reached at the individual levels are referred to and extrapolated in the standard version.

The following predefined forms (smart forms) are included in the standard package:

- Corrective actions
- Question list
- Audit report
- Audit plan

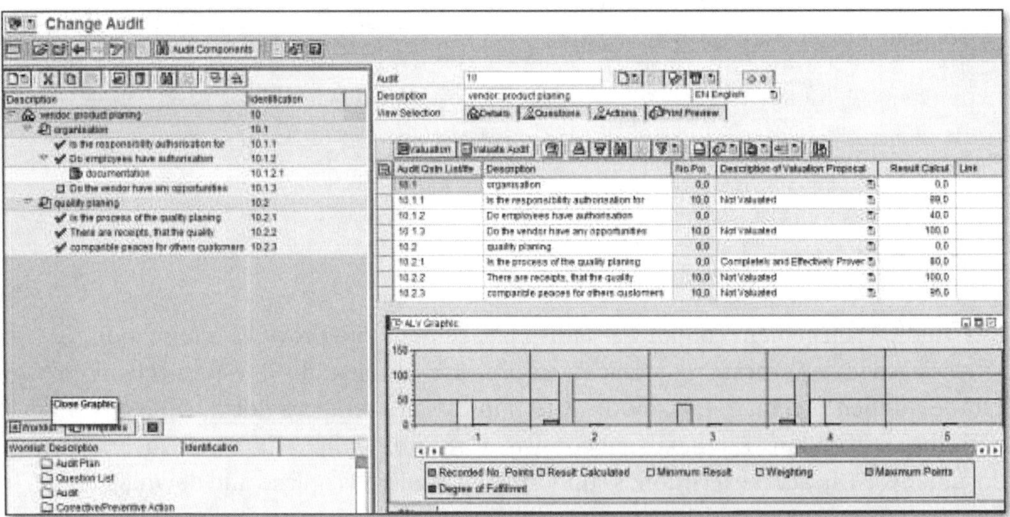


**Figure 12.4** Audit Report

All forms can be converted into a format that is accepted as an official document format (Adobe Acrobat; see Figure 12.5). You can integrate Microsoft Office documents such as drawings, inspection reports, tables, or the audit report in the audit documentation using the enhanced object services.

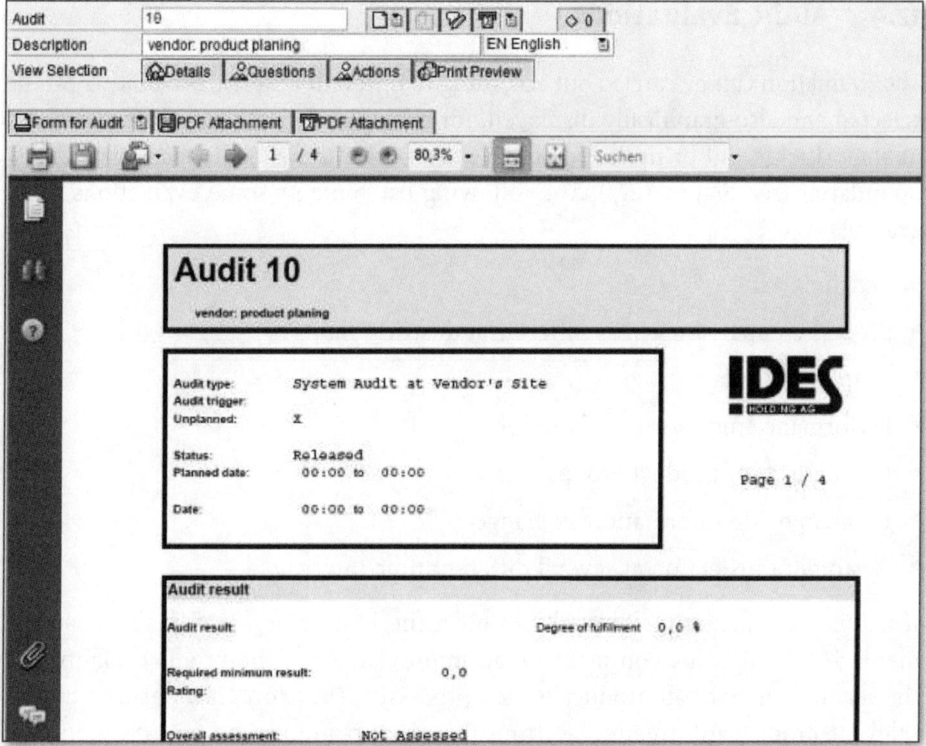


**Figure 12.5** Audit Form

## 12.8 Corrective and Preventive Actions

Action management is carried out in a similar manner as it is in quality notification. The action is created and contains catalog-supported coding, as well as a description of the action, which means that evaluations can be carried out through the same actions. Afterward, those responsible and possibly other partners are assigned. The action is completely defined after the scheduling and release have taken place. All actions can be individually compiled and completed in the worklists (see Figure 12.6).

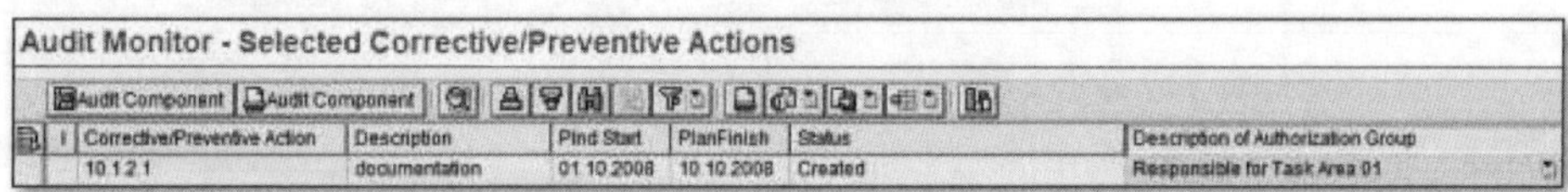


**Figure 12.6** Action Worklist

## 12.9 Audit Evaluations

The evaluation can be carried out according to different criteria. The objects can be selected and also graphically displayed, for example, the audit results of a vendor in a specific period or the comparison of several internal audits across company boundaries (see Figure 12.7). The following list contains some evaluations as an example:

- Benchmarking
- Process comparison across different industries/plants
- Graphical display
- Performance monitoring of vendors
- Comparison of product groups
- Companywide information exchange
- Customer satisfaction at several different time intervals

If audits are efficiently executed and meet the requirements of quality management, SAP PLM helps you facilitate an improvement of the product quality and the seamless flow of all product-related processes. Therefore, it is ensured that all relevant product information — from the product innovation and development to production preparation and change management to service and maintenance processing — is globally available at any time. This reduces product development times and costs, while the quality of the products and services rises.

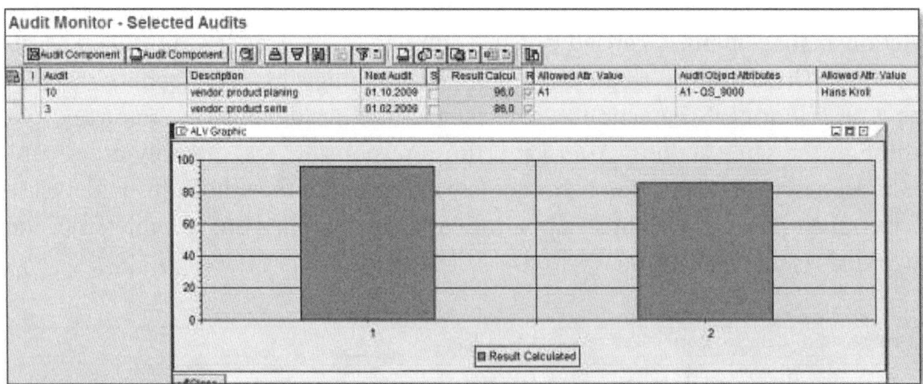


Figure 12.7 Audit Evaluation

## 12.10 Mobile Audit

Although the web interface enables you to have access at any time and from any place to all functions of audit management, for some audits, online execution is neither feasible nor desirable. In such cases, you can export the audit question list via an intermediate step (XML format) from the SAP ERP system to Excel and transfer this file to a mobile device (PDA). You can also enter the audit results on this device and transfer the processed audit question list in the reverse way, that is, back into the system. SAP provides an Excel template for exports and imports whose layout you can customize to meet your own requirements.

## 12.11 Scenario — Vendor Audit

In this scenario, a vendor audit is to be planned. The following information must be provided:

- Audit type
- Audit trigger
- Audit object (business partner)
- Texts describing the audit in detail
- Participants

With this information, you fill in the details of the audit mask (see Figure 12.8). Essential parts of preparing an audit are the question lists that are assigned via a general worklist (see Figure 12.9). Here, you only create the questions valid for the respective audit.

| Description | Identification |
|---|---|
| vendor: product serie | 3 |
| organisation | 10.1 |
| quaility planing | 10.2 |
| general view about the company | 10.3 |
| production area | 10.3.1 |
| envirement | 10.4 |

**Figure 12.8** Audit Details

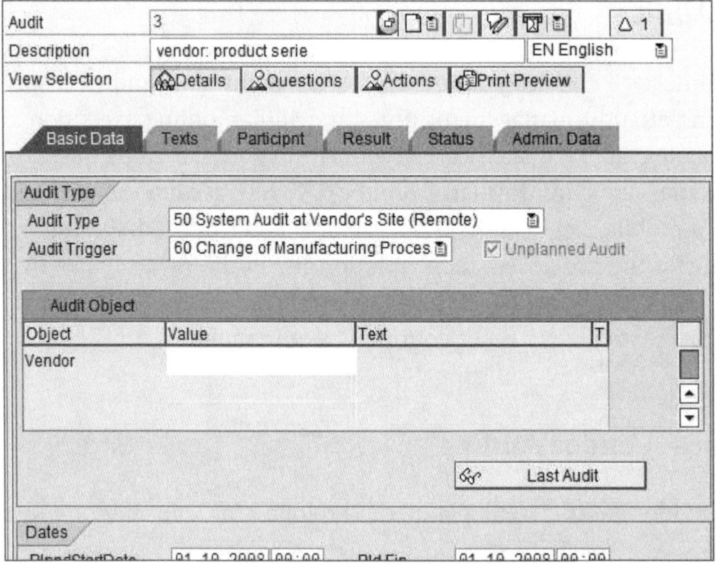


Figure 12.9 Audit Overview

The processor specifies an evaluation parameter for each question (see Figure 12.10).

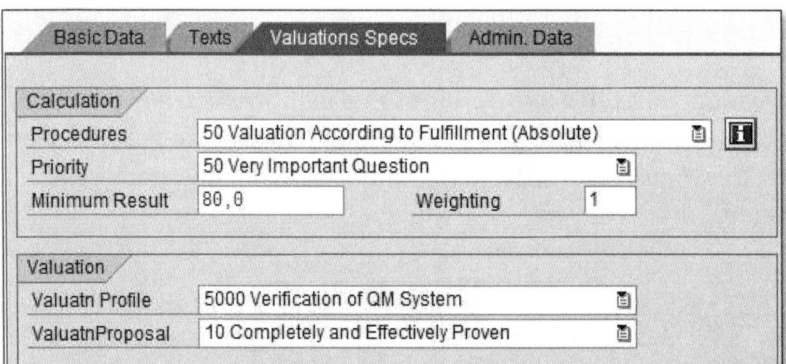


Figure 12.10 Valuation Specifications for a Question

After planning has been completed and the audit has been released, the audit is implemented. An overview of all questions can be printed as a support onsite. After you evaluate all results of the questions, the entire audit is calculated based on the underlying procedure. If a requirement is not entirely fulfilled, corrective actions are created or assigned (see Figure 12.11).

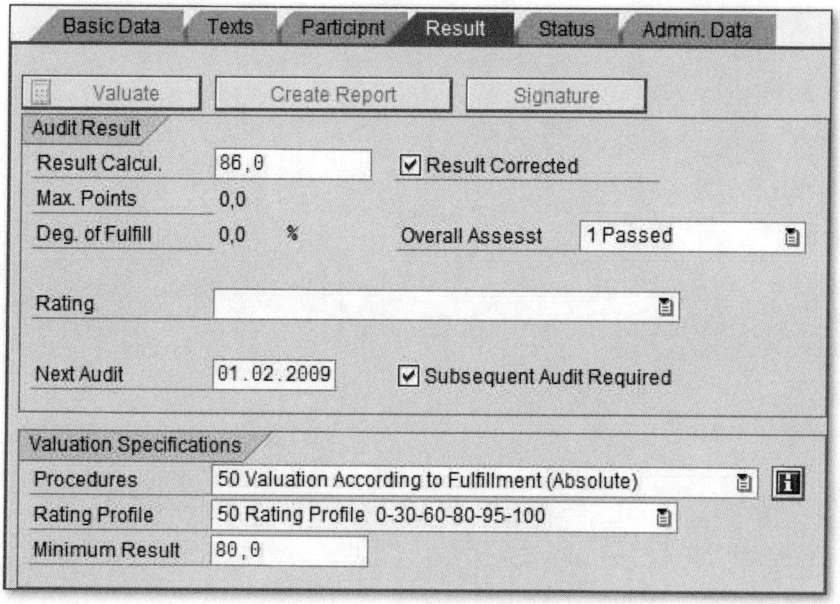

Basic Data | Texts | Participnt | Result | Status | Admin. Data

Valuate | Create Report | Signature

Audit Result

Result Calcul. 86,0 ☑ Result Corrected

Max. Points 0,0

Deg. of Fulfill 0,0 %  Overall Assesst 1 Passed

Rating

Next Audit 01.02.2009 ☑ Subsequent Audit Required

Valuation Specifications

Procedures 50 Valuation According to Fulfillment (Absolute)

Rating Profile 50 Rating Profile 0-30-60-80-95-100

Minimum Result 80,0

**Figure 12.11** Result

The system creates a report. The assigned actions are displayed in the audit's worklist, which enables you to monitor the timely implementation of corrective or improvement actions. The overview of the evaluation for the individual questions (see Figure 12.12) can be transferred to Excel at any time using the automatic calculation so that they can be processed outside the system or be provided to the vendor in case of vendor audits.

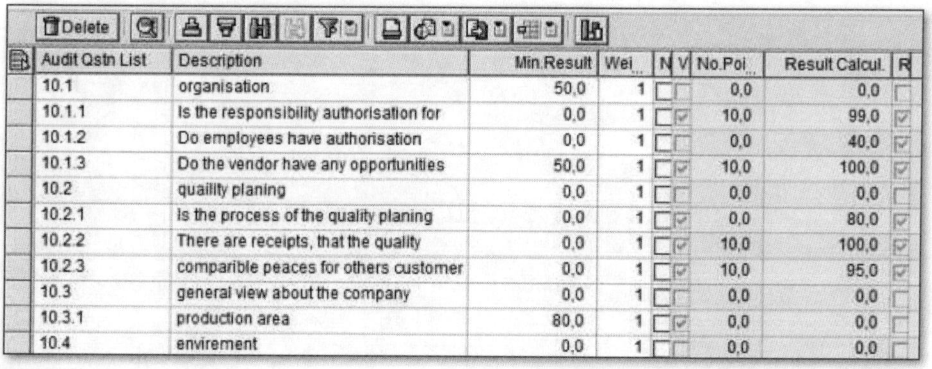

Delete

| Audit Qstn List | Description | Min.Result | Wei... | N | V | No.Poi... | Result Calcul. | R |
|---|---|---|---|---|---|---|---|---|
| 10.1 | organisation | 50,0 | 1 | ☐ | ☐ | 0,0 | 0,0 | ☐ |
| 10.1.1 | Is the responsibility authorisation for | 0,0 | 1 | ☐ | ☑ | 10,0 | 99,0 | ☑ |
| 10.1.2 | Do employees have authorisation | 0,0 | 1 | ☐ | ☐ | 0,0 | 40,0 | ☑ |
| 10.1.3 | Do the vendor have any opportunities | 50,0 | 1 | ☐ | ☑ | 10,0 | 100,0 | ☑ |
| 10.2 | quaility planing | 0,0 | 1 | ☐ | ☐ | 0,0 | 0,0 | ☐ |
| 10.2.1 | Is the process of the quality planing | 0,0 | 1 | ☐ | ☑ | 0,0 | 80,0 | ☑ |
| 10.2.2 | There are receipts, that the quality | 0,0 | 1 | ☐ | ☑ | 10,0 | 100,0 | ☑ |
| 10.2.3 | comparible peaces for others customer | 0,0 | 1 | ☐ | ☑ | 10,0 | 95,0 | ☑ |
| 10.3 | general view about the company | 0,0 | 1 | ☐ | ☐ | 0,0 | 0,0 | ☐ |
| 10.3.1 | production area | 80,0 | 1 | ☐ | ☑ | 0,0 | 0,0 | ☐ |
| 10.4 | envirement | 0,0 | 1 | ☐ | ☐ | 0,0 | 0,0 | ☐ |

**Figure 12.12** Result List

*This chapter deals with the principles, tools, and functions of Customizing, and describes the procedure based on a real-life example.*

# 13 Customizing

*Customizing* is a standard term in the vocabulary of SAP implementations. First, you are provided with the basic principles of Customizing.

## 13.1 Basic Principles

When you compare this task with the activities you perform in everyday life, you will see that you perform Customizing tasks relatively often. For example, think about when you're choosing a new car, kitchen, or house. Let's consider the "buying a car" example. In this case — in a very general sense — the car dealer acts in the same capacity as a consultant, informing you of the different vehicle mix options. He describes which features can be combined, which combinations make sense, and the cost of implementing your Customizing decisions. It is therefore easy to imagine that interaction between customers and consultants will run far more smoothly if the following practices can be ensured:

- The consultant can understand the customer's requirements.
- The customer is informed on all of the options.
- The customer formulates his requirements precisely.
- Experts assess the feasibility of the requirements.
- The resources are available for the Customizing tasks.

Of course, this is only possible if customers and consultants are "speaking the same language." In the "buying a car" example, the shared context of consultant and customer has usually developed over many years, facilitating successful communication. In an SAP implementation project, Customizing-specific communication is harder because neither the main procedure nor the available options in Customizing are clear to the customer. You have already learned how to use the method described in Chapter 2, Modeling QM Business Processes Using the EPC Method.

Another common point of reference consists of the work packages and activities that accompany the Customizing functions (called the SAP Procedure Model). This is where business know-how meets system-specific knowledge. You could even describe this as a human interface, that is, a communication platform that enables cross-area exchange. Customers who really want to understand the system and the implementation concept must therefore learn to understand Customizing.

The "Customizing a new car" example that was used earlier can also be applied to a QM implementation project, although the content would be more far-reaching and a little more complicated. The main difference is that a QM project consists of many business processes and functions. The "buying a car" process is relatively simple from the perspective of the buyer, and the combination options are generally quite clear.

The method for completing the Customizing tasks is usually iterative, approaching the objective in individual steps across several project phases. In the "buying a car" example, after Customizing has been completed, it usually takes only a few steps to complete and close the order.

To implement customer-specific requirements in an SAP ERP system, you use the *Implementation Guide* (IMG). For the QM area alone, the IMG has more than 200 different settings, many of which interact within QM and other components. Figure 13.1 displays an "expanded" IMG reference for the area of QM.

### Characteristics of Customizing Functions

Customizing the SAP ERP system is roughly divided into two main areas:

- Customizing business settings
- Customizing operative (QM) processes

Particularly when configuring business-specific basic data in the area of QM, you should check possible interactions with other logistics components. In Customizing, although this content is not separated, we recommend that you check every configuration within the framework of a QM implementation to ensure that related processes are not affected.

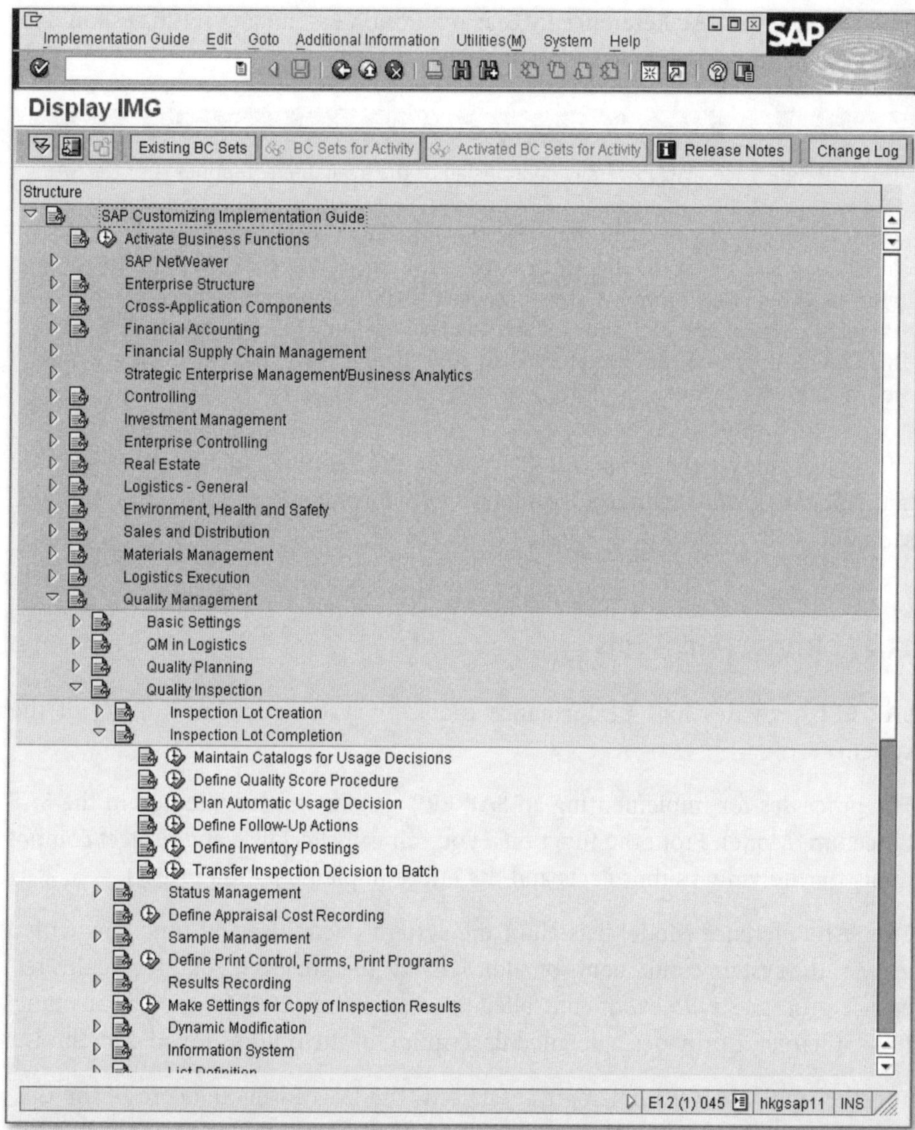


**Figure 13.1** IMG Excerpt for QM

### Implementation Guide (IMG)

The Customizing model is created in graphical format as a structure tree and is managed in the system as the SAP REFERENCE IMG. You can create individual projects from the SAP Reference IMG as required. Customizing settings should be performed and documented in the projects.

> **Tip**
>
> The SAP Reference IMG generally contains all of the available components of the SAP ERP system. At the beginning of a QM project, however, not all QM components might be visible, so you might think that the installation is not complete. But, in this case, it just means that the QM component is not part of the IMG project. The program is definitely on your system because the QM component belongs to the standard range of every logistics system. To make the QM work packages visible, all that your SAP system administrator has to do is to regenerate the SAP Reference IMG for the QM area in a new project.

The setup follows the Component View of the reference models that you are familiar with from Chapter 2, Modeling QM Business Processes Using the EPC Method.

## 13.2 Important Tools

SAP ERP provides high-performance tools for systematic Customizing of the system.

The processes for implementing an SAP ERP system are documented in the SAP Procedure Model. From the functions, you can call checklists and project components for individual subprojects and the entire implementation project.

The SAP Reference Model lists all of the system's activities and functions with a view of the system components or, alternatively, the process layout. It contains reference processes with event-controlled process chains (EPC) for the various functions. Chapter 2 provides a detailed description of the options for EPC methods.

Together with the Customizing transactions, the IMG forms the core of the Customizing activities. The structure is identical to that of the component view of the reference model. The work packages describe the configuration activities that combine to form the IMG.

In the IMG structure, you can access the Customizing Transactions by clicking on the Execute icon. This is where you make the necessary settings directly in the system according to the information from the IMG.

The PROJECT MANAGEMENT functions are the most important tools provided by SAP ERP for project management directly in Customizing. You can specify resources, time specifications, and the corresponding status for the SAP Procedure Model and the Project IMG. You can also assign PROJECT DOCUMENTATION to the Customizing activities and project work steps.

Because Customizing settings are initial prototype settings, they remain in the test or development system until completion. They are transferred to the consolidation system and then the productive system using *transport requests* (see Figure 13.2). The transport requests for a resource are listed here and are assigned a status such as "released," to indicate the transport level.

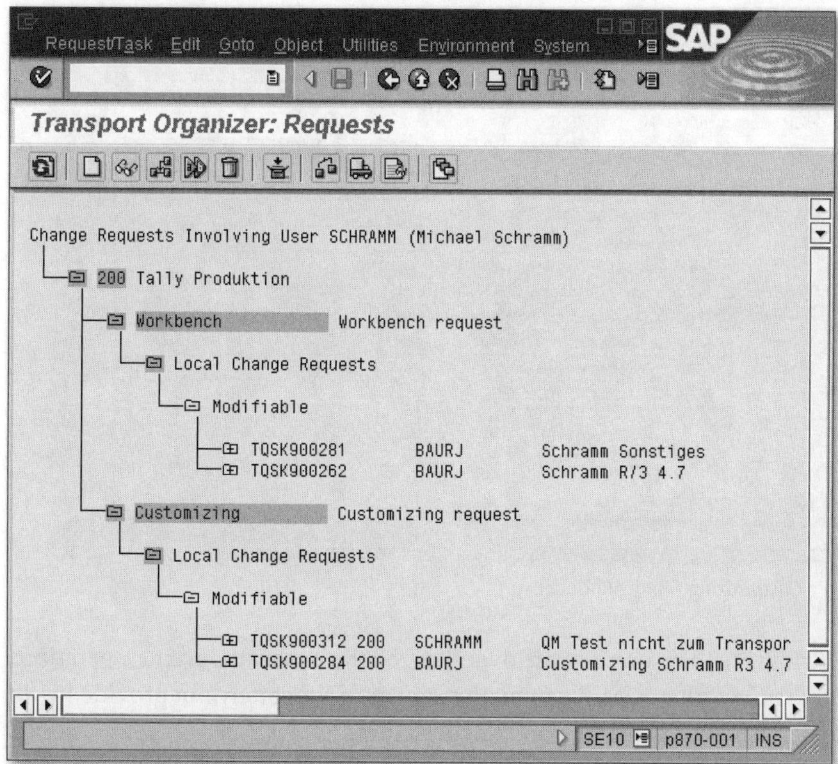


**Figure 13.2** Transferring Customizing Requests

## 13.3 Functions in Customizing

You access the Customizing overview via TOOLS • CUSTOMIZING • IMG • EDIT PROJECT. The system displays the initial screen (see Figure 13.3). The main window provides an overview of the available projects. You double-click on the project to display the Project IMG (refer to Figure 13.1). The IMG will be described in greater detail later on in this chapter.

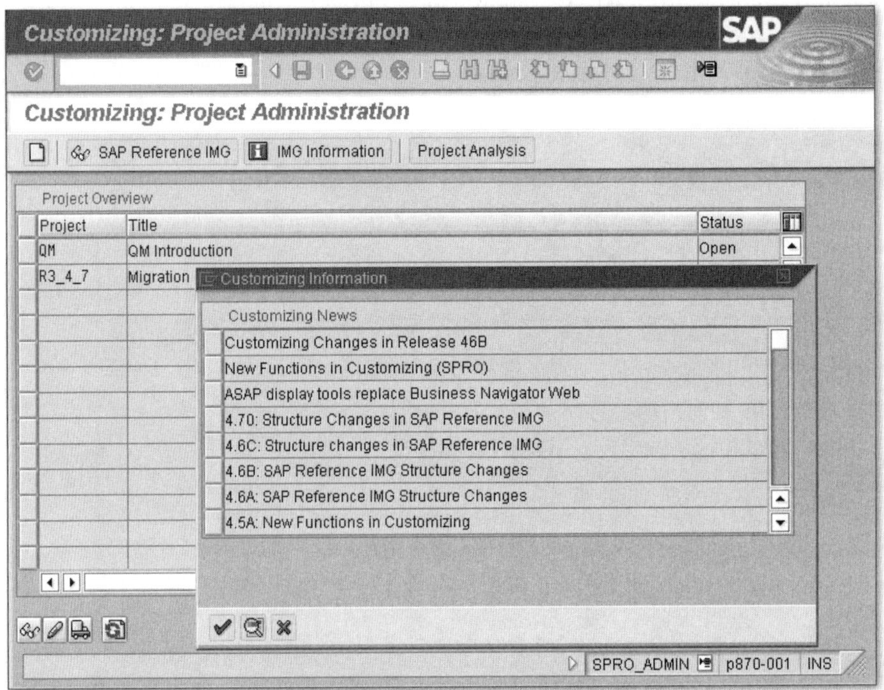


**Figure 13.3** Customizing Main Window

The following sections provide an overview of the most important operations within the framework of QM Customizing. You are deliberately not provided with a specific description of QM Customizing functions.

### 13.3.1 SAP Procedure Model

The procedure planned by SAP ERP can be divided into the four phases of a classic IT project (excerpt from the SAP Procedure Model). By continuing to develop customer-specific implementation concepts, SAP has merged the SAP Procedure Model with technical configurations in a component-related implementation model, that is, Solution Manager, ASAP.

### 13.3.2 Implementation Guides (IMGs)

In standard software systems, SAP IMGs certainly play a pioneering role in the area of customer-oriented configuration. It used to be necessary to create configuration variants for software systems in better-quality external text editors, but the SAP ERP system provides its own application. The central functions of Customizing run in the IMG in process-oriented form. The structure is based on the component view of the reference model. The IMG contains the IMG documents. The implementation activities are supported with the following functions:

- Direct execution of Customizing transactions for editing the configuration parameters
- Accompanying project documentation for every step in Customizing, including editing of your own notes on individual activities
- Status management for every work step in Customizing for project controlling
- Accompanying documentation with the IMG

#### IMG Versions

All IMG versions are represented as a structure, the lines of which are nodes or activities. The nodes can be clicked on to "expand" additional structures. At the lowest level, the EXECUTE icon indicates actual Customizing activities. The functions in the structure screen can be selected according to the key in Table 13.1.

| Icon | Meaning |
|---|---|
| | Expand by single-clicking on this icon or using the EXPAND/COLLAPSE function. |
| | Collapse by single-clicking on the icon or using the EXPAND/COLLAPSE function. |
| | Node without subnodes. |
| **Customizing-specific icons** | **Node Title** |
| | Double-click to navigate to the activity description. |
| | Click to navigate to the maintenance of the node's notes. |
| | This node includes an executable function. Click on the icon to navigate to the corresponding function. |
| | Click on the field to navigate to the status maintenance. |
| | This node includes a release note. Click on the field to display the release note. |

**Table 13.1** Functions in the Customizing Structure

Depending on the IMG selected, the line will contain additional information. Customizing includes the IMG with different scopes:

- **Reference IMG**
  You select the Reference IMG via TOOLS • CUSTOMIZING • IMG • EDIT PROJECT and the REFERENCE IMG button. Just like the reference model, this contains all functions for all components. The Reference IMG is used as the starting point for project activities and is included only once in the delivery package for every SAP ERP system. No changes are made in the Reference IMG, and no user documentation is created there. It is predominantly used as a template for the Enterprise IMG and the Project IMG. If settings in the Enterprise IMG or the Project IMG have unwanted consequences, you can use the Reference IMG to recreate the original status.

- **Enterprise IMG**
  The Enterprise IMG is a subset of the Reference IMG and also applies to the entire company. This IMG exists only once in the system. In the Enterprise IMG, the IMG structure is stocked at the client level with the necessary components and activities from the Reference IMG. This ensures that the individual projects contain only the components required for the implementation of the SAP ERP system. At any time, however, you can regenerate components in the Enterprise IMG without losing existing information.
- **Project IMG**
  Where possible, actual Customizing tasks should be performed in the Project IMG. For this purpose, IMG projects can be divided according to the requirements of project organization. For every subproject, the required components and activities are created based on the Enterprise IMG. Depending on its scope, the project structure for QM can include all activities or just subareas, such as QM in production. It is also possible to run projects solely for a specific project stage (e.g., to install a prototype stage or test operation). If, as recommended, you work in several systems and have access to a test system, you can experiment with different settings without harming the productive operation that is running in parallel.

### 13.3.3 Creating a Project IMG

You access the window for maintaining the project IMG via CUSTOMIZING • IMG • EDIT PROJECT (see Figure 13.4).

The mandatory fields are highlighted in color and are filled according to their definitions. In the PROJECT ADMINISTRATION area, it is recommended that you select YES because this allows you to activate the functions here. In the Customizing activities, you make particular use of status information and resource assignment. You can change the projects created at any time.

When you select the GENERATE PROJECT IMG function, the system displays the selection structure of the components and activities. You select the required components by clicking on them and then create a Project IMG by choosing SAVE. The result is a new project with the selected components and the areas required for executing the project. The system creates these IMG areas automatically. The project management overview now displays a line with the project number and the name of the newly added project.

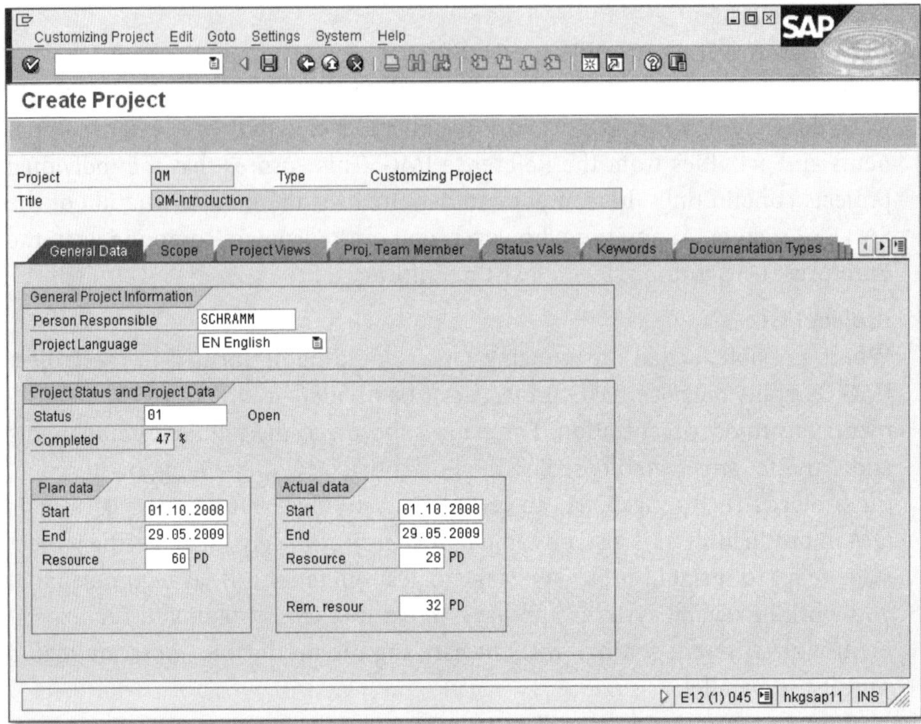


**Figure 13.4** Creating a Project IMG

## Tip

Users of Microsoft Project can use the function for forwarding project activities and their status information to Microsoft Project. When you choose the UPLOAD/DOWNLOAD function in the PROJECT MANAGEMENT window, the system displays the subsequent dialog window, in which you specify the required file name, the directory, and other selection criteria. The system creates an MPX file with the activities from the IMG. This can be processed further with Microsoft Project from Version 3.0 onward.

## Tip

If you created a new project as displayed in the example, project management content will still be empty because the new project is still "in process," however, this shouldn't lead you to believe that the settings made in other projects are already contained in this new project. Furthermore, changes to the newly created project are reflected in all of the other projects in the same system.

## Working in the Implementation Guides

The functions described here are available in all IMGs. The icons in the IMG application toolbar are self-explanatory and can also be accessed simply by clicking with the mouse (see Figure 13.5). The IMGs can be printed at various levels of detail and can be individually configured via the STANDARD SETTINGS menu item. When you select the INFORMATION menu item in Customizing, the system displays different additional information on Customizing activities (see Figure 13.6), such as the assigned status from the project notes or the link to the corresponding activities in the SAP Procedure Model.

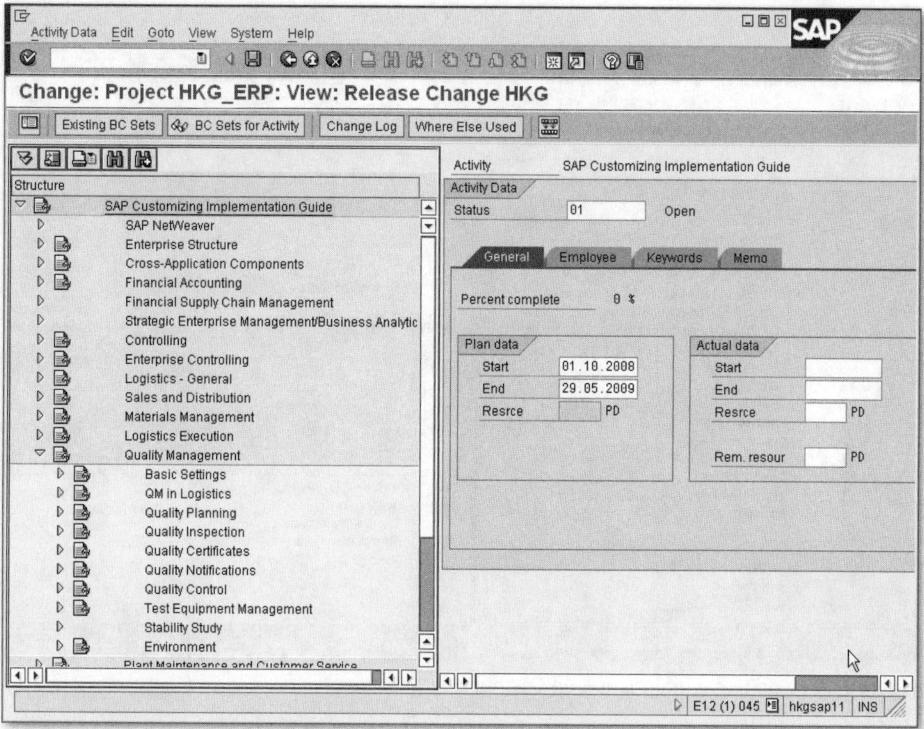


**Figure 13.5** Project IMG for Quality Management in Production

The following are the most important functions in the CHANGE: PROJECT window menu in greater detail:

- **Menu: Edit • Display IMG Activity**
  You can perform targeted searches for texts and entries in the structure.

- **Button: "Where Else Used"**
  This is a particularly useful function that you can use to check which activities use identical Customizing objects. This enables you to check any functional and business-related consequences for other components to prevent inconsistent settings.
- **Menu Information • Title and IMG Info Notes**
  If a note has been created, then it is displayed here.
- **Release Notes**
  You can use the blue i icon to check the availability of this additional information, and use this function to display the Release Notes.

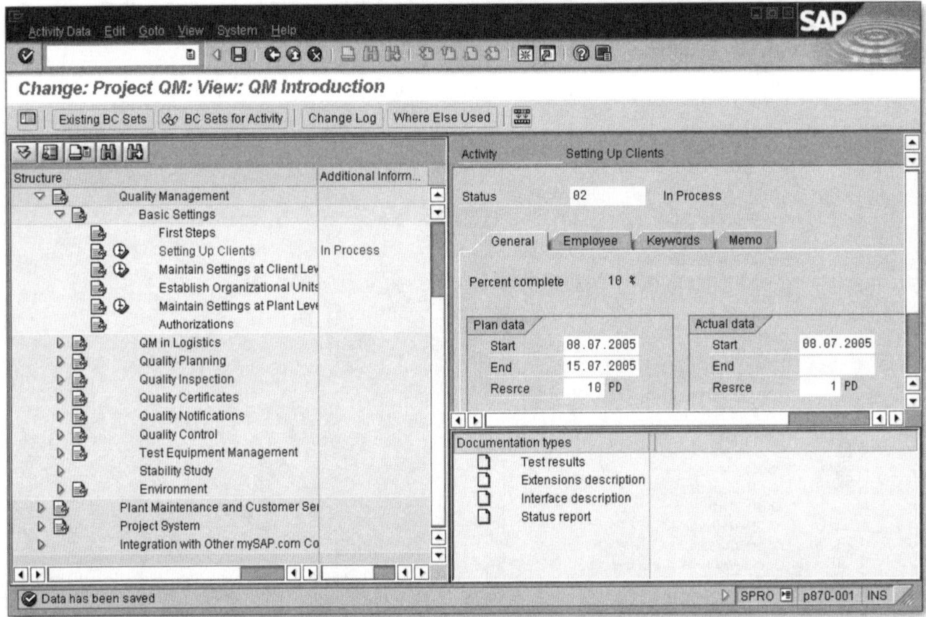


**Figure 13.6** Additional Information on Customizing Activities

- **Activity Importance**
  This divides activities into *mandatory activities* and *optional activities*.
- **Critical Activity**
  This divides activities into *critical activities* and *noncritical activities*.
- **Assignment**
  This displays assignments to activities from the ASAP Roadmap.

- **Country assignment**
  This displays the assignment to a country if you selected this when creating the project. If no country is displayed, the settings apply for all countries.
- **Application components**
  This displays the assignment to a module of an application component.
- **Business Add-In (BAdI)**
  In the right-hand column, the system displays the IMG activities in which customer-specific function enhancements are possible.

**Tip**

This is either a question of existing function modules or user exits, in which a change or docking of an in-house program is already preplanned on the SAP ERP side. During SAP release upgrades in particular, these enhancements are not as critical as enhancements to SAP original programs or function modules for which no customer enhancements are planned. SAP continuously maintains the program interfaces specified here for release upgrades.

- **Client dependence**
  The right-hand column displays which Customizing tables are client-dependent.
- **Transport type**
  The right-hand column displays which Customizing tables are included in the transport:
  - **Manual transport**
    In this case, there is no transport connection, that is, changes to Customizing tables are not automatically listed in a change request. You must copy the change manually to a change request.
  - **Automatic transport**
    In this case, there is a transport connection; that is, changes to the Customizing tables are automatically included in a change request.
  - **Language dependence**
    The right-hand column displays which Customizing tables may need to be translated and where they are required:
  - **Non-language-dependent tables**
    This means that you do not need to translate this Customizing table.
  - **Translate via standard translation process**
    You must translate these tables. You perform the translation using SAP ERP's

own translation transaction. You can access this transaction via TOOLS • ABAP WORKBENCH • UTILITIES • TRANSLATION • SHORT AND LONG TEXTS.

- **Employees**
  This displays the use of resources from the entry in project management.
- **Selection field**
  The right-hand column displays which selection fields have been assigned to your project.

## 13.4 Project Controlling with IMG and the SAP Procedure Model

The structure models provide many options for monitoring and controlling the activities in Customizing and general project processes. Most functions for project controlling can be seen directly in the structural representation of the SAP Procedure Model and the IMG:

- You use the SAP Procedure Model for project flow control.
- You control technical activities in the IMGs.

The different projects can then be evaluated according to activities, status information, and individual criteria.

### 13.4.1 Project Controlling with Status Information

You define the status depending on the processing status of a work package or an activity. To display the STATUS icon (blue checkmark with pencil), you must activate PROJECT ADMINISTRATION, as described in Section 13.3.3., Creating a Project IMG. If no project status is maintained yet, then you must enter one here. To do this, go to the PROJECT ADMINISTRATION path in the CUSTOMIZING window, and double-click on the project. Under ADMINISTRATION • ASSIGN STATUS, you assign the required status in the STATUS VALS tab (see Figure 13.7). The standard SAP delivery already contains some useful status values, but you can also create your own status values and store them here.

#### Processing Status Information

You can click on the STATUS icon in the IMG or SAP Procedure Model structure to open the input screen for status information (see Figure 13.8).

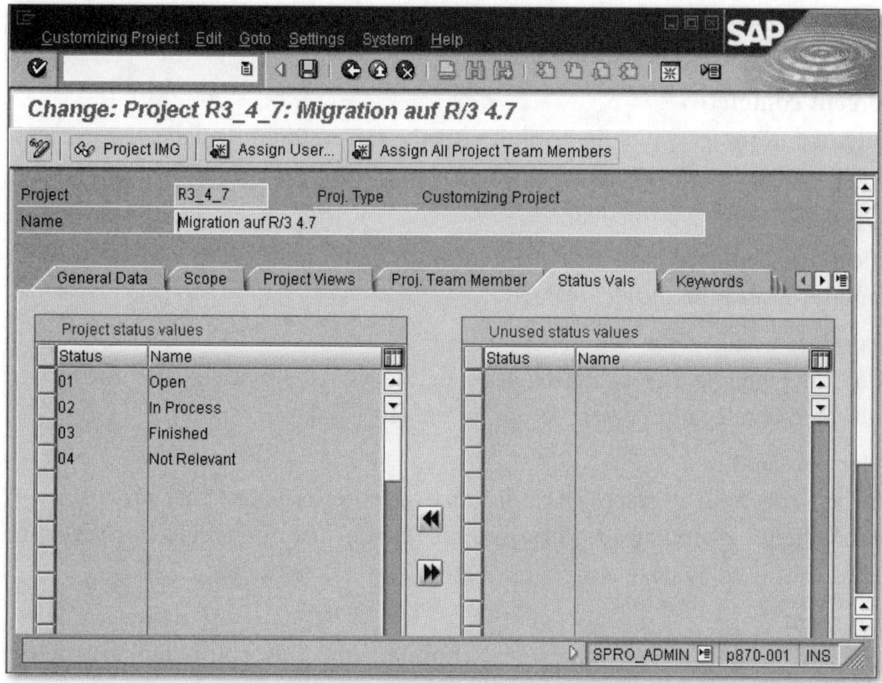


Figure 13.7 Maintaining Possible Status Values for a Project

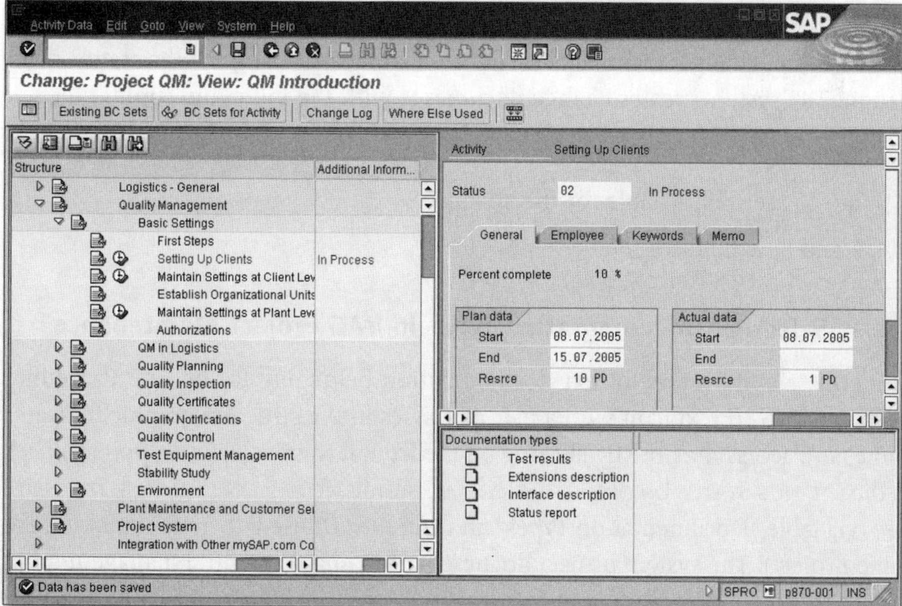


Figure 13.8 Status Information for Customizing Settings

- **Status**
  Select the required status from project maintenance.
- **Percent complete**
  Enter a percentage value here. Alternatively, the system calculates the percentage if you just enter the actual and remaining work.
- **Resources**
  Select the required resource from project maintenance. This is usually an employee from the project team.
- **Plan data actual data, remaining work**
  You can schedule the tasks/activities in the fields provided. The remaining workload is calculated when you press the [Enter] key.
- **Selection field**
  You use this field to select an additional selection criterion that provides you with a better overview in a given area. You can use these selection fields to make your own evaluations.
- **Comment**
  You can provide a short additional comment for this point in the activity/procedure.

#### Change Logs

In the system, change documents are written for every change to the status information. The system creates change documents with the following content:

- Change date
- Name of user responsible for the change
- Age and new field content

### 13.4.2 Selecting Documentation Types in IMG Project Maintenance

The term "Notes" refers to text documentation belonging to the SAP Procedure Model or IMG. A text icon with a pair of glasses in the structure graphic indicates a note. You access the note by clicking on the icon. If there is no note, you can click on the CHANGE STATUS INFORMATION ICON • CHANGE NOTE ICON • CHOOSE THE NOTE TYPE (via table "Documentation Types" and add the "Unused documentation types" to the project). The system project documentation enables central management of written records, notes, and other information in relation to project work. You also process the allowed note (documentation) types in IMG project maintenance. A selection of two or three note types is usually sufficient. Otherwise, management can quickly become too complicated.

When you select a note type, the system displays a window in which the texts are edited (see Figure 13.9). Don't be afraid to use the standard SAPscript line editor! After you have become familiar with this type of editor, it is actually quite practical. Alternatively, you can use Microsoft Word as an editor. To do this, choose BASIC FUNCTIONS • EDITOR FOR MS-WORD from the Customizing menu.

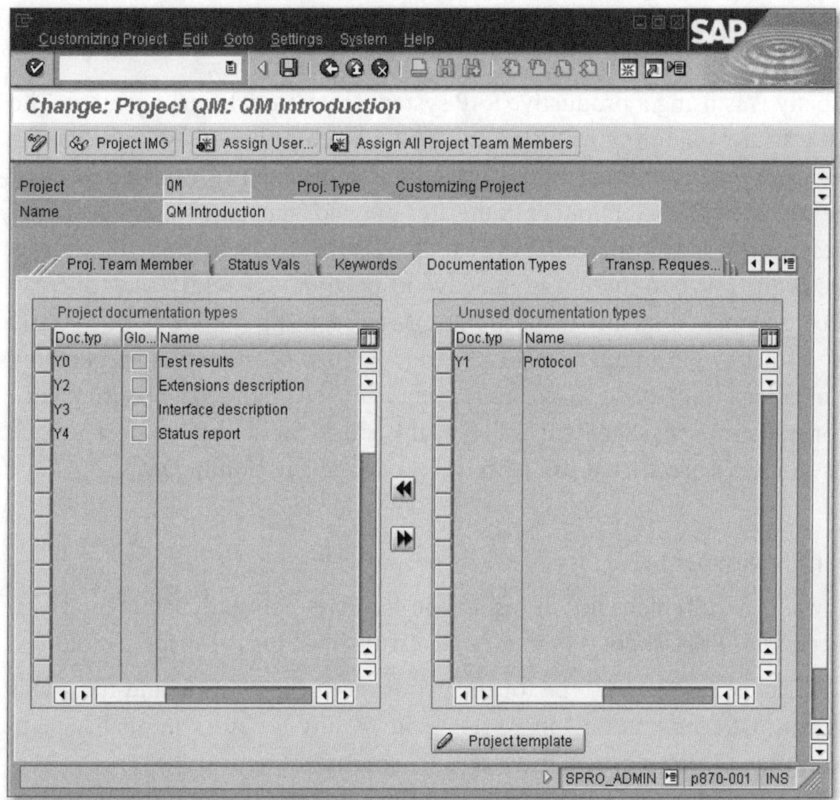


**Figure 13.9** Selecting Note Types in IMG Project Maintenance

Another advantage of SAP editors is that you will not be tempted to experiment with the numerous layout/formatting variants of an Office application, which can often drive you to distraction. Also, when using Word, most functions are deactivated, so the main advantage lies in the familiar menu commands.

## 13.5 Scenario

There is a good reason that this chapter has not yet provided any details on QM Customizing: The QM IMG alone, without the other SAP online documentation, comprises nearly 200 pages and is intended for individual configuration of an SAP QM implementation project. To provide you with a practical explanation of the basic Customizing procedure, a "real" example is used from an implementation project with Release status 4.0/4.5 at a large automotive supplier. Read the example carefully because it describes the dangers of certain Customizing settings.

### 13.5.1 Analyzing the Boundary Conditions

The company was using a productive SAP system for materials management. The company was also planning to install the SAP QM component. After analyzing interfaces from quality management to the other components, it turned out that the influence of the QM component in the area of goods movements was problematic for a stock-relevant inspection type (01, INSPECTION UPON GOODS RECEIPT FOR PURCHASE ORDER). When there was an active inspection type with CONTROL INDICATOR "Post to stock in quality inspection," QM posts using the STOCK IN QUALITY INSPECTION stock type and opens an inspection lot. The operation was triggered by goods movement 101, GOODS MOVEMENT FOR PURCHASE ORDER. The consequence of this for inventory management was that this stock could only be posted back from this stock to unrestricted-use stock via the usage decision in QM.

#### Customer Requirement

1. There was a requirement for an inspection lot that enables dynamic modifications and sampling schemes at the characteristic level for the inspection lot.
2. With the active inspection type for the goods receipt inspection and the goods movement, QM must not assume sole responsibility for stock in quality management (due to postings and interfaces to external systems)!
3. A goods movement 101 should, however, still be posted automatically to stock in quality management and allow manual postings to UNRESTRICTED or OTHER stock.
4. Where possible, original programs should be used.

### Problems with Implementation in the System

At first glance, it did not seem possible to meet the customer requirements for the following reasons:

- Non-stock-relevant inspection types have no "Goods receipt" inspection lot origin and therefore do not create an inspection lot during goods receipt. The standard inspection types with stock relevance do not allow dynamic modification at the characteristic level.
- With the standard inspection types, stock in quality management is inventory managed as soon as it exists. This means that transfer posting via goods movement transactions is no longer allowed.

### Solution with the Customizing Settings?

Via Customizing, an inspection type was provided with settings that met all of the criteria from the customer requirements. Using various tests, it could be determined that one criterion (i.e., "automatic posting to stock in quality management") was not possible with the other criteria. To enable automatic posting, it was decided to install a small supplementary program, which posts the supplied quantity with movement type 321, directly to stock in quality management. This program was triggered in every goods movement 101, GOODS RECEIPT FOR PURCHASE ORDER.

Inspection type 01, INSPECTION UPON GOODS RECEIPT FOR PURCHASE ORDER, was not used because this inspection type will always take over management of stock in quality management.

Inspection type 89, OTHER INSPECTION, was used because dynamic modifications and sampling schemes were already provided for, and the first criterion was met. The short text for the inspection type was changed to "Goods receipt inspection." To make the special Customizing settings, it was necessary to navigate in the Project IMG, as displayed in Figure 13.10, to MAINTAIN INSPECTION TYPES.

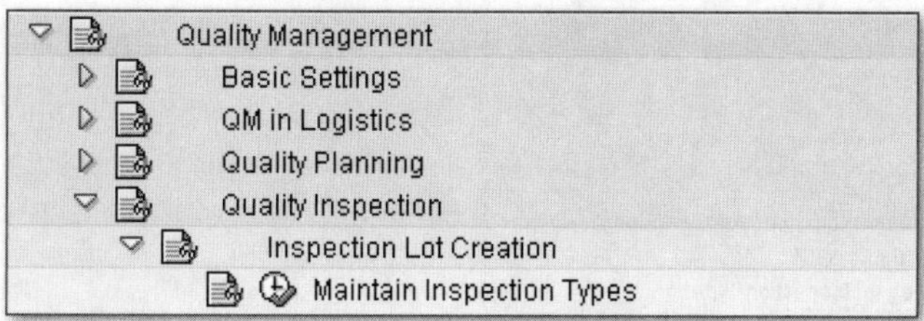


**Figure 13.10** Menu Tree to Maintain Inspection Types

In the Customizing transaction MAINTAIN INSPECTION TYPES, the short text was changed, and the entries were made in the required control functions (see Figure 13.11).

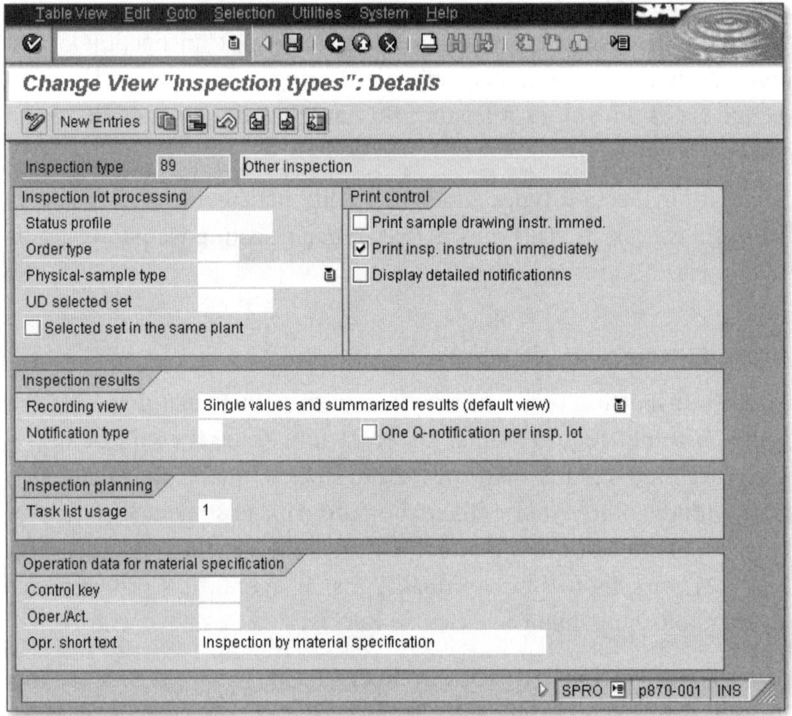


**Figure 13.11** Changing Inspection Types in Customizing

It was attempted to meet the second criterion with Customizing settings using INSPECTION FOR GOODS MOVEMENTS, as shown in Figure 13.12. This resulted in an inspection lot generation with inspection type 89 and inspection lot origin 89, OTHER.

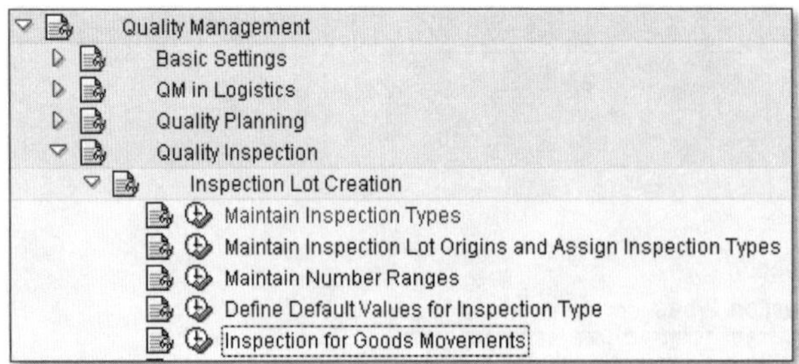


**Figure 13.12** Navigating to Inspection for Goods Movements

After selecting EDIT MOVEMENT TYPES IN INVENTORY MANAGEMENT, then MOVEMENT TYPE, the system displays the selection window for the movement types. Entering "101" and selecting EXECUTE causes the system to select all variants of movement type 101. If BACK is clicked, the DEFINE NEW MOVEMENT TYPES screen disappears, and the system displays an overview of the maintenance functions for movement type 101. Next, UPDATE CONTROL/WMS MOVEMENT TYPES was selected. The system then displayed the window shown in Figure 13.13, CHANGE VIEW "UPDATE CONTROL."

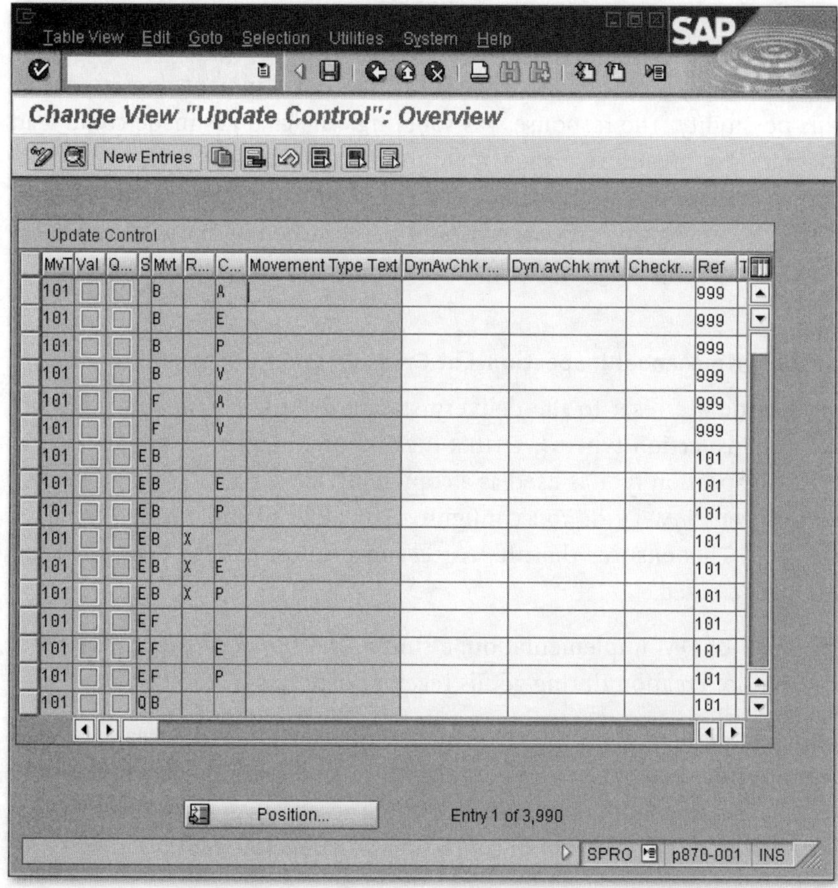


| MvT | Val | Q... | S | Mvt | R... | C... | Movement Type Text | DynAvChk r... | Dyn.avChk mvt | Checkr... | Ref | T |
|---|---|---|---|---|---|---|---|---|---|---|---|---|
| 101 | | | | B | | A | | | | | 999 | |
| 101 | | | | B | | E | | | | | 999 | |
| 101 | | | | B | | P | | | | | 999 | |
| 101 | | | | B | | V | | | | | 999 | |
| 101 | | | | F | | A | | | | | 999 | |
| 101 | | | | F | | V | | | | | 999 | |
| 101 | | | E | B | | | | | | | 101 | |
| 101 | | | E | B | | E | | | | | 101 | |
| 101 | | | E | B | | P | | | | | 101 | |
| 101 | | | E | B | X | | | | | | 101 | |
| 101 | | | E | B | X | E | | | | | 101 | |
| 101 | | | E | B | X | P | | | | | 101 | |
| 101 | | | E | F | | | | | | | 101 | |
| 101 | | | E | F | | E | | | | | 101 | |
| 101 | | | E | F | | P | | | | | 101 | |
| 101 | | | Q | B | | | | | | | 101 | |

**Figure 13.13** Change Update Control

The system contains a total of 77 variants of movement type 101. Fortunately, it is possible to use various selection functions from the menu bar to select, maintain, or switch multiple entries with the required inspection lot origin simultaneously.

All entries with inspection lot origin 01, GOODS RECEIPT are replaced with inspection lot origin 89, OTHER. When saving the settings, the system issues a warning "Caution when changing [entry belongs to SAP]," but it allows the user to perform the changes with the comment "Only for absolutely required changes."

Further tests provide preliminary confirmation of the success of the measures and prove that all of the requirements have been met. In the next step, the settings are released for an integration test. To ensure that the settings do not have any unwanted consequences, a request was sent to the development department to test for this possibility. The response was sobering. The changes made could lead to inconsistencies in inventory management. At the same time, a perfectly acceptable proposal is made for a separately purchased enhancement to the desired requirements. However, this procedure would have clashed with the basic project goal that was to use only original programs.

#### New Solution with Manual Inspection-Lot Creation and Additional Program

The settings made are reset to the delivery standard. At the moment, it is only possible to use inspection type 89, OTHER INSPECTIONS because this is not stock-relevant. This inspection type is used as a copy template for an additional inspection type 90, FIRST SAMPLING. You configure a separate planned usage for each inspection type. This ensures that the correct inspection plan is used when an inspection lot is created.

For a later phase of QM implementation, a simple additional program then takes over inspection-lot creation during goods receipt posting.

This example should show how interconnected the Customizing areas are with the different business operations. When difficult changes are involved, it is very important that you discuss the integration with representatives from the technical departments involved, in addition to contacting SAP development.

### 13.5.2 Customizing of "Maintaining Number Ranges"

An important task when configuring a new system is the setup of various number ranges. Among others, the following number ranges are particularly important for QM:

- Material numbers
- Inspection plan numbers
- Task list numbers
- Equipment numbers
- General task list numbers
- Maintenance plan numbers
- Quality notification numbers

In general, a distinction is made between *internal number assignment* and *external number assignment*. "Internal" number assignment means that the system assigns numbers from a specific range (from the reserved number range) in ascending order. "External" number assignment, however, means that the user assigns the numbers, although the allowed number range can still be preconfigured.

To ensure a clear and logical assignment, as well as an easy transition from any previously existing system to the new system, you should consider the following:

- Is there already a defined number range in the existing system?
- Do I want to keep using these numbers?
- Do I want to use "key numbers"?
- Are there relationships between the different number categories?

When investigating solution options, you can also consider mixed solutions. This means that you can adopt the numbering from the existing system first, and then continue working with the internal number assignment.

You have already seen an example of "key numbers" and learned about the mutual relationships between number categories in Chapter 11, Test Equipment Management. In the scenario presented there, the number of the maintenance plan was assigned externally (i.e., by the user), so that it consisted of both the material and the serial number.

A well-planned and structured system for number ranges and a careful combination of internal and external number assignment makes your work in the system much easier later on and increases acceptance with employees.

*During the transition from an already existing system (legacy system) to an SAP ERP system, you need to consider how data is transferred to the new system. This chapter outlines how you should proceed and which options are available.*

# 14 Migration Concepts

The transition of a high volume of master data should be ensured at an early stage by the overall project management because this data is interesting for the Quality Management department and many other persons within the enterprise. This does not apply to inspection plans. Provided that such inspection plans have already been created in the legacy system, they should not be reentered manually. This chapter outlines the options to effectively migrate existing inspection plans into the SAP ERP system.

## 14.1 Basic Principles

Implementation of SAP QM means that you must now transfer your previous data stock from the environment of quality planning to the SAP ERP system. The most important objects are inspection plans and possibly the vendor quality level. There is a precondition, however, that the structures of the transfer objects should be similar to a certain degree. You should check this point upfront with particular care. In most cases, transferring results from inspections is not absolutely necessary and is also very difficult.

Data transfer requires a well thought out concept. The following sections should be understood as tasks to be processed in the listed sequence as far as possible. Other tools are the SAP guidebook SAP *Initial Data Transfer Made Easy* [SAP AG99], the *Initial Batch Input Program* (IBIP) described in this chapter, and the Legacy System Migration Workbench.

## 14.2 Creating a Detailed Definition for the Data Transfer

The purpose of this task is to gain an overview of the data transfer. You define which application system is to be replaced and which data is to be copied.

You must consider the following points:

- Data objects to be transferred
- Transfer method, manual or automatic
- Data quantity and quality in legacy systems
- Throughput and performance of data transfer
- Availability of SAP ERP standard data transfer programs
- Authorization of detailed data transfer draft proposal
- Procedure

You must have a good knowledge of your SAP ERP system to differentiate between which data needs to be transferred (e.g., you need the material with the inspection data but not open inspection orders); and you must also have a good knowledge of the data in your previous system.

If, for example, you want to use the quality level (dynamic modification level) of the SAP ERP system, then you must translate the last status and copy it to the system. You should check the database of your previous system to determine whether this information is available. Knowledge of which data is available can help you to decide how to transfer data to the SAP ERP system. If, for example, you have 5 vendors and 50,000 items in your material master, you enter the vendors manually and transfer the quality level automatically.

This task is described by the automatic data transfer as an effective method for transferring large data quantities to your new system. This method ensures that data is error-free when it is moved to the SAP ERP system. Figure 14.1 displays the steps required for data transfer.

The data from your legacy system must exist in a format that can be read by the SAP ERP system and must be saved in a flat text file. As soon as the data has been formatted, you can import it automatically into the SAP ERP system. This is done by using an *SAP data transfer program* that reads the formatted data and moves it to the SAP ERP system.

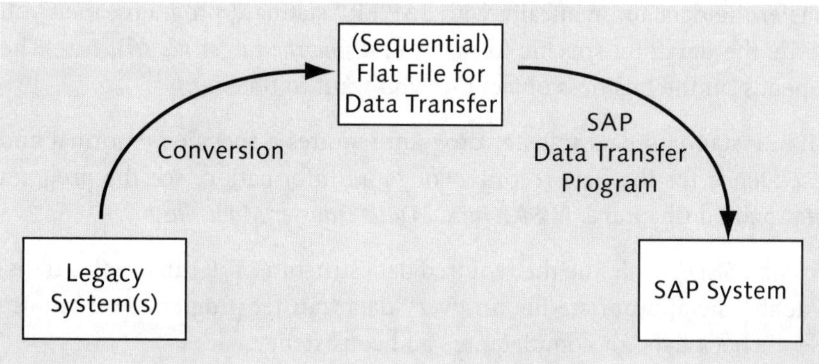


**Figure 14.1** Conversion

Based on conversion requirements, the *transfer method* must be defined for every business object. The following data transfer options are available for each business object:

- Use SAP standard data transfer programs.
- Enter data manually via online transactions.
- Create batch input programs for the data transfer.

SAP *Initial Data Transfer Made Easy* contains advice on how to decide which method to use (Chapter 3, Section "How To"). The data transfer method you choose determines the required resources (e.g., personnel for manual data entry or programmers who write routines). The "How To" section provides an assessment of the time required for each transfer method. You must know what data the previous system contains, and you must be familiar with the SAP application assigned to the business objects to be transferred.

Create a business object (e.g., an inspection plan) in the SAP ERP system to determine which data needs to be transferred. Working with the system and with the field help documentation will familiarize you with the business object. This makes it easier for you to *define fields*.

When you are creating the object, you will learn which fields are required. If you do not enter data in these fields, then you cannot save the object or proceed to the next screen.

If you transfer the data automatically with SAP ERP standard programs, then you must provide the data in a specific format and *define the target file structure*. The format depends on the business object that you want to transfer.

Every SAP ERP standard data transfer program requires a specific file format and a certain sequence for the data records. For more information, see the program documentation and Chapter 2 in SAP *Initial Data Transfer Made Easy*.

Use Transaction SXDA to define the required data structure. You can use this transaction to define the appropriate file for every data transfer program. You can use the flat file to check data for completeness and consistency.

You have two options for the value of each field: define a value or don't make an entry. There are two methods for not entering a value in a field:

- Entering a RESET value that will initialize or delete the value of a field
- Entering a NODATA value to retain the original value of the field

The SAP ERP standard data transfer programs use "/" for the NODATA value and a space for the RESET value.

When you define the target file structure, you must adapt the required fields in every screen to the *fields in the flat file*. The flat file uses the same or similar field names as the online transaction.

Because of the wide variety of possible systems, SAP cannot provide expert knowledge on every single legacy system. Consequently, you must define which data is relevant and available for your purposes. Your previous system may contain functions or a Report Writer that enables you to retrieve data in the required flat format. The quality of the data in your legacy system is important. If, for example, it contains data fields that have not been maintained, errors may occur during the execution of the data transfer program. Pay attention to the number of data records. This influences the runtime of the data transfer programs. The number of data records can serve as the basis for calculating the entire runtime if you perform speed tests with a portion of the data records.

If you are familiar with the data in both systems, you can *assign legacy data to the SAP fields*. Legacy data is used to assign matching fields, as well as field values that need to be changed. For example, in the SAP ERP system, you use "lb" for "pound" instead of "1" in the legacy system. If you're using the manual entry method, you do not assign the data to the flat file; instead, you format the data so that someone can enter it in the system.

After the preceding analysis you will get the following results:

- Data transfer method
- Detailed definition of the data fields to be transferred
- Legacy data assigned to the SAP ERP data objects
- Number of data records to be copied
- Data quality
- Detailed data transfer concept

## 14.3 Creating Data Transfer Programs

The purpose of this task is to develop the programs required for automatic data transfer. Extract the data from your legacy system and provide it in the structure required by the SAP ERP system transfer program. Note that creating and testing transfer programs can take a long time.

Decide how you want the data to be extracted from the legacy system to transfer every business object automatically. If there is no standard data transfer program (see Appendix A to SAP *Initial Data Transfer Made Easy*), you must develop a batch input program to transfer the data to the SAP ERP system.

You can use a *programming language* (ABAP, COBOL, etc.) to provide the required data format. If you use ABAP/4, you must define the appropriate structure to add the data to the ABAP Dictionary. Appendix B of SAP *Initial Data Transfer Made Easy* contains an example (pseudo code9).

If you are using C, COBOL, PL/1, or P_RPG, you can use Report RDDSRCG0 to define the required flat file structures in the required language format.

An ABAP data transfer program consists of the following three steps:

- **The flat file is read from the legacy system.**
  The flat file from the legacy system is provided in text format or stored in a Microsoft Excel table, and the data is saved in sequential data records with the

specified structure. It is imported record-by-record by the ABAP/4 conversion program from a PC or UNIX directory to an internal table. The structure of the internal table is the same as the flat file structure and allows direct access to individual fields in each data record.

- **All of the data fields in a data record are assigned to the corresponding data fields in the SAP ERP system.**
  During this process, field formats can be changed, and you can include subprograms that confirm data validity or convert data values. In this way, you can adapt units of measure, for example, to the Customizing settings. This ensures the proper operation of batch input or direct input programs.

  The program documentation describes the data formats required by batch input or direct input programs. They require a precise sequence of data records with different data structures. The different data record formats are defined by the SAP ERP tables (e.g., BGR00).

- **A flat file is issued for batch input or direct input.**
  The data records created by the conversion programs are saved in another flat file, which is used by SAP ERP batch input or direct input programs.

Chapter 2 of SAP *Initial Data Transfer Made Easy – Guidebook* describes data structures for business objects. You can also use Transaction SXDA to create an example of a data record sequence. This helps you become familiarize with the required formats and the sequence of data records created by the data transfer program. The appendix to *SAP Initial Data Transfer Made Easy* provides an example of a data transfer program.

Make use of any *database tools* that the existing system might have for converting data into the correct format. Choose an external tool that meets your requirements. If an automatic transfer is required, and no standard program is provided, you should develop a batch input program. As a result, you can now use data conversion programs that correspond to the definitions given in Section 14.2, Creating a Detailed Definition for the Data Transfer.

**Tip**

Make sure that every data field is converted correctly. Correct field formats are important (e.g., to prevent fields from being truncated).

## 14.4 Performing Manual Data Transfers

The purpose of this task is to develop reliable procedures for manual data transfer. Some of the old data must be transferred manually to your SAP ERP system. You must ensure the correctness and completeness of all manually transferred data.

The process for transferring manual data is as follows:

1. Create a list of data records for every business object that must be entered manually in the SAP ERP system.
2. Use the SAP ERP transactions for the data entry. Sort the data list in the same sequence as the sequence in which the data must be entered into the SAP ERP system.
3. Ensure that all required data is contained in the list.

The data records must have the format required by the SAP ERP transaction to prevent errors in data entry. The result is a detailed, manual conversion procedure.

## 14.5 IBIP Program for Data Transfer

Transaction IBIP is used in the Plant Maintenance (PM) and Service components for transferring master data. In QM, you can use the functions of IBIP, if you make your own adjustments for migrating test equipment, inspection plan data, and quality notifications. The following description contains the most important information from the original SAP ERP documentation.

#### Description Validity

This description applies to the following transactions/functions:

- Transaction IBIP
- Function module IBIP_BATCH_INPUT_RFC
- IBIP_BATCH_INPUT
- Transaction SA38 with ABAP RIIBIP00

The functions listed provide the same options but are started/called differently.

### General Use of Transaction IBIP

In general, follow these steps to use Transaction IBIP:

1. Create source data. You can do this either with external tools, such as Microsoft Access, or by using the data maintenance functions.
2. Define an execution mode. You have the following options:
   - Call Transaction starts the application transaction immediately to perform the data transfer.
   - BDC session (indirect) first creates a session.
   - You must then use Transaction SM35 (see the PROCESS SESSION option in Figure 14.2) to download the session to perform the data transfer. Direct input creates the required object directly with the help of function modules. This system does not generally display a dialog box. Error-free data is written directly from the function module to the database.

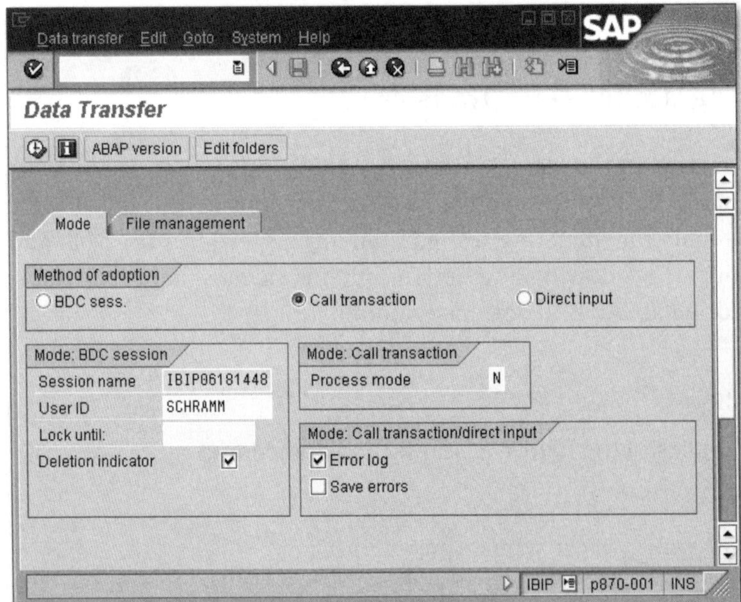


**Figure 14.2** Data Transfer with IBIP

3. Define the source file and the target file. This definition must include the path of your file and the data origin (see Figure 14.3). If you want to save the transactions with errors, you must specify a target file.
4. Execute the transaction.

For more detailed information, select the corresponding field, and press F1.

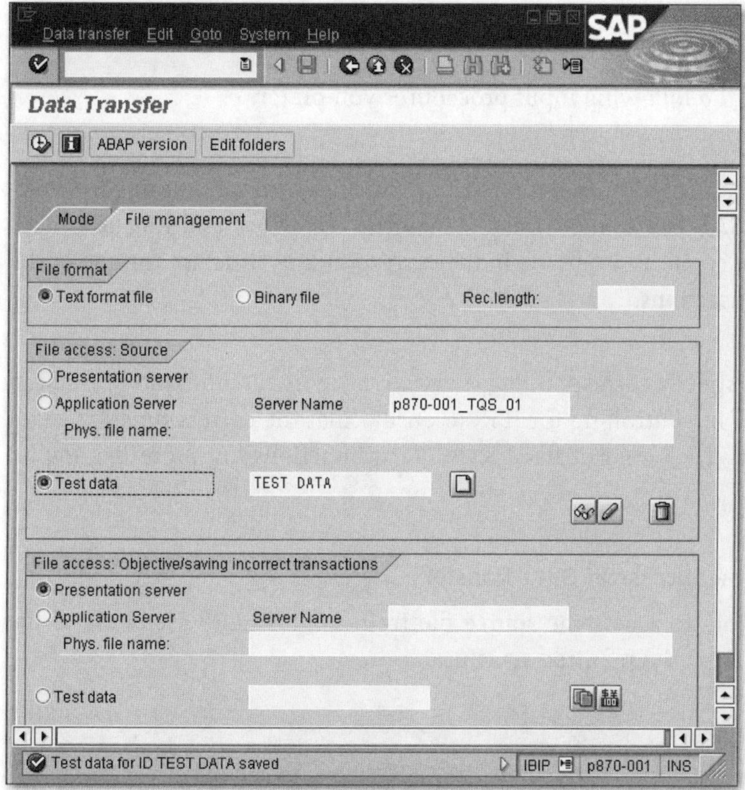


**Figure 14.3** File Management for Test Data (Source File)

### Differences Between Transaction IBIP and ABAP Version RIIBIP00

Transaction IBIP provides test tools and allows you to work interactively with data. Incorrect input data can be corrected immediately. ABAP version RIIBIP00 enables you to create a background job to perform data transfer regularly and with a fixed configuration.

#### Note on the Source File

Remember that it is neither useful nor possible to use the presentation server as a source if you start RIIBIP00 as a batch job. In this case, there is no active presentation server and therefore no active dialog box. This means that in this case files cannot be read directly from the presentation server. In the event of a batch job, you must select a source file from an application server.

#### Batch Input or Direct Input?

Decide which of the following input procedures you prefer:

- **Batch input**
  RIIBIP00 is a general tool for data transfer, which is used for entering information into the SAP ERP system using standard transactions and function modules. You must create an input file in the corresponding structure for one of the supported transactions.
- **Direct input**
  You must also specify corresponding transactions in direct input mode. You can use these keys in controlling for IBIP to ensure that the correct function modules are called. They are not fixed SAP ERP transactions but more like logical transactions.

#### Prerequisites for a Successful Data Transfer

It must be possible to access the source file from the SAP ERP system, and the source file must have the required structure.

> **Tip**
>
> If you select the TEST DATA option in FILE MANAGEMENT and then double-click on the paper icon right next to the TEST DATA input field, the system will display the next screen for transferring test data. You must fill the fields TRANSACTION CODE and RECORD NAME with the appropriate catalog entries. When you select EDIT RECORD, the system displays an input screen with the fields from the selected record name (in this example, this is TASK LIST HEADER) (see Figure 14.4). The record name IBIPTLST can be used as a template for transferring inspection plan data because the structures are quite similar (see Section 14.5, Customer Exit).

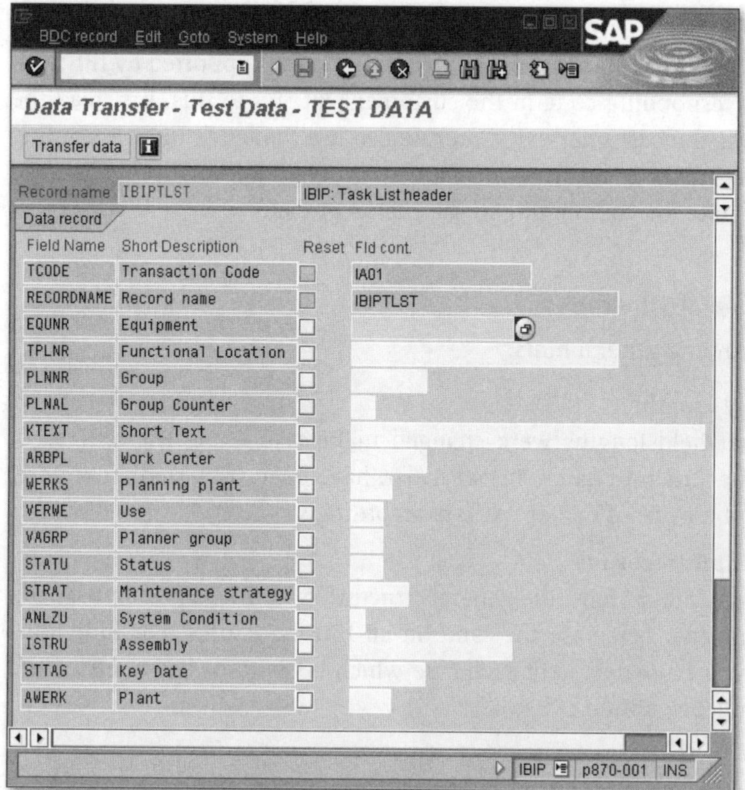


**Figure 14.4** Structure of a Test Data Record

## RFC

If you are using function module IBIP_BATCH_INPUT_RFC via RFC, make sure that DIALOG is supported because this is frequently not enabled. This often requires a local SAP GUI. If DIALOG is not supported, then you must set the parameter IBIPPARMS-DARK to X (see the function module interface). When using RFC, problems can arise if the source file is not INT_TAB. For this reason, you should use the INT_TAB option, where possible.

## Output

To save the records immediately, the system outputs a batch input group with the corresponding name, a call transaction, or direct input.

### Customer Exit

If you prefer to use a transaction for data transfer that is not supported by IBIP, you can enter the corresponding code in the customer exit. To do this, first read the documentation for the customer exit. You can also use the batch input recording tool (Transaction SHDB) to create a data transfer program automatically. You can use this as a template for your coding in the customer exit.

### Notes on the General Structure

Consider the following general hints:

- **Change to field lengths**
  Remember that field lengths were changed in Release 4.0A. The lengths of TCODE and the structure name, in particular, have been increased. Therefore, you must adapt files from earlier releases accordingly.
- **Structure of input records**
  All input records should have the general structure of IBIPREC (see Transaction SE12). The first two fields are the same in all IBIP structures. For individual transactions, you must decide in each case which fields must have entries and which you can leave unfilled.
- **TCODE**
  The TCODE (transaction code) can be specified only for the first record of the transaction.
- **RECORDNAME**
  The RECORDNAME must be specified for every record of the input file. The sequence of the records in the input file is important. Make sure that you follow the hierarchical structures in exactly the same way as specified in Section 14.5, under Direct Input as well as Batch Input and Call Transaction.
- **Initial fields**
  Initial fields in structures are generally not transported to the corresponding screen field. Therefore, empty fields are usually ignored. If you want to explicitly reset the value of a field to <empty>, you must indicate the field in the batch input structure with the value "!". This is the reset character and means that a field is reset to its initial value. These rules also apply to radio buttons and checkboxes.

- **General naming conventions**
  The structure of the individual transactions follows the general naming convention IBIP*xxxx* for direct input IBIP_. As a rule, the change transactions use the same structure as the create transactions. *xxxx* is a general code and represents the record type.

### Date and Time Fields

Date fields in the batch input structures must be entered in the format YYYYMMDD. The system checks the date format defined for the currently logged-on user (e.g., DD.MM.YYYY), and this is reflected on the screen. Time fields must have the format HHMMSS and are also changed in accordance with user-specific settings.

### Size Restrictions

If you want to transport several thousand records using this ABAP report, contact your system administrator to discuss the available PAGING area for the machine on which you are going to run the report. Every record requires 2KB. If the report terminates due to size, paging, or roll area problems, try loading several smaller input files, rather than one big one.

### Case Sensitivity

Transactions and record names must be in capital letters.

### Key to Direct Input, Batch Input, and Call Transaction Descriptions

The key for the following sections is as follows:

- "0 or more occurrences of an expected/allowed record"
- "0 or exactly 1 occurrence of an expected/allowed record"

### Direct Input

- Transaction NOTI_CREATE – Create Notification
  - Structure – IBIP_NOTI_CREATE – single record, single notification
  - IBIP_TEXT – Long text for the notification header
  - IBIP_PART – Partner for the notification

- IBIP_NOTI_ACTIVITY – Activities for the notification header
- IBIP_TEXT – Long text for the activity
- IBIP_NOTI_TASK – Tasks for the notification header
- IBIP_TEXT – Long text for the task
- IBIP_NOTI_ITEM – Items for the notification
- IBIP_TEXT – Long text for the item
- IBIP_NOTI_CAUSE – Cause for the item
- IBIP_TEXT – Long text for the cause
- IBIP_NOTI_ACTIVITY – Activities for the item
- IBIP_TEXT – Long text for the activity
- IBIP_NOTI_TASK – Tasks for the item
- IBIP_TEXT – Long text for the task
- Comment for IBIP_TEXT: The field TEXT_MARK is not needed here.

- Transaction EQUI_CREATE – Create equipment
- Structure – IBIP_EQUI_CREATE – Equipment record
- Transaction ONF_CREATE – Create confirmation for PM order
- Structure – IBIP_CONF_CREATE
  - IBIP_CONF_CREATE
  - You can make several confirmations within a transaction. For this reason, IBIP_CONF_CREATE can be used several times.
- Transaction CONF_CANCEL – Cancel confirmation for PM order
- Structure – IBIP_CONF_CANCEL
- Transaction MEDO_CREATE – Create measurement document
- Structure – IBIP_MEDO_CREATE

**Note**

If you want to transfer data with direct input, you must format your data in the internal format (pay attention to leading zeros and capitalization). Transaction IBIP allows you to call a conversion tool in FILE MANAGEMENT. You can use this tool to convert your data into the internal data format.

**Batch Input and Call Transaction**

- Transaction IE01 – Create equipment
- Transaction IE02 – Change equipment
  - Structure – IBIPEQUI – Equipment record
  - IBIPNSTA – New status profile, if necessary
  - IBIPSTAT – User status records
  - IBIPDOCU – Document Management System (DMS)
  - IBIPPART – Partner details
  - IBIPTEXT
  - For the long text: TEXT_MARK = " " (blank)
  - For internal memo: TEXT_MARK = "1"
  - IBIPCLAS – Classification record (EqmtClass)
  - IBIPFEAT – Class attributes, that is, all characteristics for class IBIPBDCD (see below; from dynpro 102)
- Transaction IL01 – Create functional location
- Transaction IL02 – Change functional location
  - Structure – IBIPFLOC – Functional location
  - IBIPNSTA – New status profile, if necessary
  - IBIPSTAT – User status records
  - IBIPDOCU –DMS
  - IBIPPART – Partner details
  - IBIPTEXT
  - IBIPCLAS – Classification record
  - IBIPFEAT – Class attributes, that is, all characteristics for the class
  - BIPBDCD (from dynpro SAPMILO0 2120)
- Transaction IN04 – Create object link (functional locations)
- Transaction IN05 – Change object link (functional locations)
- Transaction IN07 – Create object link (equipments)
- Transaction IN08 – Change object link (equipments)

- Structure — IBIPOLNK — Object link
- IBIPNSTA — New status profile, if necessary
- IBIPSTAT — User status records
- IBIPDOCU —DMS
- IBIPTEXT
- IBIPCLAS — Classification record
- IBIPFEAT — Class attributes, that is, all characteristics for the class

- Transaction IP04 — Create maintenance plan item
  - Structure — IBIPMPOS — Maintenance plan item
  - IBIPTEXT
  - IBIPOLST — Object list
  - IBIPBDCD (from item data)
- Transaction IP01 — Create maintenance plan
  - Structure — IBIPMPLA — Maintenance plan
  - IBIPMPOS — Maintenance plan item
  - IBIPTEXT
  - IBIPOLST — Object list
  - IBIPBDCD (from maintenance plan item)

**Tip**

The system supports only maintenance plan types for which the call object is first. The data for the data transfer must comply with the corresponding view of the reference object specified in the maintenance plan type definition. The view of the reference object using IBIP cannot be changed.

- Transaction IP10 — Schedule maintenance plan
  - Structure — IBIPCALL — Maintenance call (standard IP30)
  - Structure — IBIPMPST — Restart maintenance plan/start in cycle
- Transaction IA01 — Create equipment task list
- Transaction IA11 — Create functional location task list

- Transaction IA05 – Create general task list
  - Structure – IBIPTLST – Task list header
  - IBIPTEXT
  - IBIPTLOP – Operations
  - IBIPTEXT
  - IBIPTMAT – Material for an operation
  - IBIPPRTS – Production resource/tool
  - LONGTEXT
  - IBIPMPAC – Maintenance packages/up to 32
  - IBIPBDCD – From operation overview
- Transaction IK01 – Create measuring point
- Structure – IBIPMEAS – Measuring point details
  - IBIPTEXT
  - IBIPBDCD
- Transaction IK11 – Create measurement document
  - Structure – IBIPMVAL – Measurement document
  - IBIPTEXT
  - BIPBDCD (from dynpro SAPLIMR0 5210)
- Transaction MB11 – Goods movement
- Structure – IBIPGISS – Goods movement. Supported movement types are: the following
  - 221 Use for project from warehouse
  - 222 Use for project from warehouse – cancellation
  - 261 Use for order from warehouse
  - 262 Use for order from warehouse – cancellation
  - 281 Use for network from warehouse
  - 282 Use for network from warehouse – cancellation
  - 501 Receipt without purchase order to unrestricted-use
  - 502 Receipt without purchase order to unrestricted-use – cancellation

- 531 Receipt of by-product to unrestricted-use
- 532 Receipt of by-product to unrestricted-use – cancellation
- 581 Receipt of by-product to unrestricted project from network
- 582 Receipt of by-product from network – cancellation

Ensure that you always set the movement type and that you also transfer either the reservation number or the material number and corresponding account assignment (e.g., movement type 261 with an entry in the field for the order number [AUFNR]).

### IBIPBDCD for Batch Input and Call Transaction

IBIPBDCD is used for direct delivery of BDCDATA or input of BDCDATA commands (IBIPFUNCT field for commands). If you want to use screens or functions that are not supported by the standard, you can enter the BDCDATA directly in the source file. The IBIPBDCD records are not processed but are forwarded as BDCDATA in unchanged format. This means that you can enhance the standard batch input processes without having to change or create new programs. Batch input sets up records with structure BDCDATA. These records describe which screens and which fields are going to be sent. You can specify the formatted dynpros directly using IBIPBDCD. For example, IBIPBDCD has the structure TCODE_SPAC, RECORDNAME, IBIPFUNCT, and BDCDATA.

To use IBIPBDCD records, proceed as follows:

1. Leave TCODE_SPAC empty.
2. Set RECORDNAME to IBIPBDCD.
3. Provide the DATA_AREA with the structure of BDCDATA.

You can either leave the field IBIPFUNCT empty, or you can fill it with the following commands:

- **" " (blank)**
  No function. This is the usual case. IBIPBDCD is interpreted purely as BDCDATA and is used unchanged as BDCDATA for the transaction call. For more information, see structure BDCDATA.

- **GOTO**
  With function code in IBIPBDCD-FVAL, go to dynpro IBIPBDCD-PROGRAM IBIPBDCD-DYNPRO. This means that the function IBIPBDCD-FVAL is triggered. The subsequent dynpro is IBIPBDCD-PROGRAM IBIPBDCD-DYNPRO. If you do not set IBIPBDCD-PROGRAM or IBIPBDCD-DYNPRO, the running DYNPRO (e.g., PROGRAM) is used. You can use PUSH and POP to flag and retrieve a dynpro.
- **DYNP**
  The subsequent dynpro is IBIPBDCD-PROGRAM IBIPBDCD-DYNPRO.
- **FUNC**
  The function IBIPBDCD-FVAL is executed. The subsequent dynpro is the running dynpro.
- **FLD**
  In the running dynpro, FIELD IPBDCD-FNAM should be filled with the value IBIPBDCD-FVAL.
- **ENTR**
  Data is released to the running dynpro. The subsequent dynpro is the running dynpro.
- **PUSH**
  Flag the running dynpro in stack
- **POP**
  Fetch the running dynpro from stack
- **CURS**
  Position the cursor on field IBIPBDCD-FVAL.

You can use structure IBIPTEXT or IBIP_TEXT to transfer the individual text lines of a *long text*.

**Note**

The IBIPTEXT records (IBIP_TEXT records) must follow the corresponding object in the text file. A long text for a header record should, for example, follow immediately after the header record in the source file for the data transfer. If an additional comment TEXT_MARK is defined, more than one long text is possible for a structure. This text ID is used to separate the texts. In this case, the field TEXT_MARK must be set. In all other cases, the field TEXT_MARK is ignored because only one long text is possible.

If you specify an IBIPPART record, then all existing *partners* are deleted. Therefore, you must specify all partners every time, as soon as a partner (IBIPPART record) is involved.

#### Classification: Classes and Attributes

The structure IBIPCLAS only enables the assignment of a new class. If you want to change the attributes for an existing class, you must first delete the class with the record IBIPCDEL and then, in another transaction, reassign the class using IBIP-CLAS and the attributes using IBIPFEAT.

> **A Note on the Class Type**
>
> Within a transaction, you can edit only the classes for one class type. You cannot change the class type. For classification and attribute transfer, you can also use the corresponding data transfer programs. You can find these programs in Transaction sxda, under data transfer objects 0130, 0140, and 0150.

#### Test Help 1

Transaction IBIP (data transfer) allows you to record test data. You can use this option to test values in the input structures immediately and to find out which values belong to which fields. You can export the test data as a text file and then compare it with your data transfer file.

#### Test Help 2

Transaction IBIP allows you to create test data. You can use Report RIACCESS to download DDIC structures to a Microsoft Access database. You can then create simple test data and export it (see menu option EXPORT TABLE in Access). You must use the DEFINED FORMAT option to get the expected structure (i.e., your test file should have a structure that corresponds to that of the preceding example). You cannot format the source file for batch input with " " (space) or other *delimiters*.

## 14.6 Legacy System Migration Workbench for Data Transfer

The Legacy System Migration Workbench (LSMW) can be reached using Transaction LSMW. You don't require any programming knowledge to work with this workbench. All basic functions can be called via the menu. However, a migration project may quickly involve more complex requirements that require individual ABAP programming.

In LSMW, you are provided with various standard input objects that you can use to migrate master and transaction data. For the QM module, the object 0240 Inspection Plan (QM) is available. Note the following restrictions that apply if you work with the standard SAP objects for inspection plans (QM):

- For importing long texts, the number of characters is limited to a maximum of 72 per line. If the text is longer, you must distribute it to multiple lines.
- Fields that are displayed depending on control indicators, for example, limits or characteristic attributes, cannot be filled if the control indicator is not set already in a master inspection characteristic. Control indicators in inspection plans are only set after the settings for quantitative or qualitative data have been implemented.

Additional QM data objects can be loaded into the SAP ERP system by means of individual recordings.

Using LSMW, data is not directly written in the respective tables of the database. Instead, all inspections are performed for batch input and direct input, which are also implemented in online transactions. Invalid data is not transferred into the system. For batch input, the system creates sessions that can then be processed. Here, the individual screen templates are implemented, and the data is checked through the dynpro logic. The use of sessions allows for a relatively easy rework because they can be reprocessed. For direct input, data is checked by means of function modules and then written in the database.

Before you initiate the data migration, you should familiarize yourself with the transaction for creating the respective migration object. For inspection plans, for instance, this is Transaction QP01.

### 14.6.1 Working with the Standard Object for Inspection Plans

In the initial screen of LSMW, enter the Project, Subproject, and Object of the migration. These fields can be filled with any content. You should consider in advance how you want to structure your migration project.

The standard object for inspection plans works with a batch input and includes 14 main steps. However, you can readily supplement this view with additional steps under EXTRAS • PERSONAL MENU. Among others, you can also display the ABAP conversion program.

### 14.6.2 Data Migration in 14 Steps

In the following section, you are provided with a description of the most important steps for data migration using LSMW (see Figure 14.5).

Process Step

- 1 Maintain Object Attributes
- 2 Maintain Source Structures
- 3 Maintain Source Fields
- 4 Maintain Structure Relations
- 5 Maintain Field Mapping and Conversion Rules
- 6 Maintain Fixed Values, Translations, User-Defined Routines
- 7 Specify Files
- 8 Assign Files
- 9 Read Data
- 10 Display Read Data
- 11 Convert Data
- 12 Display Converted Data
- 13 Create Batch Input Session
- 14 Run Batch Input Session

**Figure 14.5** Work Steps in LSMW

#### Maintain Object Attributes

Select Standard batch/direct input as the OBJECT TYPE AND IMPORT TECHNIQUE, and enter the value "0240 Inspection Plan (QM)" for the OBJECT. By using the F4 help for the next field, all other fields are filled automatically.

#### Maintain Source Structures

The source structure is used to introduce the import files and their interrelations in SAP ERP. The source structure can appear as follows: the topmost level includes the plan header to which the material assignment is subordinated. The material assignment, in turn, includes operations, and the lowest level contains the inspection characteristics (see Figure 14.6). If you want to import long texts, you require a separate source structure.

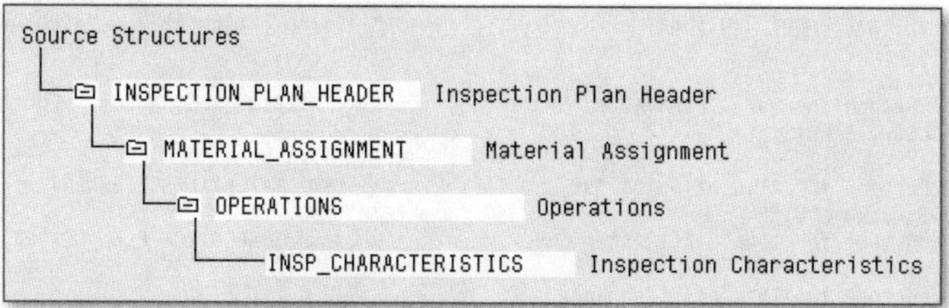


**Figure 14.6** Defining the Source Structures

> **Tip**
>
> By means of LSMW, you cannot import inspection plans without material assignment. You may need to use a dummy material number (pseudo material for data migration without any further function), if no material assignment exists.

### Maintain Source Fields

The source fields are all fields from the legacy system that you want to load into the SAP ERP system. These are assigned to the respective source structure. If an extract already exists, the simplest option is to copy the source fields from this data file. The file must include the field names in the first line, and the data must be separated by tabulators. You can also enter all source fields manually.

If a source field is saved, its length is saved as well. It is therefore important to always update the source fields if a new extract was created. Otherwise, old lengths are used, and information may be truncated. Before you can copy the source fields again, you must first delete the old source fields. The fastest way to delete them is to use the table view.

> **Tip**
>
> Double-clicking a source fields takes you to the CHANGE SOURCE FIELD window. In this window under SELECTION PARAMETER set the checkmark for IMPORT/CONVERT DATA to limit the data based on this parameter during import and conversion.

### Maintain Structure Relations

You must select the first four target structures. Assign the material-routing assignment to BI000, BI001 (see Figure 14.7). All other assignment result from the descriptions.

```
BI000 Session Record for Data Transfer of Routings                <<<< MATERIAL_ASSIGNMENT    Materia
      Select Target Structure BI000 .

-⊟ BI001 Transaction Header Record for Data Transfer of Routings       <<<< MATERIAL_ASSIGNMENT    Mat
 |        Select Target Structure BI001 .
 |
 |----BIMPL Batch Input Structure for Allocation of Mat. to Task Lists   <<<< MATERIAL_ASSIGNMENT
 |          Select Target Structure BIMPL .
 |--⊞ BIPKO Batch Input Structure for Task List Header                   <<<< INSPECTION_PLAN_HEADER
 |          Select Target Structure BIPKO .
 |--⊞ BIPFL Batch Input Structure for Task List Sequence
 |--⊞ BIPPO Batch input structure for task list operation                <<<< OPERATIONS
 |--⊞ BIPFH Batch Input Struct. for Task List Object Prod. Resource/Tool
 |----BIPMZ Batch input structure for component allocation to task list
 |--⊞ BIPMK Inspection characteristics for batch input of task lists      <<<< INSP_CHARACTERISTICS
```

**Figure 14.7** Defining the Structure Relations

## Maintain Field Mapping and Conversion Rules

Here, you assign the fields of the import file to the fields of the standard object. If the source fields have the same name as the target fields, you can automatically assign them via EXTRAS • AUTO FIELD MAPPING. Under EXTRAS • CHECK NON-ASSIGNED SOURCE FIELDS, you can then check whether a target field was found for every source field. To assign an individual field, position the cursor on a target field, and click the SOURCE FIELD button.

The most important conversion mechanisms are *1:1 transfer* (MOVE), *constants*, which you can determine using the F4 help, and individual *ABAP codes*. MOVE is the default conversion rule after field mapping has been implemented. Double-clicking a target field opens the ABAP Editor.

In the following paragraphs, these functions are described in more detail based on some examples. After mapping, LSMW automatically creates an ABAP code for a 1:1 transfer, in this case, the upper limit (see Figure 14.8).

```
TOLERANZOB                  Upper Specification Limit
                   Source:  INSP_CHARACTERISTICS-TOLERANZOB (TOLERANZOB)
                   Rule  :  Transfer (MOVE)
                   Code:    BIPMK-TOLERANZOB = INSP_CHARACTERISTICS-TOLERANZOB.
```

**Figure 14.8** 1:1 Transfer

Because the input field is displayed on the dynpro for the upper limit only depending on a control indicator, it makes sense to set the checkmark for the ONLY IF SOURCE FIELD IS NOT INITIAL checkbox that is located above the RULE button. This prevents that a nonexisting dynpro field is called which would result in an error message. The code shown in Figure 14.9 is generated.

```
TOLERANZOB          Upper Specification Limit
          Source:   INSP_CHARACTERISTICS-TOLERANZOB (TOLERANZOB)
          Rule :    Transfer (MOVE)
          Code:     if not INSP_CHARACTERISTICS-TOLERANZOB is initial.
                      BIPMK-TOLERANZOB = INSP_CHARACTERISTICS-TOLERANZOB.
                    endif.
```

**Figure 14.9** Conditional Transfer

Values that apply to all plans don't have to be in the data extract but can be entered as constants (see Figure 14.10).

```
PLNTY               Task List Type
          Rule :    Constant
          Code:     BIPKO-PLNTY = 'Q'.
```

**Figure 14.10** Working with Constants

You can select the plan's unit of measure from the assigned material master (see Figure 14.11). Prior to selecting data from the database, you should check in which format data is provided, for example, with leading zeros. The global function SKIP_TRANSACTION enables you to skip the current transaction. This means that if you have created a hierarchical structure, all elements of the structure for this data record are not transferred. The global function SKIP_RECORD is similar and cancels the transfer of the current record.

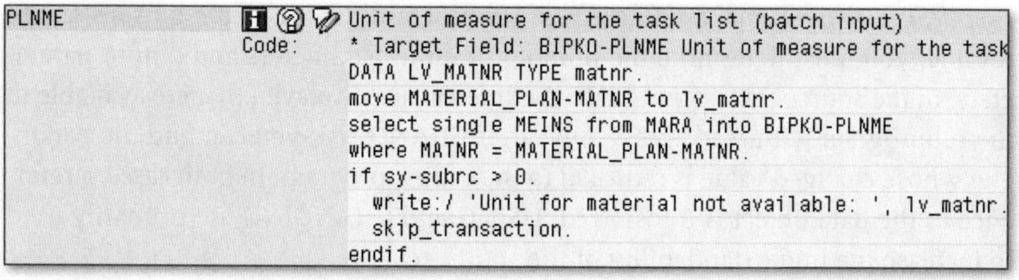

```
PLNME               Unit of measure for the task list (batch input)
          Code:     * Target Field: BIPKO-PLNME Unit of measure for the task
                    DATA LV_MATNR TYPE matnr.
                    move MATERIAL_PLAN-MATNR to lv_matnr.
                    select single MEINS from MARA into BIPKO-PLNME
                    where MATNR = MATERIAL_PLAN-MATNR.
                    if sy-subrc > 0.
                      write:/ 'Unit for material not available: ', lv_matnr.
                      skip_transaction.
                    endif.
```

**Figure 14.11** Selecting the Database

The fields in Table 14.1 need to be maintained as well.

| Target Field | Value |
|---|---|
| START | Lock date of the session in Format YYYYMMDD or 00000000. |
| TCODE | QP01. |
| PLNTY | Q (must be maintained in multiple locations). |
| PROFIDNETZ | Profile with input help. This profile can be created in Customizing under QUALITY MANAGEMENT • QUALITY PLANNING• INSPECTION PLANNING • GENERAL • MAINTAIN PROFILE FOR DEFAULT VALUES. |

**Table 14.1** Mandatory Fields in LSMW

Although LSMW provides comprehensive options for preparing and adapting data, you should consider how you can partly convert it into an SAP ERP format already during the extraction. This way, you can check loaded data more easily and reduce the complexity of programming.

### Maintain Fixed Values, Translations, and User-Defined Routines (Optional)

The central conversion rules are available in all data objects of a project. The definition of these conversion rules must be completed before you can use them in step 5.

*Fixed values* are global constants for a migration object. Here, you must define the length, data type, and value.

*Translations* enable you to work with 1:1 translation values and interval translation values. By cascading the variant, first alternative, and second alternative, it is possible to specify complex rules for data transformation.

*User-defined routines* make up an ABAP subprogram. If you create a user-defined routine, you must determine the number of input parameters and output parameters. In the source text, after USING parameters are displayed that are available in the subprogram with read access only; after CHANGING, you can find the parameter whose changed value is returned to the calling program. In both cases, a reference to the data object is transferred. USING and CHANGING are primarily used to increase the understandability of the source text.

### Specify Files

In this step, you must define the source files and specify the path to all files that are to be read by SAP ERP (see Figure 14.12).

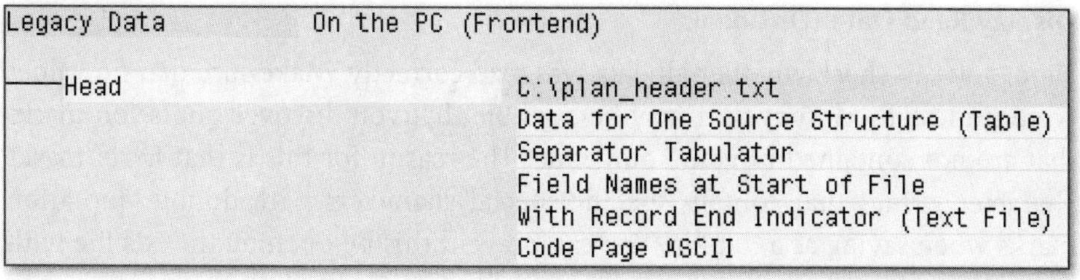

```
Legacy Data            On the PC (Frontend)

——Head                              C:\plan_header.txt
                                    Data for One Source Structure (Table)
                                    Separator Tabulator
                                    Field Names at Start of File
                                    With Record End Indicator (Text File)
                                    Code Page ASCII
```

**Figure 14.12** Publishing the Source Files

It is recommended to use the tabulator as a separator in the source file because other separators, such as commas or semicolons, are often contained in texts. If these are used, they may lead to errors in the identification and separation of individual data records.

### Assign Files

Select one of the previously defined files and assign it to a source structure. Only one file can be assigned to each source structure. If data for a source structure is distributed over multiple files, you must combine it into one file first.

### Read Data

In this step, the source data is imported into the SAP ERP application server. If you only want to read a specific number of data, you can limit the data using the selection parameters. If you marked a source field as a selection parameter during the source fields' definition, this field is now provided as a selection parameter.

If some of the desired data records are not read, this may have several reasons. It is possible that the source data partly does not match due to its structure. For example, there may be a material-routing assignment for which no plan header exists. Furthermore, an unwanted line break in the source file can change the data structure. Because LSMW processes a text file on a line basis, the data set is considered as completed if a line break appears in the text. In Excel, you can find line breaks via the Find and Replace dialog box and key combination Ctrl+J (no search text is displayed).

### Display Read Data (Optional)

Here, you can check whether all data was read correctly. Make sure that no values were truncated. Moreover, it may be possible that you discover quotation marks that are not contained in your source file. The reason for this is that Excel masks character strings that contain specific special characters with double quotation marks when saving as a .txt file. You can prevent this by opening the .xls file with OpenOffice.org Calc and saving it as a .csv file (see Figure 14.13). Any entries in the input field for TEXT DELIMITER must be removed.

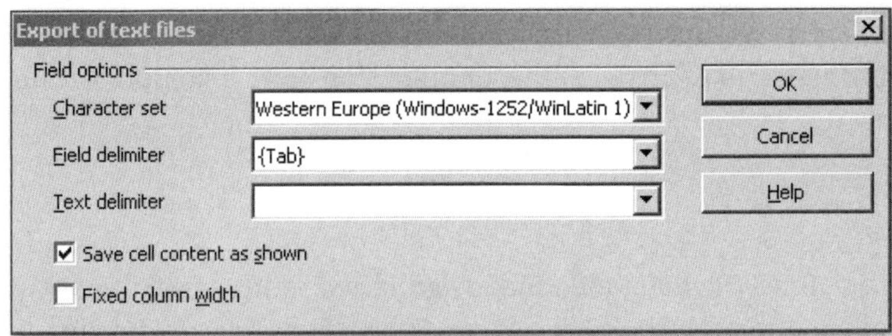


**Figure 14.13** Saving with OpenOffice

Then, you must change the file extension to .txt. A free download of OpenOffice is available under *http://www.openoffice.org/*.

### Convert Data

The read data is now converted according to specified conversion rules. Check your conversion rules if not all data is converted.

### Display Converted Data (Optional)

Here, you check whether all data was converted correctly. Run an example for each conversion rule. Fields in the target structure to which no source field was assigned are filled with the no data character ("/" [slash] by default). The value for the no data character is saved in the variable G_NODATA. If a field in the input file is filled with "/", the corresponding dynpro field is not called during data import. If the field is empty, however, the field is reset to INITIAL in the data record.

### Create Batch Input Session

In this step, you create a batch input session based on the converted data. If, during the inspection plan import, you rely on data that must be maintained separately, for example, master inspection characteristics or a change number, it must now be created at the latest. The error message "Characteristic has not been created yet" can also mean that no plant for the master inspection characteristic was assigned to the target field QPMK_ZAEHL.

### Run Batch Input Session

If you select this step, you navigate to Transaction SM35. Here, select a session, and click the PROCESS button. A window is opened in which you can specify the processing mode (see Figure 14.14).

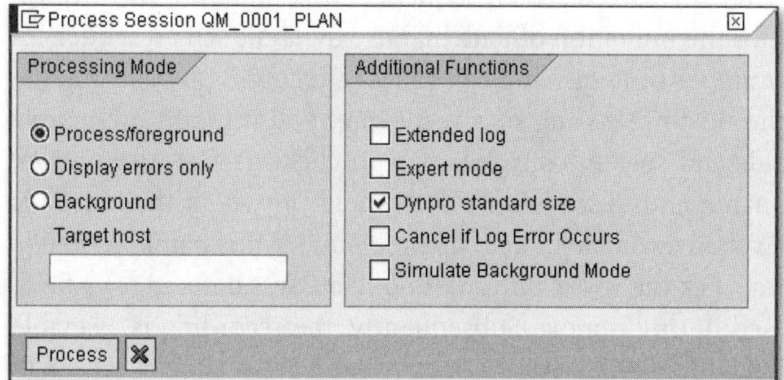


**Figure 14.14** Starting the Batch Input

If you select the PROCESS/FOREGROUND mode, you can view on the screen how the individual dynpro fields are filled. Initially, you can process some records in the foreground to discover possible errors. You can cancel the processing onscreen for a session at any time using Transaction /BEND.

When working with the standard object for inspection plans, you should run sessions in the DISPLAY ERRORS ONLY mode because you can confirm warning messages that would result in errors in the BACKGROUND mode.

If errors occur while processing a session, you can examine them by clicking on the ANALYSIS button. After you have remedied the error, for example, missing Customizing, you can run the session again with the remaining data records.

**Tip**

If you run the PROCESS/FOREGROUND or DISPLAY ERRORS ONLY mode and leave the processing, the system still waits for your input. In this case, you can cancel processing via SESSION • RELEASE and start the session again from the current point.

### 14.6.3 Individual Recordings

The recording function enables you to create user-defined migration structures for almost every transaction. You can find this function on the initial screen of LSMW under GOTO • RECORDING. Use a transaction (e.g., QP02) to select all fields that you want to load by means of LSMW. This way, the number of target fields remains relatively manageable in contrast to standard objects that must consider all fields of a transaction. Note that all entries are updated in the system. If you create a recording, you always record a fixed screen sequence. It is therefore rather difficult to use recordings for the migration of data that use dynamic screen sequences or contain a variable number of items. You can cancel a recording by clicking the disk icon (save). In the post-processing of a recording, you can add or remove individual dynpro fields and specify constants. If you click the DEFAULT button, the system assigns a name and description for the field on which the cursor is positioned. This field is then available in field mapping under this name. To delete a name and description, click the RESET button. If no name was defined for a field, the default value is used during import. Subsequently, the recording is available in the *work step overview* under MAINTAIN OBJECT ATTRIBUTES • OBJECT TYPE AND IMPORT TECHNIQUE • BATCH INPUT RECORDING.

If you want to add data for an inspection plan in Transaction QP02, during the recording creation, you need to set the plan group counter, the operation, and the inspection characteristic to the correct record in the list via the entry selection in the lower part of the screen.

### 14.6.4 Import of Long Texts

In the standard object for migration of inspection plans, you also have the option to import long texts. Additional long texts can be imported using the direct input object 0001 Long Texts. For importing long texts, the number of characters is limited to a maximum of 132 per line. If the text is longer, you must distribute it to multiple lines. The actual content of a long text can be displayed in Transaction

SE37 using the function module READ_TEXT. You obtain the import parameter (ID/LANGUAGE/NAME/OBJECT) for this function module by selecting GOTO • HEADER in the long text display (see Figure 14.15).

| Text Header | | |
|---|---|---|
| Text Name | 310Q5000000100000002 002000000000 | |
| Language | DE | |
| Text ID | QM | Inspection feature long text |
| Text Object | QSS | Inspection feature texts |

**Figure 14.15** Key Fields of an Inspection Feature Long Text

# Appendices

# A Glossary

**ABAP (Advanced Business Application Programming)** SAP-specific programming language used to program the application programs for the SAP ERP system as well as system enhancements and reports. ABAP/4 represents the fourth-generation programming language that is, among other things, object-oriented. From Release 4.6 on, ABAP became ABAP Objects.

**Advanced Planner and Optimizer (APO)** Planning and organization tool from SAP for supply chain management.

**Application Link Enabling (ALE)** Interface tool for asynchronous data exchange.

**Application Service Providing (ASP)** Consulting companies provide preconfigured and quickly usable applications based on SAP ERP modules. To a certain extent, they can be used over the web. Business processes are often completely mapped.

**Balanced Scorecard** Controlling of the company strategy. Summary of financial and process figures and results from the measurement of customer satisfaction and complaints or newly developed products.

**batch** A subset of the total quantity of a material in stock, managed separately from other subsets of the same material.

**batch input** Name for the interface for data transfer. Primarily for the transfer of large quantities of data from the legacy system before the productive start but also for large-scale data imports at a later stage.

**batch master record** If a supplied material or a material from a company's own production is subject to batch management, a batch master record is created. The relevant data for the batch is stored in this master record.

**Business Add-In (BAdI)** A programming interface defined by the developer on which further software layers (e.g., from partners) can be based without changing the original object.

**Business Intelligence (BI)** Summary of all IT instruments. The Data Warehousing, Online Analytical Processing, Data Mining, and Alerting, as well as Business Planning and Solution functions have been summarized in SAP NetWeaver Business Intelligence and are part of SAP NetWeaver.

**business process** A process/business process is a chain of business activities with individual results.

**business-to-business procurement** Procurement between companies via the Internet.

**catalog** Catalogs are used for uniform descriptions of defects, decisions, tasks, and much more. In SAP ERP, there are a great many catalogs in which the user can enter codes and written texts. In addition to the catalog types created by SAP ERP in the standard version, other user-specific catalogs can be added.

**client** A group or composition of legal, organizational, commercial, and administrative units with one shared purpose (e.g., a corporate group). In the context of client-server configurations, the client is the workstation (or PC) on which the graphical user interface (SAP GUI) is installed.

**collaboration** Stronger integration of business transaction processing between companies. This can be achieved by using SAP ERP. The Internet is increasingly incorporated here.

**company code** Smallest organizational unit for which a complete, self-contained set of accounts can be drawn up for purposes of external reporting.

**completion (business)** A function that is executed for a maintenance order if no more cost postings are expected. The business completion of a maintenance order results in the order receiving the status "Completed" indicating that it is locked for all changes in the processing. Business completion can only be performed when the maintenance order has been technically completed.

**completion (technical)** A function that is performed for a maintenance order if the planned tasks it contains have been executed.

The technical completion of a maintenance order results in the following:

- Only certain changes can be made to the order.
- The data is fixed and can no longer be changed.
- Outstanding purchase requisitions, reservations, and so on are deleted.

Maintenance notifications for the order are completed.

**confirmation** Function used to record the drawn materials, working hours used, additional materials required, travel costs incurred, technical findings, and changes made.

**confirmation (technical)** Recording of technical confirmation data. This data includes, for example:

- Cause of damage
- Location of damage on object
- Data about machine failure
- Data about plant availability

Performed actions and findings

**controlling area** Organizational unit within a company used to represent a closed system for cost accounting purposes. A controlling area may include single or multiple company codes that may use different currencies. The associated company codes must use the same operative chart of accounts.

**cost center** Organizational unit within a controlling area representing a defined location of cost incurrence.

**customer master record** This master record contains all of the necessary information about a customer from the point of view of sales and accounting. The customer appears in accounting among accounts receivable.

**Customizing** Setting the SAP ERP system according to company-specific requirements.

**Data Warehouse** Summary of enterprise data.

**dynamic modification, Dynamic modification rule** This permits changes to the inspection severity and sampling scope for an inspection.

**Enterprise Resource Planning (ERP)** Integrated business EDP system (e.g., SAP R/3, now SAP ERP).

**Equipment** An individual, physical object that is maintained as an autonomous unit and that can be installed in a technical asset or subasset. Each piece of equipment is managed in a separate equipment master record. Apart from maintenance, equipment is used in the following areas:

- Production (production resources/tools)
- Quality Assurance (test equipment and measuring devices)
- Material Management (MM) (serialized materials)
- Sales and Distribution (SD) (customer devices)

**Executive Information System (EIS)** Management information system.

**general task list** Standardized sequence of work processes for the execution of specific maintenance work to equipment. The maintenance task list is not connected to a specific item of equipment. It contains all processes, materials, and operating resources that are required for a specific maintenance action.

**histogram** Display of quantitative measured values as a frequency distribution.

**IDES (International Demonstration and Education System)** IDES is the sample company in the SAP ERP system that is set up for training and demonstration.. Some of the screenshots in this book were created using IDES.

**IMG (Implementation Guide).** Tool for customer-specific adjustment of the SAP ERP system. The IMG contains all steps for the implementation of the system, all standard settings, and all activities needed to customize the system.

**inspection instruction** Work paper specifying the inspection characteristics and test equipment for each inspection operation.

**inspection lot** Order to inspect a certain quantity of a material or equipment. Inspection lots can be created automatically or manually. The inspection lot contains important information (e.g., creation date, lot size, sample size, and vendor). It summarizes the data involved in the inspection, such as inspection specifications, inspection results, appraisal costs, and usage decisions.

**inspection plan** Inspection planning records all elements from the area of quality inspection in this plan category. These include, for instance, the inspection steps (operations and characteristics), sampling procedures, test equipment, equipping and inspection times, and inspection work centers.

**inspection severity** Generic term for the different scopes of the inspection depending on the quality level. A distinction is made among reduced, normal, and increased inspections.

**logistics** The logistics chain stretches from raw materials production and procurement across many processes, leading ultimately to the sale of the final product, whether goods or services.

**maintenance plan** A method of describing the scope and schedule for the maintenance and inspection tasks to be performed on technical objects.

A distinction is made between three types of maintenance plans:

- Time-dependent maintenance plans
- Output-dependent maintenance plans
- Multiple counter plans

**A maintenance plan consists of the following:**

- Maintenance schedule
- Maintenance item(s)

**material** Goods that are the subject of a business activity. A material can be purchased, sold, produced, maintained, repaired, or replaced.

**material number** Number that uniquely identifies a material in the SAP ERP system.

**material specification** The material specification can be used instead of an inspection plan or as a supplement to an inspection plan.

**partner** Unit within or outside your own organization, which is of interest from a business point of view and with which a relationship can be set up within the framework of a business activity. A partner can be a person or a legal entity.

Examples of partners include the following:

- Partners within your own organization
- Sales administrators
- Test equipment management representative
- Test equipment user
- Partners outside your own organization
- Customers
- Prospective customers
- Contacts

**plant** Organizational unit in logistics that structures the company. Materials are produced, and goods and services are provided in a plant.

**production resource and tool (PRT)** An operating resource used to shape a material (such as a tool or fixture) or to check its dimensional accuracy, composition, and functional efficiency (such as measurement and test equipment). A PRT can also be a document (such as a drawing) or a program. PRTs are assigned in plans to operations.

**profit center** Organizational unit in accounting, which divides the company with a management orientation, that is, for internal control.

**purchasing organization** Organizational unit within logistics, subdividing an enterprise according to the requirements of purchasing. A purchasing organization procures materials and services, negotiates conditions of purchase with vendors, and bears responsibility for such transactions.

**quality level (Q level)** The quality level is a data record, in which the inspection stage for the next inspection is stored. It creates a reference among the material, dynamification level, and vendors, and contains information such as the number of inspections that were OK, and the number of inspections since the last stage change.

**quality score (QS)** A number calculated for the quality delivered by a vendor. It is determined from the code of the usage decision or from the proportion of defects. Typically, the score is between 1 and 100, where 100 is a very good valuation.

**report** ABAP program that reads data from the database, usually prepares the data, and prepares an output in list form.

**Report Writer** A utility that can be used to create reports for various applications on an individual basis.

**routing** Work preparation collects all elements from the area of work scheduling in this plan category. This includes the work steps (processes), the production resources and tools (PRT), setup and work times, and work centers.

**run chart** Display of the development of values as a curving graph.

**SAA (System Application Architecture) standard** A standard created by IBM, which, among other things, also standardizes the user interface and the arrangement of menu items.

**sample-drawing instruction** Work paper with important information required for the drawing of random samples or physical samples from an inspection lot.

**sampling inspection** Quality inspection based on a sampling instruction for evaluation of an inspection lot.

**sampling instruction** Instruction on the scope of the sample to be drawn.

**sampling procedure** Rule for calculation of the sampling scope.

**sampling scheme** Collection of sampling instructions according to higher-order factors resulting from the sampling system. For example, the acceptable quality limits and the inspection level are used as higher-order factors.

**sampling system** Collection of sampling schemes with rules for their application.

**SAP Business Suite** A complete package of open enterprise solutions that networks all participants, information, and processes to increase the effectiveness of the business relationships. The basis of this solution is SAP NetWeaver.

**SAP Customer Relationship Management (SAP CRM)** This solution maps the business relationships between companies (service, sales, marketing) and their customers.

**SAP Enterprise Resource Planning (SAP ERP)** A comprehensive solution to map financial accounting, human resources management, logistic business processes, and corporate services. The SAP ERP solution forms the foundation for further incremental expansion of the IT landscape. It is possible to supplement SAP ERP with functions for Customer Relationship Management (CRM), Product Lifecycle Management (PLM), Supply Chain Management (SCM), and Supplier Relationship Management (SRM). With SAP NetWeaver as the technological foundation, SAP ERP supports portal technology, business intelligence, knowledge management, and mobile applications.

**SAP NetWeaver** A comprehensive integration and application platform that forms the basis for SAP business solutions and composite applications. SAP NetWeaver enables an Enterprise Services Architecture that combines SAP's decades of enterprise application experience with the flexibility of Web Services and open technologies. With SAP NetWeaver, you can create integrated, service-focused business solutions. The technology brings structured and unstructured information together. Datasets that were previously isolated in various standalone systems can be harmonized using solutions for business intelligence, knowledge management, and SAP Master Data Management (MDM). SAP NetWeaver also uses Internet standards such as HTTP, XML, and Web Services.

**SAP Product Lifecycle Management (SAP PLM)** Control of the entire lifecycle of a product – from its development to procurement and production to customer service.

**SAP Supply Chain Management (SAP SCM)** SAP covers all processes in the entire supply chain with this solution, from supplier to customer.

**SAP Supplier Relationship Management (SAP SRM)** With this tool, SAP provides a range of functions for an optimal supplier management. SAP SRM lets you evaluate your procurement strategy, connect to suppliers, and integrate them in the procurement process, to the benefit of both sides.

**SAPscript** Page description language for structuring texts and forms.

**serial number** A number you assign to an item of material in addition to the material number, to differentiate that item from other items of the material. The combination of material and serial number is unique.

**standard plan** The standard plan contains virtually all of the objects of the task list and the inspection plan. It is used mainly as a plan profile for variations of a plan or as a general template.

**stock type** There are three possible stock types for a material:

- Unrestricted-use stock
- Inspection stock

Blocked stock

**storage location** Organizational unit allowing a differentiation between various material stocks within a plant.

**Strategic Enterprise Management (SEM)** Strategic management on the basis of enterprise data.

**supply chain management** The integration of the entire supply chain from vendor to customer.

**test equipment and measuring devices** Facilities, objects, documents, or substances required before or during the inspection. Test equipment can be fixed facilities of a work center, portable devices, or objects.

In the inspection plan of the SAP ERP system, test equipment can be defined on different levels of detail:

- Group level (product group)
- Material level (material number, type)

**Individual item (equipment)** Test equipment can be maintained using maintenance plans.

**transaction** Logically concluded process in the SAP R/3 system or in the SAP ERP system. From the point of view of the user, a transaction represents a completed application on the user level (e.g., the creation of a list of inspection lots or inspection-lot creation).

**variable inspection** Quality inspection based on quantitative characteristics.

**vendor** Business partner who supplies materials or services for payment. The vendor appears in accounting among accounts payable.

**vendor master record** Data record containing all information necessary for business activities with a vendor. This data includes address data and bank data.

**work center** Organizational unit that defines when and by whom an operation must be performed. The work center has a certain available capacity. The activities performed at or from the work center are valuated by charge rates that are determined by the cost centers and activity types. The following units can be defined as work centers:

- Machines
- People
- Production lines
- Maintenance groups

# B Abbreviations

The acronyms for the SAP components are provided in Table 3.1 of Chapter 3.

| | |
|---|---|
| **ABAP** | Advanced Business Application Programming |
| **ALE** | Application Link Enabling<br>Loose coupling of distributed applications |
| **APO** | Advanced Planner and Optimizer |
| **AQAP** | Allied Quality Assurance Publications |
| **AQL** | Acceptable Quality Level |
| **ASP** | Application Service Providing |
| **BAdI** | Business Add-In |
| **BAPI** | Business Application Programming Interface |
| | Programming interface |
| **BEx** | Business Explorer |
| **BOR** | Business Object Repository |
| **BSC** | Balanced Scorecard |
| **CAQ** | Computer Aided Quality Assurance |
| **CATT** | Computer Aided Test Tool |
| | Utility for testing individual software developments |
| **CIP** | Continuous Improvement Process<br>(KAIZEN) |
| **CRM** | Customer Relationship Management |
| **CSP** | Complementary Software Program<br>Program enhancements provided by software partners |
| **DRM** | Distributor Reseller Management |
| **EAM** | Enterprise Asset Management |
| **eCATT** | Extended Computer Aided Test Tool |
| **EDP** | Electronic Data Processing |
| **EFQM** | European Foundation for Quality Management |

| | |
|---|---|
| **EIS** | Executive Information System |
| **EPC** | Event-driven process chain |
| **ERP** | Enterprise Resource Planning |
| **ESD** | Electro Static Discharge |
| **FDA** | Food and Drug Administration |
| **FIS** | Financial Information System |
| **FMEA** | Failure Mode and Effects Analysis |
| **GMP** | Good Manufacturing Practice<br>Quality requirements of the process industry |
| **GPSG** | German Devices and Product Safety Law |
| **GR** | Goods Receipt |
| **HIS** | Human Resources Information System |
| **IAC** | Internet Application Component<br>SAP transactions for Internet applications |
| **IDES** | International Demo and Education System<br>Completely configured SAP model company |
| **IDI** | Inspection Data Interface<br>Interface for exchanging inspection data |
| **IMG** | Implementation Guide |
| **ISO** | International Organization for Standardization |
| **IT** | Information Technology |
| **JEE** | Java Platform, Enterprise Edition |
| **KVP** | Continuous improvement process (KAIZEN) |
| **LAN** | Local Area Network |
| **LDAP** | Lightweight Directory Access Protocol |
| **LIL** | Logistics Information Library |
| **LIMS** | Laboratory Information and Management System |
| **LIS** | Logistics Information System |
| **MES** | Manufacturing Execution Systems |
| **NOK** | Rejection (error) |

| | |
|---|---|
| **OK** | Acceptance (no defect identified) |
| **OLAP** | Online Analytical Processing |
| **OLTP** | Online Transactional Processing |
| **PDA** | Personal Digital Assistant (Handheld PC) |
| **PDF** | Portable Document Format<br>Adobe Acrobat file format |
| **PRT** | Production resource/tool |
| **QM** | Quality Management |
| **QMIS** | Quality Management Information System |
| **QRK** | Control chart |
| **QS** | Quality score |
| **RFC** | Remote Function Call |
| **SAA** | System Application Architecture |
| **SEM** | Strategic Enterprise Management |
| **SPC** | Statistical Process Control |
| **SQL** | Structured Query Language<br>Query language for relational databases |
| **SSL** | Secure Sockets Layer |
| **STI** | Statistical Data Interface<br>Interface for exchanging statistical data |
| **TLGC** | Task-list group counter |
| **UD** | Usage decision |
| **VDA** | Association of German Automobile Manufacturers |
| **WAN** | Wide Area Network |
| **XML** | Extensible Markup Language |

# C Bibliography

[Hartmann05] Hartmann, G., Schmidt, U. *Product Lifecycle Management with SAP*. Galileo Press, Fort Lee (NJ); Bonn (Germany), 2005.

[ISO00] ISO, International Organization for Standardization. *ISO 9001:2000. Quality Management Systems – Requirements.* Geneva (Switzerland), 2000.

[ISO02] ISO, International Organization for Standardization. *ISO/TS 16949:2002. Quality Management Systems – Particular Requirements for the Application of ISO 9001:2000 for Automotive Production and Relevant Service Part Organizations.* Geneva (Switzerland), 2002.

[ISO04] ISO, International Organization for Standardization. *ISO 14001:2004. Environmental Management Systems – Requirements with Guidance to Use.* Geneva (Switzerland), 2004.

[Karch05] Karch, S., Heilig, L. *SAP NetWeaver Roadmap*. Galileo Press, Fort Lee (NJ); Bonn (Germany), 2005.

[Keller97] Keller, G., et al. *SAP R/3 Process Oriented Implementation, Iterative Process Prototyping*. Addison-Wesley (Germany), 1998, p. 154.

[SAP AG99] SAP AG. *Initial Data Transfer Made Easy – Step by Step Guide to SAP Initial Data Transfer*. Walldorf (Germany), 1999.

[SAP AG02] SAP AG. *QM Quality Management SAP R/3 Enterprise Release 4.70 Release Notes.* Walldorf (Germany), 2002.

[SAP AG04] SAP AG. *QM Quality Management SAP ERP Central Component Release 5.0 Release Notes.* Walldorf (Germany), 2004.

[SAP AG06] SAP AG. *QM Quality Management SAP ERP Central Component Release 6.0 Release Notes.* Walldorf (Germany), 2006.

[SAP AG07] SAP AG. *Online Documentation – SAP Library – SAP ERP Central Component, Release 6.0, SAP NetWeaver 7.0.* Walldorf (Germany), 2007.

[SAP AG08] SAP AG. *Functions in Detail – Quality Management with SAP ERP.* Walldorf (Germany), 2008.

[Taucher99] Taucher, F. *Neues Denken in Prozessen*. QZ, Volume 44 (1999), p. 1197. Munich (Germany). (Only available in German language.)

# D The Authors

**Michael Hölzer** who was born in 1962 studied mechanical engineering at the technical college in Hagen, Germany. He has led various projects in the areas of plant engineering and construction, as well as mechanical engineering. Since 1990, Michael has been working as a freelance consultant and supervised numerous CAQ-IUMS implementations in industrial enterprises. He is an SAP-certified AcceleratedSAP (ASAP) and Quality Management (QM) consultant, and for the past ten years, he has provided support in the implementation and rollout of SAP Product Lifecycle Management (PLM), SAP Quality Management (QM), SAP Plant Maintenance (PM), and SAP Customer Service (CS) in global projects for various enterprises and industries.

**Michael Schramm**, M. Eng., was born in 1953 and studied electrical engineering at the Technical University of Darmstadt, Germany. Having worked for several years as a development engineer at Philips Peripherals in Siegen, Germany, he joined TallyGenicom Computerdrucker GmbH in Ulm, Germany, in 1987. From 1994 on, he was responsible for quality assurance and quality management at TallyGenicom. When Michael managed the implementation of the Quality Management (QM) module and the optimization of workflows and customizing, he acquired a profound knowledge of the SAP system. That knowledge was continuously enhanced during rollouts in several subsidiaries and in a plant located in China. Since 2006, Michael has held the position of Quality Manager at Epsilon Gesellschaft für technische Informatik mbH in Villingen-Schwenningen, Germany.

# Index

## D

## K



## L



## M

## R



## S

## T

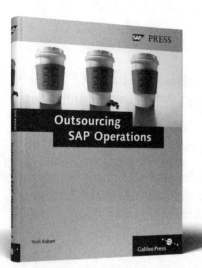

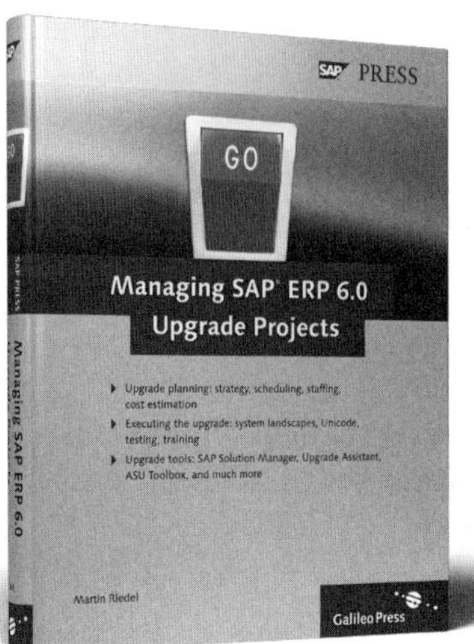


Upgrade planning: strategy, scheduling, staffing, cost estimation

Executing the upgrade: system landscapes, Unicode, testing, training

Upgrade tools: SAP Solution Manager, Upgrade Assistant, ASU Toolbox, and much more

Martin Riedel

# Managing SAP ERP 6.0 Upgrade Projects

This book is the consultant's and project team's guide to smooth and successful SAP upgrade projects. It guides you through all phases of the project and gives insight on project management approaches, best practices, possible errors, resources and tools.
After explaining how to determine the value of an upgrade, the authors start covering the individual phases of an upgrade: You'll learn how to plan for, how to manage, and finally how to execute the upgrade project in detail. A chapter on the upgrade tools, including coverage of SAP Solution Manager, rounds off this unique resource.
The many tips, tricks, checklists, and best practices presentend in a reader-friendly and practical style will make this book your ultimate resource while preparing for the project.

approx. 362 pp., 69,95 Euro / US$ 69.95, ISBN 978-1-59229-268-4, April 2009

**>> www.sap-press.de/2050**

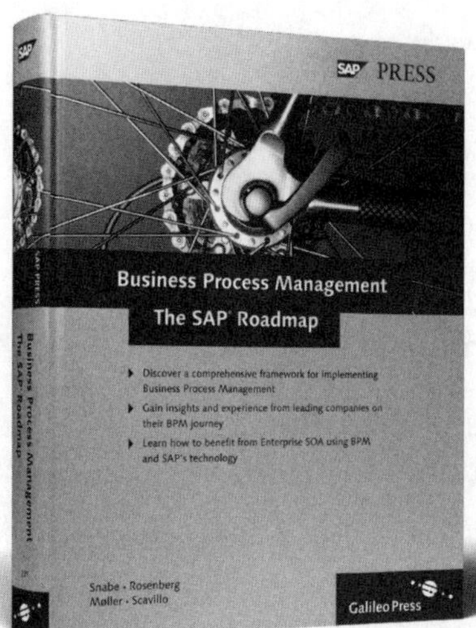


Discover a comprehensive framework for implementing Business Process Management

Gain insights and experience from leading companies on their BPM journey

Learn how to benefit from Enterprise SOA using BPM and SAP's technology

Jim Hagemann Snabe, Ann Rosenberg, Charles Møller, Mark Scavillo

# Business Process Management - the SAP Roadmap

This unique book finally sheds light on Business Process Management - a term often misunderstood and misused. It explains what BPM is, how to implement it in your company, and it gives real-life examples of BPM implementations. The authors explain the phase model and the building blocks of the BPM approach (both, for the business and the IT perspective), and they also cover the important topic of aligning BPM and SOA concepts.

411 pp., 2009, 69,95 Euro / US$ 69.95
ISBN 978-1-59229-231-8

**>> www.sap-press.de/1849**

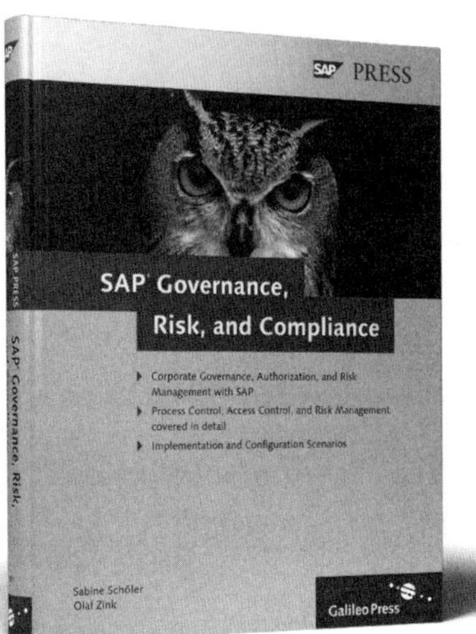


Corporate governance and risk management with SAP

Detailed view on process control, access control and risk management

Business user scenarios and configuration

Sabine Schöler, Olaf Zink

## SAP Governance, Risk and Compliance

**The Complete Resource**

This book is a roadmap for mastering the processes and configuration of the essential components of SAP Governance, Risk & Compliance. Business processes, use cases and configuration scenarios are presented in detail, with a focus on the three most important components: Process Control, Access Control, and Risk Management. Each chapter starts off with a relevant business scenario. Then it describes the configuration of the software using many step-by-step screenshots. Finally, business processes relevant to the configuration are discussed.A consistent use-case scenario is presented throughout the book to bring each of the topics.

312 pp., 2009, 79,95 Euro / US$ 79.95
ISBN 978-1-59229-191-5

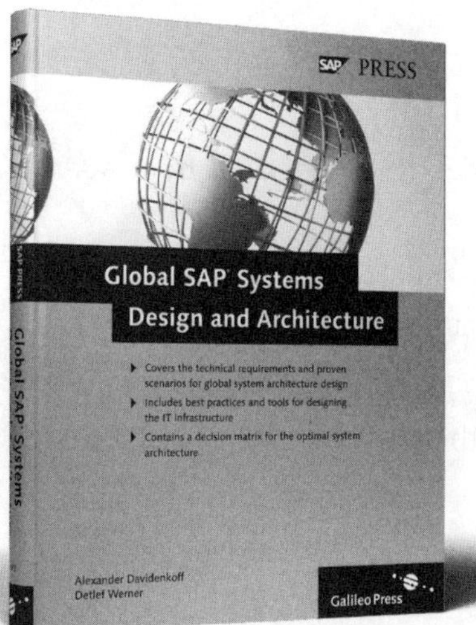

Covers the technical requirements and proven scenarios for global system architecture design

Includes best practices and tools for designing the IT infrastructure

Contains a decision matrix for the optimal system architecture

Alexander Davidenkoff, Detlef Werner

# Global SAP Systems – Design and Architecture

When planning an international SAP system implementation, the central question is often whether one global SAP system or several distributed local systems will work best. To answer this question in the best possible way, project managers, IT managers, and other key decision makers can use this book as their comprehensive guide. The book provides the business-relevant facts and technical details necessary to design and bring to realization successful international SAP system implementation projects, and readers will learn about system requirements, the factors that influence the system architecture, and the available options for various different system architectures. And that's just for starters: the book also includes valuable tips, best practices, exclusive customer reports, and much more.

317 pp., 2008, 69,95 Euro / US$ 69.95
ISBN 978-1-59229-183-0

**>> www.sap-press.de/1665**

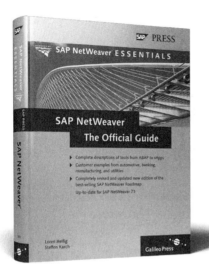

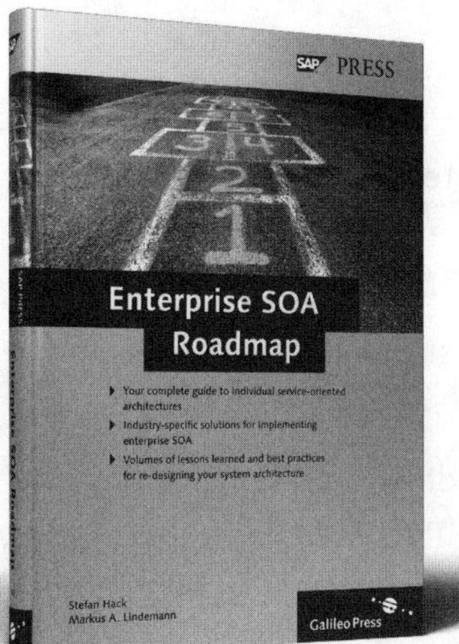


Your complete guide to individual service-oriented architectures

Industry-specific solutions for implementing enterprise SOA

Volumes of lessons learned and best practices for re-designing your system architecture

Stefan Hack, Markus A. Lindemann

# Enterprise SOA Roadmap

This book, intended for business leaders, IT managers and consultants, guides you step-by-step along the path to enterprise service-oriented architecture. Using a detailed analysis of more than 500 SAP Consulting projects in different industries as a basis, the authors deliver concrete recommendations on how best to roll out enterprise SOA in your own organization. You'll learn how SAP supports enterprises along their individual adoption paths, and benefit from the many lessons learned that are described in the book. In addition, you'll discover how to apply specific implementation options, arguments and best practices in your enterprise and how to sidestep potential implementation risks.

417 pp., 2008, 69,95 Euro / US$ 69.95
ISBN 978-1-59229-162-5

**>> www.sap-press.de/1586**

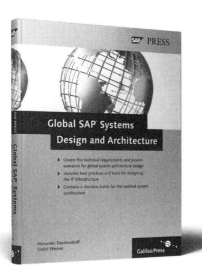